Lecture Notes of the Institute for Computer Sciences, Social Informatics and Telecommunications Engineering 316

More information about this series at http://www.springer.com/series/8197

Bo Li · Jie Zheng · Yong Fang ·
Mao Yang · Zhongjiang Yan (Eds.)

IoT as a Service

5th EAI International Conference, IoTaaS 2019
Xi'an, China, November 16–17, 2019
Proceedings

 Springer

Editors
Bo Li
Northwestern Polytechnical University
Xi'an, China

Yong Fang
Chang'an University
Xi'an, China

Zhongjiang Yan (iD)
Northwestern Polytechnical University
Xi'an, China

Jie Zheng
Northwest University
Xi'an, China

Mao Yang (iD)
Northwestern Polytechnical University
Xi'an, China

ISSN 1867-8211   ISSN 1867-822X   (electronic)
Lecture Notes of the Institute for Computer Sciences, Social Informatics
and Telecommunications Engineering
ISBN 978-3-030-44750-2   ISBN 978-3-030-44751-9   (eBook)
https://doi.org/10.1007/978-3-030-44751-9

This Springer imprint is published by the registered company Springer Nature Switzerland AG
The registered company address is: Gewerbestrasse 11, 6330 Cham, Switzerland

Preface

IoTaaS is endorsed by the European Alliance for Innovation, a leading community-based organization devoted to the advancement of innovation in the field of ICT. The 5th International Conference on IoT as a Service (IoTaaS 2019) aimed to contribute to the discussion on the challenges posed by the Internet of Things (IoT). The IoTaaS conference series aims to bring together researchers and practitioners interested in IoT from academia and industry. IoTaaS 2019 attendees presented novel ideas, exchanged points of view, and fostered collaborations. The city of Xi'an, a famous historical and cultural city of China, hosted this edition of IoTaaS.

IoTaaS 2019, consisted of two technical tracks and three workshops: Networking and Communications Technologies for IoT, IoT as a service, the International Workshop on Edge Intelligence and Computing for IoT Communications and Applications, the International Workshop on Wireless automated networking for Internet of Things, and the International Workshop on Ubiquitous Services Transmission for Internet of Things. IoTaaS has become one of the major events in these areas in the Asia-Pacific region. It has been successful in encouraging interactions among participants, exchanging novel ideas and disseminating knowledge.

Following the great success of the past IoTaaS conferences, held during the years 2014–2018, IoTaaS 2019 received 106 submitted papers, out of which 63 papers were selected for presentation. The Technical Program Committee (TPC) did an outstanding job in organizing a diverse technical program consisting of 12 symposia that covered a broad range of research areas in IoT technologies. Under the excellent leadership of TPC co-chairs Prof. Yong Fang, Prof. Jie Zheng, and Prof. Daqing Chen, TPC members handled the peer review of papers with more than three reviews per paper on average.

The technical program featured two outstanding keynote speakers, who presented their vision of IoT in theory and practice: Prof. Yingzhuang Liu, Huazhong University of Science and Technology (HUST), China, and Prof. Ba-Zhong Shen, Xidian University, China.

We would like to thank the TPC co-chairs, TPC members, all the reviewers, the workshop co-chairs, the web chairs, the publication chair, the local chairs, and all the members of the Organizing Committee, for their assistance and efforts in making the conference a success. The continuing sponsorship by EAI and Springer is gratefully acknowledged. We also express our appreciation to the conference keynote speakers, paper presenters, and authors.

February 2020   Bo Li

Organization

Steering Committee

Imrich Chlamtac   University of Trento, Italy
Bo Li   Northwestern Polytechnical University, China

Organizing Committee

General Chair

Bo Li   Northwestern Polytechnical University, China

General Co-chairs

Xiaoguang Gao   Northwestern Polytechnical University, China
Jinye Peng   Northwest University, China
Huansheng Song   Chang'an University, China

TPC Chair and Co-chair

Yong Fang   Chang'an University, China
Jie Zheng   Northwest University, China
Daqing Chen   London South Bank University, UK

Sponsorship and Exhibit Chair

Xiaoya Zuo   Northwestern Polytechnical University, China

Local Chair

Zhongjiang Yan   Northwestern Polytechnical University, China

Workshop Chair

Yong Li   Tsinghua University, China

Publicity and Social Media Chair

Hongwei Zhao   Northwestern Polytechnical University, China

Publications Chair

Jie Zheng   Northwest University, China

Web Chair

Mao Yang   Northwestern Polytechnical University, China

Tutorial Chair

Shaohui Mei   Northwestern Polytechnical University, China

Conference Manager

Radka Pincakova   EAI

Technical Program Committee

Marco Anisetti	Università degli Studi di Milano, Italy
Zhengwen Cao	Northwest University, China
Xiang Chen	Sun Yat-sen University, China
Zhengchuan Chen	Singapore University of Technology and Design, Singapore
Hua Cui	Chang'an University, China
Yongqian Du	Northwestern Polytechnical University, China
Rongfei Fan	Beijing Institute of Technology, China
Yongsheng Gao	Northwestern Polytechnical University, China
Chen He	Northwest University, China
Yongqiang Hei	Xidian University, China
Bin Li	Northwestern Polytechnical University, China
Guifang Li	Northwestern Polytechnical University, China
Jingling Li	China Academy of Space Technology in Xi'an, China
Zhan Li	Northwest University, China
Ni Liu	Chang'an University, China
Wei Liang	Northwestern Polytechnical University, China
Zhanwen Liu	Chang'an University, China
Zhongjin Liu	Coordination Center of China, China
Xin Ma	Northwestern Polytechnical University, China
Laisen Nie	Northwestern Polytechnical University, China
Yong Niu	Beijing Jiaotong University, China
Xiaoyan Pang	Northwestern Polytechnical University, China
Bowei Shan	Chang'an University, China
Zhong Shen	Xidian University, China
Jiao Shi	Northwestern Polytechnical University, China
Xiao Tang	Northwestern Polytechnical University, China
Jing Wang	Chang'an University, China
Jun Wang	Northwest University, China
Wei Wang	Chang'an University, China
Zhenyu Xiao	Beijing University of Aeronautics and Astronautics, China
Jian Xie	Northwestern Polytechnical University, China
Mingwu Yao	Xidian University, China
Daosen Zhai	Northwestern Polytechnical University, China
Yongqin Zhang	Northwest University, China
Zhou Zhang	China Electronic System Engineering Company, China

Xuan Zhu	Northwest University, China
Jiang Zhu	Zhejiang University, China
Min Zhu	Xidian University, China
Xiaoya Zuo	Northwestern Polytechnical University, China

Contents

Ubiquitous Services Transmission For Internet of Things

Wireless Automated Networking for Internet of Things

Networking Technology for IoT

IoT as a Service

Accelerating Q-ary Sliding-Window Belief Propagation Algorithm with GPU

Bowei Shan$^{(\boxtimes)}$ (iD), Sihua Chen, and Yong Fang (iD)

School of Information Engineering, Chang'an University, Xi'an, China
{bwshan,fy}@chd.edu.cn,1543275321@qq.com

Abstract. In this paper, we present a parallel Sliding-Window Belief Propagation algorithm to decode Q-ary Low-Density-Parity-Codes. The bottlenecks of sequential algorithm are carefully investigated. We use MATLAB platform to develop the parallel algorithm and run these bottlenecks simultaneously on thousands of threads of GPU. The experiment results show that our parallel algorithm achieves 2.3× to 30.3× speedup ratio than sequential algorithm.

Keywords: SWBP · LDPC · GPU · MATLAB

1 Introduction

As a very good error-correcting code [1], Low-Density-Parity-Codes (LDPC) codes are wildly used in Fifth Generation (5G) telecommunication and Internet of Things as s Service (IoTaaS). It was first invented by Gallager [2] in 1962, and unfortunately ignored by information society for more than 30 years. The renaissance of LDPC was triggered by MacKay and Neal in 1996.

Originally, binary LDPC has been decoded by belief propagation (BP) algorithm (also known as "sum-product" algorithm) [1]. In 1998, MacKay $et\ al.$ [3] generalized the binary LDPC to finite fields GF ($Q = 2^q$) and proposed a Q-ary LDPC. The Q-ary BP algorithm is used to decode Q-ary LDCP. To improve the performance of BP algorithm, Fang presented a Sliding-Window Belief Propagation (SWBP) algorithm. A lot of experiments [6] show that SWBP achieves better performance with less iteration times. In addition, it is very easy to implement and insensitive to the initial settings. Incorporating fast Q-ary BP with SWBP is a nature way to attain better performance and robustness, while it still suffers from heavy computing complexity.

Invented by NVIDIA, Graphics Processing Unit (GPU) [7] has demonstrated powerful ability for general-purpose computing. NVIDIA also presented a C-like languages interface named Compute Unified Device Architecture (CUDA) which is a useful tool for researchers to develop the parallel algorithms. Inspired by GPU's amazing ability, we propose a parallel algorithm of Q-ary SWBP and accelerate it by GTX 1080Ti. Although we has used GPU to accelerate parallel

© ICST Institute for Computer Sciences, Social Informatics and Telecommunications Engineering 2020
Published by Springer Nature Switzerland AG 2020. All Rights Reserved
B. Li et al. (Eds.): IoTaaS 2019, LNICST 316, pp. 3–8, 2020.
https://doi.org/10.1007/978-3-030-44751-9_1

binary SWBP algorithm developed by CUDA C++ [8], to our best knowledge, parallel Q-ary SWBP algorithm has still not been presented.

The rest of this paper is organized as: Sect. 2 describes the sequential Q-ary SWBP algorithm. Section 3 analyses the bottlenecks of sequential algorithm and presents the parallel algorithm. Section 4 uses GPU to accelerate the parallel algorithm and gives the experiment results. We concludes this paper in Sect. 5.

2 Q-ary SWBP Algorithm

2.1   Correlation Model

Let $\mathcal{A} = [0 : Q)$ denote the alphabet. Let $x, y \in \mathcal{A}$ denote the realization of X and Y, which are two random variables. Let X^n be the source to be compressed at the encoder. Let Y^n be the Side Information (SI) that resides only at the decoder. Let $X^n = Y^n + Z^n$. We model the correlation between input X^n and output Y^n as a virtual channel with three properties:

(1) Additive: Y^n and X^n are independent with each other;
(2) Memoryless: $p_{Z^n}(z^n) = \prod_{i=1}^{n} p_{Z_i}(z_i)$, where $p_X(x)$ denotes the Probability Mass Function (pmf) of discrete random variable X;
(3) Nonstationary: pmfs of Z_i's may be different, where $i \in [0 : n]$.

We use Truncated Discrete Laplace (TDL) distribution to model Z_i:

$$p_{X_i|Y_i}(x|y) \propto \frac{1}{2b_i} \exp\left(-\frac{|x-y|}{b_i}\right) \tag{1}$$

where b_i is the local scale parameter. Since $\sum_{x=0}^{Q-1} p_{X_i|Y_i}(x|y) = 1$, we can obtain

$$p_{X_i|Y_i}(x|y) = \exp\left(-\frac{|x-y|}{b_i}\right) \Big/ \mathcal{L}_Q(b_i, y) \tag{2}$$

where $\mathcal{L}_Q(b,y) = \sum_{x=0}^{Q-1} \exp(-|x-y|/b_i)$. To reduce the computing complexity, we use integration to approximate the summation. When b and Q are reasonably big, this approximation is precise enough by

$$\begin{aligned}
\mathcal{L}_Q(b,y) &\approx \int_0^{Q-1} \exp\left(-\frac{|x-y|}{b}\right) dx \\
&= 2b\left(1 - \frac{1}{2}\exp\left(\frac{y-(Q-1)}{b}\right) - \frac{1}{2}\exp\left(-\frac{y}{b}\right)\right)
\end{aligned} \tag{3}$$

The encoder uses Q-ary LDPC codes to compress source $\mathrm{x} \in [0 : Q)^n$ to get syndrome $\mathrm{s} \in [0 : Q)^n$. The decoder seeds source nodes x according to SI y, and runs Q-ary BP algorithm to recover x. For the belief propagation between source nodes and syndrome nodes, we give following definitions: $\xi_i(x)$ is intrinsic pmf of source node x_i; $\zeta_i(x)$ is overall pmf of source node x_i; $r_{i,j}(x)$ is the pmf passed from source node x_i to syndrome nodes s_j; and $q_{j,i}(x)$ is the pmf passed from syndrome nodes s_j to source node x_i, where $j \in \mathcal{M}_i$ and $i \in \mathcal{N}_j$. The encoding and decoding process of $Q - ary$ BP has been stated in [6], and we omit it in this paper.

2.2 SWBP Algorithm

In Q-ary BP, the source nodes need be seeded with local scale parameter b of virtual correlation channel. In [4] and [5], the parameter of virtual correlation channel is estimated by SWBP algorithm. In this paper, we will use expected L_1 distance between each source symbol and its corresponding SI symbol defined as

$$\mu_i \triangleq \sum_{x=1}^{Q} (\zeta_i(x) \cdot |x - y_i|) \tag{4}$$

Then, the estimated local scale parameter $\hat{b}$ is calculated by averaging the expected L_1 distances of its neighbors in a window with size-$(2\eta + 1)$

$$\hat{b}_i(\eta) = \frac{t_i(\eta) - \mu_i}{\min(i + \eta, n) - \max(1, i - \eta)} \tag{5}$$

where

$$t_i(\eta) \triangleq \sum_{i'=\max(1,i-\eta)}^{\min(i+\eta,n)} \mu_{i'} \tag{6}$$

To calculate (13), we first calculate $t_1(\eta) = \sum_{i'=1}^{1+\eta} u_{i'}$. Then for $i \in [2 : n]$,

$$t_i(\eta) = \begin{cases} t_{i-1}(\eta) + \mu_{i+\eta}, & i \in [2 : (\eta + 1)] \\ t_{i-1}(\eta) + \mu_{i+\eta} - \mu_{i-1-\eta}, & i \in [(\eta + 2) : (n - \eta)] \\ t_{i-1}(\eta) + \mu_{i-1-\eta}, & i \in [(n - \eta + 1) : n] \end{cases} \tag{7}$$

Same as [4] and [5], the main purpose of SWBP is to find a best half window size $\hat{\eta}$. We define an expected rate:

$$\begin{aligned} \gamma(\eta) &\triangleq -\sum_{i=1}^{n} \sum_{x=0}^{Q-1} \zeta_i(x) \cdot \ln \frac{\exp(-|x - y_i|/\hat{b}_i(\eta))}{\mathcal{L}_Q(\hat{b}_i(\eta), y_i)} \\ &= \sum_{i=1}^{n} \left(\ln \mathcal{L}_Q(\hat{b}_i(\eta), y_i) + \frac{\mu_i}{\hat{b}_i(\eta)} \right) \end{aligned} \tag{8}$$

where $\mathcal{L}_Q(\hat{b}_i(\eta), y_i)$ is defined by (3). The best half window size $\hat{\eta}$ is chosen by

$$\hat{\eta} = \arg \min_{\eta} \gamma(\eta), \tag{9}$$

It is a natural idea that best half window size should minimize the expected rate. The flowchart of Q-ary SWBP algorithm was illustrated in Fig. 1.

3   Parallel SWBP Algorithm

In sequential SWBP algorithm, each window size setup iteration generates an expected rate $\gamma(\eta)$, which is calculated by (15). Any two expected rate $\gamma(\eta_1)$ and $\gamma(\eta_2)$ $(\eta_1 \neq \eta_2)$ are uncorrelated, and can be computed in parallel. In our

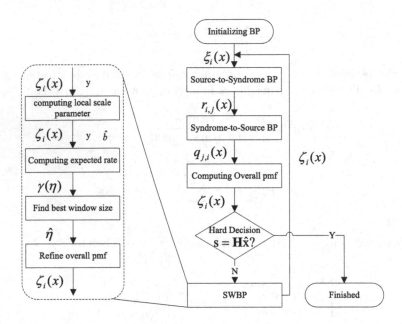

Fig. 1. Flowchart of Q-ary SWBP

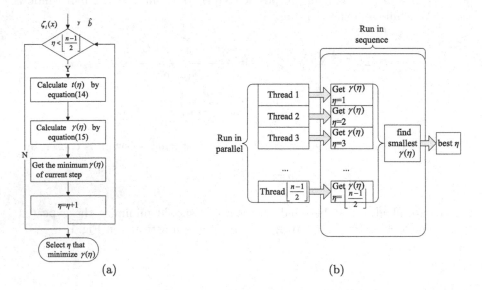

Fig. 2. (a) Sequential SWBP algorithm, (b) parallel SWBP algorithm

parallel algorithm, all $\gamma(\eta)$, $\eta \in \left\{1, 2, \ldots, \lfloor \frac{n-1}{2} \rfloor\right\}$ are calculated simultaneously by thousands of threads on GPU. Once $\gamma(\eta)$, $\eta \in \left\{1, 2, \ldots, \lfloor \frac{n-1}{2} \rfloor\right\}$ are obtained, we use $min()$ function in MATLAB to get the smallest γ and corresponding best η from array $\gamma(\eta)$. The sequential and parallel algorithm are illustrated in Fig. 2.

4   Experiment Results

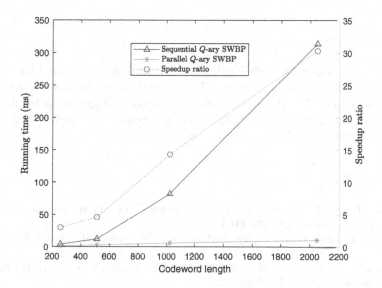

Fig. 3. Running time and speedup ratio under Q=256

In our experiments, we use Intel Core i7 with 3.60Ghz as our CPU and NVIDIA GTX 1080Ti as our GPU. We use MATLAB 2014b as our development platform. We perform numerical experiments to evaluate the performance of our parallel algorithm.

We set Q=256, and use 4 different regular LDPC codes as our input. The parameters of these LPDC codes are listed in Table 1. To eliminate the random errors, we perform 100 tests and average these outputs as our final results. The experiment result is illustrated in Fig. 3, which shows that parallel Q-ary SWBP algorithm achieves 2.9× to 30.3× accelerating ratio than sequential Q-ary SWBP algorithm. The longer the codeword length, the higher the accelerating ratio.

Table 1. Different LDPC code parameters (N is codeword length, K is information bit number)

Test	1	2	3	4
N	256	512	1024	2048
K	128	256	512	1024
Maximum degree	4	4	4	4
Code Type	Regular	Regular	Regular	Regular

5   Conclusion

We propose a parallel Q-ary SWBP algorithm to decode regular LDPC codes with different codelength and Q value. This algorithm can address the bottlnecks of sequential Q-ary SWBP and be accelerated by GPU. Experiment results show that parallel algorithm achieves 2.9× to 30.3× speedup ratio under $Q=256$. The longer codeword length leads to higher speedup ratio.

References

1. MacKay, D.J.C.: Good error-correcting codes based on very sparse matrices. IEEE Trans. Inf. Theory **45**(2), 399–431 (1999)
2. Gallager, R.: Low-density parity-check codes. IRE Trans. Inf. Theory **8**(1), 21–28 (1962)
3. Davey, M.C., MacKay, D.: Low-density parity check codes over GF(q). IEEE Commun. Lett. **2**(6), 165–167 (1998)
4. Fang, Y.: LDPC-based lossless compression of nonstationary binary sources using sliding-window belief propagation. IEEE Trans. Commun. **60**(11), 3161–3166 (2012)
5. Fang, Y.: Asymmetric Slepian-Wolf coding of nonstationarily-correlated M-ary sources with sliding-window belief propagation. IEEE Trans. Commun. **61**(12), 5114–5124 (2013). https://doi.org/10.1109/TCOMM.2013.111313.130230
6. Fang, Y., Yang, Y., Shan, B., Stankovic, V.: Joint source-channel estimation via sliding-window belief propagation. IEEE Trans. Commun. (2019, submitted)
7. NVIDIA. http://www.nvidia.com/object/what-is-gpu-computing.html
8. Shan, B., Fang, Y.: GPU accelerated parallel algorithm of sliding-window belief propagation for LDPC codes. Int. J. Parallel Program. (2019). https://doi.org/10.1007/s10766-019-00632-3

A Simple and Reliable Acquisition Algorithm for Low-Orbit Satellite Signal

Hongwei Zhao and Yue Yan[✉]

Northwestern Polytechnical University, Xi'an, China
13359237963@163.com

Abstract. In recent years, the global low-orbit communication and Internet constellation have entered a period of vigorous development. Low-orbit satellites have the advantages of high landing level and fast satellite geometry change, and the enhancement function of low-orbit navigation can complement the current mid-high-rail GNSS implementation and promote the deep integration of navigation communication, which is an important direction for the future development of the navigation system. Hongyan Navigation System is a low-orbit mobile communication and broadband internet constellation independently developed by China, which integrates navigation enhancement functions, and has real-time communication capability in full-time and complex terrain conditions to provide users with real-time global data communication and integrated information services. However, the Hongyan satellite has the characteristics of fast moving speed, short single-visible time, and greater doppler dynamics received by the users, which is not suitable for the traditional capturing methods. Therefore, it is of great research value and practical significance to study the Hongyan navigation signal. This paper studies the spread spectrum modulation and the synchronous acquisition of the transmitting signal based on the Hongyan constellation. On the Matlab platform, the excellent characteristics of the transmission signal of Hongyan system and the time-sequence capture method are verified.

Keywords: Hongyan navigation enhancement system · Low-orbit communication · Direct sequence spread spectrum · Code acquisition

1 Introduction

In modern times, the development of the Internet faces serious challenges such as scalability, security, mobility, controllability and manageability. In the future, the network will develop in the direction of deep integration with the real economy and the integration of communication and navigation functions is the construction direction of satellite navigation system in the intelligent era, aiming to establish a converged network architecture of sea, land and air to support the development of communication, navigation and surveillance network applications.

Global navigation satellite system receivers play a crucial role in variety of fields including navigation, positioning, and civilian surveying areas [1, 2], but due to the

B. Li et al. (Eds.): IoTaaS 2019, LNICST 316, pp. 9–19, 2020.
https://doi.org/10.1007/978-3-030-44751-9_2

natural vulnerability of GNSS, the application in complex environments may be limited, and the positioning accuracy may be reduced or even unable to be located [3, 5]. In order to meet the higher requirements of precision, integrity, continuity, availability and other performances, various enhanced navigations have been generated on the basis of basic GNSS systems, and global low-orbit communication and internet constellation have become a research hotspot [6]. Low-orbit satellites, as space-based monitoring stations combined with GNSS and LEO satellites, can significantly improve the accuracy of precision single-point positioning and significantly improve the convergence of precision single-point positioning [7]. Low orbit satellite can also be used to enhance RTK, which can improve the speed of long baseline fuzziness calculation and fixed success rate, and can serve high-precision industries such as surveying and mapping, ocean and fine agriculture.

The 'Hongyan Project' of the Aerospace Science and Industry Group is based on global coverage assurance, national aviation and navigation applications, and mainly uses the downlink L-band communication link of Hongyan to broadcast real-time navigation enhancement information such as precise orbit, clock difference and code deviation, and provides global precise single point positioning service [8, 9]. The overall goal is to build a real-time, high-precision, space-based, low-track navigation enhancement system around 2021, that provides global military and civilian users with dynamic decimeter-level, static centimeter-level positioning and global seamless, fast Internet communication services.

However, the research of low-orbit satellite constellation on the user receiving terminal also increases the following difficulties: low-orbit satellite has low orbit, fast motion speed, short single-star visibility time, larger doppler dynamics received by the user, which put forwards higher requirements for signal acquisition and tracking. Therefore, it is necessary to provide more studies on the synchronization of Hongyan downlink signal. We aim to test the feasibility of the Hongyan spread system and simulate the code capture of the signal using accurate, controllable and reproducible simulation signals to develop and verify the "Hongyan Constellation" hardware receiver, enabling the development time and efficiency of the receiver to be guaranteed. The research of this project will help accelerate the development of China's enhanced navigation technology, the construction of high-precision integrated PNT, deeply integrated system data fusion technology of GNSS/INS deeply integrated navigation under the complex environment and synchronization between the GNSS systems and INS system. The research results will be used in air-sea surveillance, aircraft precision approach and other fields.

The structure of the paper is as follows: in Sect. 2, direct sequence spread system model of "Hongyan Constellation" and the methods of code synchronization are presented. Section 3 illustrates and analyzes the simulation results. Section 4 summarizes the conclusions.

2 Materials and Methods

2.1 The Composition and Principle of Direct Sequence Spread System

Hongyan Constellation is a typical direct sequence spread spectrum system, it's communication model is presented in Fig. 1.

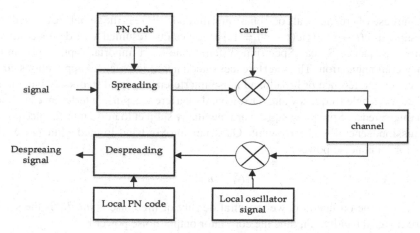

Fig. 1. Direct sequence spread spectrum system communication model

The system consists of a transmitting part and a receiving part. Generally speaking, its working mode is as follows:

The binary information code sequence that is input at the transmitting end is modularly added with the high speed code sequence to generate a spreading sequence with the same rate as the pseudo random code rate. Obviously, the bandwidth of the spreading sequence is higher than the original information bandwidth, thus completing the spectrum expansion of the information. Then, the spread spectrum sequence is subjected to carrier modulation, and the obtained radio frequency signal is amplified by power amplification. At the receiving end, the received spread spectrum signal is amplified by power and sent to the mixer. In the mixer, the signal is multiplied by the carrier, the signal is down-converted to the baseband, and the baseband signal is sent to the demodulator through the baseband filter to complete the demodulation. And then the demodulation signal is multiplied by the local PN code sequence to complete the dispreading. This restores the original data information [10].

Taking the PSK signal as an example, the signal of the direct expansion system can be expressed as:

$$s(t) = \sqrt{2P}d(t)c(t)\cos(w_0 t + \theta_0) \tag{1}$$

where $d(t)$ is the information data, and $c(t)$ is the spreading code, which is a rectangular wave signal a value of $+1$ or -1.

At the receiving end, it is assumed that the received signal contains useful signals and noise introduced by the system, which can be expressed as

$$s'(t) = \sqrt{2P}d(t)c(t)\cos(w_0 t + \theta_0) + n(t) \tag{2}$$

In the despreading process, the locally generated spreading code $c(t - \tau)$ is used to correlate with the received signal, and the related signal is expressed as

$$s'_c(t) = \sqrt{2P}d(t)c(t)c(t - \tau)\cos(w_0 t + \theta_0) + n(t)c(t - \tau) \tag{3}$$

In the case where the local code phase and the code phase in the signal are aligned,$c(t)$ is the same as $c(t - \tau)$,$c(t)c(t - \tau) = 1$, so $d(t)$ can be resumed after demodulation.

Direct Sequence Spread Spectrum system is the most important application in the military communication. The interferences encountered in practical applications cover white noise interference or broadband noise interference, partial frequency band noise interference, single frequency and narrowband interference, pulse interference and multipath interference. Spreading signals are inevitably subject to noise interference during transmission, generally additive white Gaussian noise or band-limited white noise. The correlator input noise power is

$$N_i = n_0 B_c \tag{4}$$

Wherein, the unilateral power spectral density of the noise is n_0, B_c is the spread spectrum signal bandwidth, thus the correlator output noise power is

$$N_0 = \frac{1}{2\pi} \int W_a G_{nI}(w)dw \tag{5}$$

where W_a is the information bandwidth of $2\pi B_a$. Considering that $B_a \ll B_c$ and the noise power is near f_I, we can know $G_{nI}(w)$ is approximately K_{n0}, where K is a constant related to the modulation scheme. For PSK modulation, $K = 0.903$, so

$$N_0 = \frac{1}{2\pi} K n_0 W_a = K n_0 B_a \tag{6}$$

Since the amount of information before and after despreading is constant, the processing gain of the direct-spreading system for white noise interference is

$$G_{pn} = N_i / N_0 = B_c / K B_a = G_p / K \tag{7}$$

2.2 Code Synchronization

The acquisition based on code synchronization is essentially the reception process of despreading and demodulation. Since its purpose is to perform time synchronization, it is only necessary to find the position of the correlation peak, and it is not necessary to use the demodulation and decoding link to extract the information carried by the carrier phase. Therefore, a relatively simple method is often used to eliminate the influence of the phase offset. The transmitting end modulates the synchronized code sequence, and the receiving end receives the mutually orthogonal I and Q baseband signals by orthogonal down-conversion. According to the trigonometric identity, the I and Q the two baseband signals are matched by the matched filter and the output correlation values are squared, and the obtained sum value no longer contains the carrier random phase information. Choosing this value as a statistical decision eliminates the effects of phase shift. Finally, it is compared with a certain threshold value to make a capture decision [11, 12]. The capture decision methods adopted in this paper are all based on time-domain analysis for serial search. The block diagram of serial capture principle circuit is shown as Fig. 2.

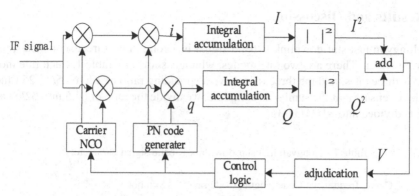

Fig. 2. Serial capture principle circuit

After the signal received by the antenna is down-converted, the digital intermediate frequency signal after sampling at the sampling interval T_c is

$$S(n) = aD(n)C(n) \exp j[2\pi(F_{IF} + F_D)nT_C + \phi] + n \qquad (8)$$

In the formula, the amplitude of the received signal is a, the navigation message data code is D_n, C_n is the C/A code, F_{IF} is the intermediate frequency, F_D is the doppler frequency, ϕ is the initial phase of the received signal and n is the noise, which is the summary of two white noises n_I and n_Q.

After demodulating and dispreading with the use of local carrier NCO and pseudo-code generator respectively, coherent accumulation is performed, and the integrated values of I and Q are calculated as follows

$$I(n) = AD(n)R[\varepsilon(n)]\mathrm{sinc}(\pi F_D T) \cos(\phi_e) + n_I \qquad (9)$$

$$Q(n) = AD(n)R[\varepsilon(n)]\mathrm{sinc}(\pi F_D T) \sin(\phi_e) + n_Q \qquad (10)$$

Wherein, A is the signal amplitude, ε_D is the chip phase difference, F_D is the carrier frequency difference, $R[\varepsilon(n)]\mathrm{sinc}(\pi F_D T)$ is the frequency difference, $\phi_e = 2\pi F_D(n - 1/2)T + \varphi$ is the carrier phase difference, φ_n is the initial phase difference. Regardless of noise, we can develop (11) from (9) (10).

$$\sqrt{I^2(n) + Q^2(n)} = aR[\varepsilon(n)]|\mathrm{sinc}(\pi F_D T)| \qquad (11)$$

The above equation shows that the phase difference between the received carrier and the replica carrier does not affect the non-coherent detection. If the number of non-coherent integrations is N_{nc}, the detection amount can be expressed as:

$$V = \frac{1}{N_{nc}} \sum_{n=1}^{N_{nc}} \sqrt{I^2(n) + Q^2(n)} \qquad (12)$$

The time domain serial capture algorithm is the most basic capture algorithm, and its hardware design is very simple.

3   Results and Discussion

The Hongyan first star downlink L-band signal is a continuous direct sequence spread spectrum signal. There are two rate modes, which is shown as Table 1. Each rate mode includes three rates, and the three rates have a spreading ratio of 125/62.5/31.25 times. In order to ensure that the symbol is complete, we divide the ratio of 62.5 into 62/63 and 31.25 is divided into 31/31/31/32.

Table 1.   Hongyan first star downlink L-band signal parameters.

Center frequency (MHz)	Code length	Code rate (Mbps)	Symbol rate
1521.5 MHz	125	Mode 1:1.2	Rate 1: 9.6/19.2/38.4 Kbps
		Mode 2:0.15	Rate 2: 1.2/2.4/4.8 Kbps

Using Matlab as a platform, the simulation of the first star downlink signal of Hongyan Constellation was carried out. According to the signal parameters, we selected the code length of 125, the code rate of 1.2 MHz and the information rate is 9.6kbps during our simulation.

3.1   Simulation of Transmitted Signal

Generation of Information Code
To build a direct expansion system, we firstly use a small number of symbols to generate an information code sequence. Let the information code rate be 9.6 kHz, the sampling frequency be 7.68 MHz, and the information code length be 20, then each information code contains 800 sampling points. The information code is shown as Fig. 3.

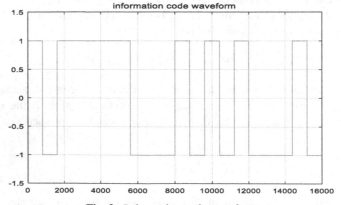

Fig. 3.   Information code waveform

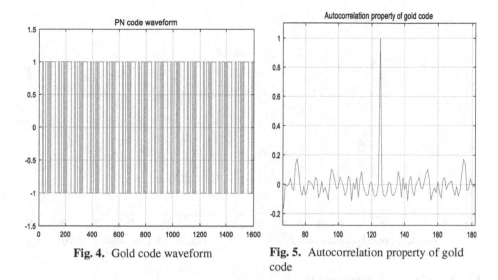

Fig. 4. Gold code waveform   **Fig. 5.** Autocorrelation property of gold code

Generation of Pseudo-Random Code Sequences

The codeword of the spreading code of Hongyan system is generated by the gold code, which is obtained by two m sequences of the same length and the same rate but of different code words.

The generator polynomial is:

$$f_1(x) = 1 + x + x^2 + x^3 + x^5 + x^6 + x^7 \tag{13}$$

$$f_2(x) = 1 + x^4 + x^5 + x^6 + x^7 \tag{14}$$

The initial phase of G1 is: [1 1 1 0 0 1 1].
The initial phase of G2 is: [0 1 0 1 1 1 0].
The pseudo-code is shown as Fig. 4. The code frequency is set to 1.2e6, so each information code contains 125 pseudo codes, that is, the generated pseudo random code sequence contains 2000 symbols.

From Fig. 5, it is clear to see that gold code has a sharp autocorrelation function to facilitate capture tracking and fast synchronization.

Spreading and Modulation

Multiply the sampled information code sequence and the pseudo-random code sequence corresponding point, the spread spectrum signal is generated in Fig. 6. Then we obtained the modulated wave shown as Fig. 7 by multiplying the corresponding point of the carrier and the spreading signal.

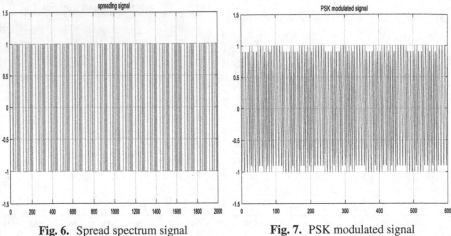

Fig. 6. Spread spectrum signal   **Fig. 7.** PSK modulated signal

3.2 Simulation of Received Signal

PSK Demodulation

Demodulation is equivalent to the inverse process of modulation, and it includes generating a local oscillator in phase with the same frequency of the carrier and then removing the high frequency component through the low pass filter, ready for the next dispreading. Demodulation signal is shown as Fig. 8.

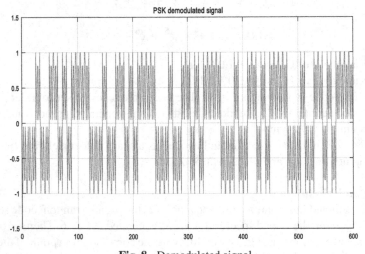

Fig. 8. Demodulated signal

Despreading

After the modulated signal is filtered by a low-pass filter, by multiplying the local pseudo-random sequence synchronized with the originator with the corresponding point of the demodulated sequence, the dispreading signal was restored. As can be seen from Fig. 9, the restored information code is basically the same as the source information code.

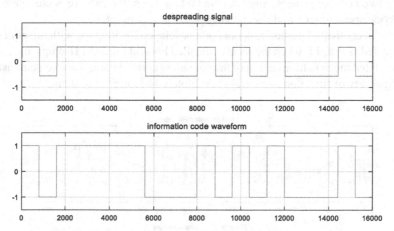

Fig. 9. Comparison of restored signal and information code

However if the noise is added, there is a big difference between the output code and the original information code, mainly because the local code inevitably has an unsynchronized phenomenon during dispreading. Figure 10 shows the comparison of dispreading signal and information code, there are a large number of burrs in the dispreading signal but the shape is roughly the same as the information code.

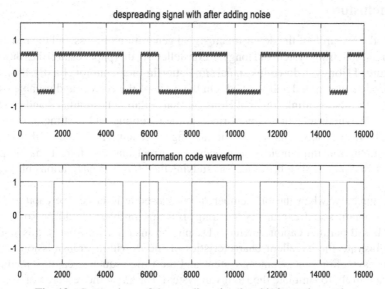

Fig. 10. Comparison of dispreading signal and information code

3.3 Time-Domain Analysis for Serial Search

In the process of code synchronization, equivalent to two codes sliding to each other, when the two code sequences coincide, the sliding stops, the capture is completed, the normal code speed enters, and the tracking phase is synchronized.

The local controlled pseudo random code is delayed by 50 chips with the gold code. As is revealed as Fig. 11, when the local controlled PN code slided 118 chips, the capture loop completed the synchronization of the spreading code. Analysis above demonstrates the applicability of time domain serial code capture to Hongyan system.

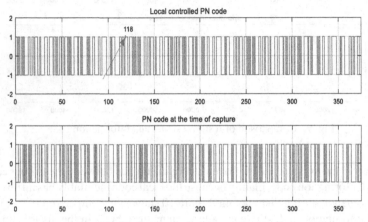

Fig. 11. The process of code synchronization

4 Conclusions

Based on the research of the downstream signal generation process and the principle of direct spread spectrum system of Hongyan constellation, this paper establishes the overall architecture of Hongyan downlink signal simulation implementation. Firstly, the pseudo-random code is generated and verified. On the basis of the correct and reliable pseudo-random code, the downlink signal of Hongyan constellation is simulated and generated, and the code synchronization is performed at the receiving end by time domain serial search. The results show that the simulation signal scheme is correct and reasonable, and the simulation implementation process is correct and credible. It has important theoretical and practical significance for studying the Hongyan navigation enhancement system.

Unfortunately, when the bit number of pseudo-code is large, the capture time of the time domain serial capture is too long. But this problem could be solved if we use FFT-based parallel capture method. Despite its insufficient aspects, this study can clearly illustrate the excellent characteristics of the downlink transmission signal of Hongyan navigation enhancement system and the time-sequence capture method can be used surefirely to simulate the Hongyan system. Based on the research of this paper, the enhancement of the Hongyan constellation combined with GNSS navigation will be summarized in our next study.

Acknowledgements. This work was supported by the National Natural Science Foundation of China (Grant No. 61771393 and 61571368), and the seed Foundation of Innovation and Creation for Graduate students in Northwestern Polytechnical University.

References

1. Abbasian, S.: Implementation of a dual-frequency GLONASS and GPS L1 C/A software receiver. J. Navig. **63**(2), 269–287 (2016)
2. Dow, J.M.: The international GNSS service in a changing landscape of global navigation satellite systems. J. Geodesy **83**, 191–198 (2009). https://doi.org/10.1007/s00190-008-0300-3
3. Borio, D.: GNSS acquisition in the presence of continuous wave interference. Electron. Syst. **46**(1), 47–60 (2016)
4. Morton, Y.T., Miller, M., Tsui, J., Lin, D., Zhou, Q.: GPS civil signal self-interference mitigation during weak signal acquisition. IEEE Trans. Signal Process. **55**(12), 5859–5863 (2007)
5. Yang, R., Xu, D.Y., Morton, Y.: An improved Adaptive Multi-Frequency GPS carrier tracking algorithm for navigation in challenging environments. In: Position Location and Navigation Symposium, pp. 899–907 (2018)
6. Navigation using the broadband low earth orbit (LEO) constellation, 20 November 2018. https://mp.weixin.qq.com/s/ijzN92JhM8f-XbVwBtlROQ
7. Li, X.: PPP for rapid precise positioning and orbit determination with zero-difference integer ambiguity fixing. J. Geophys., 833–840 (2012)
8. Lei, W.: Space-based navigation backup with single Hongyan LEO satellite and GEO satellites. Space Electron. Technol., 47–51 (2017)
9. Xu, J.: 'Hongyan' constellation shines on the mobile communication or seamlessly covers the whole world. Aerosp. China, 35–36 (2018)
10. Pany, T., Kaniuth, R., Eissfeller, B.: Deep integration of navigation solution and signal processing, pp. 13–16 (2015)
11. Yang, R.: Generalized GNSS signal carrier tracking: Part I modeling and analysis. IEEE Trans. Aerosp. Electron. Syst. **53**(4), 1781–1797 (2017)
12. Yang, R.: Generalized GNSS signal carrier tracking-Part II: optimization and implementation. IEEE Trans. Aerosp. Electron. Syst. **53**(4), 1798–1811 (2017)

An FPGA Based Reconfigurable MAC Architecture for Universal Short Range Communication Networks

Hongyu Zhang, Bo Li, Zhongjiang Yan$^{(\boxtimes)}$, Mao Yang, and Ding Wang

School of Electronics and Information, Northwestern Polytechnical University, Xi'an, China
chong@mail.nwpu.edu.cn, {libo.npu,zhjyan,yangmao,wangd}@nwpu.edu.cn

Abstract. The wireless universal short-distance network refers to a heterogeneous network that combines multiple wireless short-distance networks such as wireless local area networks and wireless personal area networks. Users can choose to use different multiple access protocols to access the network according to the characteristics of the service. This paper proposes an FPGA-based reconfigurable MAC architecture, which uses a combination of software and hardware to select the working mode of the universal MAC in the FPGA through ARM, so as to achieve fast switching between different networks. The proposed universal MAC module includes a control module based on finite state machine and a data frame transceiver module, it implements the function of switching between different networks by configuring the control module as different finite state machine of different MAC protocols. A universal MAC module combining ALOHA protocol and CSMA/CA protocol is designed and implemented in this paper. The simulation results show that the designed universal MAC module is equivalent to the CSMA/CA protocol in terms of resource utilization, and can be flexibly switching between ALOHA protocol and CSMA/CA protocol.

Keywords: Universal MAC · Reconfigurable · FPGA · Universal short range communication networks

1 Introduction

With the continuous development of network technology, wireless short-range networks gradually show its superiority. A variety of wireless network technologies such as Bluetooth, Wi-Fi, 2G, 3G, etc. greatly infiltrate people's lives, and bear more and more user traffic [1]. In the short-distance network, users have various needs, and users often need to switch networks according to different needs. Therefore, it is necessary to design a universal MAC for wireless short-range networks.

Wireless universal short-distance network refers to a heterogeneous network that combines multiple wireless short-distance networks such as wireless local

B. Li et al. (Eds.): IoTaaS 2019, LNICST 316, pp. 20–36, 2020.
https://doi.org/10.1007/978-3-030-44751-9_3

area networks and wireless personal area networks. Users can choose to use different multiple access protocols to access the network according to the characteristics of the service, which can effectively solve the above problem. So far, there have been few cases where the MAC protocol has been integrated through an integrated approach on a unified platform.

In the existing research on UMAC, Ref. [3] based on the European Omega project [2], introduced an integrated programming model of a Universal Media Access Controller (UMAC), which is capable of implementing TMAC and some InterMAC functions [3]. As shown in Fig. 1, this UMAC architecture has many features such as protocol agnosticity, high flexibility, ease of operation, scalability, and high efficiency. Compared with the traditional MAC, the flexibility is greatly improved, which provides the possibility of cross-layer optimization and function improvement of the MAC layer. At the same time, TMAC now provides customized information about link status and channel for better InterMAC functionality.

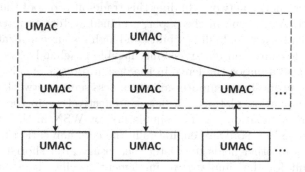

Fig. 1. Omega node architecture [4].

However, the establishment of the UMAC model in this article is implemented in Click using software programming language, which brings the problem of low efficiency.

In the case of program analysis and performance evaluation of the MAC protocol, the theoretical model is mathematically easy to handle, but usually lacks physical layer accuracy. The actual evaluation protocol can be achieved under actual PHY layer conditions through experimental prototyping and testing [5]. There are two types of experimental platforms based on commercial NICs and hardware-based customizations that can implement the actual testing of the MAC protocol, but there exist many problems such as design difficulty and high cost. The OpenMAC platform proposed in Ref. [3] is implemented on a hardware platform based on reconfigurable field programmable gate array (FPGA). The MAC protocol designed by C++ simplifies the prototyping process, thereby reducing the burden of the protocol designer on the hardware and timing. At the same time, the OpenMAC platform introduces a hardware/software partitioning concept based on a shared memory architecture, which simplifies the task, and reduces software latency by concentrating packet processing load on the HW MAC and preventing SW MAC to access to large data payloads. Therefore, in addition to the flexibility and reconfigurability brought by the hardware, the OpenMAC platform simplifies and accelerates the process of implementing the MAC protocol. The concept of hardware and software partitioning has great significance for the design of UMAC.

Compared with the rapid development of mobile device performance, the development of battery capacity is much slower. The energy consumption of the terminal needs to be solved [6]. The Green-T project in Ref. [4] optimizes energy consumption problem by effectively utilizing multiple radio interfaces to solve energy efficiency problems. This provides a reference for the idea of switching between multiple MAC protocols. At the same time, the implementation of the Green-T project still faces multiple challenges. For example, there is a need to balance the trade-off between performance and energy savings. For vertical switching scenarios, if the terminal is able to increase the investment when searching for available networks, then the terminal will have the opportunity to switch to a lower energy network, finding this trade-off is one of the goals of the Green-T project. At the end of the paper, a unified system architecture is proposed. It is hoped to achieve high flexibility and high resource utilization through OpenMAC architecture and energy-saving, flexible baseband physical interface design. This is also a major challenge in the design process of this paper.

Reference [5] proposes a computer-aided wireless sensor network (WSN) evaluation and optimization platform, which can effectively help the simulator to perform network simulation [7]. The simulators for WSN in the existing work are mainly designed for software engineers in the communication field. It is difficult for experts in other fields to master their usage after short-term training, and it is difficult for the simulator to implement specific site simulation. The middleware designed in the article is independent of the specific target architecture. It solves the above problem by abstracting objects in the WSN. The operator only needs to define the characteristics and network of the node in the user interface, then the middleware can realize the process of automatic modeling, data conversion, simulator implementation and network optimization. With this middleware, anyone can easily perform network simulations.

This paper proposes an FPGA-based reconfigurable MAC architecture that uses hardware and software to encapsulate several MAC protocols (Multiple Access Protocols) in reconfigurable field-programmable gate arrays (FPGA). In the development board, the choice of these protocols is written into ARM using a software programming language. This enables flexible use of multiple protocols, and is suitable for coping with the increasing heterogeneity of the network. At the same time, this architecture has the characteristics of high flexibility, low resource consumption rate, and high speed compared to other existing projects.

This paper is divided into five chapters. The first chapter briefly introduces the research content of this paper from research background, main ideas and existing related work. The second chapter specifically designs the FPGA-based reconfigurable MAC architecture proposed in this paper. The third chapter details the design and implementation steps of the universal MAC module based on ALOHA protocol and CSMA/CA protocol, and analyzes its simulation results and performance in all aspects in the fourth chapter. The fifth chapter looks forward to the follow-up research of this article.

2 FPGA-Based Reconfigurable MAC Architecture

2.1 FPGA-Based Reconfigurable MAC Overall Architecture

The following figure shows the integrated programming model of FPGA-based reconfigurable MAC architecture (UMAC) proposed in this paper (Fig. 2).

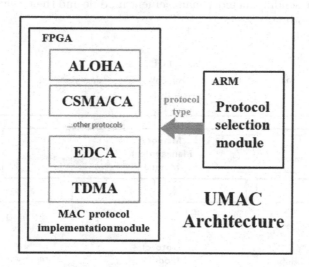

Fig. 2. UMAC Architecture.

The UMAC model is mainly divided into two parts: the protocol selection module and the protocol storage module.

(1) UMAC protocol selection module: the module is recorded into the ARM processor using software programming. The communication protocol is selected according to specific rules, and the selected protocol type is transmitted to the protocol storage module.
(2) UMAC protocol implementation module: this module is used to store the implementation flow of multiple communication protocols. The implementation of the protocol storage module is accomplished by encapsulating several MAC protocols (Multiple Access Protocols) in FPGA board using a hardware programming language.

This paper mainly discusses the UMAC protocol implementation module in the UMAC model.

2.2   UMAC Protocol Implementation Module

Figure 3 shows the system architecture of the MAC layer networking protocol module. The MAC layer networking protocol module is mainly divided into two parts: the MAC protocol module and the memory management module. The MAC protocol module mainly implements the logic function of the MAC protocol. The memory management module buffers and transmits data according to the requirements of the MAC protocol, and decides whether to send the data to the data group frame sending module or the upper layer module. In addition, the memory management module also supports for retransmission of completed data. The MAC protocol module is mainly divided into the sending module and the receiving module, and the memory management module is also divided into the sending memory management module and the receiving memory management module.

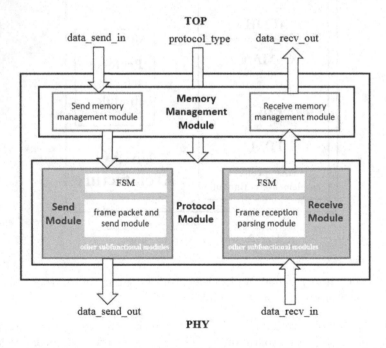

Fig. 3. System architecture of the MAC layer network protocol module.

After data arriving from the upper layer, it first enters the sending memory management module for buffering, and then transmits to the sending module of the MAC protocol with the protocol type signal transmitted by the protocol selection module. The transmitting finite state machine control module in the sending module schedules the corresponding multiple function modules to cooperate according to the protocol type signal, and finally completes data encapsulation and sends the data to the PHY layer.

After the data of the PHY layer enters the receiving module of the MAC protocol, the receiving finite state machine control module in the receiving module also cooperates according to the protocol type signal to coordinate the corresponding multiple function modules to work together, completes the receiving and parsing of the data and transmits it to the receiving memory management module for buffering, then finally outputs to the upper layer.

3   Design and Implementation of General MAC Module Based on ALOHA Protocol and CSMA/CA Protocol

In the design of the UMAC protocol implementation module, this paper cites the FPGA design and implementation method of complex communication system based on flow chart proposed in Ref. [7], which is in response to the problem that existing communication protocol and algorithm design is very complicated and lack of general FPGA design and implementation method [8]. FPGA design and implementation methods based on flow chart significantly reduce FPGA development time. The method is mainly divided into the following three parts. Firstly, a modular architecture for control and data phase separation of FPGA is designed [9, 10]. Secondly, a flow chart based finite state machine design method is proposed. Finally, a method for packaging a finite state machine into a reusable IP core in FPGA is designed. According to this flowchart-based FPGA design method, this paper takes the simple UMAC protocol implementation module including ALOHA protocol and CSMA/CA protocol as an example to verify and analyze the performance of the UMAC model envisaged in this paper.

First of all, according to the workflow of ALOHA protocol and CSMA/CA protocol, this paper draws its flow chart and divides the state, and then determines its state transition diagram.

3.1   ALOHA Protocol

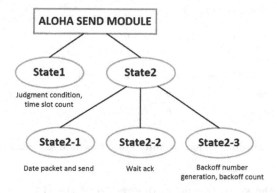

Fig. 4. ALOHA send module tree.

Sending Module. According to the workflow of the ALOHA sending module, combined with the method described in Ref. [7], the tree diagram of the ALOHA protocol sending module shown in Fig. 4 can be obtained. The single functional module consists of five parts:

1. A fixed length data frame encapsulation transmitting module;
2. Time slot division counting module;
3. Random backoff generation counting module;
4. ACK sending module;
5. NAK sending module;

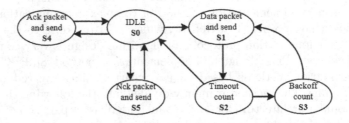

Fig. 5. ALOHA send module main control module finite state machine.

According to the transmission flow chart and the module tree diagram, the state machine transition diagram of the finite state machine as shown in Fig. 5 can be further drawn. The slot division counting module and the data buffer module are not shown in the figure, but should be added in the actual process to control data transmission and data frame buffering. The transition conditions between states are shown in the transition matrix shown in the figure below (Fig. 6).

$$
\begin{pmatrix}
0 & \text{There is data to send and} & 0 & 0 & \text{Ack send} & \text{Nck send} \\
 & \text{new time slot start} & & & \text{enable coming} & \text{enable coming} \\
0 & 0 & \text{Data send over} & 0 & 0 & 0 \\
\text{Ack coming} & 0 & 0 & \text{Count timeout} & 0 & 0 \\
 & & & \text{or nck coming} & & \\
0 & \text{Backoff over} & 0 & 0 & 0 & 0 \\
\text{Ack send over} & 0 & 0 & 0 & 0 & 0 \\
\text{Nck send over} & 0 & 0 & 0 & 0 & 0
\end{pmatrix}
$$

Fig. 6. ALOHA transmitter module finite state machine state transition matrix.

According to the state transition diagram and the state transition matrix, the state machine control module [2] of the ALOHA transmitting module and other sub-function modules can be determined.

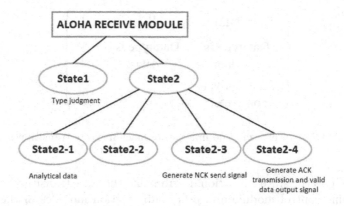

Fig. 7. ALOHA receive module tree.

Receiving Module. In the same way, according to the workflow of the ALOHA receiving module, combined with the method described in Ref. [7], the tree diagram of the ALOHA protocol receiving module shown in Fig. 7 can be obtained. The functional module is composed of two parts:

1. Data type judgment;
2. Data frame parsing module;

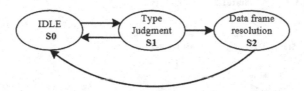

Fig. 8. Receive module main control module finite state machine.

A finite state machine state transition diagram as shown in Fig. 8 can be further drawn according to the reception flow chart and the state division tree diagram. The data cache module is not shown in the figure, but it should be added in the actual process. The transition conditions between states are shown in the transition matrix shown in the figure below (Fig. 9).

$$\begin{pmatrix} \text{Data coming} & 0 & 0 \\ \text{Datatype is} & \text{Datatype is} & 0 \\ \text{not data} & \text{data} & \\ \text{Data analysis} & 0 & 0 \\ \text{completed} & & \end{pmatrix}$$

Fig. 9. ALOHA receive module finite state machine state transition matrix.

According to the state transition diagram and the state transition matrix, the state machine control module and other sub-function modules of the ALOHA receiving module can be determined.

3.2   CSMA/CA Protocol

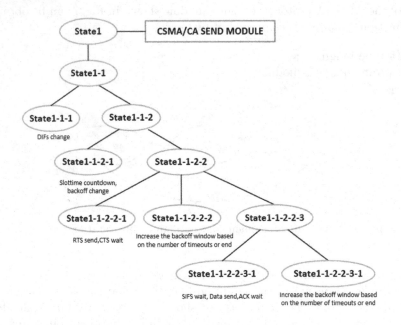

Fig. 10. CSMA/CA send module tree.

Sending Module. Similarly, according to the workflow of the CSMA/CA transmission module, combined with the method described in Ref. [7], the tree diagram of the CSMA/CA protocol transmission module shown in Fig. 10 can be obtained.

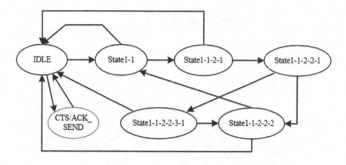

Fig. 11. CSMA/CA send module main control module finite state machine.

According to the transmission flow chart and the module tree diagram, the finite state machine state transition diagram shown in Fig. 11 can be further drawn. The transition conditions between states are shown in the transition matrix shown in the figure below (Fig. 12).

$$
\begin{pmatrix}
0 & \begin{matrix}\text{There is data to send and} \\ \text{channel is idle}\end{matrix} & 0 & 0 & 0 & 0 & \begin{matrix}\text{CTS/RTS need} \\ \text{to be send}\end{matrix} \\
\text{Channel is busy} & 0 & \text{DIFS=0} & 0 & 0 & 0 & 0 \\
\text{Channel is busy} & 0 & 0 & \text{BACKOFF=0} & 0 & 0 & 0 \\
0 & 0 & 0 & 0 & \text{time out} & \text{CTS receives right} & 0 \\
\begin{matrix}\text{The number of timeouts} \\ \text{exceeds the maximum}\end{matrix} & 0 & 0 & 0 & 0 & 0 & 0 \\
\text{Ack receive right} & 0 & 0 & 0 & \text{time out} & 0 & 0 \\
\text{CTS/ACK send over} & 0 & 0 & 0 & 0 & 0 & 0
\end{pmatrix}
$$

Fig. 12. CSMA/CA transmitter module finite state machine state transition matrix.

According to the state transition diagram and the state transition matrix, the state machine control module and other sub-function modules of the CSMA/CA transmission module can be determined.

Receiving Module. Similarly, the receiving module tree diagram shown in Fig. 13 can be made according to the working process of the receiving module, and then the state transition diagram is made. As shown in Fig. 14, the jumping conditions between the states are showed in state transition matrix of Fig. 15.

According to the state transition diagram and the state transition matrix, the state machine control module and other sub-function modules of the CSMA/CA receiving module can be determined.

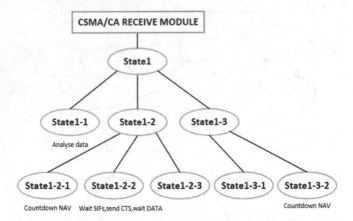

Fig. 13. CSMA/CA receive module tree.

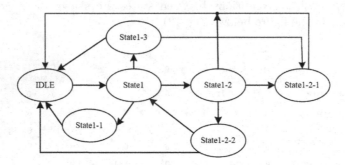

Fig. 14. Receive module main control module finite state machine.

$$
\begin{pmatrix}
\text{Frame is coming} & 0 & 0 & 0 & 0 & 0 & 0 & 0 \\
0 & 0 & 0 & 0 & 0 & \text{type is data} & 0 & \text{type is rts} & \begin{smallmatrix}\text{type is}\\ \text{cts/ack}\end{smallmatrix} \\
\text{Nav=0} & 0 & 0 & 0 & 0 & 0 & 0 & 0 & 0 \\
0 & 0 & 0 & 0 & \text{Sifs wait over} & 0 & 0 & 0 & 0 \\
\text{Data wait over} & \text{Data is coming} & 0 & 0 & 0 & 0 & 0 & 0 & 0 \\
0 & 0 & 0 & 0 & 0 & \begin{smallmatrix}\text{data receive over}\\ \text{and data is valid}\end{smallmatrix} & 0 & 0 \\
0 & 0 & 0 & 0 & 0 & 0 & 0 & 0 & 0 \\
\begin{smallmatrix}\text{Rts receive over and}\\ \text{rts is valid}\end{smallmatrix} & 0 & \begin{smallmatrix}\text{rts is valid and send}\\ \text{to this node}\end{smallmatrix} & \begin{smallmatrix}\text{rts is valid but not}\\ \text{send to this node}\end{smallmatrix} & 0 & 0 & 0 & 0 & 0 \\
\begin{smallmatrix}\text{cts/ack receive over}\\ \text{and rts/ack is valid}\end{smallmatrix} & 0 & \begin{smallmatrix}\text{cts/ack receive over}\\ \text{but not rts/ack is valid}\end{smallmatrix} & 0 & 0 & 0 & 0 & 0 & 0
\end{pmatrix}
$$

Fig. 15. Receive module finite state machine state transition matrix.

3.3   UMAC Protocol Implementation Module Based on ALOHA Protocol and CSMA/CA Protocol

The expected function of the UMAC protocol implementation module based on ALOHA protocol and CSMA/CA protocol designed in this paper is: the current working protocol can be selected according to the input protocol type signal. If the protocol type is 0, the ALOHA protocol is used for data interaction. When the protocol type is 1, the CSMA/CA protocol is used for data interaction. The overall workflow of the module is shown in Fig. 16.

After the memory management module transmits the data and the protocol type signal to the protocol module, it first enters the state machine control module of the sending module. The module selects a corresponding protocol transmission state machine according to the protocol type signal, and connects the state and state transition conditions included in the protocol to the state machine IP core, so that the involved sub-module completes the data transmission according to the protocol.

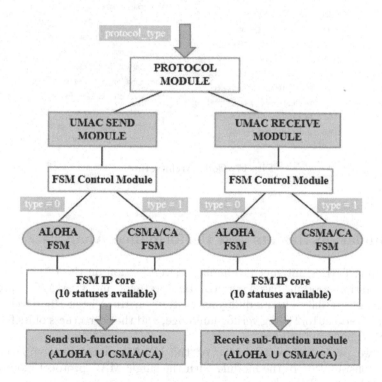

Fig. 16. UMAC Protocol Architecture.

Similarly, when data arrives, the memory management module transmits the data and protocol type signals that need to be received to the protocol module, and then first enters the state machine control module of the receiving module. The module selects a corresponding protocol receiving state machine according to the protocol type signal, and connects the state and state transition conditions included in the protocol to the state machine IP core, so that the involved sub-module completes the data reception according to the protocol.

The overall module code architecture is shown in Fig. 17, where the sub-function module section contains all the sub-function modules of a single ALOHA project and CSMA/CA project.

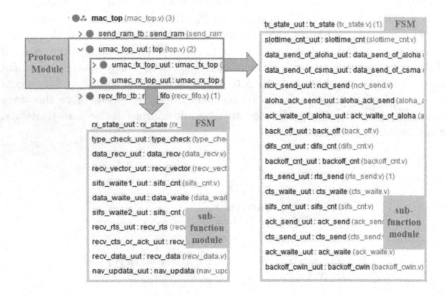

Fig. 17. Code Architecture.

4   Simulation Results and Performance Analysis

This chapter carries out specific simulation verification on the UMAC protocol implementation module based on ALOHA protocol and CSMA/CA protocol designed in Sect. 3.3. The module was written on the Virtex-707 development board of Vivado 2015.2 using verilog language, and the correctness of its function was verified by simulation test.

Now we prove the performance of the UMAC model by comparing the resource consumption of the module with the single MAC protocol module and the UMAC protocol.

By analyzing the resource consumption of the after comprehensive designed ALOHA project that implements the ALOHA protocol, the resource utilization table shown in the following figure can be obtained (Fig. 18).

Resource	Utilization	Available	Utilization %
Slice LUTs	844	303600	0.28
Slice Registers	533	607200	0.09
Memory	3	1030	0.29
IO	189	700	27.00
Clocking	1	32	3.12

Fig. 18. Resource Utilization Percentage of ALOHA.

Similarly, the resource consumption analysis of the after comprehensive designed CSMA/CA project can be obtained as shown in Fig. 19.

The resource utilization of the UMAC protocol implementation module designed and implemented in this paper is shown in Fig. 20.

Thus, we can get a comparison of resource utilization as shown in the Fig. 21.

By comparing the resource consumption rates of various aspects of ALOHA project, CSMA/CA project and UMAC protocol in the comparison table, it can be seen that although the consumption rate of the UMAC protocol implementation module in Slice LUTs is twice that of the ALOHA project, it is slightly lower than that of the CSMA/CA project. The situation of Slice Registers is similar. Although the UMAC protocol implementation module is slightly higher than the ALOHA project, it is still lower than the CSMA/CA project. At the same time, the consumption of the UMAC protocol implementation module in IO is slightly higher than that of the ALOHA and CSMA/CA projects, because

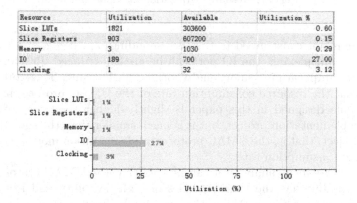

Resource	Utilization	Available	Utilization %
Slice LUTs	1821	303600	0.60
Slice Registers	903	607200	0.15
Memory	3	1030	0.29
IO	189	700	27.00
Clocking	1	32	3.12

Fig. 19. Resource Utilization Percentage of CSMA/CA.

Summary

Resource	Utilization	Available	Utilization %
Slice LUTs	2396	303600	0.79
Slice Registers	1083	607200	0.18
Memory	3	1030	0.29
IO	222	700	31.71
Clocking	1	32	3.12

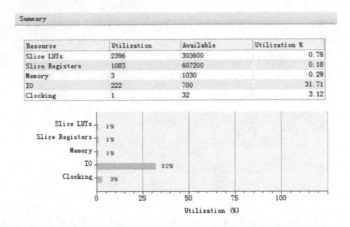

Fig. 20. Resource Utilization Percentage of UMAC.

Utilization (%)	ALOHA Project	CSMA/CA Project	UMAC Protocol implementation module
Slice LUTs	0.28	0.60	0.79
Slice Registers	0.09	0.15	0.18
Memory	0.29	0.29	0.29
IO	27	27	31.71
Clocking	3.12	3.12	3.12

Fig. 21. Resource Utilization Comparison.

the IO here is not constrained to the corresponding pin. If it is constrained to the pins by multiplexing, the IO port can be greatly reduced. In addition, the resource consumption in Memory and Clocking is the same. Therefore, we can conclude that the resource consumption rate of the UMAC protocol implementation module designed in this paper is slightly higher than that of a single protocol implementation project, but it is much smaller than the sum of a single protocol project, that is, the UMAC protocol implementation module can reduce the resource consumption rate.

Based on the above analysis, it can be seen that the UMAC protocol implementation module has the characteristics of high flexibility and low resource consumption rate while realizing the switchable functions of ALOHA and CSMA/CA protocols. This paper takes the simple UMAC protocol implementation module including ALOHA protocol and CSMA/CA protocol as an example to verify the performance of the UMAC model envisaged in this paper. If the state machine can be deeply integrated with multiple protocols, more inter-protocol switching can be achieved, which greatly reduces the resource consumption rate. This will be the future direction of this paper.

5 Conclusion

In this paper, an FPGA-based reconfigurable MAC architecture is proposed for network heterogeneity. The combination of software and hardware is adopted to select the working mode of the general MAC in the FPGA through ARM, so as to achieve fast switching between different networks. In order to verify the feasibility of the above ideas, this paper designs and implements a general MAC protocol implementation module combining ALOHA protocol and CSMA/CA protocol, which can quickly switch between ALOHA protocol and CSMA/CA protocol by controlling an external signal. The simulation results show that the module is equivalent to the CSMA/CA protocol in terms of resource utilization, which indicates that the module has the characteristics of high flexibility, high speed and low resource consumption rate.

Acknowledgement. This work was supported in part by the National Natural Science Foundations of CHINA (Grant No.61771392, 61771390, 61871322, 61501373 and 61271279), the National Science and Technology Major Project (Grant No. 2015ZX03002006-004 and 2016ZX03001018-004), and Science and Technology on Avionics Integration Laboratory (Grant No. 20185553035).

References

1. O'Brien, D.C., et al.: Home access networks using optical wireless transmission. In: IEEE International Symposium on Personal (2008)
2. Javaudin, J., Bellec, M., Varoutas, D., Suraci, V.: Omega ICT project: towards convergent gigabit home networks. In: 2008 IEEE 19th International Symposium on Personal, Indoor and Mobile Radio Communications, pp. 1–5, September 2008
3. Loeb, H., Liß, C., Rckert, U., Sauer, C.: UMAC a universal MAC architecture for heterogeneous home networks. In: 2009 International Conference on Ultra Modern Telecommunications Workshops, pp. 1–6, October 2009
4. Gallego, F.V., Alonso-Zarate, J., Liss, C., Verikoukis, C.: OpenMAC: a new reconfigurable experimental platform for energy-efficient medium access control protocols. IET Sci. Meas. Technol. **6**(3), 139–148 (2012)
5. Antonopoulos, A., et al.: Green-T: enabling techniques for energy efficient mobile terminals. In: 2012 IEEE 17th International Workshop on Computer Aided Modeling and Design of Communication Links and Networks (CAMAD), pp. 206–210, September 2012
6. Liang, Y., Ying, R., Liu, P.: Efficient middleware for network evaluation and optimization in wireless sensor network design. In: 2013 IEEE International Symposium on Circuits and Systems (ISCAS 2013), pp. 1749–1752, May 2013

7. Hangchao, J.: Design and implementation of a hybrid frequency hopping multiple access protocol for wireless ad hoc network. Master's thesis, Northwestern Polytechnical University (2018)
8. Burgun, L., Dictus, N., Lopes, E.P., Sarwary, C.: A unified approach for FSM synthesis on FPGA architectures. In: Proceedings of Twentieth Euromicro Conference. System Architecture and Integration, pp. 660–668, September 1994
9. Mihhailov, D., Sudnitson, A., Tarletski, K.: Web-based tool for FSM encoding targeting low-power FPGA implementation. In: International Conference on Microelectronics (2010)
10. Sudnitson, A., Mihhailov, D., Kruus, M.: Advanced topics of FSM design using FPGA educational boards and web-based tools. In: 2010 East-West Design Test Symposium (EWDTS), pp. 514–517, September 2010

Research on Unambiguous Acquisition of BOC Modulated Navigation Signal

Chunyang Liu$^{(\boxtimes)}$, Hongwei Zhao, and Li Li

School of Electronics and Information, Northwestern Polytechnical University,
Xi'an, China
lcy_nwpu@126.com

Abstract. BOC (Binary-Offset-Carrier) modulation is widely used in the new generation of satellite navigation system. It has been used in GPS, Galileo and Bei-Dou systems. Compared with the traditional BPSK (Binary Phase Shift Keying) modulation, it has sharper correlation characteristics and stronger anti-multipath performance. The spectrum relocation caused by its splitting frequency can effectively solve the current frequency band congestion problem. But BOC modulation has multiple peak characteristics in the time domain, and the existence of sub-peak increases the difficulty of acquisition. Adding a pseudo-code correlation branch to the original BOC code correlation branch by using autocorrelation side-peak cancellation technique (ASPeCT) can effectively weaken the sub-peak of the correlation function and avoid wrong acquisition. This paper applies this ASPeCT acquisition algorithm to the parallel pseudo-random code FFT acquisition strategy to acquire the BeiDou-3 navigation signals. And the research object is the BOC (1,1) signal of the pilot component in BeiDou-3. Experimental results show that the method adopted in this paper can ensure the acquisition time and the acquisition accuracy reaches half a chip.

Keywords: BeiDou-3 · ASPeCT · FFT · Unambiguous acquisition

1 Introduction

China's BeiDou-3 satellite navigation system has released a modern civilian GNSS signal called B1C [1]. Compared to the satellite signal of BDS-2, the B1C signal of BDS-3 has been changed from the signal structure, encoding mode and navigation message structure. It introduces the pilot signal, secondary coding, BOC modulation, LDPC encoding and B - CNAV1 navigation message structure, etc. On the one hand, these changes improve signal performance, such as anti-multipath, signal acquisition and tracking accuracy, etc. But on the other hand, they also bring a series of problems, which put forward new requirements for signal acquisition technology of receivers, such as dealing with larger data streams, solving the problem of multi-peak autocorrelation function caused by secondary coding and BOC modulation.

The BOC (1,1) signal in the pilot component of BDS-3 is studied in this paper. The spread spectrum code used here is Weil code, whose code period is 10230 and lasts for

B. Li et al. (Eds.): IoTaaS 2019, LNICST 316, pp. 37–44, 2020.
https://doi.org/10.1007/978-3-030-44751-9_4

10 ms. Such a long code period will make the amount of data to be processed very large during the acquisition process. The acquisition technique based on FFT is recognized to be computationally efficient. However, the price of the long FFT arithmetic module is very high, which limits the development of the actual receiver. When the sampling rate of 40 MHz is adopted in the modern navigation receiver, in order to complete the operation of a cycle, FFT operation must be performed on the data of more than 400,000 points, which cannot be realized by cheap FPGA resources selected by civilian receivers.

Secondly, although the peak value of the autocorrelation function of BOC modulated signal is more sharp than that of BPSK signal, it has multi-peak autocorrelation function, which can lead to the receiver to make mistakes in the acquisition procedure, resulting in a large error in the code phase estimation and difficulty getting into the tracking state. In the process of tracking phase, the tracking loop will be mistakenly locked to the side peak, which will lead to a large tracking error and cause the ambiguity of synchronous reception. Therefore, it is necessary to improve the search resolution as much as possible in order to avoid the false locking in the acquisition and tracking procedure.

Aiming at these two problems, this paper adopts the ASPeCT acquisition algorithm based on the parallel pseudo-random code FFT acquisition strategy. In the process of acquisition, firstly, partial accumulation of input data is used to reduce the rate of input data through average correlation technique [2, 3], and then ASPeCT algorithm [4] is used to realize the unambiguous acquisition of BOC (1,1) signal.

2   B1C Signal Structure

BOC modulation signal is obtained by multiplication of pseudo-random code and sub-carrier. It can be expressed as BOC (fs, fc), where fs is the ratio of rate between the carrier frequency and reference frequency, fc is the ratio of rate between pseudo random code and reference frequency. During modulation, the navigation data is firstly multiplied by pseudo random code, and then through subcarrier modulation, the signal is finally multiplied by the high frequency carrier signal, and the output is the satellite signal. The general expression of BOC modulation signal is:

$$s(t) = e^{-i\theta} \sum_k a_k \mu_{nT}(t - knT - t_0)c_T(t - t_0) \tag{1}$$

Where a_k is the navigation data, μ_{nT} is the satellite PRN code, c_T is the BOC sub-carrier, t_0 and θ is the time and phase delay.

We can obtain the autocorrelation function of BOC modulated signal by numerical method. Figure 1 shows its autocorrelation function compared with that of BPSK modulated signal. We can see it clearly that BOC modulation has multiple peak characteristics.

The carrier frequency of B1C signal which we studied in this paper is 1575.42 MHz, and it shares the frequency band with GPS L1 and Galileo E1, with a bandwidth of 32.736 MHz. A modern signal structure with orthogonal data and pilot frequency is adopted. The data component is generated by navigation message and ranging code through sub-carrier modulation, and sin-BOC (1, 1) modulation is adopted. The pilot component is generated by the ranging code via subcarrier modulation using QMBOC

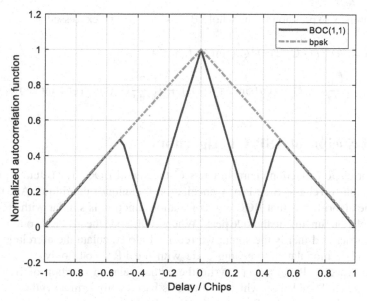

Fig. 1. BPSK and BOC (1,1) normalized autocorrelation function

(6,1,4/33) modulation. The power ratio between the data component and the pilot component is 1:3, and the designers place emphasis on the pilot component of signal power, which conforms to the design principle that the demodulation performance is sufficient, and the higher the ranging accuracy, the better, which is conducive to improving the overall performance of B1C signal.

The B1C signal can be written as a complex form:

$$S_{B1C}(t) = S_d(t) + jS_p(t) \tag{2}$$

Where, $S_d(t)$ is the data component of B1C signal, and $S_p(t)$ is the pilot component.

The mathematical expressions of data component and pilot component are:

$$S_d(t) = \frac{1}{2}D_d(t) \cdot C_d(t) \cdot sc_d(t) \tag{3}$$

$$S_p(t) = \frac{\sqrt{3}}{2}C_p(t) \cdot sc_p(t) \tag{4}$$

For the data component, due to the use of BOC (1,1) modulation, the sub-carrier is:

$$sc_d(t) = sign(\sin(2\pi f_{sc1})t) \tag{5}$$

For the pilot component, QMBOC (6,1,4/33) modulation is adopted, and its sub-carrier is composed of BOC (1,1) and BOC (6,1), with mutually orthogonal phase and power ratio of 29:4:

$$sc_p(t) = \sqrt{\frac{29}{33}}sign(\sin(2\pi f_{sc1})t) - j\sqrt{\frac{4}{33}}sign(\sin(2\pi f_{sc2})t) \tag{6}$$

The complex expression of the whole B1C signal can be expressed as:

$$S_{B1C}(t) = \frac{1}{2}D_d(t) \cdot C_d(t) \cdot sign(\sin(2\pi f_{sc1})t) +$$

$$\sqrt{\frac{1}{11}}C_p(t) \cdot sign(\sin(2\pi f_{sc2})t) + j\sqrt{\frac{29}{44}}C_p(t) \cdot sign(\sin(2\pi f_{sc1})t) \quad (7)$$

3   The Principle of ASPeCT Algorithm

For autocorrelation function characteristics of the signal BOC (1, 1), Julien proposed ASPeCT (Autocorrelation Side-Peak Cancellation Technique) algorithm1. And the principle of the algorithm is that BOC autocorrelation function is similar with BOC/PRN cross-correlation function in the side peak. Where BOC code means PRN code × square-wave subcarrier and that is the signal we received. To calculate the correlation of the sine-BOC (1,1) modulated spreading code with the PRN code only. And we write this consequence as $R_{BOC/PRN}(\tau)$, write the autocorrelation function of BOC signal as $R_{BOC/BOC}(\tau)$. The idea on which ASPeCT is based is to form a synthesized correlation function by subtracting $R_{BOC/PRN}^2(\tau)$ from $R_{BOC/BOC}^2(\tau)$ to remove the undesired side peaks. The mathematical expression of ASPeCT method is as follows:

$$R_{ASPeCT} = R_{BOC/BOC}^2(\tau) - \beta R_{BOC/PRN}^2(\tau) \quad (8)$$

Where β is a coefficient in the combination of the two squared correlation functions in order to eliminate any small remaining peak caused by a narrow front-end filter. This is successfully shown in Fig. 2.

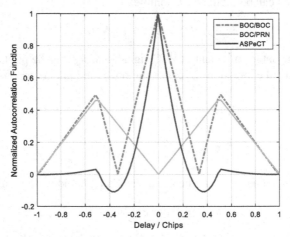

Fig. 2. Sine-BOC (1,1)/sine-BOC (1,1), sine-BOC (1,1)/PRN squared normalized correlation functions and ASPeCT modified correlation function

Figure 2 shows the output of the ASPeCT correlator of BOC (1,1) modulated signal. It can be seen that the side peak is completely reduced, and the new negative peak does not bring ambiguity. Figure 3 shows ASPeCT discriminator output for a sine-BOC (1,1) signal. It also shows the traditional BOC discriminator output using the same early-late discriminator. We can see the error locking point disappears, and the phase discriminator gain increases slightly, and the noise performance improves.

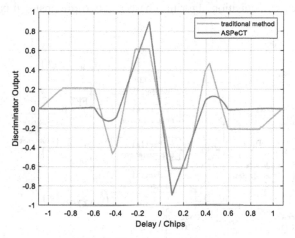

Fig. 3. Discriminator output

Figure 4 shows the multipath-induced error envelope for traditional sine-BOC (1,1) tracking, as well as for ASPeCT, in which the spacing of early and late correlators is 0.1 chip. ASPeCT algorithm reduces the envelope amplitude of multipath error and minimizes the maximum delay affected by multipath signals, thus improving the anti-multipath performance. The ASPeCT algorithm not only removes the ambiguity of BOC (1,1) signals, but also further improves the acquisition accuracy and anti-multipath performance.

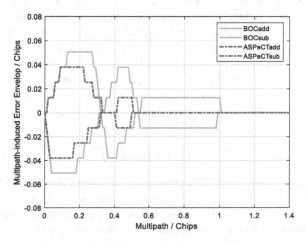

Fig. 4. Multipath-induced error envelope

4 Parallel Code Phase Search Acquisition Algorithm Based on FFT

ASPeCT algorithm has been shown to be reliably unambiguous for BOC (1,1) signal acquisition. Therefore, next, ASPeCT algorithm is applied to the traditional acquisition algorithm to realize the unambiguous acquisition of BOC signal. Figure 5 is the flow chart of the ASPeCT acquisition algorithm based on two-dimensional parallel and fast search [5].

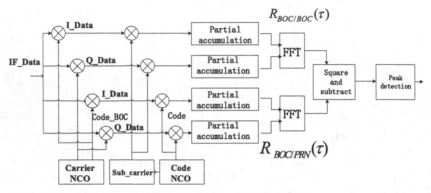

Fig. 5. The flow chart of the ASPeCT acquisition algorithm based on two-dimensional parallel and fast search

Firstly, the BOC signal received was multiplied with the sines and cosines of the local carrier to generate the zero-IF signals, written as I_Data and Q_Data. And then they were correlated with the locally generated pseudo-code sequence, Code without sub-carrier and Code_BOC modulated by the sub-carrier. Since the sampling frequency in the simulation is 40 MHz and the number of sampling points in a pseudo-code period is about 400,000, the time and resources required to directly carry out FFT will be very large, so before carrying out FFT, we can conduct 40 times reduction sampling and partial accumulation to reduce the data volume. After FFT, square the transformation results of the two relevant branches and subtract $R^2_{BOC/PRN}(\tau)$ from $R^2_{BOC/BOC}(\tau)$ to generate the detection value. If there is a peak value, the acquisition is successful. If there is no peak value, change the local code phase and repeat the above steps until the acquisition is successful. In the FPGA design, we can add more correlator resources to search multiple code phases at one time in the code phase dimension.

In the operation of FFT, frequency resolution is as follows:

$$\Delta f = \frac{1}{N\_FFT * X * T_S} \tag{9}$$

Where, N_FFT is the points of FFT, X is the length of partial accumulated data, and T_S is the time length of a pseudo-code. In this matlab simulation, the expected doppler frequency search range is −50–50 kHz. According to BeiDou Navigation Satellite System Signal In Space Interface Control Document [1], symbol rate Rb of BeiDou-3 navigation signal is 100 sps, pseudo-code period N is 10230, pseudo-code rate Rc is $1.023 * 10^6$

Mbps, pseudo-code period Tc equals 1/Rc, so the range of each FFT point which can be searched is

$$\frac{1}{N \cdot T_C} = R_b = 100 \text{ Hz} \tag{10}$$

Therefore, the number of FFT points, N_FFT, is 100 k/100=1000. To facilitate FFT operation, take 1024 points. Then, the number of partial accumulators, X=N/N_FFT, and take X=10.

The three-dimensional acquisition of BOC (1,1) using ASPeCT algorithm is shown in the figures. Figure 6 shows the acquisition result of the traditional approach when

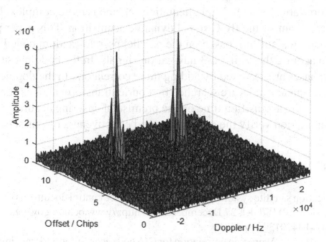

Fig. 6. The acquisition result of the traditional algorithm

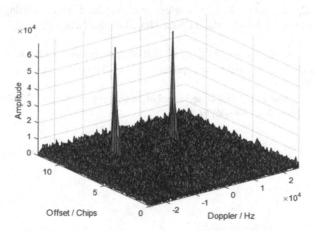

Fig. 7. The acquisition result of the ASPeCT algorithm

BOC (1,1) code phase offset is 8.5 chips, doppler frequency shift is 10 kHz, and signal-to-noise ratio is –21 dB. Figure 7 shows the acquisition result of the ASPeCT algorithm under the same conditions.

It can be seen from the figure that the ASPeCT algorithm can well eliminate the side peak, and ensure that the chip search accuracy reaches half a chip and the frequency resolution reaches 100 Hz.

5   Conclusion

In order to eliminate the side peak of BOC modulation signal, avoid the wrong acquisition, the ASPeCT algorithm, on the basis of the original BOC code related branch, adds a pseudo code correlation branch. Implementation scheme is more complex. Each search only one unit can't satisfy the BOC signal dynamic acquisition. This paper presents the ASPeCT acquisition algorithm based on the parallel pseudo-random code FFT acquisition strategy to acquire the BeiDou-3 navigation signals. In the code phase dimension, multiple code phases are searched by adding more correlators. In the doppler frequency dimension, all frequency units are searched by Fourier transform at one time, which significantly reduces the acquisition time on the premise of ensuring accuracy. Theoretical analysis and simulation verify the correctness and effectiveness of this scheme.

References

1. BeiDou navigation satellite system signal in space interface control document open service signal B1C (Version 1.0) [S/OL], 27 December 2017. http://www.beidou.gov.cn/xt/gfxz/201712/P020171226741342013031.pdf
2. Starzyk, J.A., Zhu, Z.: Averaging correlation for C/A code acquisition and tracking in frequency domain. In: Proceedings of the 44th IEEE 2001 Midwest Symposium on Circuits and Systems. MWSCAS 2001 (2001)
3. Yan, S., Ding, C.: A novel engineering implementation technique for acquiring B1C signal in the BeiDou-3 receiver. GNSS World of China 44(1), 1–9 (2019). Signal acquisition techniques and performance
4. Julien, O., Macabiau, C., Cannon, M.E., et al.: ASPeCT: unambiguous Sine-BOC(n, n) acquisition/tracking technique for navigation applications. IEEE Trans. Aerosp. Electron. Syst. 43(1), 150–162 (2007)
5. Iswariya, B.R., Kumar, H.N.: FFT based acquisition techniques of GPS L2C signals. ICTACT J. Commun. Technol. 4(4), 849–853 (2013)

Distributed Network Resource Allocation Protocol Based on Collision Scattering and Push-Pull Cascading Mechanism

Baodi Jiang, Ding Wang, Bo Li, Zhongjiang Yan[(✉)], and Mao Yang

School of Electronics and Information, Northwestern Polytechnical University,
Xi'an, China
jbd24@mail.nwpu.edu.cn, {wangd,libo.npu,zhjyan,yangmao}@nwpu.edu.cn

Abstract. Wireless directional ad hoc networks has attracted much attention from academic area in recent years due to its large antenna gain, small multipath interference, long propagation distance and space reusability. However, since the signal in other directions cannot be well sensed, the environment of the communication channel cannot be predicted, thus causing interference between multiple concurrent transmission links. Therefore, it is extremely important to study the wireless directional ad hoc networks and use its advantages to overcome its shortcomings. In this paper, the concurrent link interference problem in the wireless directional ad hoc networks is analyzed. Firstly, this paper analyzes the advantages and disadvantages of the classical Push mechanism and Pull mechanism. Then, a network resource allocation protocol, CSPC (Collision Scattering and Push-Pull Cascading), is proposed for the transmission and reception of network resources. CSPC protocol mainly uses the idea of collision scattering to increase the proportion of data transmission success by using frequency division of the time slot in the time slot where data transmission fails. The simulation results show that using CSPC protocol can efficiently increase the network throughput and solve the collision problem between concurrent transmission links.

Keywords: Wireless directional ad hoc networks · Push mechanism · Pull mechanism · CSPC

1 Introduction

The wireless directional ad hoc networks is a technology different from the traditional wireless communication network technology [1]. It doesn't need fixed equipment and base stations' support. A wireless directional ad hoc networks is a multi-hop mobility peer-to-peer network consisting of tens to hundreds of nodes and using wireless communication. Each node can be either a sending node or a receiving node. Nodes can also act as routers which make communication faster, more efficient, and more flexible [2].

© ICST Institute for Computer Sciences, Social Informatics and Telecommunications Engineering 2020
Published by Springer Nature Switzerland AG 2020. All Rights Reserved
B. Li et al. (Eds.): IoTaaS 2019, LNICST 316, pp. 45–57, 2020.
https://doi.org/10.1007/978-3-030-44751-9_5

The wireless directional ad hoc networks utilizes directional antennas compared to the wireless omnidirectional ad hoc networks, so it has more advantages. For example, the effectiveness of the radiated power is improved, the confidentiality is enhanced, and the strength of the transmitting power and the anti-interference can be increased. Frequency reuse can be used to increase the spatial reuse rate of the wireless communication network. The transmission distance is long and the number of node forwarding can be reduced.

Since the development of wireless directional ad hoc networks technology, researchers at home and abroad have proposed a number of DMAC (directional media access control) protocols and made full use of the advantages of wireless directional ad hoc networks to improve spatial reuse rate and network throughput [3].

In an actual network, each node is independent. That is, each node can only send and receive data in a specific direction, but cannot detect and avoid interference of concurrent links in other directions. So, during the transmission of network resources [4]. It is easy to occur for collision conflicts, which causes conflicts between links and makes resource allocation efficiency of the entire network very low.

In view of the above problems, relevant research has been conducted. In [5], a multi-channel access method based on collision thinning is proposed for the link collision problem. The core idea is to use multiple channels to scatter single channel collisions and not only allocate one time slot but also allocate a random channel for each node. That is, each node is assigned a time-frequency resource block. Although this algorithm can reduce the link conflict to a certain extent, it still keeps the known traffic and service type of the sending node in the whole process. This algorithm actively sends the data transmission request, but the interference situation at the receiving node is not clear. In [6], a multi-channel MAC protocol based on pseudo-random sequence is proposed for link collision problem. The links for simultaneous data transmission are organized in different pseudo-random sequences, and the receiving node receives the service of the sending node. When the conflict between the concurrent links are perceived and estimated, the collision between the links is reduced. However, the algorithm does not know the traffic and service type that the sending node needs to send, and does not know how to allocate the resource block. The two algorithms in the above two papers correspond to the existing push mechanism and pull mechanism respectively.

The push mechanism refers to the process of data transmission and reception signaling interaction initiated by the sending node. The physical meaning is to push the data generated at the sending node to the receiving node. The advantage of this mechanism is that the sending node knows the amount of traffic that needs to be sent and service type. Therefore, according to its traffic volume and service type, it can actively initiate data transmission request to the receiving node on multiple network resource blocks. The disadvantage of this mechanism is that the sending node does not know its receiving node or even multiple receiving the interference situation at the node, so the receiving node needs to feed back information such as whether the concurrent link conflicts on some resource blocks. After that, the sending node can get better network resources according to the conflict information fed back by the receiving node. The pull mechanism refers to the process of data transmission and reception signaling interaction initiated by the receiving node. The physical meaning is that the data generated at the sending node is pulled from the sending node. The advantage of this mechanism is that the data transmitted by the sending node on different network resource blocks is used to obtain various information, including, the allocation of the network resource block in which the sending node data is successfully transmitted, the situation of other sending nodes that are detected, and the situation in which the network resource block conflicts. Based on these information, the receiving node can estimate and perceive the concurrent link conflict situation around it, and the information can be used by the receiving node for protocol design or network resource allocation. The disadvantage of this mechanism is that the receiving node does not know the service that needs to be sent at the sending node. For example, quantity and type of business. So it only needs to obtain such information before it can allocate network resources.

Although both of the above mechanisms can reduce the link conflict problem to a certain extent, they are only for the protocol proposed by the receiving node or the sending node. The conflict problem is viewed from the perspective of the entire network of multiple nodes. It directly affects the throughput of the overall network. Therefore, we need to unite the transceiver nodes and propose a new protocol to further optimize the interference of the entire link. Therefore, this paper proposes the CSPC protocol. The core idea of this protocol is to overcome the shortcomings of the two mechanisms by combining the advantages of the push mechanism and the pull mechanism. When the sending node knows the traffic volume and type, but does not know the interference situation at the receiving node, it sends a data transmission request to the receiving node. Then the receiving node records the concurrent link interference and collision problem of the receiving end in the whole communication process, and returns the recorded interference condition to the sending node after the data transmission is completed, so that the sending node can know the sending service. The quantity and type can clearly understand the concurrent link interference of the receiving node, and solve the problem of concurrent link conflict.

The main contributions of this paper are as follows. (1) The CSPC protocol is proposed, which cascades the existing push mechanism and pull mechanism. (2) Effectively solve problems such as concurrent link interference. (3) Perform simulation to verify the improvement of network throughput by the CSPC protocol proposed in this paper.

The sections in this paper are organized as follows. The first section mainly introduces the wireless directional ad hoc networks, and the CSPC protocol is derived from the concurrent link interference problem. The second section establishes the system model of the algorithm. The third section describes the specific protocol, and introduces the central implementation of the CSPC protocol in detail. The fourth section carries out simulation verification, and the simulation results are obtained and analyzed. The fifth section is a summary of this article and some expectations for future work.

2   System Model

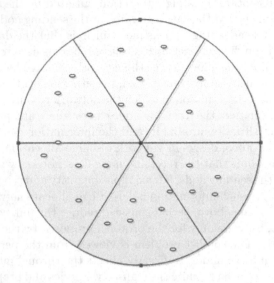

Fig. 1. Wireless directed ad hoc network node distribution.

In the directional ad hoc networks, N sending nodes and M receiving nodes are randomly distributed in the circular area shown in Fig. 1. The position coordinates of each node are represented by two-dimensional rectangular coordinates. Each node is equipped with directional antenna. The communication area divides into 6 sectors and each sector being covered by one beam. The sectors and beams are the same concept in this paper. It is assumed that the radiation intensity within the antenna radiation range is the same.

Table 1. Beam configuration

Beam number	Beam width(○)
1	0–60
2	60–120
3	120–180
4	180–240
5	240–300
6	300–360

Before introducing the specific protocol, the paper also made the following assumptions. All nodes are randomly distributed in each sector, that is, the position coordinates of each node are random. Each transceiver node has 6 beams, and the beam range is as shown in Table 1. The protocol is based on the three-way handshake protocol of the DTRA (the Directional Transmission and Reception Algorithms) scanning stage. This paper utilizes the pre-existing settings for the scanning stage and the appointment stage. In the scanning stage, not only the time slot of the reservation stage but also a random channel is allocated for the node pair. Each node pair is assigned a time-frequency resource block. In the appointment stage, the transceiver node reserves a plurality of network resource blocks organized in time series. Therefore, when the protocol is specifically described, we mainly introduce the data transmission stage. It is assumed that in all the nodes set by the wireless directional ad hoc networks, the sending nodes scan the sending nodes, and the receiving nodes are all scanning receiving nodes. All nodes communicate on the same channel. The total number of time slots set by the entire protocol is adjustable. The CSPC protocol mainly solves the conflict problem of concurrent links. Through the above model, the interference conflict between links is more clear, which is convenient for recording and optimization, and the model improves the network performance of the entire network, mainly represented by throughput.

3   CSPC Protocol Description

In this paper, we mainly describe the data transmission stage, in which the transceiver node performs data transmission on the basis of the reserved resource block sequence. Here, the channel number sequence is chiefly reflected by the resource block sequence. The multi-channel access mean previously used in the scanning stage and appointment stage. Scattering link conflicts have improved the probability of correct reception of each link [6]. At the same time, the fairness of each node will also increase. However, in order to improve fairness, this paper uses frequency division in the data transmission stage. The rule is actually to classify the time slots according to the transmission state, performing two-index frequency division where the data transmission fails, and frequency-divide the resources occupys more resources until the data can be realized. The transfer was successful. The specific agreement is divided into the following three stages.

3.1   Scanning Stage

The process of the scanning stage is accord with this paper [7]. Moreover, the scanning course is conducted on a single channel. After several rounds of scanning, most nodes are found and recorded in the neighbor node table of the corresponding node, and the table mainly includes neighbor nodes address and the sector ID of the neighboring node. At the same time, the resources in the appointment stage make an appointment here, and each scan updates the reservation allocation table of the appointment stage, which mainly includes the reserved initiation node address, the reserved receiving node address, the used channel number, and the time slot. Finally, every node is going to get one neighbor node table and one reservation allocation table at the end of the scanning stage.

3.2 Appointment Stage

In the appointment stage, every node performs resource reservation in the data transmission stage according to neighbor nodes information table and the reservation allocation table acquired in the scanning stage. After the appointment is completed, node pairs which made the appointment are going to create a resource distribution table for a data transmission of the third stage.

Based on the literature [8], this paper comes up with a new idea. The prime procedures of the algorithm are presented in Fig. 2. In this picture, node S indicates the sending node, node D expresses the receiving node, REQ indicates that sending nodes send a request to receiving nodes, REP carries the information that the receiving node replies to the serial number which selected by sending nodes, that is, whether the next data transmission can be performed, and DATA indicates that the selected serial number is based on the data that needs to be communicated. After receiving the DATA, ACK indicates the data packet sent by the receiving node (the latter DATA and ACK are chiefly embodied in the data transmission stage in this paper). After the receiving node replies to the sending node with an ACK, the receiving node reports the link collision problem and the contradiction problem that it has heard through the TRG (trigger) frame to the sending node, and the sending node performs better resource allocation according to the received TRG frame. The following are the basic steps of the push-pull cascading mechanism, as shown in Fig. 2.

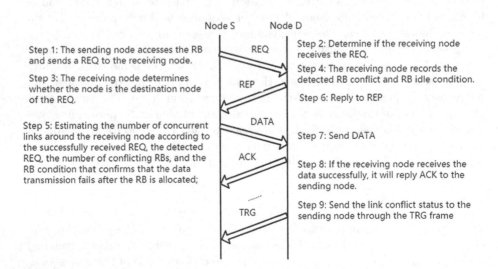

Fig. 2. Step diagram based on the push-pull cascade mechanism.

Step 1: The sending node contends to access multiple resource blocks according to the traffic volume and service type to be sent to different receiving nodes, and sends a REQ data transmission request frame to the receiving node on each resource block, and requests to allocate these resource block resources as subsequent data transmission resource block.

Step 2: If the receiving node successfully receives the REQ on a certain resource block, go to step 3. Otherwise, go to step 4.

Step 3: The receiving node determines whether the node is the destination node of the REQ. If yes, go to step 6. Otherwise, record the REQ transceiver node and mark the REQ link as the concurrent interference chain road (the sending node of the node and the node), then go to step 5.

Step 4: The receiving node records the detected resource block conflict and resource block idle condition, and then proceeds to step 5.

Step 5: Estimate the number of concurrent links around the receiving node according to the successfully received REQ, the detected REQ, the number of conflicting resource blocks, and the resource block condition that confirms the data transmission failure after the resource block allocation. Afterwards, go to step 6.

Step 6: Perform resource allocation based on the dynamic resource block number configurable according to the optimal resource block utilization rate, the estimated number of concurrent links at the local node, and whether the number of resource blocks in the network system can be dynamically changed. The algorithm, or the resource allocation algorithm based on the fixed resource block number, respectively obtains the resource block allocation situation in the new configuration, or the access probability P of the conflicted resource block in the fixed configuration, and then replies on the corresponding resource block according to the REQ information of the sending node. The REP data transmission request acknowledgement frame includes the resource block allocation condition under the new configuration or the access probability P of the conflicted resource block. Go to step 7.

Step 7: Receive the data information DATA sent by the sending node. If the data on all the allocated resource blocks is successfully received, feed back the ACK on the corresponding resource block, and then go to step 8. Otherwise, record the resource block that confirms the data transmission failure after the resource block allocation, situation, and link information for transmission failure.

Step 8: Wait for the next round of channel access. If the sending node has channel access right, go to step 1. If the receiving node has channel access right, then according to which node is waiting to send, send TRG to trigger the corresponding transmission of the frame scheduling. The node accesses the channel, and then proceeds to step 9.

Step 9: If the sending node successfully receives the TRG frame, go to step 1, otherwise go to step 8. In this paper, the resource block sequence is mainly the channel number. If two links choose resource block sequences are fully orthogonal, there are not collision occur even within the mutual communication range. If two links choose partially overlapping resource blocks sequence, the link conflict is going to exist.

3.3 Data Transmission Stage

When the appointment stage is finished, all nodes are going to create a data resource distribution table. The data transmission stage receives and sends information based on the resource distribution table and the neighbor node table. Considering the simulation behind, our data transmission stage is mainly composed of the following three parts.

(a) The first part is to generate a directional link [9]. It has been clarified in the front system model that the sending node and the receiving node contain 6 beams. Now each sending node establishes a link with all receiving nodes, and each sending node A and receiving node B need to be recorded (Fig. 3). In the case of beam activation when forming a link, the activation here refers to the beam that the two nodes cover each other when forming a link, that is, the calculation angle determines the beam.

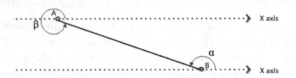

Fig. 3. Transceiver node activation beam confirmation map.

Record the information in beam activation confirmation table (two-dimensional table with rows and columns, for example, table (a, b)). That is, it is determined that each sending node needs to activate a beam when establishing a link with all receiving nodes, wherein the row of beam activation confirmation table represents all sending nodes, the column represents all receiving nodes, and a is a beam that the sending node needs to activate when establishing a link, b is the beam that the receiving node needs to activate. Here, the resource block is regarded as a time slot, and a directional link needs to be generated. For each of the sending nodes n, m of the receiving nodes of the sending node n are randomly selected from the M receiving nodes, and each of the selected receiving nodes is allocated [T/m] time slots (T is the total number of time slots). The m receiving nodes are allocated time slots in a random manner to form a data transmission time slot allocation table. Each row of the table indicates the destination node of the sending node in the relevant time slot, and each column indicates the corresponding time. The receiving node of the slot, in the case that one receiving node corresponds to multiple sending nodes, there will be conflicts between the links, so the data transmission time slot allocation table should be sorted. Check each column of the table, whether the receiving node m is in multiple rows. When it appears, only one of the repetitions is randomly reserved, and all the remaining repetitions are set to any other identical value. The time slot allocation table after the sorting does not theoretically have any interference between the links.

(b) The data transmission of the push mechanism is performed in the second part. For each sending node n, in each of the digital transmission time slots t, check the receiving node of the time slot, that is, forming a two-dimensional table (n, t). For each receiving node m, look for the t-th time column of this table to know who is the sending node. If table (n, t) not equal to 0 and n not equal to 0, it is determined that the nodes n, m point to each other. At this time, look up beam activation confirmation table to determine the beam activation of node n, m and go to set. The command is activated. In short, it is to clarify the situation of the sending and receiving nodes of each time slot and activate the beam where the sending and receiving nodes are located. Checking whether there is the same b in the column of the receiving node m in beam activation confirmation table, and if so, checking the receiving node m. There is a plurality of sending nodes pointing to m in the beam pointing to the sending node n. The result indicates that DATA fails. Otherwise, it means that DATA is successful. If table(n, t) not equal to 0 and n not equal to 0 is not satisfied, it is in somewhere. If no m and n are pointed to each other in the time slot (for example, if a time slot column is 0), then any beam of a receiving node p needs to be randomly activated to listen, and the receiving node p is randomly activated in the beam. Whether there are multiple sending nodes pointing to the receiving node p, you can check whether the column of the receiving node p in the beam activation confirmation table contains the randomly activated beam. If it is not judged to be idle, it is judged to be busy. After the interception, the result is recorded in the status situation record table to display the four cases of data transmission: DATA failed, DATA succeeded, free, busy. At this point the completion of the data transmission stage of the push mechanism.

(c) The third part is the push-pull cascading mechanism. In the place where the DATA fails in the push mechanism, the corresponding time slot is frequency-divided. The frequency division rule (collision scatter process): the 2 exponential frequency division, assign e + 1 to e, that is, the a's direction is set to the correspondence data transmission time slot allocation table, table (n, t) is matched with three parameters: m, e, c. Parameter e is an index of 2 (set e equal to 0 at the beginning), parameter c is between 0 and half of 2 to the power of e. The proportion of the sub-slots obtained when the frequency is successfully succeeded is filled in the corresponding failed place of the status situation record table generated by the push mechanism, and the other busy, free, and correct places are the same as before. The second status situation record table, at this time, completes the data transmission part of the push-pull cascading mechanism.

4   Simulation Performance

The performance of the proposed CSCP is compared with the push mechanism. The simulation results are as follows.

The number of time slots set in Figs. 4 and 5 is 20. As can be seen in Fig. 4, when the number of transceiver nodes is 1:1, the one-hop throughput of both mechanism nodes decreases with the number of nodes, but with the number of nodes increases, the node-hop throughput decreases. The lower

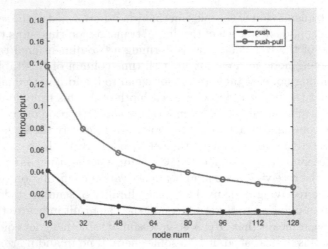

Fig. 4. The throughput of the two mechanisms in the case of 1:1 transceiver node ratio.

the throughput is. However, the push-pull mechanism has a higher through-put than the push mechanism, because the link collision increases as the num-ber of nodes increases. The frequency division method can effectively scat-ter conflicts. It can be obtained through simulation. When the number of nodes is small, the throughput can be increased by at least 3 times, and when the number of nodes is large, at least 14 times can be improved.

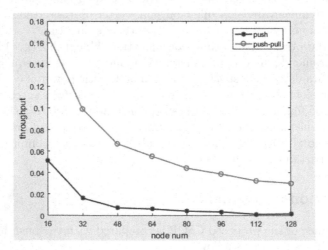

Fig. 5. The throughput of the two mechanisms in the case of 2:1 transceiver node ratio.

In Fig. 5, it can be seen that when the ratio of the number of transceiver nodes is 2:1, the overall trend of the two mechanisms is similar to that of the ratio of 1:1, but the throughput of the two mechanisms is 2:1. Compared with the ratio of 1:1, the throughput is improved. When there are fewer nodes, the throughput can be increased by at least 3 times. However, when there are many nodes, the throughput can be increased by at least 21 times. Therefore, the appropriate configuration of the number of transceiver nodes can improve the throughput of the network further.

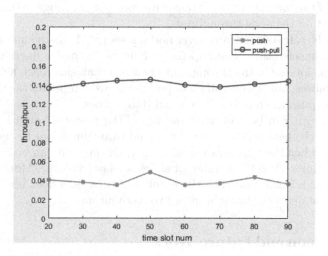

Fig. 6. Throughput of two mechanisms with different time slot values (N = M = 16).

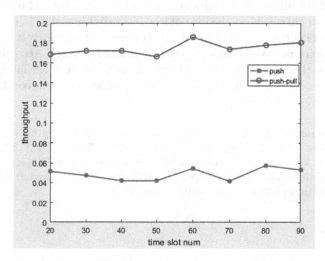

Fig. 7. Throughput of two mechanisms with different time slot values (N = 16, M = 32).

Figures 6 and 7 show the throughput comparison of the two mechanisms under different time slot values. The simulation results only show the case of a small number of transceiver nodes. Because through simulation, the number of transceiver nodes is larger than when the number of nodes is small.

In Fig. 6, the number of sending nodes and receiving nodes is the same. It can be obtained that the throughput of one-hop of the push-pull mechanism node changes relatively smoothly with the increase of the number of time slots, and the push mechanism is slightly ups and downs, but the amplitude is not large. It can be seen that, if the same number of transceiver nodes, the change of the internship has little effect on the node throughput.

In Fig. 7, the ratio of the transceiver nodes is set to 2:1. As the number of slots increases, two mechanisms' one-hop throughput of the nodes fluctuates. When the number of slots is 60, the throughput of two mechanisms reach a small peak, and then stabilizes, but the overall push-pull mechanism improves the throughput relative to the push mechanism. It is about 3 to 4 times.

In summary, it can be seen that the use of the protocol could improve the throughput of the network node one-hop. And throughput can be increased by about 3 times when the number of nodes is low. Of course it can be increased by more than 15 times when the number of nodes is relatively large. Moreover, it can be found through simulation that the number of time slots does not have much influence on the network throughput of two mechanisms.

5   Conclusion and Future Work

In order to address the link conflict problem as well as the link starvation problem in wireless directional ad hoc networks, this paper proposes one push-pull cascade-based coordinating network resource allocation protocol for transceiver nodes. The protocol considers the idea of frequency division, that is, collision scattering to deal with the proposed problems. It includes three stages: the scanning stage, the appointment stage and the data transmission stage. According to simulation results, the protocol could obviously increase network throughput. In the future, further research on neighbor discovery problems or link conflicts during the scanning stage is needed.

Acknowledgement. This work was supported in part by the National Natural Science Foundations of CHINA (Grant No. 61771392, 61771390, 61871322, 61501373 and 61271279), the National Science and Technology Major Project (Grant No. 2015ZX03002006-004 and 2016ZX03001018-004), and Science and Technology on Avionics Integration Laboratory (Grant No. 20185553035).

References

1. Huang, Z., Shen, C. C.: A comparison study of omnidirectional and directional MAC protocols for ad hoc networks. In: Global Telecommunications Conference, GLOBE-COM 2002, vol. 1, pp. 57–61. IEEE (2002)

2. Li, Q., Li, B., Yan, Z., Yang, M.: Multi-channel multiple access protocol based on classified time slots for directional ad hoc networks. In: 2018 IEEE International Conference on Signal Processing, Communications and Computing (ICSPCC) (2018)
3. Wong, D., Qian, C., Francois, C.: Directional medium access control (MAC) protocols in wireless ad hoc and sensor networks: a survey. J. Sens. Actuator Netw. **4**(2), 67–153 (2015)
4. Chlamtac, I., Conti, M., Liu, J.N.: Mobile ad hoc networking: imperatives and challenges. Ad Hoc Netw. **1**(1), 13–64 (2003)
5. Liang Y., Li B., Yan Z., Yang M.: Collision scattering through multichannel in synchronous directional ad hoc networks. In: 13th International Conference on Heterogeneous Networking for Quality, Reliability, Security and Robustness (QSHINE 2017) (2017)
6. Tu, Y., Zhang, Y., Zhang, H.: A novel MAC protocol for wireless ad hoc networks with directional antennas. In: IEEE International Conference on Communication Technology, pp. 494–499. IEEE (2013)
7. Bazan, O., Jaseemuddin, M.: A survey on MAC protocols for wireless ad hoc networks with beamforming antennas. IEEE Commun. Surv. Tutor. **14**(2), 216–239 (2012)
8. Zhang, H., Li, B., Yan, Z., Yang, M., Jiang, X.: A pseudo random sequence based multichannel MAC protocol for directional ad hoc networks. In: Wang, L., Qiu, T., Zhao, W. (eds.) QShine 2017. LNICST, vol. 234, pp. 172–182. Springer, Cham (2018). https://doi.org/10.1007/978-3-319-78078-8_18
9. Bai, Z., Li, B., Yan, Z., Yang, M., Jiang, X., Zhang, H.: A classified slot re-allocation algorithm for synchronous directional ad hoc networks. In: Wang, L., Qiu, T., Zhao, W. (eds.) QShine 2017. LNICST, vol. 234, pp. 194–204. Springer, Cham (2018). https://doi.org/10.1007/978-3-319-78078-8_20

Edge Intelligence and Computing for IoT Communications And Applications

Acoustic Frequency Division Based on Active Metamaterial: An Experimental Demonstration of Acoustic Frequency Halving

Ping Zhao, Junyi Wang, Xihan Gu, Kangzhou Suo, Yun Chen$^{(\boxtimes)}$, and Xiaoyang Zeng

State Key Laboratory of ASIC and System, Fudan University, Shanghai 201203, China
chenyun@fudan.edu.cn

Abstract. In this paper, an acoustic filter with low frequency bandstop and a broadband (0.3–3 kHz) bandstop filter are presented. In this paper, control algorithm and related equipment are integrated with piezoelectric ceramic thin film, ADC and FPGA to study a system which can mix acoustically in the process of acoustic transmission and only allow one-way transmission of sound waves.

Keywords: Piezoelectric · Mix acoustically

1 Introduction

Metamaterials have offered an entirely new route to understand and control the properties of broad kinds of materials [1]. Controlling acoustic transport at will has been pursued for many years in modern physics and applications [2]. Active acoustic metamaterial (AAMM) with tunable properties brings new potentials into acoustics [3]. For example, an acoustic second harmonic generator has been achieved with a highly nonlinear AAMM [4]. By further investigating the behavior of the signal processing system in [4], we propose an AAMM scheme for acoustic frequency division.

2 Active Control of Acoustic Transmission

By connecting the change of sound pressure with the change of electrical quantity in piezoelectric materials, part of the response function of the material to sound waves will be replaced by the response function of the circuit. The response of acoustic metamaterials to sound waves determines their equivalent acoustic parameters, so the equivalent acoustic parameters of active acoustic metamaterials are a quantity controlled by a circuit.

Consider a cavity with a piezoelectric ceramic film at one end (as shown in Fig. 1). At this point, the formula can be rewritten in the Laplace transform domain [5]

$$
\begin{bmatrix} \Delta V_O l_p \\ q \end{bmatrix} = \begin{bmatrix} C_d & d_A \\ d_A & 1/Z_p s \end{bmatrix} \begin{bmatrix} \Delta p_p \\ V_P \end{bmatrix} \tag{1}
$$

© ICST Institute for Computer Sciences, Social Informatics and Telecommunications Engineering 2020
Published by Springer Nature Switzerland AG 2020. All Rights Reserved
B. Li et al. (Eds.): IoTaaS 2019, LNICST 316, pp. 61–70, 2020.
https://doi.org/10.1007/978-3-030-44751-9_6

Where, ΔVol_p is the volume change of the piezoelectric ceramic film, q is the accumulated charge on the surface, Δp_p is the pressure difference on both sides of the piezoelectric ceramic film, V_P is the voltage on the piezoelectric ceramic, C_d is the flexibility coefficient of the film, d_A is the effective piezoelectric coefficient, Z_p is the impedance of the piezoelectric ceramics and its subsidiary circuit.

For mechanical vibration, there is also a similarity with the circuit components. For example, the behavior of the material's compliance coefficient is similar to that of the capacitor. The quality of the material has the effect similar to that of the inductor. Thus, the system shown in Fig. 1 can be fully represented as a circuit form. As shown in Fig. 2, the final circuit form is the acoustic domain, and the mechanical vibration domain and the electrical domain together form a structure. Through this equivalent circuit, we can directly control the behavior of the piezoelectric ceramic (mainly its voltage) by solving its transfer function, and then control the sound pressure change to obtain the required acoustic parameters.

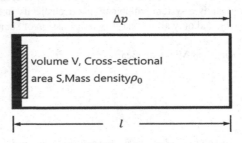

Fig. 1. Piezoelectricity

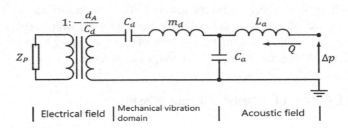

Fig. 2. Equivalent circuit of a thin film cavity of piezoelectric ceramics

3 One-Way Active Acoustic Mixer Based on Metamaterial

The above investigation shows that the desired acoustic parameters can be obtained by introducing piezoelectric materials and reasonable control of electrical quantity. Further, if the desired filtering function is achieved directly by the circuit connected with the piezoelectric material, the range of functions of the acoustic metamaterial can be greatly extended. Cummer et al. proposed a method that can realize the transformation of incident sound wave into its second-order harmonic, and this material has directional selectivity. Only the sound wave incident from the "positive direction" can be converted and amplified, so it is a one-way nonlinear acoustic metamaterial [6].

The structure of the material is two back-to-back Helmholtz resonators, which use a piezoelectric ceramic film as the common surface. Figure 3 is a schematic diagram of the piezoelectric ceramic film. It has three electrodes: ground, main and a sensing electrode. As shown in Fig. 4, the two Helmholtz resonators in this material have similar structures. They are all cylindrical cavities with only one opening, and the structural parameters are the same except for the different diameter of the opening.

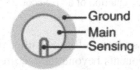

Fig. 3. Schematic diagram of piezoelectric ceramic film

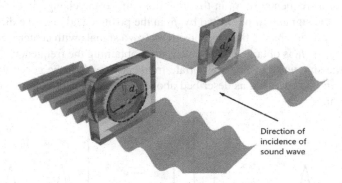

Direction of
incidence of
sound wave

Fig. 4. Functional diagram of unidirectional acoustic frequency multiplier material [6]

This design has some disadvantages in practical use. For example, in circuit design, the isolation of electrical signals between the measuring electrode and the main electrode must be considered, which requires that the resonant frequencies of the two Helmholtz resonators are far apart from each other. Since the method to produce second order harmonic is to use a full wave rectifier, it can only produce an even number of times frequency signal, and the higher the intensity of the signal is lower, which makes the material has poor universality.

With the acoustics of the corresponding part of the process in the operation process analog circuit alternative ideas are similar, we can realize the corresponding function in the digital domain, and through the AD/DA converter (AD/DA) implementation between analog signal and digital signal conversion, is shown in Fig. 5 the analog signal processing to replace as shown in Fig. 5 the digital signal processing. The adoption of digital signal processing not only achieves good isolation between input and output signals through the conversion process of AD/DA, but also allows us to not stick to the full-wave rectifier, but to use more general frequency conversion strategies.

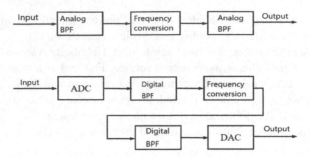

Fig. 5. Analog and digital implementation of active acoustic metamaterial control circuits

Since there are two bandpass filters before and after the frequency change module to filter out the frequency components beyond the required frequency, the input signal can be multiplied by the sine wave of a certain frequency and then the signal can be passed through the bandpass filter with the required frequency as the center frequency. As shown in Fig. 6, A signal with a center frequency of f_c is superimposed with a sine wave with a frequency of f_0 in the time domain, so the change in the frequency domain is that the signal will be shifted by f_0 in the positive and negative directions of the frequency domain, that is, the superposition of two signals with center frequency of $|f_c - f_0|$ and $f_c + f_0$ is obtained. In this way, after obtaining the frequency of the input signal, only the sine wave of the appropriate frequency needs to be generated and the input signal can be processed as described above to transform the input signal to any frequency point.

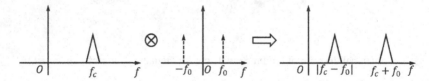

Fig. 6. Schematic diagram of general spectrum

4 Manufacturing, Implementation and Testing of Active Acoustic Mixer

The design of active acoustic metamaterials needs to consider both the material and the circuit at the same time. Therefore, the preparation of the materials, the design and implementation of the circuit system and the construction of the test system should be considered comprehensively when testing the corresponding materials.

4.1 Material Preparation

The same piezoelectric ceramic thin film in [6] is used here (as shown in Fig. 7). It is manufactured by Murata, and its corresponding model is 7bb-35-3cl0.

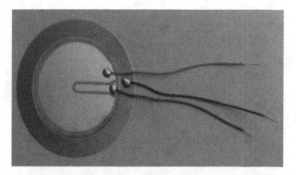

Fig. 7. Physical picture of piezoelectric ceramic film

The dimensions of two back-to-back cylindrical Helmholtz resonators are: the cavity body diameter is 33 mm, the height is 1.5 mm, the opening depth is 1.5 mm, and the opening diameter is 3 mm and 9 mm, respectively. The material used is acrylic. Through simulation of the two sized Helmholtz resonators in Sect. 2, the absorption coefficient curve shown in Fig. 8 can be obtained. It can be seen that their corresponding resonant frequencies are about 1350 Hz and 2700 Hz respectively.

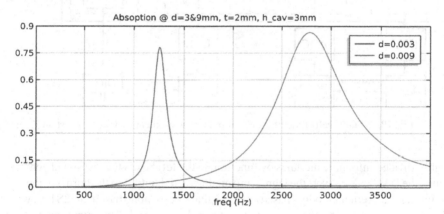

Fig. 8. The absorption coefficient curve of Helmholtz resonator

The specific manufacturing method is to carve the required cavity or hole on the 1.5 mm thick acrylic board, and then bind the acrylic board and the piezoelectric ceramic film together. In order to control the simplicity of piezoelectric ceramic thin films, two piezoelectric ceramic thin films are used, one specially for measuring incident acoustic signals and the other specially for producing output acoustic signals. The final material is shown in Fig. 9.

4.2 System Block Diagram and Module Realization

Figure 10 is the FPGA implementation block diagram of the test system and control circuit. Both the test and metamaterial control circuits are on the FPGA, which can be

Fig. 9. The resulting active acoustic metamaterials

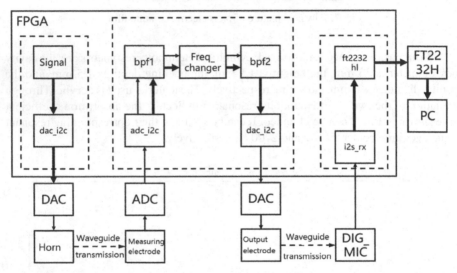

Fig. 10. FPGA realization block diagram of measurement and control system

roughly divided into three modules by function. In the left box is the test signal generator circuit, the DAC will convert the signal into analog signal output to the horn. On the right is a signal measurement module based on the digital microphone based on I2S bus, which will measure the acoustic wave transmitted from the material. The intermediate block diagram is the control circuit of acoustic metamaterial, which obtains the corresponding input sound wave signal through ADC, and then transmits the output sound wave signal to the piezoelectric ceramic film through DAC. Figure 11 is the physical picture of the whole system

4.3 Module Implementation

ADC/DAC Control Module. The ADC and DAC functions are implemented via Philips semiconductor's PCF8591 chip, which integrates AD/DA functions on a single chip. The PCF8591 chip provides an I2C bus interface for communication with the outside world, and its sampling frequency is up to 11 kHz with 8-bit digits. Two DAC and one ADC are required for the entire test system.

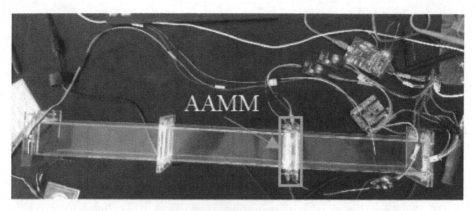

Fig. 11. Test system physical map

Digital Microphone Module. The system USES digital microphone as signal collector when collecting the final result. The digital microphone circuit module made by Adafruit is used here. Its core chip is the MEMS digital microphone made by Knowles, sph0645lm4h-b. The chip is based on the I2S audio bus, which has a sampling precision of 18 bits signed number. Its sampling frequency is adjusted by setting the frequency of the clock that controls microphone operation. The sampling frequency adopted in this paper is 46.875 kHz.

Data Transmission Module. The digital signal measured by the digital microphone is first sent by the FPGA to the FT2232H chip, which then transmits the data to the computer through the USB port. On the computer, the C program written by the corresponding driver needs to read the measurement results from the USB port. FT2232H is a USB serial port chip made by FTDI. FPGA can send data to the USB port in bytes or read data from the USB port. After obtaining the measurement results of digital microphone, FPGA needs to send the data to FT2232H chip through the data transmission module ft2232hl.

Design of Bandpass Filter. The bandpass filter module is one of the bandpass filters with central frequency of 1350 Hz and 2700 Hz respectively. Their amplitude spectrum and phase spectrum are shown in Figs. 12 and 13. According to the different functions of octave or half frequency, the positions of them will be interchanged before and after the frequency conversion module. Half frequency is just the opposite. The filter coefficient is quantified by the number of eight symbols.

Frequency Conversion Module. The frequency conversion module is a module taking the absolute value in frequency multiplication. For the number of symbols represented by binary complement, we can carry out different processing according to the different symbol bits. This paper adopts a unified approach, namely: the use of any a binary number of which is "1" exclusive or invert, and the characteristics of "0" or stay the same, the complement says first every bit binary number and its exclusive or the sign bit, and then will get the results of the exclusive or plus the sign bit, and the final result is obtained.

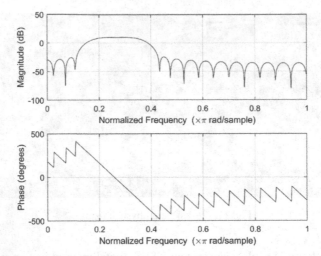

Fig. 12. The amplitude and phase spectrum of a bandpass filter with a central frequency of 1.35 kHz

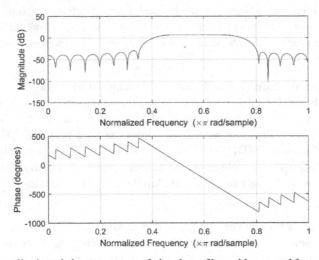

Fig. 13. The amplitude and phase spectrum of a bandpass filter with a central frequency of 2.7 kHz

In half-frequency conversion, the frequency conversion module includes a peak position control square wave generator and a multiplier. The peak position is determined by whether the current signal is larger than the previous signal and the latter signal at the same time. If the detection determines the peak position, a flag will be flipped. So, the flag signal is a pseudo-square wave. Because multiplication and square wave multiplication is actually and, so the actual implement the operation of the time and take the absolute value of similar methods: will take the sign bit of absolute value operation substitute flag bit can achieve the desired effect, and also is the data of each flag and exclusive or, then add flag will be the final result. Therefore, the square wave generator and multiplier mentioned here are corresponding to their actual effects, and the actual circuit will not actually realize a square wave generator and multiplier.

System Operation Flow Chart. The flow diagram of the whole system is shown in Fig. 14. Since active control, including test signal generation, result measurement and metamaterials, is performed on the FPGA, there are three independent processes on the FPGA after it starts and initializes the ADC/DAC module, data transfer module and several shift registers.

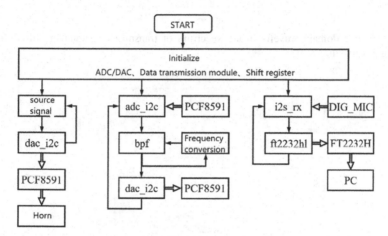

Fig. 14. System operation flow chart

Firstly, the source signal generation module and dac_i2c module cooperate to continuously convert the source signal into DAC and drive the horn to generate the initial sound wave required for testing. Secondly, the i2s_rx module and ft2232hl module cooperate to continuously read the final results from the digital microphone and send them to the upper computer through the USB chip. Thirdly, the adc_i2c module continuously reads the response of the piezoelectric ceramic film under the action of acoustic wave, and then drives the piezoelectric ceramic film to generate the corresponding target sound wave after being processed by bandpass filter - frequency conversion - bandpass filter.

5   Test Results

The half-frequency function is tested. The signal output to the horn is the sound wave input signal with center frequency of 2700 Hz. After the acoustic wave passes through the material in the forward direction, the time-domain waveform and spectrum of the signal measured at the digital microphone are shown in Fig. 15. When the sound wave enters the material from the opposite direction, the time-domain waveform and spectrum of the signal measured at the digital microphone are shown in Fig. 16. It can be seen from Figs. 15 and 16 that the unidirectional half-frequency material has a good effect in frequency conversion and a unidirectional inhibition rate of 44.8 dB is achieved.

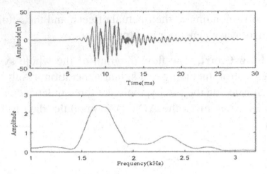

Fig. 15. The time domain waveform and spectrum of transmission signal of half frequency material in positive direction

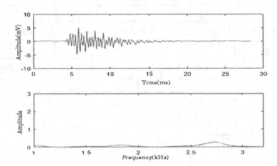

Fig. 16. The time domain waveform and spectrum of the transmission signal of the frequency multiplier material in the opposite direction

Acknowledgment. This work is supported by the National Natural Science Foundation of China (Grant No. 61525401, 61774049), the Shanghai Pujiang Talent Science funding (Grant No. 16PJD008), the Shanghai international co-operation Science funding (No. 16550720600), the Program of Shanghai Academic/Technology Research Leader under Grant 16XD1400300.

References

1. Liu, Y., Zhang, X.: Metamaterials: a new frontier of science and technology. Chem. Soc. Rev. **40**, 2494 (2011)
2. Zhu, X., Ramezani, H., Shi, C., Zhu, J., Zhang, X.: PT-symmetric acoustics. Phys. Rev. X **4**, 031042 (2014)
3. Baz, A.M.: An active acoustic metamaterial with tunable effective density. J. Vib. Acoust. **132**, 041011 (2010)
4. Popa, B.-I., Cummer, S.A.: Non-reciprocal and highly nonlinear active acoustic metamaterials. Nat. Commun. **5**, 1–5 (2014)
5. Prasad, S.A.N., Gallas, Q., Horowitz, S., et al.: Analytical electroacoustic model of a piezoelectric composite circular plate. AIAA Journal **44**(10), 2311–2318 (2006)
6. Popa, B.I., Cummer, S.A.: Non-reciprocal and highly nonlinear active acoustic metamaterials. Nat. Commun. **5**(2), 3398 (2014)

Computation Offloading and Security with Q-Learning

Songyang Ge[1,2], Beiling Lu[3], Jie Gong[3], and Xiang Chen[1,2(✉)]

[1] School of Electronics and Information Technology, Sun Yat-sen University,
Guangzhou 510006, China
chenxiang@mail.sysu.edu.cn
[2] Key Lab of EDA, Research Institute of Tsinghua University in Shenzhen (RITS),
Shenzhen 518075, China
[3] School of Data and Computer Science, Sun Yat-sen University,
Guangzhou 510006, China

Abstract. With the rapid development of the technology and wireless communication, the user cannot support the computation-intensive applications, owing to the restricted computation resources, energy supply, limited memory space and communication resources. The emerging computation mode, called mobile edge computing (MEC), provides a solution that the user can unload parts of tasks to edge servers. This communication process should be finished in the wireless network. However, computation offloading in the wireless network can encounter many kinds of attacks. Specifically, edge servers located in the edge of network are vulnerable to these security threats, such as spoofing, jamming and eavesdropping. Moreover, the computation offloading has much time latency and energy consumption. Then, how to minimize this consumption is the another problem to be solved. To improve the security and minimize the consumption, we formulate a system containing a primary user (PU), a second user (SU), an attacker and several edge servers. They communicate with each other by multiple input multiple output (MIMO) technology. In this system, the SU chooses an MEC server from the set of not being occupied by PU, determines an offloading rate and a transmission power, then the attacker selects the action of attack. The aim of this system is to optimize the utility of SU. To solve this problem, a Q-learning based optimal offloading strategy is proposed in dynamic environments. Simulation results show that our proposed scheme can improve the capacity of SU and efficiently decrease the attack rate of the attacker.

Keywords: Computation offloading · System security · Q-learning

The work is supported in part of Science, Technology and Innovation Commission of Shenzhen Municipality (No. JCYJ20170816151823313), NSFC (No. U1734209, No. 61501527), States Key Project of Research and Development Plan (No. 2017YFE0121300-6), The 54th Research Institute of China Electronics Technology Group Corporation (No. B0105) and Guangdong Provincial Special Fund For Modern Agriculture Industry Technology Innovation Teams (No. 2019KJ122).

B. Li et al. (Eds.): IoTaaS 2019, LNICST 316, pp. 71–81, 2020.
https://doi.org/10.1007/978-3-030-44751-9_7

1   Introduction

With the rapid development of mobile internet and interest of thing (IoT), many kinds of new services are constantly emerging, which makes the explosive growth of mobile communication outflow possible. The mobile terminals and smart phones, are gradually replaced by personal computer which is the main tool in the daily work, study, entertainment and social association. Meanwhile, a large number of IoT terminal devices, such as smart watches, cameras and a variety of sensors, are comprehensively applied in plenty of industries, including traffic, smart home, education, health care and agriculture.

In order to meet the demand above, different types of solutions are born at the right moment, such as Cloud computing, fog computing and mobile edge computing. Cloud computing characterizes its centralization of computing and storing data and network management by making use of cloud center [1]. Though it is convenient for humans that terminal devices access cloud computing center directly, it brings heavy network burdens, long computation delay and higher requirements for bandwidth. MEC gives a good scheme to solve the serious problems above by putting servers into the edge of network. Thus, MEC is one of the most popular schemes and regarded as a vital promoter of evolution for cellular base station. Besides, MEC can be applied in many scenarios [2], comprising of dynamic connect optimization, computational offloading in IoT, mobile big data analytic and smart transportation.

With computation Offloading, user terminals in the mode of MEC can unload tasks to the edge MEC servers, such as base stations, access points and laptops, to decrease the delay of computation, prolong the life of battery and save the computing resources [3]. There are two ways of offloading, including binary offloading and partial offloading. In this paper, the partial offloading is considered. The task can be divided into two parts in partial offloading, in which one part is for computing locally and the other is for offloading to edge servers [4,5].

In addition, owing to the fast process of development of technology, it is a challenge for MEC server to face complex wireless network. Firstly, terminal users do not know the action of other users. For instance, compared with secondary user (SU), the primary user (PU) has a priority of using spectrum is referred to [6]. Secondly, There are more and more attackers and types of smart attacks. The interaction between a smart attacker and an end-user by using prospect theory is formulated in [7]. Because MEC servers are located in the edge of network, they are closer to attackers. Besides of the advanced persistent threats to cloud storage researched in [8,9], mobile edge computing can meet more classes of attacks. In order to provide secure offloading to MEC servers, the solution to different kinds of attacks by applying reinforcement learning methods are summarized in [10].

In this paper, we propose a computation offloading game against smart attacks under the condition of existence of one primary user and a second user. Besides, we propose a Q-learning [11] based scheme for SU by choosing proper MEC server, an offloading rate and a transmission power to optimize the utility.

The main contributions of this work is summarized as follows:

(1) We investigate the computation offloading of SU with multi-antennas in the wireless network. For simplicity, we set two states of MEC server, occupied by PU and not. SU chooses the proper MEC server from the idle set. Next, SU terminal allocates the accurate amount of task to server and ensures the transmission power.

(2) A Q-learning based optimal computation offloading strategy is developed to improve the utility of SU, after observing the time varying channel information. The simulation results show that our proposed scheme can improve the utility and decrease the attack rate.

The organization of the rest is as follows. We review the related work in Sect. 2 and formulate a computation offloading game against smart attacks in Sect. 3. Moreover, a Q-learning algorithm based computation offloading with unknown channel model is proposed in Sect. 4. Then, we provide the simulation results in Sect. 5 and make conclusions in Sect. 6.

2 Related Work

Multiple input and multiple output (MIMO) is one of popular research directions nowadays. We assume that one SU, several MEC servers and an attacker are all with multiple antennas. The interaction between the receiver with multi-antennas and one spoofing node is formulated as a zero-sum physical-layer authentication game in [12]. But it only investigates one type of attack. To reduce the speed of attack and improve the secrecy capacity, one noncooperative MIMO transmission against smart attacks game, including eavesdropping, jamming, and spoofing, is proposed in [13].

In the scene of computation offloading, some researchers focus on the attack defense. By jointly optimizing the energy transmit beamforming at access point, the frequency of central process unit and offloading rate, a solution to minimize the energy consumption and time delay of a single user is derived in [14]. For the computation offloading model, a reinforcement learning based offloading frame is formulated in [15], after observing the battery level, the previous radio bandwidth and the amount of energy harvested. In this paper, We combine the MIMO scenario and computation model to simulate more complex communication environment. Furthermore, in the dynamic MEC network with varying channel state, SU cannot optimize the offloading policy against various types of smart attacks quickly and accurately. We use one of reinforcement learning algorithms, Q-learning, to derive the optimal offloading strategy.

3 Computation Offloading Game Against Attacks

3.1 System Model

We consider a mobile edge offloading system with MIMO transmissions as shown in Fig. 1, consisting a PU, a SU with N_u antennas, M MEC servers with N_m antennas and an attacker with N_a antennas. Because of the limited computation ability and battery level, SU cannot compute total task. SU chooses one specific MEC server to offload tasks, which is not occupied by PU. Besides, when MEC servers receive the signals from SU or PU, it might be attacked by attacker in the way of 4 types, including keeping silent, spoofing, jamming and eavesdropping.

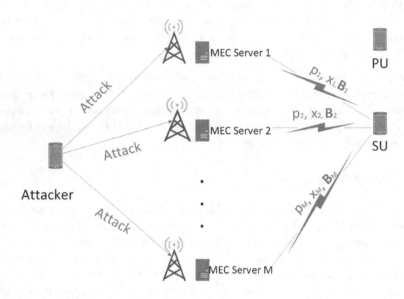

Fig. 1. Sytem model.

3.2   Offloading Model

With the development of wireless communication, the task to be computed by user becomes lager and larger. Generally, mobile device cannot meet this demand due to limited computing resources. The primary user can occupy MEC server. Therefore, MEC server has two states, being occupied or not. SU can choose an MEC sever from the idle server set to offload partial tasks, which can lighten the load greatly. Assuming that the time structure of computation offloading process is slotted, we denote the time slot index by k, with $k \in \mathcal{K} = \{0, 1, \dots\}$. The size of computing task generated by SU at time slot k is denoted by $L^{(k)}$ (in bits). The index of the MEC server selected is i, which satisfies $1 \leq i \leq M$. The proportion of the offloading task, called offloading rate, is denoted by $x_i^{(k)}$, with $0 \leq x_i^{(k)} \leq 1$. More specifically, if $x_i^{(k)} = 0$, the whole task would be computed by SU; if $x_i^{(k)} = 1$, then the task would be handled by MEC_i totally; if $0 < x_i^{(k)} < 1$, the task $x_i^{(k)} L^{(k)}$ would be computed by MEC_i, the left $(1 - x_i^{(k)})L^{(k)}$ is to be operate by SU locally. Simply, we quantize the offloading rate into $N_x + 1$ levels, i.e., $x_i^{(k)} \in \{l/N_x\}_{0 \le l \le N_x}$.

For local-computing model, we first ensure that the task computed locally is $(1 - x_i^{(k)})L^{(k)}$. The CPU cycles required for computation are denoted by ϕ. The CPU frequency of mobile device of SU, i.e., the computing speed of operator, is represented by f_j, with $f_j \le f_{max}$. We denote the computing energy efficiency of operator chip as k_j. Then, the energy consumption of local computation e_0 [3] is represented as

$$e_0 = \sum_{j=1}^{(1-x_i^{(k)})L^{(k)}\phi} k_j f_j^2. \tag{1}$$

The computing time can be written as

$$t_0 = \sum_{j=1}^{(1-x_i^{(k)})L^{(k)}\phi} \frac{1}{f_j}. \tag{2}$$

For computation-offloading model, we should be clear about the task to be offloaded is $x_i^{(k)}L^{(k)}$. Moreover, SU chooses the appropriate power $p_i^{(k)}$ to transmit signals to MEC_i, where the transmission power has bounds, i.e. $0 \le p_i^{(k)} \le p_{max}$. The bandwidth between SU and MEC is B_i. We only consider the time and energy overhead in the process of transmission. The energy consumption can be denoted as

$$e_1 = \frac{p_i^{(k)} x_i^{(k)} L^{(k)}}{B_i C_g}. \tag{3}$$

The total time of offloading computation t_1 is

$$t_1 = \frac{x_i^{(k)} L^{(k)}}{B_i C_g}. \tag{4}$$

In the analysis above, we neglect the time required in the back transmission of computation results from MEC server to SU. It is due to the reality that the amount of result data of computation task is much smaller than the size of input data. Thus, we only take the offloading time into account rather than the time delay in the back transmission.

3.3 Attack Defense Model

In this computation offloading system with MIMO transmission, SU sends M-dimensional signal vector with power $p_i^{(k)}$. From the transmitting antennas at SU to the receiving antennas at MEC_i, the channel gains can be described as channel matrix $\mathbf{H}_{um}$. In the same way, The channel matrix between SU and attacker (or between MEC server and attacker) is $\mathbf{H}_{ua}$ (or $\mathbf{H}_{ma}$). We assume that the distribution of each channel matrix follows independently and identically distributed (i.i.d) complex Gaussian distribution, i.e., $\mathbf{H}_n \sim \mathcal{CN}(\mathbf{0}, \sigma_n^2 \mathbf{I})$, with $n = um, ua, ma$.

There is an attacker generating attack to SU in the way of 4 types, including keeping silent, spoofing, jamming and eavesdropping. The attack mode can be denoted as g, with $g \in \mathcal{A}_a = \{0, 1, 2, 3\}$. The secrecy capacity C_g is formulated as [13].

For ease of reference, we list the key notation of our system model in Table 1.

Table 1. Summary of symbols and notation

Notation	Definition
N_u	Number of antennas at SU
N_m	Number of antennas at MEC server
N_a	Number of antennas at attacker
M	Number of MEC server
$L^{(k)}$	Total task of SU in time slot k
$x_i^{(k)}$	Offloading rate on MEC_i in time slot k
$p_i^{(k)}$	Transmission power to MEC_i in time slot k
f_j	CPU frequency in j-th cycle
ϕ	CPU cycles required for local computation
B_i	Bandwidth between SU and MEC_i
$t_{0/1}$	Computing time of SU or MEC
$e_{0/1}$	Energy consumption of SU or MEC
$\mathbf{H}_{um/ma/ua}$	Channel matrix
C	Secrecy Capacity
$\omega_{0/1/2/3}$	Attack cost
U_a	Utility of SU
α	Learning rate
δ	Discount factor

3.4 Game Model

We formulate the relationship between the attacker and SU as a computation offloading game against smart attacks in the MIMO wireless environment. In this process, SU is firstly constrained by PU. As a result of the limited spectrum resource, PU has priority over utilizing MEC server to unload computation task. Next, SU should select the idle server to take offloading with some transmission power. Furthermore, attacker chooses attack model to launch different kinds of smart attacks. In each time slot, attacker takes action to decrease the cost and improve the utility. Meanwhile, SU tries its best to maximize utility. In a word, we provide the game with two players maximizing their own utilities.

In the computation offloading game above, SU chooses MEC_i from idle server set, suitable transmission power and offloading rate under smart attacks. This process of choice surely makes some cost and energy consumption. We divide the total cost to 3 parts. We assume that the results of three parts have no units. We regard each part as a factor which influences the utility in the different degree and direction. The first part is about the amount of offloading computation task. Due to its beneficial property, we make it a positive number. The second section is energy consumption consisting of local computation and transmission energy consumption. In addition, we add a coefficient to the front of the sum of energy consumption to represent the impact, denoted as ρ. In order to meet the time delay constraint, SU is supposed to reduce its utility. Thus, the third portion is the overhead of time behind the corresponding coefficient ν. Obviously, the second and third parts are overhead of SU, and decrease the utility of mobile user. Therefore, we add a negative sign in the front of the value. Thus, the utility of SU in the game, denoted by U_u, relies on offloading rate, energy consumption, and delay constraint. We write the utility of SU as

$$U_u = x_i^{(k)} L^{(k)} - \rho(e_0 + e_1) - \nu(t_0 + t_1). \tag{5}$$

At the same time, attacker selects one attack mode g from $\{0, 1, 2, 3\}$, corresponding to keeping silent, spoofing, jamming and eavesdropping respectively. But attacker cannot launch blind attack for the cost. We classify the cost into 4 types according to different attacks, represented as $\{\omega_0, \omega_1, \omega_2, \omega_3\}$. Thus the utility of attacker is defined as

$$U_a = (-C_g - \omega_g), \quad g = 0, 1, 2, 3. \tag{6}$$

4 Offloading Strategy of SU in the MIMO System Based on Q-Learning

In a dynamic computation offloading computing game, it is hard for SU to estimate the current environment state, including dynamic channel condition, the action of PU and attacks of diverse types. We model the system as a Markov Decision Process, which has a finite state set and is continuous. Moreover, we represent the process as $<\mathcal{S}, \mathcal{A}_u, \mathcal{P}(s, a, s'), \mathcal{R}(s, a, s')>$, where $\mathcal{S}$ is the state set of SU and $\mathcal{A}_u$ denotes action set. $\mathcal{P}(s, a, s')$ indicates the transition probability, i.e., the agent in the current state s by choosing action a would arrive the next state s'. Moreover, $\mathcal{R}(s, a, s')$ represents the direct reward in the time of choosing action a in the current state s.

The process of seeking optimal strategy is summarized in Algorithm 1. Based on the communication environment, SU chooses one specific action $a^{(k)}$, comprising of MEC_i, $x_i^{(k)}$ and $p_i^{(k)}$, from the action set $\mathcal{A}_u$ in time slot k. Assume that SU regards the attack type of last time slot as its system state, represented as $s^{(k)} = g^{(k-1)}$. We define the direct reward as the utility discussed in the last section.

Since the transition probability is unknown in the system, we apply a kind of reinforcement learning method, called Q learning algorithm. With the reinforcement learning methods emerging as the time requires, SU can make the best of one of these methods, Q-learning algorithm, to achieve optimal mobile edge offloading strategies and get the most gain. Moreover, Q-learning algorithm can obtain the optimal strategy via trial-and-error under the condition of not assuming any probability model. The contents above are the main elements of process of Q-learning algorithm. Besides, they are also basic components of decision making process.

We write the Q function of SU as $Q(s^{(k)}, a^{(k)})$, which is the state-action value function of SU. The value function defined as $V(s^{(k)})$ is the highest value of the current state in time slot k, called state value function. Then we have the iteration equation denoted as

$$Q(s^{(k)}, a^{(k)}) \longleftarrow (1-\alpha)Q(s^{(k)}, a^{(k)}) + \alpha(U_a(s^{(k)}, a^{(k)}) + \delta V(s^{(k+1)})), \quad (7)$$

$$V(s^{(k)}) = \max_{a \in \mathcal{A}_u} Q(s^{(k)}, a), \quad (8)$$

where α is the learning rate of this algorithm, $\delta \in [0,1]$ is the discount factor about future reward. By the iteration in the learning, SU can find the optimal policy. In the current state, agent can choose the best action, observe next state and direct reward value. Lastly, Q function updates according to (7) and value function renews by (8). It can be shown that given sufficient number of iterations Q learning can converge to optimal result and max long term reward.

Because of the advantage of the policy, it is favorable for SU to choose the best action based on the system state and improve convergence performance. Consequently, SU applies the ε-greedy policy in the process of learning. That is, SU selects action with highest probability from the optimal Q function, gains the maximum of direct reward and selects the other action randomly. Thus, the learning process can balance exploration and exploitation. The probability equation above can be given by

$$\Pr(a_i^{(k)} = \tilde{a}) \begin{cases} 1-\varepsilon, & \text{if } \tilde{a} = \arg\max_{a \in \mathcal{A}_u} Q(s^{(k+1)}, a) \\ \frac{\varepsilon}{N_x}, & \text{otherwise.} \end{cases} \quad (9)$$

During the process of learning, SU learns the system state and unloads partial task $x_i^{(k)} L^{(k)}$ to MEC_i with transmission $p_i^{(k)}$ to increase the long-term reward. The mobile edge offloading scheme against smart attacks with Q-learning is summarized in Algorithm 1.

Algorithm 1. Q-learning based Computation Offloading Scheme

1: **Initialize** $g^{(0)} = 0$, $Q(s,a) = 0$, $V(s) = 0$, $\forall s$, a.
2: **for** each episode **do**
3:     **for** $n = 1, 2, 3, \cdots$ **do**
4:         Update the state $s^{(k)} = g^{(k-1)}$;
5:         Choose $a^{(k)}$ with $\varepsilon-$ greedy policy;
6:         Observe the attack type $g^{(k)}$ and U_u ;
7:         Update the Q function and value function,
8:         $Q(s^{(k)}, a^{(k)}) \longleftarrow (1 - \alpha)Q(s^{(k)}, a^{(k)}) + \alpha(U_a(s^{(k)}, a^{(k)}) + \delta V(s^{(k+1)}))$,
9:         $V(s^{(k)}) = \max_{a \in \mathcal{A}_u} Q(s^{(k)}, a)$.
10:     **end for**
11: **end for**

---

5 Simulation Results

We evaluate the performance of the computation offloading computing scheme via simulations with $L = 100$, $P = 6 : 10$, $M = 3$, $N_u = 5$, $N_m = N_a = 2$. As shown in Fig. 2, the average utility of SU increases with the growth of time slot. It raises by 173.8% over 500 time slots. Between 0-th and 500-th time slot, the utility has a rapid development and converge at 384-th time slot gradually. The reason why the curve of mobile edge offloading computing in MIMO systems changes is SU can choose different transmission powers and offloading rates according to diverse MEC server.

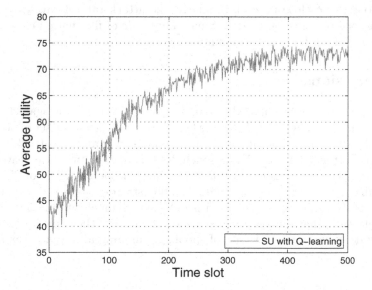

Fig. 2. Performance of computation offloading computing utility of SU for $5 \times 2 \times 2$ MIMO system with $L = 100$, $P = 6 : 10$, $M = 3$.

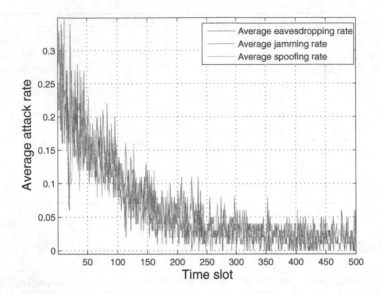

Fig. 3. The attack rate of three attacks in computation offloading scheme with $L = 100$, $P = 6 : 10$, $M = 3$.

As shown in Fig. 3, the proposed computation offloading scheme in the MIMO systems reduces rapidly the attack rate of different types of smart attack, including spoofing, jamming and eavesdropping. For instance, the scheme decreases the attack frequency of spoofing from 0.3 to 0.01 after 200 time slots. Besides, it is the first one to be close to zero. Similarly, the attack rate of eavesdropping is the second one to converge to zero. Small amplitude of fluctuation close to zero was shown in the attack rate of jamming.

6   Conclusions

In this paper, we have formulated a computation offloading game against attacks in MIMO systems, in which SU chooses the MEC server from the set of not being occupied by PU, offloading rate and transmission power and the attacker selects the action of attack. The attack types includes spoofing, jamming and eavesdropping. Besides, the object is to optimize the utility and performance of SU. Then, a Q-learning algorithm based optimal offloading strategy is proposed, under the condition of dynamic environment with unknown channel information. Simulation results show that our proposed scheme can improve the capacity of SU and efficiently decrease the attack rate of spoofing, jamming and eavesdropping.

References

1. Zhang, Q., Cheng, L., Boutaba, R.: Cloud computing: state-of-art and research challenges. J. Internet Serv. Appl. **1**(1), 7–18 (2010)

2. Ahmed, A., Ahmed, E.: A survey on mobile edge computing. In: 2016 10th International Conference on Intelligent System & Control Intelligent Systems and Control (ISCO), Coimbatore, India, pp. 1–2 (2016)
3. Mao, Y., You, C., Zhang, J., et al.: A survey on mobile edge computing: the communication perspective. IEEE Commun. Surv. Tutor. **19**(4), 2322–2358 (2017)
4. Li, Y., Li, Q., Liu, J., et al.: Mobile cloud offloading for malware detections with learning. In: IEEE International Conference on Computer Communications (INFO-COM), BigSecurity, Hongkong (2015)
5. Wan, X., Sheng, G., Li, Y., et al.: Reinforcement learning based mobile offloading for cloud-based malware detection. In: IEEE Global Communications Conference (GLOBECOM), Singapore (2017)
6. Duan, L., Gao, L., Huang, J.: Cooperative spectrum sharing: a contract-based approach. IEEE Trans. Mob. Comput. **13**(1), 174–187 (2014)
7. Xie, C., Xiao, L.: User-centric view of smart attacks in wireless networks. In: IEEE International Conference on Ubiquitous Wireless Broadband (ICUWB), invited talk, Nanjing, China (2016)
8. Xiao, L., Xu, D., Xie, C., et al.: Cloud storage defense against advanced persistent threats: a prospect theoretic study. IEEE J. Sel. Areas Commun. **35**(3), 534–544 (2017)
9. Abass, A., Xiao, L., Mandayam, N.B., et al.: Evolutionary game theoretic analysis of advanced persistent threats against cloud storage. IEEE Access **5**, 8482–8491 (2017)
10. Xiao, L., Wan, X., Dai, C., et al.: Security in mobile edge caching with reinforcement learning. IEEE Wirel. Commun. Mag. **25**(3), 116–122 (2018)
11. Sutton, R.S., Barto, A.G.: Reinforcement Learning: An Introduction. MIT Press, Cambridge (1998)
12. Xiao, L., Chen, T., Han, G., et al.: Game theoretic study on channel-based authentication in MIMO systems. IEEE Trans. Veh. Technol. **66**(8), 7474–7484 (2017)
13. Li, Y., Xiao, L., Dai, H., et al.: Game theoretic study of protecting MIMO transmission against smart attacks. In: IEEE International Conference on Communications (ICC), Paris (2017)
14. Wang, F., Xu, J., Wang, X., et al.: Joint offloading and computing optimization in wireless powered mobile-edge computing. IEEE Trans. Wirel. Commun. **17**(3), 1784–1797 (2018)
15. Min, M., Xu, D., Xiao, L., et al.: Learning-based computing offloading for IoT devices with energy harvesting. IEEE Trans. Veh. Technol. **68**(2), 1930–1941 (2019)

Distributed Resource Allocation Policy for Network Slicing with Inter-operator Bandwidth Borrowing

Jiajia Chen[1,2], Jie Gong[3], Xiang Chen[1,2(✉)], and Xijun Wang[4,5]

[1] School of Electronics and Information Technology, Sun Yat-sen University,
Guangzhou 510006, China
chenxiang@mail.sysu.edu.cn
[2] Key Lab of EDA, Research Institute of Tsinghua University in Shenzhen (RITS),
Shenzhen 518075, China
[3] School of Data and Computer Science, Sun Yat-sen University,
Guangzhou 510006, China
[4] School of Electronics and Communication Engineering, Sun Yat-sen University,
Guangzhou 510006, China
[5] Key Laboratory of Wireless Sensor Network and Communication, Shanghai
Institute of Microsystem and Information Technology, Chinese Academy of Sciences,
865 Changning Road, Shanghai 200050, China

Abstract. Network slicing is a novel technology to effectively provide solutions for heterogeneous mobile service requirements in 5G network. Meanwhile, the shortage of spectrum resources becomes more severe with massive access requirement of Internet-of-Things (IoT) applications. In this paper, we study how to allocate spectrum resources to satisfy the diversified traffic requirements with network slicing and improve the utilization of spectrum resources. A spectrum resource allocation model with three layers is considered, including operator layer, slice layer and user layer. At the mobile operator layer, mobile operators can borrow frequency bandwidth from one another to improve the spectrum efficiency. Then, the mobile operator allocates its frequency bandwidth to the slices according to users' demand. At last, the slice assigns bandwidth to users. A network utility maximization problem is formulated and a distributed resource allocation algorithm is proposed based on alternating direction method of multipliers (ADMM). Simulation results show that the proposed algorithm

The work is supported in part of Science, Technology and Innovation Commission of Shenzhen Municipality (No. JCYJ20170816151823313), NSFC (No. U1734209, No. 61501527, No. 61771495), States Key Project of Research and Development Plan (No. 2017YFE0121300-6), The 54th Research Institute of China Electronics Technology Group Corporation (No. B0105) and Guangdong Provincial Special Fund For Modern Agriculture Industry Technology Innovation Teams (No. 2019KJ122), Fundamental Research Funds for the Central Universities of China (SYSU: 19lgpy79), The Research Fund of the Key Laboratory of Wireless Sensor Network and Communication (Shanghai Institute of Microsystem and Information Technology, Chinese Academy of Sciences) under grant 20190912.

can quickly converge to the optimal solution. In addition, the overall network utility can be effectively improved by lending or borrowing spectrum resources among operators. By adding the slice layer, the network can meet different types of service requirements.

Keywords: Spectrum leasing · Network slicing · Alternating direction method of multipliers (ADMM)

1 Introduction

The fifth generation (5G) wireless networks are envisioned to interconnect a massive number of miscellaneous end devices (e.g., smartphones, remote monitoring sensors, and home appliances) generating both mobile broadband data and machine-to-machine (M2M) services/applications (e.g., video conferencing, remote monitoring, and smart homing), to realize the ubiquitous Internet-of-Things (IoT) architecture [10]. Therefore, the communication networks must be able to adapt to different application scenarios. However, the traditional communication network mainly serves the mobile broadband users, and cannot adapt to the diversified traffic requirements of 5G in the future. A promising approach to address this need is the novel concept of network slicing, which aims at allocating portions of network resources to specific tenants, such as enhanced mobile broadband (eMBB), IoT, e-health, etc [9]. In [8], network slices were defined as end-to-end (E2E) logical networks running on a common underlying (physical or virtual) network with independent control and management. Such networks can simultaneously accommodate diverse business-driven use cases from multiple players, and hence it can solve the problem of multi-scenario services in 5G.

The appearance of multi-scenario services in 5G triggers the increasing demand of spectrum resources, which however, are limited due to the scarcity of frequency bands. How to improve resource utilization in a sliced network to meet the requirement of multi-scenario services is an urgent challenging problem to be solved. Nowadays, the resource allocation problem in network slicing system has attracted a lot of research interests from both academia and industry. The authors in [5] introduced a slicing plane for radio access network to enable innovative sharing of network resources. However, the resource allocation in [5] is a static solution, which can not adapt to the dynamics of slicing. Flexible slicing design is presented in [4] and [3]. The proposed algorithm flexibly shares the radio resources among multiple tenants, but does not consider the different service requirements of slices. In [7], an IoT-oriented architecture was proposed to enable the IoT applications and services with diverse requirements based on dynamic 5G slice allocation. And in [6], a dynamic wireless resource allocation scheme considering the different service requirements of slices was proposed. Besides, a dynamic slicing and trading framework is developed in [1] that not only determines the size of the network resource slices required for various active services, but also adapts resource prices in accordance with the microeconomic laws of supply and demand. However, the exist works do not take into account the shortage of spectrum resources and the spectrum resources owned by mobile operators are static.

In this paper, we consider a resource allocation problem in a network slicing system. The spectrum resources are owned by different mobile operators in a communication network. Unlike previous works, to deal with the shortage of spectrum resources, we assume that the spectrum bandwidth can be borrowed among mobile operators. When the spectrum resource of a certain mobile operator is abundant and while the others are in short supply, the utilization of spectrum resources can be improved by spectrum leasing. Meanwhile, mobile operators are motivated to lend spectrum resources to increase their incomes by charging the borrowed spectrum. Then, the mobile operator allocates spectrum resources to the slice according to traffic requirements. In order to solve the problem of spectrum leasing and resource allocation among multiple operators, a distributed resource allocation algorithm is proposed based on alternating direction method of multipliers (ADMM) [2]. In this algorithm, the resource allocation policy is iteratively and distributively calculated by each mobile operator in the network slicing system. Simulation results illustrate the efficiency of the proposed algorithm.

2   System Model and Problem Formulation

In this section, the system model is introduced and the optimization problem is formulated by jointly considering the spectrum resource leasing among mobile operators and spectrum resource allocation to slices and users. As shown in Fig. 1, the whole network can be divided into three layers: the mobile operator layer, the slice layer and the user layer. The mobile operator layer is in charge of allocating resources to slices, then the slice layer provides specific services to its users. Different from previous works, in order to improve the utilization of

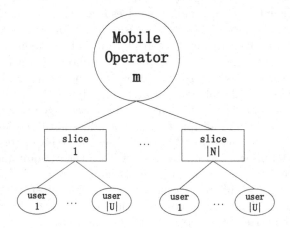

Fig. 1. Three layers of the network.

spectrum resources, we assume that the resource-lacked mobile operators can borrow spectrum bandwidth from other mobile operators.

Consider a set of mobile operators $\mathcal{M}$. At any given time, the mobile operator m $(m \in \mathcal{M})$ has a set of slices $\mathcal{N}_m$. Denote $\mathcal{U}_{n,m}$ as a set of users that belong to slice n $(n \in \mathcal{N}_m)$. The total bandwidth that is owned by mobile operator m is B_m and the amount that mobile operator i borrows from mobile operator j is $q_{i,j}$ $(i,j \in \mathcal{M}, i \neq j)$, therefore the total amount of available bandwidth of mobile operator m is

$$b_m = B_m - \sum_{i \neq m} q_{i,m} + \sum_{j \neq m} q_{m,j}, \tag{1}$$

where

$$\sum_{i \neq m} q_{i,m} \leq B_m. \tag{2}$$

Denote p_m as the price per unit of spectrum bandwidth lent by mobile operator m and C_m as the total budget of mobile operator m. The cost for borrowing spectrum from other mobile operators minus the income of lending spectrum to others should not exceed the total budget. We have

$$\sum_{j \neq m} q_{m,j} p_j - \sum_{i \neq m} q_{i,m} p_m \leq C_m. \tag{3}$$

Furthermore, the spectrum ratio of mobile operator m allocated to slice n is denoted by $f_{m,n}$ $(m \in \mathcal{M}, n \in \mathcal{N}_m)$, where $0 \leq f_{m,n} \leq 1$. Likewise $0 \leq s_{m,n,u} \leq 1$ $(m \in \mathcal{M}, n \in \mathcal{N}_m, u \in \mathcal{U}_{m,n})$ represents the spectrum ratio of slice n allocated to user u. The spectrum efficiency of the user u $(u \in \mathcal{U}_{m,n})$ is

$$c_{m,n,u} = log_2(1 + SNR_{m,n,u}), \tag{4}$$

where $SNR_{m,n,u}$ is signal to noise ratio. The transmission rate of the user u $(u \in \mathcal{U}_{m,n})$ is

$$r_{m,n,u} = b_m f_{m,n} s_{m,n,u} c_{m,n,u}. \tag{5}$$

Denote $L_{m,n}$ as the service requirement of users in slice n of operator m, then we have

$$r_{m,n,u} \geq L_{m,n}. \tag{6}$$

The overall network utility is defined as

$$W = \sum_{m \in \mathcal{M}} \sum_{n \in \mathcal{N}_m} \sum_{u \in \mathcal{U}_{m,n}} log_2(r_{m,n,u}). \tag{7}$$

We aim to maximize the overall network utility while satisfying users' requirements and operators' cost constraint. The problem is formulated as

$$\max_{q_{m,j}, f_{m,n}, s_{m,n,u}} W \tag{8a}$$

subject to

$$\sum_{j\neq m} q_{m,j}p_j - \sum_{i\neq m} q_{i,m}p_m \leq C_m, \quad \forall m, \tag{8b}$$

$$r_{m,n,u} \geq L_{m,n}, \quad \forall m,n,u, \tag{8c}$$

$$\sum_{u\in\mathcal{U}_{m,n}} s_{m,n,u} \leq 1, \quad \forall m,n, \tag{8d}$$

$$s_{m,n,u} \geq 0, \quad \forall m,n,u, \tag{8e}$$

$$\sum_{n\in\mathcal{N}_m} f_{m,n} \leq 1, \quad \forall m, \tag{8f}$$

$$f_{m,n} \geq 0, \quad \forall m,n, \tag{8g}$$

$$\sum_{i\neq m} q_{i,m} < B_m, \quad \forall m, \tag{8h}$$

$$q_{m,j} \geq 0, \quad \forall m, \; j\neq m. \tag{8i}$$

3   ADMM-Based Distributed Resource Allocation

The problem (8) is a convex problem, therefore lots of classical algorithms can solve this problem, such as simplex method and lagrangian multiplier method. However, these methods are all centralized, which are not suitable for our problem as mobile operators make divisions individually based on their own benefits and costs. Therefore, we consider a distributed algorithm to solve problem (8).

The alternating direction method of multipliers (ADMM) is a powerful tool that is well suitable for distributive convex optimization. It takes the form of a decomposition-coordination procedure, in which the solutions to small local subproblems are coordinated to find a solution to a large global problem [2]. To apply ADMM algorithm, we rewrite the problem as a standard minimization problem. It's obvious that to maximize the utility of network, (8d) and (8f) must be satisfied with equality. Hence, the problem can be rewritten as follows

$$\min_{q_{m,j},f_{m,n},s_{m,n,u}} -\sum_{m\in\mathcal{M}} \sum_{n\in\mathcal{N}_m} \sum_{u\in\mathcal{U}_{m,n}} log_2(b_m f_{m,n} s_{m,n,u} c_{m,n,u}) \tag{9a}$$

subject to

$$\sum_{u\in\mathcal{U}_{m,n}} s_{m,n,u} = 1, \quad \forall m,n, \tag{9b}$$

$$\sum_{n\in\mathcal{N}_m} f_{m,n} = 1, \quad \forall m, \tag{9c}$$

$$\sum_{j\neq m} q_{m,j}p_j - \sum_{i\neq m} q_{i,m}p_m \leq C_m, \quad \forall m, \tag{9d}$$

$$r_{m,n,u} \geq L_{m,n}, \quad \forall m,n,u, \tag{9e}$$

$$\sum_{i\neq m} q_{i,m} < B_m, \quad \forall m, \tag{9f}$$

$$q_{m,j} \geq 0, \quad \forall m, \ j \neq m, \tag{9g}$$

$$s_{m,n,u} \geq 0, \quad \forall m, n, u, \tag{9h}$$

$$f_{m,n} \geq 0, \quad \forall m, n. \tag{9i}$$

By adding complement variables and penalties, the augmented problem of (9) can be given as follows

$$\min_{\substack{q_{m,j},\, f_{m,n},\, s_{m,n,u} \\ x_m,\, y_{m,n,u},\, z_m \\ u_{m,j},\, v_{m,n,u},\, w_{m,n}}} \quad -\sum_{m\in\mathcal{M}} \sum_{n\in\mathcal{N}_m} \sum_{u\in\mathcal{U}_{m,n}} log_2(b_m f_{m,n} s_{m,n,u} c_{m,n,u})$$

$$+\frac{\rho}{2}\Bigg[\sum_{m\in\mathcal{M}} \sum_{n\in\mathcal{N}_m} \Big(\sum_{u\in\mathcal{U}_{m,n}} s_{m,n,u} - 1 \Big)^2 + \sum_{m\in\mathcal{M}} \Big(\sum_{n\in\mathcal{N}_m} f_{m,n} - 1 \Big)^2$$

$$+ \sum_{m\in\mathcal{M}} \Big(\sum_{i\neq m} q_{i,m} - B_m + z_m \Big)^2 + \sum_{m\in\mathcal{M}} \sum_{n\in\mathcal{N}_m} \sum_{u\in\mathcal{U}_{m,n}} (s_{m,n,u} - v_{m,n,u})^2$$

$$+ \sum_{m\in\mathcal{M}} \Big(\sum_{j\neq m} q_{m,j} p_j - \sum_{i\neq m} q_{i,m} p_m - C_m + x_m \Big)^2 + \sum_{m\in\mathcal{M}} \sum_{j\neq m} (q_{m,j} - u_{m,j})^2$$

$$+ \sum_{m\in\mathcal{M}} \sum_{n\in\mathcal{N}_m} \sum_{u\in\mathcal{U}_{m,n}} (r_{m,n,u} - L_{m,n} - y_{m,n,u})^2 + \sum_{m\in\mathcal{M}} \sum_{n\in\mathcal{N}_m} (f_{m,n} - w_{m,n})^2 \Bigg] \tag{10a}$$

subject to

$$\sum_{u\in\mathcal{U}_{m,n}} s_{m,n,u} = 1, \quad \forall m, n, \tag{10b}$$

$$\sum_{n\in\mathcal{N}_m} f_{m,n} = 1, \quad \forall m, \tag{10c}$$

$$\sum_{j\neq m} q_{m,j} p_j - \sum_{i\neq m} q_{i,m} p_m - C_m + x_m = 0, \quad \forall m, \tag{10d}$$

$$r_{m,n,u} - L_{m,n} - y_{m,n,u} = 0, \quad \forall m, n, u, \tag{10e}$$

$$\sum_{i\neq m} q_{i,m} - B_m + z_m = 0, \quad \forall m, \tag{10f}$$

$$q_{m,j} - u_{m,j} = 0, \quad \forall m, \ j \neq m, \tag{10g}$$

$$s_{m,n,u} - v_{m,n,u} = 0, \quad \forall m, n, u, \tag{10h}$$

$$f_{m,n} - w_{m,n} = 0, \quad \forall m, n. \tag{10i}$$

where $\rho > 0$ is the penalty parameter and x_m, $y_{m,n,u}$, z_m, $u_{m,j}$, $v_{m,n,u}$, $w_{m,n}$ ($m \in \mathcal{M}$, $n \in \mathcal{N}_m$, $u \in \mathcal{U}_{m,n}$) are slack variables.

The dual problem of (10) is given as follows

$$\max_{\substack{a_{m,n},\,d_m,\,e_m,\,g_{m,n,u} \\ h_m,\,k_{m,j},\,l_{m,n,u},\,t_{m,n}}} \left\{ \min_{\substack{q_{m,j},\,f_{m,n},\,s_{m,n,u} \\ x_m,\,y_{m,n,u},\,z_m \\ u_{m,j},\,v_{m,n,u},\,w_{m,n}}} -\sum_{m\in\mathcal{M}}\sum_{n\in\mathcal{N}_m}\sum_{u\in\mathcal{U}_{m,n}} log_2(b_m f_{m,n} s_{m,n,u} c_{m,n,u}) \right.$$

$$+\frac{\rho}{2}\left[\sum_{m\in\mathcal{M}}\sum_{n\in\mathcal{N}_m}\left(\sum_{u\in\mathcal{U}_{m,n}} s_{m,n,u}-1\right)^2+\sum_{m\in\mathcal{M}}\left(\sum_{n\in\mathcal{N}_m} f_{m,n}-1\right)^2\right.$$

$$+\sum_{m\in\mathcal{M}}\left(\sum_{i\neq m} q_{i,m}-B_m+z_m\right)^2+\sum_{m\in\mathcal{M}}\sum_{n\in\mathcal{N}_m}\sum_{u\in\mathcal{U}_{m,n}} (s_{m,n,u}-v_{m,n,u})^2$$

$$+\sum_{m\in\mathcal{M}}\left(\sum_{j\neq m} q_{m,j}p_j-\sum_{i\neq m} q_{i,m}p_m-C_m+x_m\right)^2+\sum_{m\in\mathcal{M}}\sum_{j\neq m}(q_{m,j}-u_{m,j})^2$$

$$\left.+\sum_{m\in\mathcal{M}}\sum_{n\in\mathcal{N}_m}\sum_{u\in\mathcal{U}_{m,n}} (r_{m,n,u}-L_{m,n}-y_{m,n,u})^2+\sum_{m\in\mathcal{M}}\sum_{n\in\mathcal{N}_m}(f_{m,n}-w_{m,n})^2\right]$$

$$+\sum_{m\in\mathcal{M}} e_m\left(\sum_{j\neq m} q_{m,j}p_j-\sum_{i\neq m} q_{i,m}p_m-C_m+x_m\right)$$

$$+\sum_{m\in\mathcal{M}}\sum_{n\in\mathcal{N}_m}\sum_{u\in\mathcal{U}_{m,n}} g_{m,n,u}(r_{m,n,u}-L_{m,n}-y_{m,n,u})$$

$$+\sum_{m\in\mathcal{M}} h_m\left(\sum_{i\neq m} q_{i,m}-B_m+z_m\right)+\sum_{m\in\mathcal{M}}\sum_{m\neq j} k_{m,j}(q_{m,j}-u_{m,j})$$

$$+\sum_{m\in\mathcal{M}}\sum_{n\in\mathcal{N}_m} a_{m,n}\left(\sum_{u\in\mathcal{U}_{m,n}} s_{m,n,u}-1\right)+\sum_{m\in\mathcal{M}} d_m\left(\sum_{n\in\mathcal{N}_m} f_{m,n}-1\right)$$

$$\left.+\sum_{m\in\mathcal{M}}\sum_{n\in\mathcal{N}_m}\sum_{u\in\mathcal{U}_{m,n}} l_{m,n,u}(s_{m,n,u}-v_{m,n,u})+\sum_{m\in\mathcal{M}}\sum_{n\in\mathcal{N}_m} t_{m,n}(f_{m,n}-w_{m,n})\right\}$$

$$(11)$$

where $a_{m,n}$, d_m, e_m, $g_{m,n,u}$, h_m, $k_{m,j}$, $l_{m,n,u}$, $t_{m,n}$ ($m\in\mathcal{M}$, $n\in\mathcal{N}_m$, $u\in\mathcal{U}_{m,n}$) are dual variables. In addition, we define $\mathbf{Q}_m=\left(q_{m,1},\cdots,0,\cdots,q_{m,M}\right)^T$ with only the m-th element being zero to represent the resource array of mobile operator m borrowing from other mobile operators. And $\mathbf{Q}'_m=\left(q_{1,m},\cdots,0,\cdots,q_{M,m}\right)^T$ with the m-th elements being zero to represent the resource array that mobile operator m lends to other operators. We have

$$(\mathbf{Q}_1^T,\mathbf{Q}_2^T,\cdots,\mathbf{Q}_M^T)^T=(\mathbf{Q}'_1\,\mathbf{Q}'_2\cdots\mathbf{Q}'_M). \qquad (12)$$

As each operator decides the amount of resource borrowed from others distributively, $\mathbf{Q}_m$ will be updated in each subproblem. Then, by (12), $\mathbf{Q}'_m$ will be updated by sharing information among operators.

Let $\mathbf{F}_m=\left(f_{m,1},f_{m,2},\cdots,f_{m,N}\right)^T$, $\mathbf{P}_m=\left(p_1,p_2,\cdots,p_m\right)^T$ and $\mathbf{S}_m=\begin{pmatrix} s_{m,1,1} & \cdots & s_{m,1,U} \\ \vdots & \ddots & \vdots \\ s_{m,N,1} & \cdots & s_{m,N,U} \end{pmatrix}$. To apply ADMM algorithm to solve the problem distributively, we decompose the minimization problem into $|\mathcal{M}|$ subproblems. In particular, each operator optimizes $\mathbf{Q}_m$, $\mathbf{F}_m$, $\mathbf{S}_m$ by solving the following sub-problem separately.

$$(\mathbf{Q}_m^{(k+1)}, \mathbf{F}_m^{(k+1)}, \mathbf{S}_m^{(k+1)}) = arg\Big\{ \min_{\mathbf{Q}_m, \mathbf{F}_m, \mathbf{S}_m} -\sum_{n\in\mathcal{N}_m}\sum_{u\in\mathcal{U}_{m,n}} log_2(b_m^{(k)} f_{m,n} s_{m,n,u} c_{m,n,u})$$

$$+ \frac{\rho}{2}\Big[(\sum_{i\neq m} q_{i,m}^{(k)} - B_m + z_m^{(k)})^2 + \sum_{n\in\mathcal{N}_m}(\sum_{u\in\mathcal{U}_{m,n}} s_{m,n,u} - 1)^2$$

$$+ (\mathbf{Q}_m^T\mathbf{P} - \sum_{i\neq m} q_{i,m}^{(k)} p_m - C_m + x_m^{(k)})^2 + \sum_{j\neq m}(q_{m,j}^{(k)} - u_{m,j}^{(k)})^2$$

$$+ \sum_{n\in\mathcal{N}_m}\sum_{u\in\mathcal{U}_{m,n}}(r_{m,n,u}^{(k)} - L_{m,n} - y_{m,n,u}^{(k)})^2 + (\sum_{n\in\mathcal{N}_m} f_{m,n} - 1)^2$$

$$+ \sum_{n\in\mathcal{N}_m}\sum_{u\in\mathcal{U}_{m,n}}(s_{m,n,u}^{(k)} - v_{m,n,u}^{(k)})^2 + \sum_{n\in\mathcal{N}_m}(f_{m,n}^{(k)} - w_{m,n}^{(k)})^2\Big]$$

$$+ e_m^{(k)}(\sum_{i\neq m} q_{i,m}^{(k)} p_m - \sum_{j\neq m} q_{m,j}^{(k)} p_j - C_m + x_m^{(k)})$$

$$+ \sum_{n\in\mathcal{N}_m}\sum_{u\in\mathcal{U}_{m,n}} g_{m,n,u}^{(k)}(r_{m,n,u}^{(k)} - L_{m,n} - y_{m,n,u}^{(k)})$$

$$+ h_m^{(k)}(\sum_{i\neq m} q_{i,m}^{(k)} - B_m + z_m^{(k)}) + \sum_{j\neq m} k_{m,j}^{(k)}(q_{m,j}^{(k)} - u_{m,j}^{(k)})$$

$$+ \sum_{n\in\mathcal{N}} a_{m,n}^{(k)}(\sum_{u\in\mathcal{U}_{m,n}} s_{m,n,u}^{(k)} - 1) + \sum_{n\in\mathcal{N}_m} t_{m,n}^{(k)}(f_{m,n}^{(k)} - w_{m,n}^{(k)})$$

$$+ \sum_{n\in\mathcal{N}_m}\sum_{u\in\mathcal{U}_{m,n}} l_{m,n,u}^{(k)}(s_{m,n,u}^{(k)} - v_{m,n,u}^{(k)}) + d_m^{(k)}(\sum_{n\in\mathcal{N}_m} f_{m,n}^{(k)} - 1)\Big\}$$

$$(13)$$

After the matrix $\mathbf{Q}_m$ is update, the matrix $\mathbf{Q}'_m$ can be updated by the mobile operators sharing how much bandwidth to be borrowed with one another. Later, each operator solves the following problems distributively to update the slack variables:

$$x_m^{(k+1)} = arg\min_{x_m} \frac{\rho}{2}((\mathbf{Q}_m^{(k+1)})^T\mathbf{P} - (\mathbf{Q}'_m^{(k+1)})^T\mathbf{P} - C_m + x_m)^2 + e_m^{(k)}x_m \quad (14a)$$

$$y_{m,n,u}^{(k+1)} = arg\min_{y_{m,n,u}} \frac{\rho}{2}(r_{m,n,u}^{(k+1)} - L_{m,n} - y_{m,n,u})^2 - g_{m,n,u}^{(k)}y_{m,n,u} \quad (14b)$$

$$z_m^{(k)} = arg\min_{z_m} \frac{\rho}{2}(\sum_{i\neq m} q_{i,m}^{(k+1)} - B_m + z_m)^2 + h_m^{(k)}z_m \quad (14c)$$

$$u_{m,j}^{(k+1)} = arg\min_{u_{m,j}} \frac{\rho}{2}(q_{m,j}^{(k+1)} - u_{m,j})^2 - k_{m,j}^{(k)}u_{m,j} \quad (14d)$$

$$v_{m,n,u}^{(k+1)} = arg\min_{v_{m,n,u}} \frac{\rho}{2}(s_{m,n,u}^{(k+1)} - v_{m,n,u})^2 - l_{m,n,u}^{(k)}v_{m,n,u} \quad (14e)$$

$$w_{m,n}^{(k+1)} = arg\min_{w_{m,n}} \frac{\rho}{2}(f_{m,n}^{(k+1)} - w_{m,n})^2 - t_{m,n}^{(k)}w_{m,n} \quad (14f)$$

In the end, the dual variables are also updated distributively:

$$a_{m,n}^{(k+1)} = a_{m,n}^{(k)} + \rho(\sum_{u \in \mathcal{U}} s_{m,n,u}^{(k+1)} - 1) \tag{15a}$$

$$d_m^{(k+1)} = d_m^{(k)} + \rho(\sum_{n \in \mathcal{N}} f_{m,n}^{(k+1)} - 1) \tag{15b}$$

$$e_m^{(k+1)} = e_m^{(k)} + \rho((\mathbf{Q}_m^{(k+1)})^T \mathbf{P} - (\mathbf{Q}'^{(k+1)})^T \mathbf{P} - C_m + x_m) \tag{15c}$$

$$g_{m,n,u}^{(k+1)} = g_{m,n,u}^{(k)} + \rho(r_{m,n,u}^{(k+1)} - L_{m,n} - y_{m,n,u}^{(k+1)}) \tag{15d}$$

$$h_m^{(k+1)} = h_m^{(k)} + \rho(\sum_{i \neq m} q_{i,m}^{(k+1)} - B_m + z_m^{(k+1)}) \tag{15e}$$

$$k_{m,j}^{(k+1)} = k_{m,j}^{(k)} + \rho(q_{m,j}^{(k+1)} - u_{m,j}^{(k+1)}) \tag{15f}$$

$$l_{m,n,u}^{(k+1)} = l_{m,n,u}^{(k)} + \rho(s_{m,n,u}^{(k+1)} - v_{m,n,u}^{(k+1)}) \tag{15g}$$

$$t_{m,n}^{(k+1)} = t_{m,n}^{(k)} + \rho(f_{m,n}^{(k+1)} - w_{m,n}^{(k+1)}) \tag{15h}$$

In summary, the algorithm is given as Algorithm 1.

Algorithm 1. Proposed ADMM-based Resource Allocation Algorithm

---

1: Fix a penalty parameter $\rho > 0$; Initialize $q_{m,j}^{(0)}$, $f_{m,n}^{(0)}$, $s_{m,n,u}^{(0)}$, $x_m^{(0)}$, $y_{m,n,u}^{(0)}$,

   $z_m^{(0)}$, $u_{m,j}^{(0)}$, $v_{m,n,u}^{(0)}$, $w_{m,n}^{(0)}$ $a_{m,n}^{(0)}$, $d_m^{(0)}$, $h_m^{(0)}$, $k_{m,j}^{(0)}$, $l_{m,n,u}^{(0)}$, $t_{m,n}^{(0)}$; Set k=0;

2: **repeat**

3:     Each operator updates $\mathbf{Q}_m^{(k+1)}$, $\mathbf{F}_m^{(k+1)}$, $\mathbf{S}_m^{(k+1)}$ according to (13);

4:     Each operator m propose its intended amount of bandwidth $q_{m,j}^{(k+1)}$ to

       borrow to every other operator j to update $\mathbf{Q}'_m^{(k+1)}$

5:     Each operator updates slack variables $x_m^{(k+1)}$, $y_{m,n,u}^{(k+1)}$, $z_m^{(k+1)}$,

       $u_{m,j}^{(k+1)}$, $v_{m,n,u}^{(k+1)}$, $w_{m,n}^{(k+1)}$ according to (14)

6:     Each operator updates dual variables $a_{m,n}^{(k+1)}$, $d_m^{(k+1)}$, $h_m^{(k+1)}$, $k_{m,j}^{(k+1)}$, $l_{m,n,u}^{(k+1)}$,

       $t_{m,n}^{(k+1)}$ accroding to (15)

7:     $k := k + 1$

8: **until** a predefined convergence criterion is satisfied.

In this algorithm, each operator firstly determines whether to borrow bandwidth from others according to their own spectrum bandwidth and users' requirements and updates $\mathbf{Q}_m$. Then, each operator allocates bandwidth to its slices and users and updates $\mathbf{F}_m$ and $\mathbf{S}_m$. After $\mathbf{Q}_m$ is updated, mobile operators tell one another how much bandwidth is needed to be borrowed. Thus, $\mathbf{Q}'_m$ is updated according. Next, each mobile operator updates slack variables and dual variables according to (14) and (15). Since the problem is convex, the optimality of the proposed algorithm can be guaranteed. Therefore, by iterating until a predefined convergence criterion is satisfied, the maximum network utility can be obtained.

4   Simulation Results

In this section, the performance of the proposed algorithm is evaluated by simulations. In our simulations, each operator has 2 slices and each slice has 2 active users. The rate requirements specified by users in slicing are referred to [1]. The simulation parameters are listed in the Table 1.

Table 1. Simulation parameters and values

Mobile operator	1	2	3	4
Spectrum bandwidth	50 MHz	20 MHz	50 MHz	20 MHz
The price per unit of spectrum	15	30	15	20
The limitation of cost	200	150	200	300
Service requirement of users in slice 1	20 MHz	10 MHz	15 MHz	60 MHz
Service requirement of users in slice 2	1 MHz	40 MHz	30 MHz	1 MHz

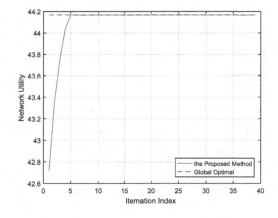

Fig. 2. The optimal network utility of the proposed method versus iterations, $|\mathcal{M}| = 2$.

The optimal network utility of the system versus iterations is depicted in Figs. 2 and 3, with 2 and 4 operators respectively. Simulation parameters of Fig. 2 are based on mobile operator 1 and 2 in Table 1. In order to evaluate the performance of proposed algorithm, the global optimal solution of problem (8) is given for comparison. According to Figs. 2 and 3, we can see that the proposed algorithm can achieve the global optimal solution quickly. When there are 2 operators in the system, the proposed method converges in 5 iterations. When there are 4 operators in the system, the proposed method needs 9 iterations to converge.

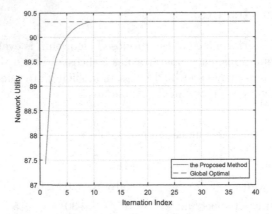

Fig. 3. The optimal network utility of the proposed method versus iterations, $|\mathcal{M}| = 4$.

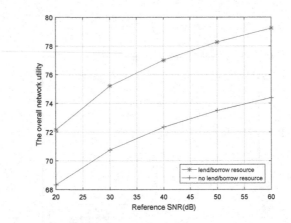

Fig. 4. The optimal network utility with and without spectrum resource leasing versus reference SNR.

The optimal network utility when there is no spectrum leasing between operators is also compared, as shown in Fig. 4. As can be seen that with the increasing of SNR, the network utility of the system enabling spectrum resource leasing changes from 72 to 79. However, without spectrum resource leasing, the network utility of the system only change from 68 to 74.2. It validates that when there are operators lacking of spectrum resources, our model can effectively solve the problem and improve the network efficiency.

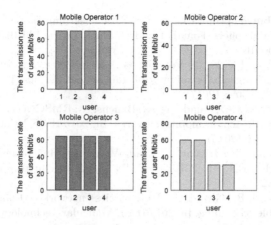

Fig. 5. The users'data rate with the proposed algorithm.

The users' data rates are shown in Fig. 5. Comparing with the service requirements specified by the slices in Table 1, it can be seen that the transmission rates of users of each mobile operator meet the service requirements specified in the slices. Among them, mobile operators 1 and 3 have adequate spectrum resources. In order to achieve maximum network utility, their bandwidth is evenly allocated to each slice, then each slice allocates resources to its users evenly. Therefore, the users' transmission rates of different slices are the same. Mobile operators 2 and 4, however, do not have sufficient spectrum resources to meet the service requirements, so they borrow spectrum resources from operator 1 and 3. In order to maximize network utility, the slices allocate the spectrum resources to users equally. Therefore, the proposed model can effectively adapt to various service requirements in 5G.

5   Conclusion

In this paper, a network utility maximization problem is formulated and solved by a distributed resources allocation method based on ADMM in a three-layer network consisting of mobile operator layer, slicing layer and user layer. As the problem is convex, the optimality of the proposed algorithm can be guaranteed. By comparing with the global optimal solution, simulations validate the effectiveness and optimality of the proposed algorithm. Meanwhile, on the premise that spectrum resources between operators can be rented, the network spectrum utilization has been significantly improved, and the users' data rates can be guaranteed through network slicing.

References

1. Akguel, O.U., Malanchini, I., Suryaprakash, V., Capone, A.: Service-aware network slice trading in a shared multi-tenant infrastructure. In: 2017 IEEE Global Communications Conference, GLOBECOM, pp. 1–7 (2017)

2. Boyd, S.: Distributed optimization and statistical learning via the alternating direction method of multipliers. Found. Trends® Mach. Learn. (2010). https://doi.org/10.1561/2200000016
3. Caballero, P., Banchs, A., de Veciana, G., Costa-Pérez, X.: Multi-tenant radio access network slicing: statistical multiplexing of spatial loads. IEEE/ACM Trans. Netw. **25**(5), 3044–3058 (2017)
4. Garces, P.C., Perez, X.C., Samdanis, K., Banchs, A.: RMSC: a cell slicing controller for virtualized multi-tenant mobile networks. In: 2015 IEEE Vehicular Technology Conference, pp. 1–6 (2015)
5. Gudipati, A., Labs, B., Lucent, A.: RadioVisor: a slicing plane for radio access networks. In: HotSDN, pp. 237–238. ACM (c) (2014). https://doi.org/10.1145/2620728.2620782
6. Kamel, M.I., Le, L.B., Girard, A.: LTE wireless network virtualization: dynamic slicing via flexible scheduling. In: 2014 IEEE Vehicular Technology Conference, pp. 1–5 (2014)
7. Kapassa, E., Touloupou, M., Stavrianos, P., Kyriazis, D.: Dynamic 5G slices for IoT applications with diverse requirements. In: 2018 Fifth International Conference on Internet of Things: Systems, Management and Security, pp. 195–199 (2018)
8. Ordonez-Lucena, J., Ameigeiras, P., Lopez, D., Ramos-Munoz, J.J., Lorca, J., Folgueira, J.: Network slicing for 5G with SDN/NFV: concepts, architectures, and challenges. IEEE Commun. Mag. **55**(5), 80–87 (2017)
9. Sciancalepore, V., Cirillo, F., Costa-Perez, X.: Slice as a service (SlaaS) optimal IoT slice resources orchestration. In: GLOBECOM 2017 - 2017 IEEE Global Communications Conference, pp. 1–7 (2017)
10. Ye, Q., Zhuang, W., Zhang, S., Jin, A., Shen, X., Li, X.: Dynamic radio resource slicing for a two-tier heterogeneous wireless network. IEEE Trans. Veh. Technol. **67**(10), 9896–9910 (2018)

Power-Efficient Communication
for UAV-Enabled Mobile Relay System

Long Chen[1,2], Shu Cai[1,2(✉)], Weidong Zhang[1,2], Jun Zhang[1,2],
and Yongan Guo[1,2]

[1] Jiangsu Key Laboratory of Wireless Communications, Nanjing University of Posts
and Telecommunications, Nanjing, China
caishu@njupt.edu.cn
[2] Engineering Research Center of Health Service System Based on Ubiquitous
Wireless Networks, Nanjing, China

Abstract. This paper studies a unmanned aerial vehicle (UAV)-enabled
wireless relay communication system, where a UAV provides relay services
to a source node and a destination node. To minimize the total power consumption of UAV, we jointly design the trajectory of UAV and transmission power of both UAV and source node, under the constraints on minimum data rate, transmission power, UAV's mobility, and information-
causality. The obtained problem is non-convex and difficult to solve in
general. Hence, a successive convex approximation based optimization
method is proposed to solve the problem approximately. Numerical simulations are performed to show effectiveness of the proposed method.

Keywords: UAV communication · Mobile relay system · Trajectory
design · Optimization

1 Introduction

In current wireless communication networks, based stations are usually built
and fixed on the ground, which can be costly and lack of flexibility. For this reason, the communication network assisted by unmanned aerial vehicle, which is
cheaper and can adjust its position flexibly, becomes an attractive research direction. Compared with conventional static networks, the UAV-assisted network
offers new opportunities for performance improvement through the adjustment
of the UAV's locations or trajectories [1–3].

According to the features of UAV, the existing works can be roughly divided
into two categories: UAV-enabled base station (BS) [4–6] and UAV-enabled
mobile relay [7,8]. The authors of [4] use a UAV-BS to provide public information
to a group of users. For this multicast channel, the achievable rate maximization

Supported by the National Key R&D Program of China (2018YFC1314900), the Natural Science Foundation of China under Grant U1805262, 61671251, and 61871446,
NUPTSF (Grant No. NY217033).

problem is studied by jointly design the transmit power allocation and UAV trajectory, subject to UAV speed and power constraints. In [5], TDMA technology is applied on the UAV for user access control, and then a minimum throughput maximization problem is considered. In [6], the UAV is used to serve multiple ground nodes simultaneously, under the framework of downlink orthogonal frequency division multiple. And the minimum average throughput of users is maximized by transmit power and trajectory optimization. In the UAV-enabled relay network, the authors in [7] study the throughput maximization problem, where UAV trajectory and both source and relay transmit power are optimized jointly, subject to the constraints of UAV mobility and information causality. A multi-hop relay system containing multiple UAVs is considered in [8].

Another key difference between a ground based system and the UAV-enabled one is that the total energy budget of a UAV is strictly limited by its battery capacity, which is the reason for a power-efficient UAV-enabled communication system. Some early results consider only the transmission power of drones, but ignore the flight power consumption. However, in practice, flight power consumption may be higher than that of data transmission, and is thus not negligible. Therefore, the trade-off between network throughput and total energy consumption is studied in [9], based on which, a comprehensive energy consumption model for UAV was established. Based on this model, an energy-efficient drone is also studied in the wireless sensor network [10].

To the best of our knowledge, the power-efficient communication for a UAV-enabled relay has not been studied until now. In this paper, the UAV power consumption minimization problem is considered, where the UAV trajectory and transmit power of both UAV and source node are optimized, subject to the constraints of link transmission rate, UAV mobility, power budget, and information causality. Since the flight power consumption and information causality constraints are non-convex, the optimization problem is non-convex in general. We thus propose a successive convex approximation (SCA) based method to solve it approximately.

2   System Model and Problem Formulation

Consider a wireless communication network, which is composed of a source node S, a destination node D, and a UAV-enabled aerial relay. The UAV need to fly from a starting point to a terminal point in a given time duration T. During this time, it receives signal from S and then forwards it to D, where the locations of S and D are fixed. For ease of expression, we divide the period T into N equal time slots, which are indexed by $n = 1, ..., N$. Here, N is chosen such that the duration $\delta = T/N$ is small enough and thus the UAV's location in each time slot can be approximated by $[q^T[n], H]^T$, $n = 1, \cdots, N$, where $q[n] = (x[n], y[n])^T$ denotes a point in Cartesian coordinate system.

Let us first consider the channel between UAV and the destination node D, which is assumed to be dominated by the line-of-sight (LoS) link. Then, the channel power gain at time slot n is given by

$$h_{ud}[n] = \frac{\beta_0}{d[n]^2} = \frac{\beta_0}{\|q[n] - w_D\|^2 + H^2} \tag{1}$$

where β_0 represents the reference channel gain at $d = 1$ m and w_D denotes the horizontal coordinate of node D. Obviously, the achievable rate from the UAV to node D is

$$R_{ud}[n] = \log_2\left(1 + \frac{p_u[n]h_{ud}[n]}{\sigma^2}\right) \tag{2}$$

$$= \log_2\left(1 + \frac{p_u[n]\gamma_0}{\|q[n] - w_D\|^2 + H^2}\right). \tag{3}$$

where $p_u[n]$ denotes the transmission power of UAV relay, $\gamma_0 = \beta_0/\sigma^2$, and σ^2 denotes the noise power spectrum density.

Similarly, one can obtain the channel power gain from the node S to the UAV in the n-th time slot and the corresponding achievable rate, which are given by

$$h_{su}[n] = \frac{\beta_0}{\|q[n] - w_S\|^2 + H^2}, \tag{4}$$

$$R_{su}[n] = \log_2\left(1 + \frac{p_s[n]h_{su}[n]}{\sigma^2}\right) \tag{5}$$

$$= \log_2\left(1 + \frac{p_s[n]\gamma_0}{\|q[n] - w_S\|^2 + H^2}\right) \tag{6}$$

where w_S denotes the horizontal coordinate of node S, $p_s[n]$ denotes the transmission power of node S at time slot n.

Note that in the n-th time slot, the UAV can only forward the data that has already been received from node S, which is referred to as information-causality constraint [6]. By assuming that the processing delay at UAV is one slot, this constraint can be expressed by

$$R_{ud}[1] = 0, \quad \sum_{i=2}^{n} R_{ud}[i] \leq \sum_{i=1}^{n-1} R_{su}[i], \quad n = 2, ..., N \tag{7}$$

The flight power consumption of UAV is given by [9]

$$P_p = \sum_{n=1}^{N}\left(k_1\|v[n]\|^3 + \frac{k_2}{\|v[n]\|}\left(1 + \frac{\|a[n]\|^2}{g^2}\right)\right), \tag{8}$$

where k_1 and k_2 are constant numbers depend on the UAV's structure and flight environment, $a[n]$ and $v[n]$ denote acceleration and speed of the UAV in the n-th time slot, and g the gravity acceleration.

Further define the transmit power of UAV in the n-th time slot by $p_u[n]$, then the total transmit power consumption is $P_t = \sum_{i=1}^{N} p_u[i]$. Finally, we can obtain the power-efficient communication (PEC) problem

$$(P) \min_{\{q[n],p_s[n],p_u[n],v[n],a[n]\}} P_t + P_p \tag{9a}$$

$$s.t. \quad \eta \leq \frac{1}{N} \sum_{n=2}^{N} R_{ud}[n], \tag{9b}$$

$$\sum_{n=2}^{k} R_{ud}[n] \leq \sum_{n=1}^{k-1} R_{su}[n], k = 2, ..., N, \tag{9c}$$

$$0 \leq p_s[n] \leq p_{smax}, \tag{9d}$$

$$0 \leq p_u[n] \leq p_{umax}, \tag{9e}$$

$$q[1] = q_0, q[N+1] = q_f, \tag{9f}$$

$$v[1] = v_0, v[N+1] = v_f, \tag{9g}$$

$$q[n+1] = q[n] + v[n]\delta + \frac{1}{2}a[n]\delta^2, n = 1, ..., N, \tag{9h}$$

$$v[n+1] = v[n] + a[n]\delta, n = 1, ..., N, \tag{9i}$$

$$\|v[n]\| \leq V_{max}, n = 1, ..., N, \tag{9j}$$

$$\|a[n]\| \leq a_{max}, n = 1, ..., N, \tag{9k}$$

where (9b) is the rate requirement at destination, (9c) is the information-causality constraint, (9d) and (9d) are the transmission power constraints for node S and UAV, respectively, (9f)–(9k) are constraints related to UAV's flight trajectory.

Note that the objective function and constraints (9b) and (9c) are nonconvex, so is problem (9). Therefore, solving it directly is computationally inefficient. Next, we will propose a SCA based method [11] to solve it approximately.

3 Proposed Solution

To deal with the objective function, we first introduce slack variables $\{\tau_n\}$, and modify (9) into

$$(P1) \min_{\{q[n],p_s[n],p_u[n],v[n],a[n],\tau_n\}} P_t + P_p', \tag{10a}$$

$$s.t \quad (9b), (9c), (9d), (9e), (9f), (9g), (9h), (9i), (9j), (9k), \tag{10b}$$

$$\|v[n]\|^2 \geq \tau_n^2, n = 1, ..., N, \tag{10c}$$

$$\tau_n \geq 0, n = 1, ..., N, \tag{10d}$$

where

$$P_p' = \sum_{n=1}^{N} (k_1\|v[n]\|^3 + \frac{k_2}{\tau_n} + \frac{k_2\|a[n]\|^2}{g^2\tau_n}) \tag{11}$$

Obviously, problem (9) and (10) are equivalent in the sense that optimal solution of the latter must satisfy $\|v[n]\| = \tau_n$.

To deal with the nonconvex constraint (10c), we apply the first-order Taylor expansion to $\|v[n]\|^2$ and obtain

$$\|v[n]\|^2 \geq \|\bar{v}^r[n]\|^2 + 2\bar{v}^r[n]^{\mathrm{T}}(v[n] - \bar{v}^r[n]) \triangleq f^{lb}(v[n]) \tag{12}$$

where $\bar{v}^r[n]$ is the solution of the previous iteration. Note that $f^{lb}(v[n])$ is a concave lower bound of $\|v[n]\|^2$, therefore one can safely replace (10c) by the convex constraint

$$f^{lb}(v[n]) \geq \tau_n^2. \tag{13}$$

To deal with the non-convex constraint (9b), we define

$$\bar{a}_u^r[n] = \sqrt{\bar{p}_u^r[n]}, \ \bar{d}_u^r[n] = H^2 + \|\bar{q}^r[n] - w_D\|^2, \tag{14}$$

$$a_u[n] = \sqrt{p_u[n]}, \ d_u[n] = H^2 + \|q[n] - w_D\|^2, \tag{15}$$

where $\bar{p}_u^r[n]$ and $\bar{q}^r[n]$ denote some feasible transmit power and location of the UAV in n-th slot. Then, $R_{ud}[n]$ can be written as

$$R_{ud}[n] = \log_2\left(1 + \frac{a_u^2[n]\gamma_0}{d_u[n]}\right). \tag{16}$$

Note that x^2/y is convex whenever $x \in \mathbb{R}$ and $y > 0$, and $\frac{x^2}{y} \geq \frac{2x'}{y'}x - \frac{x'^2}{y'^2}y$ is always satisfied for any x', y' in the function domain. Thus, $R_{ud}[n]$ can be lower bounded by a concave function

$$R_{ud}^{lb,r}[n] = \log_2\left(1 + \gamma_0\frac{2\bar{a}_u^r[n]}{\bar{d}_u^r[n]}a_u[n] - \gamma_0\frac{(\bar{a}_u^r[n])^2}{(\bar{d}_u^r[n])^2}d_u[n]\right), \tag{17}$$

where $R_{ud}^{lb,r}[n]$ is a concave in $(a_u[n], q[n])$ [12].

Then, the constraint (9b) can safely replaced by

$$\eta \leq \frac{1}{N}\sum_{n=2}^{N} R_{ud}^{lb,r}[n]. \tag{18}$$

Next, we tackle the non-convex constraint (9c). First, for the left hand side, $R_{ud}[n]$ can be written as

$$R_{ud}[n] = \log_2(1 + \frac{p_u[n]\gamma_0}{\|q[n] - w_D\|^2 + H^2}) \tag{19}$$

$$= R_{lud}[n] - R_{rud}[n], \tag{20}$$

where

$$R_{lud}[n] = \log_2(H^2 + \|q[n] - w_D\|^2 + p_u[n]\gamma_0), \tag{21}$$

$$R_{rud}[n] = \log_2(H^2 + \|q[n] - w_D\|^2). \tag{22}$$

Given a feasible point $(\bar{p}_u^r[n], \bar{q}^r[n])$, a global upper bound of $R_{lud}[n]$ and lower bound of $R_{rud}[n]$ can be obtained by

$$
R_{lud}^{ub,r}[n] = \log_2(\bar{d}_u^r[n] + (\bar{a}_u^r[n])^2 \gamma_0)
$$
$$
+ \frac{(d_u[n] + (a_u[n])^2 \gamma_0 - \bar{d}_u^r[n] - (\bar{a}_u^r[n])^2 \gamma_0) \log_2 e}{\bar{d}_u^r[n][n] + (\bar{a}_u^r[n])^2 \gamma_0}, \tag{23}
$$

$$
R_{rud}^{ub,r}[n] = \log_2(\bar{d}_u^r[n] + 2(q[n] - w_D)^{\mathrm{T}}(\bar{q}^r[n] - w_D)). \tag{24}
$$

Hence, the global upper bound of $R_{ud}[n]$ is given by

$$
R_{lud}[n] = R_{lud}^{ub,r}[n] - R_{rud}^{ub,r}[n], \tag{25}
$$

Second, the right-hand-side of (9c) can be transformed similar to that of (9b). Denote

$$
\bar{a}_s^r[n] = \sqrt{\bar{p}_s^r[n]}, \ \bar{d}_s^r[n] = H^2 + \|\bar{q}^r[n] - w_S\|^2, \tag{26}
$$
$$
a_s[n] = \sqrt{p_s[n]}, \ d_s[n] = H^2 + \|q[n] - w_S\|^2, \tag{27}
$$

where $(\bar{p}_s^r[n], \bar{q}^r[n])$ is given feasible point. Then a global lower bound of $R_{su}[n]$ can be obtained by

$$
R_{su}^{lb,r}[n] = \log_2 \left(1 + \gamma_0 \left(\frac{2\bar{a}_s^r[n]}{\bar{d}_s^r[n]} a_s[n] - \frac{(\bar{a}_s^r[n])^2}{(\bar{d}_s^r[n])^2} d_s[n] \right) \right), \tag{28}
$$

where $R_{su}^{lb,r}[n]$ is concave in $(a_s[n], q[n])$ [12]. Then, the constraint (9c) can be safely replaced by

$$
\sum_{n=2}^{k} (R_{lud}^{ub,r}[n] - R_{rud}^{ub,r}[n]) \leq \sum_{n=1}^{k-1} R_{su}^{lb,r}[n], k = 2, ..., N, \tag{29}
$$

which is convex [11].

Based on all the above approximations, an SCA sub-problem of (10) can be obtained by

$$
(P2) \quad \min_{\{q[n], a_s[n], a_u[n], v[n], a[n], \tau_n\}} \sum_{n=2}^{N} (a_u[n])^2 + P_p' \tag{30a}
$$

$$
s.t \quad (9f), (9g), (9h), (9i), (9j), (9k), \tag{30b}
$$

$$
\eta \leq \frac{1}{N} \sum_{n=2}^{N} R_{ud}^{lb,r}[n], \tag{30c}
$$

$$
\sum_{n=2}^{k} (R_{lud}^{ub,r}[n] - R_{rud}^{ub,r}[n]) \leq \sum_{n=1}^{k-1} R_{su}^{lb,r}[n], k = 2, ..., N, \tag{30d}
$$

$$
0 \leq a_s[n] \leq \sqrt{p_{smax}}, \tag{30e}
$$

$$
0 \leq a_u[n] \leq \sqrt{p_{umax}}, \tag{30f}
$$

which is convex and can be efficiently solved by using optimization tools such as CVX [5].

Finally, the proposed SCA-based method for the PEC problem is summarized in Algorithm 1.

Algorithm 1. SCA-based algorithm for the PEC problem

1: **Initialize** $\bar{p}_u^r[n], \bar{p}_s^r[n], \bar{q}^r[n], \bar{v}^r[n], \bar{a}^r[n]$ and set r=0, tolerance $\epsilon > 0$.
2: Obtain objective function value F^r
3: Obtain $\{\bar{a}_u^r[n], \bar{a}_s^r[n]\}$ based on (14) and (26).
4: **repeat**
5: Update $\{\bar{d}_u^r[n], \bar{d}_s^r[n]\}$ based on (14) and (26).
6: Update $\{\bar{a}_u^{r+1}[n], \bar{a}_s^{r+1}[n], \bar{q}^{r+1}[n], \bar{v}^{r+1}[n], F^{r+1}\}$ by solving the problem (P2).
7: Set $r = r + 1$.
8: **until** $F^{r-1} - F^r < \epsilon$
9: **Output** $\{\bar{p}_u^r[n], \bar{q}^r[n], \bar{v}^r[n], \bar{a}^r[n], F^r\}$

---

4   Numerical Results

In this section, experiments are performed to evaluate the proposed algorithm. The simulation settings are similar to those in [7], which are UAV parameters $H = 100\,\text{m}$, $a_{max} = 30\,\text{m/s}^2$, $V_{max} = 30\,\text{m/s}^2$, $k_1 = 0.002$, $k_2 = 70.698$, $p_{umax} = 0.1\,\text{W}$, $v_0 = (1, 0.4)$, $v_f = (0, 0)$, and $\delta = 1\,\text{s}$, channel power gain $\beta_0 = -50\,\text{dB}$, source transmit power $p_{smax} = 0.2\,\text{W}$, noise power spectrum density $\sigma^2 = -110\,\text{dBm}$, data rate requirement $\eta = 5\,\text{bps/Hz}$.

The Algorithm 1 is initialized as follows: the initial trajectory is a straight line between the starting and terminal points, the accelerations of the first and last four time slots are a_1 and a_2, which are related to total duration T, respectively, and those of the other time slots are $\mathbf{0}$. The tolerance for convergence is $\varepsilon = 0.1$.

In Fig. 1, the UAV's trajectories varying with total duration T is plotted, where the marker "o" denotes the locations of nodes S and D and the marker "□" denotes the location of UAV with a sampling interval $5\,\text{s}$. In the figure, we see that when $T = 90$, the trajectory is a straight line. And it curves to node D, when T becomes large. The reason is that when T is large enough, the rate constraints can be satisfied easily and the UAV tries to fly at the speed with lowest propulsion power.

The corresponding transmission power of UAV is shown in Fig. 2. It is seen that the transmission power of UAV decreases with the increase of T. In Fig. 3, the speed and acceleration are also given out. We see that the UAV's acceleration is large at the first and last several time slots, and is zero in the other slots. When the time T is large enough, the speed of UAV is stable.

In Fig. 4, the total power consumption varying with time for $T = 270\,\text{s}$ is illustrated, where "initial" denotes power consumption of UAV with its flight

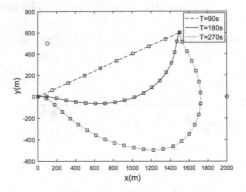

Fig. 1. UAV trajectories for different periods T, starting point is (0, 0), ending point is (1500, 600). The sampling interval of the path is 5 s and is marked as a '□'.

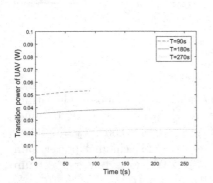

Fig. 2. Transmission power of the UAV

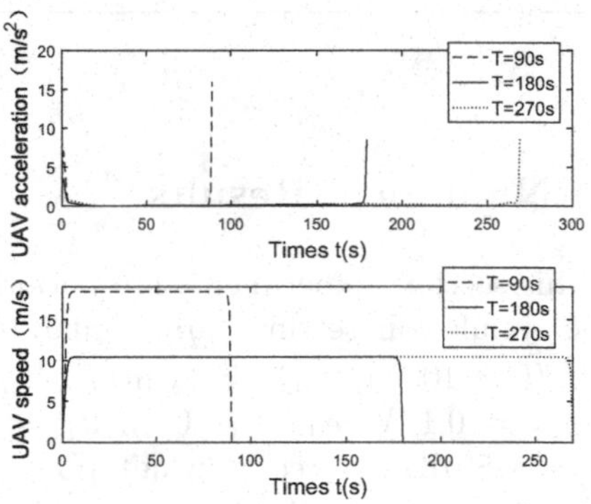

Fig. 3. UAV speed and acceleration

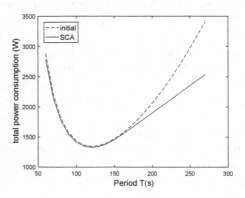

Fig. 4. The power consumption

path as a straight line, while "Algorithm 1" denotes those given by Algorithm 1. We see that the proposed method is more energy efficient, which is remarkable when $T > 200\,\mathrm{s}$.

5 Conclusion

This paper considers power-efficient communication for a UAV-enabled mobile relay system. A rate constrained power-efficient relay-UAV trajectory and transmit power joint design problem is considered, which is non-convex and difficult to deal with. Hence, an SCA-based optimization method is proposed to solve the problem approximately. Numerical experiments are performed to show the effectiveness of the proposed method.

References

1. Zeng, Y., Zhang, R., Lim, T.J.: Wireless communications with unmanned aerial vehicles: opportunities and challenges. IEEE Commun. Mag. **54**(5), 36–42 (2016)
2. Chen, Y., Feng, W., Zheng, G.: Optimum placement of UAV as relays. IEEE Commun. Lett. **22**(2), 248–251 (2018)
3. Azari, M.M., Rosas, F., Chen, K., Pollin, S.: Optimal UAV positioning for terrestrial-aerial communication in presence of fading. In: 2016 IEEE Global Communications Conference (GLOBECOM), December 2016, pp. 1–7 (2016)
4. Wu, Y., Jie, X., Ling, Q., Rui, Z.: Capacity of UAV-enabled multicast channel: joint trajectory design and power allocation (2017)
5. Wu, Q., Yong, Z., Rui, Z.: Joint trajectory and communication design for UAV-enabled multiple access (2017)
6. Wang, H., Ren, G., Chen, J., Ding, G., Yang, Y.: Unmanned aerial vehicle-aided communications: joint transmit power and trajectory optimization. IEEE Wirel. Commun. Lett. **7**(4), 522–525 (2018)
7. Zeng, Y., Zhang, R., Lim, T.J.: Throughput maximization for UAV-enabled mobile relaying systems. IEEE Trans. Commun. **64**(12), 4983–4996 (2016)
8. Wang, C., Ma, Z.: Design of wireless power transfer device for UAV. In: 2016 IEEE International Conference on Mechatronics and Automation, August 2016, pp. 2449–2454 (2016)
9. Zeng, Y., Zhang, R.: Energy-efficient UAV communication with trajectory optimization. IEEE Trans. Wireless Commun. **16**(6), 3747–3760 (2017)
10. Hua, M., Wang, Y., Zhang, Z., Li, C., Huang, Y., Yang, L.: Power-efficient communication in UAV-aided wireless sensor networks. IEEE Commun. Lett. **22**(6), 1264–1267 (2018)
11. Marks, B.R., Wright, G.P.: A general inner approximation algorithm for nonconvex mathematical programs. Oper. Res. **26**(4), 681–683 (1978)
12. Shen, C., Chang, T.-H., Gong, J., Zeng, Y., Zhang, R.: Multi-UAV interference coordination via joint trajectory and power control (2018)

Reliable Index Modulation Aided Spatial M-ary DCSK Design

Zuwei Chen[1], Lin Zhang[1($\boxtimes$)] , and Zhiqiang Wu[2,3]

[1] School of Electronics and Information Technology, Sun Yat-sen University,
Guangzhou 510006, China
isszl@mail.sysu.edu.cn
[2] Department of Electrical Engineering, Tibet University, Lhasa 850012, China
[3] Department of Electrical Engineering, Wright State University, Dayton 45435, USA

Abstract. Higher order modulation and spatial modulation schemes improve the data rate for differential chaos shift keying (DCSK) systems by transmitting more bits in one time slot, however, the reliability performances become worse respectively due to more dense signal distributions and bad channel condition of active antenna. In this paper, we propose to utilize the antenna and symbol indexes to improve both the data rate and the reliability performances for DCSK systems with aid of antenna selection. Therein the information is modulated cooperatively using the antenna index and the symbol index. Then with the aid of the feedback channel state information (CSI) from receivers, the antenna with the best CSI is selected to transmit modulated symbols, which helps to improve the reliability performance. At the receiver, reverse operations are performed. Furthermore, we provide the theoretical symbol error rate (SER) and bit error rate (BER) over the multi-path Rayleigh fading channel. Simulation results demonstrate that the proposed scheme achieves better reliability performances than the counterpart schemes with the same data rate.

Keywords: Differential chaos shift keying (DCSK) · Index modulation · Multiple input multiple output (MIMO) · Spatial modulation (SM) · Reliability performances

1 Introduction

Differential chaos shift keying (DCSK) schemes have aroused a lot of research interests since no chaotic synchronization circuits are required at the receiver, which is attractive for practical implementations. Although DCSK systems inherit the benefits of chaotic communications including secure and robust transmissions, they sacrifices the data rate performances owing to the transmission of reference chaotic signals.

© ICST Institute for Computer Sciences, Social Informatics and Telecommunications Engineering 2020
Published by Springer Nature Switzerland AG 2020. All Rights Reserved
B. Li et al. (Eds.): IoTaaS 2019, LNICST 316, pp. 104–115, 2020.
https://doi.org/10.1007/978-3-030-44751-9_10

In order to achieve high data rate, higher modulation and spatial multiplexing have been utilized. Specifically, quadrature chaos shift keying [1] (QCSK) utilizes Hilbert transform to convey one more bits on one chaotic sequence. Then [2,3] exploit the idea of a round constellation similar to phase shift keying (PSK) to further improve QCSK scheme to transmit more bits, and [4] utilizes orthogonal chaotic sequences to generate the QCSK-based M-ary DCSK signals based on a square constellation similar to the quadrature amplitude modulation (QAM). In addition, [5] uses M-order Walsh code (WC) to increase the data rate.

On the other hand, the spatial multiplexing provided by multiple input multiple output (MIMO) antennas is also exploited to improve the data rate. [6] presents a DCSK system using space-time coding based on Alamouti scheme, while [7] applies the orthogonal space-time block coding aided DCSK scheme. Moreover, [8] combines the high order modulation with the spatial multiplexing, and presents a MIMO M-ary DCSK scheme to be used when the channel state information (CSI) can hardly be obtained, and the spatial modulation (SM) is proposed in [9] to further improve the efficiency with a low complexity. However, due to more dense signal distributions and bad channel condition of active antenna, high order M-ary and SM aided DCSK systems may suffer from reliability performance degradations, especially when channel varies dramatically.

In order to achieve a better tradeoff between the reliability and data rate performances, in this paper, we propose to jointly utilize the antenna index and the symbol index to modulate the information, and present an index modulation-aided spatial M-ary DCSK (IM-S-M-DCSK).

To be more explicit, at the transmitter, the input information is modulated and embedded into the symbol index and the antenna index jointly. Then the index modulated symbols are modulated by the reference chaotic sequence and its orthogonal version obtained from Hilbert transform to generate high order chaotic modulated symbols. The resultant modulated chaotic symbol is then transmitted via the antenna with the best CSI, which can be easily obtained from the receiver via the feedback channel. At the receiver, reverse operations are performed with a low complexity since only one signal received from the antenna with the best CSI is required to be processed.

Briefly, the main contributions include: (1) both the antenna index and the symbol index are exploited to modulate the same transmitted symbol and the feedback CSI is utilized to identify which antenna is selected to transmit chaotic modulated symbols; (2) the complexity of the receiver is reduced compared with other scheme adopting SM technology; (3) we provide the theoretical bit error rate (BER) and symbol error rate (SER) expressions over multi-path Rayleigh fading channels.

The remainder of the letter is organized as follows. The IM-S-M-DCSK scheme is presented in Sect. 2, then in Sect. 3, we derive theoretical BER and SER expressions. Simulations and corresponding results are provided in Sect. 4. Finally, we conclude this paper in Sect. 5.

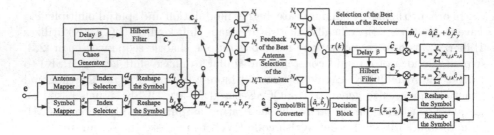

Fig. 1. IM-S-M-DCSK transceiver.

Table 1. Mapping rule.

	Bits	Selected Antenna or Symbol	Select-ed Index	Reshape the Symbol	$m_{i,j} = \tilde{a}_i c_x + \tilde{b}_j c_y$
$N_T = 2, \tilde{M} = 2$	0	T_1 s_1	1	$-d$	$d \begin{bmatrix} -c_x - c_y & c_x - c_y \\ -c_x + c_y & c_x + c_y \end{bmatrix}$
$M = 4$	1	T_2 s_2	2	d	
$N_T = 4$	00	T_1 s_1	1	$-3d$	$d \begin{bmatrix} -3c_x - 3c_y & -3c_x - c_y & -3c_x + c_y & -3c_x + 3c_y \\ -c_x - 3c_y & -c_x - c_y & -c_x + c_y & -c_x + 3c_y \\ c_x - 3c_y & c_x - c_y & c_x + c_y & c_x + 3c_y \\ 3c_x - 3c_y & 3c_x - c_y & 3c_x + c_y & 3c_x + 3c_y \end{bmatrix}$
$\tilde{M} = 4$	01	T_2 s_2	2	$-d$	
$M = 16$	11	T_3 s_3	3	d	
	10	T_4 s_4	4	$3d$	

2   IM-S-M-DCSK Scheme

2.1   Structure of the Scheme

In this section, we will elaborate the structure of the IM-S-M-DCSK scheme. Figure 1 illustrates the transceiver structure of the proposed scheme.

At the transmitter, the input information is firstly modulated by the symbol index and the antenna index jointly. Then the signals bearing index modulated symbols are further modulated by orthogonal chaotic sequences alternately. Subsequently, the resultant chaotic modulated signals are transmitted through the channel with the best CSI selected from $N_T \times N_R$ MIMO channels.

At the receiving end, after the transmission over independently and identically distributed (i.i.d.) fading channels, the receiver mounted with N_R antennas activate the specific selected antenna corresponding to the channel with the best CSI, and perform reverse operations to retrieve the information. More details about the IM-S-M-DCSK design are given as below.

2.2   Transmitter

At the transmitter side, the chaos generator module outputs the chaotic sequences to modulate the symbols obtained from the index modulators to formulate the spatial M-DCSK signals for transmissions.

Chaos Generator. Here we adopt the second order Chebyshev polynomial function to generate the chaotic sequences of length β, which is expressed as

$$u_{v+1} = 1 - 2u_v^2 \tag{1}$$

where u_v denotes the v-th chip of the chaotic sequence. Based on Eq. (1), we use $c_x = (c_{x,1}, \ldots, c_{x,\beta})$ to denote the first part of chaotic sequences output from the chaos generator, and $c_{x,k}(k = 1, 2, \cdot, \beta)$ is the k_{th} generated chip of the chaotic sequence.

Then we use Hilbert transform to generate another quadrature chaotic sequence, which is represented by $c_y = (c_{y,1}, \ldots, c_{y,\beta})$ [1]. Thus, we have $\sum_{k=1}^{\beta} c_{x,k} c_{y,k} = 0$. Then the resultant chaotic sequence is normalized to achieve $\sum_{k=1}^{\beta} c_{x,k}^2 = \sum_{k=1}^{\beta} c_{y,k}^2 = 1$.

Index Modulation-Aided Spatial M-DCSK. As shown in Fig. 1, the input bit sequence $\mathbf{e}$ is divided into two parts, the first $\log_2(N_T)$ bits are mapped onto a selected antenna denoted by T_n $(n = 1, \ldots, N_T)$, while another $\log_2(\tilde{M})$ bits of the second part are mapped into a selected symbol denoted by $S_m \left(m = 1, \ldots, \tilde{M} \right)$ where $M = N_T \times \tilde{M}$. Notably, the mapping rule from the bits to T_n and S_m follows the Gray decoding.

Subsequently, the subscripts n and m in T_n and S_m are transformed to the decimal number a_i $(i = 1, \ldots, N_T)$ and b_j $\left(j = 1, \ldots, \tilde{M} \right)$, which respectively correspond to the antenna index and the symbol index.

To be more explicit, as shown in Table 1, the index modulation is carried out by transforming the data bits to a_i and b_j by applying the Gray decoding. Then we reshape the indexes, i.e., $\tilde{a}_i = (2a_i - (N_T + 1))\,d$, $\tilde{b}_j = (2b_j - (M + 1))\,d$, which are used respectively as the x-axis coordinate and y-axis coordinate of a specific constellation point in the modulation constellation, where d denotes the unit distance between two constellation points in the constellation map.

After the index modulation, the resultant $\tilde{a}_i$ and $\tilde{b}_j$ are separately modulated by chaotic sequences c_x or c_y. The resultant chaotic modulated symbol is expressed as $m_{i,j} = \tilde{a}_i c_x + \tilde{b}_j c_y$, which is transmitted during the q-th symbol duration via the antenna with the best channel gain as follows

$$s(k) = \begin{cases} c_{x,k}, k = 2\,(q-1)\,\beta + 1, \ldots, (2q-1)\,\beta \\ \tilde{a}_i c_{x,k} + \tilde{b}_j c_{y,k}, k = (2q-1)\,\beta + 1, \ldots, 2q\beta \end{cases} \tag{2}$$

Furthermore, Fig. 2 illustrates the constellation diagram. It can be seen that thanks to Gray decoding, each symbol has only one bit different from the neighbor constellation point and hence the received symbol intruding the neighbor point's decision area would cause only one bit error.

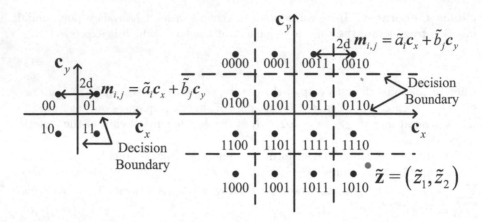

Fig. 2. Constellation diagram.

2.3 Receiver and Decision

As shown in Fig. 1, after the channel transmission, corresponding to the k_{th} chip in the q-th symbol duration, the received signal is obtained as

$$r(k) = h(k) \otimes s(k) + n(k) \tag{3}$$

where $\otimes$ is the convolution operator, and $n(k)$ is a wideband additive white Gaussian noise (AWGN) with zero mean and variance $N_0/2$. We consider a multipath slow Rayleigh fading channel, which is commonly used in spread spectrum systems [3,4,10], with the impulse response function of

$$h(k) = \sum_{l=1}^{L} \alpha_l \delta(k - \tau_l) \tag{4}$$

where L is the number of paths, α_l and τ_l are respectively the channel coefficient and the path time delay of the l-th path.

As shown in Fig. 1, corresponding to the two components of sequentially transmitted signals, the received signals can be easily separated into two parts. One is the first β chips denoted by $\hat{c}_x$ and the other is the last β chips denoted by $\hat{m}_{i,j} = \hat{a}_i \hat{c}_x + \hat{b}_j \hat{c}_y$ where $\hat{c}_y$ is similarly obtained by performing Hilbert transform on $\hat{c}_x$.

Then the correlation demodulation is carried out respectively on the antenna index modulated symbols and the symbol index modulated symbols, and the corresponding decision variable are respectively determined by

$$z_a = \sum_{k=1}^{\beta} \hat{m}_{i,j,k} \hat{c}_{x,k} \quad z_b = \sum_{k=1}^{\beta} \hat{m}_{i,j,k} \hat{c}_{y,k} \tag{5}$$

where $\hat{m}_{i,j,k}$ is the k-th chip of $\hat{m}_{i,j}$. Then, we reshape the decision variable and the resultant decision variables can be denoted by $\tilde{z}_a = z_a / \sum_{l=1}^{L} \alpha_l^2$ and $\tilde{z}_b = z_b / \sum_{l=1}^{L} \alpha_l^2$.

Subsequently, demapping operations are performed based on Fig. 2, and the estimates of the user information, which is represented by $\hat{\mathbf{e}}$, can be obtained by evaluating the distance from a specific symbol to the constellation point. For example, as shown in Fig. 2, assuming that $M = 16$ and the decision vector is $\tilde{\mathbf{z}} = (\tilde{z}_1, \tilde{z}_2)$, we can naturally obtain the estimates as "1010" since $\tilde{\mathbf{z}} = (\tilde{z}_1, \tilde{z}_2)$ has the nearest distance with the point $(3d, -3d)$.

Next, based the above signal expressions, we will evaluate the theoretical error rate performances and derive SER and BER expressions.

3   Performance Analysis

In this section, we apply the Gaussian approximation method to derive the theoretical SER and BER expressions, which are dependent on the probability density distribution (PDF) of the channel with the best gain given as below.

3.1   Probability Density Function Derivation

For L independent Rayleigh fading channels having the equal variances, the PDF of the symbol SNR γ_s is given by [11]

$$f_{\gamma_k}(\gamma_s) = \frac{\gamma_s^{L-1}}{(L-1)! \bar{\gamma}_p^L} \exp\left(-\frac{\gamma_s}{\gamma_p}\right) \tag{6}$$

where γ_s is determined by $\gamma_s = \left(\sum_{l=1}^{L} \alpha_l^2\right) \frac{E_s}{N_0}$, where $\sum_{l=1}^{L} \mathrm{E}\left[\alpha_l^2\right] = 1$, E_s is the average transmitted energy per symbol, and N_0 is the variance of the complex AWGN, and $\bar{\gamma}_p$ is the average symbol SNR per channel, which can be calculated by $\bar{\gamma}_p = \left(\frac{E_s}{N_0}\right) \mathrm{E}\left[\alpha_l^2\right] = \left(\frac{E_s}{N_0}\right) \mathrm{E}\left[\alpha_o^2\right], l \neq o$.

In addition, based on the properties of the chi-square distribution, the corresponding cumulative density function (CDF) is derived as

$$\Pr\left(\gamma_p \leq \gamma_s\right) = 1 - \exp\left(-\frac{\gamma_s}{\bar{\gamma}_p}\right) \sum_{k=0}^{L-1} \frac{1}{k!} \left(\frac{\gamma_s}{\bar{\gamma}_p}\right)^k \tag{7}$$

In our IM-S-M-DCSK system, the PDF of the MIMO channel that is selected to transmit the signal with the best CSI is given as follows [12]

$$f_{\gamma_s}(\gamma_s) = \sum_{g=1}^{N_T \times N_R} f_{\gamma_g}(\gamma_s) \prod_{p=1, p \neq g}^{N_T \times N_R} \Pr\left(\gamma_p \leq \gamma_s\right) \tag{8}$$

3.2   Theoretical SER Expression

Without loss of generality, we assume that the largest multipath delay is much shorter than the symbol duration and the inter-symbol interference (ISI) can be accordingly neglected. In addition, we also assume that the channel coefficient is constant during each symbol duration. Then we approximate the decision variables in Eq. (5) as approximated as

$$
\begin{aligned}
z_a \approx \sum_{k=1}^{\beta} & \left[\left(\sum_{l=1}^{L} \alpha_l c_{x,k-\tau_l} + n_k \right) \right. \\
& \left. \times \left(\sum_{l=1}^{L} \alpha_l \left(a_i c_{x,k-\tau_l} + b_j c_{y,k-\tau_l} \right) + n_{k+\beta} \right) \right] \\
z_b \approx \sum_{k=1}^{\beta} & \left[\left(\sum_{l=1}^{L} \alpha_l c_{y,k-\tau_l} + n'_k \right) \right. \\
& \left. \times \left(\sum_{l=1}^{L} \alpha_l \left(a_i c_{x,k-\tau_l} + b_j c_{y,k-\tau_l} \right) + n_{k+\beta} \right) \right]
\end{aligned}
\tag{9}
$$

where n_k is additive white Gaussian noise (AWGN) [1], and n'_k is obtained by performing Hilbert transform on n_k. Notably, when ideal Hilbert transform is performed, n'_k has the same statistics as n_k.

For large spreading factor, considering that the chaotic sequence has the property of $\sum_{k=1}^{\beta} c_{x,k-\tau_l} c_{x,k-\tau_p} \approx 0$, $l \neq p$ [10], Eq. (9) can be further simplified as

$$
\begin{aligned}
z_a \approx & \sum_{k=1}^{\beta} \sum_{l=1}^{L} \alpha_l \left(a_i c_{x,k-\tau_l} + b_j c_{y,k-\tau_l} \right) n_k + \sum_{k=1}^{\beta} n_k n_{k+\beta} \\
& + \sum_{l=1}^{L} a_i \alpha_l^2 \sum_{k=1}^{\beta} c_{x,k-\tau_l}^2 + \sum_{k=1}^{\beta} \sum_{l=1}^{L} \alpha_l c_{x,k-\tau_l} n_{k+\beta} \\
z_b \approx & \sum_{k=1}^{\beta} \sum_{l=1}^{L} \alpha_l \left(a_i c_{x,k-\tau_l} + b_j c_{y,k-\tau_l} \right) n'_k + \sum_{k=1}^{\beta} n'_k n_{k+\beta} \\
& + \sum_{l=1}^{L} b_j \alpha_l^2 \sum_{k=1}^{\beta} c_{x,k-\tau_l}^2 + \sum_{k=1}^{\beta} \sum_{l=1}^{L} \alpha_l c_{y,k-\tau_l} n_{k+\beta}
\end{aligned}
\tag{10}
$$

Recall that in M-order square constellation, $\tilde{M} = N_T = \sqrt{M}$, and the amplitudes of constellation points are respectively $\pm d, \ldots, \pm \left(\sqrt{M} - 1 \right) d$, the energy of a specific symbol determined by

$$
\begin{aligned}
E_s &= \frac{1}{M} \sum_{i=1}^{N_T} \sum_{j=1}^{\tilde{M}} \left(a_i^2 + b_j^2 + 1 \right) \sum_{k=1}^{\beta} c_x^2 = \mathrm{E} \left(a_i^2 + b_j^2 + 1 \right) \\
&= \frac{2 \left(M - 1 \right) d^2 + 3}{3}
\end{aligned}
\tag{11}
$$

Then we can derive the mean and the variance of decision variables as

$$E\left[z_a\right] = a_i \sum_{l=1}^{L} \alpha_l^2 \quad E\left[z_b\right] = b_j \sum_{l=1}^{L} \alpha_l^2$$

$$\operatorname{var}\left[z_a\right] = \sum_{l=1}^{L} \alpha_l^2 \, E\left[a_i^2 + b_j^2 + 1\right] \frac{N_0}{2} + \frac{\beta N_0^2}{4}$$

$$\approx \sum_{l=1}^{L} \alpha_l^2 \frac{E_s N_0}{2} + \frac{\beta N_0^2}{4} \tag{12}$$

$$\operatorname{var}\left[z_b\right] \approx \sum_{l=1}^{L} \alpha_l^2 \frac{E_s N_0}{2} + \frac{\beta N_0^2}{4}$$

For transmissions over AWGN channel, based on Eq. (12), we can be derive that both decision variables have the variance of $\frac{E_s N_0}{2} + \frac{\beta N_0^2}{4}$ before and after reshaping. Thus the conditional probability that the decision variable $\tilde{z}$ exceeds the boundaries in the constellation map is determined by

$$P_e = \Pr\left(\left|\tilde{z}_a - a_i\right| > d\right) = 2Q\left(\frac{d}{\sqrt{\frac{E_s N_0}{2} + \frac{\beta N_0^2}{4}}}\right) \tag{13}$$

Accordingly, we can derive the SER expression based Eqs. (11) and (13) as

$$P_s^{AWGN}\left(\gamma_s\right) = 1 - \left[1 - \frac{\sqrt{M}-1}{\sqrt{M}} P_e\right]^2 \tag{14}$$

$$= 1 - \left[1 - \frac{2\left(\sqrt{M}-1\right)}{\sqrt{M}} Q\left(\frac{6d\gamma_s/\left(2\left(M-1\right)d^2+3\right)}{\sqrt{2\gamma_s+\beta}}\right)\right]^2$$

where $Q\left(x\right) = 1/\sqrt{2\pi} \times \int_x^\infty \exp\left(-t^2/2\right)dt$, for $x \geq 0$.

When transmitted over slow and flat Rayleigh fading channels, the SER expression is expressed as

$$P_s^{Rayleigh} = \int_0^{+\infty} P_s^{AWGN}\left(\gamma_s\right)f\left(\gamma_s\right)d\gamma_s \tag{15}$$

where $f\left(\gamma_s\right)$ is given by Eq. (8).

3.3   Theoretical BER Calculation

Based on Eq. (14), by referring to [13], we can get the BER expression over the AWGN channel as

$$P_b^{AWGN}\left(\gamma_s\right) = \frac{\sum_{p=1}^{\log_2\sqrt{M}} \sum_{w=0}^{W} T_w^p \operatorname{erfc}\left(\frac{F_w \gamma_s}{\sqrt{2\gamma_s+\beta}}\right)}{\sqrt{M}\log_2\sqrt{M}} \tag{16}$$

where $T_w^p = (-1)^{\left\lfloor \frac{w \times 2^{p-1}}{\sqrt{M}} \right\rfloor} \left(2^{p-1} - \left\lfloor \frac{w \times 2^{p-1}}{\sqrt{M}} + \frac{1}{2} \right\rfloor \right)$, $W = (1 - 2^{-p})\sqrt{M} - 1$, and $F_w = \frac{6(2w+1)d}{\sqrt{2}(2(M-1)d^2+3)}$, where $\lfloor x \rfloor$ denotes the largest integer of x, and $\mathrm{erfc}\,(x) = 2/\sqrt{\pi} \times \int_x^\infty \exp\left(-t^2\right) dt$.

Then similar to Eq. (15), the BER expression over Rayleigh fading channels can be obtained as

$$P_b^{Rayleigh} = \int_0^{+\infty} P_b(\gamma_s) f\left(\gamma_s\right) d\gamma_s. \tag{17}$$

4   Simulation Results

In this section, we provide simulation results to verify the effectiveness of the theoretical analysis and to demonstrate the outstanding performances of our design under different parameter settings. In the simulations, $d = \sqrt{3/(2(M-1))}$, and we assume that perfect CSI and the same channel parameters are shared between the pair of transceivers.

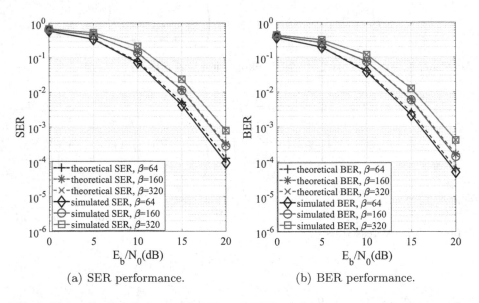

(a) SER performance.   (b) BER performance.

Fig. 3. Theoretical and simulated SER and BER performance comparisons over the single-path Rayleigh fading channel. $N_T = 2$, $N_R = 2$, $\tilde{M} = 2$, $M = 4$.

Firstly, Fig. 3(a) compares the theoretical SER and BER over the single-path Rayleigh fading channel when $\beta = 64, 160, 320$. It can be observed from Fig. 3(a) and (b) that for larger β such as $\beta = 320$, the theoretical SER and BER approximately overlap with the simulated ones, and are more consistent with the simulation results thanks to higher Gaussian approximation precision with more samples than the case that $\beta = 64$ and $\beta = 160$. Moreover, it is noticeable that for smaller β, the SER and BER performances are better than those with larger β since the interferences may increase when the value of β increases [4].

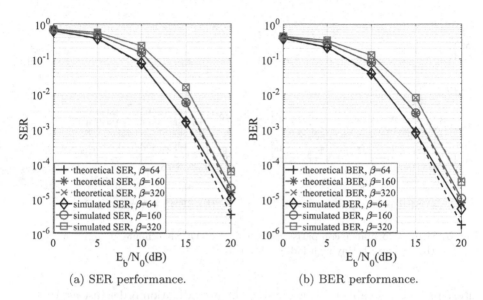

(a) SER performance.   (b) BER performance.

Fig. 4. Theoretical and simulated SER and BER performance comparisons over the 2-path Rayleigh fading channel. $N_T = 2$, $N_R = 2$, $\tilde{M} = 2$, $M = 4$.

Subsequently, Fig. 4 verifies the effectiveness of theoretical SER and BER expressions over 2-path Rayleigh fading channels with $\mathrm{E}\left[\alpha_1^2\right] = \mathrm{E}\left[\alpha_2^2\right] = 1/2$, $\tau_1 = 0$, $\tau_2 = 1$. Similar to Fig. 3(a), we can observe that the theoretical results match the simulated ones not well for small β, and the reliability performances degrade with the increasing β.

Figure 5(a) and (b) respectively compare the presented IM-S-M-DCSK scheme with the benchmark spatial modulation DCSK (SM-DCSK) scheme [9] when $\beta = 64$, and another benchmark square-constellation-based M-ary DCSK (S-M-DCSK) [4] over a 2-path Rayleigh fading channel under different configuration parameters of antennas. The channel parameters are assumed as $\mathrm{E}\left[\alpha_1^2\right] = \mathrm{E}\left[\alpha_2^2\right] = 1/2$, $\tau_1 = 0$ and $\tau_2 = 1$. It can be seen from Fig. 5(a) and (b) that our IM-S-M-DCSK systems achieve better reliability performances than benchmark schemes while providing higher data rate transmissions with higher order modulations. Moreover, for different N_T and N_R, IM-S-M-DCSK MIMO systems can achieve better reliability performances than those of the single input single out (SISO) S-M-DCSK systems [4]. In the Fig. 5(a), there is a performance lower bound for $M = 16$ case because the inter-path interference cannot be ignored for the modulation order $M = 16$ leading to a closer distance between symbols and a small spreading factor $\beta = 64$ leading to a larger correlation value of signals over different paths. When β is enough large, the interpath

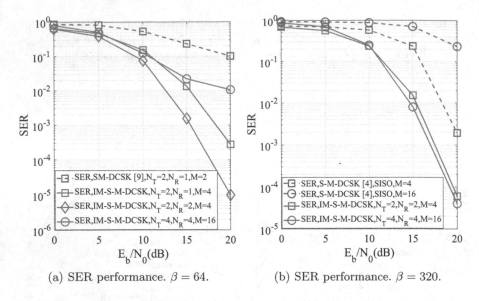

(a) SER performance. $\beta = 64$.   (b) SER performance. $\beta = 320$.

Fig. 5. SER performance comparisons with the SM-DCSK scheme [9] and S-M-DCSK [4] over the multipath Rayleigh fading channel.

interference is also able to be ignored for high modulation order just as $M = 16$ case in Fig. 5(b).

5   Conclusion

In this paper, we address the issue of reliability performance degradation for high order or spatial modulation DCSK systems. In our design, we propose to use the antenna index and the symbol index modulating the symbol to ensure the data rate. The resultant chaotic modulated symbols are then transmitted over the channel with the best channel gain to eliminate the bad effect of the channel assignment for the traditional SM scheme and obtain well channel condition. Then we derive theoretical SER and BER expressions which have been verified via the performance comparisons with the simulation results. More over, the simulation results over fading channels under different parameter settings demonstrate that the presented IM-S-M-DCSK scheme achieves better reliability performances than the benchmark schemes while providing higher data rate transmissions. Last but not the least, it's worth pointing out that the presented index modulation aided design can be easily integrated with the MIMO-DCSK system and its low-complexity receiver and the high security of chaos signal is suitable for the devices in the Internet of things (IoT).

Acknowledgements. This work was supported by the National Natural Science Foundation of China (Grant No. 61602531) and State's Key Project of Research and Development Plan under (Grant 2017YFE0121300-6).

References

1. Galias, Z., Maggio, G.M.: Quadrature chaos-shift keying: theory and performance analysis. IEEE Trans. Circuits Syst. I Fundam. Theory Appl. **48**(12), 1510–1519 (2001)
2. Cai, G., Fang, Y., Han, G.: Design of an adaptive multiresolution M-ary DCSK system. IEEE Commun. Lett. **21**(1), 60–63 (2017)
3. Wang, L., Cai, G., Chen, G.R.: Design and performance analysis of a new multiresolution M-ary differential chaos shift keying communication system. IEEE Trans. Wireless Commun. **14**(9), 5197–5208 (2015)
4. Cai, G., Fang, Y., Han, G., Lau, F.C.M., Wang, L.: A square-constellation-based M-ary DCSK communication system. IEEE Access **4**, 6295–6303 (2016)
5. Kolumbán, G., Kis, G.: Reception of M-ary FM-DCSK signals by energy detector. In: Proceedings of the NDES 2003, Scuol, Switzerland, pp. 133–136 (2003)
6. Kaddoum, G., Vu, M., Gagnon, F.: Performance analysis of differential chaotic shift keying communications in MIMO systems. In: 2011 IEEE International Symposium of Circuits and Systems (ISCAS), Rio de Janeiro, Brazil, pp. 1580–1583. IEEE (2011)
7. Wang, S., Lu, S., Zhang, E.: MIMO-DCSK communication scheme and its performance analysis over multipath fading channels. J. Syst. Eng. Electron. **24**(5), 729–733 (2013)
8. Wang, S., Wang, X.: M-DCSK-based chaotic communications in MIMO multipath channels with no channel state information. IEEE Trans. Circuits Syst. II Exp. Briefs **57**(12), 1001–1005 (2010)
9. Kumar, A., Sahu, P.R.: Performance analysis of spatially modulated differential chaos shift keying modulation. IET Commun. **11**(6), 905–909 (2017)
10. Xia, Y., Tse, C.K., Lau, F.C.M.: Performance of differential chaos-shift-keying digital communication systems over a multipath fading channel with delay spread. IEEE Trans. Circuits Syst. II Exp. Briefs **51**(12), 680–684 (2004)
11. Proakis, J.G., Salehi, M.: Digital Communications, 5th edn. McGraw-Hill, New York (2007)
12. Aydin, E., Ilhan, H.: A novel SM-based MIMO system with index modulation. IEEE Commun. Lett. **20**(2), 244–247 (2016)
13. Cho, K., Yoon, D.: On the general BER expression of one- and two-dimensional amplitude modulations. IEEE Trans. Commun. **50**(7), 1074–1080 (2002)

A Contract-Based Incentive Mechanism for Resource Sharing and Task Allocation in Container-Based Vehicular Edge Computing

Siming Wang, Xumin Huang, Beihai Tan[✉], and Rong Yu

Guangdong Key Laboratory of IoT Information Processing,
Guangdong University of Technology, Guangzhou, China
bhtan@gdut.edu.cn

Abstract. Vehicular edge computing (VEC) has emerged as a promising paradigm to provide low-latency service by extending the edge computing to vehicular networks. To meet the ever-increasing demands of computation and communication resources, utilizing vehicles as augmented infrastructure for computation offloading is an appealing idea. However, due to the lack of effective incentive and task allocation mechanism, it is challenging to exploit vehicles as infrastructure for computation offloading. To cope with these challenges, we first propose a container-based VEC paradigm by using efficient, flexible and customized resources of the vehicles. Then, we present a contract-based incentive mechanism to motivate vehicles to share their resources with service requesters (SRs). The optimal contract items are designed for multiple types of vehicles while maximizing the expected utilities of the SRs. Numerical results demonstrate that the proposed contract-based incentive mechanism is efficient compared with conventional schemes.

Keywords: Container-based vehicular edge computing · Resource sharing · Task allocation · Contract-based incentive mechanism

1 Introduction

With the rapid advance of the Internet of Vehicles (IoV), smart vehicles with vehicular networks access have experienced ever-increasing growth in number and variety [1,2]. According to the recent report, nearly a quarter billion vehicles will be connected by 2020 [3]. These vehicles with different communication modes such as vehicle-to-vehicle (V2V) and vehicle-to-infrastructure (V2I) are regarded as the important component of the future IoT-based infrastructure for providing various applications and services [4,5]. The emerging vehicular applications are computation-intensive and have low-latency requirements, such as augmented reality (AR), self-driving, and intelligent navigation service etc. [6]. Unfortunately, this poses huge challenges to the resource-limited vehicles to guarantee

© ICST Institute for Computer Sciences, Social Informatics and Telecommunications Engineering 2020
Published by Springer Nature Switzerland AG 2020. All Rights Reserved
B. Li et al. (Eds.): IoTaaS 2019, LNICST 316, pp. 116–129, 2020.
https://doi.org/10.1007/978-3-030-44751-9_11

the low-latency requirements and the quality of service (QoS). To handle the ever-increasing demands of computation resources, vehicular edge computing (VEC) supported by container-based technology constitutes a new computation offloading paradigm in vehicular networks and improves the system performance [7,8].

To deal with the ever-increasing demands of computation resources, it is promising to utilize vehicles as augmented infrastructure with container-based virtualization for computation offloading. Nowadays, smart vehicles are installed with powerful computing units, advanced communication devices and sensors [9]. It is practicable to leverage such large amount of on-board resources to perform computation offloading in vehicular networks [10]. Furthermore, compared with heavyweight virtual machines (VM), container-based virtualization technology is more available in vehicular networks. With the characteristics of short time implementation, efficient resource utilization and low maintenance cost, the onboard units (OBUs) customization can be implemented by container-based virtualization and offers high flexibility in platform management [11]. Existing studies have exploited container-based virtualization technologies in edge computing. The authors in [11] integrated light weighted virtualization with IoT edge networks. They presented container-based VEC and exploited task offloading among different vehicles. A parked vehicle edge computing with container-based virtualization was proposed to utilize the computing resources of parked vehicles [12]. The authors in [3] proposed a novel architecture for task selection and scheduling at the edge of network using container-as-a-service.

However, there are still many issues in the implementation of computation offloading in container-based VEC. First, existing studies assume that the vehicles serve as infrastructure for computation offloading voluntarily [13,14]. However, this assumption is not available in the practical situation. Because the vehicles are selfish, they may reject to contribute their onboard resource without any payment. The challenge is to design an efficient incentive mechanism to motivate vehicles to share their computation resources with SRs. Second, the information asymmetry between SRs and vehicles is necessary to be considered. The vehicles can be dishonest, and they are not willing to reveal their private information to others. The vehicles are intended to maximize their own payoffs and cheat SRs by charging more payment. Third, with multiple vehicles and multiple SRs, it is not easy to design an efficient task allocation scheme to reduce service delay and maximize the saved delay utility. Thus, it is necessary to design an efficient incentive mechanism to address the resource sharing and task allocation problem and overcome the asymmetric information scenario between vehicles and SRs.

To solve the challenges mentioned above, we propose a contract-based incentive mechanism to encourage the vehicles to share their onboard resources and help offload tasks from SRs. Furthermore, the proposed novel contract-based framework solves the task allocation problem. A set of resource-reward contract items is designed for maximizing the SRs utilities and stimulating each type of vehicle to accept the contract item that is intently designed for its type. The vehicles with different energy cost efficiency are classified into multiple types. The asymmetric information scenario between SRs and vehicles can be overcome by solving the contract-based optimization problem. Numerical results demonstrate that the proposed contract-based incentive mechanism is efficient compared with conventional schemes.

The rest of this paper is organized as follows. Section 2 introduces the system model with network entities in container-based VEC. The contract formulation and simplification is presented in Sect. 3. The solution is given in Sect. 4. Performance evaluation results are shown in Sect. 5 before the paper is concluded in Sect. 6.

2   System Model

2.1   Network Entities

The system model of container-based VEC is shown in Fig. 1. There are existing multiple vehicles and multiple SRs in VEC. Due to the limited computation resources, the potential SRs have great demands for computation resources in various applications, such as data mining, image processing and natural language translation. Each SR generates a task which can be offloaded to a vehicle. To offer low-latency services to the SRs, the vehicles with rich onboard resources can serve as infrastructure by offloading tasks from SRs. The vehicular containers deployed on OBUs share hardware infrastructure and host operation system. Compared with traditional virtual machines (VM), the main benefits of applying container-based virtualization in OBUs' resource customization include light weight, increased performance, higher efficiency, and no need for privilege

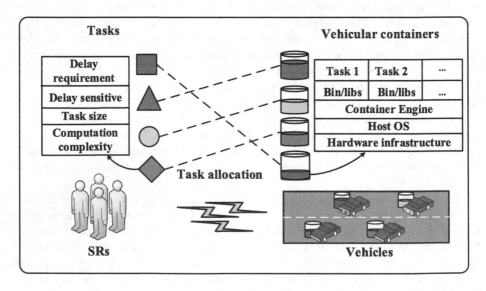

Fig. 1. System model of container-based VEC.

instruction trapping [3]. Each vehicle can accept multiple computation offloading tasks from the SRs, and the vehicular container will allocate computation resources to the tasks efficiently according to the demands of the SRs. In the container-based VEC paradigm, the SRs can reduce service delay by offloading computation tasks to proximate vehicles with rich computation resources. Each vehicle has freedom to decide whether to accept the tasks from the SRs according to its utility.

2.2 Utility Functions of SRs

The set of SRs is denoted as $\mathcal{I}$. The tasks from the SRs are described in four terms as $\alpha_i = \{T_i^{\max}, \lambda_i, s_i, \kappa_i\}, i \in \mathcal{I}$. Here, $T_i^{\max}$ denotes the maximum delay tolerance of the task, s_i denotes the size of the task, and κ_i represents the amount of required computation resource of unit size of task. The tasks are delay-sensitive, and the SRs can get utility $\lambda_i \Delta t_i$ by finishing the task α_i, where λ_i is the unit revenue of saved delay of task α_i and Δt_i is the saved delay in completing the task α_i compared to $T_i^{\max}$. We assume that an orthogonal spectrum is allocated to each vehicle, and thus we can ignore the co-channel interference among vehicles. For a single link between the i-th SR and the type-j vehicle, the signal-to-noise ratio (SNR) at the type-j vehicle can be represented by

$$\gamma_{i,j} = \frac{p_i d_{i,j}^{-\varepsilon} |h_{i,j}|^2}{N_0}, \tag{1}$$

where p_i is i-th SR's transmitting power, $d_{i,j}$ represents the transmission distance between the i-th SR and the type-j vehicle, ε represents the path-loss exponent, $h_{i,j}$ denotes the Rayleigh channel coefficient with a complex Gaussian distribution and N_0 is the power noise. The transmission time for uploading the task α_i to type-j vehicle can be denoted by

$$t_{i,j}^{up} = \frac{s_i}{r_{i,j}} = \frac{s_i}{B \log_2 (1 + \gamma_{i,j})}, \tag{2}$$

where $r_{i,j}$ is the transmission rate between the i-th SR and the type-j vehicle, B denotes the bandwidth of the link. Because of the fast mobility of the vehicles, the task uploading process will fail if the vehicles run out of the communication range of the SRs. According to [14], we denote the dwell time of type-j vehicle inside the communication range of i-th SR as $t_{i,j}^d$. The task uploading process will fail if $t_{i,j}^{up} > t_{i,j}^d$. We assume that the SRs are distributed along the road and their communication range as a circle with a diameter, and $t_{i,j}^d$ can be computed as

$$t_{i,j}^d = \frac{\widetilde{d}_{i,j}}{\overline{v}_j}, \tag{3}$$

where $\widetilde{d}_{i,j}$ is the distance between the type-j vehicle and the endpoint of the i-th SRs communication diameter in the vehicle heading direction [14] and $\overline{v}_j$

denotes the average velocity of type-j vehicle. If the task α_i is offloaded to type-j vehicle, the task execution time $t_{i,j}^{com}$ is denoted as

$$t_{i,j}^{com} = \frac{\kappa_i s_i}{f_{i,j}}, \tag{4}$$

where $f_{i,j}$ is the amount of computation resources contributed by the type-j vehicle. The saved delay in completing the task α_i compared to the maximum delay tolerance T_i^{max} is given as

$$\Delta t_{i,j} = T_i^{max} - t_{i,j}^{com} - t_{i,j}^{up}, \tag{5}$$

We introduce a binary variable $x_{i,j}$ as follows,

$$x_{i,j} = \begin{cases} 1, & \text{if task } \alpha_i \text{ allocated to type-} j \text{ vehicle,} \\ 0, & \text{otherwise,} \end{cases} \tag{6}$$

Similar to [1]. The utility of i-th SR is defined as the revenue minus the payment, which is written by

$$U_i = \sum_{j \in \mathcal{J}} x_{i,j} \left(\lambda_i \Delta t_{i,j} - \pi_{i,j} \right). \tag{7}$$

where π_i^j is the reward paid by i-th SR for the task offloading to the type-j vehicle.

2.3 Utility Functions of Vehicles

If the tasks from SRs are offloaded to the vehicles, there will be energy cost when the vehicles executes the tasks. For the task $\alpha_i, i \in \mathcal{I}$, the utility of the type-j vehicle can be defined as

$$V_j = \sum_{i \in \mathcal{I}} x_{i,j} \left(\pi_{i,j} - e_j \kappa_i s_i \eta f_{i,j}^2 \right), \tag{8}$$

where e_j is the energy cost coefficient, η represents the constant determined by the switched capacitance of type-j vehicle and $e_j \kappa_i s_i \eta f_{i,j}^2$ denotes the energy cost of type-j vehicle when finishing the task α_i.

Definition 1. *Because the SRs are not aware of vehicles' private information, such as energy cost coefficient, the SRs can sort the vehicles into multiple discrete types. Based on (8), we define the type $\theta_{i,j}$ as follows*

$$\theta_{i,j} \triangleq \frac{1}{e_j \kappa_i s_i \eta}, \tag{9}$$

which suggests that the lower energy cost coefficient, the higher type of vehicles. The set of vehicles' types is denoted as $\Theta_i = \{\theta_{i,1}, \theta_{i,2}, ..., \theta_{i,J}\}, \forall i \in \mathcal{I}$. The types of vehicle are sorted in an ascending order and classified into J types, which are denoted by $\theta_{i,1} < ... < \theta_{i,j} < ... < \theta_{i,J}, \forall i \in \mathcal{I}$.

According to (9), the utility functions of vehicles can be rewritten as

$$V_j = \sum_{i \in \mathcal{I}} x_{i,j} \left(\pi_{i,j} - \frac{f_{i,j}^2}{\theta_{i,j}} \right). \tag{10}$$

2.4 Social Welfare

Based on (7) and (10), social welfare is defined as the summation of the utility functions of the SRs and the vehicles, which is denoted by

$$W = \sum_{i \in I} \sum_{j \in J} x_{i,j} \left(\lambda_i \Delta t_{i,j} - \frac{f_{i,j}^2}{\theta_{i,j}} \right). \tag{11}$$

The payment $\pi_{i,j}, \forall i \in I, \forall j \in J$ are cancelled out in the social welfare. The social welfare is the profit of saved delay minus the vehicles' energy cost, which is equivalent to optimize the whole system's efficiency, i.e., earning more profits from saved delay at the less cost of energy cost.

3 Problem Formulation

3.1 Contract Formulation

There exists an asymmetric information scenario between SRs and vehicles, the SRs can optimize their expected utilities by using the statistical distributions of vehicles' types from historical data. The SRs are only aware of the probability of the vehicles belong to type-$\theta_{i,j}$ from statistical data. We denote $\beta_{i,j}$ as the probability that the vehicles belong to the type-$\theta_{i,j}$, and $\sum_{j \in J} \beta_{i,j} = 1, \forall i \in I$. By considering the heterogeneity among different vehicles, the SRs offer different contract items to multiple types of vehicle. The vehicles can accept or reject the offering contract items according to their utility functions. The contract-based optimization problem is to optimize the expected utilities of the SRs, which is formulated as

$$\max_{(x_{i,j}, f_{i,j}, \pi_{i,j})} \sum_{i \in I} \sum_{j \in J} N \beta_{i,j} U_i$$

$$\text{s.t.} (12a) \ x_{i,j} \in \{0, 1\}, \sum_{j \in J} x_{i,j} \leq 1, \forall i \in I, \forall j \in J,$$

$$(12b) \ \sum_{i \in I} x_{i,j} f_{i,j} \leq f_j^{\max}, \forall j \in J,$$

$$(12c) \ t_{i,j}^{up} \leq t_{i,j}^d, \forall i \in I, \forall j \in J,$$

$$(12d) \ \pi_{i,j} - \frac{f_{i,j}^2}{\theta_i^j} \geq \pi_{i,j} - \frac{f_{i,j}^2}{\theta_{i,j}}, \forall i \in I, \forall j, k \in J,$$

$$(12e) \ \pi_{i,j} - \frac{f_{i,j}^2}{\theta_{i,j}} \geq 0, \forall i \in I, \forall j \in J. \tag{12}$$

where N denotes the total number of vehicles, and $N\beta_{i,j}$ represents the number of the vehicles that belong to type-$\theta_{i,j}$. (12a) indicates that the variable $x_{i,j}$ is defined as a binary value, and one SR can be allocated with at most one vehicle. (12b) denotes the limit of computation capacity of the vehicle. The constraint

(12c) denotes the delay constraints of task uploading. (12d) is incentive compatibility (IC) constraints which ensure that the vehicles can optimize their utilities by choosing the contract items that are designed for their types. (12e) is individual rationality (IR) constraints which ensure that each type of vehicle's utility is positive.

3.2   Problem Simplification

It is difficult to solve the optimization problem (12) with so many complicated IC constraints and IR constraints which are not-convex and coupled among different types of vehicle. Since the optimization problem (12) is not a convex optimization problem, the complicated constraints in optimization problem should be simplified through following lemmas.

Lemma 1. *For any feasible contract* $(\pi_{i,j}, f_{i,j}), \forall i \in \mathcal{I}, \forall j, k \in \mathcal{J}, \pi_{i,j} > \pi_{i,k}$ *if and only if and* $\theta_{i,j} > \theta_{i,k}$, *and* $\pi_{i,j} = \pi_{i,k}$ *if and only if* $\theta_{i,j} = \theta_{i,k}$.

Proof. Please refer to [15].

Lemma 2. *For any feasible contract* $(\pi_{i,j}, f_{i,j}), \forall i \in \mathcal{I}, \forall j, k \in \mathcal{J}, \pi_{i,j} > \pi_{i,k}$ *if and only if* $f_{i,j} > f_{i,k}$ *and* $\pi_{i,j} = \pi_{i,k}$ *if and only if* $f_{i,j} = f_{i,k}$.

Proof. Please refer to [15].

Lemma 3. *Given that the IC constraints of all types of vehicle are satisfied, if the utility of the SR is maximized under asymmetric information scenario, the IR constraints of vehicles can be replaced by*

$$\pi_{i,1} - \frac{f_{i,1}^2}{\theta_{i,1}} = 0, \forall i \in \mathcal{I}, \tag{13}$$

Proof. From Definition 1, the types of vehicle satisfy $\theta_{i,1} < \theta_{i,2} < \cdots < \theta_{i,j} < \cdots < \theta_{i,J}, \forall i \in \mathcal{I}$. According to the IC constraints in (12d), we can obtain

$$\pi_{i,j} - \frac{f_{i,j}^2}{\theta_{i,j}} \geq \pi_{i,1} - \frac{f_{i,1}^2}{\theta_{i,j}} \geq \pi_{i,1} - \frac{f_{i,1}^2}{\theta_{i,1}} \geq 0, \tag{14}$$

If the IR constraint of type-1 vehicle is guaranteed, the IR constraints of all type of vehicles are satisfied. This completes the proof.

Lemma 4. *The IC constraints of vehicles can be reduced as the local downward incentive compatibility (LDIC):*

$$\pi_{i,j} - \frac{f_{i,j}^2}{\theta_{i,j}} \geq \pi_{i,j-1} - \frac{f_{i,j-1}^2}{\theta_{i,j}}, \forall i \in \mathcal{I}, \forall j \in \{2, ..., J\}, \tag{15}$$

and the local upward incentive compatibility (LUIC):

$$\pi_{i,j} - \frac{f_{i,j}^2}{\theta_{i,j}} \geq \pi_{i,j+1} - \frac{f_{i,j+1}^2}{\theta_i^j}, \forall i \in \mathcal{I}, \forall j \in \{1, ..., J-1\}, \tag{16}$$

Proof. Please refer to [16].

Lemma 5. *If the utility of SR is maximized, the IC constraints of vehicles can be reduced as*

$$\pi_{i,j} - \frac{f_{i,j}^2}{\theta_{i,j}} = \pi_{i,j-1} - \frac{f_{i,j-1}^2}{\theta_{i,j}}, \forall i \in \mathcal{I}, \forall j \in \{2, ..., J\}. \tag{17}$$

Proof. Please refer to [16].

According to Lemmas 3 and 5, the complicated IR and IC constraints can be reduced. Thus the optimization problem (12) can be rewritten as

$$\max_{\{x_{i,j}, f_{i,j}, \pi_{i,j}\}} \sum_{i \in \mathcal{I}} \sum_{j \in \mathcal{J}} N\beta_{i,j} U_i$$

$$s.t.(18a) \ x_{i,j} \in \{0, 1\}, \sum_{j \in \mathcal{J}} x_{i,j} \le 1, \forall i \in \mathcal{I},$$

$$(18b) \ \sum_{i \in \mathcal{I}} x_{i,j} f_{i,j} \le f_j^{\max}, \forall j \in \mathcal{J},$$

$$(18c) \ t_{i,j}^{up} \le t_{i,j}^d, \forall i \in \mathcal{I}, \forall j \in \mathcal{J}, \tag{18}$$

$$(18d) \ \pi_{i,j} - \frac{f_{i,j}^2}{\theta_{i,j}} = \pi_{i,j-1} - \frac{f_{i,j-1}^2}{\theta_{i,j}}, \forall i \in \mathcal{I}, \forall j \in \mathcal{J},$$

$$(18e) \ \pi_{i,1} - \frac{f_{i,1}^2}{\theta_{i,1}} = 0, \forall i \in \mathcal{I},$$

$$(18f) \ f_{i,1} \le \cdots \le f_{i,j} \le \cdots \le f_{i,J}, \forall i \in \mathcal{I}.$$

4   Solution

We solve the optimization problem (18) by using a standard method. We first resolve the relaxed problem without monotonicity constraint (18f). The solutions are then verified whether to satisfy the monotonicity constraint (18f). By iterating the (18d) and (18e), we have

$$\pi_{i,j} = \frac{f_{i,1}^2}{\theta_{i,1}} + \sum_{n=2}^{j} \frac{f_{i,n}^2 - f_{i,n-1}^2}{\theta_{i,n}}$$

$$= \frac{f_{i,j}^2}{\theta_{i,j}} + \sum_{n=2}^{j} \left(\frac{1}{\theta_{i,n-1}} - \frac{1}{\theta_{i,n}} \right) f_{i,n-1}^2, \tag{19}$$

where $\forall i \in \mathcal{I}, \forall j \in \{2, ..., J\}$. Substitute (18e) and (19) into optimization problem (18), and all $\pi_{i,j}, \forall i \in \mathcal{I}, \forall j \in \mathcal{J}$ can be removed from the optimization problem (18), which becomes

$$\max_{\{x_{i,j}, f_{i,j}\}} \sum_{i \in \mathcal{I}} \sum_{j \in \mathcal{J}} N \beta_{i,j} x_{i,j} \left[\lambda_i \left(T_i^{max} - \frac{\kappa_i s_i}{f_{i,j}} - \frac{s_i}{r_{i,j}} \right) \right.$$

$$\left. - \sum_{j=1}^{J-1} \left(\frac{1}{\theta_i^j} \sum_{n=j}^{J} \beta_{i,n} - \frac{1}{\theta_{i,j+1}} \sum_{n=j+1}^{J} \beta_{i,n} \right) f_{i,j}^2 - \frac{\beta_{i,J}}{\theta_{i,J}} f_{i,J}^2 \right] \tag{20}$$

$$\text{s.t.} (20a)\ x_{i,j} \in \{0,1\}, \sum_{j \in \mathcal{J}} x_{i,j} \le 1, \forall i \in \mathcal{I},$$

$$(20b)\ \sum_{i \in \mathcal{I}} x_{i,j} f_{i,j} \le f_j^{max}, \forall j \in \mathcal{J},$$

$$(20c)\ t_{i,j}^{up} \le t_{i,j}^d, \forall i \in \mathcal{I}, \forall j \in \mathcal{J},$$

First, we can use standard convex optimization tools in [17] to solve it to get $f_{i,j}^*$. Then $\pi_{i,j}^*$ can be calculated by (18e) and (19). After that, we need to check whether the solutions satisfy the monotonicity constraint (18f). If the solutions $\widehat{f_{i,j}}^*, \forall i \in \mathcal{I}, \forall j \in \mathcal{J}$ satisfy the monotonicity constraint (18f), the solutions are our optimal solutions. However, if the solutions $\widehat{f_{i,j}}^*, \forall i \in \mathcal{I}, \forall j \in \mathcal{J}$ do not satisfy the monotonicity constraint (18f), the solutions are infeasible solutions. Thus, we need to make some adjustments as follows. Since $U_i, \forall i \in \mathcal{I}$ are concave functions on $\widehat{f_{i,j}}^*, \forall i \in \mathcal{I}, \forall j \in \mathcal{J}$, the infeasible solutions can be replaced by feasible solutions iteratively [18]. When there exists an infeasible solution $\left\{ \widehat{f_{i,m}}^*, \widehat{f_{i,m+1}}^*, ..., \widehat{f_{i,n}}^* \right\}$, set

$$f_{i,j}^* = \arg\max_{\{f\}} \sum_{s=m}^{n} U_s, i \in \{m, m+1, ..., n\}, \tag{21}$$

After obtaining the feasible solutions $f_{i,j}^*, \forall i \in \mathcal{I}, \forall j \in \mathcal{J}$, we can derive the optimal price $p_{i,j}^*$ as follow

$$\pi_{i,j}^* = \begin{cases} \frac{f_{i,1}^{*2}}{\theta_{i,1}}, & j = 1, \\ \frac{f_{i,j}^{*2}}{\theta_{i,j}} + \sum_{n=2}^{i} \left(\frac{1}{\theta_{i,n-1}} - \frac{1}{\theta_{i,n}} \right) f_{i,n-1}^{*2}, & j = \{2, 3, ..., J\}. \end{cases} \tag{22}$$

Then, $x_{i,j}^*$ can be calculated iteratively by the constraints (20a), (20b) and (20c). So far, we have derived the optimal contract $(f_{i,j}^*, \pi_{i,j}^*), \forall i \in \mathcal{I}, \forall j \in \mathcal{J}$ which can optimize the expected utilities of the SRs and satisfy the IR and IC constraints.

Table 1. Simulation parameters

Parameter	Setting
Radius of the SRs communication coverage	200 m
Number of SRs I	15
Number of vehicles' type J	10
Bandwidth of SRs B	10 MHz
Transmission power of SRs p_i	30 dBm
Noise power N_0	-114 dBm
Path loss exponent ε	3.4
Maximum delay tolerance T_i^{max}	$8-10$ s
Mapping from bit to cycles κ_i	$1*10^3 - 1.5*10^3$ cycle/bit
Size of task s_i	$3*10^6 - 4*10^6$ bit
Saved delay profit coefficient λ_i	$0.1-1$
Effective switched capacitance η	10^{-28}
Energy cost coefficient e_j	$0.1-1$
Velocity of vehicles $\bar{v}_j$	$2-20$ m/s
Maximum computation resource of vehicle f_j^{max}	$2.5-3$ GHz

5 Numerical Results

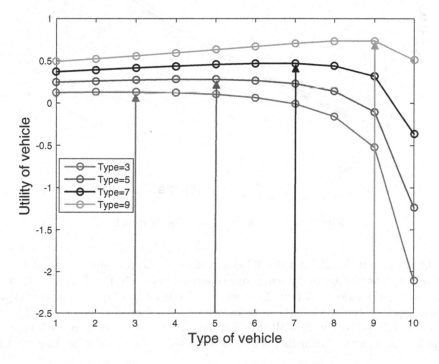

Fig. 2. Utility of vehicle versus type of vehicle.

We consider a two-lane two directional road randomly distributed with 10 vehicles and 15 SRs. We assume that the SRs are distributed along the road and their communication range as a circle with a diameter. The number of vehicle types is equal to the number of vehicles. Without loss of generality, the vehicle types are following a uniform distribution. In our simulation, we first give an analysis about the feasibility (IC and IR constraints) of the proposed contract-based incentive scheme. Second, we conduct the comparisons of social welfare with different types of vehicles. Finally, we compare the social welfare by varying the number of SR. For comparisons, the numerical results are performed by solving the problem by using the proposed contract-based scheme under asymmetric information scenario (CA), contract-based scheme under complete information scenario (CC) [16], Stackelgerg game scheme (SG) [19] and take-it-or-leave scheme (ToL) [20]. The system performance is being simulated using MATLAB with system parameters in Table 1.

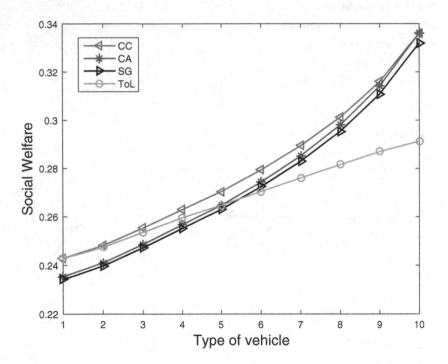

Fig. 3. Social welfare versus type of vehicle.

The feasibility of IR and the IC constraints of the proposed contract-based scheme under asymmetric information scenario is shown in Fig. 2. A SR (i.e., $i = 10$) is selected randomly. Figure 2 shows that the utilities of type-3, type-5, type-7, and type-9 vehicles when the vehicles select all the contract items $(\pi_i^j, f_i^j), i = 10, j \in \mathcal{J}$ offered by the i-th SR. We can observe that the utility of each type of vehicles can maximize its utility when the vehicles select the contract item that is designed for their types, which suggests the IC constraints are satisfied. Further, the utilities of vehicles are non-negative when they choose the best contract item that fits their corresponding types, which means that the IR constraints are guaranteed. After the vehicles select the contract items, the types of vehicles will be known by the SRs. Therefore, the information asymmetry between SRs and vehicles can be overcome.

We illustrate social welfare with respect to different types of vehicle under four schemes in Fig. 3. We set the threshold type of ToL scheme is 5. It can be seen from Fig. 3 that the social welfare achieved by all schemes increase with type of vehicle. It is profitable to employ higher type of vehicles to help execute computation tasks from SRs. The higher type of vehicles are with higher energy efficiency to share resources with SRs. Furthermore, the CC scheme achieves the maximum value of social welfare as the upper bound. The social welfare achieved by the proposed CA scheme is better than SG scheme and ToL scheme. Due to the information asymmetry between SRs and vehicles, SRs have no acknowledgment of the type of vehicle, the designed IC constraint-based CA scheme can only bring a approximate optimal social welfare, which is upper bounded by CC scheme under complete information scenario. The SRs are fully aware of the types of vehicle under complete information scenario and tries to extract all profit from the vehicles. The gap between social welfare and that of CA scheme increases along with the type of vehicles.

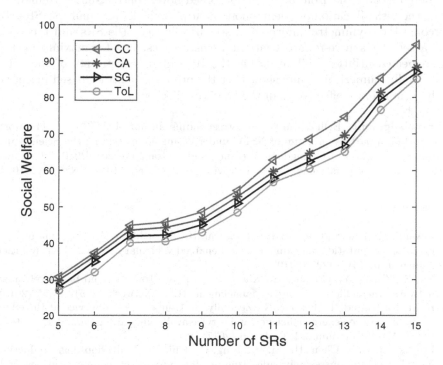

Fig. 4. Social welfare versus number of SRs.

Figure 4 shows the performance of social welfare as a function of the number of SRs under all four schemes. It can be observed from Fig. 4 that social welfare achieved by all four schemes increase with the number of SRs. As shown in Fig. 4, the CC scheme gives the highest performance of social welfare among all four schemes, followed by the CA scheme, SG scheme and ToL scheme. That because SRs extract revenue from the vehicles as much as possible under complete information scenario, and less benefits are left to the vehicles. While in CA scheme, vehicles have limited contract items to select from SRs under asymmetric information scenario. However, the vehicles have freedom to optimize their own utility in SG scheme, and they can reserve more benefits from SRs. Therefore, the social welfare achieved by contract-based scheme are better than that of SG scheme. ToL scheme achieves the lowest social welfare among four schemes. The reason is that any vehicle whose type larger than the threshold type will reject the contract offered by SRs. In this case, only the vehicles higher than the threshold type can achieve non-negative utilities.

6   Conclusion

In this paper, we propose a container-based VEC paradigm with efficient and flexible customization of vehicles' resources. Then, we present a contract-based incentive mechanism to motivate vehicles to share their computation resource and help offload tasks from SRs. The proposed novel contract-based framework solves the task allocation problem among multiple vehicles and multiple SRs. To overcome the asymmetric information scenario between the SRs and the vehicles, a set of resource-reward contract items are designed for maximizing the SRs expected utilities while ensuring the IR and IC constraints of the vehicles. Finally, numerical results show that the proposed contract-based incentive mechanism is more effective than the traditional schemes.

Acknowledgment. Beihai Tan is the corresponding author of this paper. The work is supported in part by program of NSFC under Grant no. 61971148, the Science and Technology Program of Guangdong Province under Grant no. 2015B010129001, and Natural Science Foundation of Guangxi Province under Grant 2018GXNSFDA281013.

References

1. Liwang, M., Dai, S., Gao, Z., Tang, Y., Dai, H.: A truthful reverse-auction mechanism for computation offloading in cloud-enabled vehicular network. IEEE Internet Things J. **6**, 4214–4227 (2019)
2. Yu, R., Zhang, Y., Gjessing, S., Xia, W., Yang, K.: Toward cloud-based vehicular networks with efficient resource management. IEEE Network **27**(5), 48–55 (2013)
3. Kaur, K., Dhand, T., Kumar, N., Zeadally, S.: Container-as-a-Service at the edge: trade-off between energy efficiency and service availability at fog nano data centers. IEEE Wirel. Commun. **24**(3), 48–56 (2017)
4. Li, X., Hu, B.-j., Chen, H., Li, B., Teng, H., Cui, M.: Multi-hop delay reduction for safety-related message broadcasting in vehicle-to-vehicle communications. IET Commun. **9**(3), 404–411 (2015)

5. Li, X., Hu, B.-J., Chen, H., Andrieux, G., Wang, Y., Wei, Z.-H.: An RSU-coordinated synchronous multi-channel MAC scheme for vehicular ad hoc networks. IEEE Access **3**, 2794–2802 (2015)
6. Dai, Y., Xu, D., Maharjan, S., Zhang, Y.: Joint load balancing and offloading in vehicular edge computing and networks. IEEE Internet Things J. **6**, 4377–4387 (2019)
7. Yang, C., Liu, Y., Chen, X., Zhong, W., Xie, S.: Efficient mobility-aware task offloading for vehicular edge computing networks. IEEE Access **7**, 26652–26664 (2019)
8. Liu, Y., Yu, H., Xie, S., Zhang, Y.: Deep reinforcement learning for offloading and resource allocation in vehicle edge computing and networks. IEEE Trans. Veh. Technol. **68**(11), 11158–11168 (2019)
9. Abdelhamid, S., Hassanein, H., Takahara, G.: Vehicle as a resource (VaaR). IEEE Network **29**(1), 12–17 (2015)
10. Huang, X., Yu, R., Liu, J., Shu, L.: Parked vehicle edge computing: exploiting opportunistic resources for distributed mobile applications. IEEE Access **6**, 66649–66663 (2018)
11. Morabito, R., Cozzolino, V., Ding, A.Y., Beijar, N., Ott, J.: Consolidate IoT edge computing with lightweight virtualization. IEEE Network **32**(1), 102–111 (2018)
12. Huang, X., Li, P., Yu, R.: Social welfare maximization in container-based task scheduling for parked vehicle edge computing. IEEE Commun. Lett. **23**(8), 1347–1351 (2019)
13. Arif, S., Olariu, S., Wang, J., Yan, G., Yang, W., Khalil, I.: Datacenter at the airport: reasoning about time-dependent parking lot occupancy. IEEE Trans. Parallel Distrib. Syst. **23**(11), 2067–2080 (2012)
14. Xu, C., Wang, Y., Zhou, Z., Gu, B., Frascolla, V., Mumtaz, S.: A low-latency and massive-connectivity vehicular fog computing framework for 5G. In: 2018 IEEE Globecom Workshops (GC Wkshps), pp. 1–6. IEEE (2018)
15. Bolton, P., Dewatripont, M.: Contract Theory. MIT Press, Cambridge (2005)
16. Hou, Z., Chen, H., Li, Y., Vucetic, B.: Incentive mechanism design for wireless energy harvesting-based Internet of Things. IEEE Internet Things J. **5**(4), 2620–2632 (2017)
17. Boyd, S., Vandenberghe, L.: Convex Optimization. Cambridge University Press, Cambridge (2004)
18. Gao, L., Wang, X., Xu, Y., Zhang, Q.: Spectrum trading in cognitive radio networks: a contract-theoretic modeling approach. IEEE J. Sel. Areas Commun. **29**(4), 843–855 (2011)
19. Liu, T., Li, J., Shu, F., Tao, M., Chen, W., Han, Z.: Design of contract-based trading mechanism for a small-cell caching system. IEEE Trans. Wireless Commun. **16**(10), 6602–6617 (2017)
20. Zhou, Z., Liu, P., Feng, J., Zhang, Y., Mumtaz, S., Rodriguez, J.: Computation resource allocation and task assignment optimization in vehicular fog computing: a contract-matching approach. IEEE Trans. Veh. Technol. **68**(4), 3113–3125 (2019)

A New Method for Deriving Upper Bound of OCR-TDMA Performance

Xinyu Liu, Qingfeng Zhou[✉], and Min Peng

School of Computer and Information, Hefei University of Technology, Hefei, China
liuxinyu@mail.hfut.edu.cn, enqfzhou@ieee.org, pengmin@hfut.edu.cn

Abstract. With the rapid development of flash memory technology, the buffer capacity of device becomes higher. In this case, infinite buffer could be introduced to derived the upper bound of system performance. In this paper, a new method which considers Enqueue rate and Dequeue rate of buffer is proposed to derive the performance of OCR-TDMA when buffer length of relay $L = \infty$. In simulation part, buffer lengths from 1 to ∞ are considered as parameters to compare system performances, and the theoretical results and simulation results match well. Therefore, the proposed method can be applied in other similar model to simplify the derivation of system performance.

Keywords: Cooperative MAC · TDMA · Throughput · Buffer

1 Introduction

In modern 5G era, the applications of edge computing and content enhance the experiences of end users in cellular network, which has less redundant transmissions, more efficient bandwidth resources and faster service response.

Actually the concept of edge computing has been proposed for several year, and one of the key points to achieve this scheme is to design reliable tactics. In [1,2], many technologies and tactics for mobile edge computing (MEC) are studied. The idea of collaboration is a significant concept in edge computing, which utilizes the distributed end users to save and run their own demands [3,4]. However in future cellular network, end users are not just clustered around macro base station. Micro cells and femto cells are deployed everywhere and the topology of cellular network could be multi-hop. In this case, the tactics of edge computing should be considered in a scene which contains source node, destination node and relay nodes.

The study of relay channel have over forty years history. But what made it be focused by the worldwide is some cooperative communication schemes which proposed in the end of last century. Cooperative communication utilize the available resource near the transmission link and make use of the diversity gain of Multiple-Input Multiple-Output (MIMO). Cooperative technique is able to harvest spatial diversity, increase the reliability of transmission and the throughput of whole system [5,6].

© ICST Institute for Computer Sciences, Social Informatics and Telecommunications Engineering 2020
Published by Springer Nature Switzerland AG 2020. All Rights Reserved
B. Li et al. (Eds.): IoTaaS 2019, LNICST 316, pp. 130–140, 2020.
https://doi.org/10.1007/978-3-030-44751-9_12

Cooperative communication need a cooperative group work together not like the point-to-point transmission scheme. Thus a good cooperative Media Access Control (MAC) scheme can collect great performance gain. Based on 802.11 MAC system, several cooperative MAC, such as CoopMAC [7,8], Distributed Cooperative MAC [9,10], Cooperative Aloha [11]. However, these MAC scheme are designed for packet-based (or contention-based) networks like Ad Hoc networks or WLANs, but not for cellular networks or some other networks with high dense nodes.

Channel-based MAC schemes are widely applied in high dense network. C-TDMA [12] and CR-TDMA [13] are two TDMA-based cooperative MAC scheme proposed for this kind of network. The former use the MISO technique to improve the uplink transmission, in which many mobile devices forward their data to base station. The latter works for a mesh network, in which few helper nodes exist near the default relay nodes and they can help transmitting packets if they have empty buffer. In previous work [14], we proposed a new TDMA-based MAC scheme Opportunistic Cooperative Relaying TDMA (OCR-TDMA), which provides superior throughput performance compared with CR-TDMA in theoretical analysis and simulation results. But there is a improper special case in our previous analysis. In this paper, we set the buffer capacity $L = \infty$, which means R would not have full buffer anymore. This case is more practical and can be applied to some situations of which relay node has low traffic or large buffer capacity. And we also treat the performance of this model as the upper bound of OCR-TDMA.

2   System Model

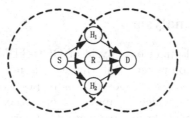

Fig. 1. System model of a two-hop relay network containing a default relay and several helpers

In this two-hop network model, there are four types of nodes, a source S, a destination D, a single relay R surrounded by a few available helpers H_i, $i \in \{1, \cdots, n_h\}$, as shown in Fig. 1. Each node has only one antenna and works in half-duplex mode. R is default relay which means R will save the new relay packet from S if the buffer of R is not full while H_i have intention to receive relay packet for cooperation only if H_i is idle (empty buffer).

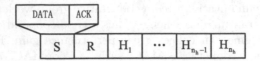

Fig. 2. Structure of a time frame containing $n_h + 2$ identical time slots

Let E_s, E_r and E_h be the transmission powers of S, R, H_i respectively. The channel from node i to node j has an channel coefficient h_{ji} and it suffers the Rayleigh fading. So the signal-to-noise ratio in receiving node is given by $SNR_{ji} = |h_{ji}|^2 E_i / N_0$, where N_0 means the power density of AWGN.

Each node has its own buffer, of which capacity for packets is L. Without considering about channel coding, each packet has N BPSK-Modulated bits. So the average BER of transmission from node i to node j can be calculated as $p_{ji} = 0.5(1 - \sqrt{\gamma_{ji}/(1 + \gamma_{ji})})$, where the average received SNR $\gamma_{ji} = E[|h_{ji}|^2]E_i/N_0$. Therefore, the probability of successful transmission is $P_{succ,ji} = (1 - p_{ji})^N$, while the probability of occurring error is $P_{err,ji} = 1 - P_{succ,ji}$.

Considering this is a TDMA-based system, as shown in Fig. 2, each node of S, R, H_i is allocated to a time slot in every frame. These nodes could only send packet in their own time slot. After transmitting, each time slot reserves a very short period for returning ACK. Thus each frame contains $n_h + 2$ time slots.

In the first time slot of each frame, we assume that the buffer of S is not empty and all packets in buffer are addressed to D. Actually, besides receiving the relay packets from S, R and H_i will generate non-relay packets by themselves and these packets are not forwarded to D. σ_{nr} is the generating rate of non-relay packet in each time slot at R while it is simplified in H_i that the probability of empty buffer is P_{idle}.

3 Performance Analysis

Previously [14], the performance analysis of OCR-TDMA with a special case that $P_{succ,dh} = 1$. has completed. But this case is not practical in a realistic environment. In this paper we proposed a more practical case that the buffer of R has infinite capacity which means $L = \infty$ ("the buffer of R" would be replaced by "buffer" in the following passage). Comparing with limited buffer, R can have more opportunities to transmit relay packet. In this section we divide the analysis into two situations, Infinite packets in buffer and Almost no packet in buffer.

Before discussing these two circumstances, we propose two variables, Enqueue rate and Dequeue rate. Enqueue rate means the rate when packet enters the buffer and Dequeue rate refers to the rate when packet goes out of the buffer. In this paper, the packets, which will access the buffer, are composed of relay packets and non-relay packets. Meanwhile, there are two approaches that packets leave the buffer, one is transmitted by R itself and another is cooperated by helper nodes (Fig. 3).

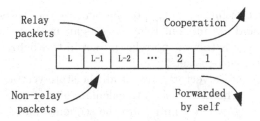

Fig. 3. The situations of packets entering and leaving R's buffer

When the buffer capacity is limitless, Enqueue rate and Dequeue rate will not be influenced by L. So if Enqueue rate is larger than Dequeue rate, buffer would be filled frame by frame and the length will be infinite finally, otherwise the buffer length would always fluctuate above zero.

3.1   Infinite Packets in Buffer

Analyze Features. Although the buffer is empty in the beginning, which is only a very short period during the whole working time, it has little impact on the sum throughput if Enqueue rate is faster than Dequeue rate. So we assume this system start working with infinite buffer. In this case, the system possesses two features:

(a) The packets which at the tail of Buffer cannot reach the head of buffer if this packet was held by H_i. Because the probability, of which H_i didn't help transmit the relay packet to D successfully before this packet reach the head of buffer, is nearly 0 (maybe it could happen after a very very long time about 10000 years, this situation can be neglected now).

(b) The packets which at the head of buffer will not be held by H_i. On the one hand, H_i will absolutely not get any non-relay packets. On the other hand, the relay packet, as mentioned in (a), can be held by H_i with nearly 0 probability.

When ensuring these two features, we can separate the throughput into two parts. Here are the packet at the head of buffer which could be forwarded by R only, as well as a new relay packet which can only be transmitted by H_i as long as H_i get it, or it will get into the buffer as normal if R get it while H_i not.

Analyze the Situation at Buffer's Tail. If R received a new relay packet but H_i didn't, this packet would be a member of buffer and it would distribute steadily all over the buffer in accompanied with other relay packets and non-relay packets. After a very long time it will reach the head of buffer and be forwarded by R. But if H_i received this relay packet, we consider this packet will certainly be transmitted by H_i and it will not exist in Buffer whether R has received it or not.

We propose a vector $[y_1, y_2, ..., y_{n_h}]$ to characterize the states of helper nodes. Helper nodes can hold n_h different relay packets at most so the range of y_i can be $[0, n_h]$, where 0 means there is no relay packet in this helper node and $[1, n_h]$ represents disparate relay packets.

After deriving all state vectors, we put all the state vectors in one collection $\mathbf{y}$ with a fixed order. The next task is to calculate all the transition probability from state i to state j, where i and j are the sequence numbers of the i_{th} and the j_{th} state vectors in $\mathbf{y}$ respectively. In order to simplify the calculation, we construct two transition sub-matrix $\mathbf{B}_{hs}$ and $\mathbf{B}_{dh}$ to characterize the procedures of S → H and H → D. The final matrix $\mathbf{B}$ is given by:

$$\mathbf{B} = [\mathbf{B}_{j,i}]_{N \times N}) = \mathbf{B}_{hs}\mathbf{B}_{dh} = [P_{hs(j,i)}]_{N \times N}[P_{dh(j,i)}]_{N \times N} \tag{1}$$

where N is the number of state vectors.

To calculate P_{hs} and P_{dh}, we propose another two vectors $[t_{h_1 s}, \cdots, t_{h_{n_h} s}]$ and $[t_{dh_1}, \cdots, t_{dh_{n_h}}]$ which represent whether S → H or H → D is successful or not respectively. For instance, if $[t_{h_1 s}, t_{h_2 s}, t_{h_3 s}] = [1, 0, 1]$, that means S → H_1, S → H_3 are successful but S → H_2 is failed. Meanwhile the probability of procedure S → H_i can be calculated as:

$$P_{s \to h}(t_{h_1 s}, \cdots, t_{h_{n_h} s}) = \prod_{i=1}^{n_h} [P_{succ,hs}(t_{h_i s} = 1) + P_{err,hs}(t_{h_i s} = 0)] \tag{2}$$

Therefore the algorithm of generating matrix $\mathbf{B}_{hs}$ is given by Algorithm 1. where $\mathbf{y}[i]$ is the i_{th} vector element in $\mathbf{y}$ and $Index(\mathbf{y}, \mathbf{x})$ is a function which find the sequence number of $\mathbf{x}$ in $\mathbf{y}$, and then return this number as result.

As same as the above, the probability of procedure H_i → D can be calculated as

$$P_{h \to d}(t_{dh_1}, \cdots, t_{dh_{n_h}}) = \prod_{i=1}^{n_h} [P_{succ,dh}(t_{dh_i} = 1) + P_{err,dh}(t_{dh_i} = 0)] \tag{3}$$

and the algorithm of generating matrix $\mathbf{B}_{dh}$ is given by Algorithm 2.

After finishing the construction of $\mathbf{B}_{hs}$ and $\mathbf{B}_{dh}$, we derive the final matrix $\mathbf{B}$. Let $\Pi_h = [\pi_1, \pi_2, \cdots, \pi_N]$ be the vector of the steady probability of state vectors. Then we can derive the results Π_h from solving the equation $\Pi_h \mathbf{B} = \Pi_h$.

In this system model, if H_i has received relay packets, we consider these packets will certainly reach D. Then the throughput is given by

$$Th_{A,tail} = P_{recv,H} \tag{4}$$

where $P_{recv,H}$ represent the probability that helper nodes could receive a new relay packet, which is given by

$$P_{recv,H} = \sum_{i=1}^{N} \pi_i \left[1 - (1 - P_{succ,hs} P_{idle})^{N_0(\mathbf{y}[i])} \right] \tag{5}$$

in this formula, $N_0(\mathbf{y}[i])$ represent the number of 0 in the i_{th} state vectors of $\mathbf{y}$.

Algorithm 1. Calculation of $P_{hs(j,i)}$

1: *Previous State:* (i)
   Initialization:
2: **for** $j = 1$ **to** N **do**
3:     $P_{hs(j,i)} = 0$
4: **end for**
   Calculation:
5: **for** $index = 0$ **to** $2^{n_h} - 1$ **do**
6:     $(t_{h_1 s}, \cdots, t_{h_{n_h} s}) = dec2bin(index)$
7:     $\mathbf{x} = \mathbf{y}[i]$
8:     $x_{max} = max\{\mathbf{x}\}$
9:     **for** $k = 1$ **to** n_h **do**
10:        **if** $t_{h_k s} = 1$ **then**
11:            $\mathbf{x}[k] \leftarrow (x_{max} + 1)(\mathbf{x}[k] = 0) + \cdots$
                 $\mathbf{x}[k](\mathbf{x}[k] > 0)]$
12:        **end if**
13:    **end for**
14:    $j = Index(\mathbf{y}, \mathbf{x})$
15:    $P_{hs(j,i)} \leftarrow P_{hs(j,i)} + P_{s \rightarrow h}(t_{h_1 s}, \cdots, t_{h_{n_h} s})$
16: **end for**

Algorithm 2. Calculation of $P_{dh(j,i)}$

1: *Previous State:* (i)
   Initialization:
2: **for** $j = 1$ **to** N **do**
3:     $P_{dh(j,i)} = 0$
4: **end for**
   Calculation:
5: **for** $index = 0$ **to** $2^{n_h} - 1$ **do**
6:     $(t_{h_1 s}, \cdots, t_{h_{n_h} s}) = dec2bin(index)$
7:     $\mathbf{x} = \mathbf{y}[i]$
8:     $x_{max} = max\{\mathbf{x}\}$
9:     **for** $k = 1$ **to** n_h **do**
10:        **if** $t_{h_k s} = 1$ **then**
11:            $x_k = \mathbf{x}[k]$
12:            **for** $m = 1$ **to** n_h **do**
13:                $\mathbf{x}[m] \leftarrow (\mathbf{x}[m] - 1)(x_k > 0)(\mathbf{x}[m] > x_k) \cdots$
                     $+\mathbf{x}[m](\mathbf{x}[m] < x_k)]$
14:            **end for**
15:        **end if**
16:    **end for**
17:    $j = Index(\mathbf{y}, \mathbf{x})$
18:    $P_{dh(j,i)} \leftarrow P_{dh(j,i)} + P_{h \rightarrow d}(t_{dh_1}, \cdots, t_{dh_{n_h}})$
19: **end for**

Analyze Situation at Buffer's Head. We consider the packets which at the head of buffer will not exist in H_i, so both of these relay packets and non-relay packets have to experience an enough long period to make themselves distribute steadily. So the ratio of both non-relay packets and relay packets is given by

$$(n_h + 2)\sigma_{nr} : (1 - P_{recv,H})P_{succ,rs} \tag{6}$$

Then the throughput can be given by

$$Th_{A,head} = \frac{(1 - P_{recv,H})\,P_{succ,rs}}{(1 - P_{recv,H})\,P_{succ,rs} + (n_h + 2)\,\sigma_{nr}}P_{succ,dr} \tag{7}$$

where the fraction is the probability that the first packet is a relay packet and $P_{succ,dr}$ refers to the probability of successful transmission.

Final Throughput. In this system model, since a relay packet could only be transmitted by R or H_i, the final throughput can be calculate as follow

$$Th_A = Th_{A,tail} + Th_{A,head} \tag{8}$$

All the analysis above are based on the special case that the length of buffer will always keep infinite. The next section we will discuss the situation on the contrary.

3.2   Almost No Packet in Buffer

Condition of Classification. Before discussing the new case, we need to know, what is the requirement of numerical relationship that could generate a result, which Enqueue rate would slower than Dequeue rate.

Enqueue rate is composed of two parts, which are the access of both relay packets and non relay packets to the buffer. Therefore we propose a formula of Enqueue rate which can be described as

$$R_{in} = P_{succ,rs} + (n_h + 2)\sigma_{nr} \tag{9}$$

where $P_{succ,rs}$ is the probability of receiving relay packet successfully and $(n_h + 2)\sigma_{nr}$ represent the expected rate of generating non-relay packets in each frame.

Due to our obtaining of $P_{recv,H}$, Dequeue rate consists of R's transition and H_i's help. So it can be given by

$$R_{out} = P_{succ,dr} + P_{succ,rs}P_{recv,H} \tag{10}$$

Obviously, $P_{succ,dr}$ represents the transition ability of R itself, and $P_{succ,rs}P_{recv,H}$ refers to the probability of H_i's successful cooperation. The reason why $P_{recv,H}$ need to multiply $P_{succ,rs}$ is that in last section, we didn't consider about R's receiving when calculating $P_{recv,H}$.

The new case is under certain condition when $R_{out} > R_{in}$.

Acquirement of New B'. In this section, we use an approximate method to get a new transition matrix B'. New B' can be derived by updating matrix B_{hs} to B'_{hs}. The updating method is shown below

$$P'_{hs(j,i)} = \begin{cases} P_{hs(j,i)} + [1 - (n_h + 2)\sigma_{nr}] \times \cdots \\ \quad P_{succ,rs}P_{succ,dr} \sum_{k>j} P_{hs(j,k)} & i = j \\ P_{hs(j,i)}\{1 - [1 - (n_h + 2)\sigma_{nr}] \times \cdots \\ \quad P_{succ,rs}P_{succ,dr}\} & i > j \\ 0 & i < j \end{cases} \qquad (11)$$

where $P_{hs(j,i)}$ is the transition probability which transfers from state i to state j in B_{hs}. Unlike the case that buffer has lower Dequeue rate, in the procedure S → H, R may get the same relay packet in S slot and transmit this packet successfully in its own slot. If that happened, we consider state vectors $[y_1, y_2, ..., y_{n_h}]$ didn't change so that the values of diagonal line in B'_{hs} should be larger than it in B_{hs}.

The updating factor possessed three parts as listed below:

1. The probability R has no non-relay packet in its buffer is $1 - (n_h + 2)\sigma_{nr}$;
2. The probability R receive relay packet successfully is $P_{succ,rs}$;
3. The probability R forward this packet successfully is $P_{succ,dr}$;

In each line of B'_{hs}, case $i = j$ represent H_i didn't change it states after this transition, so we use the sum of the other state vectors' probability multiplies the updating factor and add this value to the element of diagonal line.

Throughput. As same as above, we can easily use the same method to get $\Pi'_h = [\pi'_1, \pi'_2, \cdots, \pi'_N]$ by $\Pi'_h B' = \Pi'_h$ after deriving $B' = B'_{hs}B_{dh}$. And $P'_{recv,H}$ can be calculated by

$$P'_{recv,H} = \sum_{i=1}^{N} \pi'_i \left[1 - (1 - P_{succ,hs}P_{idle})^{N_0(\mathbf{y}[i])}\right] \qquad (12)$$

Finally we propose the formula of calculating throughput which is given by

$$Th_B = P'_{recv,H} + (1 - P'_{recv,H})P_{succ,rs} \qquad (13)$$

Throughput can be increased in the following three situations, both of R and H_i received a same relay packet, H_i got one packets while R didn't or R got that but H_i didn't. $P'_{recv,H}$ includes the first two situations because in this section we updating the B to B' by considering the influence of R. And it is no difficult task to understand that $(1 - P'_{recv,H})P_{succ,rs}$ is the third situation.

4   Simulations and Results

To make simulation more practical, we assume transmission powers of S, R and H_i are the same, represented by $E_i = E$. All the channels suffer the Rayleigh fading with different distance between every two nodes, resulting different SNR for each link. In the following comparison, we set the packet length $N_{bit} = 1024$, and the number of helpers $n_h = 3$.

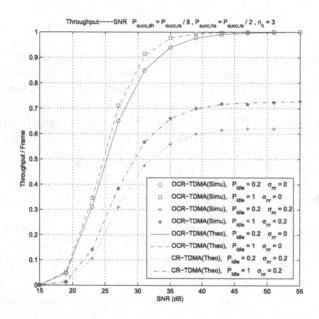

Fig. 4. The throughput curves of OCR-TDMA given different σ_{nr} and P_{idle}

Figure 4 shows the throughput of OCR-TDMA with P_{idle} chooses 0.2 or 1 and σ_{nr} chooses 0 or 0.1. The x axis is SNR, or equivalent $P_{succ,rs}$. In this simulation, buffer has infinite capacity and we set $P_{succ,dh} = P_{succ,hs}/8$, which make us control the Enqueue rate is larger than Dequeue rate or not more easily. In this figure, the red line is the case that Enqueue rate is lower than Dequeue rate and the blue line is on the contrary. The numerical results, which calculated in Part III, match the simulation results very well.

Figure 5 shows the influence of buffer capacity on the throughput and the other parameters are same as above. We set 5 simulations with L given $1, 10, 100, 1000, 100000$, which represent the very small, small, medium, large and nearly infinite buffer capacity. The results present the gap between our special case and the normal case. This figure show us the numerical results with the case $L = \infty$ can be treated as proper upper bound of OCR-TDMA.

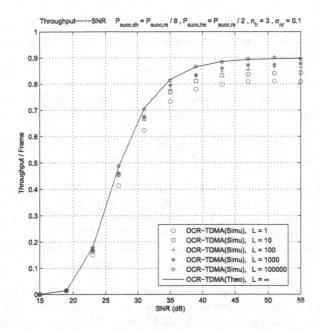

Fig. 5. The throughput curves of OCR-TDMA with different L

5   Conclusion

In this paper, we propose a more practical case $L = \infty$ to approximately calculate the throughput of OCR-TDMA and the results of this case can be treated as upper bound of OCR-TDMA. The numerical results and simulation results match very well. Meanwhile we provide a new method to solve the problem of analyzing buffer, which is very direct and useful. However, the method to evaluate the performance of OCR-TDMA with normal case still need to be explored, and this will be our future work.

Acknowledgement. This work was supported by the National Natural Science Foundation of China No. 61601164, No. 61971138 and the Science and Technology Planning Project of Guangdong Province under Grant 2016B010108002.

References

1. Mach, P., Becvar, Z.: Mobile edge computing: a survey on architecture and computation offloading. IEEE Commun. Surv. Tutor. **19**(3), 1628–1656 (2017)
2. You, C., Zeng, Y., Zhang, R., et al.: Asynchronous mobile-edge computation offloading: energy-efficient resource management. IEEE Trans. Wireless Commun. **17**(11), 7590–7605 (2018)
3. Shi, W., Cao, J., Zhang, Q., Li, Y., Xu, L.: Edge computing: vision and challenges. IEEE Internet Things J. **3**(5), 637–646 (2016)

4. Tran, T.X., Hajisami, A., Pandey, P., et al.: Collaborative mobile edge computing in 5G networks: new paradigms, scenarios, and challenges. IEEE Commun. Mag. **55**(4), 54–61 (2017)
5. Sendonaris, A., Erkip, E., Aazhang, B.: User cooperation diversity. Part I. System description. IEEE Trans. Commun. **51**(11), 1927–1938 (2003)
6. Laneman, J.N., Tse, D.N.C., Wornell, G.W.: Cooperative diversity in wireless networks: efficient protocols and outage behavior. IEEE Trans. Inf. Theory **50**(12), 3062–3080 (2004)
7. Liu, P., Tao, Z., Panwar, S.: A cooperative MAC protocol for wireless local area networks. In: Proceedings of the IEEE International Conference on Communications (2005)
8. Liu, P., Tao, Z., Narayanan, S., et al.: CoopMAC: a cooperative MAC for wireless LANs. IEEE J. Sel. Areas Commun. **25**(2), 340–354 (2007)
9. Shan, H., Zhuang, W., Wang, Z.: Distributed cooperative MAC for multihop wireless networks. IEEE Commun. Mag. **47**(2), 126–133 (2009)
10. Shan, H., Cheng, H.T., Zhuang, W.: Cross-layer cooperative MAC protocol in distributed wireless networks. IEEE Trans. Wireless Commun. **10**(8), 2603–2615 (2011)
11. Bharati, S., Zhuang, W.: Performance analysis of cooperative ADHOC MAC for vehicular networks. In: Global Communications Conference. IEEE (2012)
12. Yang, Z., Yao, Y.D., Li, X., et al.: A TDMA-based MAC protocol with cooperative diversity. IEEE Commun. Lett. **14**(6), 542–544 (2010)
13. Lee, J.K., Noh, H.J., Lim, J.: TDMA-based cooperative MAC protocol for multihop relaying networks. IEEE Commun. Lett. **18**(3), 435–438 (2014)
14. Liu, X., Chen, C., Huang, A., et al.: A new TDMA-based cooperative MAC scheme. In: 2015 22nd International Conference on Telecommunications (ICT). IEEE (2015)

Task Migration Using Q-Learning Network Selection for Edge Computing in Heterogeneous Wireless Networks

Yi Liu[1], Jie Zheng[1(✉)], Jie Ren[2], Ling Gao[1], and Hai Wang[1]

[1] Northwest University, Xi'an, China
jzheng@nwu.edu.cn
[2] Shaanxi Normal University, Xi'an, China

Abstract. For edge devices, pushing the task to other near devices has become a widely concerned service provision paradigm. However, the energy-constrained nature of edge devices makes optimizing for Quality of Service (QoS) difficult. We choose three factors as QoS: the delay limitation, the CPU usage of terminal and energy consumption. Due to the delay limitation of different tasks for edge computing and the different rates in heterogeneous wireless networks, we propose a network selection task migration algorithm based on Q-learning that captures the trade-off between QoS and energy consumption. Our approach can automatically choose a suitable network to perform task migration reasons about the task's QoS requirements and computing rate in 4G network, Wi-Fi, Device-to-device (D2D). We demonstrate a working prototype using the YOLOv3 on the Vivo X9 devices. Based on real hardware and software measurements, we achieve 27.79% energy saving and 35% reduction in delay.

Keywords: Edge computing · Heterogeneous wireless networks · Network selection · Task migration · Q-learning

1 Introduction

1.1 A Subsection Sample

Due to the limited computing and memory resource of mobile edge devices (e.g. drone, smartphone, wearable device, and automobile), they are not able to process compute-intensive tasks in time, such as image recognition, traffic navigation, and the violation of QoS may cause the economic loss, threat the human life [1]. Generally, the heavyweight tasks of edge devices are migrated to the cloud servers which equipped with high-performance computing power and large storage [2]. With the increasing network traffic and unstable network conditions, the cloud server cannot guarantee the QoS for each task. To solve this problem, researchers Jinming Wen and Hong Xing try to take advantage of other idle edge devices to process the part of the heavyweight tasks. Such as [3, 4] they focus on the D2D conditions, but miss opportunity of a wider range of devices under the heterogeneous network, and cannot achieve a global optimal results.

© ICST Institute for Computer Sciences, Social Informatics and Telecommunications Engineering 2020
Published by Springer Nature Switzerland AG 2020. All Rights Reserved
B. Li et al. (Eds.): IoTaaS 2019, LNICST 316, pp. 141–150, 2020.
https://doi.org/10.1007/978-3-030-44751-9_13

In this paper, we propose a network selection task migration algorithm based on Q-learning. The goal of network selection task migration algorithm based on Q-learning is to implement network selection. In this paper, we define QoS to represent the delay of the task [5]. Our approach selects the optimal network access. Through this network, we migrate tasks that cannot be completed by the edge device to the appropriate server. Our approach focuses on the performance energy consumption of the edge device and the task delay. Because of the performance limitations of the edge device, the task with high-performance requirements cannot be completed; the size of the task delay also has a great impact on the user experience. Therefore, we choose the edge devices energy consumption and the task delay as feedback variables and input them into the algorithm. The algorithm performs self-learning based on feedback. In the end, we get the most optimal network selection strategy based on Q-learning and automatically access the network. We conducted an experimental evaluation using the mobile phone Vivo X9 as an edge device. We use YOLOv3 [6] as a task model for experimental verification. Through experiments, our algorithm is compatible with edge computing heterogeneous wireless network.

The main contribution of this paper is the network selection task migration algorithm based on Q-learning, which can use data feedback to optimize the network selection strategy. Our algorithm considers the problem of resource utilization, the impact of edge device energy consumption and the task's QoS requirements. Our algorithm is compatible with edge computing. We have solved some of the problems in the network selection algorithm of heterogeneous wireless network. Our results show that based on our strategy when performing task migration in edge computing, the energy consumption of the terminal can be reduced, and the change of task delay also improves the user experience. Our technology can be widely applied to edge computing environments for large-scale, low-energy edge device deployments. This can effectively reduce the cost of edge computing deployment.

In this paper, Sect. 2 introduces the system model, including the task model and the network model; Sect. 3 provides the detailed algorithm flow of the task migration network selection strategy; In Sect. 4, we verify the effectiveness of the task migration network selection strategy through experimental simulation. We conclude this paper in Sect. 5.

2   System Model

2.1 Task Model

In this work, we use the convolutional neural network YOLOv3 to perform image recognition tasks. YOLOv3 uses the Darknet-53 basic feature extractor, which combines Darknet-19 and deep residual networks, and has 53 convolutional layers. Compared to other more advanced classifiers, Darknet-53 handles fewer floating-point operations, is faster, and achieves the highest measured floating-point operations per second. This can make better use of system performance, improve evaluation efficiency, and thus improve recognition speed.

In the experiment of this paper, we select five sets of the coco2014 dataset [7] as our experiment dataset.

2.2 Network Model

The heterogeneous wireless network system is composed of a plurality of heterogeneous network elements, including macrocell, picocell and femtocell [8]. They distinguish between each other by transmission energy, coverage, backbone and transmission characteristics. The heterogeneous wireless network system distributes macrocells within the coverage of the picocells [9]. Inside the macrocell, the picocells are set in the communication hotspot area, and femtocell is randomly constructed by the user in the indoor area using Wi-Fi.

We use 4G and Wi-Fi to build heterogeneous wireless networks. There are two industry-developed technologies, LTE-Advanced developed by 3GPP and WirelessMAN-Advanced developed by IEEE. In China, the 4G technologies adopted by China Unicom and China Mobile are mainly LTE TDD and LTE FDD. We use LTE TDD and LTE FDD in our experiments as 4G standard. LTE Peak download is 100 Mbit/s, and peak upload is 500 Mbit/s.

There are many versions of Wi-Fi, and we are currently using Wi-Fi 4 and Wi-Fi 5 (the leading technologies are IEEE 802.11a/b/g/n and IEEE 802.11ac). The Wi-Fi network we experimented with was also based on these two Wi-Fi standards. Their theoretical maximum data transfer rates are 72–600 Mbit/s and 433–6933 Mbit/s, respectively.

The purpose of constructing a heterogeneous wireless network scenario is that the picocell can better guarantee the communication quality of the hotspot area; the home base station can make the user more convenient to access the network in real time [10].

3 Network Selection Strategy for Task Migration

Before giving the network model, we first introduce the basics of the network model, a model-free reinforcement learning algorithm. Q-learning is to record the side of the learning, so tell the agent what action to take will have the greatest reward value [11]. Q-learning tells us to adopt different strategies in different situations through self-learning which does not require a model of any environment, including agents, environment, rewards, and actions. It abstracts the problem into a Markov decision process [12]. The ultimate goal of the entire process is to find the expectation of the strategy that accumulates the most rewards:

$$
\max_{\pi} E\left[\sum_{t=0}^{H}\left(\gamma^t R(S_t, A_t, S_{t+1})|\pi\right)\right] \tag{1}
$$

in the Eq. (1), S define as set of states, A define as set of actions, $R = (s, a, s')$ is reward function, H is horizon, γ represents discount factor.

The main advantage of Q-learning is its problem-solving system. By dynamically planning the Bellman equation, each state is valuably determined not only by the current state but also the former state. The value of the current state S can be obtained by expecting the cumulative reward of the previous state $V(s)$:

$$
V_\pi(s) = E(U_t|S_t = s) \tag{2}
$$

we will formulate the Eq. (2) as follows:

$$V_\pi(s) = E_\pi\big[R_{t+1} + \gamma[R_{t+2} + \gamma[\ldots]]|S_t = s\big] \tag{3}$$

after finishing we get the following equation,

$$V_\pi(s) = E_\pi\big[R_{t+1} + \gamma[R_{t+2} + \gamma V(s')]|S_t = s\big] \tag{4}$$

we can obtain the optimal cumulative expectation:

$$V^*(s) = \max_\pi E\left[\sum_{t=0}^{H} (\gamma^t R(S_t, A_t, S_{t+1})|\pi, s_0 = s)\right] \tag{5}$$

and the optimal value action function denoted as:

$$Q^*(s) = \sum_{S'}\left(P(s'|s, a)\Big(R(s, a, s'), \gamma \max_{a'} Q^*(s', a')\Big)\right) \tag{6}$$

by (5) and (6), and after iterating over Q, Q denoted as:

$$Q(s, a) = Q(s, a) + \alpha\left[r + \gamma \max_{a'} Q^*(s', a') - Q(s, a)\right] \tag{7}$$

Where α is the learning rate, the range is 0 to 1. The larger the learning rate value, the faster the convergence of the whole algorithm, and vice versa; γ is the reward decay coefficient.

A. System status

According to the Q-learning algorithm theory, we define the state of the environment as:

$$S := (n, v, p) \tag{8}$$

Our environmental state mainly includes three parameters, the network connection state n, the network transmission rate v under the network connection state n, and the terminal energy consumption p.

B. Action selection

In this paper, the action is mainly to change the network status and find a suitable network transmission rate network. We denote a as action, and $A = \{a, a \in \{0, 1, 2, \ldots, N\}\}$ as a collection of all possible actions, the terminal accesses the network $N : a = N$.

C. Reward function

The reward function is mainly used to feedback the network selection strategy [10]. We consider the network transmission rate and terminal energy consumption as the evaluation indicators. Our reward is directly proportional to the network transmission rate and inversely proportional to the terminal energy consumption. The reward function R is denoted as:

$$R = \frac{V}{P} \tag{9}$$

Where V is the network transmission rate, and P is the terminal energy consumption.

D. Algorithm

Implementation of Network Selection Model Algorithm Based on Q-learning:

(a) Initialization. The weight of the network selection model is initialized, and α and γ in the Eq. (5) are set.
(b) Status input. When the image recognition starts, the task model is used to collect data of the current environmental state, and the current network state and network transmission rate data are collected, and finally, the state s is constructed according to Eq. (6).
(c) Action selection. Select an action with an arbitrary probability ε according to the obtained Q value.
(d) The iterative update. State s executes the action selected in step (c) and then reaches the next state s′, and the state s′ updates the Q value to $Q(s')$ by the Eq. (7); The update is convenient for the next state to obtain the Q value.
(e) Network Update. After several iterations, the state of the final moment and the corresponding Q value are obtained. Obtain the corresponding option with the highest weight and output it to get the final output result of the network (Fig. 1).

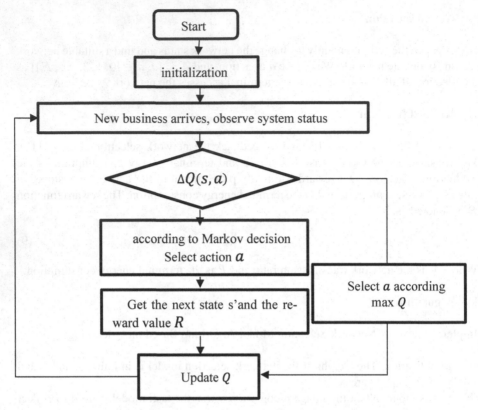

Fig. 1. Q-learning network selection algorithm flow chart

4   Experimental Results and Analysis

4.1   Experimental Platform

Our experimental platform is the Vivo X9 mobile phone. The system has an 8 cores A53 Qualcomm Snapdragon 625 running at 2.0 GHz, and Adreno 506 as GPU. We run the Android 7.1.2. We use YOLOv3 app to perform the local image recognition task test. We deploy YOLOv3 on the host as edge computing server and deploy YOLOv3 app on OnePlus 6 as another device in edge computing. Besides, we obtain the edge device's energy consumption information through the energy test tool written in our lab. We experimented with the network simulation tool Fiddler to simulate the network status of 4G, Wi-Fi and D2D [13].

4.2   Evaluation Methodology

Evaluation Method. We use the comparison experiment to evaluate our algorithm: verify the energy consumption and time-consuming of the image recognition task based on the Q-learning network selection algorithm in the edge computing, and verify the energy consumption and time-consuming of the image recognition task based on the random network selection algorithm in the edge computing. Finally, by comparing the indicators of the two strategies, we can evaluate our algorithm. Specifically, the terminal performs image recognition tasks in edge computing. We partition the images into 5 sets where each of them contains 100 images. We use our algorithm and random selection network algorithm respectively to do experiments. We repeat this process 3 times. Use the energy test tool to collect parameters during the experiment: time, CPU energy consumption.

Performance Report. We report the arithmetic mean and variance in the evaluation report. The arithmetic mean can well reflect the concentration trend within a phase. The variance can well reflect the degree of data fluctuations in a phase. For the system status, we collect three parameters: network connection status, network transmission rate, and CPU energy consumption data. To collect data, we set five different network environments including Wi-Fi (IEEE 802.11ac), 4G (LTE-TDD) and D2D (Bluetooth), then save the network connection status and network transmission rate. We excluded the impact of other apps on the experiment. To measure the energy consumption, we developed a lightweight tool to take read CPU information note running at a frequency of 100 samples per second. Then we matched the time stamps to compute the energy consumption.

4.3   Experimental Results

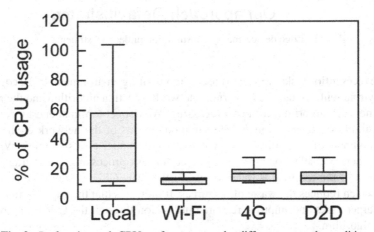

Fig. 2. Performing task CPU performance under different network conditions

In Fig. 2, we compare the performance of the CPU in four cases. Under the condition of performing the same tasks, the local image recognition task has higher requirements on the CPU, especially the energy consumption peak requires the CPU to work in a higher voltage environment. In the edge computing, that is, the task is performed in the environment of Wi-Fi, 4G, and D2D, the energy consumption of the terminal CPU is not high, and the image recognition task can be completed with only a small overhead. This diagram reinforces our works that we should make task migration when the performance of the edge device does not meet the mission requirements. The rest of the discussion in this paper explains how to solve the network selection problem when task migration in edge computing.

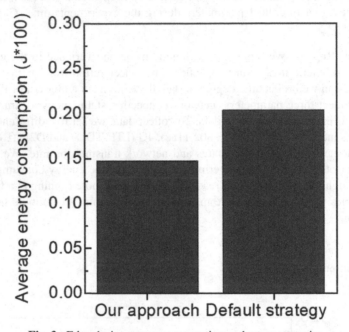

Fig. 3. Edge device energy consumption under two strategies.

Image recognition tasks are sent to the edge computing environment. In the edge computing environment, we use the Q-learning network selection algorithm and the random selection network algorithm for task processing. We collect terminal energy consumption of multiple experiments under the same conditions of the network environment. Figure 3 compares the terminal energy consumption under two strategies. When the Q-learning network selection algorithm is used for task processing, the average energy consumption of the terminal is reduced by 27.79%. The CPU usage of the terminal is reduced, which reduces the waste of resources. It indicates that the edge computing can perform larger tasks and improve resource utilization through the Q-learning network selection algorithm.

Figure 4 calculates the ratio of our approach's improvement in task delay compared to the random network selection algorithm. In short, the network selection task migration algorithm based on Q-Learning effectively reduce the task delay. In the case of the same two policy network environments, the task execution time based on our approach is reduced by an average of 35%. We also calculated variance of the task delay. The results show that the variance of the task execution time using our method is significantly smaller than the default strategy. Our approach is more robust. The result indicates that through

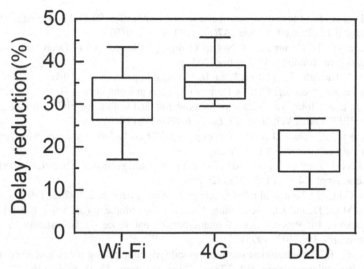

Fig. 4. Comparison of delays between the two strategies.

the monitoring of network transmission rate, our approach can make rational use of resources in the edge computing environment to avoid uneven use of network resources.

5 Conclusion

In this paper, we proposed a task migration based on Q-learning network selection for edge computing in heterogeneous wireless networks. With the proposed algorithm, we achieved nearly 30% energy savings. The performance requirements of the terminal are significantly reduced. At the same time, the delay of the task is also reduced 35%. It indicates that the edge computing based on Q-learning network selection strategy reduces the performance requirements of the terminal in terms of energy consumption, and the task with high delay requirement can also meet its requirements.

Acknowledgement. This work was supported in part by the National Natural Science Foundation of China (Grants nos. 61701400, 61572401 and 61672426), by the Project Funded by China Postdoctoral Science Foundation (Grants nos. 2017M613188 and 2017M613186), by the Natural Science Special Foundation of Education Department in Shaanxi (Grant no. 2017JQ6052), and Natural Science Special Foundation of Education Department in Shannxi (17JK0783).

References

1. Ahmed, A., Ahmed, E.: A survey on mobile edge computing. In: 10th IEEE International Conference on Intelligent Systems and Control (ISCO 2016). IEEE (2016)
2. Ahmed, E., et al.: Application optimization in mobile cloud computing: motivation, taxonomies, and open challenges. J. Netw. Comput. Appl. **52**, 52–68 (2015)
3. Wen, J., et al.: Energy-efficient device-to-device edge computing network: an approach offloading both traffic and computation. IEEE Commun. Mag. **56**(9), 96–102 (2018)

4. Xing, H., et al.: Joint task assignment and resource allocation for D2D-enabled mobile-edge computing. IEEE Trans. Commun. **67**(6), 4193–4207 (2019)
5. Qin, Q., et al.: To Compress, or Not to Compress: Characterizing Deep Learning Model Compression for Embedded Inference (2018)
6. Redmon, J., Farhadi, A.: YOLOv3: An Incremental Improvement (2018)
7. Lin, T.Y., et al.: Microsoft COCO: Common Objects in Context (2014)
8. Zheng, J., et al.: Joint load balancing of downlink and uplink for eICIC in heterogeneous network. IEEE Trans. Veh. Technol. **66**(7), 6388–6398 (2016)
9. Hu, L., Zhou, L.Q., Deng, J., et al.: A strategy of SDN based adaptive multipath load balancing. J. Xi'an Polytech. Univ. **32**(2), 243–247 (2018)
10. Zheng, J., et al.: Joint downlink and uplink edge computing offloading in ultra-dense HetNets. Mob. Netw. Appl. **24**(5), 1452–1460 (2019)
11. Watkins, C.J.C.H.: Technical note: Q-learning. Mach. Learn. **8**, 279–292 (1992)
12. Littman, M.L., Dean, T.L., Kaelbling, L.P.: On the complexity of solving Markov decision problems. In: Proceedings of International Conference on Uncertainty in Artificial Intelligence, pp. 394–402 (1995)
13. He, Y., et al.: D2D communications meet mobile edge computing for enhanced computation capacity in cellular networks. IEEE Trans. Wirel. Commun. **18**(3), 1750–1763 (2019)

Measurement and Analysis of Fading Characteristics of V2V Propagation Channel at 5.9 GHz in Tunnel

Xu Zhang[1], Mi Yang[2], Wei Wang[1(✉)], Ruisi He[2], Jun Hou[1], and Xinyi Liu[1]

[1] School of Information Engineering, Chang'an University, Xi'an, China
wei.wang@chd.edu.cn
[2] School of Electronic and Information Engineering, Beijing Jiaotong University, Beijing, China

Abstract. In this paper, we present a vehicle-to-vehicle (V2V) wireless channel measurement at 5.9 GHz in the tunnel environments. The small scale fading characteristics are analyzed for outside and inside the tunnel, and the conjunction part in between. We evaluate the received signal magnitude inside the tunnel by comparing its distribution with five typical theoretical fading distributions. The best fit among the considered fading distributions is found to be Rician distribution that has the lowest Goodness of Fit (GoF) indicator. The K-factor calculated from measurements data inside the tunnel is lower than the values obtained outside the tunnel. Further, the K-factor is found to be dependent on the transmitter (Tx)-receiver (Rx) distance in the considered scenario.

Keywords: V2V · Propagation channel · Tunnel · Fading characteristics

1 Introduction

Internet of things (IOT) is a huge network of real-world various objects linked by the internet through information sensing equipments and realize the interconnection of people, machines and objects at any time and any place [1]. Internet of vehicles (IOV) is a specific application of IOT in urban intelligent transportation system. IOV uses the technologies of wireless communication and sensing detection to collect and interaction the information of vehicles, roads, environment through the Vehicle to everything (V2X) links, so as to realize an intelligent integrated network of traffic management control, vehicle control and dynamic information service [2,3].

V2X is mainly divided into three categories: vehicle-to-vehicle (V2V) [4], vehicle-to-infrastructure (V2I) [5], vehicle-to-pedestrian (V2P) [6], which forms the vehicular ad hoc networks (VANETs) by intercommunication. V2V communication is not limited to fixed base station, but a direct wireless communication between two moving vehicles from one end to another. V2V plays an important

© ICST Institute for Computer Sciences, Social Informatics and Telecommunications Engineering 2020
Published by Springer Nature Switzerland AG 2020. All Rights Reserved
B. Li et al. (Eds.): IoTaaS 2019, LNICST 316, pp. 151–160, 2020.
https://doi.org/10.1007/978-3-030-44751-9_14

role in intelligent transportation system which can monitor "hidden" data such as the speed and position of other vehicles, and automatically predicts whether there will be a possible collision with other vehicles on the road. To better develop the V2V communication systems, it is essential to understand the V2V propagation channel.

Many measurement campaigns and channel modeling of V2V wireless channel have been performed in recent years for typical environments (e.g., rural, suburban, urban, and highway) [4, 7–9]. Other particular environments such as underground parking and tunnel have also been investigated marginally. Particularly, the small scale fading in tunnel has not been thoughtfully studied. [10] presents a study on the statistical analysis of the small-scale fading of the V2V propagation channel at 5.9 GHz inside tunnels. The results of the paper shows that the Rice distribution to fit cumulative distribution function (CDF) and the mean K factor values outside the tunnel is higher than inside the tunnel. However, an insight into the other fading characteristics, e.g., Rayleigh, Weibull, etc. is needed.

In this paper, we present a channel measurement at 5.9 GHz in the tunnel environment. Based on the measurement data the small scale fading characteristics are analyzed for outside and inside tunnel, and the conjunction part in between. We compare the statistical characteristic of the received signal magnitude with 5 typical theoretical fading distributions. Based on the GoF indicator the best fit among 5 considered fading distributions is found to be Rician distribution. The K-factor is calculated and analyzed, that K-factor depends on the Tx-Rx distance.

The paper is structured as follows: in Sect. 2, the setup of the channel measurement campaign is addressed. Section 3 presents the data processing methods and the results. Finally Sect. 4 concludes the paper.

2   Channel Measurement

2.1   Measurement Setup

The channel measurement campaign was conducted with the BJTU channel sounder, which relies on National Instrument-PXI chassis based software defined radio system [11]. The channel sounder is consist of vector signal transmitter and receiver, clock module, power supply module, data storage, transmitting antenna/receiving antenna and other modules. At the transmitter side, the chassis NIPXIE-1082 and the vector signal transmitter NIPXIE-5673 are used to continuously transmit 5.9 GHz signal. Orthogonal Frequency Division Multiplexing (OFDM) sequence is adopted as the sounding signal of channel. A power amplifier is used to amplify the sounding signal at the transmitter, and then the signal is transmitted by a single transmit antenna mounted on the top of the vehicle. The receiver is composed of the chassis NIPXIE-1082 and the vector signal receiver NIPXIE-5663. During the measurement, both single-input single-output (SISO) and single-input multiple-output (SIMO) measurement were considered. For the former case, the same antenna as the transmit antenna was used

Fig. 1. Vehicles used for measurement: the van on the left side was used for transmitter and the car on the right hand side was used for receiver.

at the receiver; and for the latter case, we used an antenna array consisting of 16-elements, each of which is dual polarized. Each antenna unit of the antenna array was controlled by electronic switch, and data of each antenna channel was collected and stored in a time division manner. In both cases, the receive antennas were mounted on the rooftop of the receiver vehicle as shown in Fig. 1, where the van on the left side was used for transmitter and the car on the right hand side was used for receiver.

The software platform of the channel sounder is based on the programming environment of Laboratory Virtual Instrument Engineering Workbench (LabVIEW), which can efficiently program and control the hardware equipment of the channel sounder. With suitable setting the software, extracting data collected by the receiver for real-time processing, storage and displaying can be achieved.

To synchronize the transmitter and receiver, Rubidium clock disciplined by the timing information obtained from Global Positioning System (GPS) receivers as the frequency norm standards were used on both sides. To provide power to the channel sounder, the high-power inverter was used to convert the 12 V DC power of the vehicle battery into 220 V AC power. To prevent the power interruption and unstable current, the uninterruptible power supply was used between the inverter and the channel sounder. Table 1 shows the 5.9 GHz channel sounding system parameters.

2.2   Measurement Environment

The measurement campaign was conducted in a tunnel in the south region of Xi'an city. Both vehicles travelled in the same direction with similar speeds. The

Table 1. 5.9 GHz channel sounding system parameters.

Centre frequency f_c	5.9 GHz
Measurement type	SISO and SIMO
Bandwidth B	30 MHz
Transmit power	max. 34 dBm
Test signal	OFDM signal
Transmit and receive antenna speed	$\sim 40^{km/h}$

Fig. 2. Rectangular tunnel with two lanes

measurement was started at the street cross shortly before the entrance of the tunnel, such that the channel propagation characteristics can be obtained for outside tunnel, inside tunnel and the conjunction part in between. During the measurement campaign, there always exists a direct line-of-sight (LoS) between the transmitter and the receiver. Figure 2 shows the picture of the rectangular tunnel consisting of a two lanes. Figure 3 visualizes the received power for the measurement where the vehicles started from the street cross. The received power is varying distributed between -55 dBm and -30 dBm. In the beginning, the received power varies insignificantly. It is due to the fact that both vehicles were waiting for the traffic light changing from red to green. It can be seen that there is a large decreasing in the received power while two vehicles traveled towards the tunnel with increasing distance between transmit and receive antennas. The fading depth of received signal outside the tunnel is smaller than inside tunnel.

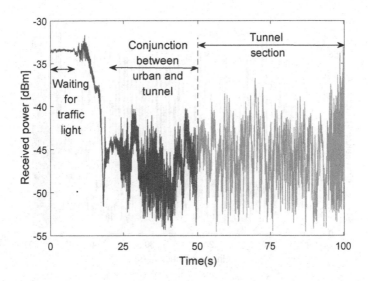

Fig. 3. Received power outside and inside the tunnel for measurement (Color figure online)

3   Small-Scale Fading Analysis

In order to evaluate the small scale fading in the tunnel, the received signal strength is normalized to mitigate the large scale fading effect, i.e., distance dependent path loss. Similar to [12–14], a sliding window is used to calculate the large scale fading by moving average method. The received power is normalized to the average power taken over a certain measurement samples where the channel is regarded to be stationary. In this paper, the window length is set to 200 consecutively measured samples. Figure 4 visualizes the normalized magnitude of the received signal inside the tunnel.

In the statistical characteristics of describing small scale fading, there are usually two probability distribution functions assumed for V2V communication channel: Rician distribution and Rayleigh distribution, but other distributions such as Nakagami-m and Weibull have also been proven to well fit the fading behavior. More specifically, the Rice and Weibull distributions have been used in paper [12]. The Weibull distribution is a more generalized distribution model, which is identical to the Rayleigh distribution when the shape parameter $k = 2$. If the shape parameter of the Weibull distribution is larger than two, the Weibull distribution becomes similar to the Rician distribution.

Within the measurement data, starting from the 50 s, both vehicles entered the tunnel. Therefore, the measured data inside the tunnel was considered to determine the small-scale fading distribution type in the tunnel. Figure 5 shows the CDF curves of the signal magnitude taking into account five typical theoretical distributions for fitting, including Normal distribution, Rayleigh distribution, Rician distribution, Weibull distribution, and Log-Normal distribution.

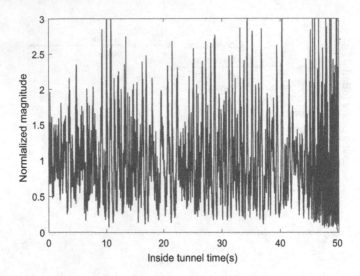

Fig. 4. Normalized magnitude of the received signal.

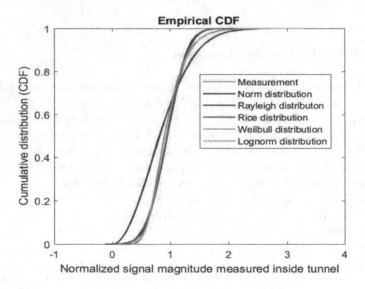

Fig. 5. Distribution conditions for fitting

A popular approach to characterize the distribution is the Kolmogorov-Smirnov (KS) test statistic serving as a GoF indicator [12–14]. The so-called test statistic ρ is calculated as:

$$\rho = \sup_x |F_X(x) - F(x)| \tag{1}$$

Table 2. GoF values of considered distributions.

Distribution	ρ
Norm	0.0269
Rayleigh	0.2049
Rice	0.0215
Weibull	0.0313
Lognorm	0.0518

where sup is the supremum operator, $F_X(x)$ and $F(x)$ are the empirical and
theoretical CDFs of x, respectively. A lower value for ρ indicates a better fit of
the distribution to the empirical CDF calculated using the measurement samples. Table 2 lists the GoF indicator ρ for the different distributions. It can be
seen that the value of ρ for the normal distribution, Rician distribution and
Weibull distribution fits are close to each other. Particularly, the value of ρ for
Rician distribution is the lowest. Considering the fact that Tx-Rx distance were
generally short during the measurement, and the LoS path existed during the
measurement, it is reasonable to consider the Rician fading to approximate the
small scale fading characteristics of the magnitude inside tunnel.

The Rician distribution can be represented as

$$f(x) = \frac{2(K+1)}{\Omega} \cdot e^{-K - \frac{(K+1)^2}{\Omega}}$$
$$\times I_0(2\sqrt{\frac{K(K+1)}{\Omega}}x) \tag{2}$$

where x stands for the magnitude, I_0 is the $0th$ order modified Bessel function of
the first kind, $\Omega = E\{x^2\}$, and K is the Rician K-factor, i.e., the power ratio of
the dominant path to the multipath components. In general, K-factor is defined
as

$$K = \frac{A^2}{2\sigma^2} \tag{3}$$

where A denotes the peak amplitude of the dominant component and σ the
root mean square value of the amplitude. To calculate K the moment-based
method [15] with

$$K = \frac{\sqrt{1-\gamma}}{1 - \sqrt{1-\gamma}} \tag{4}$$

and

$$\gamma = \frac{\text{Var}\{x^2\}}{(E\{x^2\})^2} \tag{5}$$

is widely used. The notations Var and E stand for the sample variance and
expectation estimators, respectively. To use the sample variance and expectation
estimators, a spatial window length has to be considered that is no longer than
the window length for removing the large scale fading. Therefore, a window
length of around 180 magnitude samples is used to calculate the K-factor.

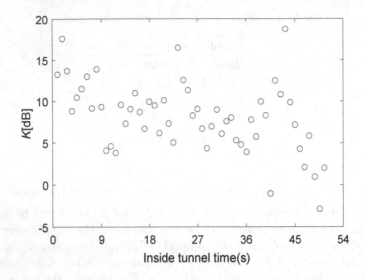

Fig. 6. Variation of the K-factor for measurement inside tunnel.

Figure 6 shows the estimated K-factor values versus the measurement index inside the tunnel. Since there exists a direct LoS component, the K-factor values are relatively large. The change of K-factor in the figure probably because the multipath component inside tunnel varies in power due to the changing environment, e.g., moving cars, resulting in the variation in power of the multipath component. While both vehicles moved inside the tunnel, the K-factor decreases in average as seen from Fig. 6. It is probably due to the fact that the distance between transmitter and receiver slightly increases. The obtained mean and standard deviation values of the K-factor are 8.1 and 4.2, respectively.

As a comparison, the K-factor estimated for outside the tunnel is calculated as well and visualized in Fig. 7. It can be noticed that in the beginning both vehicles were stable with a distance of about 5 m and, thus, the fading depth is insignificant which results in very large k-factors. While the distance between the transmitter and the receiver increased to about 50 m from the 7th second, the k-factor decreases. Thus, in considered scenario where the transmitter and the receiver is not separated far away, the k-factor shows a dependency on the distance between the transmitter and receiver.

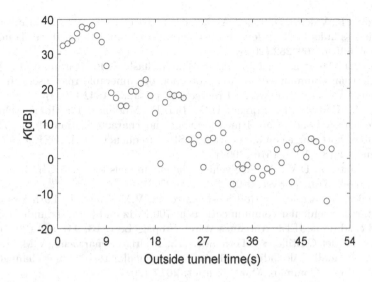

Fig. 7. Variation of the K-factor for measurement outside tunnel.

4   Conclusion

Tunnel is a safety-critical environment for applications of intelligent transportation system in terms of wireless based communications and navigation. To investigate small scale fading characteristics for in tunnel V2V propagation channel, a channel measurement campaign at 5.9 GHz with a bandwidth of 30 MHz was performed. In this paper, a detailed description of the channel measurement campaign and analysis of the small scale fading characteristics are presented. The results show that the received signal experiences a Rician fading due to the presence of a direct LoS path. Inside the tunnel the mean and standard deviation of the K-factor values are 8.1 and 4.2, respectively. As the distance between transmitter and receiver is not large, a distance dependency between the distance and the K-factor has been found. To model the distance dependent K-factor is the next research direction.

References

1. Muntjir, M., Rahul, M., Alhumyani, H.A.: An analysis of Internet of Things (IoT): novel architectures, modern applications, security aspects and future scope with latest case studies. Int. J. Eng. Res. Technol **6**(6), 422–447 (2017)
2. Contreras, J., Zeadally, S., Guerrero-Ibanez, J.A.: Internet of vehicles: architecture, protocols, and security. IEEE Internet Things J. **5**(5), 3701–3709 (2017)
3. de Ponte Mueller, F.: Survey on ranging sensors and cooperative techniques for relative positioning of vehicles. Sensors **17**(2), 271 (2017)
4. Molisch, A., Tufvesson, F., Karedal, J., Mecklenbrauker, C.: A survey on vehicle-to-vehicle propagation channels. IEEE Wirel. Commun. Mag. **16**(6), 12–22 (2009)

5. Belanovic, P., Valerio, D., Paier, A., Zemen, T., Ricciato, F., Mecklenbrauker, C.F.: On wireless links for vehicle-to-infrastructure communications. IEEE Trans. Veh. Technol. **59**(1), 269–282 (2010)
6. Anaya, J.J., Merdrignac, P., Shagdar, O., Nashashibi, F., Naranjo, J.E.: Vehicle to pedestrian communications for protection of vulnerable road users. In: IEEE Intelligent Vehicles Symposium Proceedings, pp. 1037–1042 (2014)
7. Cheng, L., Henty, B.E., Stancil, D.D., Bai, F., Mudalige, P.: Mobile vehicle-to-vehicle narrow-band channel measurement and characterization of the 5.9 GHz dedicated short range communication (DSRC) frequency band. IEEE J. Sel. Areas Commun. **25**(8), 1501–1516 (2007)
8. Sen, I., Matolak, D.W.: Vehicle-vehicle channel models for the 5-GHz band. IEEE Trans. Intell. Transp. Syst. **9**(2), 235–245 (2008)
9. Fernandez, H., Rubio, L., Rodrigo-Penarrocha, V.M., Reig, J.: Path loss characterization for vehicular communications at 700 MHz and 5.9 GHz under LOS and NLOS conditions. IEEE Antennas Wirel. Propag. Lett. **13**, 931–934 (2014)
10. Susana, L., del Castillo, A., Fernández, H., Rodrigo-Peñarrocha, V.M., Reig, J., Rubio, L.: Small-scale fading analysis of the vehicular-to-vehicular channel inside tunnels. Wirel. Commun. Mob. Comput. **2017** (2017)
11. Yang, M., et al.: A cluster-based three-dimensional channel model for vehicle-to-vehicle communications. IEEE Trans. Veh. Technol. **68**(6), 5208–5220 (2019)
12. Bernado, L., Zemen, T., Tufvesson, F., Molisch, A., Mecklenbrauker, C.: Time- and frequency-varying K-factor of non-stationary vehicular channels for safety-relevant scenarios. IEEE Trans. Intell. Transp. Syst. **16**(2), 1007–1017 (2015)
13. He, R., Zhong, Z., Ai, B., Ding, J., Yang, Y., Molisch, A.: Short-term fading behavior in high-speed railway cutting scenario: measurements, analysis, and statistical models. IEEE Trans. Antennas Propag. **61**(4), 2209–2222 (2013)
14. Wang, W., Raulefs, R., Jost, T.: Fading characteristics of maritime propagation channel for beyond geometrical horizon communications in C-band. Ceas Space J. **11**(1), 95–104 (2017). https://doi.org/10.1007/s12567-017-0185-1
15. Greenstein, L.J., Michelson, D.G., Erceg, V.: Moment-method estimation of the Ricean K-factor. IEEE Commun. Lett. **3**(6), 175–176 (1999)

Arrival Prediction Based Reservation MAC for the Next Generation WLAN

Huanhuan Cai, Bo Li, Mao Yang$^{(\boxtimes)}$, and Zhongjiang Yan

School of Electronics and Information, Northwestern Polytechnical University,
Xi'an, China
caihuanhuan@mail.nwpu.edu.cn,
{libo,yangmao,zhjyan.npu}@nwpu.edu.cn

Abstract. Wireless Local Area Network (WLAN) has been greatly developed for the last twenty years. Quality of Service (QoS) and Quality of Experience (QoE) in high-dense deployment scenario greatly challenges the next-generation WLAN [1]. To address this challenge, researchers proposed channel reservation mechanism for WLAN, but the premise of channel reservation mechanism is to know the next packets exact arrival time. This assumption is impractical since the next packets arrival time is a stochastic process. In order to solve the above problem, this paper proposes an arrival prediction based channel reservation media access control (MAC) for the next generation WLAN. Simulations show that the protocol can reduce the network collisions generated by concurrency to a certain extent and improve network throughput.

Keywords: WLAN · Prediction · Channel reservation · MAC protocol

1 Introduction

In recent years, the rapid development of wireless communication technology has brought great convenience to our lives. For example, the usual communication tools such as smart phones and Bluetooth headsets rely on wireless communication technology. Wireless communication technology plays a huge role in today's society, and all aspects of our lives are related to wireless communication technology. It can be seen that the wireless network attracts more and more users because of its high flexibility and convenience, which leads to the rapid growth of wireless data traffic worldwide. In the face of such a huge increase in wireless business, countless people in the industry have gone on to research on wireless networks. As a key component of wireless networks, WLAN has received great attention from industry and academics. It is expected that the next-generation WLAN standard IEEE 802.11ax will be officially promulgated in the second half of 2019 [2].

As the number of users continues to increase, so does the need to access wireless networks. The growing distributed wireless network allows users to access the wireless network at any time. In order to make the channel resources in the

B. Li et al. (Eds.): IoTaaS 2019, LNICST 316, pp. 161–170, 2020.
https://doi.org/10.1007/978-3-030-44751-9_15

network more fully available, the multiple access technology has long been one of the research hotspots. The WLAN multiple access is based on Carrier Sense Multiple Access with Collision Avoidance (CSMA/CA) technology [3]. For example, our most common enhanced distributed channel access access (EDCA) channel method is based on CSMA/CA. A competitive access method with service priority enables high-priority services to achieve higher quality of service. At present, there are four queues in the common EDCA mechanism, which correspond to four kinds of services: voice (VO), video (VI), best effort (BE) and background (BK), and different services enter different queues. Different competition windows and different inter-frame spacing (AIFS) are set for each queue to make the competition priority when accessing the channel [4]. When accessing a channel, there is a different priority when competing. If a site has a service that needs to access the channel, it first randomly selects a backoff value from the backoff window of its own service, and then detects whether the channel is idle. If the channel is idle, it performs a backoff process. Once it is backed off to zero, The data frame is started to be transmitted. If the channel is busy during the backoff process, the backoff does not continue. The current backoff time is suspended, and when the channel becomes idle again, the backoff is resumed. After the data frame is sent, if the destination station successfully receives the data frame, after a period of time, the destination station sends an ACK acknowledgement frame to the source station. If the source station successfully receives the ACK acknowledgement frame, the transmission is Successful, otherwise the transmission fails, and the data frame is retransmitted after waiting for a while. The above is the specific implementation process of the EDCA mechanism. It is characterized by distributed access based on random competition. If there are more users in the network and the traffic is relatively large, these users want to transmit data through CSMA/CA. It is possible to cause multiple users to simultaneously transmit data on the channel, thereby causing mutual transmission and interference between each other, causing conflicts, and data transmission failure [5]. Conflicts and interferences are mainly caused by random competition of stations and competing for shared wireless channels to transmit data [6]. Conflict and interference are important features of WLAN systems, especially for next-generation WLANs for high-density deployment scenarios. The channel reservation technology broadcasts the time of transmitting the next data packet when the current data packet is transmitted, and the neighboring node reasonably avoids the time of the reservation, Thereby alleviating the conflict of the congested channel.

Channel reservation protocol is divided into synchronous channel reservation and asynchronous channel reservation. As is shown in Fig. 1. Synchronization requires strict time synchronization. It divides the time into periodic frames, and then divides each frame into time-slots of equal length. At the beginning of each time slot, the nodes are allowed to compete to obtain channel access. Right, then this node can reserve the channel usage rights of the subsequent slots. The asynchronous mode does not need to divide the time slot, and the reservation of the next transmission time period is performed by the current node data transmission process. This paper adopts the asynchronous channel reservation method to design the protocol.

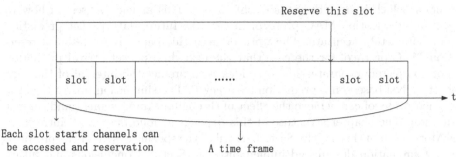

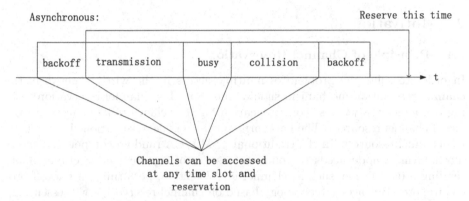

Fig. 1. The difference between synchronous and asynchronous reservation MAC protocol.

At present, there have been many researches on the channel reservation mechanism, such as A channel reservation based multi-channel MAC protocol with serial cooperation for the next Generation WLAN [7], this article focuses on two aspects of capabilities, one is cooperative relay, the other is channel reservation, will These two aspects are skillfully combined to mitigate link collisions. Such as A Cooperative Channel Reservation MAC Protocol with Adaptive Power Control and Carrier Sensing [8], the article will The time resource and space resources of the channel are used together. The main work is to do two aspects. One is to calculate the channel reservation time period, and the other is to adjust the channel reservation space. The former is calculated according to the periodicity of the real-time service, and the latter is Using a combination of power control and carrier sense, this protocol improves QOS for real-time traffic. There are many other studies as shown in the references [9–13]. Various studies have given various solutions for the channel reservation mechanism, but their premise is to know when the next data packet is transmitted, and this assumption is too strong, because the next packet is a random process. Predicting the arrival of the next data packet based on current and historical data packet arrivals is a problem worth studying, which can be done using fitting or machine learning methods, which is not the focus of this paper. This article focuses on how to design a subscription MAC protocol in case the future data packet prediction is not completely accurate. The work done in this paper is to design a reservation MAC protocol for the case that the next data packet arrival prediction is not completely accurate. The core idea is to predict the interval of the next packet arrival based on a prediction accuracy P. The simulation proves that the designed protocol can achieve the effect of throughput improvement and conflict reduction. The chapter structure of this paper is as follows: Sect. 2 introduces the Motivation of this article. Sect. 3 describes the specific design of the protocol. Sect. 4 simulation design and implementation. Sect. 5 Conclusions and future work.

2   Motivation

2.1   Principle of Channel Reservatio

In order to solve the problem of multiple access in the wireless network, the channel reservation mechanism should come out. The channel reservation technique enables the wireless communication link to achieve reliable access to the use of channel resources. The basic principle is to make reservations before using the channel resources. In the traditional CSMA/CA random competition access mechanism, a node needs to complete a series of signaling interactions before sending a data frame, such as channel idle detection, performing a backoff procedure, etc., But access technology based on channel reservation will essentially change the randomness of channel access. Its core idea is that when the node successfully accesses the channel through the CSMA/CA mechanism for the first time, it notifies the neighbor node of the time when the node uses the channel for the next time, and makes an appointment for the channel usage right in advance. when other node know the reservation time of this node and When the reservation time arrives, Other nodes do not participate in channel competition. When the reservation time arrives, this node can access the channel directly and send data in the appointed time period without competing with other nodes for channel usage.

2.2   This Article Motivation

The flow chart of traditional EDCA access channel is shown in Fig. 2. The solid line in the figure is the data normally transmitted and the dotted line is the interference received.

It can be seen that this random competitive access mode will cause multiple users to compete for access rights to the channel at the same time in the case of more users and larger traffic, thus causing transmission interference and transmission failure. This conflict is particularly serious in the case of the deployment of high-density neighbourhoods. However, this kind of conflict can be well avoided by introducing channel reservation mechanism, as shown in Fig. 3.

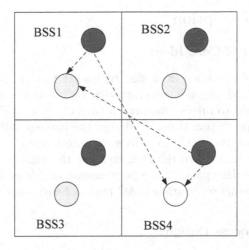

Fig. 2. Conflict occurs when users compete for the channel at the same time.

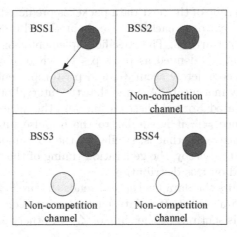

Fig. 3. Reservation mechanism avoids neighbor nodes competing to the channel at the same time.

During the period of reserved time, other nodes do not participate in the competition of the channel, so the node can obtain the right to use the channel and transmit data directly in the reserved time period. Many previous studies have designed reservation mechanism protocols on the premise of knowing when the next data packet will arrive. This paper first predicts when the next data packet will arrive. After the predicted time is obtained, the channel usage right at this predicted time will be reserved. In the appointed time period, the neighbor node will not generate the node. Interference. In order to reduce link conflicts and improve network performance.

3   Protocol Description

3.1   Introduction of Core Ideas

This protocol is mainly aimed at packet-by-packet transmission, does not use frame aggregation and can not accurately grasp when the next data packet arrives. First, we need to predict the arrival time of the next data packet. Then after knowing this prediction time, we design the corresponding channel reservation MAC protocol. Its goal is to reduce the interference and collision caused by neighbor nodes, and weaken the need to know the next one. On the premise of the arrival time of data packets, the performance of this protocol is compared with that of the channel reservation MAC protocol without prediction.

3.2   Protocol Process Design

The MAC protocol process designed in this paper is as follows:

(1) First, the arrival time of the next data packet is predicted, that is, the interval at which the next data packet arrives is predicted immediately after the current data packet arrives. The specific implementation is as follows: The prediction accuracy is defined as $p(0 \leq p \leq 1)$, where $p=1$ represents that the prediction is completely accurate, and $p=0$ represents that the prediction is completely inaccurate. Assume that the interval of the next packet is subject to Truncated Normal Distribution, and the mean is Δ. When $p=1$ represents variance $=0$, it is similar to the impulse function; when $p=0$ represents variance $=\infty$, that is, similar to the continuous Gaussian white noise distribution. Thereby, the generation timing of the next packet can be determined based on this distribution.

(2) The node transmits the data packet and sends the predicted packet interval Δ of the next data packet. If a data packet arrives before the $\Delta + \delta$ time, the data packet is sent out at the time of $\Delta + \delta$; otherwise, the data packet is not sent.

(3) Other nodes do not send packets at the time of $\Delta + \delta$ (pre-ordering packets must be guaranteed to end), and if the packet of the reserved node is not heard, the channel can be contending.

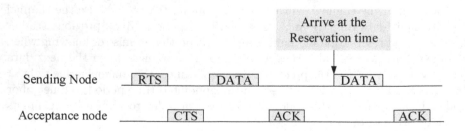

Fig. 4. Reservation mechanism protocol process.

The process is as shown in the following Fig. 4. When the transmitting node has a service request and the transmitting node first contends to the channel, it predicts the arrival time of the next data packet. The transmitting node performs the current data transmission, and carries the predicted time of arrival of the next service in the transmitted data packet, that is, the time of the next use of the channel. When the predicted time comes, I directly send the data packet.

3.3   Frame Format Design

Because it is necessary to carry the information of the reservation time when the node sends the data packet, in order to support this condition, this paper adds a 1-byte information bit in the MAC header to store the reservation information. The modified MAC frame format is designed as follows (Fig. 5):

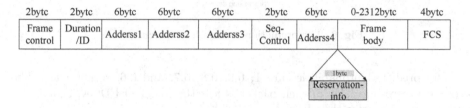

2bytc	2bytc	6bytc	6bytc	6bytc	2bytc	6bytc	0-2312bytc	4bytc
Frame control	Duration /ID	Adderss1	Adderss2	Adderss3	Seq-Control	Adderss4	Frame body	FCS

1byte
Reservation-info

Fig. 5. Frame format.

4   Simulation and Results

On the simulation platform supporting the key technologies of IEEE 802.11ax, the protocol algorithm proposed in this paper is simulated and implemented. Through the writing of the MAC layer code related functions and the simulation scenario configuration, the following simulation results are obtained, and the performance of the protocol is evaluated by the result. In the process of simulation, the EDCA mechanism is used as the basis for simulation comparison with the proposed scheme.

4.1   Simulation Scenario Configuration

Simulation scenario configuration:

- Simulation topology: Configure the cell of 1*2.
- a cell with a side length: 15 m.
- Number of STAs per cell: randomly assign a STA.
- The packet size: 1500 Bytes.
- the maximum transmission time of the data packet: Cancel RTS/CTS, 0.000236 s.
- Simulation duration: 5 s.
- Service MCS: MCS9.

4.2 Performance Analysis

Through simulation, the average DCF chart of the processing delay of each packet is shown in Fig. 6:

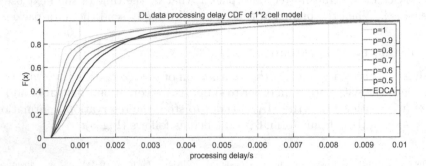

Fig. 6. The prediction is completely accurate.

The predicted probabilities are 1, 0.9, 0.8, 0.7, and 0.6, respectively. The average processing delay of each packet is less than that of EDCA, that is, its performance is better than EDCA.

Change the prediction accuracy P, which is 1 (predictive accuracy), 0.9, 0.8, 0.7, 0.6, 0.5, and count the average throughput of each packet. Compared with EDCA, the result is shown in Fig. 7:

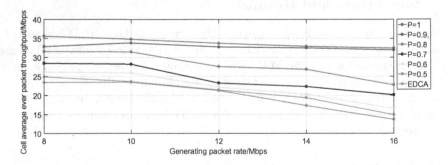

Fig. 7. Performance with different prediction accuracy.

It can be seen that at different service rates, the average throughput of each packet is calculated, $P = 1$ is greater than $P = 0.9$ is greater than $P = 0.8$ is greater than $P = 0.7$ is greater than $P = 0.6$ is greater than the EDCA mechanism, indicating the prediction accuracy. When the ratio is greater than or equal to 0.6, the performance of this prediction algorithm is better than that of the EDCA mechanism. When $P = 0.5$, its performance is the same as or better than that of EDCA, and the result is in line with expectations.

5   Conclusion and Future Works

This paper proposes a channel reservation MAC protocol based on prediction, which is used to make channel reservations. Compared with the EDCA mechanism, the join reservation mechanism reduces the link collision and reduces the packet loss rate. The prediction is added so that the reservation mechanism can still proceed without being able to accurately grasp when the next data packet arrives. The simulation results show that this protocol has certain advantages in some specific situations. However, this paper studies the case of packet without packet aggregation. In future research, we can continue to consider how to perform prediction and reservation in the case of packet aggregation.

Acknowledgement. This work was supported in part by the National Natural Science Foundations of CHINA (Grant No. 61771390, No. 61871322, No. 61771392, No. 61271279, and No. 61501373), the National Science and Technology Major Project (Grant No. 2016ZX03001018-004), and Science and Technology on Avionics Integration Laboratory (20185553035).

References

1. Bo, Y., Bo, L., Qiao, Q., Yan, Z.: A new multi-channel mac protocol based on multi-step channel reservation. In: IEEE International Conference on Signal Processing (2014)
2. Deng, D.J., Chen, K.C., Cheng, R.S.: IEEE 802.11ax: next generation wireless local area networks. In: International Conference on Heterogeneous Networking for Quality (2014)
3. Chen, Z., Khokhar, A.A.: A channel reservation procedure for fading channels in wireless local area networks. IEEE Trans. Wireless Commun. **4**(2), 689–699 (2005)
4. Alahmadi, A.A., Madkour, M.A.: Performance evaluation of the IEEE 802.11e EDCA access method. In: International Conference on Innovations in Information Technology (2009)
5. Bo, Y., Bo, L., Yan, Z., Mao, Y., Zuo, X.: A reliable channel reservation based multi-channel MAC protocol with a single transceiver. In: International Conference on Heterogeneous Networking for Quality (2015)
6. Zhang, X., Dai, Z., Zhu, H.: Channel reservation based on contention and interference in wireless ad hoc networks. In: International Conference on Computer Communication & Networks (2014)
7. Bo, Y., Bo, L., Yan, Z., Mao, Y.: A channel reservation based multi-channel MAC protocol with serial cooperation for the next generation WLAN. In: IEEE International Conference on Signal Processing (2016)
8. Yuan, Y., Bo, L., Yan, Z.: A cooperative channel reservation MAC protocol with adaptive power control and carrier sensing. In: International Conference on Connected Vehicles & Expo (2013)
9. Kai, G., Yong, S., Guo, W., Zhu, J.: Channel-hold-based reservation MAC protocol wireless packet networks. In: PIMRC IEEE on Personal, Indoor & Mobile Radio Communications (2003)
10. Jiang, Y.F., Gao, H.M., Zhu, B.H.: A distributed MAC protocol based on reservation for ad hoc networks. In: IEEE International Conference on Computer Science & Automation Engineering (2012)

11. Wong, C.M., Hsu, W.P.: A coordinated channel reservation MAC protocol for dynamic spectrum access networks. In: International Conference on Wireless Communications (2009)
12. Yuan, Y., Bo, L.: Performance evaluation of an efficient cooperative channel reservation MAC protocol in wireless ad hoc networks. In: IEEE International Conference on Signal Processing (2011)
13. Ming, M., Yang, Y.: A novel contention-based MAC protocol with channel reservation for wireless LANs. IEEE Trans. Wireless Commun. 7(10), 3748–3748 (2008)

OFDMA Based Synchronization Protocol for Distributed MIMO in the Next Generation WLAN

Luoting Gan, Bo Li, Mao Yang$^{(\boxtimes)}$, Zhongjiang Yan, and Qi Yang

School of Electronics and Information, Northwestern Polytechnical University, Xi'an, China
glt102288@mail.nwpu.edu.cn, {libo.npu,yangmao,zhjyan}@nwpu.edu.cn

Abstract. In the next generation Wireless Local Area Network (WLAN), IEEE 802.11 regards improving the throughput of the network as a major technical goal. Distributed Multiple Input Multiple Output (D-MIMO) System is an important issue to improve system capacity efficiency, but D-MIMO technology requires extremely high clock consistency between nodes. Therefore, this paper proposes a synchronization protocol based on Orthogonal Frequency Division Multiple Access (OFDMA) for D-MIMO. Firstly, this paper chooses a new clock synchronization process for the synchronization protocol (Two-Way Message Exchange), which is characterized by high synchronization accuracy. Second, we propose and refine the procedure of the synchronization protocol and design the frame structure of the protocol to make it compatible with IEEE 802.11 frame format. The simulation results show that with the increase of the number of APs in D-MIMO, proposed synchronization protocol reduces the overhead by nearly 50% compared with single user (SU) based synchronization protocol. Moreover, the clock synchronization accuracy increases with the increase of the number of information interactions.

Keywords: D-MIMO · OFDMA · Two-Way Message Exchange · Synchronization

1 Introduction

With the popularity of portable devices such as smartphones and tablet computers, and the proliferation of multimedia mobile services such as video conferencing, social applications and virtual reality, users are eager to access the network wirelessly anytime, anywhere to enjoy various business services. Under this circumstance, WLAN with the advantages of high throughput, low cost and simple network layout has been favored by users. The IEEE 802 officially established the Extremely High Throughput (EHT) Topic Interest Group/Study Group (TIG/SG) in May 2018, which will further improve throughput as a

© ICST Institute for Computer Sciences, Social Informatics and Telecommunications Engineering 2020
Published by Springer Nature Switzerland AG 2020. All Rights Reserved
B. Li et al. (Eds.): IoTaaS 2019, LNICST 316, pp. 171–181, 2020.
https://doi.org/10.1007/978-3-030-44751-9_16

major technical goal. The MIMO technology can significantly improve the system throughput [1]. In theory, by increasing the number of antennas, the system capacity and spectrum utilization can be doubled. EHT hopes to increase throughput by increasing spatial streams (such as 16 streams), but limited by device capabilities, a single access point (AP) is often difficult to provide 16 spatial streams, and due to cost issues, it is impossible to install multiple roots. The antenna and the AP will not install large number of antennas. Therefore, D-MIMO, also known as Joint Transmission, is a technical means to achieve large number of spatial streams.

D-MIMO means that the transmitting end or the receiving end of the communication is composed of a plurality of devices, that is, the antennas of the plurality of devices are integrated and used in a coordinated manner to achieve the effect of MIMO. D-MIMO has been proposed by Broadcom, Huawei, Marvell, MTK, Intel and other companies as one of the key EHT technologies [2]. However, since D-MIMO is to transmit and receive data between multiple devices, the clock between devices should be synchronized in order to transmit data accuracy and data packets transmitted or received between devices are not interfered with each other. So how to make multiple devices ensure synchronization on the clock is a technical prerequisite for implementing D-MIMO and must be solved. Unfortunately, the synchronization algorithms proposed by 802.11 are difficult to meet the synchronization requirements of D-MIMO systems.

Through the investigation of D-MIMO in the existing WLAN, the existing literature does not propose a particularly effective solution to the synchronization problem of D-MIMO system. Literature [3] introduced a new D-MIMO mechanism, but the specific process of system clock synchronization is still traditional. Literature [4] just introduced the main technology of D-MIMO, indicating that clock synchronization is a big problem for D-MIMO, but it does not propose an effective solution. Based on this, this paper proposes a new OFDMA-based synchronization protocol algorithm for the next generation wireless LAN. This is also the first in the field of WLAN to adopt the two-way message exchange method to solve the D-MIMO time synchronization problem.

This paper gives a brief overview of D-MIMO technology and an introduction to clock synchronization technology, focusing on the two-way message exchange synchronization information exchange. Then, in the D-MIMO system, this paper proposes a new synchronization mechanism protocol, OFDMA based Synchronization protocol, to achieve the extremely high precision of D-MIMO. Explain the detailed protocol flow and improve its frame structure to make it compatible with 802.11 frame structure. Finally, set up the simulation scenario and perform verification tests, explain the simulation results, and look into the future.

In the following sections of the article, we will introduce the basic principles of D-MIMO and several methods related to clock synchronization in the second chapter. In the third chapter, the basic idea and detailed flow based on the OFDMA synchronization protocol algorithm will be described in detail. Then, the simulation scenario is designed and compared with the traditional synchronization results in Chapter four. Finally, in Chapter five, we will draw conclusions and prospects.

2   Motivation

2.1   The Principle of D-MIMO

By jointly transmitting data of antennas distributed in different geographical locations, D-MIMO can transform the interference signals of other base stations into useful signals, While coordinating interference of the same frequency among base stations, it can also make full use of antennas of multiple cells to jointly transmit downlink multi-space flow and receive up-link multi-space flow. Therefore, D-MIMO can improve the number of spatial streams transmitted, thereby improving single-user throughput and system spectrum efficiency, it also can ensure the throughput per unit area grows steadily with the increase of the number of stations [5]. D-MIMO is one of the important interference resolution and capacity enhancement technologies in high-density networking scenarios [6]. However, D-MIMO requires extremely high synchronization time of the system, so how to make the clock synchronization of each AP of the D-MIMO system become a research hotspot of D-MIMO.

As shown below (Fig. 1). In high-density station network, D-MIMO combines multiple transmitting points (APs) that interfere with each other into a cluster, and the AP weights the user data to be transmitted by using orthogonal transmission vectors. The orthogonal user data is jointly transmitted in parallel, does not interfere with each other, and the interference signal of the neighboring cell becomes a useful signal [7].

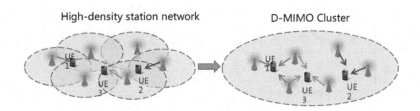

Fig. 1. Schematic diagram of D-MIMO system

2.2   The Principle of Clock Synchronous

In D-MIMO systems, nodes have their own independent clocks. Ideally, the clock for each node should be of the formula $C(t) = t$ (t is the ideal time). BHowever, due to differences in the hardware configuration of each node, the frequency, period, phase, and duty cycle of the clock signals between nodes may be different, As shown in Fig. 2, in practice, the clock model of the node should be:

$$C(t) = f * t + \theta \tag{1}$$

Where: f is the clock phase difference and is the clock offset. As can be seen from Fig. 2, the AP's clock relationship (e.g, node A and B) can be expressed as:

$$C_B(t) = f^{AB} \cdot C_A(t) + \theta^{AB} \qquad (2)$$

Where: f^{AB} and θ^{AB} represent the clock phase difference and clock offset of node B relative to node A. When $\theta^{AB} = 0$ and $f^{AB} = 1$, nodes A and B reach full synchronization. If there are N nodes in the D-MIMO system, if the clock of each node is equal to other clocks in the whole network, that is, $C_i(t) = C_j(t)$ i and j = 1, 2, 3, $\cdots\cdots$, N. The whole system clock is considered completely synchronous.

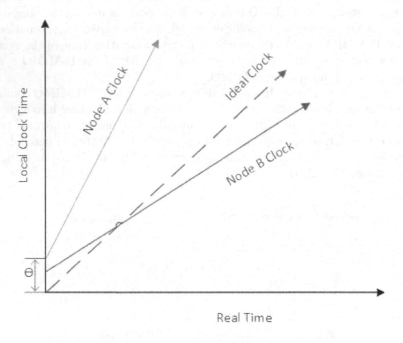

Fig. 2. Clock model of wireless nodes

In the Wireless Local Area Network, clock synchronization between nodes can be achieved by transmitting a set of timing messages to the nodes to be synchronized, and the transmitted data packets mainly contain timestamp information about the transmitting nodes. There are many algorithms for implementing system synchronization. Here, the Two-Way Message Exchange and the One-Way Message Exchange are mainly introduced.

2.3   Two-Way Message Exchange

Two-Way Message Exchange is a classic mechanism, mainly used to exchange clock information between two adjacent nodes. Protocols using this mechanism are Lightweight Time Synchronization (LTS)[8], Timing Synchronization Protocol Sensor Network (TPSN) [9], etc. As shown in Fig. 3, node A is a reference node and node B is the node to be synchronized. In the Two-Way Message Exchange process. Node B wants to be fully synchronized with the reference node A on clock [8,10]. As can be seen from the figure, After the Kth information interaction, the node B to be synchronized sends a synchronization frame to the node A at $T_{K,1}$, the node A receives the synchronization frame at $T_{K,2}$ and replies to the node B with a synchronization frame at time $T_{K,3}$, at $T_{K,4}$, the node B receives the synchronization frame sent by node A. After N rounds of synchronization information frame exchange, node B obtains a set of timestamp data$\{T_{K,1}T_{K,2}T_{K,3}T_{K,4}\}$. here, $K = 1, 2, 3, \cdots\cdots, N$. The above process can be expressed as a mathematical model [11]:

$$T_{K,2} = f(T_{K,1} + \tau + X_K) + \theta \tag{3}$$

$$T_{K,3} = f(T_{K,4} - \tau + Y_K) + \theta \tag{4}$$

where: f is the relative clock skew of node B with respect to node A, θ is the relative clock offset, we can know τ is to determine the delay time, Y_K is the transmission duration of A to B, X_K is the transmission duration of B to A.

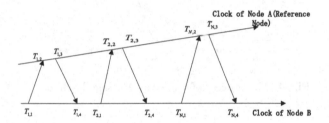

Fig. 3. The process of Two-Way Message Exchange

From Eqs. (3) and (4), it is necessary to estimate three parameters f, θ and τ. After N rounds of message exchange, an expression in the form of a matrix can be obtained according to (3) and (4) [12], as follows:

$$\begin{bmatrix} T_{1,1} \\ \vdots \\ T_{N,1} \\ -T_{1,4} \\ \vdots \\ -T_{N,4} \end{bmatrix} + \tau \cdot 1_{2N} = \begin{bmatrix} T_{1,2} & -1 \\ \vdots & \vdots \\ T_{N,2} & -1 \\ -T_{1,3} & 1 \\ \vdots & \vdots \\ -T_{N,3} & 1 \end{bmatrix} \begin{bmatrix} 1/f \\ \theta/f \end{bmatrix} - \begin{bmatrix} X_1 \\ \vdots \\ X_N \\ Y_1 \\ \vdots \\ Y_N \end{bmatrix} \tag{5}$$

Where: 1_{2N} is a column vector with a length of $2N$ and all value are 1. According to the above expression, frequency offset and phase offset can be estimated by the Maximum Likelihood Estimation (MLE) and its corresponding Kramer-law boundary [8].

2.4 One-Way Message Exchange

As shown in Fig. 4, in the One-Way Message Exchange process, the master AP will broadcast a synchronization frame carrying the timestamp of the transmission time and the number of synchronization rounds to the plurality of slave APs. When the APs to be synchronized receives the synchronization frame, it obtains the timestamp sent by the master AP. After the Kth round of information exchange, the slave APs can know the timestamp of the transmission of the master AP in the Kth round and the synchronization frame received by itself. Timestamp. it is given by:

$$T_{K,2} = f(T_{K,1} + \tau + X_K) + \theta \tag{6}$$

After the N round of synchronization information frame exchange, the node to be synchronized can estimate the value of f and θ by linear regression [13]. Thereby achieving the entire network clock synchronization.

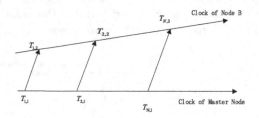

Fig. 4. The process of One-Way Message Exchange

In D-MIMO system, the requirements for clock synchronization of each node are particularly high. It can be seen from the above that the two-way message exchange can achieve higher accuracy than the one-way message exchange. Therefore, it is worth studying how to support the two-way clock synchronization method in DMIMO. This is also the research place of this paper.

3 OFDMA Based Synchronization Protocol for D-MIMO

3.1 Protocol Overview

How to make the master AP and other slave APs as synchronized as possible on the clock? This is an urgent problem to be solved in the D-MIMO system. This is also one of the basic technologies for implementing D-MIMO. Only by maximizing synchronization, D-MIMO can greatly improve the throughput of the system and eliminate some interference. On the contrary, it will cause the Master AP and the Salve AP to interfere with each other's data. This not only does not improve the throughput of the network, but causes the D-MIMO system to fail to work properly and even crashes the entire network. Therefore, this paper proposes a new synchronization protocol algorithm - OFDMA based Synchronization protocol.

Expect to be able to synchronize D-MIMO as much as possible. The general idea of the protocol is that the Master AP broadcasts a synchronization frame to Slave APs to be synchronized, and the trigger frame contains the number of two-way message exchange exchanges and the resource allocation for the Slave APs to perform the two-way message exchange process. After receiving the trigger frame, the Slave APs perform N rounds of two-way message exchanges on the already allocated resource blocks. After the N rounds of exchange, the Slave APs should obtain N sets of timestamp data$\{T_{K,1}T_{K,2}T_{K,3}T_{K,4}\}$. Finally, the relative frequency offset and relative phase offset between the Slave APs and the Master AP are estimated according to the Maximum Likelihood Estimation and its corresponding Cramer-Labor Boundary to complete accurate time synchronization. Compared with SU, the synchronization protocol based on OFDMA has obvious advantages, not only the time overhead is small, but also the clock synchronization in the same time period makes the D-MIMO system more consistent in time.

3.2 The Process of the Synchronization Protocol

In the D-MIMO system, as shown in the Fig. 5, when the Master AP wants to invoke the surrounding AP for D-MIMO transmission, the specific process is divided into the following steps:

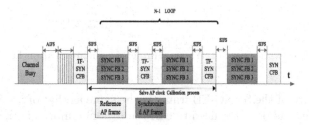

Fig. 5. The process of the OFDMA based Synchronization protocol

1. The clock reference source AP (which can be a master AP or a slave AP) sends Trigger Frame of Synchronization Feedback (TF-SYNC-FB) to trigger a synchronization feedback frame of the slave AP, where the frame carries the number N of synchronization information interactions and the APs that need to be scheduled.
2. After receiving the TF-SYNC-FB, the AP to be synchronized sends the synchronization feedback (SYNC-FB) on the corresponding RU and records the time at which the synchronization frame is transmitted.
3. The AP of the reference clock continues to transmit the TF-SYNC-FB, which carries the timestamp T2 of the AP receive SYNC-FB and the timestamp T3 of the AP send TF-SYNC-FB, and the N carried by the TF-SYN-FB is decremented by one.

4. After receiving the TF-SYNC-FB, the AP to be synchronized obtains T1, T2, T3 and the timestamp T4 of receiving the TF-SYNC-FB, then the Salve AP records these timestamps.
5. Cycling steps 2–4, after completing the N-1 TF and FB cycles, at this time, N = 0. The AP of the reference clock sends the SYNC-FB to all APs to be synchronized, and the N-way message exchange synchronization loop ends.
6. The AP to be synchronized obtains 4 N timestamps, and the accurate clock synchronization can be completed after the estimated parameter values.

3.3 Frame Structure Design

The frame structure of TF-SYNC-FB can be extended according to the MAC frame structure of 802.11. As shown in Fig. 6, the field in which the trigger frame is added is the common info field and the SYNC info field. The information carried in the SYNC field is the timestamp T2 of the SYNC FB received by the reference clock, the timestamp T3 of the TF-SYNC-FB, and the number of remaining handshaking. The Common field contains the type of trigger frame.

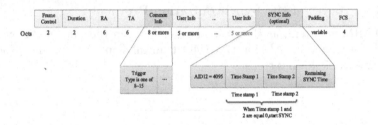

Fig. 6. Frame structure of Trigger Frame of Synchronization Feedback

The structure of the SYNC-FB frame is the same as that of the 802.11 MAC frame structure, and does not need to carry additional information, so the frame structure is not extended.

4   Simulation Design and Implementation

In the D-MIMO system, the accuracy of the clock synchronization reflects the advantages and disadvantages of the synchronization protocol. Based on this, we set up the simulation platform and design the simulation environment to verify the change of the clock synchronization accuracy of the AP to be synchronized as the number of synchronization information changes. We designed a simple scenario in which two nodes do clock synchronization. One node is the Master AP and the other is the Slave AP. The Master AP and the Salve AP use the synchronization protocol proposed in this paper to exchange synchronous frames. As shown in Fig. 7, when the number N of synchronization information interactions increases gradually, we find that the time difference between the primary

AP and the secondary AP is getting smaller and smaller, that is, the accuracy is getting higher and higher. Of course, for the universality of the results, we tested the synchronization accuracy test under different relative frequency offsets and phase offsets. It is found that the synchronization precision of the node to be synchronized is higher as the number N of synchronization information interactions increases.

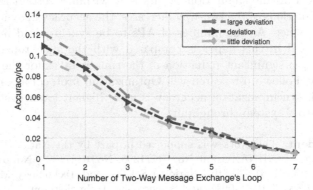

Fig. 7. Synchronization accuracy under different frequency offsets and the number of different synchronization information interactions

We have learned from the previous tests that the accuracy of clock synchronization increases rapidly as the number of interactions increases, but in wireless LANs, the overhead of an algorithm and whether the frame format designed according to the protocol is compatible with the traditional frame format prove whether the algorithm has practical possibilities. Based on the proposed synchronization protocol, we designed the frame format of the sync frame to be perfectly compatible with the 802.11 frame format. Here, we will compare the overhead of the OFDMA-based synchronization protocol proposed in this paper compared to the traditional SU-based synchronization protocol algorithm. As shown in Fig. 8, we find that the overhead of the OFDMA-based synchroniza-

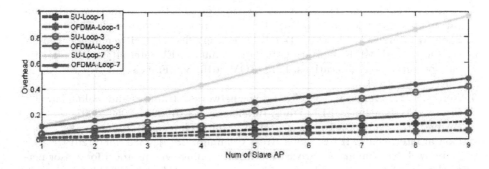

Fig. 8. Comparison of OFDMA-based synchronization protocol and SU-based synchronization protocol overhead

tion protocol algorithm is much lower than that of the traditional SU proposed synchronization protocol as the number of APs to be synchronized increases.

5   Conclusions and Future Works

It can be seen from the simulation results that within a certain range, as the number of interactions of the two-way increases, the accuracy of synchronization is higher and higher. As the number of APs to be synchronized increases, the protocol proposed in this paper is compared with the synchronization based on SU. There is a significant reduction in the time it takes for the protocol to reach accuracy. Follow-up research will Optimization protocol algorithm, So as to the network synchronization accuracy is more higher, lower overhead. So as to further improve system throughput.

Acknowledgment. This work was supported in part by the National Natural Science Foundations of CHINA (Grant No. 61771390, No. 61871322, No. 61771392, No. 61271279, and No. 61501373), the National Science and Technology Major Project (Grant No. 2016ZX03001018-004), and Science and Technology on Avionics Integration Laboratory (20185553035).

References

1. IEEE Draft Standard for Information Technology - Telecommunications and Information Exchange Between Systems Local and Metropolitan Area Networks - Specific Requirements Part 11: Wireless LAN Medium Access Control (MAC) and Physical Layer (PHY) Specifications Amendment Enhancements for High Efficiency WLAN, in IEEE P802.11ax/D4.0, February 2019, pp. 1–746, 12 March 2019
2. Balan, H., Rogalin, R., Michaloliakos, A., Psounis, K., Caire, G.: AirSync: enabling distributed multiuser MIMO with full spatial multiplexing. Netw. IEEE/ACM Trans. **21**(6), 1681–1695 (2013)
3. Hamed, E., Rahul, H., Partov, B.: Chorus: truly distributed distributed-MIMO, pp. 461–475 (2018). https://doi.org/10.1145/3230543.3230578
4. Jian, Y., Yonghui, C., Guoshun, L.: Research on D-MIMO technology and application strategy. Telecommun. Eng. Technol. Stand. **31**(249(06)), 52–55 (2018)
5. Shen, W., Lin, K.C., Chen, M., Tan, K.: Client as a first-class citizen: practical user-centric network MIMO clustering. In: 35th Annual IEEE International Conference on Computer Communications, INFOCOM 2016, San Francisco, CA, USA, 10–14 April 2016 (2016)
6. Aeron, S., Saligrama, V.: Wireless ad hoc networks: strategies and scaling laws for the fixed SNR regime. IEEE Trans. Inf. Theory **53**(6), 2044–2059 (2007)
7. Gesbert, D., Hanly, S., Huang, G., et al.: Multi-cell cooprataive networks: a new look at interference. IEEE J. Sel. Areas Commun. **28**(9), 1380–1480 (2019)
8. Ganeriwal, S., Kumar, R., Srivastava, M.B.: Timing-sync protocol for sensor networks. In: Proceedings of SenSys 03, Los Angeles, CA, pp. 138–149, November 2003

9. Sichitiu, M.L., Veerarittiphan, C.: Simple, accurate time synchronization for wireless sensor networks. In: Proceedings of IEEE WCNC, New Orleans, LA, pp. 1266–1273, March 2003

10. Van Greunen, J., Rabaey, J.: Lightweight time synchronization for sensor networks. In: Proceedings of 2nd ACM International Conference on Wireless Sensor Networks and Applications (WSNA), San Diego, CA, pp. 11–19 (2003)

11. Noh, K., Chaudhari, Q., Serpedin, E., Suter, B.: Novel clock phase offset and skew estimation two-way timing message exchanges for wireless sensor networks. IEEE Trans. Commun. 55(4), 766–777 (2007)

12. Wu, Y.C., Chaudhari, Q., Serpedin, E.: Clock synchronization of wireless sensor networks. IEEE Signal Process. Mag. 28(1), 124–138 (2011)

13. Huang, P., Desai, M., Qiu, X., Krishnamachari, B.: On the multihop performance of synchronization mechanisms in high propagation delay networks. IEEE Trans. Comput. 58(5), 577–590 (2009)

Vehicle Feature Point Trajectory Clustering and Vehicle Behavior Analysis in Complex Traffic Scenes

Xuan Wang$^{(\boxtimes)}$, Jindong Zhao, Yingjie Wang, Jun Lv, and Weiqing Yan

Yantai University, Yantai 264005, China
xuanwang_91@126.com

Abstract. Video-based analysis technology has a wide range of applications in intelligent transportation system (ITS). Vehicle segmentation and behavior analysis has become an important research area in traffic video analysis. To solve the problem of 2D video detection technology in actual traffic video scenes, a bottom-up analysis method is employed to study the related technical problems. Firstly, M-BRISK descriptor algorithm is proposed for describing local feature points, which based on the method of original BRISK. Secondly, a 3D feature analysis method based on rigid motion constraints for vehicle trajectory is proposed. With the result of camera calibration and the preset back-projection plane, the 2D trajectory points can be back-projected to the 3D space, and the back projection data of the 2D image can be reconstructed in 3D space. Thirdly, similarity measure method is proposed for achieving the trajectory clustering. The experimental results show that the proposed method not only accelerates the speed of clustering method, but also improves the accuracy of trajectory clustering at some extent. Moreover, the vehicle motion information contained in the trajectory data can be analyzed to recognize vehicle behavior. All of these provide an important data foundation for vehicle abnormal behavior detection and the identification of traffic status levels in traffic scenes.

Keywords: Vehicle segmentation · Feature point detection · Trajectory clustering · Behavior analysis

1 Introduction

Vehicle motion segmentation and vehicle behavior analysis are important research areas in complex traffic video. In the past few decades, with the increasing coverage of traffic video surveillance, a large number of research scholars have been attracted to the key technology research of traffic video analysis. Nowadays, road monitoring equipment has been spread all over traffic junctions and road sections, and video surveillance has become the most direct and effective way to monitor the real-time operation of road traffic, as shown in Fig. 1. With

B. Li et al. (Eds.): IoTaaS 2019, LNICST 316, pp. 182–205, 2020.
https://doi.org/10.1007/978-3-030-44751-9_17

the development of computer hardware devices, many video analysis methods [2,7,11,12,25,28,29] for vehicle detection can achieve the requirement of real-time detection.

Fig. 1. Traffic video scene.

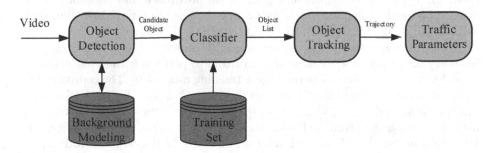

Fig. 2. Top-down traffic video analysis system model.

There are many key technologies in the intelligent development of traffic monitoring systems. These methods are used to understand how traffic video analysis works. In general, it can be summarized into two categories: the top-down approach and the bottom-up approach. The specific process is shown in Figs. 2 and 3.

The top-down approach has obvious advantages in high-definition video and smooth traffic environments. If the vehicle targets are not occluded, these methods have high detection and tracking accuracy using the appropriate classifier, but these methods have high computational complexity and low operating efficiency. They may be difficult to meet the requirement of real-time. In addition, the actual traffic scene is difficult to predict, the mutual occlusion of the vehicle

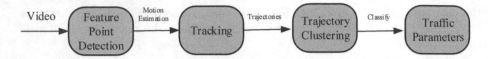

Fig. 3. Bottom-up traffic video analysis system model.

and other various environmental factors greatly affect the robustness of these methods. The bottom-up approach uses a partial-to-integral analysis method based on the feature point detection of the vehicle target, and gradually completes the object segmentation process even if the vehicle target is partially blocked during the motion. That is because the other local feature points still able to be detected, then the tracking task can be completed. After that, the behavior analysis method is needed to be performed. Moreover, the detection algorithm based on the feature point is highly efficient, and can better meet the real-time requirement in practical applications.

In the bottom-up system framework, researchers are working on various local features such as edges, corners, parts, and spots. In recent years, the local feature descriptors have a great development. The typical algorithm is SIFT proposed by Lowe [16] in 2004. The algorithm uses the gradient information around the feature point to describe it and use the image pyramid to solve the scale problem. Thus, SIFT feature descriptor has good scale invariance and rotation invariance. Subsequently, many researchers proposed some improved algorithm, such as PCA-SIFT [32], GLOH [17], SURF [3], DAISY [27] and so on.

After expressing some apparent features of the moving objects effectively, it is necessary to use a similarity measure algorithm to perform feature matching on the video sequence to complete the object tracking process [9]. The common similarity measures are including Euclidean distance, Gaussian distance, Block distance, Hamming distance, Chessboard distance, Manhattan distance, Weighted distance, Chebyshev distance, Barth Charlie coefficient, Hausdorff distance, etc. And the simplest should be the Euclidean distance. In the object tracking process, if we directly search and match the video scene globally to determine its optimal matching position, it will inevitably have to deal with a lot of redundant information, and also greatly increase the computing amount of the computer and reduce its computing speed. Therefore, it is of great significance to use a specific search algorithm to estimate and calculate the position of the object in the next moment to narrow the scope of searching.

One common way is to predict the location of the moving object in the next frame and find the best matching position in the vicinity area, such as Kalman filtering [10], extended Kalman filtering [30], and particle filtering. Another way is to continually optimize the direction of searching to speed up the process of searching and matching, such as Mean Shift [5] and Camshift [6].

Behavioral understanding of the moving object can be achieved through the trajectory pattern analysis. In the process of discriminating the trajectory mode, trajectory feature extraction and learning method of trajectory pattern are two important steps, which have an important influence on the realization of the trajectory behavior recognition. In terms of trajectory feature selection, Buzan [8] uses the method of calculating the longest common subsequence to realize the clustering and retrieval of motion trajectories; based on the Euclidean distance between trajectories, Hu et al. [31] used multi-level clustering method to perform equal-dimensional processing on vehicle trajectories in order to solve the classification problem of trajectories; There are two main methods for learning the behavior trajectory: neural network-based learning method and unsupervised clustering-based learning method. Johnson [13] and Sumpter [26] used a self-organizing feature map (SOM) neural network approach to modeling the spatial pattern of motion trajectories. Hu et al. [31] used the fuzzy SOM method to learn the motion trajectory and behavior pattern of the target to realize the detection and discrimination of abnormal events.

The bottom-up video analysis method can solve the problem of vehicle segmentation in complex traffic scenes, and it has higher operational efficiency. Therefore, based on the design ideas of this kind of video analysis method, this paper conducts related research, taking the image local feature points as the research object, using the tracking matching algorithm to obtain the 2D motion trajectory of the vehicle feature points, and analyzing the clustering problem between the trajectories based on the rigid motion constraint. The main contribution of this paper are as following:

- A feature extraction algorithm based on BRISK is proposed for complex traffic scenes. In terms of feature detection, we uses the adaptive FAST algorithm to detect the feature points in the scale space. In terms of feature description, we constructs a hybrid binary feature descriptor based on BRISK. The method can not only guarantee calculation rate, but also extract and locate the feature points effectively.
- A 3D feature analysis method of vehicle trajectory based on rigid motion constraints is proposed. Camera calibration is used to build the back projection data of the image in 3D space. Combined with the idea of back projection, the relative height between different trajectories is obtained based on the rigid motion constraint. Then, the estimated values of relevant traffic information of feature points corresponding to each trajectory in 3D space are further obtained.
- Using the extracted 3D information estimation of feature point trajectory to construct a new similarity measure between trajectories, and applying it to the framework of spectral clustering algorithm to realize the vehicle feature point trajectory clustering in 3D space.
- Based on the 3D information of vehicle feature point trajectory and its clustering results, the behavior model and semantic analysis of vehicle trajectories in traffic scene are carried out, and the traffic prevalence of actual roads is analyzed.

The rest of this paper is organized as follows. An overview of the system is presented in Sect. 2. Section 3 describes the method of feature extraction. 3D feature reconstruction is presented in Sect. 4. Section 5 displays the vehicle trajectory clustering method. Vehicle behavior analysis is given in Sect. 6. Experimental results are reported in Sect. 7 and finally Sect. 8 draws the conclusion.

2   Overview of the System

According to the specific research process of vehicle trajectory extraction and behavior analysis, the overall technical framework of this paper is shown in Fig. 4. The research content is mainly divided into three points: vehicle feature point trajectory extraction, trajectory feature extraction and cluster analysis, and vehicle behavior analysis. The vehicle feature point trajectory extraction is the basis of the latter link. It mainly studies the feature point detection and stable tracking of the vehicle target in the video sequence, and then obtains the trajectory data of the vehicle feature point in the 2D image plane. The feature extraction and cluster analysis of the trajectory are based on the camera calibration of the real traffic scene. The motion characteristics of the vehicle trajectory in 3D space are obtained by rigid motion constraint analysis, and the similarity measure is constructed to realize the clustering segmentation. Vehicle behavior analysis is based on the 3D trajectory to obtain the traffic parameters in the actual traffic scene, using the prior knowledge to semantically express the vehicle trajectory, providing a data foundation for further analysis of the individual vehicle behavior and the traffic flow behavior.

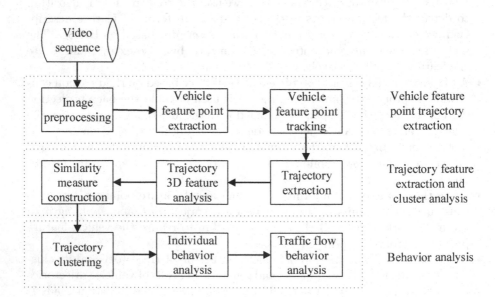

Fig. 4. Overview of the system framework.

3   Feature Extraction

In recent years, researchers have proposed several methods for binary feature description for real-time applications, such as BRIEFF [4], ORB [24], BRISK [15] and FREAK [1]. In fact, achieving high quality features and maintaining low computational costs is very challenging. This paper proposes a feature point detection algorithm based on the improved BRISK algorithm for complex traffic scenes. In the aspect of feature point detection, it uses the adaptive FAST algorithm mask to detect the feature points of the scale space. In the aspect of feature point description, it constructs a hybrid binary structure feature descriptor based on BRISK algorithm.

3.1   Feature Point Detector

FAST (Features from accelerated segment test) [22,23] is a corner detection algorithm proposed by Edward Rosten and Tom Drummond. The most outstanding advantage of this algorithm is that the computational efficiency is very high. Its computational speed is as fast as its name, and it is more efficient than other mainstream algorithms (such as SIFT, SUSAN, Harris). And if the machine learning method is applied to the FAST algorithm, it can show better results. The FAST corner detection algorithm is often used for video processing research due to its speed advantage. The principle of the FAST corner point is: if a pixel point and a specific number of pixels in its surrounding area are located in a different area, the pixel point is called a corner point. That is to say, some attributes are irrelevant. In the case of grayscale images, the gray value of the point is smaller or larger than the gray value of the point in its surrounding area, then the pixel may be a corner, as shown in Fig. 5.

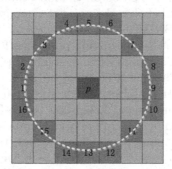

Fig. 5. FAST algorithm principle diagram.

3.2   Feature Point Descriptor

The FAST algorithm only performs feature point detection in the image, but does not further describe the feature points, so it can not apply the feature points to the process of image matching and tracking. Therefore, researchers have proposed many feature descriptors based on the feature points of FAST detection, such as ORB, BRISK, FREAK and so on. Based on the BRISK algorithm, a hybrid binary descriptor is proposed in this paper. The image pyramid is constructed by using the Brisk algorithm in the scale space. Then, the information of the BRISK algorithm is enriched by the information of the local downsampling. This method improve the robustness of the original BRISK.

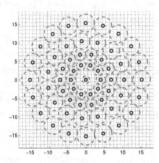

Fig. 6. Sampling mode of BRISK.

The sampling mode of BRISK is shown in Fig. 6. It can be found that the BRISK algorithm only considers the intensity relationship between the sampling points, that is, only the pairwise intensity comparison between the sampling point positions is considered. The local information of the sampling point is lost, which makes the algorithm unstable. Therefore, the basic idea of this paper is to construct feature descriptors based on the local information of the sampling points and the information between the pairs of sampling points to improve the robustness of the original BRISK.

Let $\mathbf{\Pi}$ be a set of all N sample point positions, for each sample position $\mathbf{p}_i^\alpha = (x_i, y_i) \in \mathbf{P}$, uniform sampling of four points $S(\mathbf{p}_i^\alpha) = \{s_{i,k}^\alpha, k = 1, 2, 3, 4\}$ is performed on a circle of radius R centered on $\mathbf{p}_i^\alpha$, where α is the local main direction, this paper used the Intensity Centroid [21] algorithm to calculate the main direction of the feature points. According to the LBP operator [19], local information can be encoded by the gray relationship between the sampling position $\mathbf{p}_i^\alpha$ and each local sampling point $s_{i,k}^\alpha$. However, this encoding is sensitive to the center point $\mathbf{p}_i^\alpha$, so it was not applied to binary descriptions. In order to encode local information robustly, this paper uses the gray relation between local sample points $s_{i,k}^\alpha$ for encoding.

Assuming $I(\mathbf{p}_i^\alpha, \sigma)$ is the smoothed gray value of point $\mathbf{p}_i$, and σ is the Gaussian filter variance. For each rotated sample position $\mathbf{p}_i^\alpha$, the paired gray values of the local sample points $s_{i,k}^\alpha \in S(\mathbf{p}_i^\alpha)$ are compared. A local gradient binary descriptor is constructed by combining all test results into a binary string, each bit b corresponding to:

$$b = \begin{cases} 1, & I(s_{i,k}^{\alpha}, \sigma_i) > I(s_{i,t}^{\alpha}, \sigma_i) \\ 0, & otherwise \end{cases} \quad \begin{aligned} & \forall \mathbf{p}_i^{\alpha} \in \mathbf{P} \wedge s_{i,k}^{\alpha}, s_{i,t}^{\alpha} \in S(\mathbf{p}_i^{\alpha}) \\ & \wedge k, t = 1, 2, 3, 4 \wedge k \neq t \end{aligned} \quad (1)$$

Since the local sampling position of each sample point has four points, the dimension of this feature descriptor is $N \times C_4^2 = 6N$ bits. It should be noted that the gray scale comparison between local sample points $s_{i,k}^{\alpha}$ is closely related to the local gradient operator, because they both consider the gray difference between the local sample pairs.

The feature descriptor of the above construction encodes the local information of the sampling point into a binary string. We further supplements it with the global information of the sample points, which is encoded by the gray intensity comparison between the sample points. Use set $\mathbf{A}$ to represent the all combined results of the sample point pairs:

$$\mathbf{A} = \{(\mathbf{p}_i^{\alpha}, \mathbf{p}_j^{\alpha}) | \mathbf{p}_i^{\alpha}, \mathbf{p}_j^{\alpha} \in \mathbf{P} \wedge i \neq j\} \quad (2)$$

Furthermore, a subset $\mathbf{B}$ in which it has M pairs of sample points is selected from $\mathbf{A}$, so that each bit b of the binary descriptor is constructed by:

$$b = \begin{cases} 1, & I(\mathbf{p}_j^{\alpha}, \sigma_j) > I(\mathbf{p}_i^{\alpha}, \sigma_i) \\ 0, & otherwise \end{cases} \quad \forall (\mathbf{p}_i^{\alpha}, \mathbf{p}_j^{\alpha}) \in \mathbf{B} \quad (3)$$

In this part, we construct the feature descriptor in a manner consistent with the original BRISK. The same is that the short-range pairs of sample points are used to construct the feature descriptor. The difference is that the M-sample point pairs of the shortest distance are only a supplementary part of the previous local gradient-based binary feature descriptor. The mixed BRISK descriptor (M-BRISK) is constructed by the above two steps of binary string.

4   3D Feature Reconstruction

4.1   Inverse Projection Transformation

The imaging process of the camera is a description of the loss of information in 3D real space, and this process is irreversible. At present, most of the methods for image detection, tracking and behavior analysis are based on 2D image plane. However, due to the perspective transformation of the camera imaging, the geometrical and motion characteristics inherently of the objects are no longer exist in the 2D image plane. For example, some geometric features such as symmetry, parallelism, vertical and circular will be changed due to perspective projection transformation; the same moving object has obvious scale changes at different positions in the video sequence; and vehicles with uniform motion in 3D world space are performed non-uniform motion in the 2D video sequence, and so on. All of the above situations will make the related algorithms based on 2D image facing great difficulties. In order to solve the segmentation problem of vehicles in complex traffic scenes, it is necessary to extract the 3D information of the vehicle. This paper proposes a method based on rigid motion constraints for vehicle 3D trajectory feature analysis.

Camera calibration is the important part for obtaining the 3D parameters of objects based on video/image. However, the trajectory clustering and behavior analysis under the monocular camera is based on the vehicle feature point trajectory in 3D space. It is an important precondition for the subsequent algorithm to obtain the transformation between the 2D image and the 3D space. The working process of the camera model is:

$$\lambda p = K \begin{bmatrix} R & T \end{bmatrix} P_W = H P_W \tag{4}$$

where, $H = K \begin{bmatrix} R & T \end{bmatrix}$, $p = [u, v, 1]^T$, $P_W = [X_W, Y_W, Z_W, 1]^T$, λ is the scale factor, K is the camera internal parameters, R and t compose the external parameter matrix of the camera. The internal and external parameters can be calculated accurately by the recovery method of vanishing points [14].

Camera imaging is a perspective projection process from 3D space to 2D image. Conversely, the transformation process of mapping 2D image to 3D space is called inverse perspective mapping (IPM). In order to obtain reconstructed images with perspective effects through back-projection transformation, researchers can only use existing constraints and prior knowledge to make certain reasoning and estimation [20]. A common method is to first use the transformation relationship and the constraints to achieve the location mapping, and then fill the data. In order to describe this inverse transformation process more clearly, the mapping process is marked as:

$$p_I = F \cdot P_W \tag{5}$$

where F represents a transformation matrix of the 3D world coordinate system and the 2D image coordinate system. If a certain image coordinate p_I and one of its coordinate value in the 3D world coordinate system are known, for instance, if the actual height Z_W of the coordinate point is known, the specific position P_W in the 3D world which corresponding to p_I can be obtained. The process is expressed as:

$$P_W = F^{-1} \cdot (P_I \bigoplus Z_W) \tag{6}$$

In terms of mathematical theory, if the pixel points in the 2D image plane are back-projected into the 3D world coordinate system directly, unique solution can not be obtained owing to the uncertain scale parameter. However, if a certain dimensional coordinate parameter in the 3D space is determined, the 3D coordinate corresponding to the 2D pixel coordinate can be obtained uniquely. Therefore, we can preset a back-projection plane in 3D space, that is, to determine information of a certain dimension, so that the data of inverse projection transformation can be obtained on the back-projection plane.

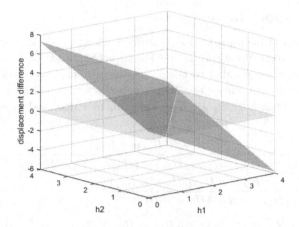

Fig. 7. Rigid motion constraint.

4.2   Rigid Motion Constraint

This section simulates the motion trajectories of feature points on a rigid body in 3D space, and they are back-projected onto several back-projection planes paralleling to the road surface. In the actual scene, the height range of the vehicles have a certain limitation. Generally, the height of vehicles is no more than 4 m. Therefore, the 3D information of the vehicle trajectory points can be obtained indirectly. Specifically, we use the enumeration method to test the trajectory height information to reconstruct the trajectory information in 3D space, and use the rigid motion constraints to calculate the height relationship between different reconstructed 3D trajectories.

$$D(P_{fi}^{h_1}, P_{fj}^{h_2}) = D(P_{Fi}^{h_1}, P_{1i}^{h_1}) - D(P_{Fj}^{h_2} - P_{1j}^{h_2}) \quad h_1, h_2 = 0, \ldots, 4 \qquad (7)$$

where, $D(P_{Fi}^{h_1}, P_{1i}^{h_1})$ is the displacement of the feature point p_i during F frame in 3D space, $P_{fi}^{h_1}$ is reconstructed 3D trajectory from the 2D trajectory point p_{fi} with the height information h_1, and $D(P_{fi}^{h_1}, P_{fj}^{h_2})$ is the displacement difference of the two reconstructed 3D trajectories. Figure 7 shows the relationship between the displacement differences of two trajectories in an ideal case (without tracking error) using the height enumeration method. It can be found that the heights of the two trajectories and their displacement are on the same plane:

$$ah_1 + bh_2 + c = Diff \qquad (8)$$

If the two trajectories belong to the same car, the displacement value is the same, that is, the $Diff$ is zero. Therefore, the height relationship of the two trajectories can be obtained:

$$ah_1 + bh_2 + c = 0 \qquad (9)$$

4.3   3D Information Reconstruction

Based on the idea of back-projection transformation, we set the vehicle moving direction (ie, the road direction) as the Y_W direction, and constructed multiple back-projection planes parallel to the Y direction. Then, we reconstructed the 3D trajectory information from the 2D trajectories with the known enumeration value of Z_W. According to Eq. 4, (X_W, Y_W) can be calculated as follows:

$$
\begin{aligned}
Y_W &= \frac{A - B(H_{31}u - H_{11})}{(H_{32}u - H_{12})(H_{31}v - H_{21}) - (H_{32}v - H_{22})(H_{31}u - H_{11})} \\
X_W &= \frac{A - Y_W(H_{32}u - H_{12})(H_{31}v - H_{21})}{(H_{31}u - H_{11})(H_{31}u - H_{21})}
\end{aligned}
\tag{10}
$$

where, $A = (Z_W H_{13} + H_{14} - v(Z_W H_{33} + H_{34}))(H_{31}v - H_{21})$, $B = Z_W H_{23} + H_{24} - v(Z_W H_{33} + H_{34})$. Thereby, it is possible to recover the 3D trajectory of the vehicle target at different height planes. As shown in Fig. 8(a), we simulated the trajectory of the same vehicle in an ideal state. The 2D image projection in the calibration scene is shown in Fig. 8(b). It can be found that the feature point trajectories of different heights have different pixel displacement and pixel speed. Therefore, the 3D trajectory can be estimated by constructing the different projection planes of different heights as shown in Fig. 8(c). Using these trajectory information and the motion characteristics of the rigid objects, this paper attempts to analyze the real position information and a series of 3D features of vehicles in 3D space, such as the actual speed, acceleration, displacement, driving direction, etc.

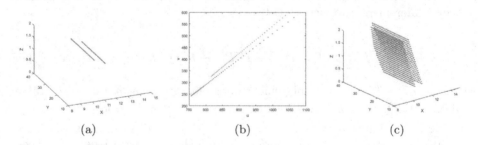

(a)   (b)   (c)

Fig. 8. 3D information reconstruction.

From the above, the specific algorithm for 3D feature extraction of vehicle trajectories in traffic scenes is as follows:

- Calibrate the camera in the traffic scene and obtain the transformation matrix H;
- Use enumeration method to set the back projection planes of different heights in the range of 0–4 m, and back-project the 2D trajectories on to the different back projection planes;

- Calculate the velocity $V(i, h)$ of each feature point trajectory on different inverse projection planes, where i represents the i-th trajectory and h represents the height of the back projection plane;
- Use the K-mean algorithm to achieve the clustering analysis, and classify the trajectory data by velocity difference;
- Perform the histogram statistics on $V(i, h)$ of each set of trajectories, and use the velocity interval with the highest frequency as an estimated value of the real velocity in 3D space;
- Calculate height information of each cluster by using the spatial relationship and the estimated velocity;
- Reconstruct the position information of the feature points in the 3D space by combining the height information of each cluster.

5   Trajectory Clustering

5.1   Clustering Algorithm

The similarity measure is an important basis for data mining techniques such as data classification, clustering and abnormal behavior recognition. This paper constructs a new similar measure relationship between the trajectories using 3D information of feature point trajectories and applies it to the spectral clustering algorithm.

The specific implementation steps of the algorithm are as follows:

- Construct a similarity matrix W between the trajectories according to the similarity measure between the trajectory data;
- Calculate its normalized Laplacian matrix $L = D^{-\frac{1}{2}}(D - W)D^{-\frac{1}{2}}$;
- Calculate the eigenvalues $\{\lambda_i, i = 1, 2, \cdots, n\}$ and eigenvectors $\{E_i, i = 1, 2, \cdots, n\}$ of L;
- Calculating an indication feature vector Q_i corresponding to E_i;
- Perform the K-means clustering using the feature vectors corresponding to the first k minimum eigenvalues of Q.

5.2   Similarity Measure

Based on the 3D feature analysis of the vehicle feature point trajectory, we performed 3D feature extraction for each feature point trajectory, and constructed an attribute feature vector $F = (H, V, X, Y)$ that can represent each trajectory information, where H represents the relative height between the trajectory and the reference trajectory, V indicates the 3D velocity of the trajectory reconstructed by the trajectory set T, and (X, Y) represents the 3D coordinate of the trajectory point at a certain time. F covers not only the feature information inherent of each trajectory, but also the relative positional relationship between the trajectories. Therefore, we use the trajectory set T to extract the eigenvector F corresponding to each trajectory, and combine the Gaussian similarity calculation model to construct a new similarity measure S:

$$S(T_i, T_j) = \exp(-\frac{d^2(F_{T_i}, F_{T_j})}{2\sigma^2}) \tag{11}$$

where, $d(F_{T_i}, F_{T_j})$ is the Euclidean distance of the attribute feature vector extracted by any two trajectories in the trajectory set T, F_{T_i} is a 1×4 feature vector which includes four parameters of the trajectory, and σ is the scale factor.

Since the research object of this paper is the vehicles, the distribution of feature points on the same vehicle is limited. It means that the X coordinate range of feature point trajectory in the same vehicle can not exceed the width of the vehicle itself. Using this property, the similarity matrix W between vehicle trajectory sets is further constructed by:

$$W(T_i, T_j) = \begin{cases} \exp(-\frac{d^2(F_{T_i}, F_{T_j})}{2\sigma^2}) & d(X_{T_i^f}, X_{T_j^f}) \leq \xi \\ 0 & otherwise \end{cases} \tag{12}$$

where, ξ is a threshold parameter according to the actual outer contour size standard of the road vehicle, but since the reconstructed trajectory 3D information is an estimated value, there is a certain error between estimated value and the real value.

In the case of a given set of trajectories, the construction process of the similar matrix is as follows:

- Calculate the 2D velocity $v = \{v_1, v_2, \ldots, v_n\}$ of each 2D trajectory of the trajectory set, and select the trajectory with the minimum 2D velocity v_p as the reference trajectory T_p;
- Calculate the relative height between each trajectory and the reference trajectory.
- Use the enumeration method to construct different heights of the back projection planes in the range of 0–4 m to recover each trajectory in 3D space;
- Calculate an estimated velocity of each trajectory in 3D space and the spatial position of the feature point at the current frame;
- Construct the attribute feature vector $F_{T_i} = (H_i, V_i, X_i, Y_i)$ of each trajectory;
- Calculate the similarity matrix W between the trajectory data set T using the Eq. (12);

6   Vehicle Behavior Analysis

6.1   Vehicle Individual Behavior Analysis

In this section, the 3D information of the vehicle trajectory is used to further analyze the behavior pattern of the individual vehicle in traffic scene, so as to detect the abnormal behavior of the vehicle. Many related threshold information are contained in this section, and for a determined traffic scene, the associated threshold information is the same. These threshold information is dependent on theoretical calculations and empirical values.

Over-Speed and Low-Speed Driving. According to China's Road Traffic Safety Law, the highway sections should identify the limits of their driving speed clearly. For example, the maximum speed of vehicles on the highway cannot exceed 120 km/h, and the minimum speed cannot be lower than 60 km/h.

Therefore, the speed limit value of the road section can be obtained for the determined road section of highway. If $V_i > V_\alpha$, the vehicle is judged to be over-speed; if $V_i < V_\beta$, the vehicle is determined to be low-speed, where V_i is the estimated value of the real speed of the i-th vehicle, V_α and V_β are the maximum speed and the minimum speed of the road section respectively.

Retrograde. The camera has a fixed installation position and angle in the traffic scene. Firstly, we determine the correct driving direction of the road manually based on the driving direction of the vehicle in the traffic video. Then, we use camera calibration technology to obtain the 3D position information of the direction marking line and its direction vector. As shown in Fig. 9, one direction vector can be set in the two-lane road section, and two or more correct direction vectors should be set according to the actual situation.

Fig. 9. Setting of the correct driving direction.

According to the 3D trajectory information of the vehicle feature point, the motion vector (X_i^f, Y_i^f) of each frame can be determined, and the information of the X direction is used to select the correct driving direction of the road for retrograde event discrimination. If (X_R, Y_R) indicates the correct direction of the road, the direction angle of the vehicle can be obtained:

$$\bar{\theta} = \frac{1}{m} \sum_{i=0}^{m} |\arccos(\frac{X_R X_i^f + Y_R Y_i^f}{\sqrt{X_R^2 + Y_R^2}\sqrt{(X_i^f)^2 + (Y_i^f)^2}})| \tag{13}$$

$$IsRetrograde = \begin{cases} true & \bar{\theta} \geq \alpha \\ false & \bar{\theta} < \alpha \end{cases} \tag{14}$$

where, (X_i^f, Y_i^f) is the direction of motion of the i-th trajectory in the same category at the f frame, and α is the empirical threshold. In the actual application process, the fault tolerance of the algorithm needs to be considered. The vehicle behavior cannot be judged according to the data at a certain moment. Instead, it should be counted whether the direction angle of the vehicle motion satisfies the retrograde condition for a period of time. This paper counts the number l that the vehicle direction angle is greater than the empirical threshold α for a period of time. If $l > \beta$, we consider the vehicle as a retrograde vehicle.

Parking. If an abnormal parking event occurs, the feature point trajectory of the vehicle has obvious characteristics. It is embodied in a state in which the speed of the vehicle gradually decreases to zero, and the position information tends to be constant. The discriminating rules are as follows:

- If $V_k^f < \xi$, the counter of abnormal speed is incremented by 1.
- If $Isstop > \eta$, the vehicle has an abnormal parking event.

where, V_k^f indicates the instantaneous speed of the k-th cluster of the vehicle at the f-th frame, ξ is the minimum speed threshold and η is the speed anomaly threshold.

Abnormal Lane Change. The lane change behavior of the vehicle occurs more frequently in actual traffic, while the road is divided by solid lines (white solid line, yellow solid line, double yellow solid line). These solid lines are forbidden to be touched during the driving.

For the normal driving vehicle, its movement trend is along the direction of the lane line, that is, its motion trajectory is approximately parallel with the road marking line. However, there is a certain angle between the trajectory of the vehicle in which the lane changing behavior occurs and the road marking line. Therefore, this paper uses the following method to determine the abnormal lane change behavior of the vehicles:

- For a specific traffic road, camera calibration is performed manually to obtain the actual 3D space coordinates of the solid line marker line on the road;
- Calculate the variance in the X direction using the 3D trajectory information of the vehicle feature points in each category:

$$\bar{S} = \frac{1}{mn} \sum_{t=1}^{m} \sum_{i=1}^{n} (X_t(i) - \bar{X}_t)^2 \tag{15}$$

- If $\bar{S} > \gamma$, it is considered that the driving behavior of the vehicle is a lane change, and it is necessary to further judge whether the behavior is a violation of the rules. If $|X_t(i) - X_{Road}| < \varepsilon$, it regards the vehicle as violation of rules.

where, $X_t(i)$ represents the X coordinate of the i-th point of the t-th trajectory in 3D space, $\bar{X}_t$ is the average of the X coordinates of the t-th trajectory; X_{Road} indicates the X coordinate of the solid line marker on the road in 3D space; γ, ε are the experience threshold, which can be determined based on the specific scene.

Traffic Flow Behavior. In this section, the 3D information of the vehicle motion trajectory and the clustering results are used to calculate the traffic flow and traffic flow speed of a certain road section, which can be used to evaluate the real-time traffic status.

Traffic Flow. In order to fully consider the time series of the trajectory points during the motion, previous clustering results is combined to filter the trajectory data of the current frame, so the attribute feature extraction and cluster analysis are only carried out for the newly added trajectory data. It not only reduces the amount of calculation, but also improves the accuracy of clustering of newly trajectory data in some extent. The specific strategy can be described as:

- Set the time interval t of the clustering based on the video rate. That means cluster analysis is performed on the feature point trajectory in the current interest region every interval t frame;
- The trajectory data is filtered twice before each run of the clustering algorithm. One is to screen out trajectory data that meets a certain length; the other is to filter out the new trajectory data.
- Count the clustering results obtained each time, then the traffic flow per hour or day of the road section is obtained.

Traffic Flow Speed. In order to facilitate the measurement and calculation, this paper selects the interval average speed as the measurement index of the traffic speed. In the selected observation section, several instantaneous moments are selected at fixed time intervals, and the average value of the instantaneous speeds of all vehicles at that moment is calculated by using the vehicle feature point trajectory 3D information. The specific formula is as follows:

$$\bar{v}_s = \frac{1}{MN} \sum_{k=1}^{N} \sum_{i=1}^{M} \frac{s_k(i)}{\triangle t} \tag{16}$$

where, $\triangle t$ is the time interval of adjacent frames, $s_k(i)$ is the distance during the time interval between the current frame and the previous frame at the ith feature point of the kth vehicle.

7   Experimental Results

In this section, we evaluate the performance of the proposed system. In Sect. 7.1, the performance analysis of feature descriptor is evaluated. The trajectory clustering results on the different traffic videos are shown in Sect. 7.2. Section 7.3 performs the application results of vehicle behavior analysis.

7.1   Performance Analysis of Feature Descriptor

The performance indicators of the feature descriptors were evaluated using the recall and $1 - precision$ curves proposed in [18]. This paper compared the M-BRISK descriptor with the SURF, ORB, BRISK and FREAK descriptors. Since SURF is a classic fast descriptor, ORB, BRISK and FREAK are recently proposed binary descriptors. For fair comparison, image blocks of the same size (31×31) are set for all test descriptors and the different images of Oxford dataset are used for correlation test. The original picture of the data set is shown in Fig. 10. Each group of images has different changing factors, including fuzzy processing, rotation and scale change, perspective change, illumination change, and image compression. Figure 11 shows the experimental results of different descriptors for different impact indicator.

Fig. 10. Test images.

For all cases, the M-BRISK descriptor is better or at least comparable to the descriptors of all other tests. This is because the discrimination of the descriptor can be improved by the combination of the local features and the information between them. As can be seen from Table 1, M-BRISK runs at the same rate level as the ORB, BRISK and FREAK algorithms, and they are all much faster than the SURF. In summary, the M-BRISK algorithm can achieve higher performance with high speed, and it suitable for real-time applications.

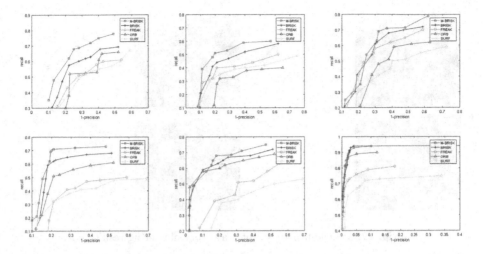

Fig. 11. Experimental results of different descriptors for each set of image pairs.

Table 1. Running time.

Methods	SURF	ORB	BRISK	FREAK	M-BRISK
Running time (ms)	0.404	0.026	0.038	0.032	0.040

7.2 Trajectory Clustering Results

We collects 1000 sets of vehicle trajectory data from 20 road sections of Hangzhou Jinqu highway for clustering algorithm test, and the trajectory datasets contains different numbers of vehicle targets, including 2 vehicles, 3 vehicles, 4 vehicles, 5 vehicles, etc. Some experimental results of clustering the trajectory set are shown in Fig. 12. It can be found that even if the vehicle has a common speed or partial occlusion, the algorithm can effectively cluster the feature point trajectories belonging to different vehicles. In addition, this paper analyzes the clustering results of the 1000 sets of data based on the number of vehicle targets, and compares them with the traditional method based on 2D trajectory methods. The results are shown in Table 2.

Table 2. Clustering precision.

Number of vehicle	2	3	4	5
3D trajectory clustering accuracy (CP)	94.75%	93.54%	89.17%	87.63%
2D trajectory clustering accuracy (CP)	90.18%	85.21%	78.32%	69.67%

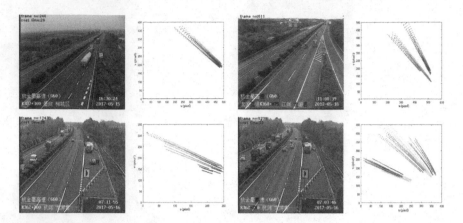

Fig. 12. Vehicle feature point trajectory clustering result.

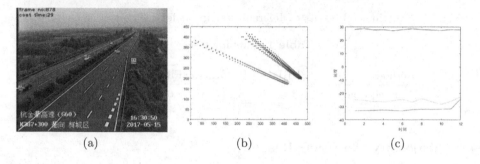

(a)   (b)   (c)

Fig. 13. Vehicle real-time velocity analysis.

In order to better evaluate the clustering effect of the proposed method, we analyzed the relevant experimental results quantitatively and defined the accuracy of the clustering. The specific formula is as follows:

$$CP = \frac{1}{N} \sum_{i=1}^{N} \frac{t_i}{n_i} \times 100\% \tag{17}$$

where, N is the number of trajectory data sets with the same number of vehicles, t_i is the number of trajectory classified correctly for the i-th trajectory data set, n_i is the total number of trajectory included in the i-th trajectory data set.

7.3   Vehicle Behavior Analysis

Vehicle Individual Behavior. By reconstructing the 2D trajectory information in 3D space, the real velocity of each trajectory can be estimated, and then the real-time real velocity of the vehicle object can be estimated, so that we can draw the velocity curve of the vehicle target at each moment in order to determine whether it occurred over-speeding, low-speeding or parking events. The following is a specific experimental analysis based on specific trajectory data.

Table 3. Vehicle real-time velocity.

Objects	Real-time velocity (m/s)										
Vehicle 1	−33.2	−33.0	−32.9	−32.6	−32.9	−33.2	32.3	−32.1	−32.2	−32.0	−31.7
Vehicle 2	27.9	28.5	27.6	27.8	27.1	27.87	28.5	27.8	27.5	27.2	27.8
Vehicle 3	−28.0	−25.4	−26.2	−26.5	−25.7	−24.6	−26.6	−24.1	−26.3	−28.3	−26.1

Table 4. Direction angle of the vehicle in real time.

Objects	Direction angle (°)										
Vehicle 1	0.038	0.043	0.045	0.578	0.800	0.484	0.029	0.103	0.625	0.182	0.333
Vehicle 2	0.021	0.016	0.078	0.051	0.338	0.110	0.386	0.245	0.311	0.086	0.028
Vehicle 3	0.315	2.383	1.509	4.215	3.121	0.705	2.065	3.174	3.322	1.419	2.373

As shown in Fig. 13, Fig. 13(a) is the 2D trajectory data extracted from the vehicles of a highway section, Fig. 13(b) is the result of cluster analysis, and Fig. 13(c) is the real-time velocity curve. The partial data results of the real-time velocity at the same time are shown in Table 3, wherein the sign indicates that the running direction of the vehicles, the speed of the upstream vehicle is marked as positive, and the speed of the descending vehicle is marked as negative. Based on the estimated real-time velocity of the vehicles, it can be used as a discriminating indicator whether the vehicle has over-speed or low-speed driving. For retrograde behavior, it is necessary to observe its real-time motion vector to determine whether it has retrograde behavior, as shown in Table 4. In addition, if an abnormal parking event occurs, the velocity curve of the vehicle is as shown as Fig. 14, where its trajectory velocity will continue to approach for a period of time. For the behavior such as lane change, in addition to the direction angle, the offset in the X direction is needed to be considered. As shown in the trajectory data of Fig. 15, we can observe the driving direction angle of the real-time. As shown in Table 5, it can be found that the direction angle of the vehicle become larger and larger, and the variance of the corresponding trajectory data in the X direction is also larger than the preset. Thus, the vehicle in Fig. 15 is judged as abnormal lane change behavior.

Table 5. Direction angle of the vehicle in real time.

	Direction angle (°)										Variance
Trajectory 1	5.01	5.49	6.40	4.69	10.57	6.75	9.45	8.51	9.95	10.1	0.54
Trajectory 2	6.08	6.34	7.28	5.42	8.57	6.91	7.71	7.17	9.01	9.46	0.52
Trajectory 3	5.24	5.95	5.40	5.07	9.37	6.93	9.11	7.55	9.73	10.41	0.50
Trajectory 4	5.02	5.75	7.46	5.12	9.28	6.44	9.48	8.76	10.94	08.92	0.55
Trajectory 5	5.35	6.24	5.99	6.43	6.27	5.23	7.43	6.47	7.92	7.95	0.54

Traffic Flow Behavior Analysis. This section used the real-time data obtained by the proposed method to analyze the traffic flow and traffic flow speed of a highway section, which can provide the data support for the real-time traffic status. This paper took the monitoring video of Jinqu highway as the test data, and analyzed the traffic flow and traffic flow speed data of the K362 road sections at 30 min intervals from 6:30 to 18:00 on May 16, 2017. According to the obtained real-time traffic flow parameters, we drawn the real-time parameter curves and observe the time-varying rule of each traffic parameter visually, as shown in Fig. 16. It can be seen that on May 16th, the traffic volume of the K362 section of the Jinqu highway was small, and the traffic flow was large in the afternoon. Meanwhile, the traffic flow speed of the whole day is at a reasonable range. Therefore, the traffic condition of this road section is good and smooth.

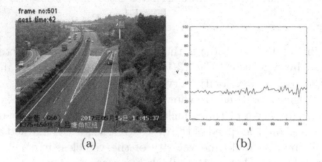

Fig. 14. Vehicle parking analysis.

Fig. 15. Trajectory data of lane change.

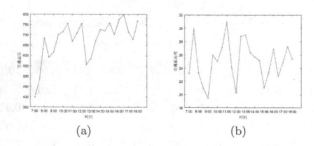

Fig. 16. Traffic flow data of No. 362 section of Hangzhou Jinqu highway on May 16, 2017.

8 Conclusion

In this paper, the problems of vehicle feature point detection, trajectory extraction, rigid motion constraint, trajectory clustering and vehicle behavior analysis are studied. We constructed a mixed binary descriptor using the local gradient of the sample point position and the intensity comparison between the sample points. The algorithm has strong robustness in the face of image blur, rotation, scale, viewing angle and illumination changes, and can meet the needs of practical applications in real-time. In order to better solve the segmentation problem of moving vehicles in complex traffic scenes, this paper proposed a method based on rigid motion constraints for vehicle 3D trajectory feature analysis, and constructed a new similarity measure between trajectory sets. It is applied to the framework of the spectral clustering algorithm to realize trajectory clustering in 3D space. In addition, this paper uses the obtained 3D information of the vehicle trajectory and its clustering results to analyze the vehicle behavior in the specific traffic scenes.

Acknowledgement. This work was supported by National Natural Science Foundation of China under Grants 61801414, Natural Science Foundation of Shandong Province under Grants ZR2017QF006, the Major Science and Technology Innovation Projects in Shandong Province 2019JZZY020131, the China Postdoctoral Science Foundation under Grant 2019T120732.

References

1. Alahi, A., Ortiz, R., Vandergheynst, P.: Freak: fast retina keypoint. In: IEEE Conference on Computer Vision and Pattern Recognition (2012)
2. Barth, A., Franke, U.: Tracking oncoming and turning vehicles at intersections. In: International IEEE Conference on Intelligent Transportation Systems (2010)
3. Bay, H., Tuytelaars, T., Van Gool, L.: SURF: speeded up robust features. In: Leonardis, A., Bischof, H., Pinz, A. (eds.) ECCV 2006. LNCS, vol. 3951, pp. 404–417. Springer, Heidelberg (2006). https://doi.org/10.1007/11744023_32
4. Calonder, M., Lepetit, V., Strecha, C., Fua, P.: BRIEF: binary robust independent elementary features. In: Daniilidis, K., Maragos, P., Paragios, N. (eds.) ECCV 2010. LNCS, vol. 6314, pp. 778–792. Springer, Heidelberg (2010). https://doi.org/10.1007/978-3-642-15561-1_56
5. Chang, C., Ansari, R.: Kernel particle filter for visual tracking. IEEE Sig. Process. Lett. **12**(3), 242–245 (2005)
6. Comaniciu, D., Ramesh, V., Meer, P.: Real-time tracking of non-rigid objects using mean shift. In: IEEE Conference on Computer Vision and Pattern Recognition CVPR (2002)
7. Dai, Z., et al.: Video-based vehicle counting framework. IEEE Access **7**, 64460–64470 (2019)
8. Dan, B., Sclaroff, S., Kollios, G.: Extraction and clustering of motion trajectories in video. In: International Conference on Pattern Recognition (2004)
9. Fang, Y., Wu, J., Huang, B.: 2D sparse signal recovery via 2D orthogonal matching pursuit. Sci. China Inf. Sci. **55**(4), 889–897 (2012)

10. Ali, N.H., Hassan, G.M.: Kalman filter tracking. Int. J. Comput. Appl. **89**(9), 15–18 (2014)

11. Jeon, G., Anisetti, M., Lee, J., Bellandi, V., Jeong, J.: Concept of linguistic variable-based fuzzy ensemble approach: application to interlaced HDTV sequences. IEEE Trans. Fuzzy Syst. **17**(6), 1245–1258 (2009)

12. Jeon, G., Anisetti, M., Wang, L., Damiani, E.: Locally estimated heterogeneity property and its fuzzy filter application for deinterlacing. Inf. Sci. Int. J. **354**(C), 112–130 (2016)

13. Johnson, N., Hogg, D.: Learning the distribution of object trajectories for event recognition. Image Vis. Comput. **14**(8), 609–615 (1996)

14. Kanhere, N.K., Birchfield, S.T.: A taxonomy and analysis of camera calibration methods for traffic monitoring applications. IEEE Trans. Intell. Transp. Syst. **11**(2), 441–452 (2010)

15. Leutenegger, S., Chli, M., Siegwart, R.Y.: BRISK: binary robust invariant scalable keypoints. In: International Conference on Computer Vision (2011)

16. Lowe, D.G.: Distinctive image features from scale-invariant keypoints. Int. J. Comput. Vis. **60**(2), 91–110 (2004)

17. Mikolajczyk, K., Schmid, C.: A performance evaluation of local descriptors. In: IEEE Computer Society Conference on Computer Vision and Pattern Recognition (2003)

18. Mikolajczyk, K., Schmid, C.: A performance evaluation of local descriptors. IEEE Trans. Pattern Anal. Mach. Intell. **27**, 1615–1630 (2007)

19. Ojala, T., Harwood, I.: A comparative study of texture measures with classification based on feature distributions. Pattern Recogn. **29**(1), 51–59 (1996)

20. Prasad, M., Fitzgibbon, A.W.: Single view reconstruction of curved surfaces. In: IEEE Computer Society Conference on Computer Vision and Pattern Recognition (2006)

21. Rosin, P.L.: Measuring Corner Properties. Elsevier (1999)

22. Rosten, E., Porter, R., Drummond, T.: Faster and better: a machine learning approach to corner detection. IEEE Trans. Pattern Anal. Mach. Intell. **32**(1), 105–119 (2008)

23. Rosten, E., Drummond, T.: Machine learning for high-speed corner detection. In: Leonardis, A., Bischof, H., Pinz, A. (eds.) ECCV 2006. LNCS, vol. 3951, pp. 430–443. Springer, Heidelberg (2006). https://doi.org/10.1007/11744023_34

24. Rublee, E., Rabaud, V., Konolige, K., Bradski, G.R.: ORB: an efficient alternative to SIFT or SURF. In: 2011 International Conference on Computer Vision (2011)

25. Sivaraman, S., Trivedi, M.M.: Combining monocular and stereo-vision for real-time vehicle ranging and tracking on multilane highways. In: International IEEE Conference on Intelligent Transportation Systems (2011)

26. Sumpter, N., Bulpitt, A.: Learning spatio-temporal patterns for predicting object behaviour. Image Vis. Comput. **18**(9), 697–704 (2000)

27. Tola, E., Lepetit, V., Fua, P.: Daisy: an efficient dense descriptor applied to wide-baseline stereo. IEEE Trans. Pami **32**(5), 815–30 (2010)

28. Wang, X., Song, H., Fang, Y., Cui, H.: Novel discriminative method for illegal parking and abandoned objects. J. Adv. Comput. Intell. Intell. Inform. **22**, 907–914 (2018)

29. Wang, X., Song, H., Guan, Q., Cui, H., Zhang, Z., Liu, H.: Vehicle motion segmentation using rigid motion constraints in traffic video. Sustain. Cities Soc. **42**, 547–557 (2018)

30. Wang, Y., Papageorgiou, M.: Real-time freeway traffic state estimation based on extended Kalman filter: a general approach. Transp. Res. Part B **39**(2), 141–167 (2007)
31. Weiming, H., Dan, X., Tieniu, T., Steve, M.: Learning activity patterns using fuzzy self-organizing neural network. IEEE Trans. Syst. Man Cybern. Part B Cybern. Publ. IEEE Syst. Man Cybern. Soc. **34**(3), 1618 (2004)
32. Yan, K., Sukthankar, R.: PCA-SIFT: a more distinctive representation for local image descriptors. In: Proceedings of CVPR, vol. 2, no. 2, pp. 506–513 (2004)

Ubiquitous Services Transmission For Internet of Things

DOS/SP: Distributed Opportunistic Channel Access with Smart Probing in Wireless Cooperative Networks

Zhou Zhang[1]($\boxtimes$), Ye Yan[1], Wei Sang[1], and Zuohong Xu[2]

[1] Tianjin Artificial Intelligence Innovation Center (TAIIC), Tianjin, China
zt.sy1986@163.com
[2] National University of Defense Technology, Changsha, China

Abstract. This paper investigates optimal distributed opportunistic channel access in wireless cooperative networks with multiple relays deployed. While probing all potential relay channels could result in significant overhead and spectrum efficiency affected, distributed OCA strategies with smart relays probing is studied in this research. To achieve reliable communications of high efficiency, number of probed relays and way to use have to be carefully decided in a dynamic manner. Finding that the sequential channel probing and access are coupled, an optimal distributed OCA is much challenging, and main difficult lies in how to exploit multi-source diversity, multi-relay diversity and time diversity in full manner. To tackle this problem, an analytical framework is built based on theory of optimal sequential observation planned decision. This decision-theoretic approach integrates the design of MAC layer and physical layer, enabling smart probing and cooperative transmissions under multiple relays. Based on it, an optimal DOCA/SP strategy is proposed to maximize average system throughput, and the optimality is rigorously proved. The implementation is described, and through numerical and simulation results effectiveness is validated.

Keywords: Opportunistic scheduling · Smart relaying · Optimal sequential observation plan decision

1 Introduction

Recently wireless network harvests an unprecedented development in fulfilling rapidly increasing demands in various applications. These demands are from enhanced quality-of-service on system performance such as transmission reliability, throughput and energy efficiency. In fulfilling network management of multiple layers orderly and efficiently, joint design viewpoint is motivated, which has led to a cross-layer design concept, generally known as *opportunistic channel access*.

In a wireless network, the channel is usually shared by multiple users, and each individual user experiences time-varying channel condition. At a time

© ICST Institute for Computer Sciences, Social Informatics and Telecommunications Engineering 2020
Published by Springer Nature Switzerland AG 2020. All Rights Reserved
B. Li et al. (Eds.): IoTaaS 2019, LNICST 316, pp. 209–227, 2020.
https://doi.org/10.1007/978-3-030-44751-9_18

instant, if channel quality of a user is poor, it is likely to drop the opportunity of accessing the channel and let others of good channel conditions access that channel. Whereas a myopic interest may be lost, more can be harvested in long run, as in the later if the user is in good channel condition, it transmits during channel access opportunities of others. In doing this, by letting nodes be aware of physical layer information, the MAC-layer mechanism coordinates channel access among multiple users more efficiently. Therefore, it is observed that, through opportunistic channel access (OCA), the average network throughput can be significantly enhanced.

In existing efforts, related works relevant to OCA are in two parts, centralized OCA (COCA) and distributed OCA (DOCA). Most of works tackle the COCA problem, where a centralized node, e.g., base station in a cellular network, can make channel-aware scheduling based on global channel state information (CSI) from all users [1,2]. In contrast, research on DOCA is still limited. In a distributed network, all users share the channel and contend for sensing and access. It is challenging to design an efficient strategy deciding how each user senses and accesses a shared channel using local and limited channel information. To address this difficulty, a study in novelty is carried out in [3] based on optimal stopping theory. Its basic idea is to let all users contend for channel access: if the winner has an achievable rate smaller than a threshold, it is optimal to *continue*, i.e., to give up access opportunity and re-contend the channel with others; otherwise, it is optimal to *stop*, i.e., to utilize the opportunity accessing the channel. Easy implementation benefits from such *pure-threshold* strategy. Extended from the work, the DOCA problem over an interference channel, which allows multiple nodes transmitting simultaneously, is investigated in [4], while the problem under delay constraints is also studied in [5] for real-time services.

To our best knowledge, a few works are concerned on DOCA for cooperative network, i.e. [6,7]. In particular, assuming channel state symmetry, two scenarios are investigated in [6]. In the first scenario, a dedicated relay node is considered, and each winner source determines whether to probe relay channel before transmission; in the second scenario, multiple un-dedicated relays are considered, and channel gain of the best relay is observed at a winner source. The best relay is used for cooperative transmission. By modeling this problem under two-level stopping approach, optimal strategies are proposed maximizing network throughput. In addition, different scenario is investigated in [7], and two cases are analysed. Particularly, in Case I a winner source knows all CSI of relays channels, and in Case II a winner source only knows a part. Maximizing the average network throughput, optimal DOCA strategies are proposed using optimal stopping theory and its extension.

As the contributions from these works, a trade-off problem is solved, and the balance is taken between the time spent in channel probing and transmission efficiency in channel access. Nevertheless, static probing pattern is considered in existing research as all relays are to probe once relay probing is decided. The flexibility in relay probing is much constrained and the benefit from multiple relays transmission is hardly obtained. Without channel symmetry, the contradiction is oblivious, as sufficient channel information offers increased transmission efficiency but results in heavy overhead. As the relay number becomes significant, a dilemma is faced. Therefore, it is naturally enlightened to design distributed scheduling strategy for managing channel probing and access of multiple sources and relays in an intelligent manner.

In this research, the DOCA problem with smart relays probing is thus investigated for distributed cooperative network, which is named as DOCA/SP problem. Within it, findings of optimal DOCA strategies, which determines how to probe two-hop channels (including both direct and relay channels), when to stop probing channels and how to access the channel, are pursued. The main contributions are listed as follows.

- An analytical framework is built up for the DOCA/SP problem based on optimal sequential observation planned decision (OSOPD) theory, and a decision-theoretic approach is proposed which guides the design of multi-source multi-relay OCA with smart channel probing in a distributed manner.
- Under the framework, an optimal DOCA/SP strategy is proposed which maximizes the average system throughput, and its optimality is rigorously proved.
- Implementations of the proposed strategy are presented enabling network operation, and through numerical simulations theoretic results are verified.

The rest of this paper is organized as follows. The network model and the protocol description of DOCA/SP are presented in Sect. 2. The analytical framework based on the OSOPD theory is established in Sect. 3, and based on it an optimal DOCA/SP strategy is derived in Sect. 4. Performance evaluation is provided in Sect. 5, followed by concluding remarks in Sect. 6.

2 Network and Protocol Model

2.1 Network Model

Supposed that in a distributed cooperative network there are K source-destination pairs, and L relays are employed to aid communications between sources and destinations, as shown in Fig. 1.

The source-destination pairs operate in a distributed manner, and a direct link between each pair is available. The sources contend to communicate with their destinations, and for transmission from a source to its destination, multiple relays are available aiding the transmission in decode-and-forward (DF) mode. The transmission power of a source and a relay is denoted as P_s and P_r, respectively. Channel reciprocity in terms of channel gain is assumed, and we denote the channel gain from the ith source to its destination (and vice versa) as h_i, the channel gain from the ith source to the jth relay (and vice versa) as f_{ij}, and the channel gain from the jth relay to the ith destination (and vice versa) as g_{ji}. It also assumes that $\sqrt{P_s}h_i$, $\sqrt{P_s}f_{ij}$ and $\sqrt{P_r}g_{ji}$ follow a Complex Gaussian distribution with zero mean and variance being σ_h^2, σ_f^2 and σ_g^2, respectively.

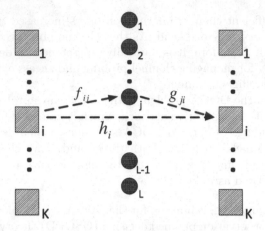

Fig. 1. Network model

In each source-to-destination transmission, say from the ith source to its destination, a relay, say the jth relay, aids the transmission. The maximal rate achieved as in [8] is that

$$\min\left(\log_2(1 + P_s|h_i|^2 + P_r|g_{ji}|^2), \log_2(1 + P_s|f_{ij}|^2)\right).$$

2.2 Basic Protocol Structure

Without delving into protocol details given in following sections, we present the basic protocol structure. In such network, all source-destination nodes follow a simplified carrier sensing multiple access with collision avoidance (CSMA/CA) mechanism and share a common channel for access. Similar mechanism is assumed in [7,9–11]. The DOCA/SP protocol, which describes the channel contention process of sources, is shown below.

At the beginning of a time slot with duration δ, each source independently contends to access the channel by sending a request-to-send (RTS) packet with probability p_0. In that time slot, there are three possible outcomes:

- **Idle:** If there is no source transmitting RTS in that slot (with probability $(1 - p_0)^K$), all sources continue to contend in next slot.
- **Collision:** If there are two or more sources transmitting RTSs (with probability $1 - (1 - p_0)^K - Kp_0(1 - p_0)^{K-1}$), a collision happens. Then in the next slot after a CTS duration, all sources continue to contend.
- **Success:** If there is only one source, say Source i, transmitting RTS (with probability $Kp_0(1 - p_0)^{K-1}$), this source is called *winner* of the channel contention.

As follows, we present the DOCA/SP protocol operation by steps upon successful channel contention slot.

On Receiving of the RTS from Source i**:** If the RTS from Source i is received by Destination i and each relay, the relays and Destination i can estimate the channel gain between Source i and itself. Then three options are available at the destination.

- *Stop:* If the channel gain of direct link is high enough, Destination i sends a CTS notifying that Source i transmits data to its destination without relaying.
- *Continue:* If the channel gain of direct link is low, Source i drops this transmission opportunity and re-contends the channel with other sources.
- *Defer:* Otherwise, Source i postpones by spending extra time for probing channels between relays and the destination, and makes subsequent decision.

Furthermore, we describe the subsequent operation when Destination i decides to defer.

1. *Send probing CTS:* Destination i decides the number of relays to probe, denoted by J, and sends a probing CTS notifying the J relays to probe second-hop channels.
2. *On receiving of the probing CTS:* If the relays receive a probing CTS, they take turns sending a probing RTS to Destination i, containing CSI of first-hop channels.
3. *On receiving of the RTS from relays:* After reception of the RTS from the relays, Destination i obtains channel gains from probed relays to itself, and collects the channel gains of both hops. Based on the information, through reward comparison between direct-link and relaying transmissions, referring to the traffic volume successfully transmitted, Destination i chooses a manner of higher reward to transmit.

Finally, Destination i decides to stop or continue.

- **Stop:** Destination i sends a CTS to Source i in designated manner as stated above.
- **Continue:** Destination i keeps silent, and other sources can detect an idle slot after the RTS-CTS exchange among Source i, the relays and Destination i. The idle slot tells other sources that Destination i decides to continue.

After a successful transmission, a new contention is started among all source nodes.

3   Decision Theoretical Approach Based on OSOPDT

In this section, based on *optimal sequential observation planned decision theory* (OSOPDT), the DOCA/SP problem is formulated as an OSOPD problem as in [12], and an analytic framework for finding optimal strategies is established, forming a whole course from observation to decision. On this basis, an optimal sequential observation plan decision rule is to be found maximizing the statistical average objective function, and further refined as an optimal strategy for the DOCA/SP problem.

3.1   Observation Process

As foundation of the analytic framework, sequential observation process is first formulated from dynamic process of multi-source channel contention and sequential probing of direct and relay channels. An observation is defined, associated with a sub-observation process.

Through problem analysis, an *observation process* is formed, and an observation starts from sources' channel contention and lasts until another channel contention. It is defined as the process of channel contention among all sources until a successful contention. In particular, for each observation, denoted as kth observation, a random time duration, denoted as $t_s(k)$ is spent until a winner source appears, denoted as $s(k)$. Channel gain in the direct link, denoted as $h_s(k)$, from itself to its destination is observed by the destination. In this respect, after kth observation, information denoted by $\mathscr{F}_k = \{s(k), h_{s(k)}(k), t_s(k)\}$ is obtained. As each round channel contention is independent, the number of contentions follows a geometric distribution with parameter $K p_0 (1 - p_0)^{K-1}$. Among all the contentions for an observation, the last contention is successful, and its total duration is $\tau_{RTS} + \tau_{CTS}$. The quantities τ_{RTS} and τ_{CTS} are durations of an RTS and CTS, respectively. Any other contention is either an idle slot (with duration δ) or a collision (with duration τ_{RTS}). The mean of the duration of an observation is thus given as $\tau_o = \tau_{RTS} + \tau_{CTS} + \frac{(1-p_0)^K}{K p_0 (1-p_0)^{K-1}} \cdot \delta + \frac{1-(1-p_0)^K - K p_0 (1-p_0)^{K-1}}{K p_0 (1-p_0)^{K-1}} \cdot \tau_{RTS}$.

After each observation, by protocol structure described in Subsect. 2.2, the destination of winner source obtains CSI from the source to itself, and then has three options: to stop, defer or continue. The information obtained also depends on these options. In particular, for kth observation, the winner source $s(k)$ could obtain at maximum full information, denoted by

$$\mathscr{G}_k(L) = \{f_{s(k)1}(k), g_{1s(k)}(k), ..., f_{s(k)L}(k), g_{Ls(k)}(k)\},$$

where h, f and g with index (k) denote channel gain realizations after kth channel contention success, respectively. With the observation index $k = 1, 2, ..., \infty$, an observation information sequence $\{\mathscr{G}_k(L)\}_{k=1,2,...,\infty}$ is defined, and $\{\mathscr{F}_k \vee \mathscr{G}_k(L)\}_{k=1,2,...,\infty}$ represents all information observed through the whole course of a successful transmission[1].

3.2   Sub-observation Process

It is found that, for each observation from successful channel contention, relay channel information to obtain for each observation is dynamic, determined by relay probing decision. In particular, after kth observation, different information $\{\mathscr{G}_k(j)\}_{j=1,2,...,L}$ of relay channels may be observed, depending on number of probed relays. The following three cases exist, as observation process couples with decision on channel probing and access.

– If to stop, observation process ends and no further information is observed.

---

[1] The symbol $\vee$ represents the union of information.

- If to continue, the winner source re-contends the channel, and next observation will be after another success of multiple sources channel contention.
- If to defer, the winner source decides relays number to probe, and further observation occurs. Upon decision to probe J relays, first J relays are probed and information $\mathscr{G}_k(J)$ is observed at cost of an extra time $J \cdot \tau_{RTS} + \tau_{CTS}$. By obtaining extra CSI of relay channels, the destination calculates the maximal achievable rate using the relays, and access the channel during duration $\tau_d - \tau_{CTS} - J \cdot \tau_{RTS}$. The duration τ_d denotes the channel coherence time minus a CTS duration, as a CTS sent after channel gain estimation of the direct link and first-hop link. Thereafter, the source has to decide to either stop or continue.

Therefore, to model the dynamic decision process as stated above, a new observation process of finer granularity is required, enabling the smart probing decision after each observation. Motivated by that, for each observation, two *sub-observations* are defined. We use n to denote the sub-observation index. For kth observation, the first sub-observation, i.e. sub-observation $n = 2k - 1$ is defined, and information $\mathscr{F}_k$ is obtained. The second sub-observation, i.e. sub-observation $n = 2k$ is also defined, and at maximum full channel information $\mathscr{G}_k(L)$ is obtained. It is worth noting that, the second sub-observation is determined by decision of smart relay probing.

Along the index n, a sub-observation process is formed from the observations along index k, and decision process of smart relays probing can be analysed on this basis. Specially, after kth channel contention success, a winner source can decide if to stop or further probe. If to observe, the number J of relays to probe is optimized based on history information of the sub-observation process until time index $n = 2k - 1$. In details, a decision $J = 0$ means not probing relay and letting sources re-contend the channel, while $J > 0$ means probing J relays, obtaining observation information $\mathscr{G}_k(J)$.

3.3   Observation Plan and Objective Function

Based on built-up sub-observation process, we are finding out an optimal sequential plan decision rule, based on which an optimal DOCA/SP strategy is derived.

We define a *sequential observation plan*, denoted by $\mathbf{a} = (a_1, a_2, ..., a_n)$ for $n \in \mathbb{N}$. The plan $\mathbf{a}$ represents a sequence with respect to the sub-observation process. Its domain is that

$$\mathbb{A} \triangleq \left\{ (a_1, a_2, ..., a_j) : j \in \mathbb{N}, a_{2k-1} = 1, a_{2k} \in \{0, 1, 2, ..., L\}, \forall k \leq \left\lceil \frac{j}{2} \right\rceil \right\}.$$

The symbol $\mathbb{N}$ denotes a set including all positive integers and 0^2. For the plan, $a_{2k-1} = 1$ means that, at sub-observation $n = 2k - 1$, sources contend the channel, and a source wins the channel and obtains CSI of the direct link. $a_{2k} \in \{0, 1, ..., L\}$ means that, at sub-observation $n = 2k$, the winner source has to

---

[2] When $j = 0$, the sequence $(a_1, a_2, ..., a_j)$ does not exit, and is denoted as ().

decide whether to probe relay channels ($a_{2k} > 0$) or not ($a_{2k} = 0$). To probe relays, how many channels to observe is further to decide, i.e. $a_{2k} \in \{1, 2, ..., L\}$. An instance of an observation plan is $(a_1, a_2, ..., a_{2k+1}) = (1, 2, 1, 1, ..., 1, 0, 1)$.

Moreover, an observation plan associates with observed information. Until nth sub-observation, the information obtained by a plan $\mathbf{a} = (a_1, a_2, ..., a_n)$ is denoted as $\mathscr{B}_{\mathbf{a}}$. In it, for $n = 2k - 1$, the information is[3] $\mathscr{B}_{\mathbf{a}} = (\vee_{m=1}^{k} \mathscr{F}_m) \vee (\vee_{m=1}^{k-1} \mathscr{G}_m(a_{2m}))$, and for $n = 2k$, the information is $\mathscr{B}_{\mathbf{a}} = (\vee_{m=1}^{k} \mathscr{F}_m) \vee (\vee_{m=1}^{k} \mathscr{G}_m(a_{2m}))$.

Based on observation plan and information observed, reward function is defined reflecting the system throughput of DOCA/SP. In particular, after nth sub-observation, observation plan $\mathbf{a}$ is experienced, and a reward is obtained after a successful transmission, which refers to the maximal total traffic volume sent by the winner source in the transmission round. We denote the reward by $Y_{\mathbf{a}}$, which is a deterministic function based on information $\mathscr{B}_{\mathbf{a}}$. Meanwhile, a time cost $T_{\mathbf{a}}$ is also spent, referring to the total waited time from the first observation until nth sub-observation plus the data transmission duration. If it is to stop after the observation plan $\mathbf{a}$, an instantaneous system throughput $Y_{\mathbf{a}}/T_{\mathbf{a}}$ is obtained.

Based on definitions above, we define the optimal DOCA/SP strategy and formulate the statistical optimization problem as follows. Symbol N aligning with previous work [7] denotes an DOCA/SP strategy. Notably, such strategy differs from the stopping rule in the research before. Particularly, under optimal stopping theory, the problem on when to stop barely matters, in which the stopping rule N takes a integer value. However, in our research an optimal strategy of a sequence plan is to find, and the optimal rule takes a plan $\mathbf{a}$.

Following an DOCA/SP strategy N, after each round successful transmission, a traffic volume Y_N and time cost T_N are obtained. In the long term, by the law of large number, the time average system throughput will converge in full probability (i.e. almost surely) to the statistical average throughput, satisfying that

$$\lim_{t \to \infty} \frac{Y_N(1) + Y_N(2) + \cdots + Y_N(t)}{T_N(1) + T_N(2) + \cdots + T_N(t)} \xrightarrow{a.s.} \frac{\mathbb{E}[Y_N]}{\mathbb{E}[T_N]}.$$

Here $\mathbb{E}[\cdot]$ means expectation.

In the following section, the goal is to find an optimal DOCA/SP strategy N^* which attains the maximal average system throughput[4] $\sup_N \frac{\mathbb{E}[Y_N]}{\mathbb{E}[T_N]}$.

4   Optimal DOCA/SP Strategy

In this section, an optimal DOCA/SP strategy for the distributed cooperative network is derived, maximizing the average system throughput in steps under the analytic framework in Sect. 3. The procedure is as follows. The objective

---

[3] The symbol $\vee_{m=1}^{n}$ can be understood as the union of information.

[4] Note that the supreme may not be attainable, while the maximum is defined as the attainable supreme.

function of fractional form is first transformed into a price-based function, upon which an optimal rule is then derived. Taking advantage of special traits of the practical problem, analysis is carried out, refining the optimal rule into an optimal DOCA/SP strategy. At last, implementation of the strategy is investigated guaranteeing feasibility and practicability.

4.1 Equivalent Transformation

Recognizing that the average throughput maximization problem is analytically intractable, it is transformed into another problem of a price-based objective function. We use $Z_{\mathbf{a}}(\lambda)$ and $Z_N(\lambda)$ to denote transformed rewards $Y_{\mathbf{a}} - \lambda T_{\mathbf{a}}$ and $Y_N - \lambda T_N$, respectively. The argument λ is the price charged on the time spent. For a given price $\lambda > 0$, a strategy for the transformed objective function is denoted by $N(\lambda)$, and an optimal strategy is denoted as $N^*(\lambda)$. The relation between the original and transformed problems is given below.

Lemma 1. *A strategy $N^*(\lambda^*)$ maximizing the expected reward $\mathbb{E}[Z_N(\lambda^*)]$ such that $\sup_N \mathbb{E}[Z_N(\lambda^*)] = 0$ is optimal which achieves the maximal average system throughput. The price λ^* is the maximal average system throughput, and uniquely exists satisfying $\sup_N \mathbb{E}[Z_N(\lambda^*)] = 0$.*

In accordance with the lemma above, the main train for solving the DOCA/SP problem is enlightened. For a given price $\lambda > 0$, an optimal strategy is first acquired achieving $\sup_N \mathbb{E}[Z_N(\lambda)]$. Then, by replacing λ with λ^*, the strategy $N^*(\lambda^*)$ is a solution for the DOCA/SP problem.

4.2 Optimal Sequential Plan Decision Rule

Based on the framework described in Sect. 2, an optimal observation plan decision rule is derived in this subsection. After kth channel contention success, at sub-observation $n = 2k-1$, the instantaneous reward $Y_{\mathbf{a}}$ is $\tau_d R_d(k)$, which refers to the traffic volume sent in direct link at rate $R_d(k) = \log_2\left(1 + P_s|h_{s(k)}(k)|^2\right)$.

And at sub-observation $n = 2k$, if relay(s) probed, i.e. $a_n > 0$, the instantaneous reward $Y_{\mathbf{a}}$ is $(\tau_d - \tau_{CTS} - a_n \cdot \tau_{RTS}) \cdot \max\left\{R_d(k), R_r(k)/2\right\}$. It refers to the maximal traffic volume transmitted over both direct and relay channels. The symbols $R_d(k)$ and $R_r(k)$ denote transmission rates by direct and relaying transmission, respectively. For instance, under single relay transmission, say a transmission from Source i to its destination and jth relay is used, the rate $R_r(k)$ is calculated as

$$\min\left\{\log_2(1 + P_s|h_i(k)|^2 + P_r|g_{ji}(k)|^2), \log_2(1 + P_s|f_{ij}(k)|^2)\right\}.$$

For multiple relays transmission, the rate $R_r(k)$ denotes the maximal achievable rate. It is attained through optimal multi-relay selection based on instantaneous channels conditions.

On the other hand, if the winner source does not probe relay, i.e. $a_n = 0$, the reward is defined as $Y_\mathbf{a} = -\infty$. In this case, the winner source will not let the source transmit, but drops transmission opportunity and re-contending the channel with other sources.

Correspondingly, the time cost until sub-observation n is calculated as

$$T_\mathbf{a} = \sum_{l=1}^{k} t_s(l) + \sum_{l=1}^{k-1} \left(\mathbb{I}[a_{2l} > 0] \cdot \tau_{CTS} + a_{2l} \cdot \tau_{RTS} \right) + \tau_d.$$

It denotes the total time spent if a source transmits.

To avoid abasement, several notations and relations are provided as necessary. For an arbitrary observation sequence $\mathbf{a} = (a_1, a_2, ..., a_j)$ and an integer m, $(\mathbf{a}, m)$ denotes a prolonged sequence $(a_1, a_2, ..., a_j, m)$. A relation between any two sequential plans is specified as that: for plans $\mathbf{a}$ and $\mathbf{b}$, $\mathbf{b} \geq \mathbf{a}$ means $b_i = a_i$ for $\forall 1 \leq i \leq |\mathbf{a}|$. We also denote $A_\mathbf{a}$ as the set of actions following the plan $\mathbf{a}$.

For a plan $\mathbf{a}$, we define $V_\mathbf{a} = \sup\limits_{j \in A_\mathbf{a}} \mathbb{E}[U_{(\mathbf{a},j)}|\mathscr{B}_\mathbf{a}]$ and $U_\mathbf{a} = \sup\limits_{\mathbf{b} \geq \mathbf{a}} \mathbb{E}[Z_\mathbf{b}|\mathscr{B}_\mathbf{a}]$.

In particular, $V_\mathbf{a}$ represents the maximal average reward if not stop at plan $\mathbf{a}$ conditioned on observed information. $U_\mathbf{a}$ represents the maximal average reward conditioned on observed information. Notably, for an observation plan with $|\mathbf{a}| = 0$ (i.e. without making any channel probing), the expected reward $U_\mathbf{a}$ (i.e. $U_{()}$) is denoted as U_0 and $U_0 = \sup\limits_{N} \mathbb{E}[Z_N]$.

Based on definitions as above, an optimal rule is derived in Theorem 1.

Theorem 1. *For any price $\lambda > 0$, an optimal sequential plan decision rule is in form that: starting from $|\mathbf{a}| = 0$, at sub-observation n, it is optimal to stop with $N^* = \mathbf{a}$ when $Z_\mathbf{a} \geq V_\mathbf{a}$, or continue otherwise. Furthermore, if continue at $n = 2k - 1$, it is optimal to update sequential plan by $\mathbf{a} = (\mathbf{a}, J^*)$ where $J^* := \min\{0 \leq j \leq L : U_{(\mathbf{a},j)} = V_\mathbf{a}\}$. If continue at $n = 2k$, sequential plan is updated by $\mathbf{a} = (\mathbf{a}, 1)$.*

4.3   Further Analysis on the Optimal Rule

Based on the optimal rule, we derive an optimal strategy for DOCA/SP problem in the distributed cooperative network. By observing the optimal rule, threshold functions are crucial, with respect to which statistical characteristics of the system model is studied to solve. Bellman equations are used to calculate these thresholds.

For a sequential plan $\mathbf{a}$, thresholds $V_\mathbf{a}$ and $U_\mathbf{a}$ can be calculated from Bellman Equation [12, Chapter 2]. In particular, thresholds $V_\mathbf{a}$ and $U_\mathbf{a}$ satisfy that

$$U_\mathbf{a} = \max\{Z_\mathbf{a}, V_\mathbf{a}\} = \max \left\{ Z_\mathbf{a}, \sup_{j \in A_\mathbf{a}} \mathbb{E}[U_{(\mathbf{a},j)}|\mathscr{B}_\mathbf{a}] \right\}. \tag{1}$$

Since the action set $A_\mathbf{a}$ for plan $\mathbf{a}$ depends on length of $\mathbf{a}$, Bellman Equation has two expressions, which are analysed respectively as follows.

Expression 1: For an odd length $|\mathbf{a}| = 2k - 1$, Eq. (1) is rewritten as

$$U_{\mathbf{a}} = \max\left\{Z_{\mathbf{a}}, \max_{j \in \{0,1,\dots,L\}} \mathbb{E}[U_{(\mathbf{a},j)} | \mathscr{B}_{\mathbf{a}}]\right\}. \tag{2}$$

Expression 2: For an even length $|\mathbf{a}| = 2k$, Eq. (1) is rewritten as

$$U_{\mathbf{a}} = \max\left\{Z_{\mathbf{a}}, \mathbb{E}[U_{(\mathbf{a},1)} | \mathscr{B}_{\mathbf{a}}]\right\}. \tag{3}$$

In accordance with expressions above, thresholds are represented by observed information $\mathscr{B}_{\mathbf{a}}$. Recalling that such information includes information on sources' channel contention, direct link and relays channel gains, and using the relation between two expressions, Expression 2 is analyzed in advance below.

Based on $U_{\mathbf{a}}$ in Expressions 1 and 2, the threshold $V_{\mathbf{a}}$ is derived by its definition.

Based on expressions analysis, thresholds $\{U_{\mathbf{a}}, V_{\mathbf{a}}\}$ in Theorem 1 are represented. According to Theorem 1, an optimal strategy is derived as follows.

Theorem 2. *For a given price $\lambda > 0$, an optimal strategy has the structure that: after kth successful channel contention with $k \in \mathbb{N}$, at sub-observation $2k - 1$,*

- *if the immediate reward $\tau_d R_d(k) - \lambda \tau_d \geq M_j\big(R_d(k)\big)$ for all $j = 1, 2, \dots, L$ and $\tau_d R_d(k) - \lambda \tau_d \geq U_0$, stop and transmit over direct link.*
- *if the expected reward $U_0 > \max\left\{\tau_d R_d(k) - \lambda \tau_d, \max_{j=1,2,\dots,L} M_j\big(R_d(k)\big)\right\}$, continue without probing relays and skip to sub-observation $2k + 1$.*
- *otherwise, continue by probing J^* relays with $J^* = \min\{j \in \{1, 2, \dots, L\}$: $M_j\big(R_d(k)\big) = \max_{l=1,2,\dots,L} M_l\big(R_d(k)\big)\}$.*

then, at sub-observation $2k$,

- *if the immediate reward $\big(\tau_d - \tau_{CTS} - J^* \cdot \tau_{RTS}\big) \max\big\{R_d(k), R_r(k)/2\big\} \geq U_0 + \lambda\big(\tau_d - \tau_{CTS} - J^* \cdot \tau_{RTS}\big)$, then stop;*
- *otherwise, to continue.*

Optimal Multi-relay Relaying Transmission. The procedure of multi-relay transmission is as follows. After each time channel contention success and relays probing, channel gains of direct and 2-hop channels are obtained by the winner source. A two-phase time division relaying transmission is used. Particularly, after kth successful channel contention, and for $J \in \{1, 2, \dots, L\}$ relays under distributed beam-forming, the maximal transmission rate $R_r(k)$ or more specifically denoted by $R_r^J(k)$. Therein, $\{\gamma_1 \geq \gamma_2 \geq \cdots \geq \gamma_J\}$ are descending ordered, from channel gains in the fist-hop $\{|f_{s(k)1}(k)|^2, |f_{s(k)2}(k)|^2, \dots, |f_{s(k)J}(k)|^2\}$. And after ordering, channel gains in the second hop are permuted, and channel gains are regenerated, denoted by $\{|g_{\sigma_1 s(k)}|^2, |g_{\sigma_2 s(k)}|^2, \dots, |g_{\sigma_J s(k)}|^2\}$. The permutation function σ maps the index j to σ_j. Also, for $u = 1, 2, \dots, J$, sets are denoted that $A_u = \left[\gamma_u \leq \sum_{j=1}^{u} P_r |g_{\sigma_j s(k)}(k)|^2 + P_s |h_{s(k)}(k)|^2\right]$ and $B_u = \big[\gamma_u \leq$ $\sum_{j=1}^{u-1} P_r |g_{\sigma_j s(k)}(k)|^2 + P_s |h_{s(k)}(k)|^2\big]$. The operator $(\bar{\cdot})$ denotes the supplement set.

Reward and Threshold Relationship. Based on the maximal rate as above, threshold comparison given in Theorem 2 is further studied. To simplify the optimal strategy in terms of complexity, relations between the instantaneous reward and thresholds are analysed. In this regard, we investigate thresholds properties.

Firstly, the monotonicity of threshold functions $M_j(R_d)$ for $j = 1, 2, ..., L$ are considered. When j relays are probed, the expected reward $M_j(R_d(k))$ conditioned on direct-link channel gain $|h_{s(k)}(k)|^2 = h_s$ is calculated as

$$M_j(R_d) = \mathbb{E}\big[\max\big\{(\tau_d - \tau^j) \cdot \max\{\log_2(1 + h_s),\ R_r^j(k)/2\} - \lambda\tau_d, U_0 - \lambda\tau^j\big\}\big]. \tag{4}$$

Since R_r increases with h_s and two-hop channel gains of relay channels are independent of R_d, function $M_j(R_d)$ is strictly increasing over h_s.

As follows, we investigate the monotonicity of threshold functions $M_j(h_s) - (R_d(h_s)\tau_d - \lambda\tau_d)$ for $j = 1, 2, ..., L$. They represent difference between the expected reward by probing j relays channels and the immediate reward by direct channel transmission. It is rewritten as

$$M_j(h_s) - (R_d(h_s)\tau_d - \lambda\tau_d) = \\ \mathbb{E}\big[\max\big\{(\tau_d - \tau^j)\max\{0, R_r(h_s)/2 - R_d(h_s)\} - R_d(h_s)\tau^j, \\ U_0 + \lambda(\tau_d - \tau^j) - R_d(h_s)\tau_d\big\}\big]. \tag{5}$$

By observing the right-side of (5), it suffices to prove decreasing monotonicity of $\frac{1}{2}R_r(h_s) - R_d(h_s)$.

When j relays are probed, there are in total 2^j combinations, which are used for cooperative transmission. We use notations $\mathcal{J}_l$ to denote lth combination with $l \in \{1, 2, ..., j\}$. The difference between rates in relaying and in direct transmission, is calculated as

$$\frac{1}{2}R_r(h_s) - R_d(h_s) = \frac{1}{2} \cdot \max_{l=1,2,...,2^j} \\ \log_2 \frac{1 + \min\big(\min_{m \in \mathcal{J}_l} P_s|f_{s(k)m}|^2, \sum_{m \in \mathcal{J}_l} P_r|g_{ms(k)}|^2 + P_s h_s\big)}{(1 + P_s h_s)^2}.$$

It is observed that the above function is decreasing over h_s. And in the right-side of (5), other components are subtracted by either $R_d(h_s)\tau^j$ or $R_d(h_s)\tau_d$ which increases with h_s. And the decreasing monotonicity of (5) over h_s is proved.

Based on the monotonicity properties, the relation between thresholds $\{M_j(R_d)\}$, $j = 1, ..., L$, rewards $R_d(h_s)\tau_d - \lambda\tau_d$ and U_0 is then investigated to refine the optimal strategy into a channel-gain threshold-based strategy.

In particular, when[5] $h_s \to -\infty$, for a number $j \in \{1, 2, ..., L\}$ of probed relays, by Eq. (4) we have $\lim_{h_s \to -\infty} M_j(h_s) = U_0 - \lambda \tau^j$, and when $h_s \to \infty$, we have $\lim_{h_s \to \infty} M_j(R_d) = \infty$.

Therefore, using increasing monotonicity, there exists a unique threshold, denoted as h_j^* such that $M_j(h_j^*) = U_0$ for $j \in \{1, 2, ..., L\}$. For $h_s \geq h_j^*$, we have $M_j(R_d) \geq U_0$, while for $h_s < h_j^*$, we have $M_j(R_d) < U_0$.

Moreover, when $h_s \to -\infty$, for $j \in \{1, 2, ..., L\}$ we have

$$\lim_{h_s \to -\infty} M_j(R_d) - \tau_d R_d(h_s) + \lambda \tau_d = \infty,$$

and when $h_s \to \infty$, we have

$$\lim_{h_s \to \infty} M_j(R_d) - \tau_d R_d(h_s) + \lambda \tau_d = -\infty.$$

Therefore, by the decreasing monotonicity, there exits a unique threshold $h_j^\dagger$ such that $M_j(h_j^\dagger) = \tau_d R_d(h_j^\dagger) - \lambda \tau_d$. For $h_s \geq h_j^\dagger$, we have $M_j(R_d) \leq \tau_d R_d - \lambda \tau_d$, while for $h_s < h_j^\dagger$, we have $M_j(R_d) > \tau_d R_d - \lambda \tau_d$.

As specified above, quantities $\{h_j^*, h_j^\dagger\}_{j=1,2,...,L}$ are interactions of the reward and threshold functions over the direct channel gain h_s, which are pure channel-gain based thresholds.

4.4 Refined Optimal Strategy for Transformed Problem

Using channel-gain based thresholds, the optimal strategy in Theorem 2 can be significantly simplified, and an optimal strategy of threshold-based structure is derived in Theorem 3.

Theorem 3. *For a price $\lambda > 0$, an optimal strategy for the transformed problem is of channel-gain based threshold structure as follows.*

Structure 1: *If $\min_{j=1,2,...,L} h_j^* \leq \max_{j=1,2,...,L} h_j^\dagger$, after kth successful channel contention where $k \in \mathbb{N}$, each winner source obtains direct link channel gain h_s and operates as that:*

- *if $h_s \leq \min_{j=1,2,...,L} h_j^*$, it is optimal to give up transmission and re-contend with other sources.*
- *if $h_s \in \left(\min_{j=1,2,...,L} h_j^*, \max_{j=1,2,...,L} h_j^\dagger \right)$, it is optimal to probe number of relays such that*
  $J^* := \min\{1 \leq j \leq L : M_j(R_d) = \max_{l=1,2,...,L} M_l(h_s)\}$. Then, if J^* relay(s) are probed, when $(\tau_d - \tau^{J^*}) \max\{R_d(h_s), \frac{1}{2} R_r(h_s)\} \geq U_0 + \lambda(\tau_d - \tau^{J^*})$, it is optimal to stop, or continue otherwise.

---

[5] It notes that, since $h_s \geq 0$ always holds, the negative value is not valid. However, the analysis makes sense for checking the monotonic property and obtaining theoretic bounds for $M_j(R_d)$.

– *if* $h_s \geq \max\limits_{j=1,2,...,L} h_j^\dagger$, *it is optimal to transmit directly without relaying.*

Structure 2: *If* $\min\limits_{j=1,2,...,L} h_j^* > \max\limits_{j=1,2,...,L} h_j^\dagger$, *the optimal strategy degrades into a simple form as that: after kth successful channel contention where* $k \in \mathbb{N}$, *it operates as that:*

– *if* $\tau_d R_d(h_s) - \lambda\tau_d \leq U_0$, *it is optimal to transmit in direct link.*
– *otherwise, to continue.*

The maximal expected reward U_0 is uniquely determined by the equation that

$$U_0 = \mathbb{E}\big[\max\big\{\tau_d R_d - \lambda\tau_d, U_0, \max\limits_{j=1,2,...,L} M_j(R_d)\big\}\big] - \lambda\tau_o.$$

Based on above theorem, we denote $h^* \triangleq \min\limits_{j=1,2,...,L} h_j^*$ and $h^\dagger \triangleq \max\limits_{j=1,2,...,L} h_j^\dagger$, respectively. They are determined by channel characteristics and number of relays to probe. Correspondingly, we also denote $\max\limits_{j=1,2,...,L} M_j(R_d)$ as $M^*(R_d)$.

Unique existence of channel-gain thresholds in Theorem 3 is guaranteed by the following Lemma.

Lemma 2. *For any price* $\lambda > 0$, *the array of solution* $\{U_0, h^*, h^\dagger\}$ *satisfying threshold relation* $h^* \leq h^\dagger$ *is unique if it exits; moreover, the solution* U_0 *is unique if* $h^* > h^\dagger$.

As the relation of h^* and $h^\dagger$ reflects structure of the optimal strategy as shown in Theorem 3, the decision criteria is given in Theorem 4. The function $M^*(y, r)$ is equivalently transferred from $M^*\big(R_d(h_s)\tau_d, r\big)$, where y represents the immediate reward $R_d(h_s)\tau_d - \lambda\tau_d$.

With F_0 denoted as cumulative distribution function (CDF) of h_s following an exponential distribution, a special factor r_0 uniquely exists, such that

$$r_0 = r_0 \cdot F_0\big(R_d^{-1}(\frac{r_0}{\tau_d} + \lambda)\big) +$$

$$\int\limits_{R_d(x)-\lambda=r_0/\tau_d}^{\infty} (R_d(x)\tau_d - \lambda\tau_d)dF_0(x) - \lambda\tau_o. \tag{6}$$

Theorem 4. *If* $M^*(r_0, r_0) > r_0$, $h^* \leq h^\dagger$ *satisfies and by the optimal strategy each winner source will probe relay(s) when* $h_s \in (h^*, h^\dagger)$; *otherwise,* $h^* > h^\dagger$ *satisfies and the optimal strategy degrades to a simple form where relay probing is discarded.*

4.5 Optimal DOCA/SP Strategy and Its Implementation

Optimal DOCA/SP Strategy. By replacing the price λ by λ^* such that $U_0(\lambda^*) = 0$, an optimal DOCA/SP strategy is obtained.

For a given price $\lambda > 0$, we solve the following equation to derive expected reward $U_0(\lambda)$:

$$U_0(\lambda) = \mathbb{E}\big[\max\big\{\tau_d R_d - \lambda\tau_d, U_0(\lambda), M^*(R_d)\big\}\big] - \lambda\tau_o. \tag{7}$$

Decision criteria $M^*(r_0(\lambda), r_0(\lambda)) > r_0(\lambda)$ by Theorem 4 needs to determine, and depending on the optimal strategy structure, two cases exist in calculating value of $U_0(\lambda)$:

– if criteria satisfied, $U_0(\lambda)$ is calculated through solving the equations, where a unique solution $\{U_0(\lambda), h^*(\lambda), h^\dagger(\lambda)\}$ is guaranteed;
– otherwise, $U_0(\lambda)$ is equal to $r_0(\lambda)$ satisfying Eq. (6).

For both cases, unique existence of $U_0(\lambda)$ is guaranteed by Lemma 2.

Then, being a specific λ such that $U_0(\lambda) = 0$, the maximal average throughput λ^* is uniquely calculated in accordance with Lemma 1. Replacing price λ with λ^*, an optimal DOCA/SP strategy is derived, and it operates as follows.

In such a distributed network with multiple DF relays, all sources randomly contend the channel. After the kth channel contention success, a source, say Source $s(k)$ wins the channel, and obtains direct link channel gain h_s, then

– if $M^*\big(r_0(\lambda^*), r_0(\lambda^*)\big) > r_0(\lambda^*)$,
  • if $h_s \leq h^*(\lambda^*)$, it gives up the transmission opportunity and re-contends the channel with other sources.
  • if $h_s \in \big(h^*(\lambda^*), h^\dagger(\lambda^*)\big)$, it spends an extra duration τ^{J^*} to probe the first $J^* := \min\big\{j \in \{1, 2, ..., L\} : M_j(R_d) = \max\limits_{l=1,2,...,L} M_l(h_s)\big\}$ relays. After probing those relays, if $\max\{R_d, \frac{1}{2}R_r(k, J^*)\} \geq \lambda^*$, the winner source transmits in cooperation; otherwise, it gives up the transmission opportunity and re-contends the channel with other sources. When the source transmits, a factor value is embedded in the CTS from the destination used for beam-forming[6]. Then, following procedure is used for channel access of duration $\tau_d - \tau^{J^*}$:
    1. in the first-half duration, the winner source transmits data to all relays and the destination;
    2. in the second-half duration, the relay(s) able to decode the transmitted data forwards its received data to the destination by signal processing using optimal beam-forming.
  • if $h_s \geq h^\dagger(\lambda^*)$, it transmits over direct link without spending extra time to probe relays.
– if $M^*\big(r_0(\lambda^*), r_0(\lambda^*)\big) \leq r_0(\lambda^*)$,
  • if $R_d \geq \lambda^*$, it transmits directly.
  • otherwise, it gives up the transmission opportunity and re-contends the channel with other sources.

---

[6] The factor is norm of beam forming vector in the second hop.

5   Performance Evaluation

This section uses computer simulation results to validate the results above. Consider 5 source-destination pairs and multiple relays in the distributed cooperative network. Channels from sources to each relay, from sources to destinations experience i.i.d. Rayleigh fading, while channels from the relays to destinations also experience i.i.d. Rayleigh fading. Channel contention parameters of source nodes are set as $p_0 = 0.3$, $\delta = 25$ μs, $\tau_{RTS} = \tau_{CTS} = 50$ μs.

The average system throughput of proposed DOCA/SP strategy for the distributed cooperative network is verified. The average received signal-to-noise ratio (SNR) of direct link is σ_h^2, the average received SNR of first-hop and second-hop relay channels are σ_f^2 and σ_g^2, respectively. We consider a scenario where $\sigma_f^2 = 4 \cdot \sigma_h^2$, $\sigma_g^2 = 2 \cdot \sigma_h^2$. By simulating based on various values on the main impact factors, the analytical system throughput and system throughput achieved by the proposed DOCA/SP strategy is compared. Firstly, when the average SNR σ_h^2 varies from 2dB to 8dB, the two-line result in the top of Table 1 shows the numerically calculated (shown as 'analytical') and simulated (shown as 'simu') system throughput achieved by the proposed strategy. Secondly, we consider the scenario where $\sigma_h^2 = 5$ dB, $\sigma_f^2 = 30$ dB and $\sigma_g^2 = 20$ dB. By varying the number of relays from single ($L = 1$) to multiple relays ($L = 7$), the two-line result in the middle of Table 1 show the numerically calculated and simulated system throughput. Thirdly, scenario with $\sigma_h^2 = 5$ dB, $\sigma_f^2 = 30$ dB, $\sigma_g^2 = 20$ dB and $L = 6$ is considered. When channel coherence time τ_d increases from 1 ms to 4 ms, the two-line result in the bottom of Table 1 show the numerically calculated and simulated system throughput. In these three scenarios, it can be seen that the analytical and simulation results match well, confirming accuracy of the analysis of the proposed strategy. As the analytical results are the optimal value, the optimality of proposed strategy s is verified. And it is also found that: (1) the average system throughput increases when SNR increases; (2) average system throughput increases when channel coherence time increases; (3) average system throughput increases if more relays are deployed.

Table 1. System throughput match

σ_h^2	2 dB	4 dB	6 dB	8 dB
analytical	1.7673	2.1626	2.6834	3.2790
simu	1.7646	2.1634	2.6823	3.2749
Duration of τ_d	1 ms	2 ms	3 ms	4 ms
analytical	2.4957	3.1688	3.4989	3.6853
simu	2.4998	3.1644	3.4904	3.6860
Number of relays	1	3	5	7
analytical	2.9521	3.3583	3.4790	3.5016
simu	2.9569	3.3574	3.4776	3.4979

To check performance enhancement by the proposed strategy, we compare system performance with alternative strategies. Two strategies are investigated: (1) No-wait strategy: a winner source has full CSI, including CSI of direct link and all relays channels, and it always transmits using the best achievable rate; (2) Optimal-single-relay (OSR) strategy: it is similar to our proposed strategy with two major differences. Each winner source will probe all relays when defer is selected, and rather than multiple relays selection, best single-relay selection is used for relaying transmission.

In simulation, we consider a scenario where relay channels statistics are $\sigma_f^2 = 6 \cdot \sigma_h^2$ and $\sigma_g^2 = 3 \cdot \sigma_h^2$. For a fixed duration of τ_d (i.e. $\tau_d = 1$ ms, 2 ms, 3 ms, 4 ms), when the direct-link average SNR σ_h^2 varies from 1 dB to 5 dB, the *stopping gain* is calculated, expressed by the ratio of performance increase by the proposed optimal strategy when compared with the average system throughput of No-wait strategy. The results are shown in Table 2. It is seen that the optimal strategy has obvious benefit in improving system throughout. Moreover, a trend shows that, when the average SNR of direct channel increases, the stopping gain decreases.

Figure 2 shows average system throughput of our proposed strategy and those of the OSR strategy. It is shown that, for the scenario with single relay deployed, the proposed optimal strategy is equivalent to the OSR strategy, and thus the same performance is obtained. For fixed number of relays from $L = 3$ to $L = 7$, the proposed OCA strategy performs better than that of OSR strategies. Particularly, the performance enhancement by the proposed strategy becomes larger when relays being deployed increase. Such phenomenon can be explained as follows. Through multiple relays selection transmission optimization, the proposed strategy exploits relays channels information better. Operated under the proposed strategy, each winner source dynamically selects the best number of relays to probe and transmit. By doing this, trade-off between channel information exploitation and overhead in such information collection is well balanced. In Fig. 2, when more relays are deployed for opportunistic transmission, average system throughput of the proposed optimal strategy remains increasing. However, as relays increase, the system throughput of the OSR strategy shows an opposite trend. The OSR strategy under scenario $L = 5$ performs better than $L = 7$, which is explained that, using the single best-relay selection, there is a sharper trade-off between relay channel exploitation and information overhead. It means that, overhead for probing most L relays channels dominates the benefit of system throughput.

Table 2. Stopping gain on average throughput

Duration of τ_d	1 dB	2 dB	3 dB	4 dB	5 dB
1 ms	84.81%	65.31%	49.10%	38.22%	33.28%
2 ms	49.12%	36.56%	24.98%	16.16%	10.77%
3 ms	52.26%	33.61%	25.45%	13.53%	8.15%
4 ms	56.47%	40.50%	24.50%	15.03%	11.14%

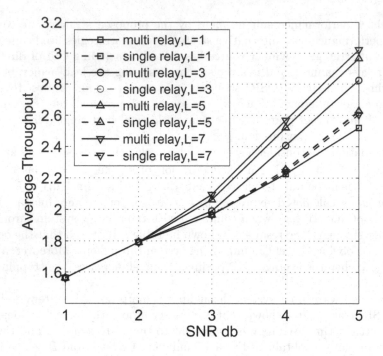

Fig. 2. Comparison between our proposed and OSR strategy

6 Conclusion

In a wireless ad-hoc cooperative network with multiple relaying, independent channel fading is experienced between all source-destination pairs and multiple relays being deployed. To improve the spectrum efficiency, a joint and efficient exploitation of the multi-source diversity, multi-relay cooperative diversity and time diversity is desired, and thus opportunistic channel access managing multiple sources and relays transmission is motivated. To harvest the full exploitation of these diversities, the DOCA problem with smart relays probing is investigated in this research. With regards to the problem, an optimal DOCA/SP strategy is proposed with its optimality rigorously proved, and the implementation is also presented. The findings will imply a novel view of jointly cross-layer design for opportunistic channel sensing and access for distributed cooperative networks.

References

1. Andrews, M., Kumaran, K., Ramanan, K., Stolyar, A., Whiting, P., Vijayakumar, R.: Providing quality of service over a shared wireless link. IEEE Commun. Mag. **39**(2), 150–154 (2001)
2. Viswanath, P., Tse, D.N.C., Laroia, R.: Opportunistic beamforming using dumb antennas. IEEE Trans. Inf. Theory **48**(6), 1277–1294 (2002)

3. Zheng, D., Ge, W., Zhang, J.: Distributed opportunistic scheduling for ad hoc networks with random access: an optimal stopping approach. IEEE Trans. Inf. Theory 55(1), 205–222 (2009)
4. Ge, W., Zhang, J., Wieselthier, J., Shen, X.: PHY-aware distributed scheduling for ad hoc communications with physical interference model. IEEE Trans. Wireless Commun. 8(5), 2682–2693 (2009)
5. Tan, S., Zheng, D., Zhang, J., Zeidler, J.: Distributed opportunistic scheduling for ad-hoc communications under delay constraints. In: Proceedings of IEEE INFOCOM (2010)
6. Gong, X., Chandrashekhar, T.P.S., Zhang, J., Poor, H.V.: Opportunistic cooperative networking: to relay or not to relay. IEEE J. Sel. Areas Commun. 30(2), 307–314 (2012)
7. Zhang, Z., Jiang, H.: Distributed opportunistic channel access in wireless relay networks. IEEE J. Sel. Areas Commun. 30(9), 1675–1683 (2012)
8. Laneman, J.N., Tse, D.N.C., Wornell, G.W.: Cooperative diversity in wireless networks: efficient protocols and outage behaviour. IEEE Trans. Inf. Theory 50, 3062–3080 (2004)
9. Bahareh, S., Kanodia, V., Kumar, P.R.: Opportunistic media access for multirate ad hoc networks. IEEE Trans. Inf. Theory 51(4), 1348–1358 (2005)
10. Poulakis, M.I., Panagopoulos, A.D., Constantinou, P.: Channel-aware opportunistic transmission scheduling for energy-efficient wireless links. IEEE Trans. Veh. Technol. 62(14), 192–204 (2013)
11. Tan, S.S., Zeidler, J., Rao, B.: Opportunistic channel-aware spectrum access for cognitive radio networks with interleaved transmission and sensing. IEEE Trans. Wireless Commun. 12(5), 2376–2388 (2013)
12. Schmitz, N.: Optimally sequentially planned decision procedures. Springer, New York (1993). https://doi.org/10.1007/978-1-4612-2736-6

Energy-Efficient Resource Allocation for Mobile Edge Computing System Supporting Multiple Mobile Devices

Song Jin[1], Qi Gu[2], Xiang Li[3], Xuming An[3], and Rongfei Fan[3(✉)]

[1] Institute of Telecommunication Satellite, China Aerospace Science
and Technology Corporation, Beijing 100094, China
390923423@qq.com
[2] Beijing Jiaotong University, Beijing 100044, China
15112094@bjtu.edu.cn
[3] Beijing Institute of Technology, Beijing 100081, China
{lawrence,fanrongfei}@bit.edu.cn, 1952590139@qq.com

Abstract. Nowadays, mobile edge computing (MEC) has become a promising technique to provide mobile devices with intensive computation capability for the applications in the Internet of Things and 5G communications. In a MEC system, a mobile device, who has computation tasks to complete, would like to offload part or all the data for computation to a MEC server, due to the limit of local computation capability. In this paper, we consider a MEC system with one MEC server and multiple mobile devices, who access into the MEC server via frequency division multiple access (FDMA). The energy consumption of all the mobile devices is targeted to minimized via optimizing the computation and communication resources, including the amount of data for offloading, the bandwidth for accessing, the energy budget for offloading data, the time budget for offloading, for each mobile device. An optimization problem is formulated, which is non-convex. We decompose it into two levels. In the lower level, a convex optimization problems is formulated. In the upper level, a one-dimensional variable is to be optimized by bisection search method.

Keywords: Edge computing · Data offloading · Multiple users · FDMA

1 Introduction

In the past decade, as smart mobile terminals is obtaining tremendous popularity, mobile users look forward to running real-time applications on their device anywhere [1]. These applications, such as augmented reality (AR), online games and face recognition, has a stringent requirement on latency and computation [2]. However, limited computation capability and battery capacity make it difficult for the mobile devices to fulfill the users' task within the rigid time constraint

B. Li et al. (Eds.): IoTaaS 2019, LNICST 316, pp. 228–234, 2020.
https://doi.org/10.1007/978-3-030-44751-9_19

alone. To solve these problems, mobile-edge computing (MEC) is emerging as a promising technique to provide cloud computing service at the mobile edge network [3]. Rather than transferring all the data for computing to the remote cloud servers, mobile users only need to offload data to the near small-cell base station with MEC server, which avoids the long propagation delay between the mobile device to the remote cloud center and insures the performance for those real-time mobile applications under stringent latency constraint [4].

In a MEC system, the computation task for each mobile users can be offloaded in two ways of scheme, binary and partial offloading. For the unpartitionable computation task, the binary offloading case should be implemented and the whole task should be either offloaded or computed locally entirely. In the partial offloading case, the partitionable task can be divided into two parts and only one of them is offloaded. In the meantime, offloading data to the base station will bring additional communication overhead. Since the battery capacity of mobile devices is limited, it is necessary to balance the tradeoff between the energy cost of local computing and offloading so as to minimize the mobile device's total energy consumption.

There are many works focusing on the energy minimizing problem of offloading scheme in a MEC system. The energy consumption minimization and latency of application execution minimization problem are studied separately under a single-user MEC scenario in [4]. Local CPU frequency, offloading power and data amount are optimized to minimize the energy consumption of the only mobile user. In [5], resource allocation for a multi-user mobile edge computation offloading system based on orthogonal frequency-division multiple access (OFDMA) is studied. Offloading data amount and the allocation of sub-channel are jointly optimized to minimize the sum mobile energy consumption of all mobile users. The problem is a mixed-integer programming problem and a sub-optimal algorithm is obtained. The authors of [6] investigate an multi-user offloading strategy to minimize the total energy consumption under the latency constraints for each user's task. The optimization variable are offloading time and data amount and optimal solution is found by applying KKT conditions. In [7], the authors consider a multi-mobile-users MEC system with unpartitionable computation tasks. To minimize the energy consumption on mobile users, the offloading selection, radio resource allocation, and CPU frequency allocation of the MEC server are optimized coordinately. However, the offloading strategy [7] is binary and is not fit for the partitionable task. The scheme in [4] is hard to apply to the multi-user scenario. [5] doesn't consider the latency constraints for each user's task. Meanwhile, [5,6] and [7] only consider the scenario with a fixed offloading bandwidth for each mobile user and ignore its influence on minimizing the total energy consumption, which leads to a suboptimal offloading scheme.

In this letter, we focus on jointly optimizing communication and computation resources for partial offloading in a MEC system with multiple mobile devices based on FDMA. A multiple mobile users scenario covered by a base station with MEC server is introduced with multiple parallel computation tasks requiring cloud computation resource. Each mobile user can access to the base station through wireless channels with different frequency bands simultaneously. The offloading time, bandwidth and data amount for each mobile user are optimized jointly to minimize overall users energy consumption under the latency constraints for different users' applications. A non-convex optimization problem is formulated. With some transformation, we are able to find the local optimal solution for the proposed optimization problem.

2   System Model and Problem Formulation

In this paper, we consider such a scenario. There are multiple mobile devices and one base station. A MEC server is mounted on the base station. The set of mobile devices are indexed as $\mathcal{K} = \{1, 2, ..., K\}$. Each mobile device, say device k, has a computation task to complete, say $\mathbb{T}_k$, for $k \in \mathcal{K}$. Task k can be described by a three-tuple vector, $\{D_k, C_k, T_k\}$, where D_k denotes the data size for computing (in unit of nat), C_k denotes the required CPU cycles for computing one data nat, and T_k indicates the maximal tolerable computation delay. In this paper, we consider the case that all the T_k are identical, i.e., $T_k = T$ for $k \in \mathcal{K}$. Every task is separable, i.e., every task can be divided into two parts: one part can be computed at the mobile device locally, and the other part can be offloaded to the base station and computed by the MEC server at the base station. For task k, suppose the amount of data nat for local computing is $d_{l,k}$ and the amount of data nat for offloading is $d_{o,k}$. Then there is

$$d_{o,k} + d_{l,k} = D_k, \forall k \in \mathcal{K}. \tag{1}$$

For local computing at mobile device k, the number of CPU cycles required is $C_k d_{l,k}$. The local computing can be completed within a time duration of T_k. Thus the associated energy consumption $E_{l,k}$ can be written as

$$E_{l,k} = c_0 f_k^3 T = \frac{c_0 C_k^3 d_{l,k}^3}{T^2} \tag{2}$$

where c_0 is a coefficient depending on mobile device's CPU structure, which is assumed to be identical over all the mobile devices without loss of generality, and f_k is the computation capability of kth mobile device, which is usually measured by the number of CPU cycles it can process in unit time.

For mobile device k's computing at the base station, the whole available time duration T is divided into three parts. The first part is for data offloading from kth mobile device to the base station, which occupies a time duration of t_o. The second part is for data processing at the base station, which occupies a time duration of t_p. It should be noticed that the data offloading time t_o and data processing time t_p are identical for every mobile user. This setup is for the ease of coordinating among base station and multiple mobile devices. The third part is for data feedback from the base station to every mobile device. Since the amount of data of computational result is generally negligible, we omit the time consumption of this part. Thus there is

$$t_o + t_p = T \tag{3}$$

For data offloading, suppose the normalized channel gain from kth mobile device to the base station is h_k, which is the ratio between the real channel gain and noise spectrum density. h_k for $k \in \mathcal{K}$ are assumed to keep fixed within time T, which is reasonable in slow fading scenario. These K mobile devices access into the base station via FDMA. Denote the bandwidth allocated to the uplink of kth mobile device as w_k, and the system bandwidth as W_T. Then there is

$$\sum_{k=1}^{K} w_k \leq W_T. \tag{4}$$

It should be noticed that the channel gain h_k for $k \in \mathcal{K}$ keeps unchanged within the system bandwidth W_T, which is reasonable in flat-fading scenario. Define the kth mobile device's available energy for offloading data is $E_{o,k}$. Hence the transmit power can be expressed $p_k = \frac{E_{o,k}}{t_o}$. According to Shannon theory, the channel capacity of mobile device k's uplink can be written as

$$\begin{aligned} R_k &= w_k \ln\left(1 + \frac{p_k h_k}{w_k}\right) \\ &= w_k \ln\left(1 + \frac{E_{o,k} h_k}{w_k t_o}\right) \end{aligned} \tag{5}$$

Then the offloaded data $d_{o,k}$ satisfies the following formula

$$\begin{aligned} d_{o,k} &\leq R_k t_o \\ &= w_k t_o \ln\left(1 + \frac{E_{o,k} h_k}{w_k t_o}\right) \end{aligned} \tag{6}$$

For data processing at the base station, the total amount of data processing can be written as $\sum_{k=1}^{K} C_k d_{o,k}$. Suppose the computation capability of base station is f_E. To process offloaded data of all the K mobile devices within time t_p, the following constraint should be satisfied

$$\sum_{k=1}^{K} C_k d_{o,k} \leq t_p f_E. \tag{7}$$

In such a system, the system energy consumption of all the K mobile devices can be written as

$$\begin{aligned} &\sum_{k=1}^{K} (E_{o,k} + E_{l,k}) \\ &= \sum_{k=1}^{K} \left(E_{o,k} + \frac{c_0 C_k^3 d_{l,k}^3}{T^2}\right) \end{aligned} \tag{8}$$

Our target is minimize the total energy consumption via optimizing t_o, t_p, $E_{o,k}$, $d_{o,k}$, $d_{l,k}$ and w_k for $k \in \mathcal{K}$. By collecting the formulated constraints in (1), (3), (4), (6), (7), and imposing non-negative constraints on all the variables to be optimized, we need to solve the following optimization problem.

Problem 1.

$$\min_{\substack{t_o,t_p,\{w_k\},\{E_{o,k}\},\\ \{d_{o,k}\},\{d_{l,k}\}}} \sum_{k=1}^{K} \left(E_{o,k} + \frac{c_0 C_k^3 d_{l,k}^3}{T^2} \right)$$

$$s.t. \qquad \text{Constraints } (1), (3), (4), (6), (7),$$
$$t_o \geq 0, t_p \geq 0, \forall k \in \mathcal{K},$$
$$w_k \geq 0, \forall k \in \mathcal{K},$$
$$E_{o,k} \geq 0, \forall k \in \mathcal{K},$$
$$d_{o,k} \geq 0, d_{l,k} \geq 0, \forall k \in \mathcal{K}.$$

Substitute t_p with $(T - t_o)$ by following 3, and replace $d_{l,k}$ with $(D_k - d_{o,k})$ in Problem 1, we only need to solve the following optimization problem.

Problem 2.

$$\min_{t_o,\{w_k\},\{E_{o,k}\},\{d_{o,k}\}} \sum_{k=1}^{K} \left(E_{o,k} + \frac{c_0 C_k^3 (D_k - d_{o,k})^3}{T^2} \right)$$

$$s.t. \qquad \sum_{k=1}^{K} w_k \leq W_T, \tag{9a}$$

$$\sum_{k=1}^{K} C_k d_{o,k} \leq (T - t_o) f_E, \tag{9b}$$

$$d_{o,k} \leq w_k t_o \ln\left(1 + \frac{E_{o,k} h_k}{w_k t_o}\right), \forall k \in \mathcal{K} \tag{9c}$$

$$t_o \geq 0, \forall k \in \mathcal{K}, \tag{9d}$$

$$w_k \geq 0, \forall k \in \mathcal{K}, \tag{9e}$$

$$E_{o,k} \geq 0, \forall k \in \mathcal{K}, \tag{9f}$$

$$d_{o,k} \geq 0, \forall k \in \mathcal{K}. \tag{9g}$$

3   Solution

In this part, we turn to solve Problem 2. It can be checked that Problem 2 is non-convex since the function $w_k t_o \ln\left(1 + \frac{E_{o,k} h_k}{w_k t_o}\right)$ in (10c) are non-concave with w_k and t_o. Hence it is difficult to get the optimal solution of Problem 2. Next we turn to develop sub-optimal solution of Problem 2. In the first step, we decompose Problem 2 into two levels. In the lower level, the variable t_o is fixed, and the rest of variables of Problem 2 are optimized. Specifically, for the lower level, by fixing t_o, Problem 2 turns to be the following optimization problem

Problem 3.

$$F(t_o) \triangleq \min_{\{w_k\},\{E_{o,k}\},\{d_{o,k}\}} \sum_{k=1}^{K} \left(E_{o,k} + \frac{c_0 C_k^3 (D_k - d_{o,k})^3}{T^2} \right)$$

$$s.t. \qquad \sum_{k=1}^{K} w_k \leq W_T, \tag{10a}$$

$$\sum_{k=1}^{K} C_k d_{o,k} \leq (T - t_o) f_E, \tag{10b}$$

$$d_{o,k} \leq w_k t_o \ln \left(1 + \frac{E_{o,k} h_k}{w_k t_o}\right), \forall k \in \mathcal{K} \quad (10c)$$

$$t_o \geq 0, \forall k \in \mathcal{K}, \quad (10d)$$

$$w_k \geq 0, \forall k \in \mathcal{K}, \quad (10e)$$

$$E_{o,k} \geq 0, \forall k \in \mathcal{K}, \quad (10f)$$

$$d_{o,k} \geq 0, \forall k \in \mathcal{K}. \quad (10g)$$

In the upper level, the variable t_o is to be optimized to minimize the function $F(t_o)$, i.e., we need to solve the following optimization problem.

Problem 4.

$$\min_{t_o} F(t_o)$$
$$s.t. \ \ 0 \leq t_o \leq T$$

It can be checked that solving Problem 4 is equivalent with solving Problem 2. For Problem 3, there is such a lemma.

Lemma 1. *Problem 3 is a convex optimization problem.*

Proof. In Problem 3, it can be easily checked that the objective function of Problem 3 is convex with $E_{o,k}$ and $d_{o,k}$, it can be also checked that the function $w_k t_o \ln \left(1 + \frac{E_{o,k} h_k}{w_k t_o}\right)$ in (10c) is concave with w_k when t_o is fixed. Hence Problem 3 is a convex optimization problem [8].

This completes the proof.

Remark: Problem 3 is a convex optimization problem. Hence it can be solved by existing numerical methods optimally.

For Problem 4, the optimization of t_o is essentially a one-dimensional search problem. We adopt bisect search method to find the optimal solution. Local optimality can be guaranteed at least.

4   Conclusion

In this paper, a MEC system with one MEC server and multiple mobile devices under FDMA mode is investigated. The energy consumption of all the mobile devices is to be minimized by optimizing various computation and communication resources. The associated optimization problems are formulated, and found to non-convex. To solve the formulated optimization problem, we decompose the formulated problem to two levels, in which a convex optimization problem need to be solved in the lower level and a bisection search need to be run in the upper level. The proposed method offer an solution at least with local optimality for the formulated optimization problem. In the future, it is of importance and interesting to study the security issue [9,10], as each mobile device offload private data to the MEC server.

References

1. Barbarossa, S., Sardellitti, S., Lorenzo, P.D.: Communicating while computing: distributed mobile cloud computing over 5G heterogeneous networks. IEEE Signal Proc. Mag. **31**(6), 45–55 (2014)
2. Mao, Y., You, C., Zhang, J., Huang, K., Letaief, K.B.: A survey on mobile edge computing: the communication perspective. IEEE Commun. Surv. Tut. **19**(4), 2322–2358 (2017)
3. Milan, P., Jerome, J., Valerie, Y., Sadayuki, A.: Mobile-edge computing introductory technical white paper. White Paper (2014)
4. Wang, Y., Sheng, M., Wang, X., Wang, L., Li, J.: Mobile-edge computing: partial computation offloading using dynamic voltage scaling. IEEE Trans. Commun. **64**(12), 4268–4282 (2016)
5. You, C., Huang, K., Chae, H., Qi, H., Kim, B.: Energy-efficient resource allocation for mobile-edge computation offloading. IEEE Trans. Wirel. Commun. **16**(3), 1397–1411 (2017)
6. Tao, X., Ota, K., Dong, M., Qi, H., Li, K.: Performance guaranteed computation offloading for mobile-edge cloud computing. IEEE Wirel. Commun. Lett. **6**(6), 774–777 (2017)
7. Zhao, P., Tian, H., Qin, C., Nie, G.: Energy-saving offloading by jointly allocating radio and computational resources for mobile edge computing. IEEE Access **6**, 11255–11268 (2017)
8. Boyd, S.P., Vandenberghe, L.: Convex Optimization. Cambridge University Press, Cambridge (2004)
9. Tu, W., Lai, L.: Keyless authentication and authenticated capacity. IEEE Trans. Inf. Theory **64**(5), 3696–3714 (2016)
10. Tu, W., Goldenbaum, M., Lai, L., Poor, H.V.: On simultaneously generating multiple keys in a joint source-channel model. IEEE Trans. Inf. Forensics Secur. **12**(2), 298–308 (2017)

Dynamic Maximum Iteration Number Scheduling LDPC Decoder for Space-Based Internet of Things

Ruijia Yuan[1(✉)], Tianjiao Xie[1,2], and Yi Jin[1]

[1] China Academy of Space Technology (Xi'an), Xi'an, People's Republic of China
yuanyuanruijia@163.com
[2] School of Electronics and Information, Northwestern Polytechnical University, Xi'an, China

Abstract. For Space-based internet of things (S-IoT) application scenario, a Dynamic Maximum Iteration Number (DMI) scheduling decoder for LDPC codes is proposed. Distinct from traditional Static Maximum Iteration Number (SMI) scheduling LDPC decoder using fixed maximum iteration number, our DMI LDPC decoder has extra circuit to obtain the dynamic maximum iteration number, which could improves BER performance only at the expense of a slightly logic resources and a small ratio of memories, compared with conventional SMI scheme. Therefore, the DMI decoder is very suitable for the fluctuation of signal-to-noise ratio of S-IoT link.

Keywords: Space-based Internet of Things (S-IoT) · LDPC decoder · Iteration · FPGA

1 Introduction

The Internet of Things (IoT) [1] is a network application mode for machine-to-machine communication and interconnection. The space-based Internet of Things (S-IoT) [2] refers to the coverage of blind areas in remote areas, oceans and other terrestrial networks, and relies on satellite communication networks to achieve reliable communication transmission. The terminals of the S-IoT are widely distributed in land, sea, air, and sky. The propagation delays of various types of terminals to satellites are not only long but also jagged, resulting in different signal losses. Therefore, the specificity of the link is that the signal-to-noise ratio (SNR) fluctuates greatly. Aiming at this channel characteristic of S-IoT, this paper proposes a variable maximum iterations design for LDPC decoder. This method can implement dynamic data for each frame of data in the decoding process according to the actual channel characteristics. The maximum iterations is allocated for different SNR to improve the BER performance of the system.

© ICST Institute for Computer Sciences, Social Informatics and Telecommunications Engineering 2020
Published by Springer Nature Switzerland AG 2020. All Rights Reserved
B. Li et al. (Eds.): IoTaaS 2019, LNICST 316, pp. 235–241, 2020.
https://doi.org/10.1007/978-3-030-44751-9_20

In current decoders [4–8], the iterations of the next block do not start until a preset maximum iteration number is reached, which is called Static Maximum Iteration Number (SMI) scheduling decoder in this paper. However, in SMI, low BER frames of decoder input can be corrected after a small number of iterations, thus the process circuit is idle. Conversely, that of high BER frames cannot be corrected until SMI is reached, thus it is potentially harmful to the overall BER performance of decoder. If the idle time saved by low BER frames can be effectively used by those high BER frames, the BER performance should be improved. Traditionally, stopping criteria [4–8] is only used to save energy in iterative decoders. However, authors in [3] apply this method only for Turbo soft-input/soft-output decoders and additional three data buffers at the decoder input is analyzed to increase the average number of iterations.

In this paper, we consider making full use of processing capability of LDPC decoders. Thus, additional more data buffers are also involved to further increase the average number of iterations. Moreover, the implementation circuit of generating dynamic maximum iteration number is also presented in this paper. Our DMI scheduling LDPC decoder could improve the BER performance while it maintains nearly the same hardware resources as the existing SMI scheme.

2   Static Maximum Iteration Number (SMI) Scheduling Decoder for LDPC Codes

2.1   LDPC Decoding Algorithm

The typical LDPC decoding algorithm is Sum-Product Algorithm (SPA) [4], which provides a powerful method for decoding LDPC codes. However, it suffers from large complexity and is very sensitive to finite word length implementation [6]. The Min-Sum decoding Algorithm (MSA) [5] is similar to the SPA, just with an approximation of check node process. The most popular derived MSA used in hardware implementation is normalized MSA (NMSA) [5], in which at the i-th iteration the Check Node processing Units (CNU) compute the Check to Variable (C2V) messages $R_{mn}^{(i)}$ as follows:

$$R_{mn}^{(i)} = \alpha \prod_{n' \in N(m) \backslash n} sign\left(Q_{n'm}^{(i-1)}\right) \min_{n' \in N(m) \backslash n} |Q_{n'm}^{(i-1)}| \tag{1}$$

Where normalized factor α is introduced to compensate for the performance loss in the MSA compared to SPA. Q_{nm} is the Variable to Check (V2C) messages, $N(m)$ denotes the set of variable nodes connected to check node m. The exclusion of an element n from $N(m)$ is denoted by $N(m) \backslash n$.

At the i-th iteration, the Variable Node processing Units (VNU) compute $Q_{nm}^{(i)}$ and $Q_n^{(i)}$ as the following:

$$Q_{nm}^{(i)} = C_n + \sum_{m' \in M(n) \backslash m} R_{m'n}^{(i)} \tag{2}$$

$$Q_n^{(i)} = C_n + \sum_{m' \in M(n)} R_{m'n}^{(i)} \qquad (3)$$

Where Q_n represent the posterior message corresponding of variable node n. $M(n)$ denotes the set of check nodes connected to variable node n. The exclusion of an element m from $M(n)$ is denoted by $M(n)\backslash m$. C_n denotes the intrinsic (channel) message associated with variable node n.

$$C_n = log(P(x_n = 0|y_n)/P(x_n = 1|y_n)) \qquad (4)$$

Here both C2V and V2C messages are called extrinsic messages. Decoding can repeat iteratively until the check equations are satisfied or a preset maximum iteration number is reached.

2.2 Static Maximum Iteration Number (SMI) Scheduling LDPC Decoder

Before we present a new DMI scheduling LDPC decoder, timing and its corresponding definitions are first analyzed.

From the above description of LDPC decoding algorithm, it can be seen that the calculations for each iteration need the channel messages of the intact one frame. So the incoming data should be stored into a buffer until one frame data is completely reached. Then the iterative decoding process can be executed. In engineering, for real-time decoding, conventional iterative decoders usually employ two independent buffers at the input of decoder. The capacity of each buffer is set to one frame size. One buffer is filled with current frame coming from the demodulator and the other is used for the iterative decoding process for last frame. Afterwards the buffers tasks are switched. As a result this method effectively avoids the previous frame data being covered with the current frame data before it is completely processed.

Therefore maximum processing time T_{mp} of each frame should be no more than the incoming time of one frame. Here T_{mp} can be calculated as

$$T_{mp} = I_m \times C_I \qquad (5)$$

where I_m is maximum iteration number and C_I is the clock cycles per iteration.

Figure 1 illustrates the timing of existing SMI method for consecutive data of LDPC iterative decoder. It can be seen that T_{mp} (or I_m multiples C_I) of each frame is a constant, which approximates to the incoming time of one frame. So it is a Static Maximum Iteration number (SMI) strategy decoding, where both we_ramf1 and we_ramf2 are write-enable signals.

3   Proposed Dynamic Maximum Iteration Number (DMI) Scheduling LDPC Decoder

In the SMI method, I_m is a constant which is proportional to the time of storing one dataframe (Eq. (5)). Decoding can repeat iteratively I_m times until the entire

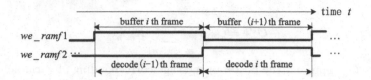

Fig. 1. The timing of SMI strategy decoding for consecutive data.

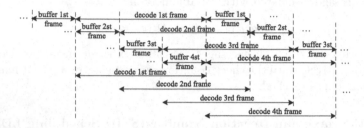

Fig. 2. The timing of DMI strategy decoding for consecutive data with F = 4 frames buffer.

codeword $\hat{x}$ (one frame) satisfy the parity check equations or the preset I_m is reached. However, some frames terminate the decoding after a small number of iterations, while other frame cannot be corrected either when I_m is reached. If the iterations frames saved idle time can be effectively used by those big iterations frames, the BER performance should be improved. By the observation, DMI strategy is proposed in this section.

In order to analyse how to use the saved idle time in DMI strategy, the timing of the DMI decoding with F = 4 frames buffers is demonstrated as an example in Fig. 2. Here the number of frames buffer F is an integer greater than 2. Because four buffers are utilized, each data frame can be retained in buffer for other three incoming frames time until a new data frame arrived. Therefore, the maximum iteration number prolongs three times more than the existing of buffering two frames case, i.e., maximum iteration number is increased up to $(F - 1) \times I_m$. Moreover, in the worst case, each frame can iterate minimum one frame incoming time, i.e., maximum iteration number is not less than I_m, which guarantees the BER performance of DMI not worse than that of SMI. This iterative time allocation method makes full use of idle time of that early termination frames to optimize the utilization of circuit resources. As a result maximum iteration number of DMI is dynamic, denoted I_{md}, which has a range from I_m to $(F - 1) \times I_m$, as shown in Fig. 2.

The main difference between SMI and DMI strategies are that the former has a predetermined constant I_m before the decoder is started, while for the latter its I_{md} of current frame should be calculated by the last previous frame. In fact, SMI specifies F = 2, which is a special case of DMI.

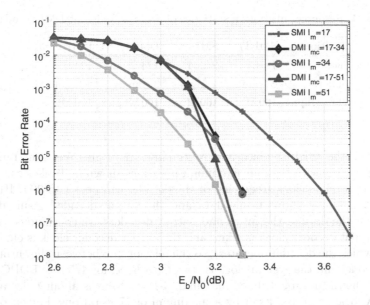

Fig. 3. BER curves of SMI and DMI for CCSDS 4/5 LDPC code

4   Simulation Results

In order to assess the performance of the above two scheduling decoding algorithms, SMI and DMI, LDPC codes in the CCSDS standard [9] was employed. AWGN channel is considered. In order to obtain a tradeoff between complexity and BER performance, the NMSA is used for check-node update. Normalization factor α is set to be 0.75.

The BER performance versus E_b/N_0 for the existing SMI and the new DMI are demonstrated in Fig. 3. It depicts the performance of SMI in solid lines with $I_m = 17$, 34 and 51, respectively. In order to make some comparisons with SMI, the DMI scheme with F = 3 and F = 4 frames buffer, corresponding $I_{md} =$ 17–34 and 17–51, respectively, are also illustrated in dashed lines in the same figure.

In Fig. 3, it can be seen that, At BER of 10^{-6}, our DMI with $I_{mc} = 17$–34 achieves the approximate BER performance as that of SMI with $I_m = 34$. The similar observations can be made that DMI with $I_{mc} = 17$–51 achieves the approximate BER performance as that of SMI with $I_m = 51$.

5   Implement Results

Based on the proposed architectures described in previous sections, we implement the CCSDS LDPC decoder. Q = 6 bits quantization scheme is adopted in our implementation. We choose the Xilinx Vertex5 xc5vlx330-1ff1760 device as the target FPGA.

Table 1. Resources utilization statistics of SMI and different DMI decoders

Iterations	SMI 17	SMI 34	DMI 17–34	DMI 17–51
Slices	12182	24364	12497	12497
Buffers	2 frames	4 frames	3 frames	4 frames
Throughput	160 Mbps	160 Mbps	160 Mbps	160 Mbps

Through the ISE10.1 place and route simulation, plus 5ns constraint, the decoder designed with the four maximum iterations shown in Table 1 can satisfy the constraint. The clock frequency of the decoder can be set to 200 MHz. The memory buffers the input frame data and the output decoded result data to ensure that the data of the input and output decoders are continuous. Assume that the input decoder clock is clkin, and the output decoder clock is clk (ie, the clock at which the decoder operates), so the relationship between the throughput of the decoder and the system clock is $clk \times CodeRate$, for 4/5 rate LDPC (5120, 4096), as shown in Table 1, fixed maximum 34 iterations is about twice as large as FPGA logic resources fixed by a maximum of 17 iterations, but encoded at a bit error rate of 10^{-6} The gain can be increased by 0.3 dB. It can be seen that for a fixed maximum number of iterations, FPGA resources can be used in exchange for high coding gain; iterative 17–34 times, iterations 17–51 times and fixed maximum 17 iterations account for the same FPGA logic resources. The throughput is the same, but the iteration is 17–34 times faster than the fixed maximum 17 iterations. When the bit error rate is 10^{-6}, the coding gain can be increased by 0.3 dB, which is equivalent to the fixed maximum 34 iterations, and the iteration is 17–51 times. The fixed maximum 17 iterations can increase the coding gain by 0.35 dB at a bit error rate of 10^{-6}, achieving a coding gain comparable to a fixed maximum of 51 iterations.

It can be seen that this section can save about half of the slice resources with the same coding gain and the same throughput than the fixed maximum iteration number of decoding schemes. In addition, for the buffer of input and output, BRAM is adopted in FPGA. In order to improve the utilization of BRAM resources, we use dual-port BRAM, which can buffer one frame with A and B ports of dual-port BRAM respectively. Therefore, buffering 3 frames and The number of BRAMs used to buffer 4 frames is the same, so iterative 17–51 times is more advantageous than FPGA iterations 17–34 times.

6   Conclusion

In this paper, to improve the code gain of LDPC decoder, we propose a DMI scheduling LDPC decoder architecture, which achieves better BER performance than the existing SMI decoder. Base on the proposed architecture, the FPGA implementation result shows the hardware resources of CCSDS decoder is a slightly more than that of SMI case. The proposed DMI scheduling LDPC decoding strategy is a promising candidate for space-based IoT link with big fluctuation of signal-to-noise ratio.

Acknowledgment. This research was supported by National Natural Science Foundation of China under Grant 61801377.

References

1. Feltrin, L., et al.: Narrowband IoT: a survey on downlink and uplink perspectives. IEEE Wireless Commun. **26**(1), 78–86 (2019)
2. Qian, Y., Ma, L., Liang, X.: Symmetry chirp spread spectrum modulation used in LEO satellite internet of things. IEEE Commun. Lett. **22**(11), 2230–2233 (2018)
3. Vogt, J., Finger, A.: Increasing throughput of iterative decoders. Electron. Lett. **37**(12), 770–771 (2001)
4. MacKay, D.J.C., Neal, R.M.: Near Shannon limit performance of low density parity check codes. Electron. Lett. **33**(6), 457–458 (1997)
5. Chen, J., Dholakia, A., Eleftheriou, E., Fossorier, M.P.C., Hu, X.Y.: Reduced-complexity decoding of LDPC codes. IEEE Trans. Commun. **53**, 1288–1299 (2005)
6. Wang, Z., Cui, Z., Jin, S.: VLSI design for low-density parity-check code decoding. IEEE Mag. Circuits Syst. **11**, 52–69 (2011)
7. Nguyen-Ly, T., Savin, V., Le, K., Declercq, D., Ghaffari, F., Boncalo, O.: Analysis and design of cost-effective, high-throughput LDPC decoders. IEEE Trans. VLSI Syst. **26**(3), 508–521 (2018)
8. Lu, Q., Fan, J., Sham, C.W., Tam, W.M., Lau, F.C.M.: A 3.0 Gb/s throughput hardware-efficient decoder for cyclically-coupled QC-LDPC codes. IEEE Trans. Circuits Syst. I, Reg. Papers **63**(1), 134–145 (2016)
9. CCSDS 131.1-O-2: Low density parity check codes for use in near-earth and deep space applications, September 2007

A Temperature Sensor System in the 4G-Based Internet of Things

Donglin Bai$^{(\boxtimes)}$ and Feng Jin

College of Information and Communication,
National University of Defense Technology, Xi'an 710106, China
baidonlin@126.com

Abstract. In order to manage real-time ambient temperature values at all times and places, this paper realizes a 4G-based temperature sensor system for the internet of things. Sensor platform gets the temperature values from wireless terminal nodes through the ZigBee coordinator, and upload it to the remote MySQL database server via 4G. In addition, an application is developed on mobile phone for users to obtain real-time temperature values, and a website for PC users is set up to realize the temperature values searching and displaying in real time.

Keywords: Temperature sensor · ZigBee · 4G · Internet of Things

1 Introduction

Since the concept of the Internet of Things (IoT) was first presented by Kevin Ashton, IoT has become one of the significant concepts that transform our surroundings more and more intelligent. During the past decades, we have witnessed IoT emerging into smart homes, healthcare system, transportation system, and other enterprises. This paper realizes a kind of temperature sensor system in IoT involving 4G telecommunications. Sensor platform gets the temperature values from wireless terminal nodes through the ZigBee coordinator, and upload it to the remote MySQL database server via 4G. In addition, an application is developed on mobile phone for users to obtain real-time temperature values, and a website for PC users is set up to realize the temperature values searching and displaying in time.

2 Description of the System

2.1 Framework

The system could be represented with four layers. Each neighboring layer interacts with each other, and they form a whole service system [1]. Figure 1 shows the framework of the system.

B. Li et al. (Eds.): IoTaaS 2019, LNICST 316, pp. 242–248, 2020.
https://doi.org/10.1007/978-3-030-44751-9_21

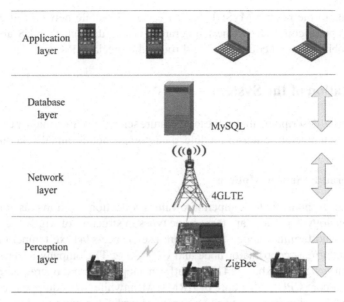

Fig. 1. Framework of the temperature sensor system

Perception Layer. ZigBee technology is used to transmit the temperature values adopted from the sensor nodes to ZigBee coordinator on this layer. ZigBee based on IEEE802.15.4 is a typical LAN protocol. It is also featured by its low-power consumption [2] and short distance of communication.

Network Layer. The data transmission between ZigBee coordinator and remote data storage units is realized by 4GLTE technology, which is widely applied by the communication operator in China. Featured by its IP routing technology, the upload rate reaches 50 Mbit/s, and the download rate is about 100 Mbit/s. The transmission demand of the system will be fully satisfied.

Database Layer. It is based on a remote MySQL database server, which is a small open-source database management system. It is widely used in small websites because of its high R/W speed and low cost. It is compatible with different operating system, such as Windows and Linux.

Application Layer. There are two types of terminal devices, personal computer and mobile terminal. Personal computer, which is based on B/S structure, obtains the temperature values from MySQL database. The mobile terminal uses the popular Android operating system and Java language to develop special temperature values gathering Android Package (APK) on the Eclipse development platform, which enables Android smart phones to obtain ambient temperature values at anytime and anyplace.

2.2 Work Flow

As shown in Fig. 1, the ZigBee nodes collect the environmental temperature values, and upload it to the ZigBee coordinator through the ZigBee network; the coordinator transmits data to the remote MySQL database via 4G mobile network; after that, the terminal computer could check the temperature values through the B/S architecture, while the mobile terminal could check it through the special APK.

3   Application of the System

According to the description above, the temperature sensor system is mainly composed of three modules: temperature sensor module, data storage module and displaying module.

3.1   Temperature Sensor Module

This module is responsible for temperature values collection and transmission based on ZigBee technology [3]. There are three node types in structure of ZigBee, coordinator, routing node and terminal node. This system uses zxbee-s4412xe temperature values gathering platform as coordinator node and CC2530 of TI Company as terminal node [4]. The main system of zxbee-s4412xe platform adopts Android operating system and provides quad-core CPU with a core of ARM9. Meanwhile, it is equipped with ZigBee wireless module, which can be used as ZigBee coordinator node to obtain data from terminal node through special APK. CC2530 is a new generation of ZigBee SOC chip, which supports IEEE802.15.4 standard [5]. DHT11 digital temperature and humidity sensor is inserted into CC2530, which is used to collect the temperature and humidity values and convert it into digital signal to transmit. The transmission distance is more than 20 m.

When network is being established, coordinators and terminal nodes use PAN_ID to identify whether they are in the same network, and the two types of nodes need to be set to the same value, otherwise the two nodes cannot communicate with each other normally.

Zxbee-s4412xe starts the special APK and searches for the node devices which have the same PAN_ID. After successful networking, the temperature and humidity value of the node could be checked. It is shown in Figs. 2 and 3.

In order to upload the values to the remote server database, network transmission function in the special APK is needed. In the original project, MyThread.java is added by the Eclipse development tools, and mysql-connector-java-5.0.88-bin.jar is added to the libs. Then asynchronous HTTP requests are executed and the MySQL database is connected by correct configuration of user name/password through the designated port of 3306.

3.2   Data Storage Module

This module is located on the remote computer server which is equipped with MySQL database. In the system construction, MySQL is built with XAMPP software. XAMPP software is a powerful integration software package, including Apache, MySQL, PHP, FileZilla, Tomcat, and so on. It can be installed under Windows, Linux and other operating systems. Navicat for MySQL software is used to operate the database. It provides a visual interface and convenient operating mode.

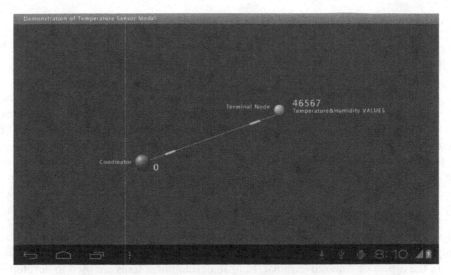

Fig. 2. Zxbee-s4412xe successfully connects to the DHT11 terminal node

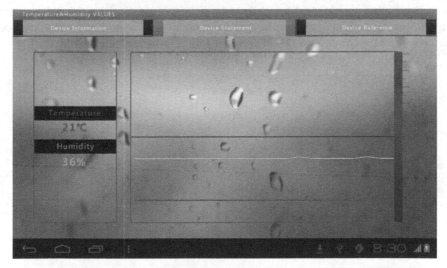

Fig. 3. Zxbee-s4412xe obtains the temperature values from DHT11 terminal node

A database (named as temptest) is created in MySQL, and two tables (named as temp and user) are created which are used to store temperature values and access user's authentication.

```
DROP TABLE IF EXISTS 'temp';
CREATE TABLE 'temp' (
'id' int(11) NOT NULL AUTO_INCREMENT,
'temp_l' float(10,2) NOT NULL DEFAULT '0.00',
```

'temp_h' float(10,2) NOT NULL DEFAULT '0.00',
'eq' varchar(50) NOT NULL,
PRIMARY KEY ('id')
) ENGINE=InnoDB AUTO_INCREMENT=10 DEFAULT CHARSET=utf8;

As the temp table shows, id represents the number of devices, temp_l means the minimum temperature, temp_h means the maximum temperature, and eq represents the device. When the coordinator has data updates, it updates the corresponding contents of the temp table in the temptest database. At the same time, MySQL is needed to be set up to allow external connection access, and the specified host is allowed to connect to the server's MySQL database via legal username/password.

3.3 Displaying Module

This module includes two parts: Android terminal and PC terminal, presenting the temperature values in different ways.

In the aspect of Android terminal, Eclipse development tools are used to develop a special APK, including data searching function for MySQL database. In the process of programming, network access is configured in Androidmanifest.xml, and the MySQL connection package is added to libs; while in the process of interface designing, Fragment is used to set the bottom of the interface with option buttons, so different operations are conducted on MySQL through different options. Figure 4 shows the details.

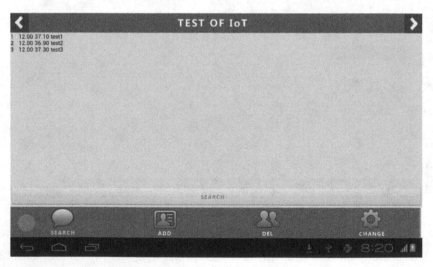

Fig. 4. Interface of the android terminal

In order to display on the PC terminal, a website is deployed on the database server. The system selects Apache to provide network access, and uses PHP language to develop the website. Other terminals (PC, mobile phones) can access the website through 4G network. As the following programming shows, data processing on the MySQL database could be performed.

```
$link_id=mysql_connect($DBHOST,$DBUSER,$DBPWD);
mysql_select_db($DBNAME);
$str="select * from temp ORDER BY id;";
$result=mysql_query($str, $link_id);
```

Figure 5 shows the interface of the website. The contents of temp table is able to be obtained from temptest database, and be sorted according to id. It presents the lowest temperature, the highest temperature and the collection device.

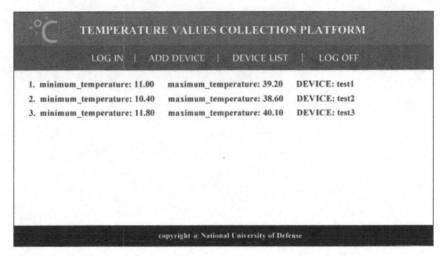

Fig. 5. The interface of the temperature values collection platform

4   Conclusion

For managing ambient temperature values at all times and places, this paper realizes a temperature sensor system involving IoT and 4G telecommunications. The system is composed of four layers. In particular, sensor platform gets the temperature values from ZigBee terminal nodes through the ZigBee coordinator, and upload it to the remote MySQL database server by 4G. In addition, an application is developed on mobile phone for users to obtain real-time temperature values, and a website for PC users is set up to realize the temperature values collecting and displaying in real time. This realization of system could be applied to other similar occasions such as environmental monitoring system or smart home system design.

References

1. Nord, J.H., Koohang, A., Paliszkiewicz, J.: The Internet of Things: review and theoretical framework. Expert Syst. Appl. **133**, 97–100 (2019)

2. Jian, L., Yupeng, L., Daqin, P.: Discussion on optimization of low power consumption protocol of communication terminal in mobile internet of things. Telecommun. Netw. Technol. **4**, 60–61 (2014)
3. Yixuan, J., Mingsheng, J.: Analysis of remote mobile monitoring system based on mobile internet of things. J. Mech. Electr. Eng. **5**, 727–728 (2015)
4. Xiaoli, N.: GAO Xiaolong: wireless temperature acquisition system based on CC2530. Comput. Knowl. Technol. **8**, 215–216 (2015)
5. Jingwei, C., Hao, H.: Wireless temperature acquisition system based on ARM and ZigBee. Electron. Sci. Technol. **4**, 12–13 (2013)

Compressive-Sensing Based Codec of the Y Color Component for Point Cloud

Weiwei Wang[1], Hui Yuan[2(✉)], Hao Liu[1], and Qi Liu[1]

[1] School of Information Science and Engineering,
Shandong University, Qingdao, Shandong, China
wangweiwei@mail.sdu.edu.cn, liuhaoxb@gmail.com, sdqi.liu@gmail.com
[2] School of Control Science and Engineering,
Shandong University, Jinan, Shandong, China
yuanhui0325@gmail.com

Abstract. The point cloud obtained by the 3D laser scanner contains a very large amount of data, in order to transmit the point cloud data as much as possible with the limited bandwidth, the effective compression of point cloud data has become a problem that needs to be solved urgently nowadays. In this paper, we use the compressive sensing theory to compress and reconstruct one of the point features, that is, the Y color component, served as the signal. We also use the K-SVD algorithm to explore the signal's sparsity according to its unique structural features, the K-SVD algorithm can learns a sparse basis matrix that is common to all point cloud models used in our experiments. For experimental results, we use rate-distortion metric. The results show that for each point cloud model, our method can achieve a higher probability to reconstruct the original data after compressed.

Keywords: Compressive sensing · K-SVD algorithm · Pointcloud

1 Introduction

In the field of computer vision, it has become more important to represent data in 3D. In recent years, point clouds have become popular to represent 3D data, as the scanners that can capture 3D data increasingly ubiquitous, 3D point clouds have widely been used in different kinds of fields in modern society, like robotics [1], autonomous driving [2], virtual/augmented reality [3], vehicular networking technology [4], internet of things [5] etc. A point cloud is a collection of points that can describe the surface of an object which can obtained by the 3D scanners, and can represented as a set of 3D points $\{p_i | i = 1, ... n\}$, where each point contains a position vector (x, y, z), and its features such as color (R, G, B), surface normal, etc. However, with the development of the scanners, point cloud can be created at very high rates which allow for efficient and compact storage as well as transfer of this data, compression of point cloud has therefore

© ICST Institute for Computer Sciences, Social Informatics and Telecommunications Engineering 2020
Published by Springer Nature Switzerland AG 2020. All Rights Reserved
B. Li et al. (Eds.): IoTaaS 2019, LNICST 316, pp. 249–258, 2020.
https://doi.org/10.1007/978-3-030-44751-9_22

been Chinese and foreign academia hot research field, which is the key driving force in the fields of immersive communication and automatic driving.

The compression of point cloud can be started from two aspects: geometry and texture. At first, the compression of geometry information gained the most concerned. Among them, the octree decomposition method [6] has been used extensively because of its efficiency and low-complexity. Given a point cloud P, we can get a cube based on its geometric information that is able to surround the entire point cloud model, then, an octree O is constructed with a maximum number of level L and the points in P are sorted into the cells of the octree. We can divide the cube by the mean value from the three directions of x, y, z, each subdivision produces eight child cells. If the current cell is occupied or does not meet the maximum number of level that we already set, it continues to be divided. At the process of encode, the existent child cells are specified in a single byte per cell subdivision, i.e. each bit specifies the occupancy of a child cell. This is the most basic principle for encoding geometric information of the point cloud with an octree.

In recent years, with the development of 3D video panorama and other technologies, for better visual effects, and recently the color feature of the point cloud received an increasing amount of attention in particular. However, for data represented in point cloud form, which is irregular, the compression of the color also faces enormous challenges. Instead of compressing the irregular data directly, [7–9] map the irregular data into regular data for convenient data processing. Mekuria et al. [7] traversed each point's color with a depth first order from the octree and then used the zig-zag scan to map them to a 8×8 blocks of a 2D grid. After that, they compressed the grids with JPEG by using the correlations between the colors. Almost the same idea with Mekuria, Tu et al. [8] map the point cloud into range images and then compressed them with either JPEG or MPEG-4. Cui et al. [9] compressed the 2D grids data by selecting two redefined models. And in this paper, we compressed one of the color attributes by exploiting compressive sensing theory.

In 2006, the theory of compressive sensing (CS) proposed by Candès and Donoho [10–13] pointed out that for signals that are sparse themselves or sparse under a certain transform basis, they can be observed by non-linear down-sampling. And then the low-dimensional observations can be used by the measurement matrix which satisfy the Restricted Isometry Property (RIP) with transform basis to perform a high probability reconstruction of the original signal. Different from the traditional Nyquist sampling theorem, the compressive sensing theory combines the sparse characteristics of the signal, and uses the measurement matrix to observe the signal, so that the sampling process of the signal does not depend on the bandwidth of the signal, but the content and structure of the signal. Therefore, the theory of compressive sensing opens a new path for the compressing and coding theories of signals. In the past decade, the CS algorithm has made great progress, especially the development of its reconstruction algorithm [14–16]. Wang et al. [17] applied this theory to the deep network of image reconstruction, which not only achieves good reconstruction effect, but also reduces the computational complexity. In order to avoid unauthorized access to multimedia content, Athira *et al.* [18] even added this theory to Encryption technology. In the automobile sensor system, radar sensors are often used to image in order to provide better visual aids for drivers. A new radar signal processing technology based on compressive sensing theory is proposed by Baselice *et al.* [19] which can image two or more targets in the same line of sight. The performance of radar DAS (DAS: Driver Assistance Systems) is greatly improved. It can be seen that the theory is widely used in various fields.

In this paper, we use compressive sensing theory to compress and reconstruct one of each point's color component, that is, Y color component. In the early data preprocessing stage, we will use the geometric information to spatially decompose the point cloud with octree firstly, after that we can obtain the Y color component values for each point in the same cell. The Y color component values are then applied as a signal in our compressive sensing theory. Simultaneously, we use the K-SVD algorithm to learn a sparse basis that can be universally used by these five models: Longdress_vox10_1300, Loot_vox10_1200, Queen_0200, Redand-black_vox10_1550 and Soldier_vox10_0690, these five models we used in the experiments are all from the new test models presented at the MPEG 125th conference.

The following contents are organized as follows: in the second part we will introduce how to use the geometric spatial characteristics and the local similarity characteristics of the point cloud to obtain the training data; the third part, as the acquired training data has some similarities, we propose to use the K-SVD algorithm to train a dictionary to obtain the sparse basis of signals; in the fourth part, we will give the experimental results and have a brief explanation; in the fifth part, we concludes the paper and provides pointers to future directions.

2   Acquisition of Training Data

Generally speaking, the points collected by the 3D laser scan are out of order, if we want to use the compressive sensing theory to have a good compression and reconstruction effect on the point cloud data, the higher the similarity of the point's Y color component value, the better, this will provide important guarantees for our subsequent dictionary learning method to obtain a good sparse basis, so we need to do some preprocessing on the point cloud data. In this paper, we use a signal matrix to train the sparse basis matrix $\mathbf{D}$ with each column of the signal matrix to be one signal. In the experiment, we take the Y color component of each point in the same cell as a signal. To ensure that the dimensions of each signal can be the same, we first decompose each point cloud model with an octree. The octree decomposition process only uses the geometric information of the point cloud model: given a point cloud model, a cuboid can be constructed according to the maximum and minimum values of its coordinate information, which can then be divided from the mean of the three coordinate axes, with each cell be divided into eight childcells. We finally want to extract the Y color component of the points in the same cell as our signal, and also try to ensure that the number of points in each cell can be the same, that is, the dimensions of our signals are the same. In experimenting we set the dimension of a signal to 512. For each cell subdivision, the number of points in each cell can be known and only cells with more than 512 points are further subdivided. However, this does not absolutely guarantee that the number of points contained in each cell is the same as 512.

Through the above octree decomposition, we can know which cell each point is located. After simple processing, we can get an index matrix. The value in each column of this matrix represents the index value of the point in the same cell. The number of columns of the index matrix is the number of cells in which the point cloud is divided by the octree. (Index value: each point cloud model is a $N \times 6$ matrix $\mathbf{I} = \{i_0, ..., i_{N-1}\}$ after reading with Matlab, regardless of the normal vector, N represents the total number of points in the model, with i_n $(n = 0, ..., N - 1)$ represents the geometric and color information of a point. n is what we said the index value). After the index matrix is obtained, to make a better use of the similarity between signals, we slice the points in the same cell, and perform a raster scan for each point on the slice. The slice operation changes only the order of the index value in the index matrix $\mathbf{I}$. Then we extract the Y color component of each point according to the index matrix and subsequently get the signal matrix $\mathbf{S}$. What needs to be mentioned is that each value in the signal matrix is de-averaged. For signals with less than 512 values, zero-padding operations is performed in the vacant place. The disadvantages of this is that it is equivalent to an increase in the amount of data, and the coding efficiency will be very low.

In our experiment, the signal matrix is obtained from five point cloud models by the method of obtaining training data proposed above. The signal matrix is then used as our training data in the K-SVD algorithm. Among the five models, the training data of the Longdress_vox10_1300 model has a dimension of 512×4777, the Loot_vox10_1200 model is 512×3824, the Queen_0200 model is 512×6131, the Redandblack_vox10_1550 model is 512×3784, and the Soldier_vox10_0690 model is 512×7385, so the dimension of the large training data $\mathbf{S}$ composed of these five models is 512×25901. The purpose of using the five point cloud models to form a large training data is to learn a dictionary $\mathbf{D}$ that is common to the five point cloud models. Under the dictionary $\mathbf{D}$, each point cloud model can have a good sparse representation.

3   Over-Complete Dictionary Training of Point Cloud Based on K-SVD Algorithm

In the existing sparse representation theory, there are usually two methods used to create a sparse representation dictionary: (1) Based on mathematical models. E.g. Fast Fourier Transform (FFT), Discrete Cosine Transform (DCT) [20], Wavelet Transform [21,22] etc. (2) Training dictionary for training sets with distinct characteristics.

For signals that do not have the properties of digital image signals, they do not necessarily have good sparsity in the DCT transform domain, so if the

DCT domain transform is still performed, the sparse coefficients obtained cannot guarantee the sparsity. In the preliminary stage of the experiment, we used the DCT transform basis for the signal, but the effect was not satisfactory. In order to get the sparsity of the more general signals, we later modified it to obtain the sparse basis matrix of the signal through the dictionary learning method. The dictionary learning learns a matrix, which is equivalent to the transformation matrix in the DCT transform, and is often called over-complete dictionary, its number of rows is much smaller than the number of columns, which is generally represented by $\mathbf{D}$. In the signal encoding and decoding algorithm based on compressive sensing, constructing a good dictionary is a very important part. The quality of the dictionary directly affects the quality of the final reconstruction effect.

The commonly used dictionary learning algorithms are K-SVD [23] and K-Means [24]. The K-SVD algorithm obtains the over-complete dictionary that is most suitable for the training set through continuous training update. Since it is adaptively obtained through training update, the signals can be decomposed according to its excellent structural features in the over-complete dictionary for better exploration of the signal's sparsity.

3.1 K-SVD Algorithm

In the K-SVD algorithm, $\mathbf{Y} = \mathbf{DX}$, with $\mathbf{Y}$ is the sample signal matrix, $\mathbf{D}$ is the dictionary, $\mathbf{X}$ is the sparse coefficient matrix, the goal of the algorithm is to train a dictionary $\mathbf{D}$ so that the product of the dictionary $\mathbf{D}$ and the sparse coefficient matrix $\mathbf{X}$ can be as close as possible to the matrix $\mathbf{Y}$, while each column of the sparse coefficient matrix $\mathbf{X}$ is as sparse as possible. In our experiment, the sample signal matrix $\mathbf{Y}$ is our training set $\mathbf{S}$ which we obtained above. During training, according to the suggestions in [23], for atoms that are used less frequently and have similarities, we replaced them with normalized vectors in the sample signal matrix that maximizes the error. In this experiment, the training set $\mathbf{S}$ is composed of five point cloud models, Longdress_vox10_1300, Loot_vox10_1200, Queen_0200, Redandblack_vox10_1550, Soldier_vox10_0690, and the learned dictionary can be universally used by this five models, then, each model is compressed through the compressive sensing methods by using the common dictionary $\mathbf{D}$ as there sparse basis.

3.2 Compressive Sensing Theory

As we stated earlier, the theory of compressive sensing (CS) proposed by Candès and Donoho [10–13] pointed out that for signals that are sparse themselves or sparse under a certain transform basis, almost exact reconstruction of the signal can be achieved by unknown observations. The focuses of this theory are measurement matrix, sparse basis matrix and the reconstruction algorithm. The measurement matrix acts as a down-sampling, reducing the original high-dimensional data to a low-dimensional, reducing the amount of data, which in turn can be encoded with fewer bits-streams. There are two requirements for the measure matrix: it can play the role of down-sampling; and together with the sparse basis matrix satisfies the Restricted Isometry Property (RIP). Therefore, the dimension of the measurement matrix must ensure that the number of rows is less than the number of columns. In our experiments, the measurement matrix $\Phi \in R^{m \times n}$, $m = a \times n$, obviously, a is the sample rate. We set the values of the two sample rates to 0.7, 0.8 and 0.5 respectively for comparison experiments, n is 512. The measurement matrix can be divided into deterministic measurement matrix and random measurement matrix. The common deterministic measurement matrix has partial orthogonal matrix, polynomial deterministic matrix, Toeplitz matrix, partial Fourier matrix, etc. and the commonly used random measurement matrix is Gaussian random measure matrix. In this experiment, a more common Gaussian random measurement matrix is adopted. Since the generation of the matrix is random, in order to ensure that the same measurement matrix can be used under different quantization steps, we first generate a $m * n$-dimensional Gaussian random measurement matrix. The measurement matrix is saved and then loaded directly into each run.

The discrete point cloud data are almost non-sparse in numerical representation, so it is impossible to directly observe and reconstruct point cloud data. Therefore, we need to find the sparse representation of point cloud data under a certain transformation basis. The so-called sparse representation of a signal means that the signal can be linearly represented by a small number of basis vectors in its space, and the basic idea of sparse representation theory based on an over-complete dictionary can be considered in a condition of reconstructing the original signal as much as possible to replace the traditional orthogonal basis by an over-complete basis. The number of rows of the over-complete dictionary is much smaller than the number of columns. The K-SVD algorithm gradually trains the redundant dictionary that is most suitable for the training set through iterative operations. That is, we can get the sparse basis of point cloud data through the K-SVD algorithm described above.

After compressing and encoding the point cloud data by the compressive sensing method in the encoder, we need to use the reconstruction algorithm at the decoder to recover the original data as much as possible. In recent years, many reconstruction algorithms have appeared in the field of compressive sensing. Among many reconstruction algorithms, the orthogonal matching pursuit (OMP) algorithm is widely used in the field of sparse representation because of its simple and easy to use. The input of this algorithm is a one-dimensional signal, that is to say, the one-dimensional signal OMP algorithm can perform sparse representation better. In this experiment, although the input is the sample signal matrix, each column of the matrix is a signal, so we adopt this reconstruction method.

4   Experiment Result

A brief review of the entire experiment process: Five point cloud models, after acquiring the training data, combine the training data of the five models to obtain a large training data, and then use the K-SVD algorithm to train a common sparse basis for the five models and finally applied to each point cloud model by compressive sensing. The models used in the experiment is the new test models given by MPEG 125th conference: Longdress_vox10_1300 with 857966 points, Loot_vox10_1200 with 805285 points, Queen_0200 with 1000993 points, Redandblack_vox10_1550 with 757691 points, Soldier_vox10_0690 with 1089091 points. In the case of compressive sensing, different sample rates and quantization steps were applied to compare experiments. The specific experimental data and RD curves are as Fig. 1:

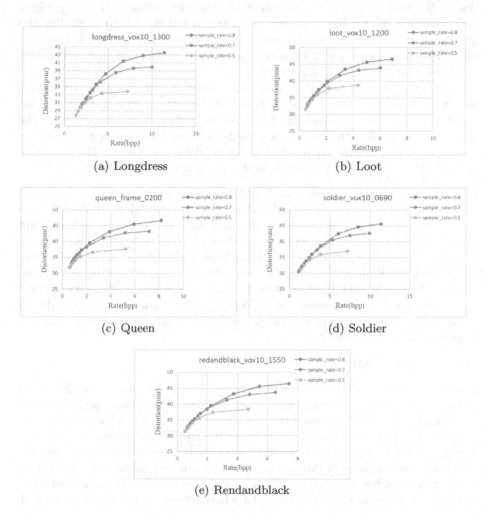

(a) Longdress   (b) Loot

(c) Queen   (d) Soldier

(e) Rendandblack

Fig. 1. Rate and distortion curves of these five models after encoding and decoding of the compressive sensing

From the experimental results, we can see that in the case of high code rate, the reconstruction effect is better. The higher the sample rate, the better the reconstruction effect.

5   Conclusion and Prospect

The rapid development of 3D scanning technology makes it possible to efficiently obtain massive point cloud data to represent real-world objects, but usually the amount of point cloud data is very large, so compressed encoding and reconstruction of 3D point cloud has become one of the research hotspots. How to perform high-efficiency compressed encoding and reconstruction without degrading the quality of the point cloud model has been a problem that the field is trying to solve. The compressive sensing theory proposed by Candès *et al.* in 2006 provides a new way for compression algorithms.

After studying the theory of compressive sensing and sparse representation theory, this paper analyzed and processed the scattered and disordered point cloud data in space, studied its sparse representation method, and used the octree to fully exploit the information inside its data. The models were spatially decomposed and finally obtained point cloud data suitable for the theory of compressive sensing. The work done in this paper can be summarized as follows:

1. Using the octree to achieve the spatial decomposition of the point cloud, and slicing the points in each cell, which improves the numerical similarity of the Y-color components of the 3D point cloud data and provides an important guarantee for sparse representation of three-dimensional point clouds.
2. Using the five models of Longdress_vox10_1300, Loot_vox10_1200, Queen_0200, Redandblack_vox10_1550, Soldier_vox10_0690 in the test models given by the MPEG 125th conference, an over-complete dictionary of these five models is trained using the K-SVD algorithm, and by using the dictionary in compressive sensing, both five point cloud models can achieve higher probability reconstruction.

The next research work mainly includes:

1. Research how to divide the point cloud surface into k-nearest neighbors. In this paper, we use the octree method to decompose the point cloud, and can't guarantee the points in each cell has the same number, and we increase the amount of data artificially for the cells with insufficient points.
2. For the K-SVD algorithm to train the over-complete dictionary part, research whether an adaptive optimization algorithm can be used to judge if the iteration has reached convergence. In this paper, we just set the number of iterations to a fixed value and did not judge whether convergence has been reached.

Acknowledgement. This work was supported in part by the National Natural Science Foundation of China under Grants 61871342; in part by the National Key R&D Program of China under Grants 2018YFC0831003; in part by the Shandong Natural Science Funds for Distinguished Young Scholar under Grant JQ201614; in part by the Shandong Provincial Key Research and Development Plan under Grant 2017CXGC1504; in part by the open project program of state key laboratory of virtual reality technology and systems, Beihang University, under Grant VRLAB2019B03; and in part by the Young Scholars Program of Shandong University (YSPSDU) under Grant 2015WLJH39.

References

1. Garrote, L., Rosa, J., Paulo, J., et al.: 3D point cloud downsampling for 2D indoor scene modelling in mobile robotics. In: IEEE International Conference on Autonomous Robot Systems & Competitions. IEEE (2017)
2. Mousavian, A., Anguelov, D., Flynn, J., et al.: 3D bounding box estimation using deep learning and geometry (2016)
3. Mekuria, R., Blom, K., Cesar, P.: Design, implementation and evaluation of a point cloud codec for tele-immersive video. IEEE Trans. Circuits Syst. Video Technol. **27**, 828–842 (2016)
4. Du, Y., ShangGuan, W., Chai, L.: Particle filter based object tracking of 3D sparse point clouds for autopilot. In: 2018 Chinese Automation Congress (CAC), Xi'an, China, pp. 1102–1107 (2018)
5. Wang, H., et al.: The research of chemical plant monitoring base on the internet of things and 3D visualization technology. In: 2013 IEEE International Conference on Information and Automation (ICIA), Yinchuan, pp. 860–864 (2013)
6. Schnabel, R., Klein, R.: Octree-based point-cloud compression. In: Eurographics. Eurographics Association (2006)
7. Mekuria, R., Blom, K., Cesar, P.: Design, implementation, and evaluation of a point cloud codec for tele-immersive video. IEEE Trans. Circuits Syst. Video Technol. **27**(4), 828–842 (2017)
8. Tu, C., Takeuchi, E., Miyajima, C., Takeda, K.: Compressing continuous point cloud data using image compression methods. In: Proceedings of the IEEE Intelligent Transportation Systems (ITSC), Rio de Janeiro, pp. 1712–1719 (2016)
9. Cui, L., Xu, H., Jang, E.S.: Hybrid color attribute compression for point cloud data. In: Proceedings of the IEEE International Conference on Multimedia and Expo (ICME), Hong Kong, pp. 1273–1278 (2017)
10. Candès, E.J., Romberg, J., Tao, T.: Robust uncertainty principles: exact signal reconstruction from highly incomplete frequency information. IEEE Trans. Inf. Theory **52**(2), 489–509 (2006)
11. Donoho, D.: Compressed sensing. IEEE Trans. Inf. Theory **52**(4), 1289–1306 (2006)
12. Candès, E.: Compressive sampling. In: International Congress of Mathematics, Madrid, Spain, pp. 1433–1452 (2006)
13. Baraniuk, R.: Compressive sensing. IEEE Signal Process. Mag. **24**(4), 118–121 (2007)
14. Metzler, C.A., Maleki, A., Baraniuk, R.G.: From denoising to compressed sensing. IEEE Trans. Inf. Theory **62**(9), 5117–5144 (2014)
15. Elad, M., Aharon, M.: Image denoising via sparse and redundant representations over learned dictionaries. IEEE Trans. Image Process. **15**(12), 3736–3745 (2006)
16. Ma, L., Bai, H., Zhang, M., Zhao, Y.: Edge-based adaptive sampling for image block compressive sensing. IEICE Trans. Fundam. Electron. Commun. Comput. Sci. **99–A**(11), 2095–2098 (2016)

17. Wang, Y., Bai, H., Zhao, Y.: Image reconstruction from patch compressive sensing measurements. In: 2018 IEEE Fourth International Conference on Multimedia Big Data (BigMM). IEEE Computer Society (2018)
18. Athira, V., George, S.N., Deepthi, P.P.: A novel encryption method based on compressive sensing. In: International Multi-conference on Automation. IEEE (2013)
19. Baselice, F., Ferraioli, G., Matuozzo, G., et al.: Compressive sensing for in depth focusing in 3D automotive imaging radar. In: 2015 3rd International Workshop on Compressed Sensing Theory and Its Applications to Radar, Sonar and Remote Sensing (CoSeRa). IEEE (2015)
20. Bai, H., Wang, A., Zhang, M.: Compressive sensing for DCT image. In: International Conference on Computational Aspects of Social Networks. IEEE (2010)
21. Wang, D.W.D., Zhang, L.Z.L., Vincent, A., et al.: Curved wavelet transform for image coding. IEEE Trans. Image Process. **15**(8), 2413–2421 (2006)
22. Cheng, G.Q., Cheng, L.Z.: A new image compression via adaptive wavelet transform. In: International Conference on Wavelet Analysis & Pattern Recognition. IEEE (2007)
23. Aharon, M., Elad, M., Bruckstein, A.: K-SVD: an algorithm for designing overcomplete dictionaries for sparse representation. IEEE Trans. Signal Process. **54**(11), 4311–4322 (2006)
24. Sahoo, S.K., Makur, A.: Dictionary training for sparse representation as generalization of K-means clustering. IEEE Signal Process. Lett. **20**(6), 587–590 (2013)

Wireless Automated Networking for Internet of Things

Channel Exploration and Exploitation with Imperfect Spectrum Sensing for Multiple Users

Zuohong Xu[1], Zhou Zhang[2(✉)], Ye Yan[2], and Shilian Wang[1]

[1] National University of Defense Technology, Changsha, China
[2] Tianjin Artificial Intelligence Innovation Center (TAIIC), Tianjin, China
zt.sy1986@163.com

Abstract. In this paper, the fundamental problem of multiple secondary users (SUs) contending for opportunistic spectrum sensing and access over multiple channels in cognitive radio networks is investigated, when sensing is imperfect and each SU can access up to a limited number of channels at a time. For each channel, the busy/idle state is independent from one slot to another. The availability information of channels is unknown and has to be estimated by SUs during channel sensing and access process. Learning loss, also referred as regret, is thus inevitable. To minimize the loss, we model the channel sensing and access process as a multi-armed bandit problem, and contribute to proposing policies for spectrum sensing and access among multiple SUs under both centralized and distributed framework. Through theoretical analysis, our proposed policies are proved with logarithmic regret asymptotically and in finite time, and their effectiveness is verified by simulations.

Keywords: Multi-user channel sensing and access · Distributed multi-armed bandit problem · Logarithmic regret

1 Introduction

As new wireless devices and applications have been rapidly deployed, the past decade has witnessed a growing demand for wireless radio spectrum resources [1]. However, the traditional static spectrum allocation policy has been reported that most of the licensed spectrum is severely under-utilized [2]. In this regard, the concept of cognitive radio (CR) is proposed and has received great attention to alleviate the spectrum shortage problem due to its great capacity for spectrum exploitation [3,4]. In a CR network, all users are categorized as primary users (PUs) and secondary users (SUs), where PUs have the licence and strict priority to use the channel in frequency and SUs have to explore and exploit channels in an opportunistic manner. In particular, when a SU detects that a PU is occupying a given channel, it releases the channel and switches to another. If no channel is available, a SU waits until a channel is available.

© ICST Institute for Computer Sciences, Social Informatics and Telecommunications Engineering 2020
Published by Springer Nature Switzerland AG 2020. All Rights Reserved
B. Li et al. (Eds.): IoTaaS 2019, LNICST 316, pp. 261–277, 2020.
https://doi.org/10.1007/978-3-030-44751-9_23

However, in a practical network environment, the information of primary channels is usually unknown to SUs, and thus channels have to be fully explored by SUs to learn the information. At the same time, the prior observations could be exploited to gain potential rewards by accessing the sensed idle channels. The requirement for on-line learning this information results in hardness for balancing a fundamental trade-off between channel exploration and exploitation. To measure the trade-off performance, the loss due to on-line learning until time t, also represented by the regret $R(t)$, is defined as the expected difference between the reward of a genie-aided rule with known statistical information of the channels and the actual reward of a specific channel access policy. To well balance the trade-off, the problem of single SU performing opportunistic spectrum access (OSA) has been studied, and formulated as a multi-armed bandit problem (MABP). Extended from those efforts, MABP with multiple players is used to formulate the OSA problem for multiple SUs [5–7]. In such a problem, multiple SUs contend for primary channels access. To minimize the regret and equivalently maximize the average system throughput, design of on-line learning policy is much desired enabling SUs to estimate the channel information and access without collisions.

Several existing studies are seminal for studying our work. Under a centralized framework, the research in [8] proposes a stochastic game framework modelling time-varying process of competition evolution for spectrum opportunities among SUs. In each stage, there is a central spectrum moderator that auctions the available resources for SUs, and a best-response learning algorithm that improves SUs bidding policy is proposed. However, the centralized framework could not be used in cognitive networks when multiple SUs operate autonomously. Motivated by that, under a distributed framework, works in [9–11] have developed algorithms under scenarios of multiple SUs and channels with perfect spectrum sensing. Specifically, in [9] Anandkumar proposes a randomized distributed policy that utilizes the collision feedback under a slotted CR network. It is proved that under any uniformly-good learning and access policy, the proposed policy can achieve order-optimal regret. The total regret is logarithmic with slot time. Liu and Zhao [10] present a time-division fair share (TDFS) policy which yields asymptotically logarithmic regret with respect to slot time. In addition, an index-type policy with coordination mechanism is proposed in [11] which achieves regret of $O(\ln t)$ uniformly over time t. To summarize, all these existing works introduce the distributed framework under perfect sensing, and each SU can sense and access only one channel.

Moreover, some studies take imperfect spectrum sensing into accounts. In works [12, 13], a scenario with imperfect sensing and channel access limitations has been investigated. Specifically, author in work [13] models the channel sensing and access process as a bi-level MAB problem, upon which several sensing and access policies are proposed with logarithmic regret asymptotically and in finite time. Additionally, [7] deals with the OSA problem for infrastructure-less CR networks, where multiple SUs collect a priori reward by sensing and accessing one channel at one time. Therein, a policy called QoS-UCB is proposed with at most logarithmic order regret.

Different from existing works, this paper considers the scenario with multiple SUs where each user can sense multiple channels and access only limited channels under imperfect sensing, which has not yet been investigated. To the best of our knowledge, this work is the first research which considers the scenario with several features in a whole view: (i) there are multiple SUs contending for the channels with imperfect channel sensing, if more than one SU access the same channel, collision occurs and no data is successfully transmitted; (ii) each SU senses up to a limited number of channels at one time, and accesses a portion of the sensed channels[1]; (iii) SUs have no knowledge on channel availability and other SUs activities, and no exchange information is assumed among SUs.

The rest of this paper is organized as follows. System model and problem formulation are described in Sect. 2. In Sect. 3, a centralized learning and access policy for multiple SUs is proposed, and in Sect. 4 a distributed learning and access policy for multiple SUs is proposed. Theoretical analysis is made in both sections. Numerical results are then illustrated verifying the performance of our proposed policies.

2   System Model and Problem Formulation

Consider a time slotted system as used in [9,13], where time is partitioned into slots, denoted by T. Let U be the number of SUs and $N \geq U$ be the number of orthogonal licensed channels for PUs. In each channel, e.g. channel i and slot j, PUs are active with probability $1 - \theta_i$, where θ_i represents idle probability. We assume idle probability satisfies $\theta_1 > \theta_2 > ... > \theta_N$, and unknown by SUs. In this work, we define $\mathcal{M}^*$ as a set of channels $\{1, 2, ..., U \cdot M\}$. Time varying channel model is considered, and for channel i, $S_i(j) = 1$ and $S_i(j) = 0$ means the channel idle and busy at slot j, respectively. The state of each channel varies independently from a slot to another. For channel access of a slot, a reward can be obtained by a SU, which is defined as the information bits successfully transmitted in a slot. For simple expression, a reward in each slot is normalized.

In such a system, SUs access the shared spectrum in an opportunistic manner. We briefly introduce the sense and access process as follows. In a time slot, each SU selectively senses M ($M < N$) channels and subsequently access up to K ($K \leq M$) sensed idle channels. Denote sensing results of N channels by SU u in slot j as $\mathbf{X}_u(j) = (X_{u,1}(j), X_{u,2}(j), ..., X_{u,N}(j))$, where $X_i(j) = 1$ and $X_i(j) = 0$ indicate that channel i has been sensed idle and busy at slot j, respectively. Taking sensing errors into accounts, we denote P_d as the detection probability of channel i (i.e., the probability of detecting the PU active if there is PU activity), and P_f as the false-alarm probability of channel i (i.e., the probability of mistakenly estimating that the PU is active when there is no PU activity). For channel i at slot j, the probability that sensed idle is expressed as

---

[1] In a wireless CR sensor network, sensors usually have the capacity to sense more than one channel at one time; and in view of hardware constraints or limited power supply for wireless devices [16], the number of channels that can be sensed and accessed in each time slot is typically limited.

$f(\theta_i) = (1 - P_f)\theta_i + (1 - P_d)(1 - \theta_i)$. Furthermore, if channel i is sensed idle and accessed at slot j, the conditional reward is obtained from channel access, calculated as $\mathbb{E}[S_i(j)|X_i(j) = 1] = \frac{(1-P_f)\theta_i}{f(\theta_i)}$. $\mathbb{E}[\cdot]$ denotes expectation. In every slot, SU updates observed information for N channels. In particular, for SU u, the information of sensed time is denoted by $\mathbf{T}_u(t) = (T_{u,1}(t), T_{u,2}(t), ..., T_{u,N}(t))$, and reward information is denoted by $\mathbf{Y}_u(t) = (Y_{u,1}(t), Y_{u,2}(t), ..., Y_{u,N}(t))$. More specifically, $T_{u,i}(t)$ represents the number of slots in which channel i has been sensed until slot t by SU u, within it $Y_{u,i}(t)$ represents the number of slots in which channel i has been sensed idle.

As multiple SUs operate in a CR system, collisions happen when more than one SU accesses the same channel simultaneously, resulting in zero reward. For multi-user access model, both centralized and distributed OSA frameworks are investigated. An illustration of sense and access policy under a centralized framework and a distributed framework are shown in Fig. 1. In particular, under a centralized CR framework, at the beginning of slot t, each SU, e.g. SU u selects M channels for sensing, and obtains the sensing results $\mathbf{X}_u(t) = (X_{u,1}(t), X_{u,2}(t), ..., X_{u,N}(t))$. Then SUs report the results to a central agent, which updates the information of $\mathbf{T}_u(t)$ and $\mathbf{Y}_u(t)$. Subsequently, some sensed-idle channels are scheduled by the agent to SUs for channel access. On the other hand, under a distributed learning framework, a central agent does not exist. Each SU records the information $\mathbf{T}_u(t)$ and $\mathbf{Y}_u(t)$, and accesses the sensed idle channels in an autonomous manner. At the end of each slot, each SU receives an acknowledgement (ACK) feedback.

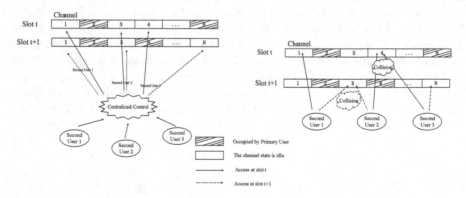

Fig. 1. An illustration of sensing and accessing policies under centralized and distributed frameworks.

Notation: For any two functions $f(n), g(n)$, $f(n) = O(g(n))$ if there exits a constant c such that $f(n) \leq c \cdot g(n)$ for all $n \geq n_0$ for a fixed $n_0 \in \mathbb{N}$, where $\mathbb{N}$ represents natural number set. Moreover, $|\cdot|$ represents the cardinality of a set.

3 Centralized Sensing and Access for Multiple SUs

In this section, we consider the scenario that multiple SUs perform joint channel sensing and access under the control of a central agent. As a fundamental metric to measure the learning policy performance, an optimal channel sensing and access policy under the ideal case where the channel information is known by the central agent, is worthwhile. In reference to the work [15], it is found that the channel set $\mathcal{M}^*$ is the optimal channel set to be sensed in each slot, which maximizes the expected system throughput. We call this sense and access policy a genie-aided rule, and regard the expected reward of this policy as the benchmark. The maximal expected reward is expressed as

$$U^*(t) = \sum_{j=1}^{t} \mathbb{E}\left[\max_{\mathcal{K}(j) \subset \mathcal{I}_{\mathcal{M}^*}(j), |\mathcal{K}(j)| \le K} \sum_{i \in \mathcal{K}(j)} \mathbb{E}\left[S_i(j) | X_i(j) = 1\right] \right], \qquad (1)$$

where $\mathcal{I}_{\mathcal{M}^*}(j)$ denotes the set of sensed idle channels under the set $\mathcal{M}^*$ at slot j, $\mathcal{K}(j)$ denotes the set of channels accessed in slot j. The inner expectation is to calculate the conditional reward of channel i while the outer expectation is for the set $\mathcal{K}(j)$.

3.1 Single Channel Access at a Slot (K = 1)

First, we consider that each SU can simultaneously sense M channels and access only one channel. Under this scenario, we propose a policy, denoted by ρ^{CENT} presented in Algorithm 1. Let ϕ denote the sensing and access policy for all U SUs, and $\phi(j)$ denote the set of channels accessed by SUs at slot j. Compared with the genie-aided rule, the regret of our proposed policy is expressed as

$$R(t, \phi) = U^*(t) - \mathbb{E}\left[\sum_{j=1}^{t} \sum_{i=1}^{N} \mathbb{E}\left[S_i(j) | X_i(j) = 1\right] \cdot \mathbb{I}\left[i \in \phi(j)\right] \right], \qquad (2)$$

where $\mathbb{I}[\cdot]$ is the indicator function, and when channel i is accessed at slot j, $\mathbb{I}[i \in \phi(j)]$ equals to 1.

Now we analyse the performance of Algorithm 1 in terms of the regret, and prove that the regret is upper-bounded logarithmically over time. Observing that the learning loss occurs when SUs do not choose the optimal channels to access, the regret comprises two components. One is from the case where a SU chooses non-optimal channels to sense and accesses the sensed idle channels. The other is from the case where a SU senses the optimal channels but not accesses the optimal sensed idle channels. By theoretical analysis, the first component is proved having an upper bound logarithmic in time as shown in Lemma 1, and the second component is also similarly bounded as shown in Lemma 2.

Algorithm 1. Single Channel Access under Centralized Learning Framework

1: For time slot $l = 1 : \lceil \frac{N}{UM} \rceil$, SU $u = 1, 2, ..., U$ senses M channels $\{(u-1)M + 1 + (l-1)UM : uM + (l-1)uM \mod N\}$, respectively. All SUs report the sensing result $\mathbf{X}_u(l)$, $u = 1, 2, ..., U$ to the central agent.

2: The central agent updates $\mathbf{T}_u$ and $\mathbf{Y}_u$, $u = 1, 2, ..., U$, and then randomly selects up to K sensed idle channels for SUs to access.

3: **for** each time t **do**

4:     The central agent estimates θ_i, $(i = 1, 2, ..., N)$ by $\hat{\theta}_i(t) = \frac{\frac{Y_i(t-1)}{T_i(t-1)} + P_d - 1}{P_d - P_f}$, sorts channels in descending order according to indexes $\hat{\theta}_i(t) + \frac{1}{P_d - P_f}\sqrt{\frac{2\ln(t-1)}{T_i(t-1)}}$, and chooses $M \cdot U$ channels of largest indexes, denoted by $\mathcal{M}(t)$.

5:     The central agent schedules SU u to sense channels set $\{(u-1)M + 1 + (l-1)UM : uM + (l-1)uM\}$, and then the SU reports the sensing result to the central agent.

6:     The central agent selects the set of sensed idle channels $\mathcal{I}(t)$, and updates $\mathbf{T}_u(t)$ and $\mathbf{Y}_u(t)$.

7:     **if** $|\mathcal{I}(t)| \geq K$ **then**

8:         it chooses K largest channels in $\mathcal{I}(t)$, and allocates them for SUs to access.

9:     **else if** $0 < |\mathcal{I}(t)| < K$ **then**

10:         it allocates channels for SUs $u = 1, 2, ..., |\mathcal{I}(t)|$ to access.

11:     **end if**

12: **end for**

Lemma 1. *For Algorithm 1, the expected number of slots where any channel $i \notin \mathcal{M}^*$ is sensed by SUs until time t has an upper bound derived as*

$$\mathbb{E}[T_i(t)] \leq \frac{8\ln t}{(\theta_{UM} - \theta_i)^2(P_d - P_f)^2} + 1 + \frac{MU\pi^2}{3}, \tag{3}$$

where $T_i(t)$ represents the number of slots that channel i has been sensed.

Proof. Recall that idle probability satisfies $\theta_1 > \theta_2 > ... > \theta_N$, for any channel $i \notin \mathcal{M}^*$, we have

$$T_i(t) = 1 + \sum_{j=\lceil \frac{N}{UM}\rceil + 1}^{t} \mathbb{I}[i \notin \mathcal{M}^*]. \tag{4}$$

Similar to the Appendix D in the work [13], it can conclude that

$$T_i(t) \leq l +$$
$$\sum_{k=1}^{UM}\sum_{j=1}^{t}\sum_{t_1=1}^{j}\sum_{t_2=l}^{j} \mathbb{I}\left[\hat{\theta}_k(t_1) + \frac{1}{P_d - P_f}\sqrt{\frac{2\ln j}{t_1}} \leq \hat{\theta}_i(t_2) + \frac{1}{P_d - P_f}\sqrt{\frac{2\ln j}{t_2}}\right]. \tag{5}$$

By doing expectation for both sides of (5) and using Chernoff-Hoeffding bound, we obtain that

$$\mathbb{E}[T_i(t)] \leq \frac{8\ln t}{(\theta_{UM} - \theta_i)^2(P_d - P_f)^2} + 1 + \frac{MU\pi^2}{3}. \tag{6}$$

From above, we can see that the expected number of slots that the channels sensed not within the set $\mathcal{M}^*$ grows as $O(\ln t)$ with finite t and $t \to \infty$.

We denote $T'(t)$ as the number of slots where optimal set is sensed but wrong channel is accessed. In the following, we present Lemma 2 which provides an upper bound for the expectation $\mathbb{E}[T'(t)]$.

Lemma 2. *For Algorithm 1, the expectation of $T'(t)$ is bounded by*

$$\mathbb{E}\left[T'(t)\right] \le \sum_{i=1}^{UM-1} \sum_{k=i+1}^{UM} \left[\frac{8 \ln t}{(\theta_i - \theta_k)^2 (P_d - P_f)^2} + 1 + \frac{\pi^2}{3} \right]. \tag{7}$$

Proof. By definition of $T'(t)$, a slot where optimal set is sensed but wrong channel is accessed happens when optimal channel set is sensed, i.e. $\mathcal{M}(j) = \mathcal{M}^*$, but central agent has a wrong top UM-order of the indexes $\hat{\theta}_i(j) + \frac{1}{P_d - P_f} \sqrt{\frac{2 \ln(j-1)}{T_i(j-1)}}$. Under such circumstance, the estimated order of indexes $\hat{\theta}_i(t) + \frac{1}{P_d - P_f} \sqrt{\frac{2 \ln(t-1)}{T_i(t-1)}}$ for the first $U \cdot M$ channels is not correct. Therefore, it suffices to analyse the bound for the event where any two channels, e.g. channel i and channel k with $i < k, i, k \in \mathcal{M}^*$ are estimated in wrong order.

Recall that $\theta_i > \theta_k$. The event happens when $\hat{\theta}_i(t) + \frac{1}{P_d - P_f} \sqrt{\frac{2 \ln(t-1)}{T_i(t-1)}} < \hat{\theta}_k(t) + \frac{1}{P_d - P_f} \sqrt{\frac{2 \ln(t-1)}{T_k(t-1)}}$. Similar to the proof in Theorem 1, the result is derived.

In accordance with two lemmas above, two components contributing to the regret are with upper bound logarithmic over time. And apparently we can conclude the regret bound in the following theorem.

Theorem 1. *The regret $R(t)$ of Algorithm ρ^{CENT} satisfies $O(\ln t)$.*

Proof. For the centralized scenario, regret has a bound by the sum of two components as shown below.

$$R(t) \le \Delta \sum_{i=UM+1}^{N} \mathbb{E}\left[T_i(t)\right] + \Delta \mathbb{E}\left[T'(t)\right], \tag{8}$$

where $\Delta \triangleq \mathbb{E}\left[\max_{i \in \mathcal{M}^*} \frac{\theta_i(1-P_f)}{f(\theta_i)} X_i(j) \right]$ is the bound for expected reward loss in each slot.

In particular, $\sum_{i=UM+1}^{N} \mathbb{E}\left[T_i(t)\right]$ represents the number of slots where SUs do not choose the optimal channels to sense while $\mathbb{E}\left[T'(t)\right]$ represents the number of slots that SUs sense the optimal channels but access non-optimal sensed idle channels. Combining results from (3) and (7), the regret satisfies the following inequality

$$R(t) \leq \triangle \ln t \sum_{i=UM+1}^{N} \frac{8}{(\theta_{UM} - \theta_i)^2 (P_d - P_f)^2}$$

$$+ \triangle \ln t \sum_{i}^{UM-1} \sum_{k=i+1}^{UM} \frac{8}{(\theta_i - \theta_k)^2 (P_d - P_f)^2} \tag{9}$$

$$+ \triangle (N - UM) \left(\frac{UM\pi^2}{3} + 1 \right) + \triangle \binom{UM}{2} \left(\frac{\pi^2}{3} + 1 \right).$$

By definition of $O(\ln t)$ in the notation above, the conclusion is derived.

3.2 Multiple Channel Access at a Slot ($K > 1$)

Then we consider the case where SUs simultaneously access multiple channels at a slot. After SUs report the sensing result to central agent, the central agent schedules the sensed idle channels. If the number of sensed idle channels is less than $U \cdot K$, all sensed idle channels will be allocated to SUs; otherwise, $U \cdot K$ channels with best expected reward are selected for SUs. Under this case, the expected reward of the genie-aided rule can be calculated in (1), while the regret is derived in (2). To design a policy, Line 7 to Line 11 of Algorithm 1 should be modified as follows: if $|\mathcal{I}(t)| \geq U \cdot K$, within set $\mathcal{I}(t)$ central agent schedules $U \cdot K$ channels with best expected reward for SUs to access; otherwise, central agent allocates all channels in $\mathcal{I}(t)$ to SUs. In an extreme case where all channels are sensed busy, no channel is accessed. In this scenario, the regret $R(t)$ of Algorithm ρ^{CENT} satisfies $O(\ln t)$, and the proof process is similar to Theorem 1.

4 Distributed Sensing and Access for Multiple SUs

Different from centralized framework, in this section, we consider a distributed framework where no information exchange or prior agreement is assumed among multiple SUs. Two challenges are thus faced. On one hand, sensing results cannot be shared by SUs, resulting in a slow convergence of estimation process in respect to channel information. On the other hand, multiple SUs accessing the same channel in one slot causes transmission collisions, resulting in additional throughput loss. To overcome these challenges, a distributed sensing and access policy with minimal regret is desired.

As follow, we propose a distributed policy by which each SU selects the channel set for sensing in a randomized manner, driven by collision feedback after channel access. In particular, different from the centralized case, SUs randomly choose one channel set for sensing, then choose sensed idle channels for access in a slot. At the end of this slot, SUs will receive a collision feedback indicating whether collisions happen. Only those SUs who receive collision feedback will randomize the channel set for sensing and access in the next slot. For simplicity, we name the proposed distributed policy $\rho^{\text{RANDOMIZE}}$.

4.1   Single Channel Access ($K = 1$)

First, we consider the genie-aided policy for optimal channel sensing and access when channel information is known by SUs. Before introducing our policies, it is necessary to analyse the benchmark, i.e., the optimal expected reward of genie-aided rule. Different from the benchmark of centralized cases, SUs make decisions based on their own sensing observations. The expected reward of distributed genie-aided rule can be given as

$$
U^*(t) = \sum_{j=1}^{t} \max_{\mathcal{M}_u(j), u=1,\dots,U} \sum_{u=1}^{U}
$$

$$
\mathbb{E}\left[\max_{\mathcal{K}_u(j) \subset \mathcal{I}_{\mathcal{M}_u(j)}, |\mathcal{K}_u(j)| \le K} \sum_{i \in \mathcal{K}_u(j)} \mathbb{E}\left[S_i(j) | X_i(j) = 1 \right] \right],
\tag{10}
$$

where $\mathcal{M}_u(j)$ denotes the set of channels sensed by SU u at slot j, $\mathcal{I}_{\mathcal{M}_u(j)}$ denotes the set of sensed idle channels in $\mathcal{M}_u(j)$ at SU u in slot j, $\mathcal{K}_u(j)$ denotes the channel set that SU u accesses in slot j.

Then, we consider how to get the best reward by genie-aided rule in the following lemma.

Lemma 3. *When SUs sense the channel set* $\{\mathcal{M}_u^*\}_{u=1,2\dots,U}$, *where* $\mathcal{M}_u^* = \{u, M(U - u) + (u + 1), \dots, M(U - u) + (u + M - 1)\}$, *and access the sensed idle channel of the smallest index, the maximal reward* $U^*(t)$ *is achieved.*

Proof. Recall that $K = 1$, the expected reward in (10) can be rewritten as

$$
U^*(t) = \sum_{j=1}^{t} \max_{u=1,\dots,U} \sum_{u=1}^{U} W_M\left(\theta_{u,1}, \theta_{u,2}, \dots, \theta_{u,M}\right) \cdot (1 - P_f),
\tag{11}
$$

where $W_n(x_1, \cdots, x_n) = x_1 + (1 - f(x_1)) x_2 + \cdots + \prod_{i=1}^{n-1} (1 - f(x_i)) x_n$. It can be proved that the function $W_n(x_1, x_2, \cdots, x_n)$ is an increasing function of variables $(x_1, x_2, \cdots, x_n)$.

To maximize the expected reward $U^*(t)$, the problem is transformed into how to allocate $U \cdot M$ channels to each SU. Assume that channel 1 is allocated to SU 1, Eq. (11) is written as

$$
U^*(t)/t = \theta_1 + \max_{u=1,\dots,U}
$$

$$
\left((1 - f(\theta_1)) W_{M-1}(\theta_{1,2}, \cdots, \theta_{1,M}) + \sum_{u=2}^{U} W_M(\theta_{u,1}, \cdots, \theta_{u,M}) \right).
\tag{12}
$$

Subsequently, we further consider how to allocate remaining channels to SU 1 and other SUs. Notably, any $i \geq 2$, we have $1 - f(\theta_1) < 1 - f(\theta_2) < 1$. Thus, $U^*(t)/t$ will become larger if optimal channels are allocated to other SUs. In particular, if the channel is allocated to SU 1, the reward $W_{M-1}(\theta_{1,2}, ..., \theta_{1,M})$ will be discounted by a coefficient $1 - f(\theta_1)$, which contributes less to $U^*(t)$). Therefore, it is optimal to allocate channels $\{M(U-1)+2, \cdots, UM\}$ (i.e., those channels with smallest availability probability in $\mathcal{M}^*$) to SU 1 and the other channels $\{2, 3, \cdots, M(U-1)+1\}$ to other SUs. By analogy, the optimal allocation rule for all SUs is derived, under which for each SU u, the optimal sensing channel set should be $\{u, M(U-u)+(u+1), \cdots, M(U-u)+(u+M-1)\}$. Here concludes the proof.

In accordance with Lemma 3, the expected reward of genie-aided rule is calculated as

$$U^*(t) = t \cdot \sum_{u=1}^{U} W_M \left(\theta_u, \theta_{(U-u)M+(u+1)}, \cdots, \theta_{(U-u)M+(u+M-1)}\right) \cdot (1 - P_f), \quad (13)$$

and the regret is derived as

$$R(t, \{\phi_u\}_{u=1,2,\cdots,U}) = U^*(t) -$$

$$\mathbb{E}\left[\sum_{j=1}^{t}\sum_{u=1}^{U}\sum_{i=1}^{N}\mathbb{E}[S_i(j)|X_i(j)=1]\mathbb{I}[\phi_u(j)=i]\prod_{v=1,v\neq u}^{U}\mathbb{I}[\phi_v(j)\neq\phi_u(j)]\right], \quad (14)$$

where $\{\phi_u\}$ represents the access policy and $\phi_u(j)$ represents the channels accessed in slot j at SU u. The term $\mathbb{I}[\phi_v(j) \neq \phi_u(j)]$ means that if there are multiple SUs choosing the same channel, collision happens and no reward is received.

In the following, to minimize the regret, we present our proposed policy in Algorithm 2 and analyse its regret bound. Note that there are multiple SUs contending for channels, collisions exist resulting in regret increase. Through analysis, the regret consists of two parts: one comes from the case where SUs do not sense or access non-optimal sensed idle channels, and the other comes from multi-user collisions.

For the first part contributing to the regret, it contains two situations, denoted by situation 1 and situation 2, respectively. In situation 1, SU u senses or accesses channels not within $\mathcal{M}^*$, while in situation 2, the channels sensed or accessed by SU u within $\mathcal{M}^*$ but not within $\mathcal{M}_u^*$. The reason for situation 2 existing is that SU u has a wrong estimation of optimal channel order, and thus SU is likely to choose wrong channels to sense and access.

Considering situation 1, the expected number of slots $T_{u,i}(t)$ where a SU u senses and accesses non-optimal channel i is derived in Lemma 4.

Lemma 4. *For Algorithm 2, the expected number of slots where any channel $i \notin \mathcal{M}^*$ is sensed by SU u until time t has an upper bound*

$$\mathbb{E}\left[T_{u,i}(t)\right] \leq \frac{8\ln t}{(\theta_{UM} - \theta_i)^2(P_d - P_f)^2} + 1 + \frac{M\pi^2}{3}. \quad (15)$$

Proof. The proof of inequality (15) is similar to that of Lemma 1.

Algorithm 2. Distributed Learning with Randomization by SU u

1: Set $Flag = 0$. SU u senses all N channels using $\lceil \frac{N}{M} \rceil$ slots. At each slot, it selects "a sensed idle channel to access, and then update $\mathbf{T}_u$ and $\mathbf{Y}_u$.

2: **for** at slot t **do**

3:     SU u estimates θ_i, $(i = 1, 2, ..., N)$ by $\hat{\theta}_{u,i}(t) = \frac{\frac{Y_{u,i}(t-1)}{T_{u,i}(t-1)} + P_d - 1}{P_d - P_f}$, and then sorts channels in a descending order by indexes $\hat{\theta}_{u,i} + \frac{1}{P_d - P_f} \sqrt{\frac{2 \ln(t-1)}{T_{u,i}(t-1)}}$. The order is recorded as $\mathcal{N}'_u$.

4:     **if** $Flag = 1$ **then**

5:         $Sel_u(t) \Leftarrow Unif(1, 2, ..., U)$.

6:     **else**

7:         $Sel_u(t) \Leftarrow Sel_u(t - 1)$.

8:     **end if**

9:     SU u calculates index of sensing channels set as $\mathcal{A}_u(t) = \{Sel_u(t), M(U - Sel_u(t)) + (Sel_u(t) + 1), \cdots, M(U - Sel_u(t)) + (Sel_u(t) + M - 1)\}$

10:     Update channel sensing set by $\mathcal{M}_u(t) \Leftarrow \mathcal{N}'_u(\mathcal{A}_u(t))$. $Flag \Leftarrow 0$.

11:     Update $\mathbf{T}_u(t)$ and $\mathbf{Y}_u(t)$, and obtains the set of sensed idle channels $\mathcal{I}_u(t)$.

12:     **if** $\mathcal{I}_u(t)$ is non-empty **then**

13:         SU u accesses channel i with largest $\hat{\theta}_{u,i} + \frac{1}{P_d - P_f} \sqrt{\frac{2 \ln(t-1)}{T_{u,i}(t-1)}}$, and waiting for ACK feedback.

14:         **if** SU u receives the ACK **then**

15:             $Flag \Leftarrow 0$.

16:         **else**

17:             $Flag \Leftarrow 1$.

18:         **end if**

19:     **else**

20:         Do not access any channel at slot t.

21:     **end if**

22: **end for**

In reference to Lemma 4, we can derive the bound for the expected time of situation 1 by taking the slots that all SUs sense and access non-optimal channels into consideration. Then, we analyse the expected number of slots for situation 2. Denote $T'_u(t)$ as the expected number of slots where SU u has a wrong estimation of optimal channel order until time t, and the conclusion is derived in Lemma 5.

Lemma 5. *For Algorithm 2, the expected number of slots where a SU u does not estimate the correct order of optimal channels until t has an upper bound*

$$\mathbb{E}\left[T'_u(t)\right] \leq \sum_{i=1}^{UM-1} \sum_{k=i+1}^{UM} \left[\frac{8 \ln t}{(\theta_i - \theta_k)^2 (P_d - P_f)^2} + 1 + \frac{\pi^2}{3}\right]. \tag{16}$$

Proof. The proof of inequality (16) is similar to that of Lemma 2.

In Lemma 5, we derive the bound for the expected number of slots where SU u has a wrong estimation of optimal channel order. Notably, when situation

1 exists, there must be a wrong estimation of optimal channel order at SU u. Therefore, we can derive an upper bound for the expected time of situation 2 by summing up $\mathbb{E}[T'_u(t)]$ at all SUs.

Subsequently, we analyse the second part contributing to regret, which comes from multi-user collisions. Define $M(t)$ as the number of collisions faced by SUs in optimal channels until time t. The bound for the expectation of $M(t)$ is given in the following lemma.

Lemma 6. *For Algorithm 2, the expectation of $M(t)$ is bounded by*

$$
\begin{aligned}
\mathbb{E}[M(t)] &\leq \sum_{u=1}^{U} \mathbb{E}[T'_u(t)] \cdot \binom{2U-1}{U} \\
&\leq U \cdot \sum_{i=1}^{UM-1} \sum_{k=i+1}^{UM} \left[\frac{8\ln t}{(\theta_i - \theta_k)^2 (P_d - P_f)^2} + 1 + \frac{\pi^2}{3} \right] \cdot \binom{2U-1}{U}.
\end{aligned}
\tag{17}
$$

Proof. Define *good events* as the events that all SUs have correct order of top $U \cdot M$ channels, while other events are defined as *bad events*. Each event consists of a consecutive time slots. Denote b as the number of *bad events* until t. $B(k)$, $k = 1, 2, ..., b$ represents the *good event* and $B^c(k)$, $k = 1, 2, ..., b$ represents the *bad event* between two adjacent *good events*. Denote $M(B(k))$ and $M(B^c(k))$ as the collision number during the event $B(k)$ and $B^c(k)$, respectively. In each slot, if there are multiple SUs accessing the same channel, collision number will increase 1.

Subsequently, we analyse collision number $M(t)$ until t. In each slot, either a *good event* or a *bad event* happens, so $M(t)$ contains two parts, one is the collisions under *good event*, which can be expressed as $\sum_{k=1}^{b} M(B(k))$, the other one is the collisions under *bad event*, which can be expressed as $\sum_{k=1}^{b} M(B^c(k))$. Therefore, $M(t)$ is written as

$$
M(t) = \sum_{k=1}^{b} M(B(k)) + \sum_{k=1}^{b} M(B^c(k)).
\tag{18}
$$

In a *good event*, collision number is bounded by

$$
\sum_{k=1}^{b} \mathbb{E}[M(B(k))] \overset{(a)}{\leq} \sum_{u=1}^{U} \mathbb{E}[T'_u(t)] \cdot \left(\binom{2U-1}{U} - 1 \right).
\tag{19}
$$

where inequality (a) comes from the Theorem 3 in work [9], $\binom{2U-1}{U} - 1$ represents the probability of having an orthogonal configuration over optimal channels by all SUs in a slot under the perfect knowledge of channel information.

In a *bad event*, by definition of $T'_u(t)$, we have the following inequality

$$
\sum_{k=1}^{b} \mathbb{E}[M(B^c(k))] \leq \sum_{u=1}^{U} \mathbb{E}[T'_u(t)].
\tag{20}
$$

Concluded from (18) to (20), the expectation of $M(t)$ is bounded by

$$
\begin{aligned}
\mathbb{E}[M(t)] &= \sum_{k=1}^{b} \mathbb{E}[M(B(k))] + \sum_{k=1}^{b} \mathbb{E}[M(B^c(k))] \\
&\leq \sum_{u=1}^{U} \mathbb{E}[T_u'(t)] \cdot \binom{2U-1}{U}.
\end{aligned}
\tag{21}
$$

In reference to (16) and (21), (17) is concluded.

In accordance with Lemmas 4, 5 and 6, we derive the regret bound in the following theorem.

Theorem 2. *The regret $R(t, \{\phi_u\}_{u=1,2,...,U})$ of Algorithm 2 satisfies $O(\ln t)$.*

Proof. Recall that the regret consists of two parts: one comes from the case where SUs do not sense or access non-optimal sensed idle channels, and the other comes from multi-user collisions. The regret resulting from the first case can be concluded from Lemmas 4 and 5, while the regret resulting from the second case can be concluded from Lemma 6. Therefore, the regret is bounded as

$$
\begin{aligned}
&R(t, \{\phi_u\}) \\
&\leq \eta \cdot \left(\sum_{u=1}^{U} \sum_{i \notin \mathcal{M}^*} \mathbb{E}[T_{u,i}(t)] + U \cdot K \cdot \sum_{u=1}^{U} \mathbb{E}[T_u'(t)] \right) + \eta \cdot U \cdot K \cdot \mathbb{E}[M(t)] \\
&\leq \eta \cdot \left(\sum_{u=1}^{U} \sum_{i \notin \mathcal{M}^*} \left[\frac{8 \ln t}{(\theta_{UM} - \theta_i)^2 (P_d - P_f)^2} + 1 + \frac{M\pi^2}{3} \right] \right. \\
&\quad \left. + U^2 \cdot K \cdot \sum_{i=1}^{UM-1} \sum_{k=i+1}^{UM} \left[\frac{8 \ln t}{(\theta_i - \theta_k)^2 (P_d - P_f)^2} + 1 + \frac{\pi^2}{3} \right] \cdot \left(\binom{2U-1}{U} + 1 \right) \right).
\end{aligned}
$$

where $\eta = \max\limits_{u=1,\cdots,U} \mathbb{E}\left[\max\limits_{i \in \mathcal{M}_u^*} \frac{\theta_i (1-P_f)}{f(\theta_i)} X_i(j) \right]$. The term $\sum\limits_{u=1}^{U} \sum\limits_{i \notin \mathcal{M}^*} \mathbb{E}[T_{u,i}(t)]$ represents the number of time slots that all SUs sense or access channels not belonging to $\mathcal{M}^*$, while the term $U \cdot K \cdot \sum\limits_{u=1}^{U} \mathbb{E}[T_u'(t)]$ represents the maximal number that channel order is incorrectly estimated and thus incorrectly accessed by all SUs. $U \cdot K \cdot \mathbb{E}[M(t)]$ describes the worst case that all SUs access the same K channels in a slot, under which all SUs have no reward.

From the expression of $R(t, \{\phi_u\})$, by definition of $O(\ln t)$, the conclusion is derived.

4.2 Multiple Channel Access ($K > 1$)

Then we consider the case where SUs simultaneously sense and access multiple channels at a slot. For each SU, if the number of sensed idle channels is less than K, all sensed idle channels will be accessed; otherwise, K channels with best expected rewards are accessed. Under this case, the expected reward of the genie-aided rule can be calculated in (11), while the expected reward of regret is derived in (14). To design a policy, Line 12 to Line 13 of Algorithm 2 can be modified as follows: if $|\mathcal{I}_u(t)| \geq K$, SU u accesses up to K channels with K-th largest $\hat{\theta}_{u,i} + \frac{1}{P_d - P_f} \sqrt{\frac{2 \ln(t-1)}{T_{u,i}(t-1)}}$ in $\mathcal{I}_u(t)$; if $|\mathcal{I}_u(t)| \leq K$, SU u accesses all channels in $\mathcal{I}_u(t)$. Then SU u waits for ACK feedback. For the scenario where SUs simultaneously access multiple channels at a slot, the regret $R(t)$ of Algorithm $\rho^{\text{RANDOMIZE}}$ also satisfies $O(\ln t)$, and the proof process is similar to that of Theorem 2.

5   Numerical Results

In this part, we perform simulations, varying the number of channels and SUs to verify the effectiveness of the proposed algorithms. Consider a cognitive radio network with U SUs and N channels, each SU can sense M channels, and access K channels. We set $P_d = 0.8$ and $P_f = 0.3$. The information of channels is listed in Table 1.

Table 1. Experimental parameters.

N	θ_i
N = 5	(0.5296, 0.4001, 0.9817, 0.1931, 0.2495)
N = 6	(0.1647, 0.7506, 0.4402, 0.9408, 0.8242, 0.6610)
N = 7	(0.8811, 0.5390, 0.3468, 0.9522, 0.7823, 0.0471, 0.7968)
N = 8	(0.6923, 0.5430, 0.3544, 0.8753, 0.5212, 0.6759, 0.8783, 0.9762)
N = 20	(0.0965, 0.1320, 0.9221, 0.9861, 0.5352, 0.0598, 0.2348, 0.3532, 0.8612, 0.0154, 0.0430, 0.1690, 0.6891, 0.7317, 0.6477, 0.4709, 0.5870, 0.2963, 0.7847, 0.1890)

First we perform simulations for ρ^{CENT}, where the results are shown in Fig. 2. We consider various scenes with $U = 2, 3$, $N = 5, 6, 7, 8$ and $K = 1, 2$. Since our proposed algorithm is bounded by $O(\ln t)$, we explore the relationship between time and normalized regret $R(t)/\ln t$. From Fig. 2, it is easy to see that $R(t)/\ln t$ is finitely bounded. Further observation finds that when the number of channels increases, $R(t)/\ln(t)$ becomes larger. This is because as the number of channels increases, the number of non-optimal channels increases, so SUs utilize more time to sense and access non-optimal channels, consequently resulting in larger regret and slower sensing speed. Additionally, as K increases, $R(t)/\ln(t)$ becomes larger. This is because when the estimation of channel order is not correct, SUs are more likely to access the non-optimal channels.

Then, we present simulations for $\rho^{\text{RANDOMIZE}}$. We consider different scenarios with $U = 2, 3$, $N = 5, 6, 7, 8$, $K = 1, 2$. From Fig. 3, it is seen that the

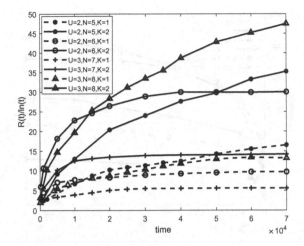

Fig. 2. Average $R(t)/\ln t$ of Algorithm ρ^{CENT}.

normalized regret $R(t)/\ln(t)$ tends to be finitely bounded as time goes, which verifies that the regret is bounded by $O(\ln t)$. From the result we find that there is no transmission loss as time goes infinitely, which means that all SUs will access the optimal channels and converge to a collision-free configuration. Similar to ρ^{CENT}, with the increasing number of channels N, regret increases. As expected from the comparison between Figs. 2 and 3, we can see centralized allocation policy has a lower regret than that of distributed allocation policy.

Further, we increase the number of channels ($N = 20$), and compare the regret with various M, K and fixed U in Fig. 4. It is seen that as time increases, $R(t)/\ln(t)$ is asymptotically limited. With fixed number of SUs and the number

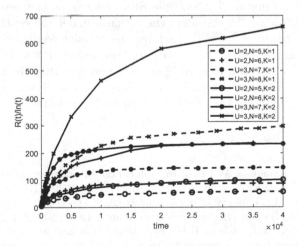

Fig. 3. Average $R(t)/\ln t$ of Algorithm $\rho^{\mathrm{RANDOMIZE}}$.

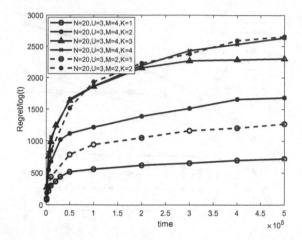

Fig. 4. Average $R(t)/\ln t$ of Algorithm $\rho^{\text{RANDOMIZE}}$ with different M and K.

of channels M, $R(t)/\ln(t)$ increases with increasing number of K. It is explained that before correctly estimating the order of channels, accessing more channels will bring out more collisions and higher probability for non-optimal channels. Another important observation is that with fixed U and K, sensing more channels simultaneously can contribute to lower $R(t)/\ln(t)$. The reason behind is that if SU can sense more channels at one time, it can not only estimate channels more quickly, but has broader chance to get access of sensed idle channels.

6   Conclusion

In this paper, we propose policies for both centralized and distributed learning of channel information for multiple SUs under imperfect sensing in a CR network. Algorithm ρ^{CENT} considers the scenario under the centralized framework while Algorithm $\rho^{\text{RANDOMIZE}}$ adapts the collision feedback to randomize the channel set for SUs under the distributed framework. Both algorithms make SUs converge to a collision-free configuration, ensuring that the regret is logarithmic asymptotically and in finite time. Theoretical analysis and simulations are presented to illustrate the efficiency of proposed algorithms.

References

1. Tanab, M.E., Hamouda, W.: Resource allocation for underlay cognitive radio networks: a survey. IEEE Commun. Surv. Tutor. **19**(2), 1249–1276 (2016)
2. Chen, Y., Oh, H.: A survey of measurement-based spectrum occupancy modeling for cognitive radios. IEEE Commun. Surv. Tutor. **18**(1), 848–859 (2016)
3. Le, T.N., Chin, W.L., Chen, H.H.: Standardization and security for smart grid communications based on cognitive radio technologies–a comprehensive survey. IEEE Commun. Surv. Tutor. **19**(1), 125–166 (2017)

4. Sexton, C., Kaminski, N.J., Marquez, J.M., Marchetti, N., Dasilva, L.A.: 5G: adaptable networks enabled by versatile radio access technologies. IEEE Commun. Surv. Tutor. **19**(2), 688–720 (2017)
5. Rai, V., Diad, I., Tholeti, T., Kalyani, S.: Spectrum access in cognitive radio using a two-stage reinforcement learning approach. IEEE J. Sel. Top. Signal Process. **12**(1), 20–34 (2018)
6. Kumar, R., Darak, S.J., Hanwal, M.K., Sharma, A.K., Tripathis, R.K.: Distributed algorithm for learning to coordinate in infrastructure-less network. IEEE Commun. Lett. **23**(2), 362–365 (2018)
7. Modi, N., Mary, P., Moy, C.: QoS driven channel selection algorithm for cognitive radio network: multi-user multi-armed bandit approach. IEEE Trans. Cogn. Commun. Netw. **3**(1), 49–66 (2017)
8. Fu, F., Schaar, M.C.D.: Learning to compete for resources in wireless stochastic games. IEEE Trans. Veh. Technol. **58**(4), 1904–1919 (2009)
9. Anandkumar, A., Michael, N., Tand, K., Swami, A.: Distributed algorithms for learning and cognitive medium access with logarithmic regret. IEEE J. Sel. Areas Commun. **29**(4), 731–745 (2011)
10. Liu, K., Zhao, Q.: Distributed learning in multi-armed bandit with multiple players. IEEE Trans. Signal Process. **58**, 5667–5681 (2010)
11. Liu, H., Liu, K., Zhao, Q.: Learning in a changing world: restless multi-armed bandit with unknown dynamics. IEEE Trans. Inf. Theory **59**(3), 1902–1916 (2013)
12. Nguyen, T.V., Shin, H., Quek, T.Q.S., Win, M.Z.: Sensing and probing cardinalities for active cognitive radios. IEEE Trans. Signal Process. **60**(4), 1833–1848 (2012)
13. Zhang, Z., Jiang, H., Tan, P., Slevinsky, J.: Channel exploration and exploitation with imperfect spectrum sensing in cognitive radio networks. IEEE J. Sel. Areas Commun. **31**(3), 429–441 (2013)
14. Wang, K., Chen, L., Liu, Q., Wang, W., Li, F.: One step beyond myopic probing policy: a heuristic lookahead policy for multi-channel opportunistic access. IEEE Trans. Wireless Commun. **14**(2), 759–769 (2015)
15. Zhang, Z., Jiang, H.: Cognitive radio with imperfect spectrum sensing: the optimal set of channels to sense. IEEE Wirel. Commun. Lett. **1**(2), 133–136 (2012)
16. Ahmad, A., Ahmad, S., Rehmani, M.H., Hassan, N.U.: A survey on radio resource allocation in cognitive radio sensor networks. IEEE Commun. Surv. Tutor. **17**(2), 888–917 (2015)
17. Auer, P., Cesa-Bianchi, N., Fischer, P.: Finite-time analysis of the multiarmed bandit problem. Mach. Learn. **47**, 235–256 (2002)

Distributed Scheduling in Wireless Multiple Decode-and-Forward Relay Networks

Zhou Zhang[1]($\boxtimes$), Ye Yan[1], Wei Sang[1], and Zuohong Xu[2]

[1] Tianjin Artificial Intelligence Innovation Center (TAIIC), Tianjin, China
zt.sy1986@163.com
[2] National University of Defense Technology, Changsha, China

Abstract. In this paper, we study the distributed DOS problem for wireless multiple relay networks. Formulating the problem as an extended three-level optimal stopping problem, an optimal strategy is proposed guiding distributed channel access for multiple source-to-destination communications under the help of multiple relays. The optimality of the strategy is rigorously proved, and abides by a tri-level structure of pure threshold. For network operation, easy implementation is presented of low complexity. The close-form expression of the maximal expected system throughput is also derived. Furthermore, numerical results are provided to demonstrate the correctness of our analytical expressions, and the effectiveness is verified.

Keywords: Distributed opportunistic scheduling · Multiple relays selection · Joint time and spatial diversity · Optimal stopping theory

1 Introduction

With explosively increasing demands on enhanced quality of service, conventional communication network faces serious challenges where the medium access control layer and the physical layer are independently designed. As the wireless medium is shared by multiple users and severe channel fading is experienced, a cross-layer design concept, channel-aware scheduling (DOS) is thus motivated. By letting the MAC layer aware of the physical layer information, users can make channel access decision depending on the channel quality, and users in good-quality link are scheduled.

Recently, existing researches have drawn much attentions on centralized scheduling [1,2] where a controller collects channel state information (CSI) of all users, and schedules those of best channel links to access. On the other hand, the research on distributed scheduling is still in its infancy. The difficulty lies in how a user decides when to access channel access. By means of optimal stopping, the problem in ad hoc network without relays was first addressed in [3], and

© ICST Institute for Computer Sciences, Social Informatics and Telecommunications Engineering 2020
Published by Springer Nature Switzerland AG 2020. All Rights Reserved
B. Li et al. (Eds.): IoTaaS 2019, LNICST 316, pp. 278–295, 2020.
https://doi.org/10.1007/978-3-030-44751-9_24

an easy implementation is benefited from the proposed pure-threshold strategy. Extended from that, the problem of opportunistic channel access in interference channel allowing multiple nodes simultaneous transmission is investigated in [4], while the problem with time constraints for real-time service is studied in [5].

Under such distributed multi-source network system, cooperative communication has great potentials to enhance system performance and thus has been studied [6–9,11]. Utilizing cooperation diversity, network performance is improved, including reliability and capacity. Recognizing the benefits, increasing interests have been observed in cross-layer design between MAC and physical layer. To say a few, the DOS problem for amplify-and-forward (AF) relay networks is investigated in [12]. Based on bi-level optimal stopping theory, optimal opportunistic channel access strategies are derived for both cases where multiple relays are coordinated and not controlled by each winner source-destination pair. In exploration of observed information influence on the network performance, opportunistic channel access problem under single relay network is also studied in literature [13], where each source has only partial CSI.

This paper differs from existing efforts by jointly considering three following aspects. First, a direct link is used, and multiple relays participle transmission by opportunistic relaying. Second, all channels, including direct channels, channels from each source to all relays, and from all relays to each destination are not necessarily reciprocal. Third, follow-up transmission in two-hop channels is taken into accounts, for which both source and relay can transmit data for duration of channel coherence time. In terms of practicality, these aspects are usually faced in wireless networking.

These considerations lead to new challenges for finding DOS strategy for wireless multi-relay network, and distributed channel access by multiple sources, relays and destinations should be managed in an orderly manner. Moreover, under help of multiple relays, each source is endowed with more flexibility in the strategy design for first-hop channel access, and the broadcast rate at first hop determines the number of relays available for data forward at second hop. Under availability of multiple relays at second hop, more benefits are expected in terms of time and capacity. Furthermore, as a direct link is available, the problem of when direct transmission dominates and how it enhances two-hop transmissions, is worth to be investigated. Thus, optimal DOS strategy is much desired to explore and exploit joint diversity in terms of multiple relays and time between two hops.

To address the challenges, a problem of DOS for multi-relay networks is investigated, and our contribution are summarized as follows.

– Extended from the two-level optimal stopping theory, the DOS problem is formulated, with the goal to maximize average system throughput. Being the novelty, after each successful channel contention, each winner source should determine how to access channel through three-step decision, which are when sources to stop, how they stop, and when relays to stop.
– As a solution to our problem, an optimal strategy for DOS with multiple relays is proposed, maximizing the average system throughput. Different from the existing results, it is in two-threshold structure. Particularly, at first hop

the optimal rule of sources is pure-threshold, and an optimal broadcast rate is calculated through a sequential threshold comparison; at second hop, the optimal rule of relays is also pure-threshold.
- The implementation of our proposed strategy is illustrated, and the effectiveness is also validated in terms of system throughput enhancement.

The rest of this paper is organized as follows. System model and problem formulation is described in Sect. 2, and an optimal DOS strategy maximizing average system throughput is proposed. Performance evaluation is provided in Sect. 4, followed by concluding remarks in Sect. 5.

2   System Model and Problem Formulation

2.1   System Model

Consider a wireless multi-source DOS network with K source-destination pairs aided by L relays in decode-and-forward (DF) mode. In such network, a direct link between each source and destination is included, and for transmission from a source to its destination, several relays are used opportunistically aiding the transmission in a half-duplex mode. The transmission power of a source and a relay is P_s and P_r, respectively.

We denote the channel gain from the ith source to its destination as h_i, the channel gain from the ith source to the jth relay as f_{ij}, and the channel gain from the jth relay to the ith destination as g_{ji}. Typically, we assume channels gains $\sqrt{P_s}h_i$, $\sqrt{P_s}f_{ij}$ and $\sqrt{P_r}g_{ji}$ are Rayleigh faded, with $\sqrt{P_s}h_i \sim CN(0, \sigma_h^2)$, $\sqrt{P_s}f_{ij} \sim CN(0, \sigma_f^2)$ and $\sqrt{P_r}g_{ji} \sim CN(0, \sigma_g^2)$. Time-varying channel environment is considered, and channel coherence time is denoted as τ_d. Channel gains remain constantly within the duration. Notably, results from this research can be extended for general channel fading environment.

The opportunistic channel access protocol by multiple sources is operated as follows. At the beginning of a time slot with duration δ, each source independently contends for the channel by sending a request-to-send (RTS) packet with probability p_0. There are three possible outcomes:

- If there is no source transmitting RTS in the time slot (with probability $(1 - p_0)^K$), then all the sources continue to contend in the next time slot;
- If there are two or more sources transmitting RTS (with probability $1 - (1 - p_0)^K - Kp_0(1 - p_0)^{K-1}$), a collision happens, and then in the next time slot after the RTS transmission, all sources continue to contend;
- If there is only one source, say Source i, transmitting RTS (with probability $Kp_0(1 - p_0)^{K-1}$), Source i is called *winner* of the contention. By reception of the RTS, each relay and Destination i can estimate CSI between Source i and itself. Then all relays send a RTS to Destination i in turn, in which CSI from the source to each relay is included. After reception of the RTSs, Destination i knows CSI from its source to itself, from the source to all relays and from all relays to itself. Then Destination i decides to *stop*, i.e. transmit data, or

continue, i.e. re-contend channel with other sources. And if stop, it requires to determine in what manner and data rate for transmission. There are three options.

- **End-to-end transmission**: Destination i sends a CTS to Source i and all relays, notifying them to transmit under optimal scheme. Upon reception of the CTS, Source i transmits to relays and destinations in the first hop, and then in the second hop a best relay is selected forwarding data to Destination i. After channel coherence time τ_d, the two-hop transmission finishes.

- **Sources contention**: Source i gives up its transmission opportunity, and other sources can detect an idle slot after the RTS and CTS exchanges among Source i, all relays, and Destination i (i.e., that idle slot tells other sources that Source i gives up its transmission opportunity). After that a new contention is started among all the source nodes.

- **First-hop broadcast**: Destination i sends a CTS to Source i, letting it transmit data at first hop within duration τ_d. Depending on the transmission rate, a subset of relays decode the data. The destination also receive the transmitted signals from the source. Then, the relays sequentially send a RTS to Destination i. After estimating the CSI of second-hop channels, Destination i has to decide whether *to stop* or not, and thus three choices are faced in the following.

  1. **Second-hop forward**: when there exists relays at good link, Destination i decide to stop by sending a CTS for selecting a single relay to forward its received data to Destination i. After that, the two-hop transmission is accomplished;

  2. **Relay termination**: when relays which can decode the first-hop transmission are all at bad link, Destination i decide to stop by sending a CTS to the relays and sources for telling them giving up the data forward;

  3. **Relays contention**: otherwise, Destination i decides to continue, and then channel coherence time τ_d is waited until the next observation.

- After Destination i stops, either second-hop forward or relay termination, new channel contention is started among all sources.

2.2   Problem Formulation

In this sub-section, we develop a decision-theoretic approach to DOS design for distributed multi-relay networks. Based on the optimal stopping theory, the DOS can be formulated as a variant of optimal stopping problem, namely two-stage optimal stopping problem (TSOSP), and the strategy correspondences to an extended stopping rule for the problem.

We illustrate the DOS dynamics of the distributed multi-relay network in Fig. 1 as specified in Sect. 2. A dynamic two-stage observation and decision model is formulated, including the main layer for sources and sub layer for relays.

Main Layer Decision Process: At beginning of each transmission between a source-to-destination pair, multiple sources contend the channel. We define

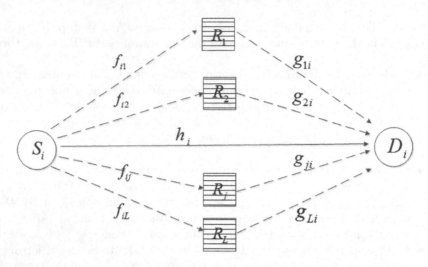

Fig. 1. System model

an *observation in the main layer* as the process of channel contention among the sources until a successful contention. In an observation, the number of contentions follows a geometric distribution with parameter $Kp_0(1-p_0)^{K-1}$. Among all the contentions in an observation, the last contention is successful, with total duration $(L+1) \cdot \tau_{RTS} + \tau_{CTS}$. The mean of an observation duration is thus given as $\tau_o = (L+1) \cdot \tau_{RTS} + \tau_{CTS} + \frac{(1-p_0)^K}{Kp_0(1-p_0)^{K-1}} \cdot \delta + \frac{1-(1-p_0)^K-Kp_0(1-p_0)^{K-1}}{Kp_0(1-p_0)^{K-1}} \cdot \tau_{RTS}$.

Given nth observation in the main layer, the winner source $s(n)$ observes information $\mathcal{F}_n = \{s(n), t_s(n), h_{s(n)}(n), f_{s(n)1}(n), ..., f_{s(n)L}(n), g_{1s(n)}(n), ..., g_{Ls(n)}(n)\}$, including those on CSI and channel contention. Based on information history until observation n, denoted by $\mathscr{F}_n := \vee_{i=1}^n \mathcal{F}_i$, the winner source decides if to stop, i.e. $N = n$, i.e. sources stop channel contention by taking some actions. Furthermore, the destination chooses an action $\phi(n) \in \{1, 2\}$. In particular, $\phi(n) = 1$ means end-to-end transmission, and $\phi(n) = 2$ means first-hop broadcast. To be further, if $\phi(n) = 1$, the winner source finishes end-to-end transmission, and receives a reward $Y_{n,\phi(n)}$; if $\phi(n) = 2$, the winner source further decides the broadcast rate R_n in first hop. After broadcast, channel access process of relays who can decode the broadcast data starts the process for data forwarding in second hop. Otherwise, new channel contention starts and the next observation is obtained.

Sub Layer Decision Process: When the main layer stops with action $\phi(n) = 2$, a subset of relays, denoted as $\mathcal{J}_n$, start *observation in the sublayer*. In each slot of channel coherence time, says observation m, each relay obtains second-hop CSI from itself to Destination $s(n)$. We denote observation information as $\mathcal{G}'_{nm} = \{g_{js(n)}(m), j \in \mathcal{J}_n\}$, and the accumulated information until observation m is denoted as $\mathcal{G}_{nm} = \vee_{i=1}^m \mathcal{G}'_{ni}$. Based on the history information in sub layer, Destination $s(n)$ decides if to stop, i.e. $M = m$, which means that relays stop forwarding by taking some actions. Then, if relays stop, an action $\psi(m) \in \{1, 2\}$ is chosen. In particular, $\psi(m) = 1$ means second-hop forward, and $\psi(m) = 2$ means terminating relays. Furthermore, if $\psi(m) = 1$, relays finish the second-hop transmission, and receives a reward $Y_{n,m,\psi(m)}$; and if $\phi(n) = 2$, relays terminate the transmission and let sources re-contend the channel. Based on this formulation, a DOS strategy is fundamentally a policy of the TSOSP.

Reward and Objective Functions: For DOS problem with multiple relays, in accordance with network protocol as described in Subsect. 2.1, utility functions are defined for the main and sub layer decision process, and are in two parts. The reward function represents transmitted data traffic, and the cost function represents time spent.

In the definitions, upon observed information until nth observation at main layer, for sources to stop by $\phi(n) = 1$, the winner source obtains a reward $Y_{n,1} = \tau_d \max\{C_h(n), C_r(n)\}$, and a cost $T_{n,1} = \sum_{l=1}^{n} t_s(l) + \tau_d$. In details, rate $C_h(n)$ represents the maximal rate in direct link, which is calculated as that

$$C_h(n) = \log_2(1 + P_s|h_i(n)|^2). \tag{1}$$

The rate $C_r(n)$ represents the achievable rate through best single-relay selection, which is calculated as

$$C_r(n) = \frac{1}{2} \max_{j \in \{1,2,\dots,L\}} \big\{ \min \big(\log_2(1 + P_s|h_i|^2 + P_r|g_{ji}|^2),$$
$$\log_2(1 + P_s|f_{ij}|^2)\big)\big\}. \tag{2}$$

Moreover, for stop by $\phi(n) = 2$, a cost is received with $T_{n,2} = \sum_{l=1}^{n} t_s(l) + \tau_d/2$, and a broadcast rate R_n (i.e., $R_n = \log_2(1 + r_n)$) is decided by the winner source. Subsequently, a relay set, denoted as $\mathcal{J}_n$, is determined, representing the relays who can decode the broadcast signal successfully.

Then, sub layer decision process of multiple relays begins, which will give a reward $Y_{n,m,\psi(m)}$ in future.

Upon observed information until mth observation at sub layer, if relays stop by $\psi(m) = 1$, a reward $Y_{n,m,1} = \tau_d R_n \mathbb{I}[g_{\mathcal{J}_n}(m) \geq r_n - P_s|h(n)|^2]$ is received as well as a cost $T_{n,m,1} = T_{n,2} + T_m$. T_m means the time spent in sub layer process, and is calculated as

$$T_m = (m-1)\tau_d + \mathbb{I}[g_{\mathcal{J}_n}(m) \geq r_n - P_s|h_{s(n)}(n)|^2]\tau_d$$
$$+ \mathbb{I}[g_{\mathcal{J}_n}(m) < r_n - P_s|h_{s(n)}(n)|^2](|\mathcal{J}_n| \cdot \tau_{RTS} + \tau_{CTS}). \tag{3}$$

Moreover, at mth observation at sub layer, if relays stop by $\psi(m) = 2$, a reward $Y_{n,m,2} = 0$ is received, and a cost $T_{n,m,2} = T_{n,2} + T_m$ is spent.

TSOSP Formulation: Based on the theoretic framework above, if winner source stops at Nth observation in main layer and relays stop at Mth observation in sub layer, an instantaneous reward $Y_{N,M}$ is obtained and a time cost $T_{N,M}$ is spent. And the corresponding instantaneous system throughput is $Y_{N,M}/T_{N,M}$. In the sequel, capital N is called stopping time in main layer, and capital M is called stopping time in sub layer. To achieve the optimal OCA strategy, our goal is to find an optimal stopping strategy $\{N^*, R_{N^*}^*, M^*\}$ maximizing the average system throughput $\sup\limits_{N,R_N,M} \mathbb{E}[Y_{N,M}]/\mathbb{E}[T_{N,M}]$. Here $\mathbb{E}[\cdot]$ means expectation.

3 Optimal OCA Strategy and Its Implementation

Enlightened by Lemma 1 in [14, Chapter 6], the maximal-expected-rate-of-return problem is transformed into a standard problem for maximal expected return in accordance with the following theorem. For a given price $\lambda > 0$, we define the reward function $V(\lambda) = \sup\limits_{N,R_N,M} \mathbb{E}[Y_{N,M} - \lambda T_{N,M}]$, representing the maximal expected reward under price λ for time cost.

Theorem 1. *The optimal OCA strategy $\{N^*(\lambda^*), R_{N^*}^*(\lambda^*), M^*(\lambda^*)\}$ achieving $\sup\limits_{N,R_N,M} \mathbb{E}[Y_{N,M}]/\mathbb{E}[T_{N,M}]$ is an optimal strategy achieving the priced expected return $V^*(\lambda^*) = \sup\limits_{N,R_N,M} \mathbb{E}[Y_{N,M} - \lambda^* T_{N,M}]$, where λ^* uniquely exits such that $V^*(\lambda^*) = 0$. The price λ^* is the maximal expected system throughput such that $\lambda^* = \sup\limits_{N,R_N,M} \mathbb{E}[Y_{N,M}]/\mathbb{E}[T_{N,M}]$.*

In accordance with Theorem 1, thought train towards finding an optimal strategy is that, for a given price $\lambda > 0$, an optimal strategy $\{N^*(\lambda), R_N^*(\lambda), M^*(\lambda)\}$ is found achieving $V^*(\lambda)$. Then, by replacing λ with λ^*, $\{N^*, R_N^*, M^*\}$ is acquired as an optimal OCA strategy maximizing the average system throughput.

Based on the relation between main layer and sub layer, reward function obtained from sub layer decision process conditioned on observation information $\mathscr{F}_n$ and broadcast rate R_n in main layer, is defined as that

$$W_n(\lambda) := \mathbb{E}[Y_{n,M^*} - \lambda T_{M^*} | \mathscr{F}_n, R_n].$$

Theorem 2. *For a given price $\lambda > 0$, finding optimal strategy $\{N^*(\lambda), R_{N^*}^*(\lambda), M^*(\lambda)\}$ is equivalent to a two-stage optimal stopping problem. In the sub layer, when main layer stops at nth observation, and $\phi(n) = 2$, an optimal stopping strategy $M^*(\lambda)$ is to find achieving W_n; in the main layer, an optimal strategy $\{N^*(\lambda), R_{N^*}^*(\lambda)\}$ is to find achieving $\sup\limits_{N,R_N} \mathbb{E}\big[(Y_N - \lambda T_N)\mathbb{I}[\phi(N) = 1] + W_N(\lambda)\mathbb{I}[\phi(N) = 2]\big].$*

Proof. We prove by deriving the two-stage optimal strategy dominates other strategy in the expected reward value.

For any strategy $\{N^\dagger, R^\dagger_{N^\dagger}, M^\dagger\}$, we analyze that[1]

$$\mathbb{E}[Y_{N^\dagger, M^\dagger} - \lambda T_{N^\dagger, M^\dagger}] =$$

$$\mathbb{E}[\overset{\infty}{\underset{n=1}{\sum}} \mathbb{I}[N^\dagger = n]\mathbb{I}[\phi(N^\dagger) = 2]\mathbb{E}[Y_{n,M^\dagger} - \lambda T_{M^\dagger}|\mathscr{F}_n]$$

$$+ (Y_{N^\dagger} - \lambda T_{N^\dagger})\mathbb{I}[\phi(N^\dagger) = 1]]$$

$$\leq \mathbb{E}[\overset{\infty}{\underset{n=1}{\sum}} \mathbb{I}[N^\dagger = n]\mathbb{I}[\phi(N^\dagger) = 2]\mathbb{E}[Y_{n,M^*} - \lambda T_{M^*}|\mathscr{F}_n]$$

$$+ (Y_{N^\dagger} - \lambda T_{N^\dagger})\mathbb{I}[\phi(N^\dagger) = 1]]$$

$$\leq \mathbb{E}[(Y_{N^*} - \lambda T_{N^*})\mathbb{I}[\phi(N^*) = 1] + W_{N^*}(\lambda)\mathbb{I}[\phi(N^*) = 2]] \qquad (4)$$

Therefore, the optimal strategy $\{N^*(\lambda), R^*_{N^*}(\lambda), M^*(\lambda)\}$ in a two-stage form can achieve $V^*(\lambda)$.

In the light of Theorem 2, optimal OCA strategy is derived as follow. A sublayer optimal strategy $M^*(\lambda)$ followed by relays is first presented in following theorem. We define upper and lower thresholds Th_l and Th_u, where $Th_l = \lambda \frac{\tau_d - \tau_{|\mathcal{J}_n|}}{\tau_d}$ and $Th_u = \lambda + \frac{\lambda(\tau_d + \tau_{|\mathcal{J}_n|})}{P_n \tau_d}$.

Theorem 3. *If main layer stops at nth observation with $\phi(n) = 2$ and broadcast rate R_n, an sub-layer optimal strategy has a one-of-three choices form:*

- *when $R_n \leq Th_l$, a myopic strategy is optimal, i.e. $M^*(\lambda) = 1$ and $\psi(M^*) = 2$;*
- *when $R_n \in (Th_l, Th_u)$, a myopic strategy is optimal, i.e. $M^*(\lambda) = 1$ and $\psi(M^*) = 1$;*
- *when $R_n \geq Th_u$, $M^* = \inf\{m > 0 : P_r \max_{j \in \mathcal{J}_n} |g_{js(n)}(m)|^2 \geq r_n - P_s|h_{s(n)}(n)|^2\}$,*

where $g_{\mathcal{J}_n} := P_r \max_{j \in \mathcal{J}_n} |g_{js(n)}(m)|^2$.

Proof. When the first-hop observation stops at observation n, an optimal stopping strategy in the second hop exists[2]. By optimal stopping theory it is of form that

$$M^* = \inf\{m \geq 0 : Y_{n,m,\psi(m)} - \lambda(T_{n,2} + T_m) \geq$$
$$\mathbb{E}[S_{n,m+1}|\mathscr{F}_n \vee \mathcal{G}_{nm}]\} \qquad (5)$$

The threshold S_{nm} is conditional reward defined as

$$\sup_{M \geq m} \mathbb{E}[Y_{n,M,\psi(M)} - \lambda(T_{n,2} + T_{M,\psi(M)})|\mathscr{F}_n \vee \mathcal{G}_{nm}]. \qquad (6)$$

---

[1] Note the superscript $\overline{\infty}$ means the summation includes term at $n = \infty$.

[2] For finite n, the existence proof is similar to Theorem 6, while $n = \infty$ means the main layer does not stop.

Based on optimal stopping theory, we have bellman equation that

$$S_{nm} = \max\{Y_{n,M,\psi(M)} - \lambda(T_{n,2} + T_{m,\psi(m)}),$$
$$\mathbb{E}[S_{n,m+1}|\mathscr{F}_n \vee \mathcal{G}_{nm}]\}. \tag{7}$$

Then, we calculate the threshold $\mathbb{E}[S_{n,m+1}|\mathscr{F}_n \vee \mathcal{G}_{nm}]$ in the right side of Eq. (5), and is shown in Eq. (8). Duration $\tau_{|\mathcal{J}_n|}$ denotes the time cost for relay channel sensing, with $\tau_{|\mathcal{J}_n|} = |\mathcal{J}_n|\tau_{RTS} + \tau_{CTS}$. The last line is from the definition of W_n, which is the maximal expected reward in sub layer.

$$\mathbb{E}[S_{n,m+1}|\mathscr{F}_n \vee \mathcal{G}_{nm}]$$

$$= \mathbb{E}\left[\sup_{M \geq m+1} \mathbb{E}\left[Y_{n,M,\psi(M)} - \lambda(T_{n,2} + T_{M,\psi(M)})\Big|\mathscr{F}_n \vee \mathcal{G}_{n,m+1}\right]\Big|\mathscr{F}_n \vee \mathcal{G}_{nm}\right]$$

$$= \mathbb{E}\left[\sup_{M \geq m+1} \mathbb{E}\left[(R_n - \lambda)\tau_d\mathbb{I}[\psi(M) = 1] - \lambda\tau_{|\mathcal{J}_n|}\right.\right.$$

$$\left.\left. -\lambda(M-m)\tau_d\Big|\mathscr{F}_n \vee \mathcal{G}_{n,m+1}\right]\Big|\mathscr{F}_n \vee \mathcal{G}_{nm}\right] - \lambda(T_{n,2} + m\tau_d)$$

$$\overset{(a)}{=} W_n(\lambda) - \lambda(T_{n,2} + m\tau_d)$$

By substituting expression in Eq. (8) into Bellman Equation (7), we have that

$$W_n - \lambda(T_{n,2} + (m-1)\tau_d) = \mathbb{E}\big[\max\{Y_{n,m,\psi(m)} -$$
$$\lambda T_{m,\psi(m)}, W_n - \lambda(\tau_{|\mathcal{J}_n|} + m\tau_d)\}|\mathscr{F}_n\big] - \lambda T_{n,2}. \tag{8}$$

And it is further simplified into the form that

$$\mathbb{E}\big[\max\{Y_{n,m,\psi(m)} - \lambda(T_{m,\psi(m)} - (m-1)\tau_d) - W_n,$$
$$- \lambda(\tau_{|\mathcal{J}_n|} + \tau_d)\}|\mathscr{F}_n\big] = 0. \tag{9}$$

The reward $-W_n$ can be derived by solving the next equation. By the sub-layer optimal stopping strategy, at each observation m, whether stop or not is decided by relation between $Y_{n,m,\psi(m)} - \lambda(T_{m,\psi(m)} - (m-1)\tau_d)$ and $W_n - \lambda(\tau_{|\mathcal{J}_n|} + \tau_d)$. And by observing the above equation, the decision on $\psi(m)$ for stop is first determined, which maximizes the reward by stop.

$$\mathbb{E}\big[\max\{\mathbb{I}[\psi(m) = 1](Y_{n,m,1} - \lambda\tau_d) + \mathbb{I}[\psi(m) = 2]Y_{n,m,2} - W_n, -\lambda\tau_d\}|\mathscr{F}_n\big] = \lambda\tau_{|\mathcal{J}_n|}.$$

Recall that reward $Y_{n,m,1} - \lambda\tau_d$ and $Y_{n,m,2} - \lambda\tau_{|\mathcal{J}_n|}$ for $\psi(m) = 1$ and $\psi(m) = 2$ respectively, it is optimal to stop by taking action as follows.

- when $(R_n - \lambda)\tau_d > -\lambda\tau_{|\mathcal{J}_n|}$ and $g_{\mathcal{J}_n}(m) \geq r_n - P_s|h(n)|^2$, we have $\psi(m) = 1$;
- otherwise, we have $\psi(m) = 2$.

Following a similar line, we analyse the Bellman Equation. For simplicity, we define $P_n := \mathbb{P}[g_{\mathcal{J}_n} \geq r_n - P_s|h(n)|^2]$.

When $(R_n - \lambda)\tau_d > -\lambda\tau_{|\mathcal{J}_n|}$, there are two cases.

Case 1: if $R_n\tau_d \geq W_n$ and $W_n \leq \lambda\tau_d$, we have

$$W_n = P_n \cdot (R_n - \lambda)\tau_d - \lambda\tau_{|\mathcal{J}_n|}. \tag{10}$$

Case 2: if $R_n\tau_d \geq W_n$ and $W_n > \lambda\tau_d$, we have

$$W_n = R_n\tau_d - \frac{\lambda(\tau_d + \tau_{|\mathcal{J}_n|})}{P_n}. \tag{11}$$

Case 3: otherwise, when $(R_n - \lambda)\tau_d \leq -\lambda\tau_{|\mathcal{J}_n|}$, we have that

$$W_n = -\lambda\tau_{|\mathcal{J}_n|}. \tag{12}$$

Based on three cases above, we further analyze the form of optimal strategy in sub layer.

1. When $R_n < \lambda\frac{\tau_d - \tau_{|\mathcal{J}_n|}}{\tau_d}$, Case 3 applies and thus it is optimal to stop at the beginning by $\phi(m) = 2$;
2. when $R_n \in \left(\lambda\frac{\tau_d - \tau_{|\mathcal{J}_n|}}{\tau_d}, \lambda + \frac{\lambda(\tau_d + \tau_{|\mathcal{J}_n|})}{P_n\tau_d}\right)$, Case 1 applies and it is optimal to stop at the beginning by $\phi(m) = 1$;
3. when $R_n \geq \lambda + \frac{\lambda(\tau_d + \tau_{|\mathcal{J}_n|})}{P_n\tau_d}$, Case 2 applies and it is optimal to stop when $g_{\mathcal{J}_n}(m) \geq r_n - P_s|h(n)|^2$ satisfies.

Theorem 3 presents an optimal strategy $M^*(\lambda)$ in the sub layer. It is conditioned on the observed information in the main layer and the broadcast rate R_n. On this basis, an optimal strategy in the main layer, denoted as $\{N^*, R_{N*}^*\}$ is focused. In the following, the problem is decomposed into two levels: the optimal stopping time N^* at higher level and its associated optimal transmission manner $\{\phi(N^*), R_{N*}^*\}$ at lower level. For finding optimal stopping time in the main layer, we define optimal expected reward $\{G_n\}_{n=1,2,\dots}$ such that $G_n := \sup_{R_n \geq 0} \{(Y_n - \lambda T_n)\mathbb{I}[\phi(n) = 1] + W_n(\lambda)\mathbb{I}[\phi(n) = 2]\}$, which represents the maximal expected reward achieved by taking optimal actions for stop in the main layer and optimal strategy in the sub layer.

Theorem 4. *In the main layer, for a price $\lambda > 0$, the problem of finding an optimal strategy $\{N^*, R_{N*}^*\}$ achieving $\sup_{N,R_N} \mathbb{E}[(Y_N - \lambda T_N)\mathbb{I}[\phi(N) = 1] + W_N(\lambda)\mathbb{I}[\phi(N) = 2]]$ is equivalently decomposed as that: in the lower level, at each observation $n > 0$, find optimal stop manner $\phi(n)$ and transmitting rate $R_n^* := \arg\sup_{R_n \geq 0} \{(Y_n - \lambda T_n)\mathbb{I}[\phi(n) = 1] + W_n(\lambda)\mathbb{I}[\phi(n) = 2]\}$; in the higher level, find optimal stopping rule $N^* := \arg\sup_{N>0} \mathbb{E}[G_N]$.*

$$\mathbb{E}[Y_{N^\dagger}(R_{N^\dagger}^\dagger) - \lambda T_{N^\dagger}]$$

$$= \mathbb{E}\Big[\sum_{n=1}^{\overline{\infty}} \mathbb{I}[N^\dagger = n]\big(Y_n(R_n^\dagger) - \lambda T_n\big)\Big]$$

$$\leq \mathbb{E}\Big[\sum_{n=1}^{\overline{\infty}} \mathbb{I}[N^\dagger = n] \sup_{R_n \geq 0} \big\{(Y_n - \lambda T_n)\mathbb{I}[\phi(n) = 1] + W_n(\lambda)\mathbb{I}[\phi(n) = 2]\big\}\Big]$$

$$= \mathbb{E}\Big[\sum_{n=1}^{\overline{\infty}} \mathbb{I}[N^\dagger = n] \cdot G_n \Big] \leq \sup_{N \geq 0} \mathbb{E}[G_N] = \mathbb{E}[G_{N^*}] \tag{13}$$

Proof. For any transmission strategy $\{N^\dagger, R_{N^\dagger}^\dagger\}$ in main layer, we derive an upper bound in Eq. (13). It is proved that $\mathbb{E}[G_{N^*}]$ is an upper bound for any feasible rules, and $\mathbb{E}[G_{N^*}]$ is achieved by following a stopping strategy N^* with its associated transmission manner such that reward G_n is attained for stop at observation n.

Based on the optimal rule's structure in Theorem 4, the optimal stopping strategy N^* in the top level relies on the reward sequence $\{G_n\}_{n \in \mathbb{N}}$, where $\mathbb{N}$ is the positive integer set. This sequence is acquired by solving problems in lower level. In this regards, for each observation n, we focus on derivation of the reward function G_n. Recognizing that the component λT_n in function G_n is independent with rate R_n, it suffices to maximize the following function, which is derived by using analytic form of $W_n(\lambda)$. Replacing W_n in Eqs. (10), (11) and (12), we have the objective function to maximize in Eq. (14).

$$\mathbb{I}[R_n < Th_l] \cdot (-\lambda \tau_{|\mathcal{J}_n|}) + \mathbb{I}[Th_l \leq R_n \leq Th_u] \cdot \Big(R_n \tau_d - \frac{\lambda(\tau_d + \tau_{|\mathcal{J}_n|})}{P_n}\Big)$$
$$+ \mathbb{I}[R_n > Th_u] \cdot \big(P_n \cdot (R_n - \lambda)\tau_d - \lambda \tau_{|\mathcal{J}_n|}\big) \tag{14}$$

For stop by $\phi(n) = 2$, i.e. two-stage transmission.

To maximize the objective in Eq. (14), we solve the problem in piece-wise region. In the following, the maximization problem is analyzed.

First, we consider the problem when $R_n \leq Th_l$.

The function $P_n \cdot (R_n - \lambda)\tau_d - \lambda \tau_{|\mathcal{J}_n|}$ is to maximized based on channels gains $\mathcal{F}_n$. Observing that the variable $|\mathcal{J}_n|$ depends on the $\{R_n, \mathcal{F}_n\}$, it requires to analyze the function when $|\mathcal{J}_n| = 1, 2, ..., L$.

Therefore, we define functions Z_k, $k = 1, 2, ..., L$ below:

$$Z_k = P_n(k) \cdot (R_n - \lambda)\tau_d - \lambda \tau_k$$

where $P_n(k) = 1 - \Big(1 - e^{-\frac{r_n - P_s|h(n)|^2}{\sigma_g^2}}\Big)^k$.

Properties of these functions are taken into accounts in the following lemma.

Lemma 1. *Function Z_k has unique maximal solution for $k = 1, 2, ..., L$, denoted as ζ_k respectively. In particular, when $r_n \le \zeta_k$, Z_k increases, and when $r_n > \zeta_k$, Z_k decreases. The maximal solutions satisfy that $P_s|h(n)|^2 \le \zeta_1 < \zeta_2 < ... < \zeta_L$.*

Proof. See Appendix A.

Second, we consider the problem when $Th_l \le R_n \le Th_u$.

The function $R_n\tau_d - \frac{\lambda(\tau_d - \tau_{|\mathcal{J}_n|})}{P_n}$ is to maximized based on channels gains $\mathcal{F}_n$. We define functions U_k, $k = 1, 2, ..., L$ below:

$$U_k = \tau_d \log_2(1 + r_n) - \frac{\lambda(\tau_d - \tau_k)}{1 - \left(1 - e^{-\frac{r_n - P_s|h(n)|^2}{\sigma_g^2}}\right)^k}.$$

Properties of functions U_k, $k = 1, 2, ..., L$ are taken into accounts in the following lemma.

Lemma 2. *For $k = 1, 2, ..., L$, function U_k is strictly concave in $r_n \ge 0$; if $P_s|h(n)|^2 > \frac{\tau_d\sigma_g^2 \log_2 e}{\lambda(\tau_{CTS}+\tau_d)} - 1$, the optimal point of U_1, denoted by η_1, is equal to $P_s|h(n)|^2$; otherwise, for $k \ge 1$, the optimal point of U_k, denoted by η_k, is equal to $x_k + P_s|h(n)|^2$ such that $\frac{\partial U_k(x)}{\partial x}\big|_{x_k} = 0$, respectively. Also, $P_s|h(n)|^2 \le \eta_1 < \eta_2 < ... < \eta_L$ is satisfied.*

Denote $Z_k^* := Z_k(\zeta_k)$ as the maximum of Z_k in $r_n \ge P_s|h(n)|^2$. As function Z_k increases with the number k of available relays in the second hop, it is obvious that $Z_1^* < Z_2^* < ... < Z_L^*$.

Moreover, by definition of functions $U_k, k = 1, 2, ..., L$, it is shown that $U_1 < U_2 < ... < U_L$ on $r_n \ge 0$. By denoting $U_k^* = U_k(\eta_k)$, $U_1^* < U_2^* < ... < U_L^*$ is satisfied.

Then, combing the function analysis above, we focus on finding the optimal broadcast rate R_n.

We first investigate the region of r_n such that $R_n \ge Th_u$.

Using properties of functions $\{Z_k\}_k = 1, ..., L$ and relations, we define an integer κ that

$$\kappa(\lambda) = \min\{k = 1, 2, ..., L : Z_k^* \ge \lambda\tau_d\}.$$

Correspondingly, regions $\{\zeta_k^-, \zeta_k^+\}$ for $k \ge \kappa'$ are further defined, and $r_n \in \{\zeta_k^-, \zeta_k^+\}$ satisfies $R_n \ge Th_u$. Also, for $\forall i \ge k$, it is proved that $\zeta_i^- \ge \zeta_{i+1}^-$ and $\zeta_{i+1}^+ \ge \zeta_i^+$.

Based on the region above, for channel information $\mathcal{F}_n$, we need to design an algorithm to determine the point maximizing the function. By sorting the first-hop channel gains in descending order as $\gamma_1 \ge \gamma_2 \ge ... \ge \gamma_L$, the region such that $R_n \ge Th_u$ is $\cup_{i=1}^{q}\{[\zeta_i^-, \zeta_i^+] \cap (\max\{\gamma_{i+1}(n), P_s|h_{s(n)}(n)|^2\}, \gamma_i(n))\}$, where integer q satisfying $\gamma_{q+1}(n) \le P_s|h(n)|^2 < \gamma_q(n)$.

As the process acquiring the optimal rate R_n^* within the region demands high complexity, further investigation is made to design an algorithm which significantly reduces the complexity. Algorithm 1 is presented in the following. In it, we define $\kappa^\dagger$ as the least integer κ such that $[\zeta_\kappa^-, \zeta_\kappa^+] \cap (\gamma_{\kappa+1}(n), \gamma_\kappa(n)) \ne \varnothing$. Moreover, for $k = 1, 2, ..., L$, truncated functions $U_k'(\gamma_k(n)) := U_k(\gamma_k(n))\mathbb{I}[\gamma_k(n) \ge \zeta_k^-]$

are defined. Also, we use $H_n := Y_{n,1} - \lambda \tau_d$ to denote the reward by instantaneous transmission.

Algorithm 1. Algorithm to determine optimal broadcast rate

1: Calculate integer q and κ' based on channel gain $\mathcal{F}_n$.
2: **if** $\gamma_q(n) \geq \max\{\eta_q, \zeta_q^+\}$ **then**
3:     $r_n^* = \arg\max\{U_q(\min(\eta_q, \zeta_q^+)), H_n\}$.
4: **else**
5:     Set $k = q - 1$.
6:     **while** $k > \kappa'$ **do**
7:         **if** $\gamma_k(n) \geq \max\{\eta_k, \zeta_k^+\}$ **then**
8:             **if** $\gamma_{k+1}(n) < \eta_k$ **then**
9:                 $r_n^* = \arg\max_{q \geq i \geq k+1}\{U_k(\min(\eta_k, \zeta_k^+)), U_i'(\gamma_i(n)), H_n\}$.
10:             **else if** $\gamma_{k+1}(n) \geq \eta_k$ **then**
11:                 $r_n^* = \arg\max_{q \geq i \geq k+2}\{U_{k+1}(\gamma_{k+1}(n)), U_i'(\gamma_i(n)), H_n\}$.
12:             **end if**
13:             $k = k - 1$.
14:         **end if**
15:     **end while**
16:     **if** $\gamma_{\kappa^\dagger}(n) < \max\{\eta_{\kappa^\dagger}, \zeta_{\kappa^\dagger}^+\}$ **then**
17:         **if** $\gamma_{\kappa^\dagger}(n) < \min(\eta_{\kappa^\dagger}, \zeta_{\kappa^\dagger}^+)$ **then**
18:             $r_n^* = \arg\max_{q \geq i \geq \kappa^\dagger}\{U_i'(\gamma_i(n)), H_n\}$
19:         **else**
20:             $r_n^* = \arg\max_{q \geq i \geq \kappa^\dagger+1}\{U_{\kappa^\dagger}(\min(\eta_{\kappa^\dagger}, \zeta_{\kappa^\dagger}^+)), U_i'(\gamma_i(n)), H_n\}$.
21:         **end if**
22:     **end if**
23: **end if**

The effective of our proposed algorithm is guaranteed by the following theorem.

Theorem 5. *Based on observed information $\mathcal{F}_n$ until observation n in main layer, Algorithm 1 solves the optimal rate R_n^* achieving G_n.*

Proof. Due to page limit, the proof is omitted.

Based on Theorem 5, the optimal transmission rate $R_n^* := \arg\sup_{R_n \geq 0}\{(Y_n - \lambda T_n)\mathbb{I}[\phi(n) = 1] + W_n(\lambda)\mathbb{I}[\phi(n) = 2]\}$is derived, which is followed by multiple sources. According to Theorem 4, it remains an optimal stopping strategy N^*. In the sequel, we target in finding an optimal stopping strategy in main layer achieving $\sup_{N > 0}\mathbb{E}[G_N(\lambda)]$.

Using the statistical characteristics of observed channel gains in the network, which are independent and identically distributed, the reward function G_n conditioned on the first-hop channel gains $\{h_{s(n)}(n), f_{s(n)1}(n), ..., f_{s(n)L}(n)\}$ remains invariant along observation n, And a following conclusion is derived.

Theorem 6. *The optimal stopping rule N^* achieving $\sup\limits_{N>0}\mathbb{E}[G_N(\lambda)]$ exists and is given by $N^* = \inf\{n > 0 : G_n(\lambda^*) \geq 0\}$, where the optimal throughput λ^* uniquely satisfies $\mathbb{E}[\max\{G_n(\lambda^*), 0\}] = \lambda^*\tau_o$.*

Notably, as the maximal average throughput λ^* is achieved by using our joint optimal strategy, according to Theorem 6 it is inferred that a unique-form second-hop optimal rule exits, which is $M^* = \inf\{m > 0 : P_r \max\limits_{j\in\mathcal{J}_n} |g_{js(n)}(m)|^2 \geq r_n\}$.

According to Theorems 2 and 4, our optimal OCA strategy is decomposed into three-level form: at the top level, an optimal stopping strategy is derived to decide when sources to stop (i.e., broadcast or directly transmit), at the medium level, an optimal transmitting rate is demanded to decide how a winner source to stop, and at the bottom level, another optimal strategy at second hop is to be decided on when relay(s) to stop (i.e., forward data to destinations).

Combing the results in Theorems 3, 5 and 6, our proposed optimal OCA strategy can be implemented as follows.

For channel access of multiple sources, upon a successful contention in the observation n, the winner source $s(n)$ obtains information $\mathcal{F}_n$, sorts the first-hop channel gains by $\{\gamma_1(n) \geq \gamma_2(n) \geq ... \geq \gamma_q(n) \geq P_s|h_{s(n)}(n)|^2\}$. If an integer q does not exist, the broadcast rate R_n is 0; otherwise, calculate $\{\zeta_k^-, \zeta_k^+\}$ for $k \in \{q, q-1, ..., 1\}$, pick up every $k' \in \{q, q-1, ..., 1\}$ such that $\gamma_{k'+1}(n) < \zeta_{k'}^+$ and $\gamma_{k'}(n) \geq \zeta_{k'}^-$; then records the minimal k' as $\kappa^\dagger$; if such k' does not exist, the broadcast rate R_n is 0; otherwise, for each step k falling from q to $\kappa^\dagger$, Source $s(n)$ acts as follows until the broadcast rate r_n^* is acquired.

- If $\gamma_k(n) \geq \max\{\eta_k, \zeta_k^+\}$
  - If $\gamma_{k+1}(n) < \eta_k$, $(r_n^*, Y_n^*) = \mathbf{v}_k^1$.
  - If $\gamma_{k+1}(n) \geq \eta_k$, $(r_n^*, Y_n^*) = \mathbf{v}_k^2$.
- If $\gamma_k(n) < \max\{\eta_k, \zeta_k^+\}$, go into next comparison until $\kappa^\dagger$.
- If $k = \kappa^\dagger$ and $\gamma_{\kappa^\dagger}(n) < \max\{\eta_{\kappa^\dagger}, \zeta_{\kappa^\dagger}^+\}$
  - If $\gamma_{\kappa^\dagger}(n) < \min(\eta_{\kappa^\dagger}, \zeta_{\kappa^\dagger}^+)$, $(r_n^*, Y_n^*) = \mathbf{v}_{\kappa^\dagger}^3$.
  - If $\gamma_{\kappa^\dagger}(n) \geq \min(\eta_{\kappa^\dagger}, \zeta_{\kappa^\dagger}^+)$, $(r_n^*, Y_n^*)) = \mathbf{v}_{\kappa^\dagger}^1$.

Then, Source $s(n)$ decides if or not to stop.

- If $\max\{Y_n^*, H_n\} < \lambda^*\tau_d$, Source $s(n)$ gives up its transmission opportunity and re-contends with other sources.
- If $\max\{Y_n^*, H_n\} \geq \lambda^*\tau_d$,
  - If $Y_n^* \leq H_n$, Source $s(n)$ transmits its data to Destination $s(n)$ in direct manner.
  - If $Y_n^* > H_n$, Source $s(n)$ broadcasts its data in rate R_n^*, and the channel probing of relays starts. The relays in $\mathcal{J}_n$ decode the signals, and based on observed channel conditions they have to decide if or not to forward data. In the mth observation, each relay, says Relay $j \in \mathcal{J}_n$, has information of channel gain $g_{js(n)}$. If $P_r|g_{js(n)}|^2 < r_n^* - P_s|h(n)|^2$, it keeps silent; otherwise, it forwards the data to Destination $s(n)$ in best single-relay transmission. After relays' transmission, a two-hop transmission is finished and a new contention is started among all sources.

It is notable that, the threshold λ^* deciding if or not to stop at first hop is calculated off-line. In the process to decide the broadcast rate, the thresholds $\{\zeta_l^+, \zeta_l^-, \eta_l\}_{l=1,2,\ldots,q}$ are calculated; also, only one of vectors $\{\mathbf{v}_k^1, \mathbf{v}_k^2, \mathbf{v}_k^3\}$ demand to obtain for the step where the condition is satisfied (i.e., it is calculated once for each-round decision).

$$\mathbf{v}_k^1 := (\arg \max_{q \geq i \geq k+1} \{U_k(\min(\eta_k, \zeta_k^+)), U_i'(\gamma_i(n))\}, \max_{q \geq i \geq k+1} \{U_k(\min(\eta_k, \zeta_k^+)), U_i'(\gamma_i(n))\}),$$

$$\mathbf{v}_k^2 := (\arg \max_{q \geq i \geq k+2} \{U_{k+1}(\gamma_{k+1}(n)), U_i'(\gamma_i(n))\}, \max_{q \geq i \geq k+2} \{U_{k+1}(\gamma_{k+1}(n)), U_i'(\gamma_i(n))\}),$$

$$\mathbf{v}_k^3 := (\arg \max_{q \geq i \geq k} \{U_i'(\gamma_i(n))\}, \max_{q \geq i \geq k} \{U_i'(\gamma_i(n))\})$$

4   Performance Evaluation

In this section, system performance for our proposed strategy is investigated through numerical simulations. We consider a wireless cooperative network with 15 source-destination pairs under the help of 6 relays. The probability that a source sends a RTS in a mini-slot is $p = 0.1$, and channel coherence time is $\tau_d = 8$ ms. RTS transmission duration is $\tau_{RTS} = 40$ µs, CTS transmission duration is $\tau_{CTS} = 40$ µs, and mini-slot duration $\delta = 20$ µs.

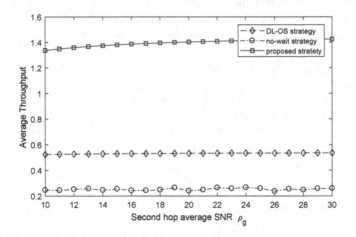

Fig. 2. Average system throughput with $\rho_g = 2 \cdot \rho_f$

Various average SNR configurations are considered. The second-hop average SNR ρ_g is from 10 dB to 30 dB, and the first-hop average SNR $\rho_f = \rho_g/2$ and $\rho_f = \rho_g/4$, respectively. To evaluate performance, the average system throughput is investigated. To verify the performance enhancement, we also compare the average system throughput with other two strategies, which are no-wait strategy and direct-link optimal stopping (DL-OS) strategy. In particular, under no-wait strategy, each source accesses the channel through direct transmission without wait, while under DL-OS strategy each source senses and accesses the direct link channel using optimal stopping strategy.

Considering different SNR configuration, two figures are shown as follows.

Figures 2 and 3 show the system performance with second-hop average SNR $\rho_g = 2 \cdot \rho_f$ and $\rho_g = 4 \cdot \rho_f$. In both figures, three curses are presented, representing the average system throughput by following our proposed strategy, no-wait strategy and DL-OS strategy, respectively. It can be seen that the average throughput with the proposed strategy performs much better than other strategies, and significant performance enhancement is harvested.

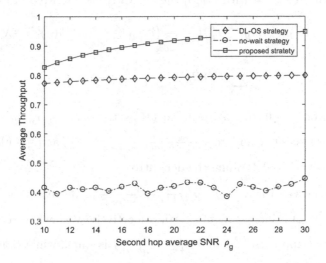

Fig. 3. Average system throughput with $\rho_g = 4 \cdot \rho_f$

5 Conclusion

In a wireless network aided by multiple relays, independent channel fading is experienced in both sources and relays. To enhance the spectrum efficiency, a joint exploitation of the multi-source diversity, multi-relay diversity, and time diversity is desired, and efficient distributed scheduling is motivated. To make a full exploitation of these diversities, the distributed DOS problem is investigated in our research. Formulating the problem as a three-level optimal stopping problem, an optimal strategy is proposed guiding distributed channel access for multiple source-to-destination communications under the help of multiple relays. The optimality of the strategy is rigorously proved, and easy implementation is presented of low complexity. The close-form expression of the maximal expected system throughput is also derived. This research should provide insights to the design of channel-aware MAC protocols in distributed cooperative network. Further research may involve the cases with quantized CSI and with QoS provision.

A   Proof of Lemma 1

For relay number $k \in \{1, 2, ..., L\}$, we define $r'_n := r_n - P_s|h(n)|^2$. For function Z_k, the first-order derivative is calculated as that

$$\frac{\partial Z_k}{\partial r'_n} = \tau_d \Big(\frac{\log_2 e}{1+r'_n+P_s|h(n)|^2} \big(1-(1-e^{-\frac{r'_n}{\sigma_g^2}})^k\big) - \frac{1}{\sigma_g^2} e^{-\frac{r'_n}{\sigma_g^2}}$$
$$(1-e^{-\frac{r'_n}{\sigma_g^2}})^{k-1} k \big(\log_2(1+r'_n+P_s|h(n)|^2) - \lambda \big) \Big).$$

By replacing $1-e^{-\frac{r'_n}{\sigma_g^2}}$ with $y(r'_n)$, the derivative is rewritten in Eq. (15).

$$\frac{\partial Z_k}{\partial r'_n} = (1-y(r'_n))ky^{1-k}(r'_n) \Big(-\frac{\tau_d}{\sigma_g^2} \big(\log_2(1+r'_n+P_s|h(n)|^2) - \lambda\big)$$
$$+\tau_d \log_2 e \frac{1}{k} \sum_{i=0}^{k-1} y^{-i}(\bar{R}_n) \frac{1}{1+r'_n+P_s|h(n)|^2} \Big). \tag{15}$$

In the region $r'_n \geq 0$, the factor in Eq. (15) satisfies $(1 - y(r'_n))y^{1-k}(r'_n) > 0$. Therefore, it suffices to compare $\frac{\tau_d \log_2 e}{1+r'_n+P_s|h(n)|^2} \sum_{i=0}^{k-1} y^{-i}(r'_n)$ and $\frac{1}{\sigma_g^2}k\big(\log_2(1+r'_n+ P_s|h(n)|^2)\tau_d - \lambda\tau_d\big)$ to determine the derivative.

It can be proved that $\sum_{i=0}^{k-1} y^{-i}(r'_n) \frac{1}{1+r'_n+P_s|h(n)|^2}$ is decreasing and $\log_2(1 + r'_n + P_s|h(n)|^2) - \lambda$ is increasing in $r'_n \geq 0$, respectively. Meanwhile, as r'_n is large, $\sum_{i=0}^{k-1} y^{-i}(r'_n)$ will approach to k and $\frac{1}{1+r'_n+P_s|h(n)|^2}$ is small, while $\{\log_2(1 + r'_n + P_s|h(n)|^2)\tau_d - \lambda\tau'_d\}$ is large. Thus, the existence of stationary point, denoted by $\zeta_k - P_s|h(n)|^2$ is guaranteed, which are unique such that $\frac{\partial Z_k}{\partial r'_n} = 0$.

As a result, function Z_k increases in $r_n < \zeta_k$, and decreases in $r_n \geq \zeta_k$. Then, relation of these points $\{\zeta_k\}, k = 1, 2, ..., L$ is further investigated. For $k > 1$, by valuing $r'_n = 0$, we have the derivative satisfy

$$\frac{\partial Z_k}{\partial r'_n}\Big|_{r'_n=0} = \frac{\log_2 e \cdot \tau_d}{1+P_s|h(n)|^2} > 0. \tag{16}$$

which means $\zeta_k > P_s|h(n)|^2$.

For $k = 1$, we have the derivative satisfy that

$$\frac{\partial Z_k}{\partial r'_n}\Big|_{r'_n=0} = \frac{\tau_d \log_2 e}{1+P_s|h(n)|^2} - \frac{\log_2(1+P_s|h(n)|^2)\tau_d - \lambda\tau_d}{\sigma_g^2}. \tag{17}$$

Suppose ζ_1 satisfies $\frac{\partial Z_k}{\partial r'_n} = 0$, we compare the points $\{\zeta_1, \zeta_2, ..., \zeta_L\}$. The situation where $\zeta_1 = P_s|h_{s(n)}(n)|^2$ is similar as $\zeta_k > P_s|h_{s(n)}(n)|^2$ for $\forall k \geq 2$.

Since ζ_k such that $\frac{\partial Z_k}{\partial R_n} = 0$, by induction it suffices from (15) to compare $\frac{1}{k} \sum_{i=0}^{k-1} y^{-i}(r'_n)$.

Based the relation shown in the following that

$$\frac{1}{k}\sum_{i=0}^{k-1} y^{-i}(r'_n) - \frac{1}{k+1}\sum_{i=0}^{k} y^{-i}(r'_n)$$

$$= \frac{1}{k(k+1)}\Big(\sum_{i=0}^{k-1} y^{-i}(r'_n) - ky^{-k}(r'_n)\Big) < 0$$

it proves that $\zeta_k < \zeta_{k+1}$ for $\forall k = 1, 2, ..., L{-}1$. In other words, $\zeta_1 < \zeta_2 < ... < \zeta_L$.

References

1. Andrews, M., Kumaran, K., Ramanan, K., Stolyar, A., Whiting, P., Vijayakumar, R.: Providing quality of service over a shared wireless link. IEEE Commun. Mag. **39**(2), 150–154 (2001)
2. Viswanath, P., Tse, D.N.C., Laroia, R.: Opportunistic beamforming using dumb antennas. IEEE Trans. Inf. Theory **48**(6), 1277–1294 (2002)
3. Zheng, D., Ge, W., Zhang, J.: Distributed opportunistic scheduling for ad hoc networks with random access: an optimal stopping approach. IEEE Trans. Inf. Theory **55**(1), 205–222 (2009)
4. Ge, W., Zhang, J., Wieselthier, J., Shen, X.: PHY-aware distributed scheduling for ad hoc communications with physical interference model. IEEE Trans. Wirel. Commun. **8**(5), 2682–2693 (2009)
5. Tan, S., Zheng, D., Zhang, J., Zeidler, J.: Distributed opportunistic scheduling for ad-hoc communications under delay constraints. In: Proceedings of IEEE INFOCOM 2010 (2010)
6. Xie, L.L., Kumar, P.R.: An achievable rate for the multiple-level relay channel. IEEE Trans. Inf. Theory **51**(4), 1348–1358 (2005)
7. Laneman, J.N., Tse, D.N.C., Wornell, G.W.: Cooperative diversity in wireless networks: efficient protocols and outage behavior. IEEE Trans. Inf. Theory **50**, 3062–3080 (2004)
8. Zhang, J., Jia, J., Zhang, Q., Lo, E.M.K.: Implementation and evaluation of cooperative communication schemes in software-defined radio testbed. In: Proceedings of IEEE INFOCOM 2010 (2010)
9. Zhang, Q., Jia, J., Zhang, J.: Cooperative relay to improve diversity in cognitive radio networks. IEEE Commun. Mag. **47**(2), 111–117 (2009)
10. Gunduz, D., Erkip, E.: Opportunistic cooperation by dynamic resource allocation. IEEE Trans. Wirel. Commun. **6**(4), 1446–1454 (2007)
11. Jing, Y., Jafarkhani, H.: Network beamforming using relays with perfect channel information. IEEE Trans. Inf. Theory **55**(6), 2499–2517 (2009)
12. Zhang, Z., Jiang, H.: Distributed opportunistic channel access in wireless relay networks. IEEE J. Sel. Areas Commun. **30**(9), 1675–1683 (2012)
13. Zhang, Z., Zhou, S., Jiang, H., Dong, L.: Opportunistic cooperative channel access in distributed wireless networks with decode-and-forward relays. IEEE Commun. Lett. **19**(10), 1778–1781 (2015)
14. Ferguson, T.: Optimal stopping and applications. Mathematics Department, UCLA. http://www.math.ucla.edu/~tom/Stopping/Contents.html

Theoretical and Experimental Comparisons of the Self-pressurization in a Cryogenic Storage Tank for IOT Application

Juan Fu$^{(\boxtimes)}$ and Jingchao Wang

China Electronic System Engineering Company, Beijing, China
fujuan0702@163.com

Abstract. The application of satellite technology in the Internet of Things (IOT) can just make up for the defects of the ground system for its wide coverage and anti-damage. More and more satellites will participate in IOT. Due to the environmental protection exhaust and high specific impulse of cryogenic propellants like liquid hydrogen and liquid oxygen, they will play an important role in satellite applications. Cryogenic liquid storage is difficult and self-pressurization phenomenon often occurs. Pressure rise prediction with high accurate is necessary when designing tank for storage. Numerical calculation of computational fluid dynamic model and experiments are always time and financial consuming. A theoretical thermal diffusion model is investigated in the paper by using a concentration parameter model in the vapor and a one-dimensional heat conduction model in the liquid. The validation of the predictive capability is conducted by comparing the predictions with experimental data. Favorable agreement is found for both the experimental cylindrical and oblate spheroidal tanks. The effect of fill level and tank size is also studied.

Keywords: Internet of Things (IOT) · Self-pressurization phenomenon · Cryogenic liquid · Theoretical thermal diffusion model

1 Introduction

The Internet of Things (IOT) is a universal network that will timely obtain, transmit, and intelligently process information such as wide area geography, environment, space, and mobile objects to achieve a comprehensive interconnection of wide areas. The inability of The conventional ground equipment and systems is failure to provide high-density, full-coverage real-time data acquisition and data transmission services for large or specific areas. It results in the lack of the necessary remote sensing and communication network support for IOT applications in these areas. Further, in disaster conditions, ground infrastructure is easily destroyed, and emergency network construction is inconvenient, so the application of the IOT and disaster emergency monitoring are greatly limited. The application of satellite technology in the IOT can just make up for the defects of the ground system, its coverage is wide and the system is persistent. The flexibility of

B. Li et al. (Eds.): IoTaaS 2019, LNICST 316, pp. 296–309, 2020.
https://doi.org/10.1007/978-3-030-44751-9_25

the space-based network determines that it will play a necessary and irreplaceable role in the IOT industry.

More and more satellites will participate in the IOT system. The propellant is needed for rocket launch and satellite attitude and orbit control. Due to the Environmental Protection exhaust and High specific impulse of cryogenic propellants like liquid hydrogen and liquid oxygen, they will play an important role in satellite applications. However, cryogenic liquid storage is difficult because the heat leak is inevitable. Thus phase change happens and the tank pressure will rise regularly. It is important to predict the pressure rise trend for the pressure control and the proper tank design.

Many methods have been developed by investigators by considering time and financial consuming besides prediction accuracy. Pressure rise tendency is often compared with experimental data to judge the methods. One-dimensional methods were used in the primary quickly tank design for its low time and financial consuming with acceptable prediction accuracy. These models often ignored heat transportation in fluid or vapor part. A homogeneous thermodynamic analysis [1] was studied assuming the energy rise rate was the same in the tank fluid. Thus, the model prediction was not well matched with the experimental data. Hochstein et al. [2] considered the transport only in liquid and compared the tendency with experiment [3]. Prediction accuracy depended on the heat location and gravity. The capability of the model proposed by Amirkhanyan and Cherkasov [4] was influenced by tank fill level. Further, CFD models were developed for computer technology development. Thermal stratification and phase change at the interface was considered in the CFD model to forecast the pressure rise [5, 6]. Results were evaluated with test data [7]. Reasonable forecast obtained only for low liquid fraction case. Other CFD models were investigated by changing condition at the interface [8] or including transport in both liquid and vapor parts [9]. The later was validated with experiment and accuracy depended on the gravity and heat leak.

Here, the self-pressurization in a closed cryogenic vessel is predicted by employing the conductivity model in liquid and lumped model for vapor phase. It is a time saving method to accurately predict the pressure rise in the enclosure tank compared with the CFD method and experiments. The performance is assessed by comparing the computing predictions with experimental self-pressurization data.

2 Mathematical Model

The partly filled cryogenic vessel is schematically illustrated in Fig. 1. The tank volume V_T is divided by the interface of the two phases into liquid volume V_L and gas volume V. Total heat leak of Q is imposed on the tank wall. Therefore, the external heat loads delivered through the dry and wetted parts of the tank are noted as Q_L and Q_V, respectively. Only liquid vapor exists in the gas part. Under these conditions, one can assume that the pressure in the vessel is unambiguously related via the saturation curve to the temperature on the interface T_S; because the pressure drops in the gas phase are small, the pressure p_V and temperature T_S may be assumed to be functions of time alone.

The governing formulas of mass, momentum, and energy are

$$\frac{\partial \rho}{\partial t} + \nabla \cdot \left(\rho \vec{V} \right) = 0 \tag{1}$$

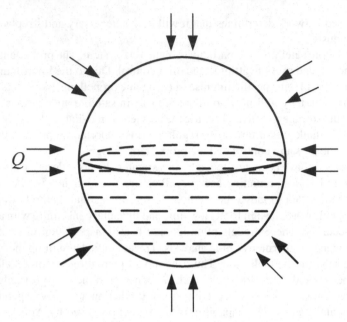

Fig. 1. Schematic diagram of the cryogenic vessel

$$\frac{\partial\left(\rho\vec{V}\right)}{\partial t} + \nabla\cdot\left(\rho\vec{V}\vec{V}\right) = -\nabla p - \nabla\cdot(S) + \rho\vec{g} \tag{2}$$

$$\frac{\partial(\rho E)}{\partial t} + \nabla\cdot\left(\vec{V}(\rho E + p)\right) = -\nabla\cdot\left(S\cdot\vec{V}\right) + \nabla\cdot(\lambda\nabla T) \tag{3}$$

Where the compressive stress $S = -\mu\left(\nabla\vec{V} + \nabla\vec{V}^T\right) + \left[(\frac{2}{3}\mu - \varsigma)\nabla\cdot\vec{V}\right]\mathbf{I}$, ρ is the fluid density, $\vec{V}$ is the fluid speed vector, p is the tank pressure, $\vec{g}$ is the acceleration of gravity, $E = h - \frac{p}{\rho} + \frac{V^2}{2} = u + \frac{V^2}{2}$ is the fluid energy per unit mass, h and u are the fluid specific enthalpy and specific internal energy respectively. λ is the fluid Thermal conductivity.

The mass rate at the interface between the two phases resulted from the evaporation or condensation is

$$j = \rho_L(\mathbf{V_L} - \mathbf{V_I})\cdot\hat{n} = \rho_V(\mathbf{V_V} - \mathbf{V_I})\cdot\hat{n} \tag{4}$$

when $\hat{n}$ pointing the liquid is positive, $\mathbf{V_L}, \mathbf{V_V}, \mathbf{V_I}$ is the speed vector of liquid, vapor and interface, respectively.

In the non-thermodynamic equilibrium state, the temperature appears at the intersection of two phases is not continuous, assuming that the interface temperature is the saturation temperature of the system. According to Fourier's law, the difference in heat flow density between the two sides of the interface is obtained:

$$\|q_s\| = \left[\left(-\lambda_L\frac{\partial T}{\partial n}\right)\Big|_L - \left(-\lambda_V\frac{\partial T}{\partial n}\right)\Big|_V\right]\mathbf{n} \tag{5}$$

n is the unit normal vector pointing to the vapor. Phase change mass flow caused by heat density is

$$j = \frac{q_s}{L} \tag{6}$$

The positive j means evaporation, negative number means condensation. The unit is kg/(m^2·s). L is the latent heat of vaporization.

The boundary conditions are as follows. The heat from the environment is $\dot{Q}$, Assuming the tank area is A, the heat flux $q = \dot{Q}/A$. At the sidewalls and interface, no slip boundary conditions are chosen. The initial condition is

$$\vec{V} = 0$$
$$T = T_0$$
$$P_0 = P_{sat}(T_0) \tag{7}$$

The initial status is the saturation state.

The control equation is nonlinear, it is difficult to solve it directly. Therefore, some assumptions are generally added to predict the pressure. The earliest applied computational model was the Uniform Thermodynamic Model [1]. The model assumes that the temperature in the vapor and liquid parts is the same, the pressure is equal to the saturated vapor pressure corresponding to the system temperature, the fluid is not pressurized, and the fluid properties do not change with the temperature. The model will be used for comparative analysis with a thermal diffusion model (TDM) combined with a gas concentration parameter model and a liquid heat conduction model proposed in this paper. The TDM takes into account the different temperature change rates of gas and liquid phase, and the two phases are mathematically modeled. The coupling solution is obtained by mass and energy transmission at the interface.

2.1 Gas Concentration Parameter Model

Mass Control Formular. Due to the volume of the tank and the total mass of the fluid medium are unchanged, there are:

$$\frac{d}{dt}(\rho_V V) = \frac{d}{dt}\left[m_p - \rho_L(V_T - V)\right]$$
$$= \frac{d}{dt}(\rho_L(V - V_T)) = \frac{d}{dt}(\rho_L V)$$
$$= J \tag{8}$$

Where $J = jA_I$ the phase transition rate (kg/s), A_I is the interface area, m_p is the total mass of the gas and liquid in the vessel, V is the gas phase volume, V_T is he total volume of the tank. ρ_V and ρ_L are the gas phase density and liquid phase density respectively. Ignoring the change in liquid density, the above formula is transferred to

$$\frac{dV}{dt} = \frac{J}{\rho_L} \tag{9}$$

The heat required for phase transition evaporation is the difference in heat flow at the interface:

$$LJ = \dot{Q}_{IL} - \dot{Q}_{IV} \Rightarrow \dot{Q}_{IV} = \dot{Q}_{IL} - LJ \tag{10}$$

Where $\dot{Q}_{IL} = \int_I (-\lambda_L \nabla T_L) \cdot \vec{n} dS$ is the heat flow on the liquid side of the interface, $\vec{n}$ refers to the unit vector perpendicular to the interface pointing to the gas phase, $\dot{Q}_{IV} = \int_I (-\lambda_V \nabla T_V) \cdot \vec{n} dS$ is the heat flow on the gas side of the interface.

Ignoring changes in liquid density, the gas volume in Eq. (8) is

$$V = V_0 \frac{\rho_L - \rho_{V,0}}{\rho_L - \rho_V} = V_0 \left(1 + \frac{\rho_V - \rho_{V,0}}{\rho_L - \rho_V} \right) \tag{11}$$

Where V_0 the initial volume of the gas, $\rho_{V,0}$ is the initial density. In the case where the gas density change value is very small relative to the density difference between the liquid and the gas density, the gas density is very close to the initial value.

The gas density obtained from the gas state equation is:

$$\rho_V = \frac{p_V}{RT} \tag{12}$$

Where R is gas constant, $R = R_M / M$, the ratio of the general gas constant R_M to the molar mass of the gas M.

Assuming that the gas phase is saturated, the temperature T is the saturation temperature T_S corresponding to the tank pressure P_V, $T = T_S$, T_S and P_V are satisfying the saturated vapor pressure:

$$\frac{1}{T_S} = \frac{1}{T_B} - \frac{R}{L} \ln \left(\frac{p_V}{p_B} \right) \tag{13}$$

T_B and p_B are the value of a reference saturation state.

Energy Control Formular. The gas energy change is:

$$\frac{d}{dt}(\rho_V V u) = \dot{Q}_V + \dot{Q}_{IV} + J \left(u + \frac{p_V}{\rho_V} \right) - p_V \frac{dV}{dt} \tag{14}$$

$\dot{Q}_V$ is the heat flow into the gas phase transmitted through the tank wall of gas part, Ju is the internal energy changes caused by evaporation, $J p_V / \rho_V$ is the pressure work due to changes in evaporation; $-p_V dV / dt$ is the External work for volume changes.

Expanding Eq. (14) and Substituting Eq. (8)–(10) into Eq. (14), Ju is eliminated, the following formula is obtained:

$$\rho_V V \frac{du}{dt} + J \left[L - p_V \left(\frac{1}{\rho_V} - \frac{1}{\rho_L} \right) \right] = \dot{Q}_V + \dot{Q}_{IL} \tag{15}$$

Further, substituting $u = c_V T_S$ and $J = \frac{d}{dt}(\rho_V V)$ into Eq. (15), there is

$$\left\{ \rho_V V c_V + \frac{\partial}{\partial T_S}(\rho_V V) \left[L - p_V \left(\frac{1}{\rho_V} - \frac{1}{\rho_L} \right) \right] \right\} \frac{dT_S}{dt} = \dot{Q}_V + \dot{Q}_{IL} \tag{16}$$

It will be abbreviated as:

$$\frac{dT_S}{dt} = B\left(\dot{Q}_V + \dot{Q}_{IL}\right) \tag{17}$$

Where B is the function of pressure.

$$B = \left\{\rho_V V c_V + \frac{\partial}{\partial T_S}(\rho_V V)\left[L - p_V\left(\frac{1}{\rho_V} - \frac{1}{\rho_L}\right)\right]\right\}^{-1} \tag{18}$$

Combing Eq. (8)–(13), there are

$$\frac{\partial p_V}{\partial T_S} = \frac{Lp_V}{RT_S^2}$$

$$\frac{\partial}{\partial T_S}(\rho_V V) = \frac{\rho_V \rho_L V}{\rho_L - \rho_V}\left(\frac{1}{RT_S^2} - \frac{1}{T_S}\right) \tag{19}$$

Then Eq. (18) is changed into

$$B = \left\{\rho_V V c_V + \frac{\rho_V \rho_L V}{\rho_L - \rho_V}\left(\frac{1}{RT_S^2} - \frac{1}{T_S}\right)\left[L - p_V\left(\frac{1}{\rho_V} - \frac{1}{\rho_L}\right)\right]\right\}^{-1} \tag{20}$$

By calculating Eq. (16), the saturation temperature T_S of the gas is obtained. Since the temperature and pressure satisfy the saturation vapor pressure equation, the pressure change p_V in the vessel can be calculated. Solving Eq. (16) the $\dot{Q}_{IL}$ needs to be known. $\dot{Q}_{IL}$ will be given by the temperature field calculation of the liquid phase. The Coupling calculation of gas and liquid phase is through $\dot{Q}_{IL}$.

2.2 Liquid Thermal Conductivity Model

There are two views on the influence of convection on the temperature field. First, convection is considered to be a forced agitation that can reduce temperature heterogeneity and therefore reduce temperature stratification. The second is that natural convection is an upward fluctuation of the heat flow. Therefore, when heat is transported from different sides into the liquid body, convection will cause overheating of the top liquid layer, thereby increasing the temperature stratification. By numerical simulation of the liquid heat leakage in the vertical cylindrical tank, the results are compared with the thermal conductivity problems, and it is found that the influence of convection on temperature is actually a combination of the above two views. Due to convection, the heat on the wall and bottom is transported into the liquid body to reduce the uneven temperature distribution. On the other hand, convection increases the temperature of the top boundary of the liquid. The temperature field is formed owing to thermal conductivity and convection. Because of the buoyancy, liquid near the heated wall moves up. When it reaches the top surface, it turns towards the center and finally reaches at the boottom. Thus circulation flow is determines in the liquid. Finally thermal stratification is formed, which means the temperature is a function of the height of the tank. This is observed by both the experiments [10] and CFD results [11, 12].

Therefore, for the specificity of the convection effect, the following assumptions are made for the calculation [4]: (1) The heat entering the liquid through the wall surface is evenly distributed in the entire liquid volume under convection, (2) The heat entering the interior of the liquid through the top interface is diffused into the liquid in the form of thermal conductivity. The vertical thermal conductivity is the fluid thermal conductivity coefficient, and the horizontal thermal conductivity coefficient is infinity, that is, the liquid at different heights. The temperature is the same in the horizontal direction. Based on the above assumptions, a one-dimensional heat conduction model of liquid is obtained.

$$\rho_L c_L A \frac{\partial T}{\partial t} = \lambda_L \frac{\partial}{\partial z}\left(A \frac{\partial T}{\partial z}\right) + A \frac{\dot{Q}_L}{V_L}$$

$$\left.\frac{\partial T}{\partial z}\right|_{z=0} = 0, \quad \left.\lambda_L\left(A \frac{\partial T}{\partial z}\right)\right|_{z=H_L} = \dot{Q}_{IL} \tag{21}$$

Where A is the heat transfer cross-sectional area at the height z of the liquid surface, H_L is the height of the liquid surface, $\dot{Q}_L$ is the heat flow into the liquid, $\dot{Q}_L / V_L$ is equivalent to heat source density. The pressure change trend of the tank can be calculated by using the temperature value calculated by the liquid thermal conductivity model and the heat transfer at the interface as the boundary condition of the gas phase change.

3 Result and Discussion

The results obtained using the foregoing thermal diffusion model (TDM) for calculations under the experimental conditions of [13] are given in Fig. 2. The experimental data were obtained in a tank of 6.75 L with liquid nitrogen for different fill levels of different external heat fluxes. A thermodynamic method with no thermal stratification is also used for the comparison. Relevant thermodynamic properties of the fluid used in the calculation model are listed in Table 1.

Table 1. Thermodynamic properties of liquid nitrogen

Symbol	Property	Value
ρ_L	Liquid density	807.7 kg/m^3
c_L	Liquid specific heat at constant volume	2041.5 J/kg K
c_V	Vapor specific heat at constant volume	1040.67 J/kg K
λ_L	Liquid thermal conductivity	0.14657 W/m K
L	Latent heat	198300 J/kg

One can see that the use of Eq. (21) instead of the condition of the absence of thermal stratification in liquid results in a considerable reduction of discrepancy between theory

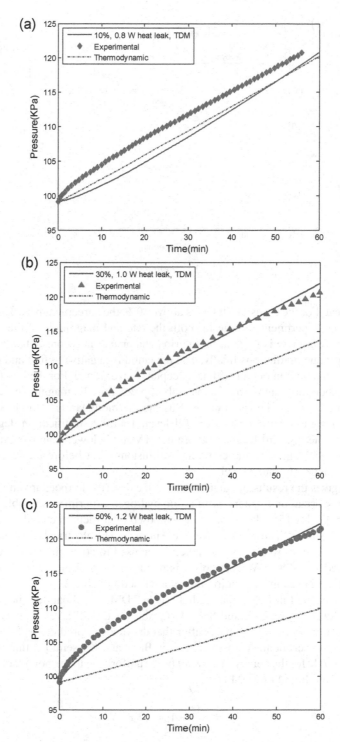

Fig. 2. Comparison of TDM, experimental data and thermodynamic; (a) fill level = 10%; (b) fill level = 30%; (c) fill level = 50%; (d) fill level = 70%.

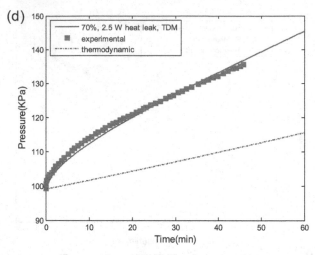

Fig. 2. (*continued*)

and experiment. For the cases of fill levels above 10%, the agreement between the TDM predictions and experiments is fine for both the rate and magnitude of the vapor rise. The rate of pressure rise is large at first period and arrives at a constant value equal to the thermodynamic predictions finally. The deviation is negative at first and positive at the end of the calculation but all with an acceptable error range. For the low fill level of 10%, TDM model does an unsatisfactory job of predicting the magnitude of the vapor pressure while captures the rise rate well as the thermodynamic. This is so because the fluid mixing more sufficient at low fill level. Thermal stratification degree is not pronounced as the high fill levels. The predicted value is lower than the experimental value because TDM ignores the convective diffusion effect before the reservoir fluid temperature reaches the same level.

Figure 3 gives the results of calculations by the described procedure and the values of the self-pressurization in a tank with liquid hydrogen experimentally obtained in the K-site facility [7, 14, 15]. The vessel was composed by a vacuum chamber enclosing a cylindrical cryoshroud. The temperatures were measured by electrical resistance heaters. The tank was covered by two MLI blankets were used to cover the tank and radiative losses were reduced. 28.08 W heat power is into the system. Relevant thermodynamic properties of fluid used in calculation model are listed in Table 2.

It is demonstrated in Fig. 3 the predictions of TDM model capture the experiment data well in fill levels of 29% and 83%. However, for the fill level 49% TDM model performs excellent at the first 6 h but after that the model's predictions becomes poor compared with experiment. It was declared by Baris and Kassemi [5] that the heating style is responsible for the deracy. It may not be the uniform heat flux boundary condition. The heat flux into liquid in TDM is

$$\dot{Q}_L = \frac{\dot{Q}}{A_{wall}} A_L = 13.86 \text{ W} \tag{22}$$

Table 2. Thermodynamic properties of liquid hydrogen

Symbol	Property	Value
ρ_L	Liquid density	70.734 kg/m^3
c_L	Liquid specific heat at constant volume	5678.2 J/kg K
c_V	Vapor specific heat at constant volume	14283 J/kg K
λ_L	Liquid thermal conductivity	0.10349 W/m K
L	Latent heat	445196.6 J/kg

where A_{wall} is the tank wall area, A_L is the tank wall area occupied by liquid Fig. 3(b). The TDM predictions exceed the experimental data means heat flux into vapor is below that heating uniformly. $\dot{Q}_V$ is

$$\dot{Q}_V = \dot{Q} - \dot{Q}_L = \frac{\dot{Q}}{A_{wall}} A_V \qquad (23)$$

Where A_V is the tank wall area occupied by vapor. Therefore, $\dot{Q}_L$ is increased to 18 W with $\dot{Q}_L$ staying at 28.08 W. Figure 4(a) shows the pressure calculated by TDM matches the experimental well. In order to verify that nonuniformly heating occurred in the fill level of 49%, the experimental data under $q_w = 3.5$ W/m^2 is used for the verification. Thus $\dot{Q}_L = 31.5963$ W with the same A_L when $\dot{Q}_L = 18$ W. The agreement is obtained in Fig. 4(b). More strict and clear experimental condition plays an important role in the validation of theory prediction model. The thermodynamic model underestimates the experimental self-pressurization due to the neglection of the conduction and convection effect in the liquid. It assumes the system is homogeneous and the saturation temperature states with that corresponding to the vapor pressure.

The experiments in Fig. 2 are carried out in different fill levels for different heat leak. Therefore, it is difficult to conclude the influence of fill level on the self-pressurization. Figure 5 gives the pressure variation in different fill levels of the same heat leak of 2 W by using thermal diffusion model. The pressurization rate decreases with increasing fill level. For a fixed heat power, as liquid volume increases due to the increasing fill level, the heat capacity increases. Thus the self-pressurization rate decreases. This phenomenon is not obvious in the NASA's experiment tank. It was observed that the pressure rise rates were lowest at middle fill levels for LH2. Pressure rise rates at varying fill level are subject to the combined effects of the liquid fill level, wall area occupied by liquid, liquid-vapor interfacial area, and system heating model.

The diameter and height of the tank are increased to 1.5 times of the experimental one. The cases of equal heat leak 2 W and equal volume energy source Q/V_T are investigated at a fixed fill level of 30%. The predicting results are shown in Fig. 6. Pressure rise is decreased as tank volume increases due to the gas volume increases with the same heat

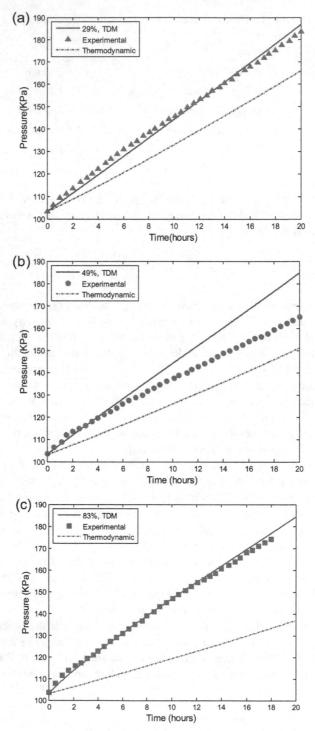

Fig. 3. Comparison of TDM, experimental data and thermodynamic; (a) fill level = 29%; (b) fill level = 49%; (c) fill level = 83%.

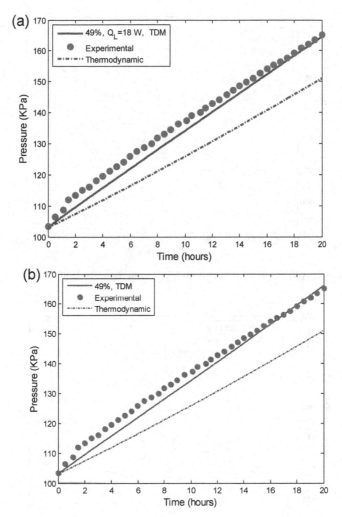

Fig. 4. Comparison of TDM, experimental data and thermodynamic of unknown heating condition (fill level = 49%).

leak. However, when the volume energy sources are equal, pressurization in the large tank increases more quickly. This is so because the interface area is larger resulting in increase of Q_{IL}.

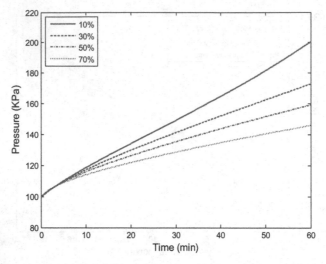

Fig. 5. Self-pressurization for different fill levels with the same heat load of $Q = 2.0$ W.

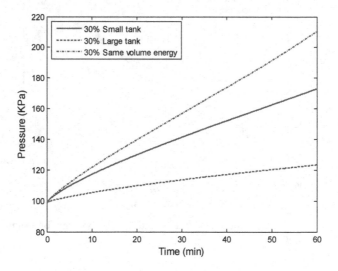

Fig. 6. Comparison of self-pressurization different tank sizes.

4   Conclusion

In this paper, a coupled thermal diffusion model is developed by employing a concentration parameter model in the vapor and a one-dimensional heat conduction model in the liquid to predict the self-pressurization in cryogenic storage tanks. The predictive capability of the model is assessed by comparing the model's predictions with cryogenic self-pressurization data obtained during experiments in Korea Advanced Institute of Science and Technology with liquid nitrogen and in NASA Glenn's K-site facility with liquid hydrogen. Comparisons between the model predictions and experimental data are conducted and agreements are reasonably acceptable. For the cylindrical tank of liquid nitrogen, the trend is that pressurization rate is lower when the fill level increases. Pressure rise is decreased as tank volume increases due to the gas volume increases with the same heat leak. Pressurization is influenced by the heat and mass exchange at the interface for two different size tanks with equal volume energy source. For the oblate spheroidal tank geometry, the effect of fill level on pressure rise is not intuitive. It is a combination of the liquid fill level, wall area occupied by liquid, liquid-vapor interfacial area, and system heating model.

References

1. Aydelott, J.: Normal gravity self-pressurization of 9-inch (23 cm) diameter spherical liquid hydrogen tanks. NASA TND-4171(1967)
2. Hochstein, J., Ji, H.-C., Aydelott, J.: Prediction of self-pressurization rate of cryogenic propellant tankage. J. Propul. Power 6(1), 11–17 (1990)
3. Abdalla, K., Frysinger, T., Androcchio, C.: Pressure-rise characteristics for a liquid hydrogen dewar for homogeneous, normal gravity, quiescent, and zero-gravity tests. NASA TM X-1134 (1965)
4. Amirkhanyan, N., Cherkasov, S.: Theoretical analysis and procedure for the calculation of thermophysical processes occurring in a cryogenic vessel under conditions of nonvented storage. High Temp. 39(6), 905–911 (2001)
5. Baris, S., Kassemi, M.: Numerical and experimental comparisons of the self-pressurization behavior of an LH2 tank in normal gravity. Cryogenics 48, 122–129 (2008)
6. Panzarella, C., Kassemi, M.: On the validity of purely thermodynamic descriptions of two phase cryogenic fluid storage. J. Fluid Mech. 484, 41–68 (2003)
7. Dresar, N.V., Lin, C., Hasan, M.: Self-pressurization of a flightweight liquid hydrogen tank: effects of fill level at low wall heat flux. NASA TM 105411 (1992)
8. Roh, S., Son, G.: Numerical study of natural convection in a liquefied natural gas tank. J. Mech. Sci. Technol. 26(10), 3133–3140 (2012)
9. Grayson, G., Lopez, A., Chandler, F., Hastings, L., Tucker, S.: Cryogenic tank modeling for the saturn AS-203 experiment. In: AIAA 2006-5258 (2006)
10. Das, S.P., Chakraborty, S., Dutta, P.: Studies on thermal stratification phenomenon in LH2 storage vessel. Heat Transfer Eng. 25, 54–66 (2004)
11. Kumar, S.P., Prasad, B.V.S.S.S., Venkatarathnam, G., Ramamurthi, K., Murthy, S.S.: Influence of surface evaporation on stratification in liquid hydrogen tanks of different aspect ratios. Int. J. Hydrogen Energy 32, 1954–1960 (2007)
12. Ren, J., Shi, J., Liu, P., Bi, M., Jia, K.: Simulation on the thermal stratification and destratifiction in liquefied gas tanks. Int. J. Hydrogen Energy 38(10), 4017–4023 (2013)
13. Seo, M., Jeong, S.: Analysis of self-pressurization phenomenon of cryogenic fluid storage tank with thermal diffusion model. Cryogenics 50, 549–555 (2010)
14. Stochl, R., Knoll, R.: Thermal performance of a liquid hydrogen tank multilayer insulation system at warm boundary temperatures of 630, 530, and 152 R. NASA TM 104476 (1991)
15. Hasan, M., Lin, C., Dresar, N.V.: Self-pressurization of a flightweight liquid hydrogen storage tank subjected to low heat flux. NASA TM 103804 (1991)

Vulnerability Analysis of Wireless Sensor Networks via Maximum Flow Interdiction

Keyu Wu[1]($\boxtimes$), Zhou Zhang[2], Xingchen Hu[1], Boliang Sun[1], and Chao Chen[1]

[1] National University of Defense Technology, Changsha 410073, China
keyuwu@nudt.edu.cn
[2] Tianjin Artificial Intelligence Innovation Center, Tianjin, China

Abstract. Due to limited resource and changing environments, wireless sensor networks are susceptible to device failures. In this paper, we evaluate network's vulnerability under potential device failures or attacking. Specifically, we model wireless sensors and their operating procedure as an S-T network, where the information rate regarding the network performance is defined. The network robustness is evaluated via considering how network capacity varies when network changes. The evaluation process turns out to be a maximum flow interdiction problem, which is then solved by transforming into a dual formation and approximating with a linear programming. Lastly, via numerical simulation, the proposed scheme is shown to be well suitable for evaluating network's robustness.

Keywords: Vulnerability analysis · Network interdiction · Maximum flow · Malicious attacking

1 Introduction

Wireless sensor networks consist of widely deployed sensors that sense environment, collect data and route information to interested users, which are essential for the Internet of things. Due to either hardware degradation and or malicious attacking, wireless sensors may fail and be out of service [1]. The performance of an improperly designed network may greatly suffer due to device failures. Therefore, robustness is an important design aspect for wireless sensor networks.

In literature, a network's robustness or vulnerability is mainly investigated from the view of the underlying graph topology. For example, in [2], the connectivity of a network is considered, where two metrics, namely "node-similarity" and "optimal connectivity", are defined to quantify network vulnerability. Similarly, work [3] considers robustness as the redundancy of routing path between two nodes, and defines a metric "natural connectivity" for measuring the network's robustness. Beside connectivity, criticality is another metric that is used for measuring network vulnerability [4,5]. The node critical value is defined via counting the number of paths that flows through a node. The edge critical value

© ICST Institute for Computer Sciences, Social Informatics and Telecommunications Engineering 2020
Published by Springer Nature Switzerland AG 2020. All Rights Reserved
B. Li et al. (Eds.): IoTaaS 2019, LNICST 316, pp. 310–317, 2020.
https://doi.org/10.1007/978-3-030-44751-9_26

is defined similarly. Therefore, a node or edge with higher criticality value contributes more to the network's throughput, and may manifest itself as a vulnerable point of a network. Furthermore, based on the definition of node and edge critical values, network criticality is defined [6,7] via averaging nodes' and edges' critical values. From the perspective of information theory, work [8] studied the vulnerability of network from the topology dissimilarities after network topology changes. The robustness metric is then calculated with the Jenson-Shannon divergence that is original from the information theory.

However, node connectivity or network topology changes does not necessarily well represent the network performance variations caused by node failures. In this paper, we will investigate the network robustness from the capacity of a sensor network. Specifically, we model wireless sensors and their operating procedure as an S-T network, where the maximum supported information rate, i.e., the capacity, of the network performance is defined. Furthermore, an intelligent attacking strategy that aims to minimize the network's capacity is considered, where the attacking strategy is solved with maximum flow interdiction methods. Finally, the network robustness is then measured in terms of capacity variations under such an attacking scheme.

The rest of this paper is organized as follows. Section 2 introduces models for representing a sensor network and its working procedure. Section 3 analyzes the network robustness with a network interdiction problem. Section 4 provides a computationally tractable algorithm for solving the interdiction problem. Section 5 shows simulations result and Sect. 6 concludes the paper.

2   Modeling the Capability of Sensor Networks

2.1   Network Topology Model

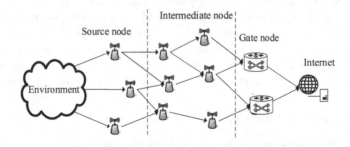

Fig. 1. An example for sensor networks under investigation.

In this paper, we investigate a sensor network as shown in Fig. 1, where some source nodes measure environment and transmit measured packets throughout intermediate nodes to gate nodes that located at the edge of network, and from gate nodes, measured information can be accessed via the Internet. Note that a measured packet can be routed to the Internet through potentially multiple paths, which is determined by underlying routing algorithms. Furthermore, since different tranceiving pairs are associated with different distance and wireless resources, edges of network have different transmission capacities.

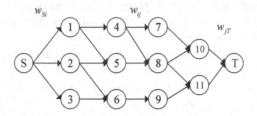

Fig. 2. S-T network induced from the sensor network.

Mathematically, the above sensor network can be modeled as a directional weighted graph, as shown in the S-T network of Fig. 2. Specifically, let $\mathcal{V} = \{1, 2, \cdots, n\} \cup \{S, T\}$ denote the sensor nodes, where $\{1, 2, \cdots, n\}$ denotes the sensor nodes in the network, S is a virtual node that represents the environment, and T is a virtual node that represents the Internet (destination of information flow). In addition, let $\mathcal{E} = \{(i, j)\}$ denote the edges that connects node i and node j with flow direction specified by underlying routing algorithm. Moreover, there is a weight associated with edge in the S-T network. Specifically, there is a weight w_{Si} associated with node S to a sensor node i, and it represents the maximum information sample rate that sensor node i is able to sense from the environment. The value of w_{Si} with $i \in \{1, 2, ..., n\}$ is determined by the capacity of sensors and the design goal of sensing tasks. In addition, there is a weight w_{jT} with $j \in \{1, 2, ..., n\}$ from a gate node j to node T, and it represents the maximum information transmitting rate from a gate node to the Internet. The value of w_{jT} is determined by the capacity of gate node and backhauls. Lastly, there is a weight w_{ij} with $i, j \in \{1, 2, ..., n\}$ from a node j to a node i, and it represents the maximum routing rate that information is transmitted from node i to node j. The value of w_{ij} is determined by nodes' transmission capability and wireless channel condition. In summary, the triple $\mathcal{G} = (\mathcal{V}, \mathcal{E}, W)$ defines a sensor network, and in the following, we evaluate the networks' performance based on the above information.

2.2 Network Capability Model

The S-T graph represented in Fig. 2 captures the network topology and capability of individual nodes (source nodes, intermediate nodes and gate nodes). In this part, we model the capability from the network point of view with network flow model, which integrates the overall ability of sensing environment, routing sensed information, and delivering information to the Internet. Specifically, we investigate the question: what is the maximum information rate can be delivered from the node S (environment) to node T (the Internet) without violating pairwise capability constraints w_{ij} with $i, j \in \{S, T, 1, 2, ..., n\}$?

The network flow model answers the question. We define a flow function $f : \mathcal{V} \times \mathcal{V} \mapsto \mathbb{R}$, such that the function f satisfying following conditions:

1. capacity constraints: for all $i, j \in \mathcal{V}$, we have $f(i,j) \leq w(i,j)$ (which means that the actual data rate cannot exceed the edge rate capacity);
2. skew symmetry: for all i, j, we have $f(i,j) = -f(j,i)$ (because edges are directional);
3. flow conservation: for all $u \in \mathcal{V}\backslash\{S,T\}$, we have $\sum_{v\in\mathcal{V}} f(u,v) = 0$ (flows into a node must equal flows out from a node).

A valid flow function f satisfying above conditions represents an assignment of data rate over different edges. The value of a flow function defined as $|f| = \sum_{i\in\mathcal{V}} f(S,i)$ represents the data rate flow over the network. Among all possible flow functions (assignments), there is an optimal flow f^* that achieve the maximum flow value, which is the best one can get under the network topology and devices' individual capacity. Hence, we can use the value of maximum flow to capture the network capacity.

There exists many algorithms for solving f^*, and Ford-Fulkerson algorithm is perhaps the most well-known one, which can solve f^* with time complexity of $\mathcal{O}(n \cdot |\mathcal{E}|^2)$ [11]. Developing fast algorithms for solving the maximum network flow is an on-going research direction in computer science. Algorithms faster than Ford-Fulkerson algorithm have been developed (see [12] and references therein).

In summary, we have developed a maximum flow model for modeling the overall network capability given sensor networks' topology and individual devices' capacity. In addition, the developed model can be solved efficiently with polynomial time complexity.

3   Vulnerability Analysis via Network Flow Interdiction

In this part, we analyze the network vulnerability under device's potential failures. Specifically, due to device degradation and potential attacks, sensors in the network may be out of service and network capability deteriorates. A robustly designed network is able to tolerate such device failures and reserve network capability as much as possible. In contrast, the performance of a vulnerable network may be severely suffered when devices are out of service.

In order to evaluate the vulnerability, we have to model the pattern of device's failures. In this paper, we analyze the network's performance changes under the worst case device failure pattern. It may correspond to an intelligent attacker that is attempting to deteriorate the network's performance by compromising the most important sensors. This problem can be modeled under network interdiction framework.

Suppose that an attacker is able to compromise k edges among the total $|\mathcal{E}|$ edges, and it selects the k edges in a way such that the maximum flow of the residual network (after removing the selected edges) is minimized. Let $x_{ij} \in \{0,1\}, \forall(i,j) \in \mathcal{E}$, indicates the decision of the attacker, i.e., if $x_{ij} = 1$ the edge (i, j) is removed from the network; $x_{ij} = 0$ otherwise. Hence, the attacker's attacking scheme can be formulated as

$$\text{MFI-K:} \quad \min_{x \in X} \quad \max_f \sum_{i \in \mathcal{V}} f(S, i) \tag{1}$$

$$\text{s.t.} \quad \sum_{(i,j) \in \mathcal{E}} x_{ij} = k \tag{2}$$

$$f(i, j) \leq w_{ij}(1 - x_{ij}) \tag{3}$$

$$\sum_{j \in FS(i)} f(i, j) - \sum_{j \in RS(i)} f(j, i) = 0, \tag{4}$$

Note that, in (1), 'max' means to find a flow assignment function that achieves network capacity (i.e., maximizes the overall network flow (see Sect. 2.2)). In addition, 'min' means to find an attacking scheme that minimizes the capacity of residual network. Lastly, constraint (3) means that a flow from node i to node j cannot exceed the capacity w_{ij}, if the edge (i, j) is not chosen by the attacker; the flow equals 0, if the edge is compromised by the attacker.

Denote the results to problem (1) MFI-K is $(x^*(k), f^*(k))$, where $x^*(k)$ means the optimal attacking decisions made by attackers, and $f^*(k)$ means the optimal flow assignment for protecting the network's performance from the attacking. We can repeatedly solve the MFI-K problem for different values of k and obtain a sequence of solutions $\{(x^*(k), f^*(k))\}_{k=1}^{K}$, from which several metrics can be defined to evaluate the network's robustness:

1. Robustness profile $\{|f^*(k)|\}_k$, which describes how the network performance changes under different attacking intensity.
2. β–quantile point $k(\beta)$ is the maximum number of edges loss such that the network can tolerate before performance drop to β percent, i.e.

$$k^\beta = \max \left\{ k \left| \frac{|f^*(k)|}{|f^*(0)|} \geq \beta \right. \right\}. \tag{5}$$

It can be seen that, for a given β, a network with larger k^β is more robust.
3. Critical edge set $\mathcal{E}^C$ is the set of edges that are susceptible to attackings, which can be defined as

$$\mathcal{E}^C = \cup_k x^*(k) \tag{6}$$

The set $\mathcal{E}^C$ describes how the vulnerable edges distributed. Given that other conditions are equivalent, a network with smaller size of $\mathcal{E}^C$ is more robust.

We have shown that the network vulnerability can be analyzed with maximum flow interdiction methods and corresponding evaluation metrics. In the following, we develop a method for solving $(x^*(k), f^*(k))$ of an MFI-K problem.

4 Solving Maximum Flow Interdiction Problems

In this part, we consider the solving of the MFI-K problem (1). It is well known that exactly solving the MFI-K is NP-hard [13], and we restore to linear approximation of MFI-K. However, due to the min-max structure, (1) manifests as a two-stage optimization problem, which hampers the solving process. By transforming the maximum flow problem into its dual formulation, the two-stage optimization problem can be transforming into a minimization problem

$$\text{MFI-K-Dual:} \quad \min_{x,u,\eta} \sum_{(i,j)\in\mathcal{E}\setminus\{(S,T)\}} w_{ij}(1 - x_{ij})\eta_{ij} \tag{7}$$

$$\text{s.t.} \quad \sum_{(i,j)\in\mathcal{E}} x_{ij} = k \tag{8}$$

$$\alpha_i - \alpha_j + \eta_{ij} \geq 0 \quad \forall(i,j) \in \mathcal{E}\setminus\{(S,T)\} \tag{9}$$

$$\alpha_T - \alpha_S \geq 1 \tag{10}$$

$$\eta \geq 0 \tag{11}$$

$$x \in [0,1]^{|\mathcal{E}|}, \tag{12}$$

where α and η are the dual variables of the constraints (3) and (4), respectively, and constraint (12) represents the linear approximation of the original problem. It can be seen that problem is a linear programming problem, which can be addressed efficiently with standard LP solver. Furthermore, from its solution, we can get $x^*(k)$, i.e., the selected attacking edges. Lastly, after removing $x^*(k)$ from the network, we can obtain $|f^*(k)|$, i.e., the performance of the residual network, by applying standard maximum flow solver [11].

5 Numerical Results

In this part, we verify our proposed evaluation methods with numerical simulation. A sensor network is generated over an area with $1000 \times 1000\,\text{m}$, where the three types of nodes are selected for representing source nodes, gate nodes and intermediate nodes, respectively. Figure 3 shows an instance of generated network. Two nodes are assumed to be able to establish connection if their distance is less than 100 m. The source node's sampling rate is fixed to 0.3 Mbps; the gate node's delivery rate is fixed to 10 Mbps; and the transmission capacity of a link is based on the distance d_{ij} between two nodes, calculated as $w_{ij} = \frac{1}{d_{ij}^2+1}$ Mbps. Links are bidirectional, and for each source node, its routing paths to gate nodes through intermediate nodes are computed via maximum flow routing algorithms [14,15].

Three different attacking schemes are considered, namely, maximum flow interdiction scheme as shown in (7); random attacking scheme that randomly removes edges in the network; greedy attacking scheme that removes edges with

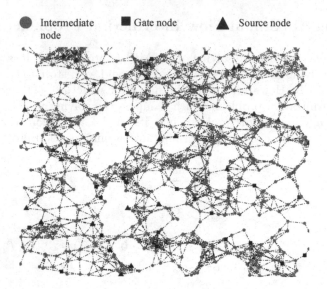

Fig. 3. Topology of a simulated sensor network instance.

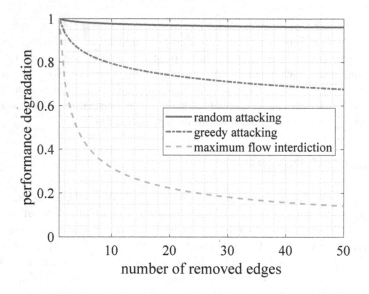

Fig. 4. Network performance degradation under different attacking schemes.

largest transmission capacity. Figure 4 shows the robustness profile of the investigated network under these three schemes averaged over 1000 network realizations. It can be seen that, as the removed edges increases, the network performance drops quickly under the maximum flow interdiction scheme. Furthermore, the network demonstrates a more robust profile against the greedy attacking scheme. Lastly, the network's performance changes slightly under random attacking scheme. In summary, different attacking schemes demonstrate significant robustness profile, while the maximum flow interdiction represents the worst case situation, and is suitable for evaluating networks' robustness.

6 Conclusion

In this paper, we have investigated network vulnerability with maximum flow interdiction methods, from which network robustness profile, the critical edges and quantile points are theoretically defined. As the maximum flow interdiction problem is NP-hard, we consider its linear approximation for solving an attacking strategy and the evaluation metrics. It is interesting to study how these metrics change under typical sensor networks' topology, which is left as future work.

References

1. Akyildiz, I.F.: A survey on sensor networks. IEEE Commun. Mag. **40**(8), 102–114 (2002)
2. Dekker, A.H., Colbert, B.D.: Network robustness and graph topology. In: Proceedings of the 27th Australasian Conference on Computer Science, vol. 26, pp. 359–368 (2004)
3. Jun, W., Barahona, M., Yue-Jin, T.: Natural connectivity of complex networks. Chin. Phys. Lett. **27**(7), 078902 (2010)
4. Tizghadam, A., Leon-Garcia, A.: LSP and back up path setup in MPLS networks based on path criticality index. In: IEEE International Conference on Communications, pp. 441–448 (2007)
5. Tizghadam, A., Leon-Garcia, A.: On congestion in mission critical networks. In: INFOCOM Workshops. IEEE (2008)
6. Tizghadam, A., Leon-Garcia, A.: On robust traffic engineering in transport networks. In: IEEE Globecom IEEE Global Telecommunications Conference. IEEE (2008)
7. Tizghadam, A., Leon-Garcia, A.: Survival value of communication networks. In: INFOCOM Workshops. IEEE (2009)
8. Schieber, T.A., Carpi, L., Frery, A.C., Rosso, O.A.: Information theory perspective on network robustness. Phys. Lett. A **380**(3), 359–364 (2016)
9. Dhuli, S., Gopi, C., Nath Singh, Y.: Analysis of network robustness for finite sized wireless sensor networks. Eprint arXiv (2016)
10. Titouna, C., Nait-Abdesselam, F., Khokhar, A.: A multivariate outlier detection algorithm for wireless sensor networks. In: IEEE ICC 2019, pp. 1–6 (2019)
11. Ford, L.R., Fulkerson, D.R.: Maximal flow through a network. Can. J. Math. **8**(3), 399–404 (1965)
12. Boykov, Y., Kolmogorov, V.: An experimental comparison of min-cut/max-flow algorithms for energy minimization in vision. IEEE Trans. Pattern Anal. Mach. Intell. **26**(9), 1124–1137 (2004)
13. Wood, R.K.: Deterministic network interdiction. Math. Comput. Model. **17**(2), 1–18 (1993)
14. Mahlous, A.R., Fretwell, R.J., Chaourar, B.: MFMP: max flow multipath routing algorithm. In: European Symposium on Computer Modeling and Simulation, Liverpool, pp. 359–368 (2008)
15. Ohara, Y., Imahori, S., Van Meter, R.: MARA: maximum alternative routing algorithm. In: IEEE INFOCOM, Rio de Janeiro, pp. 298–306 (2009)

Research on Integrated Management System of Water and Fertilizer Based on Internet of Things

Lina Zeng[✉], Huajie Lin, Tao Li, Deyun Zhou, Jianhong Yao, Zenghui Yan, and Qiang Wang

School of Electronics and Information, Northwestern Polytechnical University, Xi'an, China
zenglina@nwpu.edu.cn

Abstract. This paper designs and implements a management system of agricultural water and fertilizer integration based on Internet of Things (IOT). The design of the management system, which solves the problems of energy consumption, accuracy, stability and expansibility, is mainly composed of modules with monitoring management, water and fertilizer control, data management and remote control, while realizing greening, intellectualization, networking and digitization. The system takes SK-S7G2 microcontroller as the core to build a bidirectional data channel between the client and temperature sensor, humidity sensor and light intensity sensor by using 4-G wireless network and Ethernet communication modes. Then, the sensor parameters are sent to the client and the control instructions of the client are received to realize the remote real-time control of the motor, fan and other equipment. the production environment data collected by SK-S7G2 are transferred into the database of cloud server to construct an agricultural database of real parameters of crop growth environment. Finally, the feasibility and validity of the management system have been verified by the real environmental test, which proves that the design of the management system proposed in this paper is an effective solution of the intelligent agricultural water and fertilizer irrigation system with the characteristics of energy saving, high efficiency, accuracy and scalability.

Keywords: Internet of Things · Water and fertilizer integration · SK-S7G2

1 Introduction

Please note that the first paragraph of a section or subsection is not indented. The first paragraphs that follows a table, figure, equation etc. does not have an indent, either. China has been a big agricultural country since ancient times, agricultural technology has been inherited for thousands of years. Farmers have also occupied the vast majority of China's population so that Chinese government pay close attention to the issue

© ICST Institute for Computer Sciences, Social Informatics and Telecommunications Engineering 2020
Published by Springer Nature Switzerland AG 2020. All Rights Reserved
B. Li et al. (Eds.): IoTaaS 2019, LNICST 316, pp. 318–325, 2020.
https://doi.org/10.1007/978-3-030-44751-9_27

concerning agriculture, the country and the farmers [1, 2]. At present, there is still a certain gap between China and developed countries in agricultural level and agricultural technology [3]. Although a series of advanced technologies have been introduced and learned in recent decades, there is still much room for improvement [4], some new demands have been put forward:

Greenization: The large and long-term use of chemical fertilizers and pesticides has resulted in land salinization and environmental pollution.

Precision: The selection and use of chemical fertilizers are not precise enough, so it causes serious consequences in crops and humans.

Digitalization: The popularization of digitalization and networking of agricultural technology in China is poor, so it is not conducive to the management and analysis of agricultural data.

Internet of Things, which based on the Internet, collects information, identifies intelligently and manages decision-making by using radio frequency identification (RFID) and other sensing devices. The development of IOT technology can effectively solve the drawbacks of traditional agriculture, and provide technical support for the Greenization, precision and Digitalization of agriculture [5, 6].

This paper focuses on the design of the management system of agricultural water and fertilizer integration based on the IOT technology. The latest SK-S7G2 is used to control the relevant equipment and devices in real time and make irrigation plans. Sensors are used to detect the environment, and data are transmitted to users through 4G module for real-time monitoring of agricultural growth environment. Peristaltic pump is never used in agriculture as one of the industrial metering pump, now it is used as a liquid transfer device to solve problems of lack of pressure and Incorrect feeding of water and fertilizers in the device of fertilizer and water integration.

The stepless regulation of 0–100% can be achieved by improving the metering pump. Meanwhile, the flow can be controlled manually or by frequency regulation, remote control and computer automatic control can be realized.

Finally, the production environment data collected by SK-S7G2 are transferred into the database of cloud server to construct an agricultural database of real parameters of crop growth environment, and to achieve better agricultural production management through intelligent analysis of agricultural data.

2   Overall Design

The overall design for management system of the water and fertilizer integration based on IOT is shown in Fig. 1. The core part of the system is the microcontroller SK-S7G2, which is based on ARM Cortex-M4 processor, and it's clock speed reaches 240 MHz, all needs for development of the management system is to be Completed. Water pump and fertilizer pump is equipped for agricultural irrigation in the system, Temperature sensor, humidity sensor, light intensity sensor, PH/EC sensor and solenoid valve are also installed, and Sensing data and solenoid valve status are transmitted to S7G2 microcontroller through bus. The design mainly includes the following four modules.

2.1   Monitoring Management

In this paper, SK-S7G2 microcontroller is used to acquire environmental indicators, including air temperature, air humidity, soil humidity and light intensity, by installing various kinds sensors for agricultural production environment. All kinds of sensor data are transmitted to SK-S7G2 by CAN bus, and then these detected data are transmitted to the user's mobile device through UDP protocol for real-time monitoring by using the connected 4G module. Meanwhile, the real-time working state of every device is also transmitted to the client through this method. In addition to displaying the environmental data of farmland, the client sends commands to SK-S7G2 controller connected with 4G module through UDP protocol, which realizes the control of fan and fertilizer pump. In this process, the microcontroller judges whether the client command is valid by logical analysis. If it is reasonable, the microcontroller executes the command, otherwise the operation will not be carried out.

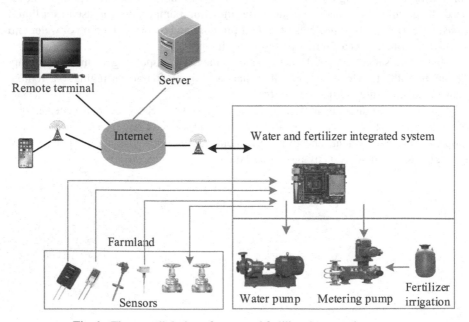

Fig. 1. The overall design of water and fertilizer integrated system.

2.2 Water and Fertilizer Control

In terms of water and fertilizer supply and control, peristaltic metering pump, which is characterized by stable pressure, precise fertilizer feeding, and the ability to transport corrosive liquids) is the main equipment. Water and fertilizer is fed into the pump as a similar peristaltic way by pipeline pressure, then be together into the mixing pipe through the different ports, and be transported to drip irrigation pipes on the farmland for irrigation by the solenoid valve. Filters will be installed in the reservoir to filter various substances such as sediment, so that The drip irrigation pipes won't clog up. Moreover, PH and EC value detectors can be installed in the pipes to detect the water and fertility quality for the import and export, which will further improve the accuracy of irrigation.

2.3 Data Management

In this paper, crop data collection is carried out in the process of farmland planting and management, and a pertinent database is constructed. The data of crop growth status are recorded in the database, which is conducive to further improving the cultivation mode of the crop. It is also convenient for scientific researchers to use the real data when they are engaged in agricultural research.

2.4 Remote Control

The control software queries the historical data from the cloud server through HTTP protocol for remote control, and sends the query instructions to the cloud server through POST method; The client sends the control commands to the cloud server through UDP protocol, and the cloud server transmits the control commands to SK-S7G2 which is equipped with 4G module by UDP protocol to controls the related equipment. Then, the communication between devices is to express their identity by sending heartbeat packets to the cloud server. The cloud server takes out the IP and port of the device and designs a list of device addresses, so that the program can be better maintained.

3 Program Testing

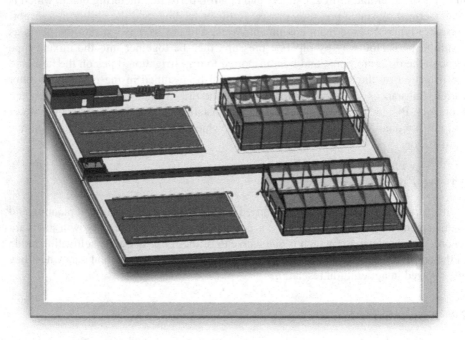

Fig. 2. The simulation diagram of the testing system.

The simulation diagram of the testing system is given in Fig. 2. Water and fertilizer integration is the main part of the testing system, which consists of metering pump, liquid savings box, mixing pipe, transmission pipe, solenoid valve, drip irrigation pipe

Table 1. The main part of the testing system.

Number	Component name	Parameter
1	Fertilizer mixing pipeline	2 lines
2	Water source pipeline	1 line
3	Metering pumps	3
4	Simulated greenhouse and field	Two pieces each (four pieces in total)
5	Solenoid valves for controlling irrigation switch	4
6	Sensors	Temperature, humidity and illumination
7	Ventilator	1
8	4G Internet Module	1
9	Transport pipelines	Some

and so on. See Table 1 for details. A reducer (small wheels drives large wheels) is used in the metering pump to ensure sufficient and stable power in irrigation, and to facilitate the realization of precision control.

Figure 3 shows the hardware devices connected to SK-S7G2 and the communication protocols used to connect the devices.

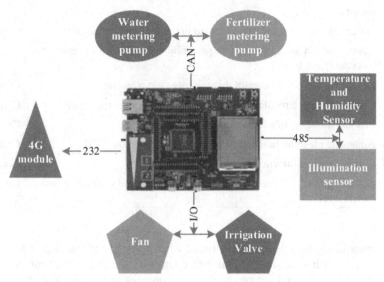

Fig. 3. Hardware system diagram.

Figure 4 shows the flow chart of the software:

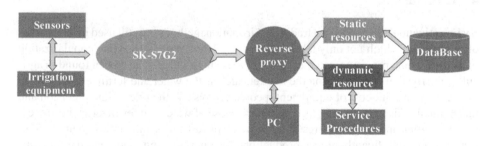

Fig. 4. Software flow chart.

After the equipment is assembled, we expect to test it according to the following scheme (Table 2):

Table 2. Test results of the water and fertilizer integration system.

Number	Test scheme	Test result
1	Observing whether SK-S7G2 can accept and display the measured data of farmland environmental sensor	Correct
2	Observing S7G2 data sent to client by changing the environment around sensor	Correct
3	Observing the historical data recorded in the database on the client	Correct
4	Control the fan and irrigation equipment by sending control commands from the client	Correct
5	Establishing expected control through irrigation planning	Correct
6	Control the speed regulation and working time of metering pump	Correct
7	Mix and transport inhaled water and fertilizer	Correct
8	Automatic cleaning function before irrigation based on S7G2	Correct
9	Getting relevant information on the web interface	Correct
10	Observing the consistency of data at the receiving and sending of the cloud server	Correct

The sensor delay is in a reasonable range when testing, and the packet loss rate of control command is low, so that the real-time control is effective. The client can acquire the real time status of farmland production environment and equipment. After setting irrigation plan, the control operation can be realized. The historical environmental data received by SK-S7G2 can also be acquired, which is conducive to the query of data.

4   Conclusion

By investigation, it is found that traditional irrigation methods are still used in many areas of our country which not only takes up too much labor, but also has low popularization of digitalization, precision and mechanization. Many problems have been found in agricultural irrigation equipment on the market, such as the water and fertilizer integration. In order to save the cost of equipment, people always use the one of low precision and mechanical. This will not only lead to excessive use of water and fertilizer in the process of fertilization and irrigation, resulting in waste of resources and environmental pollution, but also significantly reduce production efficiency, leading to increased crop costs. In order to solve this key problem, more advanced technology and modern equipment are used in the water and fertilizer integration management system, and more rational allocation and installation are carried out, giving full play to the role of each part, so as to achieve the maximum overall efficiency of the system.

Water and fertilizer integration system is based on Internet of Things technology. Firstly, the latest SK-S7G2 is used to control the equipment and devices in real time. Sensors are used to detect the environment for real-time monitoring of agricultural growth environment. Then, Peristaltic pump is never used in agriculture as one of the industrial metering pump, now it has been used as a liquid transfer device to solve problems of lack of pressure and Incorrect feeding of water and fertilizers in the device of fertilizer and water integration. In this paper, the management system of water and fertilizer integration has achieved precision and networking by design and innovation, mainly due to the stepless regulation of 0–100%. The flow can be controlled manually or by frequency regulation, and that the remote control and computer automatic control can be realized, which has the characteristics of intuitive and clear, smooth operation, no noise, small volume and convenient maintenance. Finally, the production environment data collected by SK-S7G2 are summarized into the cloud server database in order to build a database of crop growth environment requirements in order to realize the management and follow-up analysis of agricultural data.

References

1. Chen, Y., Liu, Y., Li, Y.: Agricultural development and industrial prosperity under the background of rural revitalization in China. Geogr. Stud. **38**(3), 632–642 (2019)
2. Liang, C., Cong, S., Zhiming, S., et al.: Environmental monitoring system of agricultural facilities group based on Internet of Things. Agric. Mech. Res. **41**(11), 231–234 (2019)
3. Prem, J., Yavari, A., Georgakopoulos, D., et al.: Internet of Things platform for smart farming: experiences and lessons learnt. Sensors **16**(11), 1884 (2016)
4. Liu, S., Guo, L., Webb, H., et al.: Internet of Things monitoring system of modern eco-agriculture based on cloud computing. IEEE Access **7**(99), 37050–37058 (2019)
5. Zhang, C., Shen, W.: Application of Internet of Things in agriculture. J. Northeast Agric. Univ. **82**(45734), 705–729 (2011)
6. Bai, Z., Bo, L., Mao, Y., et al.: FH-SCMA: frequency-hopping based sparse code multiple access for next generation Internet of Things. In: Wireless Communications & Networking Conference, San Francisco (2017)

Impact Analysis of Realistic Human Mobility over Wireless Network

Jianfeng Guan$^{(\boxtimes)}$ and Wancheng Zhang

State Key Laboratory of Networking and Switching Technology,
Beijing University of Posts and Telecommunications, Beijing 100876, China
{jfguan,vinciichang}@bupt.edu.cn

Abstract. Mobility management is crucial for mobile Internet services. Mobile IPv6 and many subsequent variants aim to provide network layer mobility support for mobile nodes or mobile networks, whose performance is highly dependent on user mobility model, network topology and traffic model. Several previous researches have evaluated their performance by simulations, analytical models, and experiments. However, most of them adopt classic mobility models such as RWP without considering more realistic human mobility characteristics since most of mobile devices are carried by human being. Therefore, the performance evaluation of these solutions under realistic human mobility models becomes an important issue. In this paper we investigate human mobility characteristics and evaluates their impacts on existing mobility management protocols based on a unified simulation platform which abstracts movement parameters from realistic traces and uses them to tune other mobility models. The final results show: (1) The mobility model has an important impact on performance evaluation, and the delivery costs of RD and RWP models are different from the realistic trace which may mislead the protocols design; (2) The current mobility management protocols little consider the human mobility characteristics which cannot benefit the positive of human mobility characteristics, and they should consider the impacts of human mobility and absorb human mobility characteristics in future.

Keywords: Mobility models · Mobility management · Human mobility

1 Introduction

The development of wireless and mobile technologies spurs the booming of various mobile services, and providing Internet services is becoming a big challenge. Especially, with the rapidly increasing of various IoT devices, the limitations in terms of network resource and energy consumption require the protocol design for continuous accessing for huge mobile devices to satisfy the upper service requirements and underly network characteristics. Among these protocols, many mobility management solutions have been proposed under different layers [4,9]

© ICST Institute for Computer Sciences, Social Informatics and Telecommunications Engineering 2020
Published by Springer Nature Switzerland AG 2020. All Rights Reserved
B. Li et al. (Eds.): IoTaaS 2019, LNICST 316, pp. 326–340, 2020.
https://doi.org/10.1007/978-3-030-44751-9_28

in which network layer mobility management (also called as IP mobility management) is a crucial and promising solution for global roaming of Mobile Nodes (MNs).

As a basic mobility support solution, MIPv6 [17,34] introduces Home Agent (HA) to perform the handover management and location management, and the data forwarding for each registered MNs. By extending corresponding node to maintain latest locations of MNs, it can also support optimal routing. The subsequently enhanced solutions such as Hierarchical MIPv6 (HMIPv6) [36,37] and Fast handover for MIPv6 (FMIPv6) [21–23] were proposed to optimize handover performance in terms of signaling cost and handover delay, respectively. However, all of them require the involvements of energy-limited MNs, which may aggravate the energy consumption and therefore restrict their deployment. To solve these problems, Proxy MIPv6 (PMIPv6) [11] was proposed which introduces Mobility Access Gateway (MAG) to deal with the mobility-related signaling exchange instead of MNs. It has been testified that PMIPv6 can reduce handover delay and signaling cost [10]. After that, F-PMIPv6 [42] combines fast handover with PMIPv6 to further improve its performance. The recent Distributed Mobility Management (DMM) [5] aims to make mobility management more scalable and flat to get rid of the restriction of single point failure such as HA in MIPv6 or Local Mobility Anchor (LMA) in PMIPv6.

These mobility management protocols have different characters and application scenarios [2,3,14,16,29,41]. However, how to evaluate their performance becomes an important issue before deployment. Several works have adopted simulation [6], theoretical analysis [40] and experiments [7] methods to evaluate them under different mobility models, topology models and traffic models in terms of handover latency, packet loss, signaling cost and so on. However, most of them adopt Random Walk (RW), Random WayPoint (RWP) or Random Direction (RD) due to their simplicity and tractability to model MNs' movement, while little consider the impacts of realistic human mobility characteristics. It has been verified that these traditional mobility models cannot capture human mobility characteristics [24]. Furthermore, some researches only study the performance under given topology setting by assigning the predefined distances among different mobility entities, which is difficult to emulate real application scenarios.

The recent work [39] shows that these simple mobility models are sufficient for initial testing of new schemes but insufficient for proving their viability in real-world conditions. In addition, the recent development of 5G suggests that the future mobility should support the mobility on-demand, ranging from very high mobility such as high-speed trains to low mobility or stationary devices such as smart meters. In this perspective, the mobility management should also consider the mobility characteristics of the mobility entities. Considering that many mobile device especially IoT devices move with wearable devices with humans and vehicles, and the previous work has found that the IoT devices have different characteristics in mobility from traditional mobile devices such as cellular phones [15]. Therefore, we evaluate mobility management protocols under different mobility models, and compare their performance with the realistic human mobility trace. The contributions of this paper are shown as follows: (1) we investigate the recent performance evaluation methods of mobility management protocols, and conclude their shortcomings; (2) we compare the performance of mobility management protocols under realistic trace and different mobility models; (3) we summarize the future directions of mobility management to improve its intelligence.

The organization of this paper is shown as follows. Section 2 describes typical performance evaluation methods of mobility management protocols. Section 3 summarizes the recent work of human mobility models and analyzes its features. Section 4 construct a unified simulation platform and compare performance of typical mobility management protocols under different mobility models, and analyzes their differences. Section 5 summarizes this paper.

2   Related Work

2.1   Mobility Evaluation Method

The early stage performance evaluation methods of mobility management is generally derived from the personal communication system in terms of cost and delay via analytical analysis or simulations.

Christian Makaya and Samuel Pierre [30] proposed an analytical framework to assess the performance of IPv6-based mobility management protocols under different packet arrival rates, wireless link delays, and Session-to-Mobility Ratios (SMRs). This analytical framework deduces the binding update cost, binding refresh cost, packet delivery cost, required buffer space, handoff latency and packet loss. To facilitate network design, the potential pros and cons of MIPv6, HMIPv6, FMIPv6 and F-HMIPv6 are analyzed under the given network topology and pre-defined parameters. This model, however, does not consider the message sizes and their scalability problem, and it adopts the fluid flow model which does not consider the human mobility characteristics. Besides, J-H Lee et al. evaluated the cost and handover delay in [25], respectively, which also adopts the fluid flow model. They adopted bytes*hops per second to evaluate signaling cost, and based on given topology to compare their registration delay, signaling cost and traffic intensity. More recently, Vasu et al. [40] proposed a comprehensive framework to evaluate IPv6 mobility management protocols including MIPv6, FMIPv6, HMIPv6, PMIPv6 and DMM in terms of signaling overhead, handover delay and packet loss. This framework applies transport engineering principles to derive the relation between handover delay and number of hops, and adopts the analytic results from [28] to deduce the signaling cost.

In addition to the analytical method, Guan et al. [10] studied the network-based mobility management protocols and demonstrated the experimental results of MIPv6, FMIPv6, HMIPv6 and PMIPv6 under the given test-bed, and analyzed their signaling cost and packet delivery cost under random walk model without considering the human mobility. More recently, Giust et al. [24] mainly focused on DMM especially network-based DMM, and implemented them in a

Linux-based test-bed to evaluate their handover delay in a real IEEE 802.11 scenario. Additional, they adopted the fluid flow model to derive the analytic model of signaling cost, packet delivery cost and handover latency. The above analyses show that most of existing researches adopt the fluid flow model or random walk model to capture the users' mobility. Fluid flow model can be applied when users have high mobility, while random walk is suitable for users moving in a limited area. However, both of them cannot comprehensively capture the human movement characteristics. Therefore, modeling human mobility and evaluating its impact on related network protocols have been got more concerns recently. However, there is lack of a comprehensive performance evaluation of mobility management protocols under realistic mobility models.

2.2 Human Mobility Characteristics

Different from traditional mobility models, human mobility is generally derived from realistic traces [32], and it has following statistic characteristics [33]:

- (1) Heterogeneously Bounded Mobility Area:
  Humans usually spend most of their time in several specific areas (also called as hubs) and move among them, which results in a high degree of temporal and spatial regularity of trajectories, and different people may have widely different move areas [35].
- (2) Heavy-tail Flights Length and pause times Distribution:
  Human is more likely to travel for long distances which results in that the flight distribution follows the truncated heavy-tail distribution, and the pause-time distribution follows the truncated power-law distribution [20].
- (3) Dichotomy of Inter-contact Time Distribution:
  Inter-contact time is the time elapsed between two successive meetings of the same persons. The complementary cumulative distribution function of inter-contact time of humans illustrates a dichotomy which consists of a truncated power-law head followed by an exponential tail [18].
- (4) Location Preference:
  Humans always follow simple reproducible movement patterns [13], and they spend most of time in small part of locations and repeat the same movement periodically.
- (5) Self-similar:
  The self-similar is observed at different scales such as space or time, which means that humans are always attracted to more popular places and therefore their visiting destinations tend to be heavily clustered [26]. In addition, humans like to visit destinations nearer to their current places when visiting multiple destinations in succession.
- (6) Irregular Inter-hub Movement:
  Humans do not move in a straight line from one hub to another due to the unexpected obstacles during the movement, which means humans do not take the shortest path but take a long path [27].

Due to these human mobility characteristics, the existing mobile models are not suitable to evaluate the performance of network protocols in realistic applications. In contrast, absorbing the human mobility characteristics such as predictability can benefit the protocol design. The prominent work in [8] shows that human mobility has high degree of spatial and temporal regularities. When applying the prediction into the handover [31], it can reduce the signaling cost if the prediction accuracy is higher than 40%.

2.3 Human Mobility Models

To capture these human mobility characteristics, several human mobility models have been proposed. Truncated Levy Walk (TLW) [35] is a kind of random walk which uses the truncated Pareto distributions for flight and pause-time distributions to capture the property of heavy-tail flight length distribution. In TLW model, a mobile node travels short distances in most of the time and sometimes long distances. TLW is a simple model but cannot capture the human spatial, temporal and social contexts. After that, Time-Variant Community (TVC) Model [12] captures the location visiting preferences and periodical reappearance (or spatial preference and temporal preference) by observing mobility characteristics from the traces, and sets up a time-variant community mobility model for in-depth theoretical analysis. Subsequently, SWIM [?] captures the feature that human always go to the places not very far from their home and where they can meet a lot of other people. Later on, SLAW mobility model [26] modifies Levy walk-based model and models the human waypoints as fractals. SLAW not only captures the heavy-tail flight and pause-time distributions, heterogeneously bounded mobility area of individuals and the truncated power-law inter-contact times, but also captures the additional features that the human destinations are dispersed in a self-similar manner and human more likely to choose a destination closer to its current locations. Therefore, SLAW can be viewed as a representative realistic mobility model which will be used in the following analysis.

The impacts of human mobility have been studied in term of delay torrent networks routing [19] and mobile ad hoc networks routing [38], which find out that the performance of some routing protocols becomes serious and discrepancy with the real scenarios, and they suggest to revisit mobility modeling to incorporate accurate behavioral models in future. Therefore, in this paper, we study the impact of human mobility on mobility management protocols.

3 Performance Evaluation over MM

In our performance evaluation, we first analyze realistic human mobility trace to acquire its parameters, and then tune the other mobility models to unify the simulation setting to compare them. Second, we analyze signaling and delivery costs of MIPv6, HMIPv6, PMIPv6 and DMM (including Host-DMM and Network-DMM) under different mobility models and realistic trace, and analyze their differences.

3.1   Realistic Human Mobility Trace

We select the NCSU realistic dataset [1] which records the locations of 35 nodes moving around the NCSU campuses. This realistic dataset can be viewed as a typical human mobility scenario to capture the mobility characters in campus. Its record interval is 30 seconds and the duration of each node is different. So we select a part of this dataset, which includes 34 nodes, and moves in the range of 12 * 8 km². The total moving duration is 6150 s.

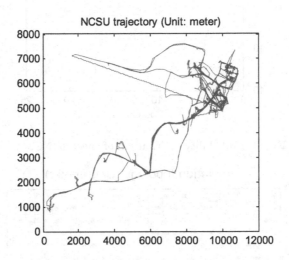

Fig. 1. The movement trajectories of NCSU.

Figure 1 shows a nodes movement trajectory (unit: meters). We can find that the trajectory is relative concentrated, and node only moves around some locations, and most moving path is not straight, which reflects the human mobility characteristics of heterogeneously bounded mobility area, location preference and irregular inter-hub movement.

Figure 2 shows the speed probability distribution. We can find out these speeds are from 0 m/s to 23 m/s, and most of speeds are below 5 m/s which are different from the traditional mobility models whose speed is generally uniform distribution between minimal speed and maximum speed. To tune the speed of other mobility models, we set the speed as [0, 21] m/s.

To simulate access networks such as MAG and domains such as LMA domain, we adopt the m * n mesh structure for the topology as shown in Fig. 3.

Each small square represents a subnet with a mobility anchor (such as AR or MAG) inside. Moreover, the topology is divided into different domains to simulate MAP domain or LMA domain where a MAP or a LMA is inside. In our simulation, we divide the topology into 24 domains which are marked as square as shown in Fig. 3. Besides, the HA is located in the center of the topology, and CMD of DMM is also located in the same location of HA.

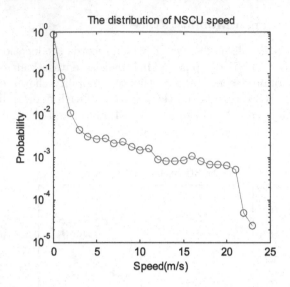

Fig. 2. Probability distribution of speed in NCSU.

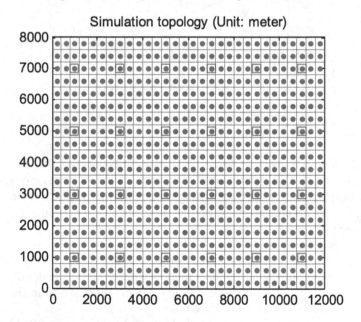

Fig. 3. The simulation topology (unit: meter).

3.2   Mobility Models Settings

In the evaluation, we adopt RW, RWP, RD to represent the typical mobility model, and SLAW to represent the human mobility model. The relevant parameters setting is based on the NCSU dataset. Table 1 shows the related parameters for each mobility models, and all simulation time is 6150 s which is same to the realistic trace.

Table 1. Simulation parameter setting.

Parameter	RW	RWP	RD	SLAW
Size (km^2)	12 * 8	12 * 8	12 * 8	12 * 8
Simulation time (s)	6150	6150	6150	6150
Velocity (m/s)	[0, 21]	[0, 21]	[0, 21]	[0, 21]
Pause time (s)	[0, 60]	[0, 60]	[0, 60]	[0, 60]
Cluster range (m)	N/A	N/A	N/A	200

First, we demonstrate the movement traces of different mobility models in the pre-defined network topology. Figure 4 shows the typical movement traces. We can get that the movement trajectories are greatly different. To be specific, RWP and RD are more diffused which are random without regularity. In contrast, RW and SLAW are more tenacious. This difference will influence the performance evaluation of mobility management protocols.

3.3 Mobility Management Analysis

Considering that handover times and location preferences are important for mobility management, we first compute the number of intra-domain and inter-domain handovers, and location distribution.

(1) The number of intra-domain and inter-domain handovers
    Figure 5 shows the numbers of intra-domain and inter-domain handover during the simulation (X axis is the simulation time). It is obvious that the number of handover is increased with simulation time. The handover numbers of RD and RWP are significantly larger than others for that their movement trajectories are more diffusible. SLAW is more close to realistic trace for that it captures some human mobility characteristics such as heterogeneously bounded mobility area of individuals and self-similar to choose destination.
    In perspective of mobility management, the more handover happens, the more signaling and delivery cost is generated. The reduction of handover derives from the glutinousness of human mobility, which reduces the handover probability.
(2) Location distribution
    Figure 6 shows the normalized location distribution of different models, where X axis is the rank of locations and Y axis is the probability of the corresponding locations. It is obvious that the realistic trace is more concentrated, and MNs only move among several locations, while other models are

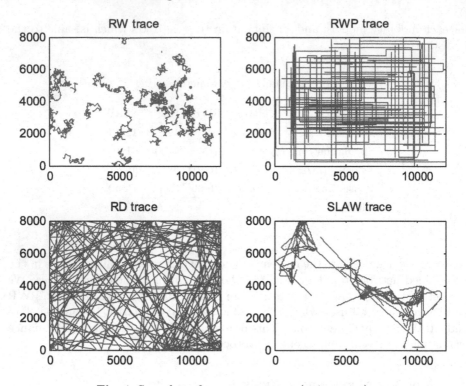

Fig. 4. Snapshot of movement traces (unit: meter).

more distributed among the total movement area. This is consistent with the fact that human beings always spend most of time in only small part of locations. Therefore, it is important to optimize mobility management in term of binding cache for that MNs are generally located in limited places.

(3) Cost analysis under different mobility models

Based on the above analyses, we compare the performance of mobility management under different mobility models. The cost analysis is based on bytes * distance and Table 2 shows the related parameters. We run each simulation for 20 times, and average them to compare with the NCSU.

Figure 7(a) shows the signaling cost of different mobility management protocols under RW, RWP, RD, SLAW and NCSU. It can get that the signaling cost under different mobility models is different, and NCSU is less than the others. And the RD has largest signaling cost, while SLAW has similar signaling cost to that of NCSU. For different mobility management protocols, their relationship of size is same under different models.

Figure 7(b) shows the delivery cost, and it is obvious that mobility model has an important impact on delivery cost. More specifically, RWP and RD have large delivery cost due to their unrealistic movements. Both RW and SLAW are similar to NCSU. More important, the size relationship of different mobility management protocols under RD and RWP is different from

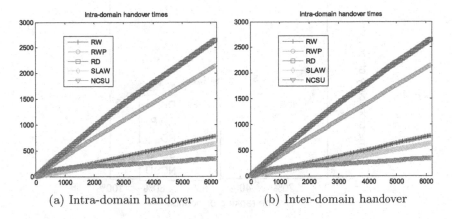

(a) Intra-domain handover   (b) Inter-domain handover

Fig. 5. The number of total handovers.

Table 2. Parameters of cost analysis.

Name	Value(s)	Description
RS	16 byte	Router solicitation
RA	64 byte	Router advertisement
BU	56 byte	Binding update, used for MIPv6
BA	40 byte	Binding acknowledgement, used for MIPv6
LBU	56 byte	Local binding update, used for HMIPv6
LBA	40 byte	Local binding acknowledgement
PBU	56 byte	Proxy binding update, used for PMIPv6
PBA	40 byte	Proxy binding acknowledgement
RtSolPr	88 byte	Proxy router solicitation, used for FMIPv6
PrRtAdv	104 byte	Proxy router advertisement, used for FMIPv6
FBU	72 byte	Fast binding update, used for FMIPv6
FBack	32 byte	Fast binding acknowledgement
HI	72 byte	Handover initiate, used for FMIPv6
HAck	32 byte	Handover acknowledgement
FNA	24 byte	Fast neighbor advertisement
ABU	56 byte	Access binding update, used for HDMM
ABA	40 byte	Access binding acknowledgement, used for HDMM
MBU	56 byte	Mobility capable access router (MAR) binding update for DMM
MBA	40 byte	MAR binding acknowledgement
MCreq	76 byte	Mobility context request, used for NDMM
MCRes	76 byte	Mobility context response, used for NDMM
Plen	500 byte	Packet length
λ	0.5	Sessions arrival rate with Poisson process
μ	30 s	Session length with exponential distribution

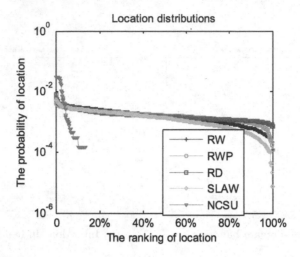

Fig. 6. Locations distribution of different models.

that of RW, SLAW and NCSU. This finding shows that using RD or RWP as the mobility model to evaluate the mobility management may get the wrong conclusion. Besides, we can also get that relative performance of each protocols follows the similar tendency, which shows that the simple mobility model can only get the qualitative results, but cannot provide the accurate quantitative results.

These evaluation results show that the performance of mobility management protocols is deeply dependent on the mobility models. However, due to the little consideration of special design for human mobility characteristics, mobility management protocols cannot absorb the positive affect of human mobility characteristics.

3.4 Discussions

Based on the above analytical results, the future mobility management design should consider the following aspects:

(1) Model the user behavior patterns and predict their future behaviors such as movement trajectory. The analytical results demonstrate that the mobile users always have the regular patterns in terms of time and space. Therefore, their movement trajectory can be predictive in advance especially in the scenarios such as high trains. Based on these findings, the mobility management protocols can be provided on-demand.

(2) Mine the social relationship among user and optimize the caching strategy. The location preference is derived from the social relationship of mobile users, which means that the mobile users only communicate with a small of part of the others. This finding can be used to optimize the binding

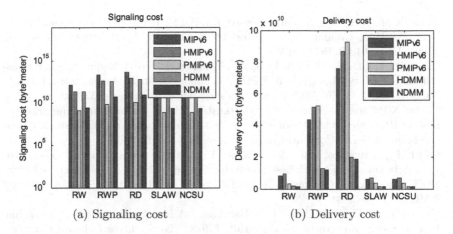

Fig. 7. The cost under different mobility models.

caching design. To improve the intelligence of mobility management, the future directions should also consider the service characteristics and social relationship to optimize design.

4 Conclusion

In this paper, we investigate the related work in term of human mobility models, and analyze their impacts on the mobility management performance evaluation. From analytical results, we can observe that although the mobility models have an important impact of performance evaluation, the compared mobility management protocols don't get the benefits from the human mobility. The future design of mobility management should absorb the human mobility characteristics such as periodic reparation and social contract relationships to further improve their performance. In this work, the domain design is simple and ideal, so the further work is to combine the real network topology and traces to analyze their performance.

References

1. Crawdad. CRAWDAD data set ncsu/mobilitymodels. Accessed 23 July 2009
2. Alsaeedy, A.A.R., Chong, E.K.P.: Mobility management for 5G IoT devices: Improving power consumption with lightweight signaling overhead. IEEE Internet Things J. **6**(5), 8237–8247 (2019). https://doi.org/10.1109/JIOT.2019.2920628
3. Balasubramanian, V., Zaman, F., Aloqaily, M., Ridhawi, I.A., Jararweh, Y., Salameh, H.B.: A mobility management architecture for seamless delivery of 5G-IoT services. In: ICC 2019–2019 IEEE International Conference on Communications (ICC), pp. 1–7, May 2019. https://doi.org/10.1109/ICC.2019.8761658

4. Bolla, R., Repetto, M.: A comprehensive tutorial for mobility management in data networks. IEEE Commun. Surv. Tutor. **16**(2), 812–833 (2014). https://doi.org/10.1109/SURV.2013.071913.00140

5. Chan, H., Liu, D., Seite, P., Yokota, H., Korhonen, J., (eds.): Requirements for Distributed Mobility Management. RFC 7333 (Informational), August 2014. https://doi.org/10.17487/RFC7333. https://www.rfc-editor.org/rfc/rfc7333.txt

6. Costa, X.P., Torrent-Moreno, M., Hartenstein, H.: A performance comparison of mobile IPv6, hierarchical mobile IPv6, fast handovers for mobile ipv6 and their combination. Mob. Comput. Commun. Rev. **7**(4), 5–19 (2003)

7. Giust, F., Bernardos, C.J., de la Oliva, A.: Analytic evaluation and experimental validation of a network-based ipv6 distributed mobility management solution. IEEE Trans. Mob. Comput. **13**(11), 2484–2497 (2014). https://doi.org/10.1109/TMC.2014.2307304

8. Gonzalez, M.C., Hidalgo, C., Barabasi, A.L.: Understanding individual human mobility patterns. Nature **453**, 779–82 (2008). https://doi.org/10.1038/nature06958

9. Guan, J., Xu, C., Zhang, H., Zhou, H.: Mobility Challenges and Management in the Future Wireless Heterogeneous Networks

10. Guan, J., Zhou, H., Yan, Z., Qin, Y., Zhang, H.: Implementation and analysis of proxy MIPv6. Wirel. Commun. Mob. Comput. **11**(4), 477–490 (2011). https://doi.org/10.1002/wcm.842

11. Gundavelli, S., Leung, K., Devarapalli, V., Chowdhury, K., Patil, B., (eds.): Proxy Mobile IPv6. RFC 5213 (Proposed Standard), August 2008. https://doi.org/10.17487/RFC5213. https://www.rfc-editor.org/rfc/rfc5213.txt, updated by RFCs 6543, 7864

12. Hsu, W., Spyropoulos, T., Psounis, K., Helmy, A.: Modeling spatial and temporal dependencies of user mobility in wireless mobile networks. IEEE/ACM Trans. Netw. **17**(5), 1564–1577 (2009). https://doi.org/10.1109/TNET.2008.2011128

13. Hsu, W., Spyropoulos, T., Psounis, K., Helmy, A.: Modeling spatial and temporal dependencies of user mobility. IEEE/ACM Trans. Netw. **17**(5), 1564–1577 (2009). https://doi.org/10.1145/1665838.1665854

14. Hwa Jung, J., Kyu Choi, D., In Kim, J., Joo Koh, S.: Mobility management for healthcare services in CoAP-based IoT networks. In: 2019 International Conference on Information Networking (ICOIN), pp. 7–12, January 2019. https://doi.org/10.1109/ICOIN.2019.8718156

15. Ishino, M., Koizumi, Y., Hasegawa, T.: A study on a routing-based mobility management architecture for IoT devices. In: 2014 IEEE 22nd International Conference on Network Protocols, pp. 498–500, October 2014. https://doi.org/10.1109/ICNP.2014.78

16. Jin, H., Jin, Y., Lu, H., Zhao, C., Peng, M.: NFV and SFC: a case study of optimization for virtual mobility management. IEEE J. Sel Areas Commun. 1 (2018). https://doi.org/10.1109/JSAC.2018.2869967

17. Johnson, D., Perkins, C., Arkko, J.: Mobility Support in IPv6. RFC 3775 (Proposed Standard), June 2004. https://doi.org/10.17487/RFC3775. https://www.rfc-editor.org/rfc/rfc3775.txt, obsoleted by RFC 6275

18. Karagiannis, T., Boudec, J.L., Vojnovic, M.: Power law and exponential decay ofintercontact times between mobile devices. IEEE Trans. Mob. Comput. **9**(10), 1377–1390 (2010). https://doi.org/10.1109/TMC.2010.99

19. Kaveh Fayazbakhsh, S.: Modeling human mobility and its applications in routing in delay-tolerant networks: a short survey, July 2013

20. Kim, M., Kotz, D., Kim, S.: Extracting a mobility model from real user traces. In: INFOCOM 2006. 25th IEEE International Conference on Computer Communications, Joint Conference of the IEEE Computer and Communications Societies, 23–29 April 2006, Barcelona, Catalunya, Spain (2006). https://doi.org/10.1109/INFOCOM.2006.173

21. Koodli, R., (ed.): Fast Handovers for Mobile IPv6. RFC 4068 (Experimental), July 2005. https://doi.org/10.17487/RFC4068. https://www.rfc-editor.org/rfc/rfc4068.txt, obsoleted by RFC 5268

22. Koodli, R., (ed.): Mobile IPv6 Fast Handovers. RFC 5268 (Proposed Standard), June 2008. https://doi.org/10.17487/RFC5268. https://www.rfc-editor.org/rfc/rfc5268.txt, obsoleted by RFC 5568

23. Koodli, R., (ed.): Mobile IPv6 Fast Handovers. RFC 5568 (Proposed Standard), July 2009. https://doi.org/10.17487/RFC5568. https://www.rfc-editor.org/rfc/rfc5568.txt, updated by RFC 7411

24. Kosta, S., Mei, A., Stefa, J.: Large-scale synthetic social mobile networkswith SWIM. IEEE Trans. Mob. Comput. 13(1), 116–129 (2014)

25. Lee, J., Bonnin, J., You, I., Chung, T.: Comparative handover performance analysis of IPv6 mobility management protocols. IEEE Trans. Ind. Electron. 60(3), 1077–1088 (2013). https://doi.org/10.1109/TIE.2012.2198035

26. Lee, K., Hong, S., Kim, S.J., Rhee, I., Chong, S.: SLAW: self-similar least-action human walk. IEEE/ACM Trans. Netw. 20(2), 515–529 (2012). https://doi.org/10.1109/TNET.2011.2172984

27. Lin, S., Tsai, W., Tsai, M., Pang, A.: IROL: A humanoid mobility model for mobile ad hoc network. In: IEEE International Conference on Communications, ICC 2014, Sydney, Australia, 10–14 June 2014, pp. 2496–2501 (2014). https://doi.org/10.1109/ICC.2014.6883698,

28. Lin, Y.: Reducing location update cost in a PCS network. IEEE/ACM Trans. Netw. 5(1), 25–33 (1997). https://doi.org/10.1109/90.554719

29. Liu, D., Huang, C., Chen, X., Jia, X.: Space-terrestrial integrated mobility management via named data networking. Tsinghua Sci. Technol. 23(4), 431–439 (2018). https://doi.org/10.26599/TST.2018.9010042

30. Makaya, C., Pierre, S.: An analytical framework for performance evaluation of IPv6-based mobility management protocols. IEEE Trans. Wirel Commun. 7(3), 972–983 (2008). https://doi.org/10.1109/TWC.2008.060725

31. Mohamed, A., Onireti, O., Hoseinitabatabaei, S.A., Imran, M., Imran, A., Tafazolli, R.: Mobility prediction for handover management in cellular networks with control/data separation. In: 2015 IEEE International Conference on Communications (ICC), pp. 3939–3944, June 2015. https://doi.org/10.1109/ICC.2015.7248939

32. Munjal, A., Camp, T., Aschenbruck, N.: Changing trends in modeling mobility. J. Electr. Comput. Eng. 2012, 16 (2012). https://doi.org/10.1155/2012/372572

33. Munjal, A., Camp, T., Navidi, W.: SMOOTH: a simple way to model human walks. Mob. Comput. Commun. Rev. 14(4), 34–36 (2010). https://doi.org/10.1145/1942268.1942281

34. Perkins, C., Johnson, D., Arkko, J., (eds.): Mobility Support in IPv6. RFC 6275 (Proposed Standard), July 2011. https://doi.org/10.17487/RFC6275. https://www.rfc-editor.org/rfc/rfc6275.txt

35. Soliman, H., Castelluccia, C., ElMalki, K., Bellier, L.: Hierarchical MobileIPv6 (HMIPv6) Mobility Management. RFC 5380 (Proposed Standard), October 2008.https://doi.org/10.17487/RFC5380. https://www.rfc-editor.org/rfc/rfc5380.txt

36. Soliman, H., Castelluccia, C., ElMalki, K., Bellier, L.: Hierarchical Mobile IPv6 (HMIPv6) Mobility Management. RFC 5380 (Proposed Standard), October 2008. https://doi.org/10.17487/RFC5380. https://www.rfc-editor.org/rfc/rfc5380.txt

37. Soliman, H., Castelluccia, C., Malki, K.E., Bellier, L.: Hierarchical Mobile IPv6 Mobility Management (HMIPv6). RFC 4140 (Experimental), August 2005. https://doi.org/10.17487/RFC4140. https://www.rfc-editor.org/rfc/rfc4140.txt, obsoleted by RFC 5380

38. Thakur, G.S., Kumar, U., Hsu, W., Helmy, A.: Gauging human mobility characteristics and its impact on mobile routing performance. IJSNet **11**(3), 179–191 (2012). https://doi.org/10.1504/IJSNET.2012.046348

39. Treurniet, J.: A taxonomy and survey of microscopic mobility models from the mobile networking domain. ACM Comput. Surv. **47**(1), 14:1–14:32 (2014). https://doi.org/10.1145/2616973

40. Vasu, K., Mahapatra, S., Kumar, C.S.: A comprehensive framework for evaluating IPv6 based mobility management protocols. Wirel. Pers. Commun. **78**(2), 943–977 (2014). https://doi.org/10.1007/s11277-014-1795-y

41. Wu, D., Nie, X., Asmare, E., Arkhipov, D., Qin, Z., Li, R., McCann, J., Li, K.: Towards distributed sdn: Mobility management and flow scheduling in software defined urban IoT. IEEE Trans. Parallel Distrib. Syst. 1 (2018). https://doi.org/10.1109/TPDS.2018.2883438

42. Yokota, H., Chowdhury, K., Koodli, R., Patil, B., Xia, F.: Fast Handovers for Proxy Mobile IPv6. RFC 5949 (Proposed Standard), September 2010. https://doi.org/10.17487/RFC5949. https://www.rfc-editor.org/rfc/rfc5949.txt

Networking Technology for IoT

Hexagram Linkage: An Ambient Assistive Living System with Healthcare for Elderly People Living Alone

Xiaohu Fan[1,2,5], Hao Huang[3,5(✉)], Qubo Xie[1,6], Xuejiao Pang[6], and Changsheng Xie[1,4]

[1] Department of Computer Science and Technology,
Huazhong University of Science and Technology,
1037 Luoyu Road, Wuhan 430074, People's Republic of China
{fanxiaohu,baidu,cs_xie}@hust.edu.cn, fanxiaohu@8hutech.com
[2] Wuhan Optics Valley Info & Tech Co., Ltd.,
888#Gaoxin Road, Wuhan, People's Republic of China
[3] School of Software Engineering, Huazhong University of Science and Technology,
1037 Luoyu Road, Wuhan 430074, People's Republic of China
thao@hust.edu.cn
[4] Wuhan National Laboratory for Optoelectronics, 1037 Luoyu Road, Wuhan 430074, China
[5] Shenzhen Research Institute,
Huazhong University of Science and Technology, Shenzhen, China
[6] Wuhan BoHuTech. Co., Ltd., 70#Guanggu Road, Wuhan, People's Republic of China
{xiequbo,pangxuejiao}@8hutech.com

Abstract. To handle the worldwide problem of aging, one of the most successful and cost-effective solutions is an ambient assisted living system. These systems integrate a collection of sensors, the Internet of Things, health management, human-computer interaction, offline medical entities and nursing services. The key technological component is a human activity recognition and anomaly detection system. We designed a platform framework that defines activity at three levels: atomic, basic and complex. Our framework process uses separate modelling with classical algorithms, so that four kinds of anomalies (point, set, scene and trend) can be detected. We implemented a real-world system and used it over two years within a scenario with nearly 200 users, thus proving the validity of the system and identifying certain deficiencies in the user's experience. Our system has the characteristics of practicability, compatibility, cost-effectiveness and robustness.

Keywords: Ambient Assisted Living · Daily activity monitoring · Abnormal behaviour pattern · Elderly healthcare

1 Introduction

The world's population of elderly people is increasing rapidly due to improvements in medical science [1], and the average life span and the proportion of older adults

© ICST Institute for Computer Sciences, Social Informatics and Telecommunications Engineering 2020
Published by Springer Nature Switzerland AG 2020. All Rights Reserved
B. Li et al. (Eds.): IoTaaS 2019, LNICST 316, pp. 343–362, 2020.
https://doi.org/10.1007/978-3-030-44751-9_29

continues to increase. High-end nursing homes with advanced medical facilities are needed to solve problems arising from this situation, but due to limited social welfare and insurance resources, more than 90% of elderly people cannot afford care or medical costs. They have no choice but to live at home, and are more likely to suffer from depression and psychosomatic disorders than the general population [2], meaning that they may require emergency attention or cause social problems; in the worst cases, they may be found dead in their homes [3]. The problem of aging has posed many challenges to society, for example:

1. The increasing burden of medical expenses: More than 40% of the US health budget is spent on the elderly, who make up only 13% of the population, resulting in an unfair distribution of social resources. Most families cannot afford private doctors, nursing care or medical services.
2. Shortages of nursing staff: In China, the number of qualified nurses is lower than 1 million, while the demand for qualified people in the elderly care/nursing industry is about 38 million.
3. Social factors: Should the government or health insurance companies be responsible for the care of these elderly people? In most cases, relatives, friends and neighbours bear this responsibility.

In order to cope with the rapid aging of society, various technologies are developing rapidly in this field. Telemedicine [4], home monitoring [5] and video surveillance [6, 7] are relatively mature solutions and are widely used. These schemes monitor dangerous situations via sensors and cameras, and send the gathered data to neighbours, relatives and health care providers for response. Although the systems themselves are effective, the actual user experience is poor, since few people are willing to be monitored unless the situation is critical. Since about 89% of elderly people prefer to live in their own homes [4] where they are comfortable, and to maintain an independent and dignified lifestyle, the use of AI technology to replace some aspects of the caregiver labour force can solve these social problems in a relatively cost-effective way. Recently, a new paradigm has been developed that aims to enhance human capabilities through digital environments, involving an intelligent technology called ambient assisted living (AAL). These digital environments are sensitive, adaptive and responsive to human needs. This innovative vision of the everyday environment includes human-computer interaction technology, and is ubiquitous, inconspicuous, and very forward-looking. The following three factors should be considered in the design of such a system:

1. Maximisation of the user's privacy;
2. Development of a compact, robust, accurate and cost-effective sensing system;
3. The ability to detect abnormal patterns and generate alerts.

The main functions of an AAL system are to prevent, treat and improve the health status of elderly people. AAL tools such as drug management reminders can allow older people to manage their own health [8, 9]. AAL technology may also include a mobile emergency response system [10], a fall detection system [11] and a video surveillance system to provide more security for the elderly. Other AAL technologies are based on the monitoring of activities of daily life (ADLs) and generating alerts to help facilitate daily activities, as well as assisting elderly people in moving around and enabling the remote control of automated home appliances [12]. Finally, such technology can enable older people to contact and communicate with their peers, family members and friends more effectively [13].

Although it is in some respects similar to a smart home, an AAL system is more targeted toward healthcare and assistive functions, and needs the participation of relevant human and entity healthcare services. Sensors rely on wireless sensor networks (WSNs) to connect home gateways to medical application systems [14]. Many sensors that are used to monitor blood sugar, blood pressure and pulse rates can send vital signs to health monitoring systems, so that nurses or doctors can monitor patients remotely [15]. With the global development of cloud computing, mobile Internet and 4G and 5G communication, these applications will continue to increase in popularity. Research [16] shows that demand from individuals for medical equipment and AAL systems is increasing; citizens are gradually beginning to participate in personal health care, in order to continue living independently and to save on nursing expenses.

The motivation of this paper is to design an AAL system with health monitoring and anomaly detection functions that is characterised by ease of use, low cost, effectiveness and robustness. Our approach provides an ecosystem of medical sensors, computers, wireless networks and software applications for medical monitoring. The main objective is to prolong the independent and dignified life of elderly people within their home environment using the personal medical information and communication technology.

2 Related Works

The development of AAL systems is mainly based on the development and popularisation of the following technologies:

1. Giant health platforms: DACAR is based on Microsoft's HealthVault platform, which provides an interface allowing users to view, define, share and manage health data [17]. Apple has also launched its HealthKit [18] to provide users with solutions via a large number of WSNs, health devices and services.
2. Pervasive computing and wearable devices: These enable people to interact with these devices as part of their daily lives. Ubiquitous sensing is an active research field, the main purpose of which is to extract useful information from data acquired by sensors and the Internet of Things [19] to achieve specific purposes.
3. Mobile Internet: The popularity of online-to-offline systems has changed the way residents live and behave on the Internet, and the utilisation rate of resources within the society as a whole has increased.

2.1   Platform, Hardware Equipment and Applications

The CASAS [20] program at Washington State University uses a large number of sensor deployments to provide a non-invasive supporting environment allowing dementia patients to live independently at home. Besides, the CASAS project provides mobile internet applications. The University of Missouri's Aging in Place project [21] aims to provide a long-term health care model for the elderly, including monitoring the parameters of their daily lives, supporting the collection of health data close to the medical level, and thus providing remote protection for their health and safety. Elite Care [22] is an assistant living facility program equipped with a large number of civil-grade sensors for monitoring various indicators such as lay status, weight and sleep disturbance, to allow monitoring of the living and health status of households. In the Aware Home [23] project at Georgia Institute of Technology, a variety of equipment is used, such as floor sensors and assistant robots, to monitor and support elderly people.

Current projects in Europe include the Grenoble Health smart home [24], PROSAFE [25], and ENABLE [26]. The Ambient Assisted Living Joint Program (AALJP) [27], sponsored by the European Commission, aims to improve the quality of life of older people across Europe through the use of AAL technology. In Asia, AAL-related home health care projects include the early Welfare Technology House project [28] and the Ubiquitous Home project [29], which measures electrocardiogram data, weight, urine volume and other indicators. Any change in activity may be an indicator of cognitive or physical decline [30]. For example, indicators such as movement patterns, walking speed, number of discharges and changes in sleep rhythms have been identified as early signs of dementia [31].

Other projects focus on wearable devices and health surveillance systems at the medical level, and are more suitable for chronic patients with certain single diseases. These wearable medical devices expand the number of dimensions of the data and the application scope of AAL systems. For example, one project [32] developed equipment for indoor positioning and structured medical health monitoring; Health Vest [33] produced smart clothes for patients; the Cushionware project [34] developed pressure sensors to recognise when a patient is in a sitting position; and Wi-Sleep [35], which did not need to be worn, monitored respiration and heart rate via WiFi signals. Apple's iWatch, Huawei and Millet have also introduced wearable devices for health monitoring. BioHarness [36] developed a chest band for the monitoring of respiration and heart rate, and applied it to patients with heart disease. There are also other ancillary functions such as the outdoor location monitoring system OutCare [37], which is an anti-vagrancy system for Alzheimer's patients, and applications and tools biased towards cognitive orthodontics [38]. The sensors used in these devices are shown in the table below (Table 1).

Table 1. General subsidiary sensors in an AAL system

Sensor type	Measurement description	Sampling frequency
Accelerometer	Multiaxial acceleration measurement	High
Gyroscope	Directional state	High
Blood pressure	Blood pressure measurement	Low, trigger
Glucose	Blood glucose measurement	High, trigger
ECG	Electrocardiogram	Very high
EEG	Electroencephalogram	Very high
Temperature	Body surface temperature	Very low
Gas	Air pressure, harmful gas	Low
Muscle	Electromyography	Very high
Eyeball	Electrooculography	Very high
Pulse oximeter	Pulse oximeter oxygen saturation	Low

2.2 Anomaly Detection

Traditional detection focuses on disasters such as fires and gas leakages, and on triggering the corresponding alarm mechanism. An AAL system is different, as it involves the analysis of abnormal activities within households, and especially dangerous situations that may indicate that these households may need help. Many of the application algorithms for abnormality detection are the same as classification algorithms, and current research fields include inactive periods [39], fall detection [40] and disease prevention [41]. The function and value of these systems can be truly reflected. For example, patients with dementia and other mental illnesses can also be monitored for abnormal activities, enabling adverse consequences to be avoided [42].

Most of the more precise algorithms adopt data-driven approaches, but for anomaly detection, a knowledge-driven approach is needed in order to define the anomaly beforehand. The anomaly detection discussed in this paper mainly involves identifying the process of change in a household daily routine. Using supervised classification algorithms for machine learning, traditional modelling technology can still perform well in anomaly detection, in which anomalous activities are identified as new activities deviating from the norm. If there are no labelled training data, an unsupervised algorithm is needed. Cluster-based anomaly detection generally uses three approaches: (i) clustering; (ii) the vicinity of cluster centres; (iii) sparse clusters, using separate sizes and thresholds of clusters to determine an anomaly [43].

There are two main methods for detecting behaviour changes, and these involve profiling and discriminating. Normal behaviour is modelled using a method based on behaviour contouring, and an identified deviation is regarded as abnormal when it exceeds a threshold value. This method of identification involves learning abnormal data from historical data, and then identifying it directly when this abnormality appears. This is a common strategy in a knowledge-driven approach. However, in a real environment, historical data containing real anomalies are very scarce, meaning that a contour-based approach has greater practical significance for applications [44].

Feature extraction includes: (i) triggering times; (ii) triggering periods; (iii) the percentage of triggering activities of the total period; and (iv) the time difference between activities, from one location to another. Features may be related to the duration of events [45]. However, the features of persistent events are difficult to quantify, so it is adopted. A Gaussian normal distribution is used to calculate the average persistent events, and the positive and negative standard deviations ($u + 2\sigma$) are then used as boundaries, as these are more theoretically supported in a mathematical sense. Human behaviour will also be affected by several other factors, such as the weather, holidays, transportation, ball games, and other variations in behaviour, so a certain rate of error is still expected.

In order to solve this problem, a model scheme based on a probability graph can effectively reduce the number of false alarms [46], and can associate activities with health status to detect anomalies, collective anomalies and changes in health trends. A location-based scheme can also be used [47]. The best way to obtain user profile data is to define the most likely and frequent changes in location in order to detect changes in abnormal behaviour. Ordonez's scheme, proposed in 2014 [48], uses Bayesian statistics to model the distribution of follow-up features. Three probabilistic features in the wireless sensor network domain are analysed: (i) sensor activation likelihood (SAL); (ii) sensor sequence likelihood (SSL); and (iii) sensor duration likelihood (SDL), which detect abnormalities based on changes in the health context. Aztiria's Concept Drift

Table 2. Analysis and comparison of anomaly detection algorithms

Algorithm	Advantages	Disadvantages	Ref.
Artificial neural network	New rules can be added adaptively Mature application	Black box model Complex network architecture Unable to explain	[49]
Hidden Markov model	Processing sequence of data is simple and clear Accurate sequence of temporary actions Effective noise handling	Cold start Large training dataset required Data independent Manual pre-defined labels	[50]
Support vector machine	Linear or planar classification	Invalid outlier data samples	[3]
Conditional random field	No cold start Longer range Effective in dealing with noise	Computing overhead Manual labelling required Cooperation with other classifiers	[51]
Semantic rules	Lowest level heading text follows	Unable to handle undefined exceptions or noise	[52]
Profile/distance similarity	Simple calculation	Only binary data Unable to handle advanced logic Only one exception	[53]

scheme is based on the profile recognition of user behaviours [47]; it compares the latest data collected by sensors with historical contours of frequent activities in the user history data, and measures the amount of modification that would be needed to match behaviour computed based on the newly captured data with frequently occurring behaviour. Indicators or thresholds are used to determine whether the latest collected data is abnormal. All of the above schemes have certain advantages and disadvantages depending on the goal and scope of application. An analysis and comparison of several anomaly detection algorithms are given in Table 2.

3 Architecture and Preliminaries

3.1 Service Architecture

A typical AAL system is a people-oriented service system that has three main aspects: intelligent family, a remote health service and a physical care service. Based on the traditional architecture of big-data-related services and information communication platform, we expect that the service capability of an offline entity is crucial to implementation. Once the deployment and configuration of an AAL system is complete, continuous monitoring of sensors is carried out, thus making the household a private space. In addition to its own objective data attributes and the particular configuration, it also needs to synthesise external information from the Internet, carry out ETL and apply it comprehensively. Numerous types of data are produced by professional services, and together with the prior experience of the experts above are used to select the most appropriate intelligent service provider for matching and processing. Guardians far away from the elderly

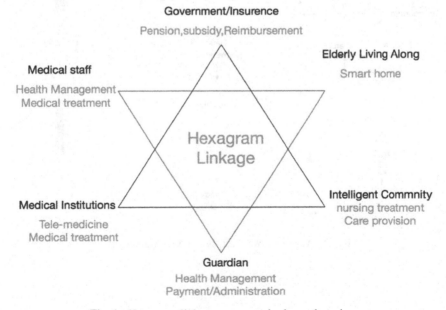

Fig. 1. Hexagram linkage: connected roles and services

person's home can purchase local or virtual services directly, anytime and anywhere, to protect their elderly loved ones living alone in their own home and to support their independent and dignified life. The architecture of these services is shown in Fig. 1. The hexagram framework connects each role with the corresponding services.

In this design framework, offline healthcare institutions provide long-term health services for residents, who are connected via telemedicine applications and the elderly person's smart home to form a complete AAL system via the Internet. With the gradual transition of the Internet to the era of mobile Internet, 4G networking and mobile computing have become available to every family, making XaaS (Everything as a Service) possible. Most computing and individual functions can remotely invoke cloud services and applications through RestFul's API. A guardian can check the status of the household anytime and anywhere via a mobile app. Based on the data shared by sensors, the Internet of Things, wearable devices and mobile medical equipment, guardians can determine a health status, price or other services that may be provided in the community or region, and can purchase entity services or third party services through mobile payment. The service can then be evaluated to promote a better experience for users. The AAL system therefore uses hardware as the carrier and entity services as support via the Internet, connecting the household and entity services together through the HAR system to facilitate automatic care. When an abnormal situation is identified, then take manual offline services, thus replacing some of the human labour in order to save costs. The abstract architecture of the overall system is shown in Fig. 2 below.

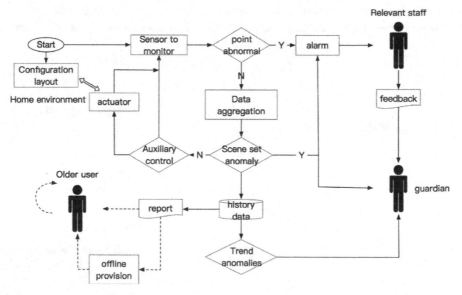

Fig. 2. Abstract flow chart for the AAL framework

3.2 Data Preliminary

In terms of equipment, we draw lessons from the deployment of the CASAS [54] project, since it has been running for five years and has been shown to be clinically effective. In terms of data attributes, we learn from MIT's PlaceLab [55], since each room has a fixed purpose within the home environment. Sensors collect basic behavioural activities, environmental parameters and corresponding timestamp information. Based on the goal of the application, we can add subjective knowledge and experience attributes, objective external data and environmental attributes to the position-aware scheme to enhance the dimensionality and validity of data. Apartment units in China are very standardised, and the living environments of most elderly people are shown in Fig. 3 below.

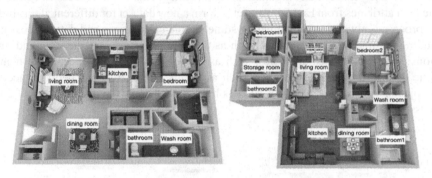

Fig. 3. Common living environments in China

An AAL system needs many different types of equipment, including MI equipment and medical equipment. These support the XML language to describe, define and link devices, provide data abstracts, and support the RESTful principle. After collecting data, we unified them via conversion to the ExADL data format, as used in our previous work [55]. The specific format is shown in Table 3.

Table 3.

Time axis	Objective attribute	Alarm	Active sensor	Subjective attribute	Behaviour description
[0]	[1:60]	[61:63]	[64:191]	[192:250]	[251:255]

The objective attributes of the data, including the device ID identification number, sensor type, timestamp, address code, data format, data sampling frequency, reading, sensor status information etc., reflect the parameter attributes of real data. In knowledge-driven schemes, subjective attributes require operators for configuration and to offer prior experience and knowledge. These attributes include: (i) ID; (ii) location, such as kitchen, living room and so on (enumerated values that machines may not necessarily understand, but human beings find very easy to understand); (iii) status and range (such as blood pressure or blood sugar values, normal range and threshold of early warning and alarms, which need professional knowledge combined with the situation in the particular household); (iv) associations (such as triggering of a smoke sensor due to an unknown fire) with the person who needs to be notified, which are solved by calling the processing module.

3.3 Data Pre-processing

The ExADL dataset is too large for the refined algorithms. In real applications, the selection of a subset of feature attributes related to the target can be used to complete the calculation and reduce the computational complexity. This is the process of selecting some data attributes from ExADL dataset to form a new dataset for different algorithms. This process is always accompanied by some simple calculations and data processing, including (i) time-related attributes, such as the time of occurrence, duration and repetitions; (ii) space-related attributes, such as the location of occurrence, room name, mobile data; (iii) complex attributes, such as events and interactions between people and objects; and (iv) state changes such as hidden attributes. The overall order of data processing is shown in Fig. 4.

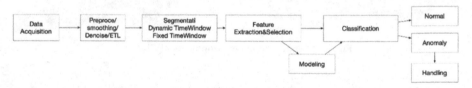

Fig. 4. Flow of data processing

We carried out the modelling of a resident's behaviour in our previous works [], in which we divided the user activity into three levels according to time granularity, corresponding to different modelling methods.

An atomic activity (AA) is the smallest unit of real human activity, i.e. one that cannot be monitored at a finer granularity. Sensor readings triggered by human activity such as swing, pressure, vibration, door opening and other attributes of active instantaneous trigger sensor, including ID, timestamp, data-driven attributes such as state readings, and the combination of knowledge-driven attributes such as the meanings and parameters of device state representation. The corresponding tags are specified in the configuration phase, and the classical ID3 algorithm is then used to model the atomic behaviour.

A basic activity (BA) is a basic unit that can independently represent possible human behaviours. It is a sequenced combination of all human-generated AAs and their attribute data within a small fixed time window (FTW). We use an unsupervised frequent pattern mining algorithm to carry out automatic labelling of black box BAs, and then use a classical hidden Markov model (HMM) to model the sequence.

A complex activity (CA) is an abstraction of real human activities. In the HAR field, it has the closest meaning to human behaviour. It refers to a sequenced set of all basic activities (BA) and other attribute information that is synthesised and formed within a specified time interval, which we call the dynamic time window (DTW). For long-term modelling of user routines, we use the classical conditional random field (CRF) model, which is generally based on a window of a day or week for offline modelling.

4 Anomaly Detection

The discovery of abnormal behaviour is of great significance in the application of AAL systems, since the living habits of the elderly are relatively routine. When abnormal behaviour occurs, it usually indicates a problem.

4.1 Definition of an Anomaly

In the actual feedback from deployment, a user's behavioural data typically obeys a normal distribution. Activity and data at each level correspond to different anomaly detection methods. We first define exceptions using four categories at the data level.

A point anomaly refers to an anomaly in data at the atomic behaviour level, including parameters exceeding a threshold range such as the time and position attributes of sensor triggering and normal habits, which have a greater statistical significance of deviation, for example a fire, getting out of bed at night or blood pressure that exceeds a standard value.

A set anomaly refers to the basic behaviour level data anomaly, including similarity matching between the sequence triggered by the sensor and the historical model exceeding the threshold. For example, when users are sick or depressed, many behaviours may deviate from historical habits.

Scenario anomalies refer to complex behavioural data anomalies, such as a user having a cold or diarrhoea, in which behavioural habits will deviate from the overall trend indicated by historical data.

Trend anomalies and others are usually calculated on the basis of specific parameters. The calculation period may be longer with fewer parameters.

The calculation process of each mode is shown in Fig. 5.

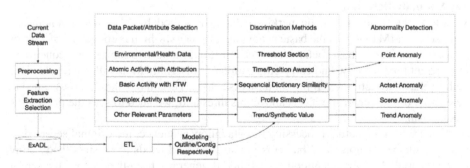

Fig. 5. Anomaly detection process at each level

4.2 Detection Methods

Point Anomaly Detection

When the system configuration is complete, we determine the alarm interval of the parameters, and start the alarm module when the data are abnormal. For abnormal behaviour, the main parameters such as the time and position of the trigger are inconsistent with the historical model, and the threshold is difficult to determine. We therefore use a simple Adaboost algorithm to carry out Boolean calculations, and beyond the part of the historical model we judge as anomalies. A detailed description is given below.

Input: Sample$(x_1,y_1),(x_2,y_2),\ldots,(x_n,y_n)$
//Is the characteristic vector of K dimension, $\forall y_i \in \{-1,1\}$;
    Initial weight of n samples $D0(i)=1/n$;
    Weak classifier $g(x) \in \{-1,1\}$; Maximum number of iterations Imax
Output: All Weak Classifiers
1: For $t=1$ to Imax do
2: Looking for $g(x)$ to minimise the weighting error
$$g_t(x) = \mathrm{argmin}_{g_t^k(x)} \sum_{i=1}^{n} D_t(i) I[g_t^k(x_i) \neq y_i]$$
$$\varepsilon_t = \sum_{i=1}^{n} D_t(i) I[g_t(x_i) \neq y_i]$$
3: Calculate the weight of $gt(x)$:$\alpha_t = \frac{1}{2}\ln\left(\frac{1-et}{et}\right)$
4: Update sample weights;
    for $i = 1$ to n do
$$D_{t+1}(i) = \frac{D_t(i)\exp[-\alpha y_1 h_t(x_i)]}{\sum_i D_t(i)\exp[-\alpha y_1 h_t(x_i)]}$$
    end for
5: end for
6: return $G(x) = \mathrm{sign}[\sum_{t=1}^{Imax} \alpha_t h_t(x)]$

Adaboost is a discriminant classifier, meaning that it needs to give a definite classification decision, and there is therefore a potential problem of uncertainty. Its statistical characteristics will select the largest number of classes in the sample as the prediction.

Set Anomaly Detection

We adopt a black box automatic marking behaviour method, based on frequent itemsets, and use an HMM to model the basic behaviour dictionary, which is composed of a series of vector matrices. In basic behaviour discrimination, we need to sample the sequence in the current time window and carry out a similarity discrimination with each behaviour in the behaviour dictionary. If the similarity is below a certain threshold, it is assumed to be normal behaviour, while if it is above this threshold, we need to start the processing mechanism.

However, in the actual processing of data inflow sequence, the original sensor data (a large number of noise and burrs) is not suitable, and needs to be smoothed before it can be used. An average smoothing method is generally used that defines the sensor attribute data sequence as i, the behaviour dictionary as Dic, and the time window as w. The mean smoothing calculation is as follows:

$$F_w(i, Dic) = \frac{1}{w} \sum_{j=i-w}^{i} SIM(Seq_j, Dic) \tag{1}$$

To calculate the distance, we adopt a cosine distance similarity. Assuming that the angle between two attribute vectors Seq_1 and Seq_2 is γ, then the similarity between the two vectors is expressed by a cosine:

$$\cos(\gamma) = \frac{Seq_1 \cdot Seq_2}{\|Seq_1\| \cdot \|Seq_2\|} = \frac{\sum_{i=1}^{n} Seq_1 \times Seq_2}{\sqrt{\sum_{i=1}^{n}(Seq_1)^2} \cdot \sqrt{\sum_{i=1}^{n}(Seq_2)^2}} \tag{2}$$

The sequence similarity of behaviour attributes (such as trigger time, duration, location, state, etc.) can be calculated using the following formula:

$$SIM(Seq_i, Dic) = \max_{Seq_j \in Dic} \left\{ SIM(Seq_i, Seq_j) \right\} \tag{3}$$

Scene Anomaly Detection

A set anomaly needs to traverse all the behaviours in the dictionary. However, a scene anomaly is relatively simple to calculate, and only needs to distinguish similarity by comparing a long-term historical contour model. We first need to determine the length of the time window, which can be expressed as a user profile in a long-term historical model trained using CRF over days, weeks or even months. Since the deployment and behaviour of users are uncertain, we use the algorithmic concept of self-organising maps (SOM) for reference in order to realise an unsupervised learning model to discriminate and to understand a user's behaviour as a hidden unknown state. If the user's behaviour deviates from the normal range, an abnormal occurrence is detected, which requires a guardian to confirm that the user is safe.

We assume that $s(t)$ is the trigger time at which the user enters the room, $D(t)$ is the duration, the hidden network node M_i is a weighted vector, and the latest data collected by the sensor are a combination of vectors $X(t) = [s(t), D(t)]$.

In order to calculate the parameters of smooth iteration nodes, we let $\gamma(t)$ be a scalar parameter factor decreasing with time t, and $N_c i(t)$ be a neighbourhood of $M_i(t)$, representing the distance $X(t)$. Then, the value of M_i calculated after I iterations can be obtained by the following formula:

$$m_i(t + 1) = m_i(t) + \gamma(t) N_c i(t)[x(t) - m_i(t)] \tag{4}$$

Input: **x(t)**, time limit **limT**
Output: Distance vector **m_i**
1:   m_1 = seed(); // Initialise random values
2:   t=1;
3:   while t < limT do
4:      for each m_i in map do
5:         d = diatance[m_i(t),x(t)]; // Computational cosine distance
6:         track mi(t) with min(d); // Use the closest similarity
7:         $m_i(t + 1) = m_i(t) + \gamma(t)N_ci(t)[x(t)-m_i(t)]$
8:      end for
9:   end while
10: return m_i ;

Based on the return value and threshold value, the processing scheme is determined by prior knowledge or manual method.

Detection of Trends and Other Anomalies

Fluctuating trends in blood pressure, heart rate and respiratory parameters indicate an abnormal health status of a user. Some parameters do not have obvious threshold limits for alarms, such as daily use of a treadmill, sleep indicators and so on. We can therefore only use the user's own historical data as a normal profile contour and calculate the difference as a reference. Taking into consideration the influence of weather-related factors and holidays, we make a concrete judgment that the user's data primarily obey a normal distribution. When the difference exceeds twice the standard deviation, an early warning is triggered, prompting the remote caregivers to pay attention. The features selected in this way are relatively simple, but the time window used is relatively large, and is typically calculated in days or weeks. Since the data features are relatively small, the same configuration can tolerate larger computational time intervals. Offline computing is normally used to calculate each feature every day.

Input: **Single feature** extraction (motion detection, heart rate, blood pressure, sleep, etc.), **time interval** [T1, T2], and sliding window interval **W**
Output: **Characteristic matrix** (with statistical indicators)
1: Establish the computational time interval T1−T2//
2: while   T1 < (T2 − W) do
         for each feature do   // Calculate for each feature.
   // Starting with T1, a sliding window with a length W is established.
3:      Process missing values ();
4:      Compute statistical indicators ();
   // Include variance, skewness, kurtosis, correlation coefficient, etc.
5:      Append(); // Write these values back to the eigenvalue matrix
6:      T2=T1+1;   //Move one day
7:      end for
8: **return** average(feature matrix);   // A smooth feature matrix is obtained.

This is handled manually when other logic or the threshold exceeds n times the standard deviation, where n = 1 or 2.

4.3 Anomaly-Handling Scheme

As described above, we define four kinds of data anomalies in AAL's information system. According to the degree of the emergency, we can divide the alarm and processing into four levels, which from high to low are as follows:

Disaster Level: For example, if a smoke alarm is triggered, this may lead to a fire, which should be dealt with by the nearest staff and 119 fire alarms.

Medical Level: Danger signs such as shortness of breath and sudden cardiac arrest are collected by mattress. It is necessary to call 120 for help from nearby medical staff and family members.

Nursing Level: Users are suspected to have health issues or danger signals, such as getting out of bed at night, instability in heart rate and blood pressure, insomnia/depression or other problems. There is a need to go to the scene to carry out a physical examination and confirmation, in order to ensure the user's safety.

Early Warning Level: Users show abnormal health trends or indicators, such as a slightly higher blood pressure, and need a guardian to contact them by telephone within a certain period of time, confirm the situation and decide on treatment. The overall exception handling process is shown in Fig. 2.

After the configuration and deployment of the AAL shown in the upper left, the system begins to monitor the data collected by sensors. According to the degree of abnormal danger and the level of the alarm, the alarm data can be distinguished from the pre-AAL gateway, which can identify abnormal data such as a fire, a gas leak, burglary, sudden respiratory arrest, rapid or slow heart rate, etc. The alarm module can then be started directly, and the relevant data can be dealt with by calling designated contact persons or emergency services such as 119 or 120. Questions, feedback on the problem and the results of the treatment are addressed by the guardian and the relevant handlers through consultation. When the gateway does not identify abnormal point data, it starts to calculate the similarity between the users and historical contours to see if there is any deviation in habits. If the distance similarity exceeds a certain threshold (that is, if it identifies an abnormal situation such as a cold or diarrhoea), it then confirms with the guardian whether this needs to be handled by the guardian. When data on a user can be accumulated for two weeks or more, trend anomalies can be calculated based on a historical weighted average. When assessing trends involving suspected insomnia, depression or forgetting to take medicine, the system should inform the guardian within a suitable period of time, and the guardian should confirm the situation as soon as possible and decide how to deal with it.

5 Case Study

In order to verify the applicability and validity of the anomaly detection methods proposed in this paper, as applied to helping elderly patients with chronic diseases, we established a demonstration base involving both medical and nursing care in Shaanxi Province, as a typical solution, with support from the government of the new urban area of Xi'an, Xi'an Mayinglong Hospital, Xi'an Mingzhong Community Service Co., Ltd., and the Information Storage Department of Wuhan Photoelectric National Laboratory. Our case study was run with 184 users for over two years, using the deployment specifications shown in Table 4 below.

Table 4. Equipment specification for the case study (per house)

Hardware	Description	Number
Temperature sensor	ZigBee, temperature and humidity at 10 min intervals	3
PIR sensor	ZigBee, motion detection at 1 min intervals	6
ECG band	BLE, steps, sleep, heart rate at 10 min intervals	1
SOS button	On demand	1
Toilet Cover	Wi-Fi, toilet time, frequency, duration	1
Leakage detector	Point alarm	1
Gas detector	Point alarm	1
Smoke alarm	Point alarm	1

With the continuous development of the electronic industry, the large-scale application of sensors makes the price of civil-grade sensors equipment wallet-friendly. Open-source hardware such as Raspberry pi and Arduino can connect different transmission

Fig. 6. Backstage management of our AAL system

protocols with various general IO interfaces. XML or JSON can quickly unify the data formats from different manufacturers, so a set of CASAS-like devices can be developed based on the above-mentioned devices, which can guarantee low cost, effective and robust (Fig. 6).

The average power consumption of the home-based part of the AAL system is about 1.8 W/h, as shown in the figure of other supporting software. The AAL project was generally effective. A total of 114 suspected safety hazards were found in time, and the guardian was notified to address these. No injuries or death occurred to the users. The warning and handling of exceptions is shown in Fig. 7.

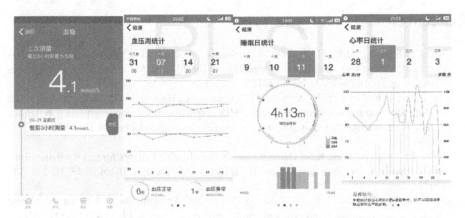

Fig. 7. Blood sugar, blood pressure, sleep status and heart rate alerts

In total, we sampled 117 sets of abnormal alarms, five of which were false alarms, and the rest were caused by the user having a cold or diarrhoea, or changes in travel behaviour. Our detection algorithm is effective, but needs to be strengthened and improved in terms of the user's experience. A visual representation of this model checking is shown in Fig. 8.

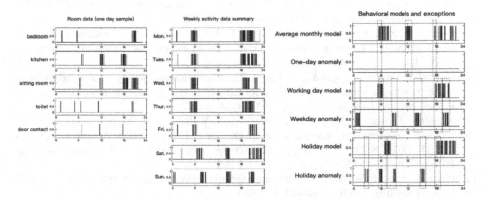

Fig. 8. Intuitive display of behaviour deviation

6 Discussion

Based on data feedback from 300 real users as part of the follow-up to this project, we conclude that the health status of working people is poorer than that of the elderly, although their physical functions are stronger. The work and rest patterns of retirees are relatively regular. Working users showed abnormal heart rates, blood pressure, sleep patterns and other aspects 20 times more frequently than the retired group. The performance of comprehensive satisfaction related to work stress and anxiety is acceptable. Some suggestions for improvement and user experience were received as feedback.

References

1. Khan, S.S., Karg, M.E., Hoey, J., et al.: Towards the detection of unusual temporal events during activities using HMMs. In: Proceedings of the 2012 ACM Conference on Ubiquitous Computing, pp. 1075–1084. ACM (2012)
2. Raymond, H.F., Chen, Y.-H., Syme, S.L., Catalano, R., Hutson, M.A., McFarland, W.: The role of individual and neighborhood factors: HIV acquisition risk among high-risk populations in San Francisco. AIDS Behav. **18**(2), 346–356 (2013). https://doi.org/10.1007/s10461-013-0508-y
3. Shin, J.H., Lee, B., Park, K.S.: Detection of abnormal living patterns for elderly living alone using support vector data description. IEEE Trans. Inf. Technol. Biomed. **15**(3), 438–448 (2011)
4. Memon, M., Wagner, S.R., Pedersen, C.F., et al.: Ambient assisted living healthcare frameworks, platforms, standards, and quality attributes. Sensors **14**(3), 4312–4341 (2014)
5. Franco, G.C., Gallay, F., Berenguer, M., Mourrain, C., Couturier, P.: Non-invasive monitoring of the activities of daily living of elderly people at home—a pilot study of the usage of domestic appliances. J. Telemed. Telecare **14**(5), 231–235 (2008)
6. Zhou, Z., Chen, X., Chung, Y.C., He, Z., Han, T.X., Keller, J.M.: Activity analysis, summarization, and visualization for indoor human activity monitoring. IEEE Trans. Circuits Syst. Video Technol. **18**(11), 1489–1498 (2008)
7. Chung, P.C., Liu, C.D.: A daily behavior enabled hidden Markov model for human behavior understanding. Pattern Recogn. **41**(5), 1572–1580 (2008)
8. Qudah, I., Leijdekkers, P., Gay, V.: Using mobile phones to improve medication compliance and awareness for cardiac patients. In: Proceedings of International Conference on Pervasive Technologies Related Assisted Environments, pp. 1–7 (2010)
9. Khan, D.U., Siek, K.A., Meyers, J., Haverhals, L.M., Cali, S., Ross, S.E.: Designing a personal health application for older adults to manage medications. In: Proceedings of International Health Informatics Symposium, pp. 849–858 (2010)
10. Eklund, J., Hansen, T., Sprinkle, J., Sastry, S.: Information technology for assisted living at home: building a wireless infrastructure for assisted living. In: Proceedings of Engineering in Medicine and Biology Society, pp. 3931–3934 (2005)
11. Aghajan, H., Augusto, J.C., Wu, C., McCullagh, P., Walkden, J.-A.: Distributed vision-based accident management for assisted living. In: Okadome, T., Yamazaki, T., Makhtari, M. (eds.) ICOST 2007. LNCS, vol. 4541, pp. 196–205. Springer, Heidelberg (2007). https://doi.org/10.1007/978-3-540-73035-4_21
12. Fleck, S., Strasser, W.: Smart camera based monitoring system and its application to assisted living. Proc. IEEE **96**(10), 1698–1714 (2008)

13. Vetere, F., Davis, H., Gibbs, M., Howard, S.: The magic box and collage: responding to the challenge of distributed intergenerational play. Int. J. Human-Comput. Stud. **67**(2), 165–178 (2009)
14. Sliwa, J., Benoist, E.: Wireless sensor and actor networks: E-health, E-science, E-decisions. In: Proceedings of the International Conference on Selected Topics in Mobile and Wireless Networking (iCOST), Shanghai, China, 10–12 October 2011, pp. 1–6 (2011)
15. Farrell, A.: ZyXEL Introduces State-of-the-Art Smart Home Gateway for Health Monitoring Applications. https://www.zyxel.com/us/en/. Accessed 16 Jan 2019
16. TeleCare. Cellular-Enabled Glucometer. http://telcare.com/. Accessed 21 Feb 2019
17. Microsoft HealthVault Platform. https://www.healthvault.com/. Accessed 24 Feb 2019
18. APPLE HealthKit Platform for Developpers. https://developer.apple.com/healthkit/. Accessed 18 Mar 2019
19. Perez, A.J., Labrador, M.A., Barbeau, S.J.: G-sense: a scalable architecture for global sensing and monitoring. IEEE Network **24**(4), 57–64 (2010)
20. Rashidi, P., Cook, D.J.: The resident in the loop: adapting the smart home to the user. IEEE Trans. Syst. Man Cybern. Part A Syst. Hum. **39**(5), 949–959 (2009)
21. Rantz, M., et al.: Using sensor networks to detect urinary tract infections in older adults. In: Proceedings of International Conference on e-Health Networking, Applications and Services (2011)
22. Adami, A., Pavel, M., Hayes, T., Singer, C.: Detection of movement in bed using unobtrusive load cell sensors. IEEE Trans. Inf Technol. Biomed. **14**(2), 481–490 (2010)
23. Abowd, G., Mynatt, E.: Designing for the human experience in smart environments. In Smart Environments: Technology, Protocols, and Applications, pp. pp. 153–174. Wiley, New York (2004)
24. LeBellego, G., Noury, N., Virone, G., Mousseau, M., Demongeot, J.: A model for the measurement of patient activity in a hospital suite. IEEE Trans. Inf Technol. Biomed. **10**(1), 92–99 (2006)
25. Chan, E.C.M., Estève, D.: Assessment of activity of elderly people using a home monitoring system. Int. J. Rehabil. Res. **28**(1), 69–70 (2006)
26. Adlam, T., Faulkner, R., Orpwood, R., Jones, K., Macijauskiene, J., Budraitiene, A.: The installation and support of internationally distributed equipment for people with dementia. IEEE Trans. Inf Technol. Biomed. **8**(3), 253–257 (2004)
27. The ambient assisted living joint program. www.aal-europe.eu. Accessed 21 Mar 2019
28. Tamura, T., Kawarada, A., Nambu, M., Tsukada, A., Sasaki, K., Yamakoshi, K.-I.: E-healthcare at an experimental welfare techno house in Japan. Open Med. Inf. **1**, 1–7 (2007)
29. Yamazaki, T.: The ubiquitous home. Int. J. Smart Home **1**(1), 17–22 (2007)
30. Franco, C., Demongeot, J., Villemazet, C., Nicolas, V.: Behavioral telemonitoring of the elderly at home: detection of nycthemeral rhythms drifts from location data. In: Proceedings of Advanced Information Networking and Applications Workshops, pp. 759–766 (2010)
31. Suzuki, T., Murase, S., Tanaka, T., Okazawa, T.: New approach for the early detection of dementia by recording in-house activities. Telemed. J. E Health **13**(1), 41–44 (2007)
32. Liu, X., Cao, J., Tang, S., et al.: A generalized coverage-preserving scheduling in WSNs: a case study in structural health monitoring. In: IEEE INFOCOM 2014, Proceedings IEEE, pp. 718–726 (2014)
33. Smart Life Technology: Healthvest (2011). www.smartlifetech.com. Accessed 27 Nov 2018
34. Liang, G., Cao, J., Liu, X., et al.: Cushionware: a practical sitting posture-based interaction system. In: CHI 2014 Extended Abstracts on Human Factors in Computing Systems, pp. 591–594. ACM (2014)
35. Liu, X., Cao, J., Tang, S., et al.: Wi-Sleep: contactless sleep monitoring via WiFi signals. In: 2014 IEEE Real-Time Systems Symposium (RTSS), pp. 346–355. IEEE (2014)

36. Zephyr: Biohraness (2011). www.zephyr-technology.com. Accessed 23 Dec 2018
37. Wan, J., Byrne, C., O'Hare, G.M., O'Grady, M.J.: Orange alerts: lessons from an outdoor case study. In: Proceedings of 5th International Conference on Pervasive Computing Technologies for Healthcare (PervasiveHealth) and Workshops, pp. 446–451 (2011)
38. Rashidi, P., Mihailidis, A.: A survey on ambient-assisted living tools for older adults. IEEE J. Biomed. Health Inform. **17**(3), 579–590 (2013)
39. Pulsford, R.M., et al.: Actigraph accelerometer-defined boundaries for sedentary behavior and physical activity intensities in 7 year old children. PLoS ONE **6**(8), e21822 (2011)
40. Abbate, S., et al.: A smartphone-based fall detection system. Pervasive Mob. Comput. **8**(6), 883–899 (2012)
41. Albinali, F., Goodwin, M.S., Intille, S.: Detecting stereotypical motor movements in the classroom using accelerometry and pattern recognition algorithms. Pervasive Mob. Comput. **8**(1), 103–114 (2012)
42. Yin, J., Yang, Q., Pan, J.: Sensor-based abnormal human-activity detection. IEEE Trans. Knowl. Data Eng. **20**(8), 1082–1090 (2008)
43. Mahmoud, S.M.: Identification and prediction of abnormal behaviour activities of daily living in intelligent environments. Thesis (2012)
44. Cardinaux, F., Brownsell, S., Hawley, M., Bradley, D.: Modelling of behavioural patterns for abnormality detection in the context of lifestyle reassurance. In: Ruiz-Shulcloper, J., Kropatsch, W.G. (eds.) CIARP 2008. LNCS, vol. 5197, pp. 243–251. Springer, Heidelberg (2008). https://doi.org/10.1007/978-3-540-85920-8_30
45. Alam, M., Reaz, M., Husain, H.: Temporal modeling and its application for anomaly detection in smart homes. Int. J. Phys. Sci. **6**(31), 7233–7241 (2011)
46. Khan, S.S., et al.: Towards the detection of unusual temporal events during activities using HMMs. In: Proceedings of the 2012 ACM Conference on Ubiquitous Computing. ACM (2012)
47. Wong, K.B.-Y., Zhang, T., Aghajan, H.: Data fusion with a dense sensor network for anomaly detection in smart homes. In: Spagnolo, P., Mazzeo, P.L., Distante, C. (eds.) Human Behavior Understanding in Networked Sensing, pp. 211–237. Springer, Cham (2014). https://doi.org/10.1007/978-3-319-10807-0_10
48. Ordóñez, F.J., de Toledo, P., Sanchis, A.: Sensor-based Bayesian detection of anomalous living patterns in a home setting. Pers. Ubiquit. Comput. **19**(2), 259–270 (2015). https://doi.org/10.1007/s00779-014-0820-1
49. Rivera-Illingworth, F., Callaghan, V., Hagras, H.: A connectionist embedded agent approach for abnormal behaviour detection in intelligent health care environments. In: 2004 IEEE International Conference on Systems, Man and Cybernetics. IEEE (2004)
50. Yan, Q., Xia, S., Shi, Y.: An anomaly detection approach based on symbolic similarity. In: Control and Decision Conference (CCDC), 2010 Chinese. IEEE (2010)
51. Cook, D., Diane, J.: Multi-agent smart environments. J. Ambient Intell. Smart Environ. **1**(1), 51–55 (2009)
52. Barsocchi, P., et al.: Monitoring elderly behavior via indoor position-based stigmergy. Pervasive Mob. Comput. **23**, 26–42 (2015)
53. Rashidi, P., et al.: Discovering activities to recognize and track in a smart environment. IEEE Trans. Knowl. Data Eng. **23**(4), 527–539 (2011)
54. Cook, D.J., et al.: CASAS: a smart home in a box. Computer **46**(7), 26–33 (2013)
55. PlaceLab. http://web.mit.edu/cron/group/house_n/data/PlaceLab/PlaceLab.htm

Message Transmission Reliability Evaluation of CAN Based on DSPN

Shujun Yong[1], Lerong Qi[2], Yunhong Ma[2(✉)], and Yifei Zhao[2]

[1] Huayin Ordnance Test Center, Weilan 710142, China
[2] Northwestern Polytechnical University, Xi'an 710072, China
mayunhong@nwpu.edu.cn

Abstract. The message transmission reliability is an important performance of CAN communication. The message transmission reliability of the CAN refers to the ability of the message to be successfully transmitted within its deadline. In order to assess the message transmission reliability of CAN, a four-node CAN communication model is set up based on the deterministic and stochastic Petri net in this paper, which is used to simulate the arbitration mechanism and error handling mechanism of CAN. The model is used to demonstrate the operation of the CAN bus in an interference environment with transient bursts which is used to simulate the external electromagnetic interference. Message transmission failure probability under the interference is used as the indicator of the message transmission reliability of CAN, and a solution method for proposed model based on the queuing theory is given to acquire the stationary value of the message transmission failure probability. The simulation gives the analysis of reliability of message transmission under different interference arrival intervals, different message priorities, different message periods and different number of nodes, which verifies the validity and feasibility of the proposed model.

Keywords: Controller area network · Reliability evaluation · Petri nets

1 Introduction

CAN-bus has the characteristics of good real-time performance because of short message frame, such as strong anti-interference ability and high cost performance. It is widely used in bus data communication between automobiles and various industrial sites. As a real-time information transmission system, CAN message failure will have a strong impact on system performance, so message transmission reliability [1] is an important indicator of CAN. The CAN message is considered to be successfully transmitted when its response time is less than its deadline. In this paper, the successful transmission probability of the CAN message is used as the indicator for evaluating the reliability of the message transmission of CAN.

There are many factors that affect the reliability of CAN data transmission, including design factors and environmental factors. With the development of electronic technology, the data communication in the industrial field is becoming more and more complex, and

© ICST Institute for Computer Sciences, Social Informatics and Telecommunications Engineering 2020
Published by Springer Nature Switzerland AG 2020. All Rights Reserved
B. Li et al. (Eds.): IoTaaS 2019, LNICST 316, pp. 363–374, 2020.
https://doi.org/10.1007/978-3-030-44751-9_30

the electromagnetic interference intensity is getting larger and larger. Electromagnetic interference can cause transmission errors, and trigger CAN error handling mechanism. With this mechanism the error message is generated and the message with error is retransmitted. The error handing mechanism effectively guarantees the successful transmission of the message. But too many errors will increase the bus utilization and delay the message response time. In severe cases, the message may miss its deadline and so the message transmission fails.

The analysis of message transmission reliability mainly evaluates whether the message response time exceeds the deadline of the message. For the response time analysis, the worst-case response time (WCRT) indicator of a message is a commonly used indicator. Tindell et al. [2] proposed a scheduling method based on fixed-priority preemption scheduling for single-processor systems in 1994. They gave a WCRT analysis method based on recursion, and concluded that the message is schedulable if the WCRT is less than the deadline. Punnekkat et al. [3] proposed a more general fault model and applied it to the WCRT analysis of CAN. Nolte et al. [4] proposed a worst-case probability response time analysis method based on the number of bits in CAN as a random variable, which reduces the conservativeness of WCRT analysis. Mubeen et al. [5] gave the WCRT analysis based on several different queues such as priority queue and FIFO queue, etc.

In addition to WCRT analysis, many researches focus on the response time distribution. As early as 1994, Muppala et al. [6] calculated the response time distribution of fixed-length periodic messages based on the stochastic reward network (SRN), but the limitation was large, which caused a big difference with the actual CAN bus. Nilsson et al. [7] considered random message lengths but did not consider bit stuffing and fault models, so the results are still too optimistic. Navet et al. [8] proposed the Worst-Case Deadline Failure Probability (WCDFP) in 2000. They believed that because of the random interference, the event that the message response time exceeded the deadline became a random event. Then give the probability algorithm of WCDFP. Portugal [9] proposed a determination of stochastic Petri nets (DSPN) model to analysis the reliability of CAN, while the model is complex and the index chosen was unable to get the required result. Kumar et al. [10] analyzed the response time distribution of CAN messages and gave an analysis model based on the (DSPN). Chen et al. [11] gave an analysis of average response time of CAN based on the queuing theory, which could only analysis the average value instead of the distribution of response time. Sun et al. [12] improved the model and compared the results obtained with the results of the simulation based on colored Petri nets (CPN) to verify the validity of the model, but the above two did not consider the fault impact.

Deterministic and Stochastic Petri Nets (DSPN) is one of the effective tools for discrete event modeling. Based on DSPN, this paper proposes a CAN communication model which simulates the arbitration mechanism and error handling process, and evaluates the reliability of CAN message transmission.

2 Working Mechanism of CAN

2.1 Bit-by-Bit Arbitration

The CAN adopts a bus topology, and all nodes are equally connected to the bus with a multi-master transmission mechanism. Since the CAN bus can only transmit one message at a time, there is a preemption of the bus when multiple messages are ready to be transmitted at the same time. The CAN bus stipulates that each message has a unique ID. Non-destructive bit-by-bit arbitration is carried out according to ID between messages. The message winning the arbitration with high priority uses the bus and transmits the message. The message that lost the arbitration waits for the next arbitration. This causes the message losing the arbitration unable to be sent immediately after the message is generated, and the message response time increases which also increases the probability of message transmission failure.

2.2 Error Handling

The CAN has a strong error detection capability. The probability of an error message being missed by the CAN bus [13] is less than 4.7×10^{-11}. Any node that detects an error will perform error signaling and recovering, which guarantee the accurate transmission of the message.

Error signaling is the process by which a node signals an error by transmitting an error flag. According to the fault confinement mechanism of CAN, the CAN node has three statuses: error active, error passive and bus-off. The error flag of the error active node is 6 dominant bits. These 6 bits will cause a bit stuffing error to abort the transmission of the message and signal the error; the error flag of the error passive node is 6 recessive bits, which can not affect the bus level; the node in the bus-off status is not allowed any interaction with the bus.

The error flag of the error active node will be superimposed. As shown in Fig. 1, if both the error bit and the previous correct bit are dominant, then for the receiving node, after monitoring the fourth dominant bit of the sending node's error flag, together with the previous two dominant bits there have already been six dominant bits monitored. Then the receiving node detects a bit stuffing error and transmits six dominant bits to signal the error, which causes the error flag on the bus to be superimposed into 10 dominant bits. Obviously, if the error bit is a recessive bit, then the two error flags will be superimposed with 12 bits, which is the maximum length of the error flag overlay. After the error flag is superimposed, 8 recessive bits are added to the error delimiter, and the transmission of the error frame is completed. In a word, in the error active status, the error signal will be an error message with length within 17 bits to 23 bits adding the 3 bits of interframe space. This error message will cause the occupation of bus and generate delay.

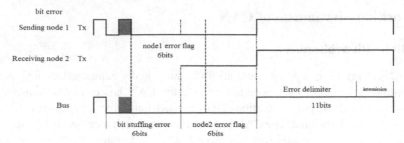

Fig. 1. Superposition of the active frame

The error recovering mechanism allows previously erroneous messages to be automatically retransmitted after the error frame is transmitted, but note that messages from other nodes are also allowed to preempt the bus. If a higher priority message is ready to be transmitted, the retransmission of the erroneous message is delayed and the probability of transmission failure increases.

3   Model Framework and Solution Method

3.1   DSPN Features

Petri nets are often used to simulate discrete events. DSPN is an improvement of the Stochastic Petri net (SPN): the forbidden arc is added to the DSPN to implement the prohibition of the transition when the place contains the number of tokens greater than or equal to the arc weight; the DSPN increases the immediate transition and can assign priorities to several conflicting immediate transitions; DSPN adds deterministic transitions to describe events that occur at a fixed time. These features of DSPN can be used to simulate the CAN communication model.

3.2   Model Framework

This paper makes the following assumptions for the model: each node transmits a periodic message, and the normal transmission times of all the messages are the same which is the maximum value; the message period is the deadline for the message. When the deadline arrives, the new message will overwrite the old message and cause the old message to fail; all nodes are in the error active status because the probability of the node being in the error passive status is very low [8]; the interference on the CAN bus is the electrical fast transient burst, which is the standard test signal of electromagnetic compatibility; the Portugal [9] founded that the change of the interference duration does not cause an order of magnitude change in the probability of message failure when other parameters are unchanged. Therefore, it is assumed that the burst signal has the same width with the bit time and affects only one bit; the interference during the error frame transmission is ignored. The error frame transmission length is the maximum length of the active error frame plus the interframe space total 23 bits.

Based on the above assumptions, a single-node CAN communication model is established as shown in Fig. 2.

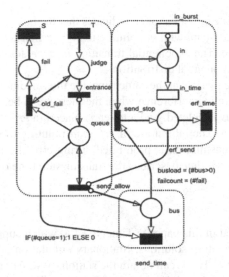

Fig. 2. Single-node model of CAN based on DSPN

The model includes the node model (the part in the dotted line on the left), the interference and error handling model (the part in the dotted line on the right), and the bus channel model (the part in the lower dotted line box).

The node model is responsible for message generating, message transmitting and message failure counting. The deterministic transition *T* represents the generation of periodic messages. The place *queue* represents the message queue. The intermediate transition *Entrance* indicates that the generated message enters the message queue *queue*, and the intermediate transition *old_fail* indicates that the old message is overwritten by the new message and so exits the message queue *queue*. Whether the two transitions mentioned before are enabled or not is determined by whether there is a token in *queue*. The token entering *queue* waits until *send_allow* is enabled, while the place *fail* and the deterministic transition *S* form a simple queuing system to count the number of failed messages.

The place *bus* and the deterministic transition *send_time* form a bus channel model. No token in *bus* indicates that the bus is idle. At this time, the intermediate transition *send_allow* will be enabled. After *send_allow* fired, a token is placed in *bus* to indicate that the bus is transmitting a message now. The deterministic transition *send_time* represents the message transmission time. After *send_time* fired, the token in *queue* and *bus* are deleted at the same time, indicating that the message in the node's message queue is already transmitted and the bus becomes idle. Note that the arc weight of *queue* to *send_time* is a logical expression, which promises that only the token in the highest priority node's queue will be deleted when *send_time* fires.

The interference and error handling model only considers the operation of the bus within the transient interference group burst interval. It is assumed that the transient interference group burst is periodic, and the conditional probability is used to extend the results of the model to the entire time domain. The exponential transition *in_burst* represents the interference of the arrival interval obeying the exponential distribution during the group burst. The place *in* with a token indicates that the bus is facing interference at this time, and the inhibiting arc with *in* pointing to *in_burst* ensures that only one interference at the same time. The exponential transition *in_time* describes the interference duration obeying the exponential distribution.

When *bus* and *in* are marked at the same time, the intermediate transition *send_stop* fires indicating that there is interference when the message is being transmitted at this time, so the token in *bus* is deleted, and a token is placed in *erf_send* to represents the error frame transmission. The inhibit arc of *erf_send* pointing to *send_allow* indicates that normal message transmission is prohibited during error frame transmission. The deterministic transition *erf_time* describes the transmission time of the error frame.

3.3 Solution Method

The simulation tool used in this paper is TimeNET4.4, which supports graphical modeling and multiple simulation solutions. Stationary simulation is a common analysis method provided in TimeNET. It can obtain the stationary value of the model when the time tends to infinity. Therefore, it is often used for probability measurement. Stationary simulation is to obtain a certain frequency value through a large number of samples. Since the number of samples is large, according to Bernoulli's law of large numbers, the frequency is infinitely close to the probability required.

In this paper, the message failure probability is obtained by solving the stationary value of the number of message failures per unit time. This value is divided by the total number of messages generated per unit time to obtain the message failure probability, and the message transmission reliability of CAN is evaluated by the message failure probability.

After experimental comparison, the Multi-trajectory stationary analysis method provided in TimeNET has higher efficiency in solving the model. Therefore, Multi-trajectory stationary analysis method is used to carry out all the simulations in the paper.

The way to solve the TimeNET model is to build a measure expression and then run the simulation to get the result of the measure expression. TimeNET gives the syntax of the measure expression, and the user can create the expression of the desired measure. The measure established in the model built in this paper is (#fail), which means the average number of tokens contained in the place *fails*. The purpose is to get the number of failed messages per unit time.

The little formula is a basic conclusion in queuing theory that describes the relationship between the average arrival rate of customers, the average number of customers in the system, and the average length of time the customer spends in the system in a stable queuing system. For this model, the place *fail* and the deterministic transition S can be considered as a queuing system. The token is regarded as the customer, the average arrival rate of the customer is the number of message failures per unit time which is defined as λ, and the average number of customers n in the system is the average number of tokens in the steady state, the average stay time of the customer in the system s is the delay of the transition S, which is determined by the little formula:

$$\lambda = n/s = E_f/delay_T \tag{1}$$

Where E_f is the average number of tokens in *fail*, that is, the stationary result of the measure: (#fail), and $delay_T$ is the firing delay of the deterministic transition T. The failure probability P_{fail} of a message with a generation period of T_g is:

$$P_{fail} = \lambda/(1/T_g) = \lambda \cdot delay_{msg} \tag{2}$$

Where $delay_{msg}$ is the delay of T of the message. Bringing the formula (1) into the formula (2):

$$P_{fail} = E_f \cdot delay_{msg}/delay_T \tag{3}$$

The message failure probability P_{fail} during the transient interference burst is obtained above and it can be extended to the entire time domain. Let the transient interference period be t_a, the duration be t_c, the probability of message failure in the entire time domain be P_a, and the probability of transient interference bursting be P_{in}, then the conditional probability is:

$$P_a = P_{fail} \cdot P_{in} \tag{4}$$

The probability of transient interference burst P_{in} is:

$$P_{in} = t_a/(t_a + t_c) \tag{5}$$

Bring Eqs. (3) and (5) into Eq. (4) to get the probability of message failure in the entire time domain P_a:

$$P_a = E_f \cdot delay_{msg} \cdot t_a/[delay_T \cdot (t_a + t_c)] \tag{6}$$

4   Simulation Analysis

4.1   Simulation Model and Parameter

A four-node model is extended by following the working mechanism of the single node model. The simulation verification of CAN message transmission reliability is carried out with the four-node model. The four-node DSPN model is shown in Fig. 3.

In the model shown in Fig. 3, there are four nodes 1, 2, 3, and 4 from left to right named queue1, queue2, queue3 and queue4 separately. The priorities of them are sequentially lowered. We have established three measurements for node 2, node 3, and node 4 to assess the probability of message transmission failure. Node 1 has the highest priority, and there is no delay caused by arbitration failure, which lead the probability of message failure to a very low level. Besides, in TimeNET, the time spent on simulation of low probability events is huge which reduces the simulation efficiency. So the node 1 is out of consideration.

The simulation was performed in the TimeNET 4.4 environment, setting a 95% confidence interval for all simulations with a relative error of 10%. Set the CAN bus communication bit rate to 125 kb/s. All nodes send data frame messages with a data field length of 8. The average frame transmission time is approximately equal to 1

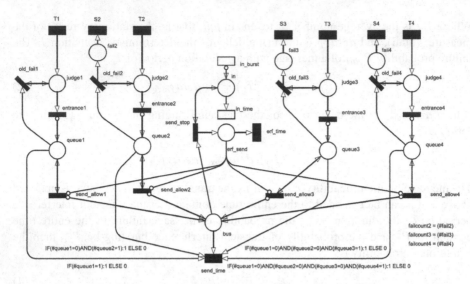

Fig. 3. Extended four-nodes model of CAN based on DSPN

ms. If an error occurs, the error frame length is 23 bits and the transmission time is approximately equal to 0.18 ms. In the simulation, the interference is assumed to be transient interference, the occurrence period is 450 ms, and the interference duration is 50 ms.

Based on the CAN model of DSPN established in this paper, the total probability P_a is simulated and counted.

4.2 Interference Arrival Interval

In order to analyze the relationship between the interference arrival interval and the message failure probability, the average interval of transient interference is set to 2 ms, 4 ms, 6 ms, 8 ms, 10 ms and then simulate separately. Other all simulation parameters are listed in the Table 1.

Table 1. Simulation parameters

Transition	Firing delay/ms
T1	6
T2	7.5
T3	7.5
T4	7.5
S2	10
S3	10
S4	10
In_time	0.008
Erf_time	0.18
Send_time	1

Note that the T2, T3, and T4 are set to the same value, which can simulate the effect of priority on failure probability when other parameters are unchanged. However, at this time, T2, T3 and T4 will fire at the same time, which will increase the probability that the three messages preempt the bus. For this reason, the delay modules are added after the transitions T3 and T4, which can effectively reduce the probability of the preemption of the bus. The message of node 3 is delayed by 2.5 ms and the message of node 4 is delayed by 5 ms, and the comparison of the failure probability of the message before and after adding the delay is analyzed. The simulation results are shown in Fig. 4.

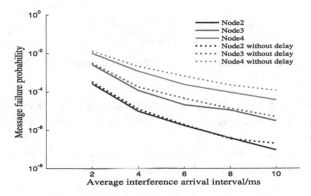

Fig. 4. The simulation results of the interference arrival interval

In Fig. 4, the vertical axis is the logarithmic axis which indicates the message failure probability, and the horizontal axis is the interference arrival interval. For all messages, as the interval of interference arrival increases, the message failure probability decreases exponentially. For the same node, the message failure probability with delay is almost always less than the value without delay, because the message generation is more uniform with delay and then the blocking and preemption phenomenon is reduced. In the case where the interference arrival interval is unchanged, the higher the priority of the node, the smaller the message failure probability, because higher priority means less waiting time, so the message is more likely to be successfully transmitted before the deadline.

4.3 Message Period

The simulation of the message period still sets the delay for node 3 and node 4. The interference arrival interval is fixed to 2 ms and the other parameters are kept unchanged. Firstly, the simulation of changing only one message period is implemented to observe the effect on all three messages failure probability. In this section, message period of node 3 is selected and changed from 7.5 ms to 15 ms with a 2.5 ms step size. The simulation results are shown in Fig. 5.

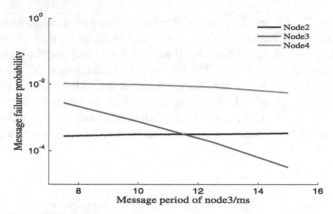

Fig. 5. The simulation results of the message period of node 3

As seen from Fig. 5, the message failure probability of node 3 decreases as the node 3 message period increases, while the failure probability of the other two messages is almost unchanged.

Secondly, all the three messages periods are changed from 7.5 ms to 15 ms with a 2.5 ms step size. The simulation results are shown in Fig. 6.

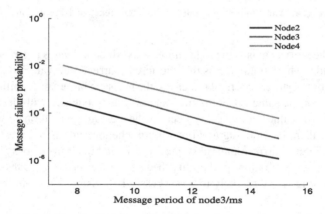

Fig. 6. The simulation results of all the three message period

It can be seen from Fig. 6 that after three message periods are changed, the failure probability of each message decreases as the message period increases, and the high priority message failure probability is always less than the low priority. From Figs. 5 and 6, we can draw a conclusion that in the case of other parameters unchanged, the message failure probability is only related to the message itself period, and the change of the message period has little effect on the failure probability of other messages.

4.4 Number of Nodes

In order to show the influence of the number of nodes on the simulation results, we performed two sets of simulations. The first group of simulations deleted the node 1 (the highest priority node) and compared the message failure probability before and after deletion while the second group deleted the node 4 (the lowest priority node) and do the same thing. The simulation parameters are the same as the Sects. 4.1 and 4.2. The simulation results are shown in the Figs. 7 and 8.

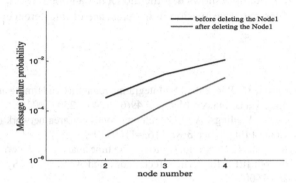

Fig. 7. The simulation results of deleting the Node1

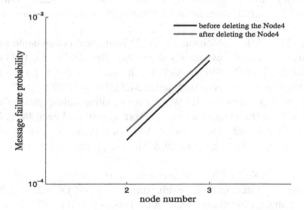

Fig. 8. The simulation results of deleting the Node4

It can be clearly seen from Figs. 7 and 8 that the message failure probability of the node 2 to node 4 is reduced after the node 1 is deleted while the message failure probability of the node 2 and node 3 do not change much after the node 4 is deleted. The results are reasonable because the node 1 as the highest priority node will hinder the transmission of node 2 to node 4. After it is deleted, other nodes send faster so the message failure probability is significantly reduced. But the node 4 has the lowest priority, so it has little influence on the transmission of other messages.

5   Conclusions

This paper establishes a CAN communication model based on DSPN, and it is used to simulate the arbitration mechanism and error handling mechanism of CAN. Based on the model, the reliability of message transmission of CAN under interference environment is evaluated. By adding transient impulse interference to the model, the influence of interference interval, message priority, message period and the number of nodes on CAN message transmission failure probability under interference environment is analyzed. The simulation example shows that the model has a good effect in evaluating the reliability of CAN message transmission in the presence of interference.

References

1. Hansson, H., Norstrom, C., Punnekkat, S.: Integrating reliability and timing analysis of CAN-based systems. IEEE Trans. Industr. Electron. **49**(6), 1240–1250 (2002)
2. Tindell, K., Burns, A., Wellings, A.J.: Calculating controller area network (CAN) message response times. Control Eng. Pract. **3**(8), 1163–1169 (1995)
3. Punnekkat, S., Hansson, H., Norstrom, C.: Response time analysis under errors for CAN. In: Proceedings of the 6th IEEE Real-Time Technology and Applications Symposium (RTAS 2000), pp. 258–265(2000)
4. Nolte, T., Hansson, H., Norstrom, C.: Probabilistic worstcase response-time analysis for the controller area network. In: Proceedings of the 9th IEEE Real-Time and Embedded Technology and Applications Symposium (RTAS 2003), pp. 200–207 (2003)
5. Mubeen, S., Maki-Turja, J., Sjodin, M.: Extending worst case response-time analysis for mixed messages in controller area network with priority and FIFO queues. IEEE Access **2**(1 Suppl.), 365–380 (2014)
6. Muppala, J.K., Trivedi, K.S., Mainkar, V., et al.: Numerical computation of response time distributions using stochastic reward nets. Ann. Oper. Res. **48**(2), 155–184 (1994)
7. Nilsson, J., Bernhardsson, B., Wittenmark, B.: Stochastic analysis and control of real-time systems with random time delays. Automatica **34**(1), 57–64 (1998)
8. Navet, N., Song, Y.Q., Simonot, F.: Worst-case deadline failure probability in real-time applications distributed over controller area network. J. Syst. Architect. **46**(7), 607–617 (2000)
9. Portugal, P.: A model based on a stochastic Petri Net approach for dependability evaluation of controller area net. In: Fieldbus Systems & Their Applications, vol. 38, no. 2, pp. 150–157 (2005)
10. Kumar, M., Verma, A.K., Srividya, A.: Response-time modeling of controller area network (CAN). In: Garg, V., Wattenhofer, R., Kothapalli, K. (eds.) ICDCN 2009. LNCS, vol. 5408, pp. 163–174. Springer, Heidelberg (2008). https://doi.org/10.1007/978-3-540-92295-7_20
11. Chen, X., Liu, L., Lu, W.: Modeling and analysis of response time of CAN bus based on queueing theory. J. Tianjin Univ. **45**(3), 228–235 (2012)
12. Sun, W., Zhang, H., Pan, C.: Analysis on real-time performance of CAN bus with improved non-preemptive M/G/1 model. J. China Railway Soc. **35**(12), 57–63 (2013)
13. ISO 11898: Road Vehicles—Interchange of Digital Information—Controller Area Network (CAN) for High-Speed Communication. International Standards Organization (1993)

Sliding-Window Belief Propagation with Unequal Window Size for Nonstationary Heterogeneous Source

Jiao Fan, Bowei Shan[ID], and Yong Fang[(✉)][ID]

School of Information Engineering, Chang'an University, Xi'an, China
{2018124056,bwshan,fy}@chd.edu.cn

Abstract. This paper presents a Sliding-Window Belief Propagation with Unequal Window Size (SWBP-UWS) algorithm to deal with the nonstationary heterogeneous source. In this algorithm, the entire source is divided into several sections according to its variation and each optimum window size is individually determined by each section. The experimental results show this algorithm outperforms the SWBP algorithm.

Keywords: SWBP algorithm · Belief propagation · LDPC code

1 Introduction

1.1 Background

Reliable communication paves the way for the development of modern IoT as a service and 5G technology. As an important error-correcting code, Low-Density Parity-Check (LDPC) codes [1,2] could protect source codes from noisy channel. Hence, LDPC codes have played a key role in various networking and communication system.

Decoding LDPC codes is a very important problem. In 2012, the Sliding-Window Belief Propagation (SWBP) technique was proposed by Fang [3] to decode LDPC codes. Thereafter, a lot of experiments [4,5] had showed that SWBP possesses many advantages compared with standard Belief Propagation (BP) algorithm. It can exactly trace time-varying channel state, demonstrate near-limit performance, is easy to be implemented, is robust to initial parameters, and is convenient to be parallelized. Recently, Shan [6] has used Graphics Processing Units (GPUs) to accelerate a parallel version of SWBP algorithm and achieved a high speed-up ratio.

All above works are based on an assumption that source are transmitted on the channel with smoothly time-varying, e.g. sinusoidally-varying, homogeneous state. Here, "homogeneous state" means the frequency of the time-varying functions keeps constant. While in the real communication system, the source and channel state usually varies arbitrarily. To better model the source, different frequency of the time-varying functions should be considered, which we name as

© ICST Institute for Computer Sciences, Social Informatics and Telecommunications Engineering 2020
Published by Springer Nature Switzerland AG 2020. All Rights Reserved
B. Li et al. (Eds.): IoTaaS 2019, LNICST 316, pp. 375–381, 2020.
https://doi.org/10.1007/978-3-030-44751-9_31

heterogeneous source. In Fang's SWBP algorithm, the *uniform sized* windows are imposed to calculate the initial local bias probability of each variable nodes for belief propagation. This set up is effective for the homogeneous source. Whether it is suitable for the heterogeneous source still need to be investigated.

1.2   Contribution

The main contribution of this paper includes: (a) A new Sliding-Window Belief Propagation with Unequal Window Size (SWBP-UWS) algorithm is proposed to deal with binary LDPC codes; (b) the size of sliding window is directly determined by the channel parameters in frequency domain; (c) smoothly sinusoidally-varying channel states with two different frequency are studied. The numerical simulated experiments demonstrate that our proposed algorithm performs better than original SWBP.

The rest of this paper is organized as follows: Sect. 2 briefly reviews the SWBP algorithm. Sect. 3 introduces our proposed model. In Sect. 4, experiment results are reported and discussed. Section 5 concludes this paper and gives the future possible development.

2   Preliminary

2.1   Notations

The LDPC code is specified by an $m \times n$ parity check matrix $\mathbf{H}$. We give the following notations to describe SWBP model.

- $\mathbf{x} = (x_1, \ldots, x_n)^T$ is the binary source, and $\tilde{\mathbf{x}}$ is the estimate of $\mathbf{x}$;
- $\mathbf{y} = (y_1, \ldots, y_n)^T$ is the Side Information (SI) available at receiver side;
- $\mathbf{s} = (s_1, \ldots, s_m)^T = \mathbf{H}\mathbf{x}$ is the syndrome;
- $\mathbf{p} = (p_1, \ldots, p_n)$, where p_i is the local bias probability, $p \triangleq \frac{1}{n} \sum_{i=1}^{n} p_i$ is the global bias probability, and $\tilde{\mathbf{p}}$ is the estimate of $\mathbf{p}$;
- α_{ij} is the belief propagated from variable node x_i to check node s_j;
- β_{ji} is the belief propagated from check node s_j to variable node x_i;
- $\boldsymbol{\sigma} = (\sigma_1, \ldots, \sigma_m)^T$ is the overall belief of variable nodes;
- $\mathcal{M}_i$ is the set of indices of check nodes connected to variable node x_i
- $\mathcal{N}_j$ is the set of indices of variable nodes connected to check node s_j

The SWBP algorithm includes three phases: the standard BP, calculating window size and refining local bias probability.

2.2   Steps of Standard BP

(1) Initialization:

$$\sigma_i^{(0)} = (1 - 2y_i) \log \frac{(1 - p_i)}{p_i}, \quad \text{and} \quad \beta_{ji}^{(0)} = 0 \tag{1}$$

(2) Variable nodes to check nodes BP:

$$\frac{1 - \alpha_{ij}}{\alpha_{ij}} = \frac{1 - \sigma_i}{\sigma_i} \Big/ \frac{1 - \beta_{ji}}{\beta_{ji}}. \tag{2}$$

(3) Check nodes to variable nodes BP:

$$1 - 2\beta_{ji} = (1 - 2s_j) \prod_{i' \in \mathcal{M}_j \setminus i} (1 - 2\alpha_{i'j}) \tag{3}$$

(4) Computing overall brief of variable nodes:

$$\frac{1 - \sigma_i}{\sigma_i} = \frac{1 - \tilde{p}_i}{\tilde{p}_i} \Big/ \prod_{j' \in \mathcal{N}_i} \frac{1 - \beta_{j'i}}{\beta_{j'i}}. \tag{4}$$

(5) Hard decision:

$$\tilde{x} = \begin{cases} 0, & \sigma_i \leq 0.5 \\ 1, & \sigma_i > 0.5 \end{cases}. \tag{5}$$

If $\mathbf{H}\tilde{\mathbf{x}} = \mathbf{s}$, the decoding process is successfully terminated; otherwise, more iteration is required.

2.3 Calculating Window Size

At the beginning of each BP iteration, all variable nodes need be seeded with local bias probability $\mathbf{p}$. Hence, estimating an appropriate $\tilde{\mathbf{p}}$ is a key issue. For a nonstationary smooth source, we can treat any segment of this source in a small window as approximately stationary. Therefore, $\tilde{\mathbf{p}}$ can be obtained by taking variable node x_i as center, and averaging it's neighbor's overall belief in a window with size h.

In fact, a suitable h is a tradeoff between two factors: on one hand, h should be large enough that neighbor nodes' information can be taken into account as much as possible; on the other hand, h should be rather small to ensure that source keeps stationary in this window. In [3], an adaptively searching algorithm was proposed to calculating window size h. In this algorithm, $\tilde{\mathbf{p}}$ is first computed by (6)

$$\tilde{p}_i = \frac{-\sigma_i + \sum_{i'=\max(1,i-u)}^{\min(i+u,n)} \sigma_{i'}}{\min(i + u, n) - \max(1, i - u)}, \tag{6}$$

where $u = \lfloor h/2 \rfloor$ is the half window size. Then, the mean squared error (MSE) between $\tilde{\mathbf{p}}$ and $\boldsymbol{\sigma}$ is computed by (7)

$$\tau = \frac{1}{n} \sum_{i=1}^{n} (\tilde{p}_i - \sigma_i)^2. \tag{7}$$

At last, an appropriate h is obtained when MSE reaches the smallest value, which is named h^*. In [3], all possible $h \in \{1, 2, \ldots, n\}$ are tested to find out the h^*.

2.4   Refining Local Bias Probability

Once h^* is determined, local bias probability can be refined by (6), which can be straightforwardly deduced to follows.

$$
\tilde{p}_i =
\begin{cases}
\tilde{p}_{i-1} + \dfrac{\sigma_{i-1} - \sigma_i + \sigma_{i+u} - \tilde{p}_{i-1}}{i + u - 1}, & 2 \le i \le (1 + u) \\[2ex]
\tilde{p}_{i-1} + \dfrac{\sigma_{i-1} - \sigma_i + \sigma_{i+u} - \sigma_{i-u-1}}{h - 1}, & (2 + u) \le i \le (n - u) \\[2ex]
\tilde{p}_{i-1} + \dfrac{\sigma_{i-1} - \sigma_i - \sigma_{i-u-1} + \tilde{p}_{i-1}}{n - i + u}, & (n - u + 1) \le i \le n
\end{cases}
\tag{8}
$$

3   Model Description

SWBP in Sect. 2 can only tackle the homogeneous source or channel state. In this section, we present the SWBP-UWS algorithm to deal with heterogeneous source. The steps of standard BP are identical with that in Sect. 2. The method of calculating window size in Sect. 2 is very time consuming. In [5], the window size was directly obtained by the frequencial characteristics of variable nodes' global bias probability. We borrow this novel idea into our new algorithm.

3.1   Calculating Different Window Size

Assuming the source is consist of l sections, i.e. $\{x_1, x_2, \ldots, x_n\} = \{x_1, \ldots, x_{n_1}\} \cup \{x_{n_1+1}, \ldots, x_{n_2}\} \cup \ldots \{x_{n_{l-1}+1}, \ldots, x_{n_l}\}$, where $n = n_l$. The frequency of time-varying function in one section is different from that in another section, but keeps constant within itself. In SWBP-UWS algorithm, the best window size for each section is independently computed by the overall beliefs within this section. Let $|\cdot|$ be the cardinality of the set. For the ith section, the algorithm first calculates the Fast Fourier Transform (FFT) of $\mathbf{r}^i$ as $f^i(\theta))$, where $\theta \in [n_i + 1 : n_{i+1}]$, and $|\theta| = W_i$. Then let $D_i = \sum_{\theta=1}^{W_i} |f^i(\theta)|$. Then the best window size for ith section is calculated by:

$$
h_i^* \approx \frac{W_i}{D_i} \sum_{\theta=1}^{W_i} |f^i(\theta)|/\theta
\tag{9}
$$

3.2   SWBP-UWS Algorithm

Once all best window sizes $h_i^*, i \in [1, \ldots, l]$ are computed, the local bias probability for each section can be computed by Eq. (8). Then we combine them to an optimum local bias probability $\tilde{\mathbf{p}}$, which will be the seeds for next BP iteration. The SWBP-UWS algorithm is summarized as follow.

Algorithm 1. SWBP-UWS Algorithm.

Require: Overall beliefs, **r**; Side information, **y**; Syndrome, **s**;
Ensure: Estimated source, $\tilde{x}$;
1: Initialization: $b_i^{(0)} = 0$, $q_{ij}^{(0)} = pmf_{ij}$
2: **for** $l = 1 :$ MAX_ITERATION **do**
3:     Steps of Standard BP [3]
4:     Computing overall beliefs $\mathbf{r} = (r_1, \ldots, r_n)^T$ for varialbe nodes:
5:     Dividing overall beliefs **r** into l sections
6:     Computing each best window size h_i^* by equation (9)
7:     Computing each optimum local bias probability by equation (8)
8:     Combining local bias probabilities in each section to optimum local bias probability $\tilde{\mathbf{p}}$
9:     Hard decision:
10:    $\tilde{x}_i = \begin{cases} 0, & \text{if } r_i \leq 0.5 \\ 1, & \text{if } r_i > 0.5 \end{cases}$
11:    **if** $\mathbf{H}\tilde{\mathbf{x}} = \mathbf{s}$ **then**
12:        quit loop
13:    **end if**
14: **end for**

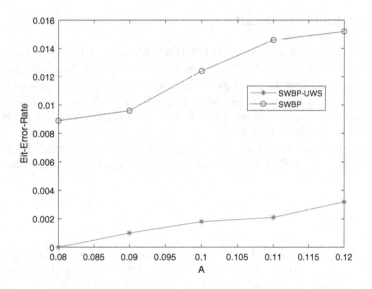

Fig. 1. Bit-error-rate under two algorithms.

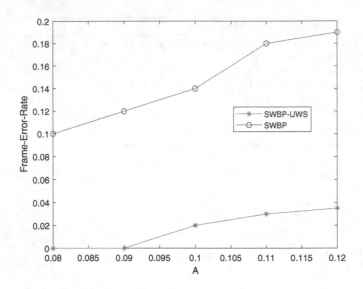

Fig. 2. Frame-error-rate under two algorithms.

4   Experimental Results

To evaluate the performance of SWBP-UWS for nonstationary heterogeneous source, a regular length n-1024 LDPC code is constructed. The local bias probability varies according to $p_i = p_{i1} + p_{i2}$, where $p_{i1} = A(1 + \sin(2\pi f_1 i_1/n))$, $i_1 \in [1, ..., 512]$ and $p_{i2} = A(1 + \sin(2\pi f_2 i_2/n))$, $i_2 \in [513, ..., 1024]$. To satisfy the heterogeneous source, we set $f1_1 : f_2 = 1 : 3$. Let five values of A be tested, i.e., $A \in \{0.08, 0.09, 0.10, 0.11, 0.12\}$.

The experimental results are illustrated in Figs. 1 and 2, from which we find that under different A SWBP-UWS outperforms SWBP algorithm in both BER and FER.

5   Conclusion

To handle the nonstationary heterogeneous source, we present a Sliding-Window Belief Propagation with Unequal Window Size (SWBP-UWS) algorithm. In this algorithm, the entire source is divided into several sections according to its variation and each optimum window size is individually determined by each section. We perform numerical experiments to evaluate our algorithm. Comparing SWBP, SWBP-UWS demonstrates better performance in both BER and FER.

References

1. Gallager, R.G.: Low-density parity-check codes. IRE Trans. Inf. Theory **8**(1), 21–28 (1962)
2. Mackay, D.J.C., Neal, R.M.: Near Sshannon limit performance of low density parity check codes. Electron. Lett. **32**(6), 457–458 (1997)
3. Fang, Y.: Ldpc-based lossless compression of nonstationary binary sources using sliding-window belief propagation. IEEE Trans. Commun. **60**(11), 3161–3166 (2012)
4. Fang, Y.: Asymmetric Slepian-Wolf coding of nonstationarily-correlated M-ary sources with sliding-window belief propagation. IEEE Trans. Commun. **61**(12), 5114–5124 (2013). https://doi.org/10.1109/TCOMM.2013.111313.130230
5. Fang, Y., Yang, Y., Shan, B., Stankovic, V.: Joint source-channel estimation via sliding-window belief propagation. IEEE Trans. Commun. (2019, submitted)
6. Shan, B., Fang, Y.: GPU Accelerated parallel algorithm of sliding-window belief propagation for LDPC codes. Int. J, Parallel Program. (2019)

Traffic Lights Detection Based on Deep Learning Feature

Changhao Wang, GuanWen Zhang$^{(\boxtimes)}$, Wei Zhou, Yukun Rao, and Yu Lv

Northwestern Polytechnical University, Xi'an 710072, China
{guanwen.zh,zhouwei}@nwpu.edu.cn

Abstract. Traffic lights detection is an important task for intelligent vehicles. It is non-trivial due to variance backgrounds and illumination conditions. Therefore, a traffic lights detection system that can apply to different scenes is necessary. In this paper, we research the traffic lights detection based on deep learning, which can extract features with representation and robustness from input image automatically and avoid using artificial features. The approach of traffic lights detection proposed in this paper includes two stages: (1) region proposal and (2) classification of traffic lights. Firstly, we propose a region proposal method based on intensity, color, and geometric information of traffic lights. Secondly, convolutional neural network (CNN) was introduced for the traffic lights classification, obtaining 99.6% average accuracy. For detection, we evaluate our system on 6804 images of different scenes, the recall and accuracy of detection achieve 99.2% and 98.5% respectively.

Keywords: Traffic lights detection · Deep learning · Region proposal · Classification

1 Introduction

Nowadays, the number of vehicles increases dramatically, which makes the traffic condition more complicated. Under this circumstance, the techniques of self-driving can be used to avoid accidents introduced by human emotion, physical condition, and qualification. The information of lanes' direction and the vehicles' or pedestrians' number and conditions nearby are crucial for self-driving cars to understand the environment so that they can make some adjustment when travelling. Therefore, the self-driving techniques include lane, vehicle and pedestrian detection. Besides, the navigating information of traffic lights also play an important role when vehicles travelling at the intersection, so traffic lights detection is one of the most important tasks for intelligent vehicles travelling safely.

Sponsored by the Seed Foundation of Innovation and Creation for Graduate Students in Northwestern Polytechnical University, zz2019140 and National College Students' innovation and entrepreneurship training program, 201810699167.

In this paper, we research traffic lights detection based on deep learning, which can extract features with representation and robustness from input image automatically, avoid using artificial features. Our approach can achieve high recall and accuracy with high processing speed in different scenes.

The approach of traffic lights detection proposed in this paper includes two stages: (1) region proposal and (2) classification of traffic lights. The layout of our approach is illustrated in Fig. 1.

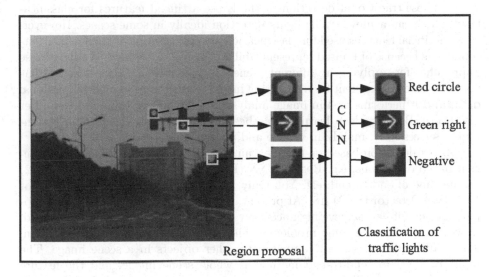

Fig. 1. Framework of the traffic lights detection

2   Related Work

Current traffic lights detection algorithm are mainly consist of two steps: extract features from images and apply a high-quality classifier or match a template for classification [12,13,28]. The most distinct features of traffic lights are color and intensity which can be used to propose the region of traffic lights from images. Omachi et al. [20] achieved traffic lights detection by using color and edge information. Their approach normalizes the RGB color space of input image, and some regions are selected as candidates of traffic lights. Then a method based on Hough transform is applied to obtain target regions. Yi et al. [17] adopted morphology filtration and statistical classification to detect traffic lights. In their method, original image is converted to a binary image by top-hat transform and threshold segmentation to obtain brighter regions firstly. Then the candidate regions that unsatisfying filtration conditions are removed by morphology and geometry features. Furthermore, a novel recognition method is carried out based on statistical analysis with amount of traffic lights image samples. It performs the color feature extracted by the Hue component in HSV color space for classifying traffic lights. In [24], a vision-based traffic lights detection method is proposed, which contains the candidates extraction and recognition. On the candidates extraction stage, they highlight the traffic lights candidate regions by perform an adaptive background suppression algorithm while suppressing the undesired backgrounds. Then, each candidate region is verified and further classified into different traffic light semantic classes. [2] uses a spot detection algorithm to detect traffic lights, and classify the detected spots with Adaptive Templates Matcher, which can avoid motion blur and illumination variations.

All those traditional detection methods use artificial features for classification, which can achieve traffic lights detection ideally in some scenes. However, those artificial features used for classification are only suitable for some fixed surroundings because of limited represent-ability. Therefore, we have to adjust those approaches for applying in different scenes. In recent years, deep learning has turned out to be excellent for discovering intricate structures in high-dimensional data, and it performs well in image analysis, speech recognition, and computer vision etc. Besides, deep learning has been applied to intelligent vehicle techniques successfully, mainly in vehicle and pedestrian detection [5,6,14,21].

Object detection based on deep learning mainly has two methods: (1) detection based on regions, e.g. Region-CNN (R-CNN) [8], Fast R-CNN [7], and (2) the method of end-to-end, e.g. You Only Look Once (YOLO) [22], Single Shot MultiBox Detector (SSD) [18]. At present, the method of end-to-end is very popular, because it can achieve high-accuracy detection with high processing speed. However, it will have some problems while applying to traffic lights detection. The traffic lights are small compared to other objects in a scene image. The input of CNN for end-to-end method is whole scene image, and the feature extracting process will downsample input image because of convolution and pooling operations. Finally, the region of traffic lights in the feature maps becomes too small to recognize. Intuitively, traffic lights has some distinct features, such as color, intensity, and shape, which can be used to distinguish traffic lights from surroundings [26,28]. Therefore, we can adopt the method of detection based on regions: proposing candidate regions according to those features firstly [3,10,11,27], and then introducing a CNN to classify candidate regions.

3   Region Proposal

We propose a region proposal method based on intensity, color, and geometric informations of traffic lights. Firstly, we employ Gaussian filtration and perform gray processing and Top-hat transform to process the intensity information of image. Secondly, we convert the image from RGB to HSI color space and filter the image according to the hue value of traffic light regions. Lastly, we restrict the regions' geometrical information to generate candidates. We can optimize the threshold of region proposal conditions to reduce the number of candidate regions, which is crucial to achieve high processing speed.

3.1   Intensity Filtration

Traffic lights are kinds of illuminant body with high intensity, this can help us to tell them from surroundings. The intensity of traffic lights varies with lighting conditions caused by weather, surroundings and other factors. In order to eliminate the effect of some small regions with high luminance, we employ Gaussian filtration. At the same time, Gaussian noise can be filtered. We achieve Gaussian filtration by using Gaussian kernel, and the kernel's values distribute according to (1).

$$G(x, y) = \frac{1}{2\pi\sigma^2} e^{\frac{-(x^2+y^2)}{2\sigma^2}} \tag{1}$$

Where x, y means relative coordinates of the points in Gaussian kernel to the central point.

After eliminating the difference of intensity, we convert the RGB image to gray level image to facilitate intensity information processing. For traffic lights detection task, we have to highlight the regions of red and green in images, which means the weights of R and G in the gray processing formula should be increased. The gray processing formula we proposed is shown as (2). Figure 2(a) shows an image after Gaussian filtration, and Fig. 2(b) is the result of gray processing.

$$Y = \max(0.9R - 0.1G - 0.3B, 0.9G + 0.1B - 0.5R) \tag{2}$$

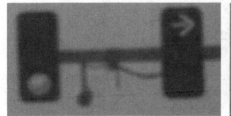 

(a) Image after Gaussian filtering   (b) Result of gray processing filtration

Fig. 2. Gray processing

We use (2) for processing the image after Gaussian filtration to highlight the regions in red or green, and then we need to distinguish them from background. The Top-hat transform [9,25], demonstrated in Fig. 3, was used to solve this problem, which is effective to obtain the bright aggregate of pixies from dark background. The top-hat transform was described as (3) in [24].

$$Tophat(f) = f - (f \circ b) = f - ((f \odot b) \oplus b) \tag{3}$$

In (3), f is an input image; b is a kernel element; $\circ$ is opening operation, and defined as (4).

$$f \circ b = (f \odot b) \oplus b \tag{4}$$

Where operator $\odot$ and $\oplus$ is defined as (5) and (6) respectively.

$$f \odot b \,|\, (x,y) = \max \{ f(x-x', y-y') - b(x',y') \,|\, (x',y') \in D_b \} \tag{5}$$

$$f \oplus b \,|\, (x,y) = \max \{ f(x-x', y-y') + b(x',y') \,|\, (x',y') \in D_b \} \tag{6}$$

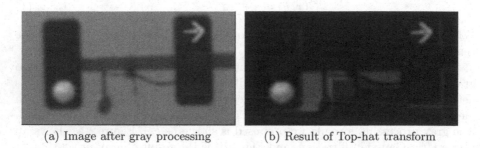

(a) Image after gray processing   (b) Result of Top-hat transform

Fig. 3. Top-hat transform

Next, we convert the image after Top-hat transform to binary image with a threshold to obtain the result of intensity filtration, the transformation uses (7).

$$Binary(x,y) = \begin{cases} 255, v(x,y) \geq T \\ 0, v(x,y) < T \end{cases} \tag{7}$$

In (7), $v(x,y)$ is the value of pixel in the image after Top-hat transform. Figure 4 shows the result of intensity filtration.

3.2   Color Segmentation

Compared with backgrounds, the color of traffic lights is also a distinctive features [1,26]. Therefore, we perform color segmentation after intensity filtration to remove background as much as possible. Since the intensity is not a concern and processing color information of an image in HSI color space is convenient, the input image is converted from RGB to HIS color space [4,23]. HSI stands for hue (H), saturation (S), and intensity (I), and H can be used to restrict the image for achieving color segmentation. To reduce computations, only the pixels of input images corresponding to the reserved regions of the result of intensity filtration are converted. The transformation from RGB to HIS uses (8), (9) and (10).

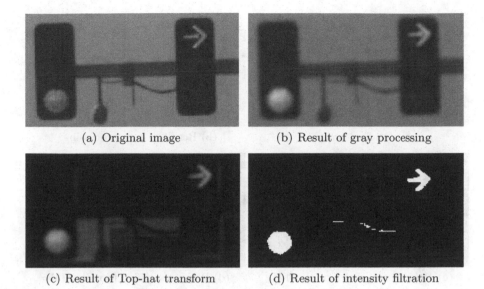

(a) Original image	(b) Result of gray processing
(c) Result of Top-hat transform	(d) Result of intensity filtration

Fig. 4. Intensity filtration

$$H = \begin{cases} \arccos\left(\dfrac{(r-g)+(r-b)}{2\sqrt{(r-g)^2+(r-b)(g-b)}}\right), b \le g \\ 360 - \arccos\left(\dfrac{(r-g)+(r-b)}{2\sqrt{(r-g)^2+(r-b)(g-b)}}\right), b \ge g \end{cases} \tag{8}$$

$$S = 1 - \frac{3\min(r,g,b)}{r+g+b} \tag{9}$$

$$I = \frac{r+g+b}{3} \tag{10}$$

Where r, g and b are the normalized values of R, G and B in RGB color space.

The value of H varies from 0 to 360, starting at the red primary at 0, passing through the green primary at 120 and the blue primary at 240, and then wrapping back to red at 360. According to the statistics, the condition of color segmentation is defined as (11), (12). Figure 5 shows the result of color segmentation.

$$\text{Red region}: 0 \le H \le 70, 340 \le H < 360 \tag{11}$$

$$\text{Green region}: 110 \le H \le 250 \tag{12}$$

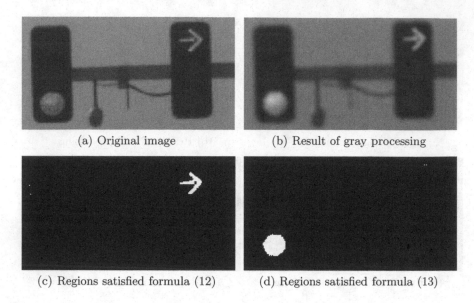

(a) Original image   (b) Result of gray processing

(c) Regions satisfied formula (12)   (d) Regions satisfied formula (13)

Fig. 5. Result of color segmentation

3.3 Geometry Filtration

The majority backgrounds of an input image can be removed after performing intensity filtration and color segmentation. However, in a scene image some objects always exist, of which intensity and color are similar to traffic lights. To solve this problem, we can utilize the geometrical information to restrict the result of color segmentation, and obtain the candidate regions. It is known that the pixels of traffic light regions should be conterminous. So, we can detect the conterminous regions and draw circumscribed rectangles of those regions firstly, and then restrict these rectangles with geometrical conditions. However, some "black holes" in the target regions will make them un-conterminous and undetectable due to the previous processing. Therefore, before we performing geometry filtration, a closing operation is employed. Closing operation can pad "black holes" to make regions conterminous. It is defined as (13). Figure 6 shows the function of closing operation.

$$f \bullet b = (f \oplus b) \odot b \tag{13}$$

Where operator $\odot$ and $\oplus$ is defined as (5) and (6) respectively.

From Fig. 6, it is clearly that the "black holes" among the arrow light are padded. Next, we can draw circumscribed rectangles of conterminous regions, with restriction of the height-width ratio ($Ratio$) and area (S), the restrict conditions are shown as (14).

$$\begin{cases} S_{\min} \leq S \leq S_{\max} \\ 1 \leq Ratio \leq \frac{\max(width, height)}{\min(width, height)} \end{cases} \tag{14}$$

Where $S_{\min}$ is the minimum area of the circumscribed rectangles; $S_{\max}$ is the maximum area of the circumscribed rectangles; $width$ is the width of the circumscribed rectangles; $height$ is the height of the circumscribed rectangles. Figure 7 shows the result of region proposal.

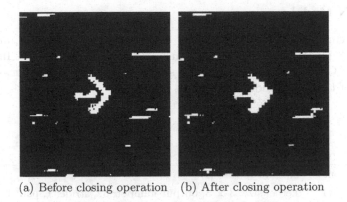

(a) Before closing operation   (b) After closing operation

Fig. 6. Closing operation

Fig. 7. Result of region proposal

4   Classification of Traffic Lights

During this stage, we use a CNN for traffic lights classification [8,15]. We can obtain a set C of candidate regions after performing region proposal. C contains the location $c_i(x_i, y_i, width_i, height_i)$ of each candidate region. In C, (x_i, y_i) is the coordinate of the top left vertex of candidate regions, $width_i$ and $height_i$ are the width and height of candidate regions respectively. According to the locations, we can cut out corresponding regions from original images as inputs of the CNN for classification. The results of classification ($label_i$) will be returned to set C and obtain set D which contains the location and label

$(d_i(x_i, y_i, width_i, height_i, label_i))$ of each candidate region. The CNN for classification only has 6 convolution layers, which can ensure high classification accuracy and fast processing speed. The data augmentation [16, 19] is performed for training the CNN.

4.1 CNN Model

The CNN can perform feature learning on the basis of input data, and it can extract multiple feature maps by convolution and pooling operation. In the output layer of CNN, we usually utilize the softmax classifier for classification. The structure of the CNN model is shown as Table 1.

Table 1. CNN model

Type	Structure
input	size: $40 \times 40 \times 3$
conv1	kernel size: 3×3, output number: 32, stride: 1, pad: 1
conv2	kernel size: 3×3, output number: 32, stride: 1, pad: 1
pooling1	max pooling, kernel size: 3×3, stride: 2
conv3	kernel size: 3×3, output number: 32, stride: 1, pad: 1
conv4	kernel size: 3×3, output number: 32, stride: 1, pad: 1
pooling2	max pooling, kernel size: 33, stride: 2
conv5	kernel size: 3×3, output number: 64, stride: 1, pad: 1
conv6	kernel size: 3×3, output number: 64, stride: 1, pad: 1
pooling3	max pooling, kernel size: 3×3, stride: 2
fc1	output number: 128
fc2	output number: 128
output	softmax, output number: 10

On the basis of region proposal, we resize the candidate regions to 40×40 as inputs of the CNN. The input images has 3 channels (R, G, B), and they are directly feed into the CNN.

The CNN model used for classification totally has six convolution layers. The first convolution layer (conv1) has 32 kernels of size 3×3 with a stride 1 pixel (for each convolution layer, we pad the border of input with 1 pixel of zero). The outputs of first convolution layer are 32 feature maps of size 40×40. The second convolution layer (conv2) is same with conv1. Then, we perform max pooling with a kernel of size 3×3 and 2-pixel stride to subsample the input feature maps, and all of the pooling layers are same. So, the output size of the first pooling layer (pooling1) is 20×20. The third and the forth convolution layers (conv3 and conv4) all have 32 kernels of size 3×3. Next, the second pooling layer (pooling2) is performed, and the size of the output data is 10×10. In the fifth and sixth convolution layers (conv5 and conv6), they both have 64 kernels of size 3×3. The last pooling layer (pooling3) reduce the size of input to 5×5. Then we introduce two fully connected layers (fc1 and fc2) with a output size of 128×1. In the output layer (classifier), we use the softmax function to predict classes.

4.2 Training

We train the CNN on a dataset made from scene images by using labeled region proposals. The dataset contains 10 categories, i.e., red circle (0), green circle (1), red left (2), green left (3), red forward (4), green forward (5), red right (6), green right (7), red negative (8), green negative (9).

During training phase, we use "step" learning rate policy, and the initial learning rate is 0.01. We carry out total 80 epochs for training and the learning rate is reduced by a factor of 10 every 20 epoch. The batch size is 100. Besides, we adopt dropout after all fully connected layers, which keeps each neuron in CNN activating with probability p to prevent overfitting.

Since the negative examples varying tremendously, the number of negative examples should be lager than positive examples in dataset. We increase the number of negative examples gradually while training the CNN to achieve high classification accuracy.

5 Experimental Results

In order to confirm the effect of proposed method, we carried out experiments of classification by CNN model and detecting traffic lights with whole system from scene images separately. We also tested the processing speed of whole system.

5.1 Region Proposal and Classification

During the region proposal stage, we convert the result of Top-hat transform into a binary image with a threshold T according formula (7). We process the image with different threshold value, and the results are shown as Fig. 8.

From Fig. 8 we can see that the backgrounds are reducing with the increasing of threshold. However, the traffic light regions will be removed partially when the threshold is overrange, so that influences the result of region proposal. According to experiments, 50 is the bast value of threshold to obtain the ideal results. For geometry filtration, the interval of S and $Ratio$ are $[144, 2000]$ and $[1, 1.5]$ respectively according to the statistics.

We used 17852 images of traffic lights and negative examples with 10 categories to test the CNN model, and the result of experiment is shown in Table 2.

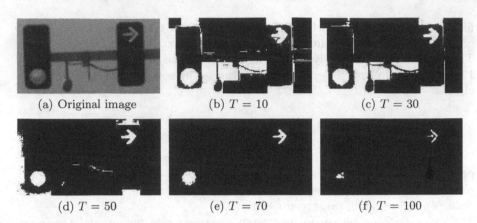

(a) Original image   (b) $T = 10$ (c) $T = 30$

(d) $T = 50$ (e) $T = 70$ (f) $T = 100$

Fig. 8. Result of intensity filtration with different threshold

Table 2. The result of classification

Label	Type	Test image (Frame)	Accuracy (%)
0	Red circle	2000	99.7
1	Green circle	1846	99.9
2	Red left	2000	100
3	Green left	2000	100
4	Red forward	1816	100
5	Green forward	1359	99.7
6	Red right	2000	99.6
7	Green right	561	99.5
8	Negative red	2000	98.8
9	Negative green	2000	98.8
Total	/	**17582**	**99.6**

5.2   Detection

The dataset for experiment of detection includes 6804 images of 10 different scenes. And we mainly consider two evaluating indicators: accuracy and recall, which are defined as (15) and (16).

$$recall = \frac{t}{s} \tag{15}$$

$$accuracy = \frac{t}{u} \tag{16}$$

Where s is the total number of traffic lights in scene images; t is the number of detected traffic lights. u is the number of all candidate regions; The result of detection is demonstrated in Fig. 9, the recall and accuracy are displayed in Table 3.

Fig. 9. Result of traffic lights detection

Table 3. The result of detection

Scene	Images	s	Recall (%)	Accuracy (%)
1	733	1344	99.9	99.3
2	427	782	100	99.9
3	636	1160	99.9	98.7
4	632	1181	99.5	99.7
5	202	287	99.0	98.6
6	876	1644	96.6	100
7	1935	2833	99.5	95.8
8	425	747	99.1	98.7
9	659	1153	99.7	99.8
10	279	279	97.5	100
Total	**6804**	**11406**	**99.2**	**98.5**

From Table 3, it is obvious that the recall and accuracy of detection achieve 99.2% and 98.5% respectively. In order to achieve high recall, we can relax some restrictions while performing region proposal. As a result, more negative regions are extracted from scene images. We can notice that the test accuracy of scene 7 is lower than others obviously. By analysing the detection results in scene 7, we found that more than one crossing are in the images, and traffic lights in the second crossing are also detected. However, traffic lights in the second crossing are too small to be classified correctly (Fig. 10(a)). Besides, the background in images are extracted as candidates regions too many so that more negative examples are classified as traffic lights (Fig. 10(b)). Therefore, the structure of the CNN can be more complicated and more training data are needed to improve the classification accuracy of negative regions.

(a)   (b)

Fig. 10. Failure result of traffic lights detection

5.3 Time Efficiency

We test 6804 images of size 922×1000 on a 2.1 GHz CPU. The average processing time of two main stages is shown in Table 4.

Table 4. Processing time of traffic lights detection

Main stage	Duration (ms)
Region proposal	39.8
Classification	27.1
Total	**66.9**

Note that the region proposal stage is time-consuming, and the processing time of classification is related to the number of candidate regions.

6   Conclusions

In this paper, we proposed a method of traffic lights detection based on deep learning features. Firstly, we take advantage of the intensity, color, and geometric information of traffic lights to perform region proposal, and obtain candidate regions. In this stage, we employ Gaussian filtration and perform gray processing and Tophat operation to process the intensity information of image. Then we convert the image from RGB into HSI color space, and filter the image according to the hue of traffic light. Next, we restrict the regions' geometrical information to generate candidate regions. Secondly, we introduce a CNN to classify the candidate regions, and combine the location and the result of classification to achieve traffic lights detection.

From the results of experiment, we obtain 99.6% average accuracy of classification by performing the data augmentation for training the network. Besides, the recall and average accuracy of detection can achieve 99.2% and 98.5% respectively, with processing time about 66.9 ms per image. Furthermore, we will optimize the region proposal algorithm to improve the processing speed for real-time application.

References

1. Chen, Z., Yang, J., Kong, B.: A robust traffic sign recognition system for intelligent vehicles. In: 2011 Sixth International Conference on Image and Graphics, pp. 975–980, August 2011
2. de Charette, R., Nashashibi, F.: Real time visual traffic lights recognition based on spot light detection and adaptive traffic lights templates. In: 2009 IEEE Intelligent Vehicles Symposium, pp. 358–363, June 2009
3. Erhan, D., Szegedy, C., Toshev, A., Anguelov, D.: Scalable object detection using deep neural networks. In: 2014 IEEE Conference on Computer Vision and Pattern Recognition, pp. 2155–2162, June 2014. https://doi.org/10.1109/CVPR.2014.276
4. Eric Hague, G.: Color segmentation in the HSI color space using the k-means algorithm. In: Proceedings of the SPIE - The International Society for Optical Engineering, vol. 3026 (1997)
5. de la Escalera, A., Armingol, J., Mata, M.: Traffic sign recognition and analysis for intelligent vehicles. Image Vis. Comput. **21**, 247–258 (2003)
6. Espinosa, J.E., Velastin, S.A., Branch, J.W.: Vehicle detection using alex net and faster R-CNN deep learning models: a comparative study. In: Badioze Zaman, H., et al. (eds.) IVIC 2017. LNCS, vol. 10645, pp. 3–15. Springer, Cham (2017). https://doi.org/10.1007/978-3-319-70010-6_1
7. Girshick, R.: Fast R-CNN. arXiv e-prints arXiv:1504.08083, April 2015
8. Girshick, R., Donahue, J., Darrell, T., Malik, J.: Rich feature hierarchies for accurate object detection and semantic segmentation. arXiv e-prints arXiv:1311.2524 (Nov 2013)

9. Horak, R., Mattioli, J.: Target detection of very dim objects using gray-level morphologic tophat (1996)
10. Hosang, J., Benenson, R., Dollár, P., Schiele, B.: What makes for effective detection proposals? IEEE Trans. Pattern Anal. Mach. Intell. **38**(4), 814–830 (2016)
11. Hosang, J., Benenson, R., Schiele, B.: How good are detection proposals, really? (2014)
12. Jensen, M.B., Philipsen, M.P., Møgelmose, A., Moeslund, T.B., Trivedi, M.M.: Vision for looking at traffic lights: issues, survey, and perspectives. IEEE Trans. Intell. Transp. Syst. **17**(7), 1800–1815 (2016)
13. John, V., Yoneda, K., Liu, Z., Mita, S.: Saliency map generation by the convolutional neural network for real-time traffic light detection using template matching. IEEE Trans. Comput. Imaging **1**(3), 159–173 (2015)
14. John, V., Yoneda, K., Qi, B., Liu, Z., Mita, S.: Traffic light recognition in varying illumination using deep learning and saliency map. In: 17th International IEEE Conference on Intelligent Transportation Systems (ITSC), pp. 2286–2291, October 2014
15. Lecun, Y., Bottou, L., Bengio, Y., Haffner, P.: Gradient-based learning applied to document recognition. Proc. IEEE **86**, 2278–2324 (1998)
16. Leng, B., Yu, K., Liu, Y., Jingyan, Q.: Data augmentation for unbalanced face recognition training sets. Neurocomputing **235**, 10–14 (2016)
17. Li, Y., Cai, Z.X., Gu, M.Q., Yan, Q.Y.: Traffic lights recognition based on morphology filtering and statistical classification, vol. 3, pp. 1700–1704 (2011)
18. Liu, W., et al.: SSD: single shot multibox detector. In: Leibe, B., Matas, J., Sebe, N., Welling, M. (eds.) ECCV 2016. LNCS, vol. 9905, pp. 21–37. Springer, Cham (2016). https://doi.org/10.1007/978-3-319-46448-0_2
19. Mas Montserrat, D., Lin, Q., Allebach, J., Delp, E.: Training object detection and recognition CNN models using data augmentation. Electron. Imaging **2017**, 27–36 (2017)
20. Omachi, M., Omachi, S.: Traffic light detection with color and edge information, pp. 284–287, January 2009
21. Ouyang, W., Wang, X.: Joint deep learning for pedestrian detection. In: 2013 IEEE International Conference on Computer Vision, pp. 2056–2063, December 2013
22. Redmon, J., Divvala, S., Girshick, R., Farhadi, A.: You Only Look Once: Unified, Real-Time Object Detection. arXiv e-prints arXiv:1506.02640, June 2015
23. Rotaru, C., Graf, T., Zhang, J.: Color image segmentation in HSI space for automotive applications. J. Real-Time Image Process. **3**(4), 311–322 (2008)
24. Shi, Z., Zou, Z., Zhang, C.: Real-time traffic light detection with adaptive background suppression filter. IEEE Trans. Intell. Transp. Syst. **17**(3), 690–700 (2016)
25. Soille, P.: Morphological Image Analysis-Principles and Applications, vol. 49. Springer, Heidelberg (2003). https://doi.org/10.1007/978-3-662-05088-0
26. Tran, T.H., Pham, C.C., Nguyen, T.P., Duong, T.T., Jeon, J.W.: Real-time traffic light detection using color density. In: 2016 IEEE International Conference on Consumer Electronics-Asia (ICCE-Asia), pp. 1–4, October 2016
27. Uijlings, J.R.R., Van De Sande, K.E., Gevers, T., Smeulders, A.W.: Selective search for object recognition. Int. J. Comput. Vis. **104**, 154–171 (2013)
28. Wang, C., Jin, T., Yang, M., Wang, B.: Robust and real-time traffic lights recognition in complex urban environments. Int. J. Comput. Intell. Syst. **4**, 1383–1390 (2011)

A Novel Algorithm for HRRP Target Recognition Based on CNN

Jieqi Li[1], Shaojie Li[2], Qi Liu[2], and Shaohui Mei[2(✉)]

[1] China Academy of Launch Vehicle Technology, Beijing 100076, China
[2] School of Electronics and Information, Northwestern Polytechnical University,
Xi'an 710129, China
meish@nwpu.edu.cn

Abstract. Compared with traditional methods, deep neural networks can extract deep information of targets from different aspects in range resolution profile (HRRP) radar automatic target recognition (RATR). This paper proposes a new convolutional neural network (CNN) for target recognition based on the full consideration of the characteristics (time-shift sensitivity, target-aspect sensitivity and large redundancy) of radar HRRP data. Using a convolutional layer with the large convolution kernel, large stride, and large grid size max-pooling, the author built a streamlined network, which can get better classification accuracy than other methods. At the same time, in order to make the network more robust, the author uses the center loss function to correct the softmax loss function. The experimental results show that we have obtained a smaller feature within the class and the classification accuracy is also improved.

Keywords: Range resolution profile (HRRP) · Radar automatic target recognition (RATR) · Convolutional neural network (CNN)

1 Introduction

Radar automatic target recognition (RATR) is an indispensable means of detection in modern information warfare. With the development of radar imaging technology and information processing technology, RATR based on high range resolution profile (HRRP) recognition has become one of the hot spots of research [7]. The HRRP is one-dimensional projection of the target in the radar observation direction obtained by wideband radar, which reflects abundant information of the scatterers contained in the target [3]. Radar HRRP target recognition refers to extracting the robust target features from HRRP which is reflected from the target and received by the radar sensor, and utilizing the features to automatically recognize the target types or models.

How to extract the robust target features from HRRP plays an important role in HRRP recognition. Features extracted using traditional methods such as sparse representation classification criteria [9] and manifold learning (ML) [8] do

© ICST Institute for Computer Sciences, Social Informatics and Telecommunications Engineering 2020
Published by Springer Nature Switzerland AG 2020. All Rights Reserved
B. Li et al. (Eds.): IoTaaS 2019, LNICST 316, pp. 397–404, 2020.
https://doi.org/10.1007/978-3-030-44751-9_33

not effectively represent the complete information of the target. These features are artificially designed and depend on actual experience and application context. In recent years, deep learning has become a research hotspot in various fields, as well as in the HRRP recognition. In [6], the proposed deep learning approach employs deep convolutional neural networks to automatically extract features from the HRRPs and experimental results show that this method achieves good recognition even at low signal-to-noise ratios. In [1], a deep network is developed to replace the shallow algorithms and Stacked Corrective Autoencoders (SCAE) is further proposed for HRRP ATR considering HRRP's characteristics. In summary, compared with the traditional pattern recognition method, the deep learning method helps to avoid over-reliance on prior knowledge to abstract features, and can automatically obtain the deep expression features of the target through feature learning.

In summary, there are traditional methods and deep learning methods in the field of radar HRRP target recognition, the deep learning methods avoid overusing hand-crafted feature, and the deep learning method can achieve better performance. However, most of deep learning based methods are designed by drawing lessons from the rules of other fields, without considering the characteristics of the data. Thus, we design a structure for radar HRRP recognition based on the characteristics of HRRP data. The advantages of this framework are:

(1) We formed the structure by several convolutional layers and max-pooling layers, and large convolution kernels are used to overcome the time-shift sensitivity of the HRRP data. Convolution operation with stride is used to reduce data redundancy, and we used max-pooing layer to overcome target-aspect sensitivity of HRRP data. This network has very few parameters (5W).
(2) When the target is transformed in full-angle domain, the use of max-pooling is not enough to overcome these changes, so we use center loss to correct the softmax loss. It can make the output of network have more reasonable distribution, which will improve the recognition accuracy of the model.

2   HRRP Target Recognition System

2.1   HRRP Data Description and Preprocessing

HRRP is the amplitude of the coherent summations of the complex time returns from target scattering points in each range cell. Accurate echo data needs to be calculated from the scattering characteristics of the electromagnetic wave according to the target, but the precise electromagnetic wave scattering characteristics are difficult to describe. When the radar resolution is much smaller than the target size, the target can be modeled as a set of independent scattering centers [2,5]. A HRRP is the amplitude of the coherent summations of the complex echoes from scattering centers of the target in each range cell onto the radar line of-sigh (LOS) [4]. The radar echoes of the ith range cell can be described as:

$$x_i = \Psi_i(f) = \sum_{k=1}^{N} a_{i,k} \exp\left(j\frac{2\pi f}{c} r_{i,k}\right) = \sum_{k=1}^{N} a_{i,k} \exp\left(j2\pi f\tau_{i,k}\right) \qquad (1)$$

where f represents the center frequency of the radar signal. N indicates the number of target scattering points in the ith range cell. $a_{i,k}$ represents the complex scattering intensity of the k scattering point in the ith range cell. c represents the speed of light. $r_{i,k}$ indicates the radial distance from the kth scattering point to the radar in the ith range cell. $\tau_{i,k}$ denotes the arrival time of the kth scattering point in the ith range cell. HRRP data can be expressed as:

$$\mathbf{x} = \left[|x_1|, |x_2|, \ldots, |x_n|\right]^T \qquad (2)$$

where n is the dimension of the HRRP data. This paper carries out HRRP identification of aircraft models. A certain type of aircraft and its scattering points model shown in Fig. 1(a) and (b), respectively.

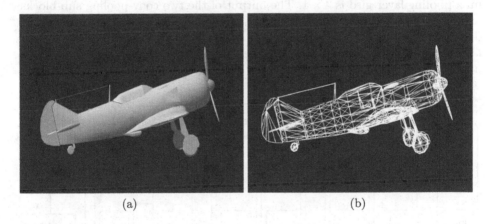

(a)   (b)

Fig. 1. HRRP model: (a) Aircraft model; (b) Scattering points model.

Due to the movement of the target and the changes in radar detection environment, there are three problems with HRRP data, namely time-shift sensitivity, amplitude-scale sensitivity, and target-aspect sensitivity of HRRP. In order to solve the problem of amplitude-scale sensitivity, we have preprocessed the data, that is, normalized amplitude.

2.2 The Simple Convolutional Neural Network with Center Loss for HRRP Recognition

Convolutional neural networks (CNN) can automatically extract the high-order abstract features of the target and have achieved great success in the field of target recognition. Generally, a CNN consist of one or more pair of convolution and pooling layers and finally ends with a fully connected layer. To our best knowledge, convolutional layers have some translation invariance and max-pooling layers have some rotation invariance. When we use radar HRRP to recognize radar targets, we will encounter several problems that need to be considered: time-shift sensitivity, amplitude-scale sensitivity, and target-aspect sensitivity of HRRP.

Architecture: As shown in Fig. 2, we used a simple network for radar HRRP recognition and adopted center loss and softmax loss as joint supervision. Loss functions introduced in Section Loss Function. In this network, we used convolutional layers to overcome the time-shift sensitivity of radar HRRP and used max-pooling layers to overcome the amplitude-scale sensitivity. In the feature mapping part, there are two conv-pooling sub-blocks which are cascaded to a fully connected layer. The convolutional layer in the first conv-pooling sub-block is 7×1 with stride 3, followed by tanh nonlinear units, and the neuron number is 32. The following max-pooling grid is 8×1. The second convolutional layer have 64 5×1 neurons with stride 2, followed by tanh nonlinear units. The Second max-pooling layer gird is 4×1. The output of the two conv-pooling sub-blocks are concatenated as the input of the first fully connected layer and the output dimension is 32, followed by relu nonlinear units. The second fully connected layer is the classification layer, and the output dimension is the target class numbers 4.

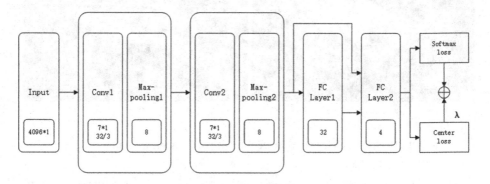

Fig. 2. Proposed simple CNN for radar HRRP recognition.

Loss Function: Generally, in image classification tasks, we use the softmax loss function to calculate the loss. The traditional softmax loss function does not restrict the distance between classes and within classes, and it is easy to produce the phenomenon that the distance within class is larger than the distance between features, leading to unsatisfactory recognition effect. Inspired by face recognition method, we use center loss function to correct softmax loss to meet the requirements of radar HRRP target recognition. The softmax loss function is presented as follows:

$$L_s = -\sum_{i=1}^{m} \log \frac{e^{\mathbf{W}_{y_i}^T \mathbf{x}_i + \mathbf{b}_{y_i}}}{\sum\limits_{j=1}^{n} e^{\mathbf{W}_j^T \mathbf{x}_i + \mathbf{b}_j}} \tag{3}$$

where $\mathbf{x}_i \in R^d$ denotes the ith deep feature, belonging to the $\mathbf{x}_i$th class. d is the feature dimension. $\mathbf{W}_j \in R^d$ denotes the jth column of the weights $\mathbf{W} \in R^{d \times n}$ in the last fully connected layer and $\mathbf{b} \in R^n$ is the bias term. n is the number of class and m is the batch size. The center loss this paper used is defined as:

$$L_c = \frac{1}{2} \sum_{i=1}^{m} \|\mathbf{x}_i - \mathbf{c}_{y_i}\|_2^2 \tag{4}$$

where $\mathbf{c}_{y_i} \in R^d$ denotes the y_ith class center of deep features. It should be updated as the deep features changed and computed by averaging the features of the corresponding classes. This formulation can characterize the intra-class variations effectively.

We used center loss to correct softmax loss to train the CNNs for discriminative feature learning. The expression of the loss function used in this paper is as follows:

$$L = L_s + \lambda L_{center} \tag{5}$$

where λ is a hyper parameter that used for balancing the two loss functions. By using this loss function in training process can make the model learn the classification features of smaller intra-class distance.

3   Experimental Results

In this paper, four aircraft HRRP data are simulated. The radar signal bandwidth is 150 MHz, the sampling frequency is 200 MHz and the center frequency is 9.7 GHz. There are 2048 samples of each aircraft and each sample contains 4096 sample points. We randomly divide the training set and test set by 50%. Take one sample for each type of aircraft, as shown in Fig. 3.

In training process, the goal is to minimize the corrected softmax loss (shown in Eq. 3). We used adaptive moment estimation optimizer, and the batch size was set to 512. The dropout regularization before the first fully connected layer was set to 0.3. The training process was stopped after 500 epochs. In testing process, the center loss did not calculate. A complete experimental process includes randomly dividing data sets, training and testing. We took the average of the results of 10 experiments as the final result. The classification results, evaluated using confusion matrix, are listed in Table 1. It is observed that the overall accuracy (OA) is 99.14%.

Figure 4 shows the distribution of deeply learned features (output of the first fully connected layer) under the supervision of different loss. The left is

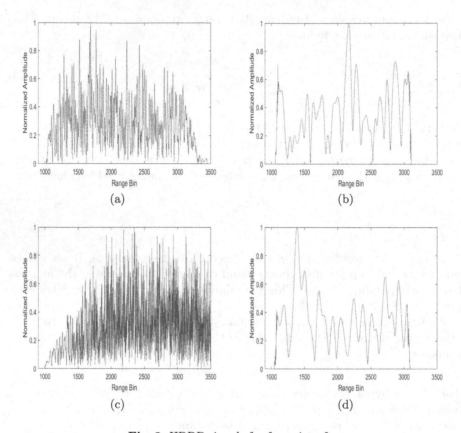

Fig. 3. HRRP signals for four aircraft.

Table 1. The results of 4 radar HRRP targets recognition

T\Pre	1	2	3	4
1	1024	0	0	0
2	0	990	0	34
3	0	0	1024	0
4	1	1	0	1022

the feature trained by softmax loss, and the right is the feature trained by softmax loss and center loss. The distance within the class in the right graph is significantly smaller than in the left graph.

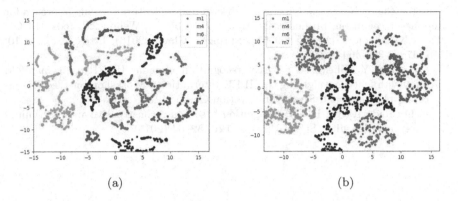

(a)   (b)

Fig. 4. The distribution of deeply learned features.

4   Conclusion

In this paper, a novel deep convolutional neural network recognition algorithm is designed and used for aircraft target recognition based on HRRP data. The proposed network has a large convolution kernel, a large stride convolution layer and large grid size max-pooling. In order to get a more robust network, the author uses the center loss function to correct the softmax loss function. The experimental results show that the method obtains the feature of smaller intra-class distance, and the recognition accuracy is very good, reaching 99.14%.

Acknowledgment. This work is supported by Fundamental Research Funds for the Central Universities (3102018AX001), National Natural Science Foundation of China (61671383), and Natural Science Foundation of Shaanxi Province (2018JM6005).

References

1. Bo, F., Bo, C., Liu, H.: Radar HRRP target recognition with deep networks. Pattern Recogn. **61**, 379–393 (2017). (Complete)
2. Guo, C., He, Y., Wang, H., Jian, T., Sun, S.: Radar HRRP target recognition based on deep one-dimensional residual-inception network. IEEE Access **7**, 9191–9204 (2019)
3. Lan, D., Wang, P., Liu, H., Pan, M., Feng, C., Zheng, B.: Bayesian spatiotemporal multitask learning for radar HRRP target recognition. IEEE Trans. Signal Process. **59**(7), 3182–3196 (2011)
4. Li, H.J., Yang, S.H.: Using range profiles as feature vectors to identify aerospace objects. IEEE Trans. Antennas. Propag. **41**(3), 261–268 (1993)
5. Liao, K., Si, J., Zhu, F., He, X.: Radar HRRP target recognition based on concatenated deep neural networks. IEEE Access **6**, 29211–29218 (2018)
6. Lunden, J., Koivunen, V.: Deep learning for HRRP-based target recognition in multistatic radar systems. In: Radar Conference (2016)

7. Wen, Y., Zhang, K., Li, Z., Qiao, Y.: A discriminative feature learning approach for deep face recognition. In: Leibe, B., Matas, J., Sebe, N., Welling, M. (eds.) ECCV 2016. LNCS, vol. 9911, pp. 499–515. Springer, Cham (2016). https://doi.org/10.1007/978-3-319-46478-7_31
8. Yue, J., Han, Y., Sheng, W.: Target recognition of radar HRRP using manifold learning with feature weighting. In: IEEE International Workshop on Electromagnetics: Applications and Student Innovation Competition (2016)
9. Zhou, D.: Radar target HRRP recognition based on reconstructive and discriminative dictionary learning. Signal Process. **126**, 52–64 (2015)

Analysis of the Influence of CAN Bus Structure on Communication Performance

Shujun Yong[1], Yunhong Ma[2(✉)], Yifei Zhao[2], and Lerong Qi[2]

[1] Huayin Ordnance Test Center, Weilan 710142, China
[2] Northwestern Polytechnical University, Xi'an 710072, China
mayunhong@nwpu.edu.cn

Abstract. CAN bus is widely used in automotive distributed embedded systems. Its protocol makes it reliable and efficient in in-vehicle communication system and industrial control system. However, the limited communication bandwidth limits its transmission efficiency. In order to improve the transmission efficiency of CAN bus, the influence of CAN bus structure to the transmission performance is analyzed in this paper. A typical CAN bus network is set and the message transmission is simulated under different CAN bus structure based on CANoe, which is widely used to study the CAN bus. The influence of different network structure on the transmission performance is analyzed. The simulation result demonstrated that the multi-level-bus CAN network using gateway reduces busload and minimize message delay effectively. It is also demonstrated that the simulation method is able to be used to find the appropriate CAN bus network structure according the busload or message delay requirement.

Keywords: CAN bus network structure · Message delay · Busload · Transmission performance

1 Introduction

The controller aerial network (CAN) bus has the advantages of real-time transmission performance and it has been widely used in various vehicles with integrated electronic systems. CAN bus provide an infrastructure of control, monitoring, and diagnostic applications in vehicle. As the functions of vehicles are becoming more and more powerful, the number of electronic control units (ECU) in the on-board CAN bus communication network is also increasing, and the network structure is becoming more and more complicated. Therefore, the bus loading is increasing and even leads to communication delivery delays in messages under the extreme situation. Accordingly, the transmission performance of the entire CAN bus system getting worse and impacts the performance of the control system, especially for the advanced drive assistance systems. Therefore, CAN bus is required to have dependability attributes, especially the real-time performance of CAN network.

The CAN network is a multi-master message broadcast system, it works with a maximum signal rate of 1 Mbps [3]. In a CAN network, many short messages are

© ICST Institute for Computer Sciences, Social Informatics and Telecommunications Engineering 2020
Published by Springer Nature Switzerland AG 2020. All Rights Reserved
B. Li et al. (Eds.): IoTaaS 2019, LNICST 316, pp. 405–416, 2020.
https://doi.org/10.1007/978-3-030-44751-9_34

broadcasted to the entire network, which provides data consistency in every node of the system [4]. When the payload is increased, the real-time performance is not ensured. Some researches were focused on modifying the protocol to improve the transmission performance [5].

In this paper, we try to analyze the impact of CAN network structure to the transmission performance through the simulation of different network. By using the hierarchical structure of different real time requirement message, minimize CAN busload to minimize the possible message latencies. The simulation is carried based on software CANoe and simulation results will provide a reference for the CAN bus structure design.

CANoe software is a CAN network application system development tool developed by Vector company [1]. It not only has network detection and analysis functions, but also can realize semi-physical simulation through CAN bus hardware interface. It is often used to build CAN network to realize full digital simulation [2] to verify the design about the CAN bus. The CANoe software comes with the database management tool CANdb++. CANoe also provides a CAPL function library, which is convenient for users to program each node and analyze bus data.

2 Multi-level-bus CAN Network Structure

2.1 Organization of CAN Node

The CAN network adopts a serial bus topology. All ECU nodes are connected on the bus, and the message is transmitted through the bus while all the nodes in the bus can received the message simultaneously.

For a CAN network system, if there are less nodes, a single bus structure is enough to guarantee the real-time of messages transmission. However, if the CAN network has so many nodes that the busload increase a lot, the high density of message even cause bus congestion due to the single bus structure. As a result, the transmission delay of the message of node is increased to cause the message packet unable to be successfully sent before the message deadline which is called the transmission fails.

In order to improve the reliability of message transmission, the multi-level-bus structure is designed according to the speed of data transmission requirement. In this structure, the messages with different real-time transmission requirements in the CAN bus are placed in different CAN bus subnets, and gateways are added between the subnets to establish communication between subnets.

The multi-level-bus structure will reduce the busload of each CAN bus subnet and satisfies the real-time performance of message transmission. Multi-level-bus networks are usually divided into high-speed subnets and low-speed subnets.

We take a typical vehicle as example. It's an in-vehicle CAN bus network whose structure is composed of two bus subnets, namely a high speed bus and a low-speed bus. In high-speed CAN subnet, eight ECU nodes are mounted on high speed bus. These ECU nodes usually sending time-critical message which is important for the in-vehicle control system. The other 6 ECU nodes are placed in low speed bus, and they have less real-time requirement and is used in mission system. The CAN network is as in Fig. 1.

In the integrated system of CAN bus, the driver mission terminal acts as a gateway in the bus network and is mounted on two buses at the same time. It is responsible for data communication between the high speed bus subnet and the bus low speed subnet. All ECU nodes in the entire network are able to communicate by sending or receiving extended frames package through gateway. If the message is only need in subnet bus, it is transmitted in local subnet. This mechanism of multi-level-bus will reduce busload effectively.

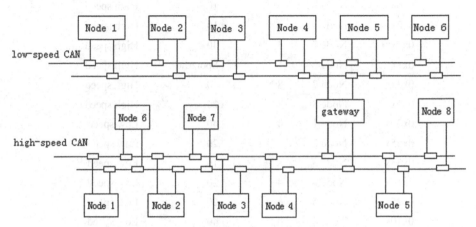

Fig. 1. Multi-level-bus CAN network structure with Gateway

2.2 Message Definition

In addition, in order to keep the communication efficiently, the different message packets sending periodic are designed to avoid bus using conflict. The packets of the nodes are sent in a periodic style with different cycle, and each message packet has a CAN ID except for the switch information interface box terminal and the driver mission terminal (gateway).

For the armored vehicle, the message packet using extended frames which the message packets with an CAN ID (identifiers) of 29 bits. The message with high priority CAN ID is in high speed subnet usually, and the lowest identifiers have the highest priority for bus contention according to the basic CAN identifier rules.

In CAN bus network, the message is sent cyclic such as message of motor rotation frequency is required to be updated every 10 ms, message of a temperature sensor is required to update every 20 ms, while some message is send sporadically. Each node may send different messages.

The sending period of some messages in the armored vehicle are listed in Table 1.

Table 1. Simulation parameters

Message ID	Node name	Data length	Send period/ms	CAN channel
0x4x	Node1	3	20	High speed
0x1x	Node2	4	40	High speed
0x6x	Node 3	5	10	High speed
0x2x	Node 4	8	10	High speed
0x7x	Node 5	5	40	High speed
0x8x	Node 6	1	Sporadic	High speed
0x3x	Node 7	8	10	High speed
0x5x	Node 8	7	20	High speed
0x35x	Node 1	4	40	Low speed
0x55x	Node 2	8	20	Low speed
0x33x	Node 3	8	10	Low speed
0x15x	Node 4	4	20	Low speed
0x25x	Node 5	6	20	Low speed
0x10x	Node 6	6	40	Low speed

3   Indicators of Transmission Performance

3.1   Busload

Busload is critical to consider the bus performance to ensure minimum delay of data. The lower busload will lead to less message delay generally. Busload is an important indicator for the CAN bus network performance.

Busload is defined as the ratio of the actual amount of data transmitted and the maximum amount of data the bus can transmit. For the CAN bus, the maximum amount of data is equal to the baud rate of the CAN bus due to the NRZ coding mechanism. Another definition is the ratio of bus busy time and bus idle time. Typically, the bus loading is expressed as the percentage of time the bus is busy for a period of time. The calculation formula of the busload is as (1):

$$\sum_{i=1}^{m} L_i / T, L_i = \left(8N_i + 47 + \left\lfloor \frac{34 + 8N_i}{5} \right\rfloor \right) \cdot T_{bit} \tag{1}$$

Here, the L_i is the size of message i, m denote the number of message in a test period of T, The term T_{bit} is the bit time of the bus, N_i denotes the data field length of message packet.

The busload is affected by many factors; the most influential is the message density. The message intensity is closely related to the transmission frequency and frame length of each message. For a special CAN bus system, the transmission frequency and frame length of each message are determined according to the protocol. In order to improve the bus transmission real-time performance, we can move to design the structure of the CAN bus network to reduce the message density under the requirement of successful message transmission.

The multi-level-bus structure with gateway can effectively reduce the pressure of transmitting packets on bus through dividing massage packets with different real-time requirement into subnets. According to the real-time requirements of the packets, nodes with different real-time requirements are placed in different transmission rate subnets, thus, for each subnet, the bus loading will reduce. The lower busload rate of the bus will be helpful for improving the real-time performance of bus data transmission.

3.2 Message Delay

Message delay is the time it takes for a message to be received from being ready to send. It is usually contain two parts, namely the transmission delay and the arbitration delay. The transmission delay is the time it taken for the message to be transmitted on the bus, which is related to the length of the message and the baud rate of the system. The arbitration delay is the time taken for the message waiting for the bus to be idle or being arbitrated. Since the CAN bus adopts the CSMA/CA communication mode, if a higher priority message is waiting to be transmitted, the bus preferentially transmits a high priority message, and the low priority message needs to wait for the next idle time of the bus and proceed on the next round. Accordingly, the message with the lower priority will have the longer arbitration delay.

In order to analyze the message transmission performance, the theoretical calculation of the response time of message transmission is analyzed firstly. The response time of message contains 3 parts as in (2):

$$R_i = C_i + J_i + W_i \tag{2}$$

The term J_i is the queuing jitter of message i, and gives the latest queuing time of the message. The term W_i represents the worst-case queuing delay of message i. The term C_i represents the longest time taken to physically send message i on the bus.

In the calculation of the C_i as in the formula of (3), N_i denotes the data field length of packet, and the filling size of the message i packets is written as $\left\lfloor \frac{34+8N_i}{5} \right\rfloor$, The term T_{bit} is the bit time of the bus [6, 8].

$$C_i = \left(8N_i + 47 + \left\lfloor \frac{34 + 8N_i}{5} \right\rfloor \right) \cdot T_{bit}, N_i = 1, 2, \ldots 8 \tag{3}$$

The W_i of a message consists both the time waiting for the higher priority messages pre-empting message and the second is the time waiting lower priority message that has already obtained the bus.

For messages with higher priority, since there is always a higher arbitration advantage, it is easier to obtain the bus usage rights, so the delay is smaller and always are easy to be successfully sent in transmission. However, for a message with a lower priority, if the bus adopts single-bus structure, the arbitration delay of the message will increase much due to the lower arbitration especially in the CAN network with many ECU nodes and high message density. If the message delay exceeds the dead-line of the message, it is called as transmission fail.

4   Simulation of Different Structure CAN Network

This paper focuses on the impact of network structure on the real-time performance of message transmission. For CAN bus with the same quantity of nodes and the same message density, the simulation is set up to analyze the real-time performance of the message in CAN network with multi-level-bus structure with the gateway. The main indicators are busload and message delay. We compare the message delay in CAN network with the single-bus structure and with multi-level bus structure separately. Furthermore, the busload is also tested in CAN network with different structures under the same situation that with the same message transmission period and the same number of ECU nodes. The influence of busload to message delay is analyzed.

4.1   Single Bus CAN Network

We outline a CAN bus network for message transmission that all nodes can send and receive messages, and the message with their own sending cycle. We study the transmission delay of the specified 7 messages with different priority in different CAN bus network.

Firstly, according to the organization of each node message, we create a CANdb++ database and define the sending cycle of each message. In addition, the relative environment variables of each node are defined. Based on the created database, a single bus CAN bus network is generated under the CANoe platform, as shown in Fig. 2.

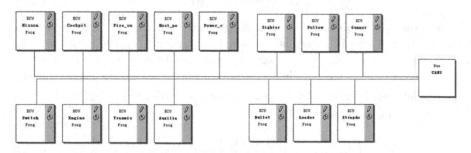

Fig. 2. Structure of Single CAN bus

4.2   Multi-level-bus CAN Network Structure

Generally, in the in-vehicle CAN bus, different message transmission periods and delay requirements are defined according to the data characteristics and real-time requirements of the nodes. For example, the real-time information of the engine needs to be transmitted at a high speed. Real-time performance of information of the entertainment comfort system is not very important. Accordingly, nodes with high real-time requirements are placed in high speed CAN subnet, and are transmitted in high baud rates. While nodes with low real-time requirements are placed in low speed CAN subnet, and messages are transmitted in with low baud rates. A multi-level-bus CAN network is built accordingly which contains CAN1 and CAN2 channels connected through a gateway. CAN1 is high speed and CAN2 is low speed subnet. Nodes in different subnets communicate with the other nodes through gateway when needed. The multi-level-bus CAN network structure is shown in Fig. 3, and the gateway will be set between the CAN1 and CAN2. In Fig. 3, the gateway is built in CAN1 named 'Mission'.

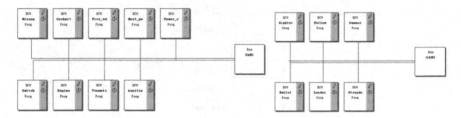

Fig. 3. Multi-level-bus CAN bus

4.3 Gateway Simulation

For the multi-level-bus CAN network, the sending and receiving of message are simulated based on the CAPL function, including the response to the environment variable, the response to the timer, and the response to the received message. In addition, the CAPL function is used to realize the information exchange function. It is used to transmit the messages from the gateway to the other subnet. The gateway node receives the message from the CAN1 channel, and transmits the data packets to the CAN2 channel.

4.4 Simulation Comparison Between Different CAN Network Structures

According to the message packet allocation of each ECU node, the sending period of each node message is set by a timer. First, the gateway node is disconnected from the chassis electrical control bus, and the bus network is work as a single-bus network. After starting the simulation, the busload of the entire chassis electrical control bus network is tested. The special 7 messages delay are also tested in the simulation of CAN network with single-bus. The busload is listed as in Table 2, and the message delay with different priority is shown in Table 3.

Table 2. Busload of single-bus network

Number of nodes	Busload
3	4.50%
4	6.82%
5	8.50%
6	13.46%
7	18.42%
8	19.34%
9	22.60%
10	25.94%
11	30.88%
12	33.75%
13	37.61%
14	40.63%
15	41.10%

Table 3. Message delays of single-bus network

The priority of message	Message delay
1	0.23
2	0.76
3	1.38
4	1.89
5	2.39
6	2.92
7	3.42

Similarly, the same message sending period and message amount is used. The communication simulation is set in the multi-level-bus CAN network and implemented. The busload of each subnet is listed in Table 4, and the specific 7 messages' delays are shown in Table 5.

Table 4. Busload of multi-level-bus network

Number of node	Low speed busload	High speed busload
3	4.00%	0.92%
4	6.32%	0.92%
5	4.50%	4.96%
6	8.96%	5.88%
7	13.92%	5.88%
8	13.92%	6.96%
9	14.83%	6.96%
10	15.98%	6.96%
11	15.98%	9.12%
12	18.85%	9.12%
13	23.79%	9.12%
14	23.79%	10.96%
15	27.65%	10.96%

Table 5. Message delays of multi-level-bus network

The priority of message	Message delay
1	0.23
2	0.31
3	0.31
4	0.82
5	1.31
6	1.85
7	2.34

5 Simulation Analysis

5.1 Experiment Data Analysis

According to the test data in the table, a trend graph showing the change of the busload with the number of nodes is as shown in Fig. 4. The busload keeps rising with the number of nodes increases. The busload is significantly higher using a single-bus network structure without a gateway than that of a multi-level-bus network structure with a gateway. If all nodes are connected on the same bus in single bus structure, the number of packets actually transmitted on the bus increases during same period of time, the busload increases accordingly. If the busload increases to a certain extent, bus congestion will occur. It will affect the real-time performance of messages transmission.

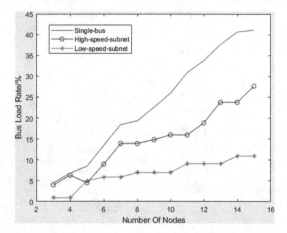

Fig. 4. Relationship between busload and number of nodes

The message transmission delay with different priority messages in both cases are shown in Fig. 5. And the improvement ratio is calculated in the Table 6. It can be seen that the message delay in multi-level-bus structure with gateway significantly reduced, especially the message with lower priority. By adding a gateway to the bus network to form a multi-level-bus structure, the pressure of transmission of a single bus message can be effectively reduced. Accordingly, the real-time performance of message is significantly enhanced. Therefore, the transmission performance of the multi-level-bus CAN network using gateway is significantly better than that of the single bus especially at the CAN network have many nodes.

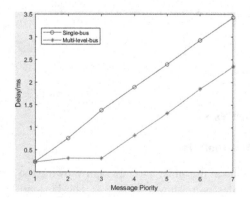

Fig. 5. Message delay in different CAN network

Table 6. Message delays reduce ratio

The priority of message	Message delays reduce ratio
1	0.00%
2	59.21%
3	77.54%
4	56.61%
5	45.19%
6	36.64%
7	31.58%

5.2 Further Discuss on Simulation

It is known that in an in-vehicle CAN bus network, there are some messages are time-critical. These messages have deadlines, if the message delay overpasses the deadline, it will cause a serious error. According to present study, it is recommended that the busload be kept below 35% on CAN bus to ensure the stable communication [6–8]. The simulation result also demonstrated that the message delay reduced to quite low over 30%.

Therefore, we can get the appropriate structure by the simulation. For the example in this paper, if the nodes in CAN network are less than 12, it is able to meet the busload requirement and need not use the multi-level-bus structure, otherwise, the multi-level-bus structure is able to improve the transmission efficiency by reducing the busload.

Accordingly, if the multi-level-bus network structure is adopted, the message transmission efficiency will be improved by reducing the busload. In addition, the multi-level-bus CAN network is able to isolate the low-speed bus from the high-speed bus to guarantee the stability of CAN bus system, especially benefit to guarantee the time-critical message transmission successfully to improve the performance of the vehicle.

6 Conclusion

This paper focuses on analyzing the influence of bus network structure to the communication performance, especially in busload and message delay. The CAN bus networks with different structure are set up and communication process is simulated. The simulation verified the transmission performance is improved by using multi-level-bus structure. The appropriate CAN bus network structure suggestion is available by the CAN bus simulation result.

References

1. Liu, J., Qu, J.: A method for testing serial bus performance of universal armored vehicles. Ordnance Ind. Autom. **35**(02), 32–34 (2016)
2. Wang, H., Miao, Q., Feng, H., Wang, T.: CAN bus fault diagnosis and analysis based on CANoe and CANScope. Mod. Comput. (Professional Version), (31), 61–65 (2015)
3. De Andrade, R., Hodel, K.N., Justo, J.F., Laganá, A.M., Santos, M.M., Gu, Z.: Analytical and experimental performance evaluations of CAN-FD bus. IEEE Access **6**, 21287–21295 (2018)
4. Navet, N., Song, Y., Simonot-Lion, F., Wilwert, C.: Trends in automotive communication systems. Proc. IEEE **93**(6), 1023–1024 (2005)
5. Cena, G., Bertolotti, I.C., Hu, T., Valenzano, A.: CAN with extensible in-frame reply: protocol definition and prototype implementation. IEEE Trans. Ind. Inform. **13**(5), 2436–2446 (2017)
6. Cao, B.: CAN bus response time analysis based on bit stuffing mechanism and scheduling algorithm research. Northeast University thesis (2014)
7. Quigley, C.P., Roxburgh, A., McLaughlin, R.T., Tang, K.H.: A low cost CAN bus transducer and its applications. In: Proceedings 7th International CAN Conference (2000)
8. Tindell, K., Burns, A.: Guaranteeing message latencies on CAN. In: Proceedings 1st International CAN Conference (1994)

Failure Reasons Identification for the Next Generation WLAN: A Machine Learning Approach

Zhaozhe Jiang, Bo Li, Mao Yang$^{(\boxtimes)}$, Zhongjiang Yan, and Qi Yang

Northwestern Polytechnical University, Xi'an 710129, China
jzz@mail.nwpu.edu.cn
{libo.npu,yangmao,zhjyan}@nwpu.edu.cn

Abstract. Artificial Intelligence (AI) is one of the hottest research directions nowadays. Machine learning is an important branch of AI. It allows the machine to make its own decisions without human telling the computer exactly what to do. At the same time, Media Access Control (MAC) is also an important technology for the next generation Wireless Local Area Network (WLAN). However, due to transmission collision, noise, interference, channel fading and other reasons, the transmission between access point (AP) and station (STA) may fail. This is limiting the overall performance. If the node can obtain the real-time failure reasons, it can adjust protocol parameters accordingly such as Modulation and Coding Scheme (MCS) and Contention Window (CW). Then, the overall performance of WLAN is improved. Therefore, a machine learning based failure reason identification approach is proposed for the next generation WLAN. In this paper, access environment is divided into four categories: nice, severe collision, deep fading and both deep fading. Different training models are used to train the data. Through our experiments, the accuracy can reach 83%, while that of Random Forest model can reach 99%.

Keywords: Machine learning · Failure reasons · Access environment state

1 Introduction

In recent years, the global communication business grows rapidly. And WLAN is one of the most important data technologies [1]. In order to meet the increasing users demands, academia and industry are devoted themselves to improving WLAN performance such as throughput, latency, Quality of Service (QoS), etc [2].

Media Access Control (MAC) is one of the key technologies in WLAN [3]. And it is also one of the focuses of communication researchers. Since WLAN is based on distributed access, reasons such as collision, interference and channel fading may affect system performance [4]. Due to the complex and time-variable

© ICST Institute for Computer Sciences, Social Informatics and Telecommunications Engineering 2020
Published by Springer Nature Switzerland AG 2020. All Rights Reserved
B. Li et al. (Eds.): IoTaaS 2019, LNICST 316, pp. 417–426, 2020.
https://doi.org/10.1007/978-3-030-44751-9_35

WLAN environment, there may be a variety of reasons leading to the transmission failures, such as collision, channel fading and so on. If the access point (AP) or STA can obtain the failure reasons, they can adopt corresponding appropriate MAC strategies to improve the access success ratio and the overall WLAN performance. Therefore, whether there exists an intelligent identification mechanism that can accurately determine the reasons for the current user access failure.

There are many studies focusing on the performance improvement of MAC. Chen etc. [5] proposed an Interference Free Full Duplex with power control (IFFD) MAC protocol to avoid Inter-Station Interference Problem (ISIP) for next generation WLAN. Tsurumi etc. [6] proposed the MAC method based on the Synchronization Phenomena of coupled oscillators (SP-MAC) to improve a total throughput of wireless terminals connected to an Access Point (AP). Kim etc. [7] proposed Adaptive Virtual Backoff Algorithm (AVBA) to improve throughput. Qu etc. [8] proposed an OFDMA based Multiple Access for IEEE 802.11ax (OMAX) protocol to increase throughput. The result indicates that OMAX protocol increases the throughput to 160%. However, few of these studies mentioned before take into account the reasons of the access failure.

This paper proposes an identification mechanism based on machine learning for access failure reasons. In this paper, access state can be totally divided into four categories: perfect environment (access success), serious collision (access failure), serious fading (access failure) and both serious channel fading and collision (access failure). The training set and test set under different conditions are obtained through simulation of NS3. After that, train the data by different machine learning models. And test the identification accuracy by the test set. Our simulation experiment shows that the accuracy of Naïve Bayes model can reach 83%. And after feature extraction, the accuracy of Random Forest model can reach 99%.

The sections of this paper are arranged as follows. Section 2 introduces the key idea of this paper. And Sect. 3 introduces the process of machine learning. The fourth section introduces the simulation configuration and performance analysis. Finally, the fifth section introduces the conclusion and future work needed to do.

2 Motivation

In this paper, the method based on machine learning is adopted to determine the reasons of user access failure. We divide access state into four types. We use the information of ACK as our data set. And we use several models to do the machine learning. Finally, we can obtain the accuracy of different models by the test set.

2.1 Access Failure Reasons

We divide STA access environment state into four types. Three of them are failure state. And the other one is successful state (Fig. 1).

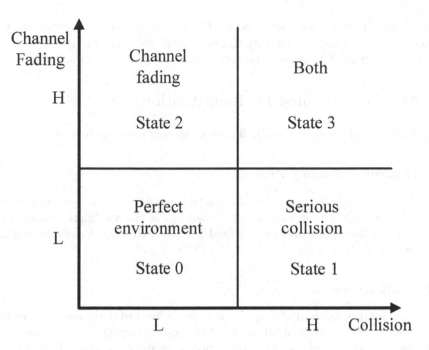

Fig. 1. Access environment state

Perfect environment means that the current state of communication is good. It is with low latency and high throughput. In our simulation configuration, the number of STAs is relatively small and it is close to AP. Therefore, the collision among STAs is relatively small. And there is almost no channel fading.

Serious collision means that the current access fails. In our simulation configuration, STA number is much more than perfect environment and STAs are close to AP. Because many STAs compete for only a channel, access failures must occur.

Channel fading is another reason of access failure. In our simulation configuration, the number of STAs is small and STAs are far away from AP. Due to the small number of STAs, the collision is not serious. It is that the distance becoming longer and the channel becoming worse, resulting in failure of access.

The last reason is both serious channel fading and collision. In our simulation configuration, the number of STAs is very large and the distance from AP to STAs is relatively long. It combines the above two reasons, so it is the worst case of communication state.

2.2   Motivation

If we can obtain the current access environment state, then we can take some steps to improve overall performance of communication. For example, when the access environment state is good, we can increase the MCS to increase the throughput. If the current collision of STAs is serious, we can increase the CW to reduce the collision probability. If the current channel fading is serious, we can reduce the MCS to ensure the successful transmission of information.

3   Machine Learning for Identification

This Section will describe the simulation process in our experiment.

3.1   Machine Learning Process

Machine learning is the use of algorithms to parse data, learn from it, and then make decisions or predictions about something in the world. It poses a deep technical revolution in almost every field [9]. The structure of machine learning is shown below (Fig. 2).

3.2   Data Generation

In this paper, the method of machine learning is used to determine the cause of STAs access failure. First of all, we need to produce enough data for the model to learn. Therefore, we use NS3 simulation software to simulate four different access environment state so as to obtain data sets.

It is well known that the Data/ACK pattern has been used in WLAN to improve the overall performance of the network. This is the foundation that we determine the cause of the current access failure. We use the ACK information in the network as training sets. We consider ACK information from two aspects. The first case is on whether the STA receives an ACK every time a packet is

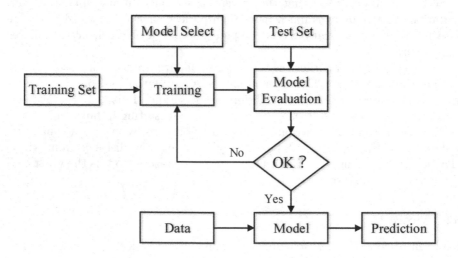

Fig. 2. Process of machine learning

transmitted. The STA will record 1 when it receives an ACK. And it records 0 when it does not receive an ACK. The other case is for each packet. It means that STA records the number of transmission times before the packet has been transmitted successfully. It will record 1 if a packet is transmitted successfully at the first time. Recording 2 means that a packet is transmitted successfully at the second time. The packet is retransmitted once. And record 0 if it exceeds the maximum number of retransmission. It indicates that the packet is abandoned.

In our simulation experiment, we configured four different access environment scenarios. They are named: Nice, Collision, Channel and Both.

Nice: It means that current access environment is perfect environment. The classification label is 0. For our simulation, there are a small number of STAs (Low Collision), low traffic rate, and close to AP (Low Channel Fading) in this scenario.

Collision: It means that current access environment is serious collision. The classification label is 1. For our simulation, there are a large number of STAs (High Collision), high traffic rate, and close to AP (Low Channel Fading) in this scenario.

Channel: It means that current access environment is channel fading. The classification label is 2. For our simulation, there are a small number of STAs (Low Collision), low traffic rate and a long distance from AP (High Channel Fading) in this scenario.

Both: It means that current access environment is channel fading and collision. The classification label is 3. For our simulation, there are as more STAs (High Collision), higher traffic rate, and nodes far away from AP (High Channel Fading) in this scenario.

The above is the overall description of the scene. And the detailed scene configuration is shown in Sect. 4.1.

After the simulation, we got a data set in the form of a matrix. There are hundreds of thousands of rows and 51 columns in the matrix. We use the first 50 transmissions or packets to determine the current access environment. A row of a matrix is called a record. The first 50 elements of a record are data, and the last is the label. There are hundreds of thousands of records in our data set. We use the data set as the training set.

Our test set is also generated by simulation. In order to validate the accuracy of the model effectively, we changed some configuration parameters to generate the test set. For example, in the scenario configuration of the training set, the distance between STA and AP is set to 150 m, 200 m and 250 m. Meanwhile, we set the distance of 180 m in the test set scenario to improve the test effectiveness. This will be closer to the real situation.

In order to further improve the accuracy of the models, we extracted the features of the data set. The mean, variance, maximum, minimum, median and mode of each record were extracted as new records. These records make up the new data set. Finally, there are hundreds of thousands of rows and 7 columns in the data set matrix. And the last column of the matrix is the label.

3.3 Data Cleaning

Due to the configuration of the simulation scenarios, a small part of data sets may be unavailable. We need to delete the unavailable data from our data set. For example, in the Channel scenario, the network performance is poor in the early stage of simulation. And it is a large packet loss ratio. However, Nice state of the network occurred in the final stage of simulation. The reason may be that other STAs no longer produce and send packets. Therefore, the STA competition pressure is reduced and the interference is also reduced. Each packet does not need to be retransmitted, which is inconsistent with the reality. Thus, it is necessary to delete this part of data set to get close to the reality.

3.4 Training Model

In the simulation of this paper, we used five different types of model to train the data respectively. They are the K Nearest Neighbor (KNN) algorithm [10], Random forest algorithm [11], Naive Bayes algorithm [12], Ensemble learning algorithm [13] and Discriminant Analysis (DA) algorithm [14]. The results of the different models are compared in the next section.

4 Simulation and Performance Evaluation

This section focuses on the detailed configuration of four simulation scenarios. And the simulation results are given and analyzed.

4.1 Simulation Scenario

WLAN is configured as a single cell uplink traffic scenario, with Distributed Coordination Function (DCF), DATA/ACK mode, without RTS/CTS interaction. There are four scenario which are Nice, Collision, Channel and Both. Under each scenario, all STAs will send 10,000 packets to AP in total. For each packet case, the data set matrix size is 40,000 *51. The data set matrix will be larger for each transmission case.

Since different parameter configurations may belong to the same scenario category. Therefore, in order to improve the completeness of the data set and the accuracy of the model, four different simulations are carried out under each scenario. The following is 4 detailed configuration tables for the four scenarios (Tables 1, 2, 3 and 4).

4.2 Results and Analysis

We use different training models in our experiment. The accuracy of different models is obtained after calculating with test set. Accuracy is shown in the Table 5.

From Table 5, we can see the experiment results of two different training sets under the same training model. As can be seen from the table, the accuracy of

Table 1. Nice scenario configuration

Parameter	1st	2nd	3rd	4th
STA number	10	20	5	10
Packets/s	100	50	50	50
Traffic rate	0.8 Mbps	0.4 Mbps	0.4 Mbps	0.4 Mbps
Distance	5 m	3 m	3 m	10 m
Packets number	4000	4000	1000	1000

Table 2. Collision scenario configuration

Parameter	1st	2nd	3rd	4th
STA number	200	100	50	200
Packets/s	1000	2000	1000	2000
Traffic rate	8 Mbps	16 Mbps	8 Mbps	16 Mbps
Distance	5 m	5 m	5 m	10 m
Packets number	4000	4000	1000	1000

Table 3. Channel scenario configuration

Parameter	1st	2nd	3rd	4th
STA number	10	10	10	10
Packets/s	100	1000	50	100
Traffic rate	0.8 Mbps	0.8 Mbps	0.4 Mbps	0.8 Mbps
Distance	200 m	150 m	250 m	250 m
Packets number	4000	4000	1000	1000

Table 4. Both scenario configuration

Parameter	1st	2nd	3rd	4th
STA number	200	200	200	100
Packets/s	1000	1000	1000	2000
Traffic rate	8 Mbps	8 Mbps	8 Mbps	16 Mbps
Distance	200 m	250 m	150 m	200 m
Packets number	4000	4000	1000	1000

Table 5. Accuracy of different models

Different model	Each transmission	Each packet
KNN	36.5%	52.4560%
Random forest	58.2756%	81.5371%
Naive bayes	60.0064%	83.7732%
Ensemble	58.2155%	81.4883%
Discriminant analysis	46.4382%	51.6129%

Naïve Bayes is highest. It can reach 83.77%. It is not a bad accuracy. However, the accuracy is not particularly high. The reason may be that the test set is obtained by adjusting the simulation parameters, which is relatively new to the training set. And the default model parameters are used in our training process. Therefore, the classification accuracy is not that high.

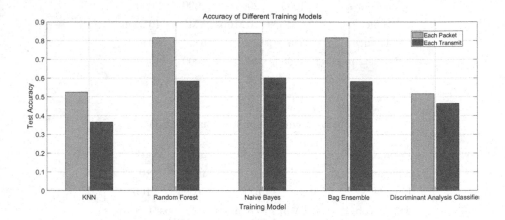

Fig. 3. Accuracy of different models

Figure 3 shows the accuracy comparison of the two training sets. It can be seen that the training set of each packet is generally better than that of each transmission. The reason might be that the total amount of information is the same in both cases. However, due to the small number of training set records in per packet case, the information content of each record is larger. Therefore, the classification accuracy of each packet case is higher (Table 6).

As can be seen from the above table, the accuracy of the model has been greatly improved after feature extraction. The accuracy of Random Forest model can reach 99%. This may because the key features of the data set are extracted. It greatly improves the classification ability of the model.

Table 6. Accuracy after features extraction

Different model	Each packet	Features extraction
KNN	52.4560%	79.5846%
Random forest	81.5371%	99.3385%
Naive bayes	83.7732%	——
Ensemble	81.4883%	95.1472%
Discriminant analysis	51.6129%	——

5   Conclusions and Future Work

In order to improve the comprehensive performance of WLAN, this paper proposes a new idea. We apply machine learning technology to WLAN. If the node can obtain current real-time access environment state, it can choose different optimization strategies accordingly. Thus, the overall performance of WLAN can be improved.

In this paper, access environment state is divided into four categories based on machine learning. They are perfect environment, serious collision, deep fading and both deep fading. Through our experiments, it is found that the accuracy of Naive Bayes model can reach 83%. And the accuracy of Random Forest model can reach 99% after feature extraction.

Due to the limited time and the author's level, there are still some parts to be improved in this paper. There is only ACK information used in the data set in this paper. It may lead to that the overall identification accuracy is not very reliable. In future studies, the author will use more information for training, such as packet time interval, CW size and other parameters. At the same time, select the appropriate model parameters. The accuracy and reliability should be further improved.

Acknowledgment. This work was supported in part by the National Natural Science Foundations of CHINA (Grant No. 61771390, No. 61871322, No. 61771392, No. 61271279, and No. 61501373), the National Science and Technology Major Project (Grant No. 2016ZX03001018-004), and Science and Technology on Avionics Integration Laboratory (20185553035).

References

1. Zheng, Y., Shi, T., Xu, X., Yuan, H., Yao, T.: Research on WLAN planning problem based on optimization models and multi-agent algorithm. In: 2017 IEEE International Conference on Cybernetics and Intelligent Systems (CIS) and IEEE Conference on Robotics, Automation and Mechatronics (RAM), Ningbo, pp. 249–254 (2017)
2. Zhou, R., Li, B., Yang, M., Yan, Z., Zuo, X.: QoS-oriented OFDMA MAC protocol for the next generation WLAN. Xibei Gongye Daxue Xuebao/J. Northwest. Polytechnical Univ. **35**, 683–689 (2017)

3. Jiang, S.: State-of-the-art medium access control (MAC) protocols for underwater acoustic networks: a survey based on a MAC reference model. IEEE Commun. Surv. Tutor. **20**(1), 96–131 (2018)
4. Firdaus, F., Ahmad, N.A., Sahibuddin, S.: Effect of people around user to WLAN indoor positioning system accuracy. In: 2017 Palestinian International Conference on Information and Communication Technology (PICICT), Gaza City, pp. 17–21 (2017)
5. Chen, Y., Chen, I., Shih, K.: An In-band full duplex MAC protocol with interference free for next generation WLANs. In: 2018 International Conference on Electronics Technology (ICET), Chengdu, pp. 407–410 (2018)
6. Tsurumi, R., Morita, M., Obata, H., Takano, C., Ishida, K.: Throughput control method between different TCP variants based on SP-MAC Over WLAN. In: 2018 IEEE International Conference on Consumer Electronics-Taiwan (ICCE-TW), Taichung, pp. 1–2 (2008)
7. Kim, J.D., Laurenson, D.I., Thompson, J.S.: Adaptive centralized random access for collision free wireless local area networks. IEEE Access **7**, 37381–37393 (2019)
8. Qu, Q., Li, B., Yang, M., et al.: An OFDMA based concurrent multiuser MAC for upcoming IEEE 802.11ax. In: Wireless Communications & Networking Conference Workshops. IEEE (2015)
9. Yang, M., Li, B., Feng, G., Yan Z.: V-CNN: When Convolutional Neural Network encounters Data Visualization (2018)
10. Staal, J., Abramoff, M.D., Niemeijer, M., Viergever, M.A., van Ginneken, B.: Ridge-based vessel segmentation in color images of the retina. IEEE Trans. Med. Imag. **23**(4), 501–509 (2004)
11. Ho, T.K.: The random subspace method for constructing decision forests. IEEE Trans. Pattern Anal. Mach. Intell. **20**(8), 832–844 (1998)
12. Peng, H., Long, F., Ding, C.: Feature selection based on mutual information criteria of max-dependency, max-relevance, and min-redundancy. IEEE Trans. Pattern Anal. Mach. Intell. **27**(8), 1226–1238 (2005)
13. He, K., Zhang, X., Ren, S., Sun, J.: Deep residual learning for image recognition. In: 2016 IEEE Conference on Computer Vision and Pattern Recognition (CVPR), Las Vegas, NV, pp. 770–778 (2016)
14. Tao, D., Li, X., Wu, X., Maybank, S.J.: General tensor discriminant analysis and gabor features for gait recognition. IEEE Trans. Pattern Anal. Mach. Intell. **29**(10), 1700–1715 (2007)

Deep Convolutional Neural Network Based Traffic Vehicle Detection and Recognition

Yukun Rao, Guanwen Zhang(✉), Wei Zhou, Changhao Wang, and Yu Lv

Northwestern Polytechnical University, Xi'an 710072, China
{guanwen.zh,zhouwei}@nwpu.edu.cn

Abstract. Traffic vehicle detection and recognition is a core technology of advanced driver assistant system (ADSD) for the intelligent vehicle. In this paper, we employ the convolution neural network (CNN) to perform the end-to-end vehicle detection and recognition.

Two vehicle classification CNNs are proposed. One is a convolution neural network consisting of four convolution layers and another is a multi-label classification network. The first networks can achieve the accuracy more than 95% while the second can achieve the accuracy more than 98%. Due to the multiple constraints, the proposed multi-label classification network is able to converge fast and achieve higher accuracy.

The vehicle detection model proposed in this paper is a model on the basis of the network model single shot multibox detector (SSD). Our network model employs the network proposed for vehicle classification as a basis network for feature extraction and design a multi-label loss for detection. The proposed network structure can achieve 77.31% mAP on the vehicle detection dataset. Compared with that of SSD network model, the obtained mAP is improved by 2.17%. The processing speed of proposed vehicle detection network can reach 12FPS, which can meet the real-time requirements.

Keywords: Intelligent vehicle · traffic vehicle classification · Multi-label classification · Traffic vehicle detection

1 Introduction

Vehicle detection and recognition is an important research course in the field of vision for unmanned (intelligent) driving technology, it is also a core technology of unmanned driving. In unmanned driving system, vehicle detection and recognition is the premise and foundation for intelligent vehicles to follow other vehicles, change lane, overtake, obstacle avoidance and other acts. The accuracy

Sponsored by the Seed Foundation of Innovation and Creation for Graduate Students in Northwestern Polytechnical University, ZZ2019140 and National College Students' innovation and entrepreneurship training program, 201810699167.

B. Li et al. (Eds.): IoTaaS 2019, LNICST 316, pp. 427–438, 2020.
https://doi.org/10.1007/978-3-030-44751-9_36

and complexity of vehicle detection and recognition directly affect the overall efficiency and performance of unmanned driving. Vehicle detection and recognition during driving can not only meet the real-time demand, but also can give some of instructions to operate the vehicle. The direction of vehicles and the type of vehicles are two important factors that affect the intelligent vehicle autonomous driving when detecting vehicles.

With the development of computer hardware and the emergence of deep learning, a new idea appears for vehicle detection and recognition in unmanned technology. Compared to the traditional methods which need manual image features extraction, the deep learning ways have better adaptability. Deep learning uses neural network for feature extraction, trains the network layer by layer, shares weights and it can enhance the speed of the image processing operations. Deep learning is mainly used in speech recognition, image recognition and so on. While dealing with these problems, the traditional feature extraction methods have limited ability to express features, but the deep learning can breakthrough these restrictions and meet the needs of computing.

Deep learning is to understand the information contained in images, sounds, and text. Deep learning has many successful cases in the face recognition [9], multi-scale image classification [1,2,6,8], object detection [12] and vehicle recognition [4,7]. Therefore, applying deep learning to the vehicle detection and recognition tasks has very significant meanings.

2   Related Works

Research on vehicle recognition mainly includes two aspects: one is the vehicle detection, another is the vehicle classification. Current vehicle detection is mainly divided into two methods, a single frame image-based method and video-based method. In this paper, we mainly study the image-based vehicle detection method. The early image-based vehicle detection methods mostly base on the appearance of the vehicle, using the edge features of image and the symmetry features to carry out vehicle position. These methods also use HOG [3] characteristics of vehicles to locate the vehicle.

Deformable parts model (DPM) [5] is mainly based on the improvement of HOG characteristics. It uses SVM [13] for classification, but needs multi-angle shooting targets while training. In 2014, Ross Grishick applied the convolution neural network to object detection [10]. In the case of insufficient dataset, pre-training of the network was required while fine-tuning the specific parts of the network. In 2015, his proposed DPM model and convolution neural network (CNN) became two widely used visual tools.

In the literature [11], Sarfraz proposed the use of the shape histogram features of the forward vehicle, and then classifies the images with the minimum distance classifier to achieve the purpose of quickly identifying the vehicle type. In the literature with the input image feature extraction, the extracted features will be compared to the characteristics in the database to find the smallest picture, and this picture corresponds to the model of the input image. In 2015, Zhang

Hongbing and others used the vehicle's HOG characteristics to position the vehicle, and then the type of vehicle was classified. His method not only reduced the computational complexity while improving the speed of calculation. 2015, Zhang [14] and others proposed a vehicle type recognition method based on convolution neural network.

In conclusion, the traditional method to vehicle detection and recognition has some disadvantages. It has huge amount of computation and pre-prepared work, besides the accuracy and detection speed can not meet the requirements of real-world application. The method based on deep learning has high accuracy and faster speed comparing to traditional ways. Besides, it does not need a lot of human pre-prepared works. So in our paper, we use deep learning ways to realize vehicle detection and recognition. On the one hand, we use tiny neural network to realize the detection task. Comparing to SSD network, we can save more time while training and increase the detection speed. On the other hand, our model can meet the requirements of multi-label task. Since in vehicle detection task, we should take vehicle type and orientation into considerations, our model can training two label at the same time. From the experiment results, we can see that with limitation of two labels, the network can converge faster and reach a higher accuracy.

We will discuss our model from following part:

Constructing CNN Network Model of Vehicle Classification: Design and train CNN network model to realize the classification task of multiple types of vehicles in CompCars (Comprehensive Car Dataset), and realize multi-label vehicle classification task. Two types of tags are trained on a network model and the training structure is compared with the training results of single labels.

Construction of Vehicle Detection and Recognition Network Model: Based on the above mentioned training model, the network structure is expanded by increasing the convolution layer, and the convolution layer Regression attribute (Regression Loss) of the candidate area rectangle is defined, to achieve an end-to-end network architecture model for vehicle detection and recognition tasks.

Do Optimized Training of Vehicle Detection and Recognition Network Model: Using the network model obtained in training in (1), the new CNN network model is initialized fine-tuned and trained, and by adjusting the network structure and training parameter the network model is further optimized to obtain higher detection and recognition accuracy and precision.

3 Proposed Approach

3.1 Constructing CNN Network Model of Vehicle Classification

For vehicle classification, we use convolution neural network which contains four convolution layer defined as four-layer convolution neural network. The four-layer convolution neural network is mainly composed of convolution layer, pooling layer, ReLU layer, full connected layer, accuracy layer and loss layer. Its structure is shown in Fig. 1.

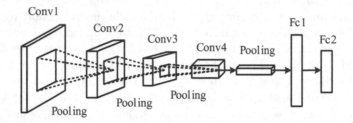

Fig. 1. Four-layer convolution neural network.

The multi-label classification network structure is obtained by modifying the structure of four convolution neural network. The network can simultaneously train a dataset with two labels. On the basis of the original four-layer convolution neural network, the multi-label classification network adds a data layer, an accuracy layer and a loss layer. The new data layer is to give the same images with another set of labels. The new accuracy layer and loss layer is to calculate the network classification accuracy and loss for the second category. Figure 2 shows the structure of the multi-label vehicle classification network model.

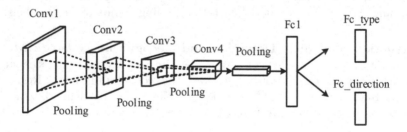

Fig. 2. Multi-label vehicle classification network model.

The accuracy layer of the network is used to calculate the accuracy which is defined as Eq. (1). The accuracy is a rate of the correct predictions and the total number of labels.

$$Ac = \frac{M}{N} \times 100\% \tag{1}$$

In Eq. (1), Ac is the classification accuracy; M indicates the number of correct labels; N indicates the total number of labels.

The loss layer of network is used to calculate classification loss. We use Softmax With Loss function which is combined by two calculation process. Softmax function $sigma(z) = (\sigma_1(z), ..., \sigma_m(z))$ is defined as Eq. (2).

$$\sigma_i(z) = \frac{\exp(z_i)}{\sum_{j=1}^{m} \exp(z_j)}, i = 1, ..., m \tag{2}$$

The next operation is the calculation of the Multinomial Logistic Loss defined in caffe, shown as Eq. (3).

$$l(y, o) = - \log(o_y) \tag{3}$$

We can obtain the Equation of Softmax With Loss by combining Eqs. (2) and (3). It is expressed by Eq. (4).

$$l(y, z) = - \log(\frac{e^{z_y}}{\sum_{j=1}^{m} e^{z_j}}) = \log(\sum_{j=1}^{m} e^{z_j}) - z_y \tag{4}$$

where m refers to the number of labels on current dataset, y means current label. This classification model is designed as a basis of vehicle detection and recognition model.

3.2 Construction of Vehicle Detection and Recognition Network Model

Vehicle detection model is mainly divided into two parts, including vehicle positioning and vehicle classification. Therefore, the most basic network structure is a vehicle classification network structure combined with a vehicle positioning network structure, the structure diagram shown in Fig. 3.

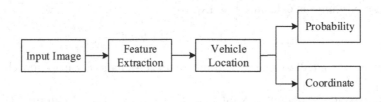

Fig. 3. The basic structure diagram of vehicle detection model.

The vehicle detection network is based on the four-layer convolutional neural network, which can generate a series of fixed-size bounding boxes on the different layers of the feature map. For each bounding box, it is necessary to determine whether it has a target and whether it is a fraction of a target, and finally a non-maximal suppression is added to produce the final test result. In each feature map of the classification network, a series of bounding box is defined. The bounding box is linked with each other in form of convolution. On each unit of the feature map, we predict each compensation value related to the bounding box shape, and assume that the image in each bounding box is the score of each object. Finally, we find out the highest score of the bounding box, and the position coordinates of the box is the position of the vehicle.

As shown in Fig. 4, for each picture, the network predicts whether the input image contains vehicle and decides the direction and type of vehicle. If it contains the vehicle in the image, the predicted vehicle coordinates should be also given at the same time. The last layer of the network is connected to two loss layers like the multi-label classification model. Each consists of two parts, including the confidence loss and the target prediction position which is the regression loss related to its true position.

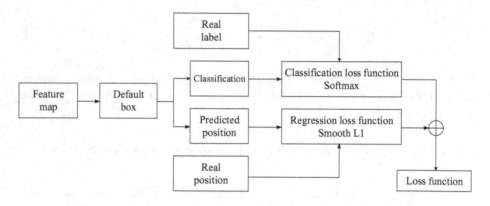

Fig. 4. The principle of vehicle detection model.

Assume that m feature maps are used for prediction, the size of default box in each feature map is calculated as Eq. (5).

$$s_k = s_{k-1} + 15 \times (k-1), k \in [2, m] \tag{5}$$

s_1 represents the smallest size of default box in the smallest feature map between the given feature map.

Then expand the default box into different shape so that it can predict different shape cars. At each location of the feature graph, the network uses multiple bounding boxes with different aspect ratios as $\alpha_r = \{1, 2, 3, 1/2, 1/3\}$, The width and height of the bounding box on different layers are shown in Eq. (6).

$$w_k^\alpha = s_k \sqrt{\alpha_r}, h_k^\alpha = \frac{s_k}{\sqrt{\alpha_r}} \tag{6}$$

When $\alpha_r = 1$, an additional frame is added, and the aspect ratio is calculated as shown in Eq. (7).

$$s_k' = \sqrt{s_k s_{k+1}} \tag{7}$$

Finally, for each position on the feature map, there are six different sizes of bounding boxes for matching. The center of each bounding box (m, n) is shown in Eq. (8).

$$m = \frac{i + 0.5}{|f_k|}, n = \frac{j + 0.5}{|f_k|} \tag{8}$$

Where $|f_k|$ is the size of k_{th} square feature map $[0, |f_k|)$. At the same time, mapping the bounding box coordinates to $[0,1]$ range.

3.3 Define the Loss Function of Multi-label Vehicle Detection and Recognition Network

As we all know, the type and direction of other cars are two important elements to decide which driving order should be executed while driving. So the loss of multi-label vehicle detection and recognition network is combined by two parts. One is the vehicle type detection part and the other is the vehicle direction detection part. We define the loss of vehicle type detection as $error_{type}$ and the loss of vehicle direction detection as $error_{dir}$. The total loss of the whole network is defined as Eq. (9).

$$loss = \alpha error_{type} + \beta error_{dir} \tag{9}$$

where α and β are influence factors of the two kinds of loss.

We set $\alpha = 0.5$ and $\beta = 0.5$ while training our multi-label vehicle detection and recognition network, which means the loss of vehicle type detection and vehicle direction detection have the same effect on the final loss.

By combining two loss, the network performs better in vehicle detection. Since there are two kinds of loss to restrict the network while training the network, the network can converge more quickly and it would be harder to diverge.

4 Experiment Results

4.1 Experiment Result of Vehicle Classification

We use the four-layer convolution neural network model to train and test the vehicle classification datasets. Vehicle classification datasets are divided into two types. One is orientation of vehicle and another is type of vehicle. In the vehicle's orientation dataset, there are 3200 front vehicle images, 3200 rear vehicle images and 3200 background images for training; 800 front vehicle images, 800 rear vehicle images and 800 background images for testing. In the vehicle's type dataset, there are 1600 car images, 1600 minibus images, 1600 bus images, 1600 truck images, 3200 backgrounds for training and 400 car images, 400 minibus images, 400 bus images, 400 truck images, 800 background images for testing.

For vehicle orientation dataset, the loss is 0.081 for final test and the accuracy is 97.75%. The accuracy of each label is shown in Table 1. For vehicle type dataset, the loss is 0.082 for final test and the accuracy is 98.04%. and the accuracy of each label is shown in Table 2.

Table 1. The accuracy of each label in vehicle orientation dataset for four-layer CNN.

Type	Total number	Correct number	Accuracy
Front car	800	792	99.00%
Rear car	800	796	99.50%
Background	800	758	94.75%
Total	2400	2346	97.75%

Table 2. The accuracy of each label in vehicle orientation dataset for four-layer CNN.

Type	Total number	Correct number	Accuracy
Car	400	393	98.35%
Minibus	400	395	98.50%
Truck	400	397	99.25%
Bus	400	398	99.50%
Background	800	771	96.38%
Total	2400	2353	98.04%

Then, the multi-label classification network model is used to train and test the vehicle classification datasets. For vehicle orientation dataset, the loss is 0.012 for final test and the accuracy is 97.91%. The accuracy of each label is shown Table 3.

For vehicle type dataset, the loss is 0.072 for final test and the accuracy is 98.34%. The accuracy of each label is shown in Table 4.

Comparing the data in Tables 1, 2, 3 and 4, we find that the multi-label classification network model can reach higher accuracy than four-layer convolution neural network in vehicle classification dataset. The accuracy increases by around 0.3%. Besides, multi-label classification network model performs better than four-layer convolution neural network. But we still need to improve our model because the accuracy of background is still too low. Due to the limitation of two series of label, multi-label classification model can converge faster and obtain higher accuracy.

Table 3. The accuracy of each label in vehicle orientation dataset for multi-label classification network model.

Type	Total number	Correct number	Accuracy
Front car	800	793	99.13%
Rear car	800	791	98.88%
Background	800	766	95.75%
Total	2400	2350	97.91%

Table 4. The accuracy of each label in vehicle type dataset for multi-label classification network model.

Type	Total number	Correct number	Accuracy
Car	400	398	99.35%
Minibus	400	396	99.00%
Truck	400	396	99.00%
Bus	400	395	98.75%
Background	800	775	96.88%
Total	2400	2360	98.34%

4.2 Experiment Result of Vehicle Detection

The four-layer convolution neural vehicle detection network is based on the four-layer convolution neural network. First, to extract the feature by using the four-layer convolution neural network in previous experiment. Then, selecting different feature layers to set the bounding box. For each bounding box, the calculation of the position error and the category error ultimately determine the position of the vehicle in the picture. When using the basic network, it is necessary to modify the basic network. The last two fully connected layers of the network are all transformed into a convolution layer. Through this operation, all the final connection layer data can be transformed into a feature map for presetting the bounding box. At the same time, to delete the original network loss layer and accuracy layer.

We select the conv4 layer, fc1 layer and the fc2 layer to set the bounding box. The bounding box size is set, as shown in Table 5. The network is trained on the vehicle test set. The training set consists 5639 images while the test set consists 1377 pictures. The final test results of the network mAP is 72.39%.

Table 5. Four-layer convolution neural network's bounding box parameter setting.

Layer	Size of feature map	The original map area	The size of bounding box
Conv4	38×38	8×8	$30 \times 30, 42 \times 21, 21 \times 42$
Fc1	19×19	16×16	$60 \times 60, 83 \times 83, 84 \times 42$ $42 \times 84, 104 \times 35, 35 \times 104$
Fc2	19×19	16×16	$60 \times 60, 83 \times 83, 84 \times 42$ $42 \times 84, 104 \times 35, 35 \times 104$

But for multi-label network, we expand the four-layer convolution neural vehicle detection network with another MultiBoxLoss layer to train two kinds of label of the vehicles. One mulitiBoxLoss layer is used to train vehicle orientation set while another is used to train vehicle type set. The bounding box setting is the same as the four-layer convolution neural vehicle detection network.

When testing the multi-label network, we first obtain the detection results of vehicle orientation. Then comparing the detection results of vehicle type with the obtained results, find the vehicle type of the bounding box where vehicle orientation is ensured. The test results of the multi-label network mAP is 77.39%. Figure 5 shows some of the picture test results.

Fig. 5. Testing results of multi-label vehicle detection network.

The comparing result is shown in Table 6. It can be concluded that the SSD network can achieve good vehicle detection effect for the data set recorded by the car camera, but the simple convolution neural network structure can achieve the same vehicle detection effect, while spending less on time costs. In the situation of the same detection effect, the four-layer convolution neural network constructed in this paper can identify the image faster because of its simple network structure and lower complexity calculation. The mAP value recognized by ResNet18 network is not high, and the reason is there are more error recognition objects. At the same time, as ResNet18 network structure is deep, the calculation complexity of the network weight updating is greater, resulting in the longer time taken to detect the picture.

Table 6. The accuracy of each label in vehicle type dataset for multi-label classification network model.

Basic network	mAP(%)
Four-layer convolution neural network	72.39
Four − layerconvolutionneuralnetwork (Multi − label)	**77.31**
VGG16(SSD)	75.14
ResNet18	74.24

In conclusion, to detect objects in the case of different situations, the network layer is not the deeper the better, but it depends on the contents of the dataset and detection requirements. If we need faster detection speed, we can use the lower convolution neural network to achieve detection. Moreover, if we need a higher accuracy, then a deeper network can be used to achieve our goals. Besides, training network with multi-label tasks can make the network work better in each task.

5   Conclusion

This paper mainly discuss about the multi-label vehicle detection network. First, a vehicle classification network is needed and it is designed as a basis network of vehicle detection and recognition network. We use four-layer convolution neural network as classification network. Small size network can reach the same accuracy as VGG net but has a higher speed than it. Next, we expand the classification network and obtain a multi-label classification network in order to meet the needs while driving. Last, we expand the multi-label classification network and obtain the multi-label vehicle detection network. From the results, training two categories on one network at same time can not only save time, but also make the network converge faster and achieve higher accuracy. So for multi-task detection, multi-label network can be considered to achieve better result.

References

1. Ciregan, D., Meier, U., Schmidhuber, J.: Multi-column deep neural networks for image classification. In: 2012 IEEE Conference on Computer Vision and Pattern Recognition, pp. 3642–3649, June 2012
2. Ciresan, D.C., Meier, U., Masci, J., Gambardella, L.M., Schmidhuber, J.: Flexible, high performance convolutional neural networks for image classification, pp. 1237–1242, July 2011
3. Dalal, N., Triggs, B.: Histograms of oriented gradients for human detection. In: 2005 IEEE Computer Society Conference on Computer Vision and Pattern Recognition (CVPR 2005), vol. 1, pp. 886–893, June 2005
4. Donahue, J., et al.: DeCAF: a deep convolutional activation feature for generic visual recognition, pp. 647–655 (2014)
5. Forsyth, D.: Object detection with discriminatively trained part-based models. Computer 47(02), 6–7 (2014)
6. Hu, Y., et al.: Algorithm for vision-based vehicle detection and classification, pp. 568–572, December 2013
7. Krause, J., Stark, M., Deng, J., Li, F.F.: 3D object representations for fine-grained categorization. In: 2013 IEEE International Conference on Computer Vision Workshops, pp. 554–561, December 2013
8. Krizhevsky, A., Sutskever, I., Hinton, G.E.: ImageNet classification with deep convolutional neural networks. Neural Inf. Process. Syst. 25, 1097–1105 (2012)
9. Lawrence, S., Giles, C.L., Tsoi, A.C., Back, A.D.: Face recognition: a convolutional neural-network approach. IEEE Trans. Neural Networks 8(1), 98–113 (1997)

10. Ren, S., He, K., Ross, G., Sun, J.: Faster R-CNN: towards real-time object detection with region proposal networks. IEEE Trans. Pattern Anal. Mach. Intell. **39**, 91–99 (2015)
11. Sarfraz, M.S., Saeed, A., Haris Khan, M., Zahid, R.: Bayesian prior models for vehicle make and model recognition, p. 35, January 2009
12. Shams, F.: Joint deep learning for car detection, December 2014
13. Vojislav, K.: Learning and soft Computing: Support Vector Machines, Neural Networks and Fuzzy Logic Models. MIT Press, Cambridge (2001)
14. Zhang, F., Xu, X., Qiao, Y.: Deep classification of vehicle makers and models: the effectiveness of pre-training and data enhancement. In: 2015 IEEE International Conference on Robotics and Biomimetics (ROBIO), pp. 231–236, December 2015

Industrial Internet of Things Interoperability Between OPC UA and OneM2M

Po-Wen Lai and Fuchun Joseph Lin[✉]

Department of Computer Science, College of Computer Science,
National Chiao Tung University, Hsinchu, Taiwan
{eric4025.cs05g,fjlin}@nctu.edu.tw

Abstract. With the emergence of the Industrial Internet of Things (IIoT), a huge amount of devices in the factory need be connected to the Internet. The use cases being considered include data exchange for inter-factory manufacturing, integrity of data collection and real-time monitoring, etc. It is important to allow seamless communications among IIoT devices of different protocols and standards. In this research, we investigate how to achieve IIoT interoperability via two popular global IIoT standards: oneM2M and OPC-UA by adopting the OPC-UA system in the field domain but connecting it to the oneM2M system in the infrastructure domain. We propose an optimized design of oneM2M Interworking Proxy Entity for resources mapping and procedures mapping between OPC-UA and oneM2M. The design contains both (1) interworking functions and (2) OPC-UA client APP, installed on the oneM2M Middle Node in the field domain, to handle the data exchange.

Keywords: OPC UA · oneM2M · Interoperability

1 Introduction

The Industrial Internet of Things (IIoT) is emerging in recent years with a huge amount of devices in the factory connected to the Internet [1–3]. The use cases being considered include data exchange for inter-factory manufacturing [4–6], integrity of data collection, real time monitoring [7–9], etc. It is important to allow seamless communications among IIoT devices with different protocols and standards.

There has been a large amount of existing research on interoperability between different protocols and standards for the Internet of Things [10–13]. However, many issues still remain about how to achieve interoperability between different IoT systems and protocols. In this research, we investigate how to achieve IIoT interoperability via two popular global IIoT standards: oneM2M and OPC-UA by adopting the OPC-UA system in the field domain but connecting it to the oneM2M system in the infrastructure domain.

The oneM2M standards already have published a technical report [14] to define the interoperability between OPC UA and oneM2M. However, many details are yet to be specified; thus more research is needed to clarify those details. Our key contribution in

© ICST Institute for Computer Sciences, Social Informatics and Telecommunications Engineering 2020
Published by Springer Nature Switzerland AG 2020. All Rights Reserved
B. Li et al. (Eds.): IoTaaS 2019, LNICST 316, pp. 439–455, 2020.
https://doi.org/10.1007/978-3-030-44751-9_37

this research includes (1) proposing a new design of IPE beyond what oneM2M specified to improve the system performance, (2) quantitatively evaluating the improvement of the new design over the oneM2M specified one by measuring the time taken in each interworking step.

The rest of this paper is organized as follows. The OPC UA and oneM2M architectures are first introduced in Sect. 2. Section 3 discusses two design alternatives of IPE: oneM2M specified one and our proposed one. Section 4 then describes the implementation and verification of each. Finally, Sect. 5 discusses our conclusion and future work.

2 Background

We first introduce OPC UA and oneM2M architectures.

2.1 OneM2M Architecture

As shown in Fig. 1, the oneM2M architecture comprises three entities:

1. *Application Entity (AE):* Application Entity is an entity that implements an M2M application service logic. Examples of AEs include remote monitoring application, machinery controlling application and power metering application.
2. *Common Service Entity (CSE):* Common Service Entity is an entity that represents a set of "common service functions" which are defined by oneM2M. Examples of common service functions include device management, group management and communication management.
3. *Network Services Entity (NSE):* Underlying Network Services Entity is an entity that provides the underlying network services to the CSEs.

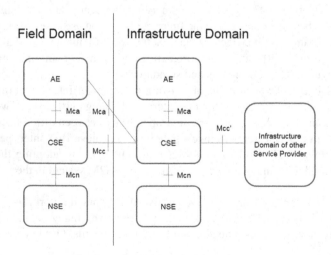

Fig. 1. oneM2M functional architecture

The communication flow between any two entities above is specified in a reference point. oneM2M reference points include the following:

1. *Mca:* specifies the communication flows between AE and CSE. These flows enable the AE to use the services support by the CSE.
2. *Mcc:* specifies the communication flows between two CSEs. These flows enable a CSE to use the services support by another CSE.
3. *Mcn:* specifies the communication flows between CSE and NSE. These flows enable the CSE to use the services support by the NSE.
4. *Mcc':* specifies the communication flows between two CSEs in different M2M service provider domains in Infrastructure Domain. These flows enable the CSE in Infrastructure Domain to use the services supported by another CSE of a different M2M service provider.

2.2 OPC Unified Architecture

The OPC (Open Platform Communications) Unified Architecture (UA) is a platform independent service-oriented architecture developed by the OPC Foundation that integrates all the functionalities of the individual OPC Classic specifications into one extensible framework [12]. There have been a lot of research focused on the performance of OPC UA [15] and the development of new applications using OPC UA. These new applications include data monitoring [16, 17], industrial automation [18], smart grid [19], etc. [20]. Moreover, interoperability between OPC UA and other standards such as BACnet [21], KNX [22], AutomationML [23], CIM [24], etc. [25, 26] has been extensively studied. This phenomenon shows that OPC UA is a popular standard in the IIoT.

2.3 OPC UA Information Model

OPC UA provides a framework that can be used to represent complex information as Objects in an Address Space which can be accessed with standard web services. Figure 2 shows how OPC UA abstracts real objects in its Address Space. This Address Space is where real objects and their components are abstracted and represented by a set of Nodes and References (the lines between Nodes); the latter are used to relate the nodes in Address Space. A View is a subset of Address Space which is used to restrict the Nodes that the Server makes visible to the Client to simplify data acquisition and control data access in the Server [14]. In summary, Address Space is where OPC-UA Servers keep its collected industrial data.

2.4 OPC UA Resource Mode

OPC UA Clients will communicate with OPC UA Servers to acquire industrial data through Defined Service Sets. All data entities are defined as "object" and located in the OPC UA servers. The OPC UA objects are represented by a set of Nodes that are only accessible through the aforementioned Address Space. Hence whenever OPC UA Clients want to browse the industrial data, they would access the Nodes in the Address Space of an OPC UA Server [14].

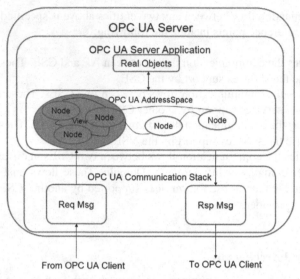

Fig. 2. OPC UA address space

3   Design of OPC UA-oneM2M Interworking IPE

In this section, we discuss the details of resource mapping and procedure mapping between OPC UA and oneM2M.

3.1   Resource Model Mapping

When the data transfer occurs between OPC UA and oneM2M, IPE should create a oneM2M <AE> resource to represent OPC UA <Root> node and map other nodes under <Root> node to the oneM2M <container> resources. An example of mapping the OPC UA resource model to the oneM2M resource tree is depicted in Fig. 3.

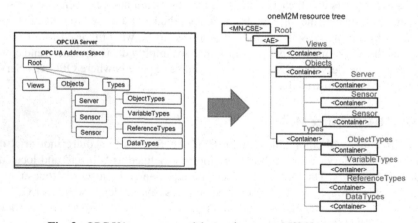

Fig. 3. OPC UA resource model mapping to oneM2M resource tree

In IIoT, there are many sensors deployed in the factory. Thus, many resources will be created in the resource model. Our goal is to design a resource structure with as minimum memory usage as possible. In [14], oneM2M recommends the use of <flexContainer> for mapping the OPC UA data to the oneM2M resource. In our approach, we use <container>/<contentInstance> instead of <flexContainer> to map the nodes under the Root of OPC UA because <container>/<contentInstance> is more suitable for our scenario. For example, if there are 10 nodes under the Root of OPC UA, according to the oneM2M specification we need to create 10 <flexContainer>'s to represent those nodes. In our approach, we use one <container> and 10 <contentInstance>'s instead of 10 <flexContainer>'s. Compared to 10 <flexContainer>'s, our approach of one <container> and 10 <contentInstance>'s uses less memory on IPE.

3.2 Procedure Mapping

The procedures of data handling in OPC UA and oneM2M are different. IPE is designed to assist OPC UA and oneM2M applications in exchanging data or requests. The concept of procedure mapping via oneM2M IPE is proposed in [14]. Nevertheless, we improve oneM2M recommendations with an optimized IPE design. To analyze the performance of both mapping methods: (1) oneM2M Specified Design of IPE and (2) Our Proposed Optimized Design of IPE, we implemented both data exchange procedures between OPC UA and oneM2M. Both methods can process data exchange successfully but exhibit different performance. In this section, we describe the details of each method. We then compare their performance in the next section.

1. *OneM2M Specified Design of IPE:* The design includes four procedures: initialization and discovery, reading, subscription and notification.

   A. *Initialization and Discovery:* To interwork with OPC UA, oneM2M needs to establish a communication session at the beginning, and represent OPC-UA device data as oneM2M resources. To achieve these objectives, the initialization and discovery procedures are proposed in oneM2M recommendations. In the initialization stage, IPE will be installed on the oneM2M MN in the field domain. In the discovery stage, IPE will connect with OPC UA devices through the OPC UA discovery mechanism and follow the mapping rules to map OPC-UA resources to oneM2M resources. As depicted in Fig. 4, the steps in the initialization and discovery procedures are:

      i. Install IPE on MN first.
      ii. After that, IPE can discover OPC UA devices utilizing OPC UA discovery mechanisms.
      iii. Map the resource on OPC UA Server to oneM2M.

   B. *Reading:* For data collection, one way to collect data from OPC UA devices is to send a <Retrieve> request from the originator AE to an OPC UA device. IPE will then translate this oneM2M <Retrieve> request to the OPC UA "Read" message in order to get data from OPC UA devices. As shown in Fig. 5, the steps in the reading procedure are:

i. The originator AE will first send the Retrieve message to IN-CSE.
ii. IN-CSE forwards the Retrieve message to MN-CSE.
iii. MN-CSE reaches IPE to map the Retrieve message to the OPC UA "Read" message.
iv. Finally, IPE will get the required data by the "Read" message.

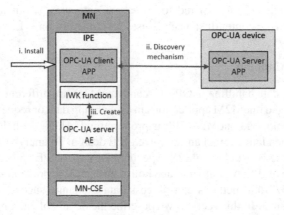

Fig. 4. Initialization and discovery procedure in non-optimized design

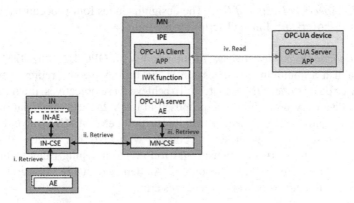

Fig. 5. Reading procedure in non-optimized design

C. *Subscription:* Another way to collect data is to use the oneM2M subscription mechanism to get notification on the change of the corresponding OPC UA resources in the address space. As shown in Fig. 6, the steps in the subscription procedure are:

i. IPE will create a subscribed-to resource for getting notifications about incoming subscription requests.

    ii. IN-CSE sends a Create request of <subscription> resource targeting at the resource under an OPC UA server AE in MN-CSE.

   iii. MN-CSE will reply a Create response message to the IN-CSE.

   iv. MN-CSE sends a Notify request message to IPE.

    v. IPE will map the Notify request message to the OPC UA Server.

   vi. When OPC UA Server APP receives this message, OPC UA Server APP will send OPC UA Client a Subscription Response message.

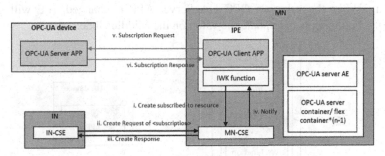

Fig. 6. Subscription procedure in non-optimized design

D. *Notification:* As shown in Fig. 7, the steps in the notification procedure are:

    i. Whenever there is an update, OPC UA Server APP will send OPC UA Client APP a notification message.

   ii. IPE will map the OPC UA notification message to an Update Request message to MN-CSE.

   iii. After receiving the message, MN-CSE will send Notify to IN-CSE.

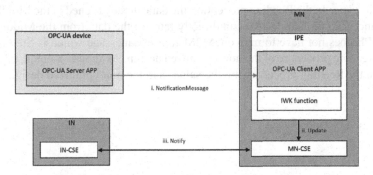

Fig. 7. Notification procedure in non-optimized design

2. *Our Proposed Optimized Design of IPE:* Compared to the oneM2M specified design of IPE, the optimized design of IPE reduces the message exchanges between IPE and the OPC UA device by caching data in the Middle Node to improve system response time. The differences between two designs are described below.

A. *Initialization and Discovery:* In the Initialization and Discovery procedure, besides the steps in the Initialization and Discovery procedure in oneM2M Non-Optimized Design of IPE, there are two more steps need to be executed as shown in Fig. 8:

   i. After IPE maps the resource on OPC UA Server to oneM2M, IPE needs to subscribes to the resource on OPC UA Server APP to keep the data up to date.

   ii. When the value on OPC UA Server APP is changed, IPE will get the notification and update the value on the Middle Node.

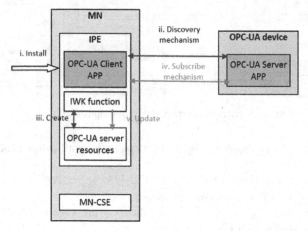

Fig. 8. Initialization and discovery procedure in optimized design

B. *Reading:* In the Reading procedure, the data already cached in the Middle Node and is up to date. IN AE can directly retrieve the data from the Middle Node, IPE does not have to map oneM2M Retrieve message which is Step iv in the Reading procedure of the non-optimized design. As shown in Fig. 9, other steps in the Reading procedure are the same as in the non-optimized design.

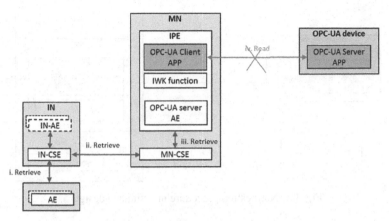

Fig. 9. Reading procedure in optimized design

C. *Subscription:* In the Subscribe procedure, we already do the subscription in the Initialization and Discovery procedure, so IPE does not need to create a subscribed-to resource and receive Notify request in order to map to the OPC-UA subscribe request which are Steps i, iv, v and vi in the Subscribe procedure of the non-optimized design. As shown in Fig. 10, other steps in the Subscribe procedure are the same as in the non-optimized design.

D. *Notification:* In the Notification procedure, we already do the update in the Initialization and Discovery procedure, so IPE does not need to map Notification message to an Update message which are Steps i and ii in the Notification procedure of the non-optimized design. As shown in Fig. 11, other steps in the Notify procedure are the same as in the non-optimized design.

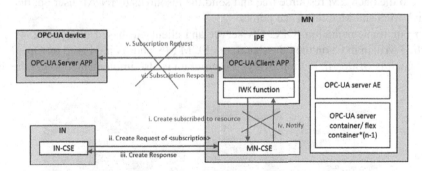

Fig. 10. Subscription procedure in optimized design

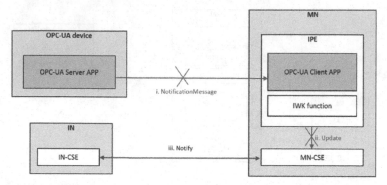

Fig. 11. Notification procedure in optimized design

4 Detailed Design and Implementation

In this section, the system implementation is explained first. Then, we describe the testing environment. Next, we show our experimental results. Finally, the testing result is analyzed.

4.1 System Implementation

Figure 12 depicts the system architecture for handling data exchange based on the scenario addressed by this research. In this system, sensors will collect the data from the environment and send the data to the OPC UA Server residing in a Raspberry Pi. OPC UA Server then sends data to OPC UA Client in the IPE on a laptop computer through the OPC UA interface. The IWK (Interworking) functions in IPE will map OPC UA data into the oneM2M resource tree and send the resources to IN-AE user applications through Mca and Mcc reference points.

In our implementation, OPC UA server and client are based on open62541 [27] which is written in C; on the other hand, oneM2M MN and IN are based on OpenMTC [28] which is written in Python. A Python program is also implemented to get the data

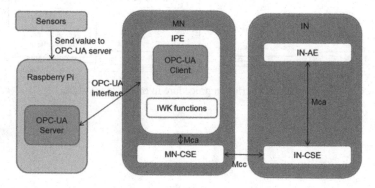

Fig. 12. System architecture design

out of the sensors. Thus we need to deal with data transmission from Python to C and from C to Python: When the sensors get the data, a Python program will store those data into a file, OPC UA Server can get the data by reading the file and manage the resource. After OPC UA Client gets the data from OPC UA Server through OPC UA interface, it will store the data into another file. IWK functions which are written in python will then get the data from this file to do the mapping procedures. After that, the data can be transmitted through Mca and Mcc reference points to the oneM2M application using RESTful communications.

In OPC UA Server, we use the functions which are provided by open62541 to create, update and transmit the data to OPC UA client. In the OPC UA client, we also use the functions provided by open62541 to subscribe the resource and send the request back to the OPC UA Server. In the IWK function, we use RESTful APIs to handle the resource in MN to fulfill the demand of mapping.

4.2 Testing Environment

Figure 13 depicts the testing environment for this research. We used a Raspberry Pi installed with OPC-UA Server APP to represent an OPC UA device that can collect the temperature and humidity data in the factory. The collected data then is sent to OPC-UA Client APP installed with the IPE. With the interworking functions in IPE, OPC-UA data can be converted to oneM2M data, then sent to oneM2M APP by OpenMTC for remote monitoring. For example, if the temperature is detected too high, oneM2M APP can send a request to turn on the fan in the factory.

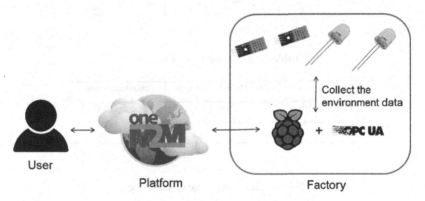

User   Platform   Factory

Collect the environment data

Fig. 13. Use case of system

4.3 Testing Results

We measure the response time of each step described in Sect. 3 to get the overall response time of a procedure under two designs. Each response time is calculated from the average of the measurements collected from 10 executions of the procedure. Besides the response time, we also count the lines of source code to estimate the cost of each system.

1. *Response time:* Table 1 shows the response times of two designs in the Initialization and Discovery procedure. If the time required for a particular step is not included in the overall response time, it will be marked with a diagonal. Table 2 shows the response times of two designs in the Reading procedure. Steps i, ii and iii compose a complete retrieve request from IN to MN. Table 3 shows the response times of two designs in the Subscribe procedure. Steps ii and iii are the request and the response of Subscribe between IN and MN. Steps v and vi are the request and the response of Subscribe between OPC UA server and client. Table 4 shows the response times of two designs in the Notify procedure. Table 5 shows the overall response times of two designs without transmission overhead. The response time of each procedure is the sum of the response times of all its steps. Table 6 shows the overall response times of two designs with transmission overhead. The response time of each procedure is the time consumed from the start to the end of each procedure including the delay of data transmission.

Table 1. Response time of initialization and discovery

	Non-Optimized Design	*Optimized Design*
Step i		
Step ii	622(ms)	Same as left field
Step iii	30(ms)	Same as left field
Step iv		55(ms)
Step v		

Table 2. Response time of reading

	Non-Optimized Design	*Optimized Design*
Step i&ii&iii	2(ms)	Same as left field
Step iv	29(ms)	

Table 3. Response time of subscribe

	Non-Optimized Design	*Optimized Design*
Step i	3(ms)	
Step ii&iii	7(ms)	Same as left field
Step iv	2(ms)	
Step v&vi	55(ms)	

Table 4. Response time of notify

	Non-Optimized Design	Optimized Design
Step i	54(ms)	
Step ii	8(ms)	
Step iii	2(ms)	Same as left field

2. *Source Line of Code:* We count the lines of source code in IPE which is composed of OPC UA Client and IWK functions to estimate the cost of our system. Table 7 shows the lines of source code in OPC UA Client and IWK functions in the non-optimized and the optimized systems, respectively, to indicate the complexity of each design.

Table 5. Overall response time (without transmission overhead)

Procedure	Non-optimized design	Optimized design
Initialization and discovery	652 (ms)	707 (ms)
Reading	31 (ms)	2 (ms)
Subscribe	67 (ms)	7 (ms)
Notify	64 (ms)	2 (ms)

Table 6. Overall response time (without transmission overhead)

Procedure	Non-optimized design	Optimized design
Initialization and discovery	674 (ms)	738 (ms)
Reading	33 (ms)	2 (ms)
Subscribe	73 (ms)	9 (ms)
Notify	68 (ms)	3 (ms)

Table 7. Source lines of code

	Non-optimized design	Optimized design
OPC UA client	240 (lines)	215 (lines)
IWK functions	121 (lines)	104 (lines)

4.4 Testing Result Analysis

The results show that all procedures of our proposed method have better response times except the Initialization and Discovery procedure because two new steps need to be added. Comparing the different steps between the optimized design and the non-optimized one, we find that most of message exchanges between IPE and the OPC UA device are removed under the optimized design without adding any new steps. Consequently, the optimized design is able to provide shorter response time.

The results of the overall response time without transmission overhead and the one with transmission overhead are about the same. This leads us to conclude that the transmission overhead does not significantly affect the overall response time. The difference of response times between two designs is primarily caused by the different numbers of message exchanges between IPE and the OPC UA device.

This research focuses on industrial IoT applications such as remote monitoring, controlling application and power metering application. As these applications require real-time processing for all incoming data, it is important to quickly respond. Consequently, our evaluation focuses mostly in the response time with an objective of shortening the response time of the system as much as possible. Therefore, we don't consider throughput, the usage of memory and CPU, or the power consumption of the system in our analysis.

We also count the lines of source code in two designs in order to estimate their complexity of software implementation. The results show that the lines of source code for the optimized design is also less than that of the non-optimized design. The reduction of complexity in the optimized design comes from the removal of some steps from the non-optimized design. Consequently, the optimized design is able to provide better software complexity than the non-optimized design.

In summary, by reducing the number of message exchanges between IPE and the OPC UA device, not only the response time of our proposed design is much faster than that of a non-optimized design, its software complexity is also improved over the non-optimized design.

5 Conclusion and Future Work

We propose an optimized IPE design to improve IIoT interoperability between oneM2M and OPC UA for the scenario where an OPC-UA system is in the field domain and oneM2M is in the infrastructure domain. For resource mapping, a new mapping method for oneM2M and OPC UA is proposed. For procedure mapping, we also propose new procedures by removing some procedural steps and thus reducing the overall response times.

To verify our optimized design, we tested our system based on a use case that simulates the scenario of data collection in the factory. In this environment, there will be many devices with different standards. Consequently, a generic standard such as oneM2M could be very useful. To achieve interoperability, we just need to make every devices communicate with oneM2M.

Our test system employs a Raspberry Pi installed with OPC-UA Server APP to represent a non-oneM2M device in the factory, designed for collecting the temperature and humidity in the room. This data is sent to OPC-UA Client APP installed in the IPE of a oneM2M Middle Node. The interworking function in the IPE then converts this OPC-UA data to oneM2M data. Finally, this data is sent to oneM2M APP by OpenMTC for remote monitoring.

As shown in the result analysis, comparing to the original oneM2M design, our optimized design improves the performance when using oneM2M in the infrastructure domain and an OPC-UA system in the field domain to collect data.

In conclusion, we propose two mapping methods which are different from the recommendation of oneM2M for resource mapping and procedure mapping, respectively. According to the result analysis, our approach improves the performance of the system where oneM2M is used in the infrastructure domain while OPC-UA is deployed in the field domain.

In our design, because the data need to be kept up to date in MN, this implies that the data need to be constantly retrieved from OPC UA devices; such operations will be costly. Also, the situation of race condition may occur which would lead to out of date data. According to the issues above, our proposed approach is more suitable for the scenario where the cost of constant data update is affordable and the race condition is acceptable.

Though the optimized design is suitable for our scenario, it may not have better performance than the original oneM2M design for other scenarios. Different resource and procedure mapping methods may be required for those other scenarios. Also, we only test our test environment with few devices, the testing scenario with a large amount of OPC UA devices should be considered for future work.

Moreover, more efficient mapping methods for other scenarios can be developed by building a test environment for each scenario. Also, the solutions of cost reduction and race condition avoidance as discussed above can be explored.

Acknowledgement. This study is conducted under the "Open Service Platform of Hybrid Networks and Intelligent Low-carbon Application Technology Project(4/4)" of the Institute for Information Industry which is subsidized by the Ministry of Economic Affairs of the Republic of China.

References

1. Derhamy, H., Eliasson, J., Delsing, J., Priller, P.: A survey of commercial frameworks for the Internet of Things. In: IEEE International Conference on Emerging Technologies and Factory Automation (EFTA) (2015)
2. Gazis, V., et al.: A survey of technologies for the Internet of Things. In: Proceedings of the International Wireless Communications and Mobile Computing Conference (IWCMC), August 2015, pp. 1090–1095 (2015)
3. Kim, J., Lee, J., Kim, J., Yun, J.: M2M service platforms: survey, issues, and enabling technologies. IEEE Commun. Surv. Tutor. **16**(1), 61–76 (2014)
4. Jung, J., et al.: Design of smart factory web services based on the industrial Internet of Things. In: Proceedings of the 50th Hawaii International Conference on System Sciences (2017)
5. De Brito, M.S., Hoque, S., Steinke, R., Willner, A.: Towards programmable fog nodes in smart factories. In: IEEE International Workshops on Foundations and Applications of Self* Systems, pp. 236–241. IEEE, September 2016

6. Lee, A., Lastra, J.: Data aggregation at field device level for industrial ambient monitoring using web services. In: 9th IEEE International Conference on Industrial Informatics (INDIN), July 2011, pp. 491–496 (2011)
7. Granzer, W., Kastner, W.: Information modeling in heterogeneous building automation systems. In: Proceedings of the 9th IEEE International Workshop on Factory Communication Systems (WFCS), Lemgo, 21–24 May 2012, pp. 291–300 (2012)
8. Schachinger, D., Kastner, W.: Model-driven integration of building automation systems into Web service gateways. In: 2015 IEEE World Conference on Factory Communication Systems (WFCS). IEEE (2015)
9. Komoda, N.: Service oriented architecture (SOA) in industrial systems. In: Proceedings of the IEEE International Conference on Industrial Informatics, August 2006, pp. 1–5 (2006)
10. Derhamy, H., Eliasson, J., Delsing, J.: IoT interoperability – on demand and low latency transparent multi-protocol translator. Trans. Serv. Comput. (2016)
11. Castellani, A.P., Loreto, S., Bui, N., Zorzi, M.: Quickly interoperable Internet of Things using simple transparent gateways. In: Interconnecting Smart Objects with the Internet Workshop, 25 March 2011 (2011)
12. Delsing, J., Rosenqvist, F., Carlsson, O., Colombo, A., Bangemann, T.: Migration of industrial process control systems into service oriented architecture. In: 38th Annual Conference on IEEE Industrial Electronics Society, IECON 2012, Montreal, Canada, 25–28 October 2012, pp. 5786–5792 (2012). https://doi.org/10.1109/iecon.2012.6389039
13. Wu, C.-W., Lin, F.J., Wang, C.-H., Chang, N.: OneM2M-based IoT protocol integration. In: IEEE Conference on Standards for Communications & Networking, Helsinki, Finland, 18–20 September 2017 (2017)
14. oneM2M, TR-0018 V2.5.0: Industrial Domain Enablement (2017)
15. Cavalieri, S., Cutuli, G.: Performance evaluation of OPC UA. In: Emerging Technologies and Factory Automation (ETFA), p. 18 (2010)
16. Verma, N.K., Sharma, T., Maurya, S., Singh, D.J., Salour, A.: Real-time monitoring of machines using open platform communication. In: 2017 IEEE International Conference on Prognostics and Health Management (ICPHM), pp. 124–129. IEEE, June 2017
17. Hästbacka, D., Barna, L., Karaila, M., Liang, Y., Tuominen, P., Kuikka, S.: Device status information service architecture for condition monitoring using OPC UA. In: 2014 IEEE Emerging Technology and Factory Automation (ETFA), pp. 1–7. IEEE, September 2014
18. Palm, F., Grüner, S., Pfrommer, J., Graube, M., Urbas, L.: Open source as enabler for OPC UA in industrial automation. In: 2015 IEEE 20th Conference on Emerging Technologies & Factory Automation (ETFA), Luxembourg, pp. 1–6 (2015)
19. Claassen, A., Rohjans, S., Lehnhoff, S.: Application of the OPC UA for the smart grid. In: 2011 2nd IEEE PES International Conference and Exhibition on Innovative Smart Grid Technologies (ISGT Europe), pp. 1–8. IEEE (2011)
20. Melik-Merkumians, M., Baier, T., Steinegger, M., Lepuschitz, W., Hegny, I., Zoitl, A.: Towards OPC UA as portable SOA middleware between control software and external added value applications. In: 17th IEEE Conference on Emerging Technologies Factory Automation (ETFA), September 2012, pp. 1–8 (2012)
21. Fernbach, A., Granzer, W., Kastner, W.: Interoperability at the management level of building automation systems: a case study for BACnet and OPC UA. In: 2011 IEEE 16th Conference on Emerging Technologies Factory Automation (ETFA), September 2011, pp. 1–8 (2011)
22. Cavalieri, S., Chiacchio, F., Di Savia Puglisi, A.: Integrating KNX and OPC UA information model. J. Comput. 9(7), 1536–1541 (2014)
23. Henßen, R., Schleipen, M.: Interoperability between OPC UA and AutomationML. Proc. CIRP 25, 297–304 (2014)
24. Kim, J.S., Park, H.J., Choi, S.H.: CIM and OPC-UA based integrated platform development for ensuring interoperability. KEPCO J. Electr. Power Energy 2(2), 233–244 (2016)

25. Cavalieri, S., Di Stefano, D., Salafia, M.G., Scroppo, M.S.: Integration of OPC UA into a web-based platform to enhance interoperability. In: 2017 IEEE 26th International Symposium on Industrial Electronics (ISIE), pp. 1206–1211. IEEE, June 2017
26. Gruner, S., Pfrommer, J., Palm, F.: RESTful industrial communication with OPC UA. IEEE Trans. Ind. Informat. **12**(5), 1832–1841 (2016)
27. open62541. https://open62541.org/
28. OpenMTC. https://www.openmtc.org/

Accuracy Analysis on GDOP
of Pseudolite Positioning System Based
on TDOA Technology

Li Li$^{(\boxtimes)}$, Yiqin Cao, and Hongwei Zhao

School of Electronics and Information, Northwestern Polytechnical University,
Xi'an 710072, China
lilinwpu@126.com

Abstract. In the case that the GNSS satellite signal is interfered and
the satellite constellation visibility is affected, an independent pseudolite
navigation and positioning system can be constructed to achieve the positioning operation of the target user. This paper proposes an independent
navigation and positioning system consisting of four pseudolites based
on the principle of Time Difference of Arrival (TDOA). In this paper,
the geometric dilution of precision (GDOP) expression of the positioning
system under the TDOA technology is derived. In view of the influence of
pseudolites geometric layout on GDOP, this paper proposes two layout
schemes, Y-type and T-type, and simulates the distribution of GDOP
values under each layout scheme. After comparing and analyzing the
simulation graphs, it is concluded that the T-shaped geometric layout
can significantly reduce the GDOP value compared with the Y-shaped
layout.

Keywords: Pseudolite · Positioning system · TDOA · GDOP

1 Introduction

The emergence of the Global Navigation Satellite System (GNSS) has driven new
developments in the field of navigation and positioning on the Earth's surface and
near the ground [1]. With the continuous improvement of hardware technology,
GNSS systems have been widely used in geodesy and measurement-oriented
industries [2], including GPS, GLONASS and Chinese Beidou satellite navigation
system (BDS). Since the availability of GNSS systems and the accuracy of the
positioning results depend on the number of visible satellites and the geometric
distribution of the satellites, poor positioning conditions such as indoors, canyons
and underground in which if the user receivers are located, can severely affect
the number and geometry of traceable satellites, and even making the GNSS
system unable to meet the needs of positioning operations. In order to solve
the above problems, the introduction of pseudolite technology can provide new
methods and approaches.

© ICST Institute for Computer Sciences, Social Informatics and Telecommunications Engineering 2020
Published by Springer Nature Switzerland AG 2020. All Rights Reserved
B. Li et al. (Eds.): IoTaaS 2019, LNICST 316, pp. 456–467, 2020.
https://doi.org/10.1007/978-3-030-44751-9_38

Pseudolites are generators that can propagate signals similar to GNSS signals. The simplest form is the GNSS signal generator and transmitter [3]. There are three main modes of operation for pseudolite technology: (a) an enhanced GNSS system based on pseudolite; (b) a completely independent pseudolite navigation and positioning system; (c) a pseudolite-based reverse positioning system [4]. Among them, a pseudolite-based navigation and positioning system, that is, a navigation constellation network composed of a sufficient number of pseudolites, in the case where the GNSS satellite signal is completely obscured by artificial and natural obstacles and GNSS technology cannot be applied for navigation and positioning, can perform independent navigation and positioning operations.

In this paper, a completely independent navigation and positioning system consisting of four pseudolites based on the principle of Time Difference of Arrival (TDOA) is proposed to achieve user receiver positioning in three-dimensional space under the circumstance that the GNSS satellite signal is interfered and the satellite constellation visibility is affected. In addition, this paper deduces the geometric dilution of precision (GDOP) expression of the positioning system based on the TDOA principle, and analyzes the main factors affecting the value of GDOP: time difference measurement accuracy, pseudolite position measurement accuracy and pseudolite geometry layout. In view of the pseudolite geometric layout, this paper proposes two layout schemes, Y-type and T-type, and simulates and analyzes the distribution of GDOP values under each layout scheme.

2 Pseudolite Independent Navigation and Positioning System

The pseudolite independent navigation and positioning system proposed in this paper adopts four pseudolites to form an independent positioning network. Each pseudolite transmits a satellite signal similar to GNSS.

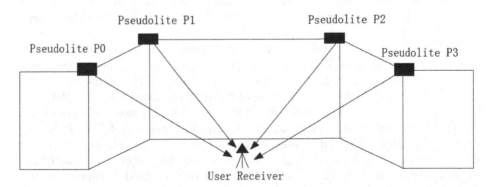

Fig. 1. The independent navigation and positioning system composition with 4 pseudolites.

The user to be located (R_T) receives the pseudolite (P_i, $i = 0, 1, 2, 3$) signal, and the receiver finally solve the three-dimensional position coordinates of its own in three-dimensional space through applying the TDOA positioning principle. The system composition diagram is shown in Fig. 1.

In different practical applications, the specific pseudolite geometric arrangement is also different, but the position information of each pseudolite itself is known in advance.

Compared with GNSS systems, pseudolite positioning systems have the following advantages [5]:

(1) The geometric distribution of the pseudolite can be designed in advance to obtain the best positioning effect.
(2) The position of the pseudolite transmitter can be arbitrarily arranged and changed in a three-dimensional space in which GNSS satellite signal is completely invisible.
(3) The economic cost of pseudolite equipment is relatively low, and a larger number of pseudolites may be considered for further research and improvement of the system.

3   TDOA Positioning Principle

Time Difference of Arrival (TDOA) [6] measures the time data of a signal sent from multiple transmitting terminals in a straight line to the receiving terminal, and obtains the distance differences between each transmitting ends and the receiving end according to the propagation speed of the electromagnetic wave in the air. So that the receiving end is able to be positioned. Considering the geometric space, in the three-dimensional space, the signal time difference between some two transmitting terminals to the receiving end determines a pair of hyperboloids with the two emitting ends as the focus. Therefore the time difference positioning technology is also called hyperbolic positioning technology.

As shown in Fig. 2, the three-dimensional time difference positioning requires at least four transmitting terminals to determine three pairs of hyperboloids, and the positioning of the user receiver is realized by the principle that the surface lines intersect to determine one point.

In this paper, four pseudolites are used to form an independent navigation and positioning system. Figure 3 shows the geometrical diagram of the positioning system. In the three-dimensional space, the position of the user to be located R_T is (x_T, y_T, z_T), the position of the four pseudolites ($P_i, i = 0, 1, 2, 3$) is (x_i, y_i, z_i), $i = 0, 1, 2, 3$, and the time difference TDOA between the pseudolite P_0 received by the user receiver and the remaining three pseudolites P_i is Δt_i, $i = 0, 1, 2, 3$. The distance difference of the user to pseudolite P_0 and to the rest three pseudolites is recorded as Δr, $i = 1, 2, 3$, and the propagation rate of the electromagnetic wave in the air is c, According to the speed distance formula, there are:

$$\Delta r_i = c \times \Delta t_i, i = 1, 2, 3 \tag{1}$$

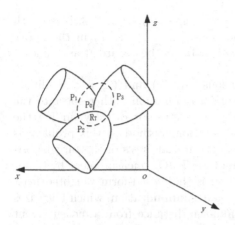

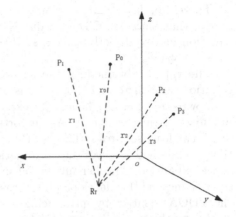

Fig. 2. Principle of three-dimensional time difference positioning.

Fig. 3. Three-dimensional time difference positioning geometry.

According to the geometric principle of three-dimensional space, the linear distance r_i, $i = 0, 1, 2, 3$ of the user to be positioned R_T to the pseudolite P_i and the distance difference between the user to the pseudolite P_0 and the other three pseudolites can be calculated by the following formula:

$$\begin{cases} \Delta r_i = r_i - r_0, i = 1, 2, 3 \\ r_0 = \sqrt{(x_T - x_0)^2 + (y_T - y_0)^2 + (z_T - z_0)^2} \\ r_i = \sqrt{(x_T - x_i)^2 + (y_T - y_i)^2 + (z_T - z_i)^2}, i = 1, 2, 3 \end{cases} \tag{2}$$

The user receiver measures the time difference of arrival (TDOA) value of the transmitted signals of each pseudolite. Then, after substituting the known position information of each pseudolite into formula (1) and formula (2) respectively, a set of equations with three unknown parameters is obtained. The equations are expressed in matrix form as:

$$AX = B \tag{3}$$

where,

$$A = \begin{bmatrix} x_0 - x_1 & y_0 - y_1 & z_0 - z_1 \\ x_0 - x_2 & y_0 - y_2 & z_0 - z_2 \\ x_0 - x_3 & y_0 - y_3 & z_0 - z_3 \end{bmatrix} \tag{4}$$

$$X = \begin{bmatrix} x_T \\ y_T \\ z_T \end{bmatrix} \tag{5}$$

$$B = \begin{bmatrix} r_0 \cdot r_1 + d_1 \\ r_0 \cdot r_2 + d_2 \\ r_0 \cdot r_3 + d_3 \end{bmatrix} \tag{6}$$

Thereinto, $d_i = \frac{1}{2}(\Delta r_i^2 + x_0^2 + y_0^2 + z_0^2 - x_i^2 - y_i^2 - z_i^2), i = 1, 2, 3$. It is worth noting that since the TDOA value is measured, $\Delta r_i(i = 1, 2, 3)$ in the above equation can be directly solved, so $d_i(i = 1, 2, 3)$ can be regarded as a known constant value.

The Eq. (3) obtained by the simultaneous Eqs. (1) and (2) is a nonlinear equation set, where r_i $i = 0, 1, 2, 3$ is a nonlinear function with respect to the unknowns x_T, y_T, z_T, hence the explicit expressions for directly finding the unknowns is more difficult. An important solution method to this problem is nonlinear least squares (NLS) [8]. Based on the initial guess of the target position, the method achieves the linearization of the TDOA measurement by taylor series expansion. Another influential method is the closed-form weighted least squares method [11] developed from least squares minimization, which linearizes the TDOA equation by introducing an unknown distance from a measurement station to the target, improves the positioning accuracy. Besides, methods such as particle filter [12] and maximum likelihood estimation [13] have also been applied to TDOA measurements.

In addition, there are two common methods for user receiver to measure the time difference of arrival of transmit signal of each pseudolite: (a) directly measuring the TOA (Time of Arrival) value of transmit signal of each pseudolite and then obtaining the difference; (b) use the cross-correlation operation technique for each pseudo-satellite signal received to obtain the TDOA value. In order to ensure the positioning accuracy, the former method requires that each pseudolite in the positioning system and the user receiver maintain time synchronization.

4   Analysis for System Positioning Accuracy

The positioning error of the pseudolite independent navigation and positioning system is related to the geometric position of the pseudolite. In order to quantitatively analyze this relationship, a conventional positioning accuracy analysis method is introduced. Define the geometric precision factor GDOP (Geometric Dilution of Precision) to describe the geometric distribution of positioning errors in three-dimensional space. GDOP in three-dimensional space is usually expressed by the following formula:

$$GDOP = \sqrt{\sigma_x^2 + \sigma_y^2 + \sigma_z^2} \tag{7}$$

where, σ_x, σ_y, σ_z respectively indicate the standard deviation of the positioning error in the x, y, and z directions.

For the distance difference $\delta r_i(i = 1, 2, 3)$ in Eq. (2), the differential is obtained:

$$\begin{aligned}
d(\Delta r_i) = &\frac{\partial \Delta r_i}{\partial x_T}dx_T + \frac{\partial \Delta r_i}{\partial y_T}dy_T + \frac{\partial \Delta r_i}{\partial z_T}dz_T \\
&+ \left(\frac{\partial \Delta r_i}{\partial x_0}dx_0 + \frac{\partial \Delta r_i}{\partial y_0}dy_0 + \frac{\partial \Delta r_i}{\partial z_0}dz_0\right) - \left(\frac{\partial \Delta r_i}{\partial x_i}dx_i + \frac{\partial \Delta r_i}{\partial y_i}dy_i + \frac{\partial \Delta r_i}{\partial z_i}dz\right)
\end{aligned} \tag{8}$$

where, $\frac{\partial \Delta r_i}{\partial x_T} = \frac{x_T - x_i}{r_i} - \frac{x_T - x_0}{r_0}$, $\frac{\partial \Delta r_i}{\partial y_T} = \frac{y_T - y_i}{r_i} - \frac{y_T - y_0}{r_0}$, $\frac{\partial \Delta r_i}{\partial z_T} = \frac{z_T - z_i}{r_i} - \frac{z_T - z_0}{r_0}$, $i = 1, 2, 3$, $\frac{\partial \Delta r_i}{\partial x_i} = \frac{x_T - x_i}{r_i}$, $\frac{\partial \Delta r_i}{\partial y_i} = \frac{y_T - y_i}{r_i}$, $\frac{\partial \Delta r_i}{\partial z_i} = \frac{z_T - z_i}{r_i}$, $i = 0, 1, 2, 3$.

To solve for dx_T, dy_T, and dz_T, the Eq. (5) is converted to a matrix form as:

$$dr = Cdx + K_0 ds_0 - K_1 ds_1 - K_2 ds_2 - K_3 ds_3 \tag{9}$$

where: $dr = \begin{bmatrix} d(\Delta r_1) \\ d(\Delta r_2) \\ d(\Delta r_3) \end{bmatrix} = \begin{bmatrix} cd(\Delta t_1) \\ cd(\Delta t_2) \\ cd(\Delta t_3) \end{bmatrix}$, $dx = \begin{bmatrix} dx_T \\ dy_T \\ dz_T \end{bmatrix}$, $ds_i = \begin{bmatrix} dx_i \\ dy_i \\ dz_i \end{bmatrix}$, $i = 0, 1, 2, 3;$

$$C = \begin{bmatrix} \frac{x_T - x_1}{r_1} - \frac{x_T - x_0}{r_0} & \frac{y_T - y_1}{r_1} - \frac{y_T - y_0}{r_0} & \frac{z_T - z_1}{r_1} - \frac{z_T - z_0}{r_0} \\ \frac{x_T - x_2}{r_2} - \frac{x_T - x_0}{r_0} & \frac{y_T - y_2}{r_2} - \frac{y_T - y_0}{r_0} & \frac{z_T - z_2}{r_2} - \frac{z_T - z_0}{r_0} \\ \frac{x_T - x_3}{r_3} - \frac{x_T - x_0}{r_0} & \frac{y_T - y_3}{r_3} - \frac{y_T - y_0}{r_0} & \frac{z_T - z_3}{r_3} - \frac{z_T - z_0}{r_0} \end{bmatrix},$$

$$K_0 = \begin{bmatrix} \frac{x_T - x_0}{r_0} & \frac{y_T - y_0}{r_0} & \frac{z_T - z_0}{r_0} \\ \frac{x_T - x_0}{r_0} & \frac{y_T - y_0}{r_0} & \frac{z_T - z_0}{r_0} \\ \frac{x_T - x_0}{r_0} & \frac{y_T - y_0}{r_0} & \frac{z_T - z_0}{r_0} \end{bmatrix}, \quad K_1 = \begin{bmatrix} \frac{x_T - x_1}{r_1} & \frac{y_T - y_1}{r_1} & \frac{z_T - z_1}{r_1} \\ 0 & 0 & 0 \\ 0 & 0 & 0 \end{bmatrix},$$

$$K_2 = \begin{bmatrix} 0 & 0 & 0 \\ \frac{x_T - x_2}{r_2} & \frac{y_T - y_2}{r_2} & \frac{z_T - z_2}{r_2} \\ 0 & 0 & 0 \end{bmatrix}, \quad K_3 = \begin{bmatrix} 0 & 0 & 0 \\ 0 & 0 & 0 \\ \frac{x_T - x_3}{r_3} & \frac{y_T - y_3}{r_3} & \frac{y_T - y_3}{r_3} \end{bmatrix}.$$

dr in Eq. (6) represents the system measurement error of the TDOA, ds_i represents the measurement error of each pseudo-satellite position information, and dx is the positioning error of the user to be located in the x, y, and z directions. The weighted least squares (WLS) method can be used to solve the positioning error:

$$d\hat{x} = (C^T C)^{-1} C^T (dr + K_1 ds_1 + K_2 ds_2 + K_3 ds_3 - K_0 ds_0) \tag{10}$$

Here let $B = (C^T C)^{-1} \cdot C^T$.

Since the TDOA value of each pseudolite signal measured by user receiver incorporates error, and the error exists in each time difference, hence the measurement error of each $\Delta r_i = c\Delta t_i$ is correlated, and the position measurement error of the pseudolite is irrelevant. Assume that after the system correction, the mean value of the measurement error is zero, and the variance of the pseudo-satellite position measurement error is the same, then the positioning error covariance matrix of the user receiver is as follows:

$$\begin{aligned} P_{d\hat{x}} = Cov(d\hat{x}) &= E[d\hat{x} \cdot d\hat{x}^T] \\ &= B(E[dr \cdot dr^T] + K_1 E[ds_1 \cdot ds_1^T] + K_2 E[ds_2 \cdot ds_2^T] \\ &\quad + K_3 E[ds_3 \cdot ds_3^T] - K_0 E[ds_0 \cdot ds_0^T])B^T \end{aligned} \tag{11}$$

where, $E[dr \cdot dr^T] = \begin{bmatrix} \sigma_{\Delta r_1}^2 & \rho_{12}\sigma_{\Delta r_1}\sigma_{\Delta r_2} & \rho_{13}\sigma_{\Delta r_1}\sigma_{\Delta r_3} \\ \rho_{21}\sigma_{\Delta r_2}\sigma_{\Delta r_1} & \sigma_{\Delta r_2}^2 & \rho_{23}\sigma_{\Delta r_2}\sigma_{\Delta r_3} \\ \rho_{31}\sigma_{\Delta r_3}\sigma_{\Delta r_1} & \rho_{32}\sigma_{\Delta r_3}\sigma_{\Delta r_2} & \sigma_{\Delta r_3}^2 \end{bmatrix},$

$$E[ds_i \cdot ds_i^T] = Cov \left(\begin{bmatrix} dx_i \\ dy_i \\ dz_i \end{bmatrix} \right) = \begin{bmatrix} \sigma_{xi}^2 & 0 & 0 \\ 0 & \sigma_{yi}^2 & 0 \\ 0 & 0 & \sigma_{zi}^2 \end{bmatrix}, i = 0, 1, 2, 3.$$

Thereinto, $\sigma_{\Delta r_i}^2 (i = 0, 1, 2, 3)$ is the variance of the measured distance difference error between pseudolite $P_i(i = 1, 2, 3)$ and pseudolite P_0, and ρ_{ij} is the correlation coefficient of the measured distance difference error between pseudolite $P_i(i = 1, 2, 3)$ and pseudolite P_0:

$$\rho_{ij} = \frac{Cov(\Delta r_{i0}, \Delta r_{j0})}{\sigma_{\Delta r_{i0}} \cdot \sigma_{\Delta r_{j0}}} \tag{12}$$

where, σ_{xi}^2, σ_{yi}^2, and $\sigma_{zi}^2 (i = 0, 1, 2, 3)$ are the variances of the measurement errors of the pseudo-satellite position information in the x, y, and z directions, respectively, and $\sigma_{xi}^2 = \sigma_{yi}^2 = \sigma_{zi}^2$.

Then the positioning error covariance matrix of the user receiver to be located can be written as follows:

$$Cov \left(\begin{bmatrix} dx_T \\ dy_T \\ dz_T \end{bmatrix} \right) = E \left(\begin{bmatrix} dx_T \\ dy_T \\ dz_T \end{bmatrix} \begin{bmatrix} dx_T & dy_T & dz_T \end{bmatrix} \right) = \begin{bmatrix} \sigma_x^2 & 0 & 0 \\ 0 & \sigma_y^2 & 0 \\ 0 & 0 & \sigma_z^2 \end{bmatrix} \tag{13}$$

Therefore, according to the definition of GDOP, the positioning geometric accuracy of the pseudo-satellite independent navigation and positioning system based on the TDOA principle in three-dimensional space can be obtained as: $GDOP = \sqrt{\sigma_x^2 + \sigma_y^2 + \sigma_z^2}$.

It can be seen from the above derivation process that reducing the measurement error variance of the TDOA and the pseudo-satellite position information can reduce the GDOP value, thereby improving the positioning accuracy of the system.

5   Simulation for Positioning Performance

In the above analysis of positioning accuracy, the final expression of the geometric dilution of precision (GDOP) in three-dimensional space shows that the GDOP of the proposed system is related to the accuracy of time difference measurement and the accuracy of pseudo-satellite position measurement. The larger both of the errors, the larger the geometric dilution of precision value, which means that the system positioning performance is worse. In addition, the geometry layout of the four pseudolites has a crucial impact on GDOP. Two kinds of pseudo-satellite layout designs are proposed below, and the GDOP distribution of the two schemes are simulated and analyzed.

Assume that the user receiver is located in a three-dimensional space of 200 m in length, 200 m in width and 10 mm in height, and establish a pseudolite positioning system in this space, setting the standard deviation of the

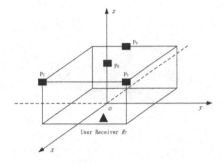

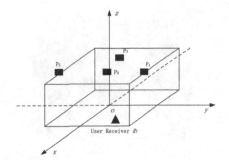

Fig. 4. Four pseudolites in Y-shaped lay-outs.

Fig. 5. Four pseudolite in T-shaped lay-outs.

time difference measurement error to 0.0075, and the standard deviation of the pseudolite absolute position measurement error is 0.5. The correlation coefficient of the measured distance difference error between pseudolite $P_i(i = 1, 2, 3)$ and pseudolite P_0 is 0.35.

The Y-shaped layout scheme is shown in Fig. 4. The three-dimensional Cartesian coordinate system is established based on the geometric center of the bottom surface of the three-dimensional geometric figure. The coordinate information of the set pseudolite $P_i(i = 0, 1, 2, 3)$ is $(0, 0, 10)$, $(100, 100, 10)$, $(100, -100, 10)$, $(-100, 0, 10)$ in turn; And assume that the user is in the horizontal plane of $z = 0$. The corresponding GDOP distribution map under this layout scheme is shown in Figs. 6 and 7.

Under the same assumptions, the T-shaped layout scheme is shown in Fig. 5. The coordinate information of the set pseudolite $P_i(i = 0, 1, 2, 3)$ is $(60, 0, 10)$, $(60, 100, 10)$, $(60, -100, 10)$, $(-60, 0, 10)$ in turn; Also assume that the user is in the horizontal plane of $z = 0$. The corresponding GDOP distribution map under this layout scheme is shown in Figs. 8 and 9.

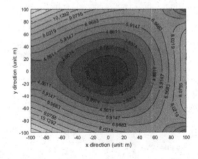

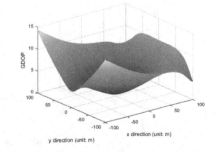

Fig. 6. GDOP contour map in Y-shaped layout.

Fig. 7. GDOP distribution in Y-shaped layout.

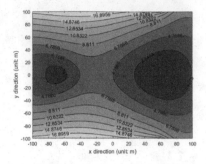

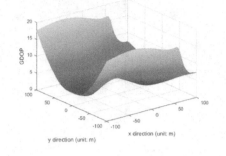

Fig. 8. GDOP contour map in T-shaped layout.

Fig. 9. GDOP distribution in T-shaped layout.

Observing Figs. 6, 7, 8 and 9, it can be seen that the GDOP contour map in Y-shaped layout is more uniform than that in T-shaped layout, and in the lower contour level, the overall growth rate of the GDOP value in the Y-shaped layout is larger than that of the T-type. When the GDOP value is less than 5, there are two parts of the contour line of the same level in the distribution map of the T-type scheme, indicating that the area with the same positioning accuracy is larger under the T-shaped layout than the Y-type scheme.

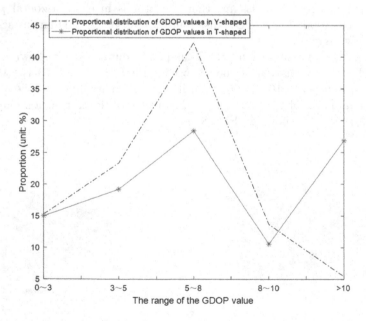

Fig. 10. Proportional distribution of GDOP values in Y-shaped and T-shaped layouts. (Color figure online)

Figure 10 shows the GDOP proportional distribution for the two layouts. The horizontal coordinate represents the range of the GDOP value in the order of 0 to 3, 3 to 5, 5 to 8, 8 to 10, and greater than 10. The blue polyline represents the proportion of the GDOP value of each point in the three-dimensional space in the Y-shaped layout, and the red polyline represents the proportion of the T-shaped layout.

Observing Fig. 10, the ratio of GDOP less than 3 is basically equal in the two layout distribution schemes, and the proportion of GDOP values in the interval of 3 to 8 in the T-shaped layout is significantly smaller than that in the Y-shaped layout, and the proportion of GDOP greater than 10 in the T-shaped layout is relatively large, reflecting the inferiority of this layout scheme. The GDOP values of each point in the Y-shaped layout are concentrated in the interval of 3–8, and the proportion of more than 10 is extremely small, indicating that the pseudo-satellite system in the Y-model has better positioning performance for the user receiver in the three-dimensional space.

It can be seen that in the pseudo-satellite independent positioning system based on the TDOA principle, a better pseudo-satellite layout scheme can significantly reduce the value of geometric dilution of precision(GDOP), thereby achieving more accurate positioning. Different geometric layouts have different advantages and disadvantages, hence it should be designed according to actual needs.

6 Analysis for Factors Affecting Positioning Accuracy

This paper makes assumptions based on the conventional pseudolites placement position height and arrangement spacing, and the four pseudolites positioning system based on TDOA technology is designed.

Next, the influence of the time measurement accuracy and the pseudolites position measurement accuracy on the final user receiver positioning accuracy will be discussed.

Assume that the timie measurement error is increased to 100 ns, the pseudo-satellite position measurement error is not considered, and the GDOP simulation of Y-shaped distribution is obtained as shown in Fig. 12.

Assume that the timie measurement error is still 50 ns, increase the pseudolite position measurement error to 10 m, and obtain the GDOP simulation diagram of Y-shaped distribution as shown in Fig. 11.

Comparing Figs. 11, 12 with Figs. 6, 7, it can be observed that:

(1) After the time measurement error increases from 50 ns to 100 ns, the GDOP increases from 3.7 to 3.9 in the range of −40 to 40 m;
(2) When the pseudolite position error is increased to 10 m, the GDOP positioning accuracy in the same range is increased from 3.7 to 6.8;
(3) The time measurement accuracy and pseudolite position accuracy have a great influence on the final user receiver positioning accuracy.

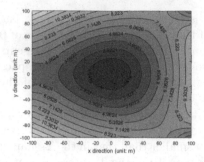

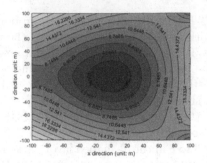

Fig. 11. GDOP contour map after the time measurement accuracy is changed.

Fig. 12. GDOP contour map after the pseudolite position measurement accuracy is changed.

7   Conclusion

In this paper, an independent pseudolite navigation and positioning system consisting of four pseudolites based on the TDOA principle is proposed in the case that the GNSS satellite signal is interfered and the satellite constellation visibility is affected. This paper introduces the mathematical principle of TDOA, deduces the geometric dilution of precision (GDOP) expression of the positioning system under the TDOA principle, and analyzes the main factors affecting the value of GDOP: time difference measurement accuracy, pseudolite position measurement accuracy and pseudolite geometry layout.

In view of the influence of pseudo-satellite geometric layout on GDOP, two layout schemes, namely Y-shaped and T-shaped, are proposed in this paper, and the distribution of GDOP values under each layout scheme is simulated. After comparing and analyzing the simulation graphs, it is concluded that the Y-shaped geometric layout can significantly reduce the GDOP value compared with the T-shaped layout, and different geometric layouts have advantages and disadvantages. In the subsequent research process, it is possible to consider selecting a larger number of pseudolites for the construction of the positioning system and designing other pseudolite layout schemes to further reduce the positioning error and improve the positioning performance.

References

1. Wang, S.: A pulsed pseudolite signal acquisition method using signal coverage recursion FFT. In: China Automation Society Control Theory Committee. Proceedings of the 36th China Control Conference, p. 6 (2017)
2. Borio, D., Odriscoll, C.: Design of a general pseudolite pulsing scheme. IEEE Trans. Aerosp. Electron. Syst. **50**(1), 2–16 (2014)
3. Shen, J., Cui, X., Lu, M.: Initial frequency refining algorithm for pull-in process with an auxiliary DLL in pseudolite receiver. Electron. Lett. **52**(14), 1257–1259 (2016)

4. Wang, J., Xu, Y., Luo, R.: Synchronisation method for pulsed pseudolite positioning signal under the pulse scheme without slot-permutation. IET Radar Sonar Navig. **11**(12), 1822–1830 (2017)
5. Yang, Y., Gao, W.: An optimal adaptive Kalman filter. J. Geodesy **80**(4), 177–183 (2006). https://doi.org/10.1007/s00190-006-0041-0
6. Shu, F., Yang, S.P., Qin, Y.L.: Approximate analytic quadratic-optimization solution for TDOA-based passive multi-satellite localization with earth constraint. IEEE Access (2016)
7. Foy, W.H.: Position-location solutions by Taylor-series estimation. IEEE Trans. Aerosp. Electron. Syst. **AES-12**(2), 187–194 (1976)
8. Torrieri, D.J.: Statistical theory of passive location systems. IEEE Trans. Aerosp. Electron. Syst. **AES-20**(2), 183–198 (1984)
9. Friedlander, B.: A passive localization algorithm and its accuracy analysis. IEEE J. Ocean. Eng. **12**(1), 234–245 (1987)
10. Huang, Y., Benesty, J., Elko, G., Mersereati, R.: Real-time passive source localization: a practical linear-correction least-squares approach. IEEE Trans. Speech Audio Process. **9**(8), 943–956 (2001)
11. Cheung, K., So, H., Ma, W., Chan, Y.: A constrained least squares approach to mobile positioning: algorithms and optimality. EURASIP J. Adv. Signal Process. **2006**, 020858 (2006). https://doi.org/10.1155/ASP/2006/20858
12. Cho, J.A., Na, H., Kim, S., Ahn, C.: Moving-target tracking based on particle filter with TDOA/FDOA measurements. ETRI J. **34**(2), 260–263 (2012)
13. Meng, C., Ding, Z., Dasgupta, S.: A semidefinite programming approach to source localization in wireless sensor networks. IEEE Signal Process. Lett. **15**, 253–256 (2008)

Research and Simulation of Physical Layer Abstraction Model for Next Generation WiFi Integrated Simulation

Kun Zhang, Bo Li, Mao Yang$^{(\boxtimes)}$, Zhongjiang Yan, and Qi Yang

School of Electronics and Information, Northwestern Polytechnical University,
Xi'an, China
zhangkun_tara@mail.nwpu.edu.cn, yangmao@nwpu.edu.cn

Abstract. In this paper, we study the physical layer (PHY) interference abstraction. First, we analyse the physical layer abstraction methods for the next generation wireless local area network (WLAN), including high frequency WLAN such as institute of electrical and electronics engineers (IEEE) 802.11ay and low frequency WLAN such as IEEE 802.11ax, and describe their implementation details. Then the received bit mutual information rate (RBIR) and the mean mutual information (MMIB) of PHY abstraction methods are studied separately. We design process of two PHY abstraction methods and implement them in the simulation platform. Some corresponding simulation results are gived. The simulation results show that the RBIR method accurately predicts link level simulation performance in a simple mapping method.

Keywords: PHY abstraction · RBIR · MMIB · WLAN

1 Introduction

With the large-scale application of smart terminal devices such as PCs and PDAs, the demand for wireless network technologies is increasing rapidly. As a product of computer network and communication technology, Wireless Local Area Networks (WLAN) has become a choice of personal communication and has developed rapidly. A number of research institutes, represented by the Institute of Electrical and Electronics Engineers (IEEE), have developed a series of protocol standards for different scenarios, which have promoted the practical use of WLAN.

With the rapid development of computer technology, the simulation technology has also undergone a leap-forward development. In modern scientific research, with the increasing difficulty of research and the increasing cost, the importance of simulation has become higher and higher. In modern scientific research, it is impossible for every experiment to be realized. Instead, advanced computer technology is used to simulate various physical realizations, which can save a lot of manpower and material resources and financial capacity. Therefore,

B. Li et al. (Eds.): IoTaaS 2019, LNICST 316, pp. 468–479, 2020.
https://doi.org/10.1007/978-3-030-44751-9_39

all scientific research institutions and equipment manufacturers conduct software simulation research when conducting scientific research, and then further improve the simulation program through actual hardware physics experiments, so that software simulation can provide simulation results to design hardware. And because of the variety of scenes, the actual products will have various complicated existing network problems at work, and the analysis of the problems requires a lot of manpower, and it is more difficult to reproduce in the laboratory environment. Therefore, a link-level and system-level integrated Wi-Fi simulation platform is required. It supports the configuration of the live network scenario model and the introduction of live network data for virtual reproduction of the network in the real environment for network performance presentation, problem root cause analysis, and algorithm design. For example, the next generation WLAN–802.11ax explicitly requires integrated simulation.

One of the biggest technical challenges of integrated simulation is the physical layer abstraction problem. The purpose of physical layer abstraction is to simulate the receiving process of data packages, to model the interference of Signal to Noise Ratio (SNR) of data packages under different subcarriers accurately, to make it more realistic, and to provide reference for system simulation. Therefore, in the simulation design, the correctness of the calculation of Packet Error Rate (PER) will greatly affect the performance of the simulation design. The computational problem of PER can be summarized as interference abstraction. There are many ways to abstract the physical layer, such as Exponential mapping (EESM), MMIB, RBIR, Constrained Capacity (CC) and so on. Among them, MMIB and RBIR are applied to next generation WLANs 802.11ay and 802.11ax respectively. Therefore, the method of interference abstraction in different forms is an important research direction.

In [1–4], using the mathematical theory of information theory, MIMO channel matrix is equivalent to multiple SISO channel matrices, and the mutual information of bits is calculated. Then the OFDM system scenario of ML receiver is modeled and the general formula of SNR mutual information on each subcarrier is calculated. According to different modulation modes, the calculation formula of mutual trust is deduced. In [5–8], OFDM system does not transmit data in the form of bits, but uses symbols as transmission tools. First, mutual information of each symbol (subcarriers) is calculated, and then the average bit mutual information is obtained. The expression derived from RBIR is too complex and usually uses mapping method. However, the existing studies only focus on specific criteria, without in-depth study of the correlation and difference between different physical layer abstraction methods.

This paper systematically analyses and studies the physical layer abstraction methods for the next generation WLAN, including high frequency WLAN and low frequency WLAN, and analyses their respective advantages and suitable methods for each protocol standard. Then the corresponding simulation results are given. The physical layer abstraction methods of 802.11ax, RBIR and 802.11ay, MMIB, are analyzed separately. Then the similarities and differences are given. The simulation implements the two abstract methods of interference and gives the corresponding simulation results.

The structure of the paper is described briefly as follows. Section 2 describes the details of PHY abstraction methods, such as RBIR and MMIB and so on. Section 3 describes how to implement PHY abstraction methods in the simulation platform and provides the simulation parameter configuration and the simulation results are given and some different methods of PHY abstraction are discussed.

2 PHY Interference Abstraction

2.1 General Introduction

The purpose of PHY abstraction is to accurately predict PER of a data packet, not simulating the actual receiving process of the physical layer which is very difficult to implement. It pays close attention to large-scale fading and small-scale fading of the every channel. The phy abstraction should base on a rule that it is computationally infeasible to simulate actual receiving process of some STAs' physical layer form APs' packet in a WLAN network simulator. The requirement for the PHY abstraction are accurate, computationally simple and easy to implement in simulation. And the PHY abstraction is independent with channel models, not closely associated with the channel. Interference models and MIMO model can be easily derived by simple by abstraction.

System-level simulation generally proves the average system performance, which helps to plan the network topology. For such simulation, the average performance of the system is reflected in the average SNR distribution of the whole cell, which is influenced mainly by the network topology and channel fading. According to modulation and coding scheme (MCS), each subscriber's average SNR was then mapped to the appropriate PER, which based on link-level SNR tables. The calculation of SNR to PER is so complicate that look-up tables is needed to use. The PHY abstraction use mapping function to get the PER of a packet.

In system-level simulation, data packets can not be sent always over AWGN channels. Wireless channel is the most complex, and its fading characteristics depend on the radio wave propagation environment. Different environments have different characteristics of transmission. Wireless channel may be very simple linear transmission, or may be interfered by many different factors. So if the modulation mode is OFDM, different frequency has different the channel gain or loss. In OFDM, the coded symbols of a data packet are sent on lots of subcarriers, so the SNR values which the receiver get are not similar. In addition, because of multipath effect, the channel gain of subcarriers can be very different.

PHY abstraction functions are designed to predict the instantaneous link performance effectively. There are different abstraction methods for kinds of systems such as OFDM, SC and so on. The final purpose of the PHY abstraction is to obtain the packet error rate of a specific fading channel which is much the same with actual receiving PER. System-level simulation will get H matrix and SNR on each subcarrier. Then the physical layer abstraction function is used to get an equivalent SNR (average or other function). The PER of the data package is obtained by SNR-PER mapping table in the Gauss channel. This is the general simulation process. as shown in Fig. 1.

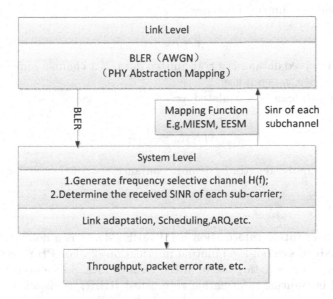

Fig. 1. Relationship of the link-level and system-level.

For all the ESM methods, the channel model and the phy layer for generalized transmission relationship:

$$Y_{output} = H_{channel}X_{input} + U_{AWGN} \qquad (1)$$

Y_{output} is the received packet signal vector X_{input} is the transmitted packet signal vector or the transmitted symbol stream, $H_{channel}$ is mimo (or siso) channel matrix, U_{AWGN} is the noise vector, also called add-Gaussian noise.

In general, The base rule is to get an equivalent average SNR ($SNR_{effective}$) in a calculated bits block. The average SNR is not different from the initial SNR. It can represent average SNR of all subcarriers symbol. So, we can not need multipath channel SNR to PER table which is more and difficult to measure, and all we need only AWGN channel SNR to PER table which can get equivalent PER using the effective SNR. The function is different according to the coding type, modulation mode and MCS value. The general expression of PHY abstraction is written as follows:

$$SNR_{effective} = Func^{-1}\left\{ \frac{1}{N}\sum_{n=1}^{N} Func(SNR_n) \right\} \qquad (2)$$

Where $SNR_{effective}$ is the equivalent or average SNR, SNR_n is the SNR of the nth sub-carrier which are equal in the AWGN channel and different in the multipath channel, N is total number of all subcarriers of a packet determined by channel bandwidth and modulation mode and $Func(\bullet)$ is an input function which is reversible.

For example, a simple SISO case:

$$y = hx + u \tag{3}$$

where y is a received data, x is a transmitted data, h is channel impulse response at each subcarrier, u is a noise.

Then, $SINR_n$ can be calculated as:

$$SINR_n = \frac{|h|^2 \varepsilon_x}{\sigma_n^2} \tag{4}$$

where ε_x is a signal strength, σ_n^2 is noise variance.

2.2 RBIR

It is also called Mutual Information ESM (MIESM). It is a nonlinear mapping from post SNR to symbol-level mutual information [2]. For PHY actual simulation, receiver receives data packets in the form of bits. So we need to calculate the received bit mutual information rate called RBIR, as shown in Fig. 2. For M-QAM, the above function can be described as follow:

$$Func(SNR; M) = \log_2 M - \frac{1}{M} \sum_{m=1}^{M} E_U \left\{ \log_2 \left(\sum_{k=1}^{M} \exp \left[\left(|U|^2 - \left| \sqrt{SNR}(s_k - s_m) + U \right|^2 \right) \right] \right) \right\} \tag{5}$$

where U is the Gaussian random variable which has best zero-mean and low variance similar to the white noise. The M of function can be 4, 6, and 8 and so on.

$$\gamma_{eff} = \alpha_1 \varphi^{-1} \left(\frac{1}{J} \sum_{j=0}^{J-1} \varphi \left(\frac{\gamma_j}{\alpha_2} \right) \right) \tag{6}$$

We should measure all SNR to PER table in the AWGN channel for different MCS and different coding type. Then these curves can be used for reference by the physical layer abstraction methods.

The PHY abstraction based on RBIR has been described in the following diagram.

2.3 MMIB

MMIB called Mutual Information based approach. Each bit experiences a different equivalent bit-channel because of the different characteristic of different modulation mode [1], as shown in Fig. 3.

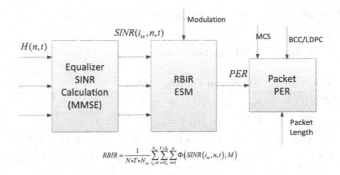

$$RBIR = \frac{1}{N \cdot T \cdot N_{ss}} \sum_{i_{ss}=1}^{N_{ss}} \sum_{t=T_0}^{T+T_0} \sum_{n=1}^{N} \Phi\left(SINR(i_{ss},n,t); M\right)$$

Fig. 2. RBIR based PHY abstraction procedure.

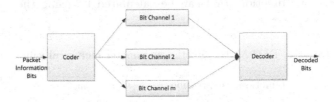

Fig. 3. MMIB based PHY abstraction procedure.

Mutual information of the equivalent channel is:

$$Infor\left(b, L\right) = \frac{1}{n} \sum_{i=1}^{n} Infor(b_i, L(b_i)) \tag{7}$$

where n is the number of bits per constellation, and $Infor(b_i, L(b_i))$ is the mutual information computational function for the input i-th bit.

Mean mutual information through N sub-carriers over the codeword:

$$MInfor = \frac{1}{mN} \sum_{n=1}^{N} \sum_{i=1}^{m} Infor(b_i^n, L(b_i^n)) \tag{8}$$

Since mutual information $I(b_i, LLR(b_i))$ is a function of constellation and SNR, mean mutual information is

$$MInfor = \frac{1}{mN} \sum_{n=1}^{N} \sum_{i=1}^{m} I\left(b_i^{(n)}, L\left(b_i^{(n)}\right)\right) = \frac{1}{N} \sum_{n=1}^{N} Infor_m\left(SNR_n\right) = \frac{1}{N} \sum_{n=1}^{N} Func\left(SNR_n\right) \tag{9}$$

Effective SNR mapping (ESM) function is derived for each modulation as follows:

$$\Phi\left(x\right) = I_m\left(x\right) = \sum_{k=1}^{K} a_k J\left(c_k \sqrt{x}\right) \tag{10}$$

Detailed values of each parameter are shown in the Table 1.

Table 1. ESM function parameter numerical value.

Modulation	Numerical approximation
BPSK	$K = 1$, $a = [1]$, $c = [2\sqrt{2}]$
QPSK	$K = 1$, $a = [1]$, $c = [2]$
16-QAM	$K = 3$, $a = [0.5\ 0.25\ 0.25]$, $c = [0.8\ 2.17\ 0.965]$
64QAM	$K = 3$, $a = [1/3\ 1/3\ 1/3]$, $c = [1.47\ 0.529\ 0.366]$

Here the above function $J(x)$ can be calculated by using the value in the Table 2:

Table 2. ESM MMIB function parameter numerical value.

Functional expression	Condition
$i_1 x^3 + j_1 x^2 - k_1 x$	$1.6363 \geq x$
$1 - \exp\left(i_2 x^3 + j_2 x^2 + k_2 x\right)$	$\infty \geq x \geq 1.63$

where $i_1 = -0.0421, j_1 = 0.2090$ and $k_1 = -0.0064$ for the first expression, and where $i_2 = 0.00181, j_2 = -0.143$ and $k_2 = 0.0550$ for the second expression.

2.4 Comparison Between RBIR and MMIB

Firstly, the advantages and disadvantages of the two PHY abstraction methods are summarized.

RBIR: The RBIR get match with AWGN results using the above parameters, but do not see results for D-NLOS or UMi channel. The mapping only needs to use AWGN curves and agreeing on AWGN curves is an easier job. Inverting the ESM function above is not that straight forward. Results for different channel models might indicate the need for channel model dependent parameters too. If the scenario is SISO models or MIMO models with linear receivers, a recommended SNR to RBIR mapping is used which is defined by a lookup table unique to each modulation. If channel dependency uses RBIR methods, RBIR functions are obtained by performing link simulations and optimizing parameters for each MCS. A different value of RBIR is obtained for each code rate, even though the modulation is fixed. Does not conform to the definition of information metric. For ML receiver, RBIR modeling needs four parameters for each MCS that are calculated by link simulations. Multiple simple examples also suggest that the RBIR approach as defined can not pass even simple sanity check or basic properties as expected from a mutual information metric.

MMIB: The MMIB can get match (with in 1 dB) with the AWGN curve for UMi channel model (both LOS and NLOS) using the above parameters, but do not see results for D-NLOS. The mapping only needs to use AWGN curves and agreeing on AWGN curves is an easier job. Inverting the ESM function above is not that straight forward. Results for D-NLOS channel might indicate the need for channel model dependent parameters too. If the scenario is SISO models or MIMO models with linear receivers, a recommended SNR to MMIB mapping is used which is defined by a function unique to each modulation. These SNR to MMIB/RBIR mapping are found to be close and hence no difference is expected in these simulations. The dealing methods are similar between MMIB with RBIR. If channel dependency uses MMIB methods, MMIB functions are generated by Numerically obtaining (by Monte-Carlo simulation and numerical integration of LLR PDFs obtained from a Gaussian matrix channel and a constellation mapping model), the theoretical true bit-level MI of a matrix channel and approximating this function with numerical approximations. No AWGN or link simulations are used at any point, as these functions are independent of the underlying system. Because the MMIB is based on mathematical theory. It is derived from information theory. So MMIB functions for ML are capacity measures defined for the underlying bit channel induced by a modulation constellation and the matrix channel. It satisfy all the properties of a bit-level mutual information metric like the SISO MI metrics and not surprisingly show good prediction for ML.

3   Simulation and Performance Evaluation

3.1   Simulation Platform NS-3

NS-3 is a open source, free and new software. It is a network simulator not only for the wireless communications but also for the cable communications. It bases on discrete event simulation which is more authentic than discrete time simulation.

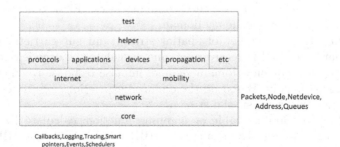

Fig. 4. NS-3 software structure.

We do not study the whole content of NS-3 which is too much and too difficult. Figure 4 shows base structure of NS-3. It is very comprehensive and can simulate many communication modes, even building a WLAN.

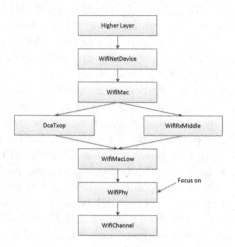

Fig. 5. NS-3 wifi model base structure.

Figure 5 shows base structure of NS-3 wifi model. At the same time, it is also a data packet transmission process. And the simulation mainly pays attention to WifiPhy model and WifiChannel model.

3.2   Implementation of RBIR and MMIB

RBIR: If receiver is receiving a packet, some other packet may be sended to receiver for interference.

(1) Channels generates not only for the both sides of communication but also for the both sides of interference communication. First generates channel impulse response in frequency domain.
(2) According to the number of spatial stream and sub-carriers and initial SNR that is got by the receiver antenna, calculate the decode output SNR. According to frequency-domain channel impulse response calculate equivalent channel matrix. Based on the deduced expression, calculate SNR each sub-carrier and every spatial stream.
(3) According to mapping table or mapping function, calculate RBIR vector through SNR vector. Then calculate RBIR vector to average RBIR.
(4) According to reverse mapping table or reverse mapping function, calculate effective SNR by average RBIR.
(5) According to AWGN channel SNR to PER table, calculate PER for the bits block.

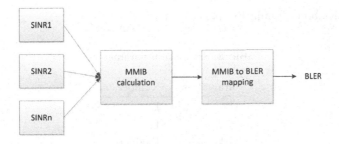

Fig. 6. MMIB produce in NS-3.

(6) Calculate the final PER of a packet and determine if this subframe is successfully received.

$$Uniform\,(0,1) \begin{matrix} > PER \to \text{transmission success} \\ \leq PER \to \text{transmission fail} \end{matrix} \qquad (11)$$

MMIB: If receiver is receiving a packet, some other packet may be sended to receiver for interference, as shown in Fig. 6.

(1) Channels generates not only for the both sides of communication but also for the both sides of interference communication. First generates time-domain channel impulse response, then calculate channel impulse response in frequency domain.

(2) According to the number of spatial stream and sub-carriers and initial SNR that is got by the receiver antenna, calculate the decode output SNR vector.

(3) According to mapping function one, calculate MMIB vector through SNR vector.

(4) According to mapping function two, calculate BLER by MMIB for the bits block.

(5) For MMIB to BLER mapping the AWGN reference fitting curves for each MCS obtained from Phy layer simulations can be stored. The function is general with some parameters to be determined.

3.3 Design of Simulation Scenarios and Configuration of Simulation Parameters

This simulation was completed on the NS-3 802.11ax platform built by our lab. The simulation scenario is set to 1 cell, 1 AP and 1 STA. The channel model is ITU Winner channel, and the scene are indoor rooms.

Table 3 is about simulation parameters.

Table 3. Simulation parameters

Parameters	Number
AP	1
STA	1
Packet length	1500byte
Data MCS	1–9
TYPE	SU-MIMO
AP Antenna	2
STA Antenna	2

3.4 Performance Evaluation

In this subsection, we analyze the simulation results. As can be seen, the thick lines represents AWGN channel, and the thin lines represents ITU channel and RBIR methods. They are not different. So it is recommended to use RBIR methods to predict the instantaneous link performance (Fig. 7).

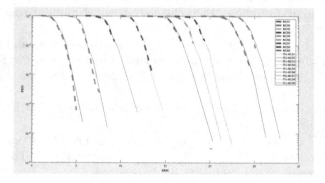

Fig. 7. SNR-PER of RBIR.

4   Conclusion

Firstly, this paper gives a general analysis of physical layer interference abstraction, and points out the main problems and solutions in wireless communication interference abstraction from link performance awareness.

For further analysis, two different interference abstraction methods used in next generation wireless communication systems are analyzed and studied in this paper. The application scope and performance of these two algorithms are compared and analyzed, and the corresponding simulation design is given.

Finally, theoretical analysis and simulation results show that RBIR is more suitable for the next generation WLAN-802.11ax and MMIB is more suitable for the next generation WLAN-802.11ay. RBIR and MMIB, Both methods are based on the average mutual information criterion and are accurate evaluation of transmission error probability.

Acknowledgement. This work was supported in part by the National Natural Science Foundations of CHINA (Grant No. 61871322, No. 61771390, No. 61771392, No. 61501373, and No. 61271279), the National Science and Technology Major Project (Grant No. 2016ZX03001018-004), and Science and Technology on Avionics Integration Laboratory (20185553035).

References

1. Lei, X., Jinbao, Z.: An accurate mean mutual information computational approach of link performance abstraction. In: IEEE International Conference on Signal Processing. IEEE (2010)
2. Meng, C., Heng, W., Wang, H.: Physical layer abstraction algorithm based on RBIR for integrations of heterogeneous networks. J. Southeast Univ. (Nat. Sci. Ed.) **42**(4), 588–592 (2012)
3. Sreenivas, B., Lal, R.J.: Physical abstraction method (RBIR) for OFDM system. In: Meghanathan, N., Nagamalai, D., Chaki, N. (eds.) Advances in Computing and Information Technology. Advances in Intelligent Systems and Computing, vol. 178, pp. 431–438. Springer, Heidelberg (2013). https://doi.org/10.1007/978-3-642-31600-5_42
4. Zhang, J., Zheng, H., Tan, Z.: A mean mutual information based algorithm for physical layer abstraction. Gaojishu Tongxin Chin. High Technol. Lett. **19**(06), 558–563 (2009)
5. Hu, L., Zhang, C.: A mutual-information based algorithm for physical layer abstraction in CMMB. Gaojishu Tongxin Chin. High Technol. Lett. **24**(7), 703–708 (2014)
6. Aguilar, F.L., Cidre, G.R., López, J.M.L., Paris, J.R.: Mutual information effective SNR mapping algorithm for fast link adaptation model in 802.16e. In: Chatzimisios, P., Verikoukis, C., Santamaría, I., Laddomada, M., Hoffmann, O. (eds.) Mobilight 2010. LNICST, vol. 45, pp. 356–367. Springer, Heidelberg (2010). https://doi.org/10.1007/978-3-642-16644-0_31
7. Tan, P., Wu, Y., Sun, S.: Link adaptation based on adaptive modulation and coding for multiple-antenna OFDM system. IEEE J. Sel. Areas Commun. **26**(8), 1599–1606 (2008)
8. Choi, Y.S., Alamouti, S.: A pragmatic PHY abstraction technique for link adaptation and MIMO switching. IEEE J. Sel. Areas Commun. **26**(6), 960–971 (2008)

Traffic Arrival Prediction for WiFi Network: A Machine Learning Approach

Ning Wang, Bo Li, Mao Yang$^{(\boxtimes)}$, Zhongjiang Yan, and Ding Wang

School of Electronics and Information,
Northwestern Polytechnical University, Xi'an, China
ningwang22668800@mail.nwpu.edu.cn, {libo.npu,yangmao,zhjyan}@nwpu.edu.cn

Abstract. At present, Wi-Fi plays a very important role in the fields of online media, daily life, industry, military and etc.

Exactly predicting the traffic arrival time is quite useful for WiFi since the access point (AP) could efficiently schedule uplink transmission. Thus, this paper proposes a machine learning-based traffic arrival prediction method by using random forest regression algorithm. The results show that the prediction accuracy of this model is about 95%, significantly outperforming the linear prediction flow. Through prediction, resources can be reserved in advance for the arrival of data traffic, and the channel can be optimally configured, thereby achieving better fluency of the device and smoothness of the network.

Keywords: Wi-Fi Network · Artificial intelligence · Big data · Machine learning · Random forest · Regression

1 Introduction

1.1 Current Status of WiFi and Artificial Intelligence

Wireless communication and network development are fast, and WiFi is one of the most important data service bearers. As one of the most important carrying methods of wireless communication services, WiFi has the following characteristics:

The main advantage of WiFi is that it is wireless, so it's not constrained by the wired environment. Therefore, it is very suitable for mobile office users and has broad application prospects.

The transmission power specified by IEEE802.11 cannot exceed 100 mW, and the actual transmit power is about 60–70 mW, which means that WiFi power is very low, it is healthy and safe to use.

To set up a wireless network, we just need a wireless network card and an AP, so that it can be combined with the existing wired architecture in a wireless mode. Sharing network resources, erection costs and complex procedures are far lower than traditional wired networks.

B. Li et al. (Eds.): IoTaaS 2019, LNICST 316, pp. 480–488, 2020.
https://doi.org/10.1007/978-3-030-44751-9_40

WIFI technology as a supplement to high-speed wired access technology, can transmit very fast and it is cheep, WIFI technology is broadly used in wired access wireless Extended field.

At present, WiFi has been widely developed and applied in various fields such as daily life, industrial development, and military development. It brings convenience to people's lives, contributes to the development of science and technology, and provides assistance for military development and industrial progress. The business volume is bound to increase gradually. In order to meet the growing needs of network development, it is imperative to update and develop the WiFi technology. The academic and industrial circles are paying attention to the key technology research and standardization promotion of the next generation WiFi.

1.2 One of the Existing Problems

Due to the characteristics of distributed random access, WiFi networks may cause collisions between data packets and interference between cells and cells. With the development of WiFi technology, the collision and interference will become more serious in the high-density deployment scenarios of the next-generation WiFi, which seriously suppresses the performance of the WiFi system (Quality of Systems, QoS) and user experience quality (Quality of Experiences, QoE).

If we can accurately estimate the arrival time of the next packet of the service based on the known arrival characteristics of the service, such as the packet length, transmission time, packet interval, and packet arrival time of the service data packet, Targeted QoS guarantees can significantly improve QoE.

1.3 Existing Literature Research

Intelligentization is a research hotspot in recent years. In particular, machine learning and deep learning have rapidly penetrated into various fields and achieved extremely beneficial effects. They have brought powerful driving forces to various industries including communications and networking. The existing research on machine learning in business arrival prediction is as follows:

Wang et al. [1] focus on the application of MLN and summarize the basic workflow for explaining how to apply machine learning technology in the network field.

Jiang et al. [2] use data-driven video quality prediction to make the best decisions to improve Internet Video Quality of Experience (QoE) through Key Feature Analysis (CFA) design and implementation.

Fadlullah et al. [3] solves the application of deep learning in network traffic control system, and points out the necessity of investigating the decentralized work of deep learning applications in various network traffic control.

Kato et al. [4] presents the appropriate input and output characteristics of heterogeneous network traffic, and describe how the modified system works and its difference from traditional neural networks.

Mao et al. [5] build systems that learn to manage resources directly from experience. They offer DeepRM, a sample solution that turns packaged task issues with multiple resource requirements into learning problems.

The rest of the articles providing ideas in the creation process of this paper are listed in the references.

However, unfortunately, the existing literature has less predictions on network traffic, and a small number of predictions of network traffic do not capture data in specific applications, and use machine learning to predict the arrival of data packets.

1.4   Work Done in This Article

In order to study and improve the QoS and QoE of WiFi in different scenarios, this paper is based on different scenarios (including scenarios with better service quality such as school library, service quality, such as school dormitory, poor service quality such as school).

The business class obtained by the canteen knows the arrival characteristics of the data packet, extracts the relevant time information, uses the machine learning method to learn and model, and predicts the arrival time of the next data packet. Found verified by simulation and real data acquired data sets, the verification test of the accuracy of the output, provided linear prediction model are compared, the results show that: under different scenarios, the established model to study the time of arrival of the data packet are better.

1.5   Article Chapter Structure

Section 1 introduces the clarification of the problem and outlines the work done in this paper.

Section 2 introduces the related techniques and resources used in this experiment.

Section 3 introduces the prediction model and accuracy of the packet arrival time based on the random forest algorithm.

Section 4 is the analysis of the experimental content, simulation prediction and results, and finally the discussion, summary and outlook.

2   Traffic Arrival Prediction Scheme

2.1   Related Introduction

In the process of obtaining data, this paper uses Huawei's packet capture interface based on test sample, and uses adb program to access the mobile phone to obtain data. In the initial information processing, Notepad++ and Wireshark software were used to extract the quintuple information and capture the stream.

In this paper, the Anaconda platform is used in the process of data processing and model building. The function library greatly reduce the lack of library support in the Python development process. It is a very rich and powerful Python development platform.

Scikit-learn is a Python library, known as Sklearn, which is widely used to solve regression problems.

2.2 Introduction of Core Ideas

The idea of the implementation is to apply the corresponding software to capture and extract the data stream, obtain the time data, use the random forest regression algorithm to model the data, and then use the established model to predict the time interval of the next packet arrival.

The random forest modeling process is Fig. 1 as follows:

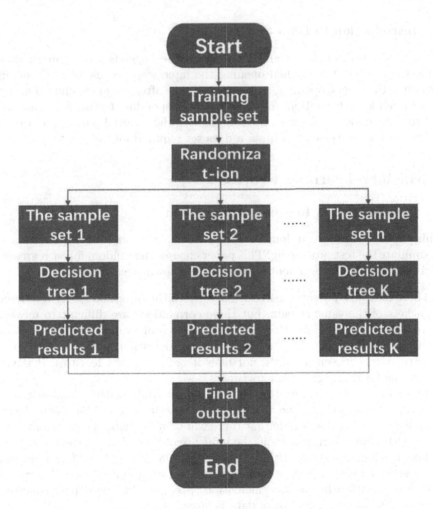

Fig. 1. The structure of the RF model

2.3 Experimental Planning and Data Collection

Under different scenarios, such as library, canteen, dormitory, the software was measured respectively, each case to ensure sufficient number of experiments, in order to get plenty of experimental data, using the control variable method, in order to better control network signal coherent condition, can use mobile phone hot manner, collection and network transmission in the process of the log information, and obtain the corresponding pcap file, get the corresponding files, through the "five yuan group" flow analysis as characteristics were caught, then for each packet received time information, and use data to establish model, to forecast the next packet arrival time.

2.4 Introduction to Data Sets

For example, in the data obtained during Mobile Legends, each game records a time (game start time) when opening the interface, records a time (opening time) after the official opening, and records a time after the game ends. Through the obtained log information and pcap file, corresponding to the start time and end time, the data is extracted, the time data of the received packet is obtained, and the data is processed to obtain a data set required for modeling.

3 Machine Learning Process

3.1 Random Forest Regression Algorithm

In this paper, we use the random forest regression algorithm to model the data set and simulate the test processing. This paper chooses the random forest regression algorithm to do the experiment based on the following reasons:

(1) There may be a potential correlation between the reception times of different packets of the same stream, but these correlations are difficult to measure correctly, so algorithms that are sensitive to multicollinearity between features are not applicable. The random forest algorithm is not sensitive to the correlation between features, nor does it need to select features. It is very suitable for this regression experiment.

(2) The random forest algorithm is very robust and relatively insensitive to discrete data points. Due to the certain interference of the received time information, it is inevitable that there will be noise data. The random forest algorithm can effectively avoid the influence of these data on the final model.

(3) The random forest algorithm aggregates a large number of classification trees, which can improve the model's prediction accuracy, and the random forest algorithm has a fast calculation speed, so the speed performance is excellent when the amount of data is large.

Random forest regression algorithm: Depend on the function of the random trees, random forests can be applied to classification and regression problems. For the regression algorithm: The cart tree is a regression tree, and the principle adopted is to gain the minimum mean square error. That is, for the arbitrary division feature F, the data sets N1 and N2 are divided into two parts according to any partition point v, to obtain the feature that makes the mean square error of each group of data N1 and N2 reach the minimum, and the sum of the mean square error of N1 and N2.

The expression is:

$$
\min_{F,v} \left[\min_{m_1} \sum_{x_i \in N_1(F,v)} (y_i - m_1)^2 + \min_{m_2} \sum_{x_i \in N_2(F,v)} (y_i - m_2)^2 \right] \tag{1}
$$

Where m1 is the sample from the N1 data set and m2 is the sample from the N2 data set.

The cart tree is predicted based on the mean of the leaf nodes, so the prediction of the forest is the average of all the predicted results of trees.

3.2 Data Preprocessing

The log information of the obtained network stream is captured, and then the log information is captured by using Notepad++ and Wireshark, and the packet length and the receiving time information of each data packet are obtained, and then the time data is normalized by programming. Make the size of the data in the range of [0, 1]. In order to satisfy the requirement that the model predicts the arrival time of the next packet according to the time of every four packets, the data is processed into a txt file of five data per line. The data set is output in txt for use. The time information is extracted by programming, and then the time information is extracted according to the obtained data set file lenandtime.txt, a total of 8406, and then the data is cleaned, in order to facilitate observation and processing, balance the influence of each input feature value, need The raw data is normalized to become the value of the [0, 1] interval, and the normalization formula is as follows:

$$
X = \frac{x_i - min(x)}{max(x) - min(x)} \tag{2}
$$

Then, through processing, a data set of five time data per line required for model training is obtained. The data set thus obtained meets the experimental requirements, and then the model training can be performed.

3.3 Model Training

Regression algorithm to model, put the data set into the model, scramble the data, use 70% of the data after the disruption as training data, and test the remaining 30%. The data is tested on the model. After training the model, you can test the data set, test the model, and visualize the test results, select the appropriate amount to evaluate the model, and ensure the readability of the results.

4   Performance Evaluation

4.1   Comparison and Analysis of Training Effects

Random forest regression model validation. Validation models need to pass appropriate evaluation indicators. The mean square error (MSE), that is, the (true value - predicted value) and then squared and then summed and then averaged, obviously, in the process of regression model prediction, the smaller the value of MSE, the higher the accuracy of the model. The formula is as follows:

$$MSE = C1m \sum_{i=1}^{m} (y_i - \hat{y})^2 \tag{3}$$

The goodness of fit R-Squared can test the fitting degree of the regression model to the sample data, the value is between 0 and 1. The higher the goodness of fit R-Squared, the higher the interpretability of the representative model:

$$R^2 = \frac{\sum_{i=1}^{n} (\hat{y}_i - \overline{y})^2}{\sum_{i=1}^{n} (y_i - \overline{y})^2} \tag{4}$$

Where: y is the actual observation, i.e. the time in the measured data; $\hat{y}$ is the predicted time value of the model; $\overline{y}$ is the average of the actual time data; m, n is the number of the samples.

Molecules are all the errors predicted by the models we train. The denominator does not consider anything else. The result we predict is the average of y. If the result is 0, then our model, the accuracy is quite poor, similar to the guess. If the result is 1, it means that our model has no errors. If the result is a number between 0–1, which is the degree of our model, the closer the value is to 1, the better the model. If the result is negative, it means that our model is not as good as guessing.

In the simulation prediction of the model, 70% of the data is used for modeling, and the remaining 30% of the data is used to train and test the model.

The predicted results were evaluated using MSE (mean square error) and R-Squared: The final model predicts that the MSE tends to be stable when the decision tree is above 31, and the MSE is on the e-6 scale. The result is very small. R-Squared is 0.98 and above, which is very close to 1. Explain that the model works well.

The result is shown in Fig. 2 as follows:
The results of multivariate linear fitting through matlab are:

$$y = 0.3119 - 0.2000 * x_1 - 0.4000 * x_2 - 0.6000 * x_3 + 0.8000 * x_4 \tag{5}$$

Comparison of the multivariate linear fit with the R-Squared results of the model in this paper is shown in Table 1.

Table 1. Model comparison

	Model of this paper	Linear fitting model
The amount of data	8401	8401
R-Squared	0.98	0.40

```
Max R Squared :
0.9999335805567419
31
Minimum MSE :
1.3994626936655444e-05
31
```

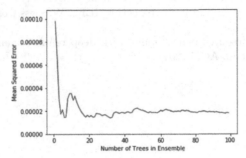

Fig. 2. Result

5   Discussion

According to the experimental data in the table, the modeling results in this paper are significantly better than the linear fitting results of Matlab, so the model built in this paper has practical significance in application.

6   Conclusions and Future Works

With the development of science and technology and the growing demand of people, WiFi will certainly develop in a more advanced, faster and more general direction in the future, and artificial intelligence will also play an important role in promoting the development of WiFi. In the future study and research life, I will pay more attention to the combination of the two, in order to make my own contribution to the development of WiFi.

Acknowledgement. This work was supported in part by the National Natural Science Foundations of CHINA (Grant No. 61771390, No. 61871322, No. 61771392, No. 61271279, and No. 61501373), the National Science and Technology Major Project (Grant No. 2016ZX03001018-004), and Science and Technology on Avionics Integration Laboratory (20185553035).

References

1. Wang, M., et al.: Machine learning for networking: workflow, advances and opportunities. IEEE Netw. **32**(2), 92–99 (2018)
2. Jiang, J., et al.: CFA: a practical prediction system for video QoE optimization. In: Usenix Conference on Networked Systems Design and Implementation USENIX Association (2016)
3. Fadlullah, Z., et al.: State-of-the-art deep learning: evolving machine intelligence toward tomorrow's intelligent network traffic control systems. IEEE Commun. Surv. Tutorials **19**, 2432–2455 (2017)
4. Kato, N., et al.: The deep learning vision for heterogeneous network traffic control: proposal, challenges, and future perspective. IEEE Wireless Commun. **24**, 146–153 (2017)
5. Mao, H., et al.: Resource management with deep reinforcement learning. In: The 15th ACM Workshop. ACM (2016)

Enabling IoT/M2M System Scalability with Fog Computing

Yuan-Han Lee and Fuchun Joseph Lin[(⊠)]

Department of Computer Science, College of Computer Science,
National Chiao Tung University, Hsinchu, Taiwan
{henry19950709.cs02g,fjlin}@nctu.edu.tw

Abstract. As increasingly more IoT/M2M devices are connected to Internet, they will cause serious congestion to IoT/M2M systems normally deployed in the cloud. Although Cloud can scale out to support more data requests, it may not be able to satisfy the low latency demanded by certain IoT/M2M applications. Fog, as an edge of Cloud, can alleviate the congested problem in the cloud and provide low latency for critical IoT/M2M applications due to its proximity to IoT/M2M devices. In this research, we propose (1) utilizing oneM2M, a global IoT/M2M standard, as the middleware to connect the cloud and the fog, (2) using Traffic Classifiers to intercept and divert IoT/M2M traffic requiring low latency to Fog and (3) deploying independent scalability mechanisms for Cloud and Fog. We demonstrate and verify our scalability design using a smart hospital use case and show that our proposed system can achieve better scalability results in terms of latency, CPU usage and power consumption compared to those with only Fog or Cloud.

Keywords: Scalability · Cloud computing · Fog computing · oneM2M · IoT · M2M · OpenStack · Kubernetes

1 Introduction

With an estimate of 20 billion IoT/M2M devices connected to the Internet in 2020 by Gartner, it is foreseen that the cloud-based IoT/M2M systems will soon face the issues of network congestion. Traditionally, an IoT/M2M system can achieve scalability solely in the cloud. Nevertheless, it may still fail to deliver the low latency demanded by some IoT/M2M applications such as those for eHealth and video streaming. In this research, we propose the utilization of "Fog Computing" [1] to help Cloud handle the data traffic that requires low latency. Also, to increase the overall system capacity, scalability mechanisms for Cloud and Fog are independently designed while assuring the demands from low latency applications are met by Fog.

Fog, as an extension of Cloud, attempts to move the cloud capacity such as compute, network and storage to the edge [2]. As such, Fog is much closer to end users and IoT/M2M devices than Cloud. The Fog node is the key component in the Fog architecture. Before data is sent to Cloud, it will be sent to Fog first for filtering and preprocessing.

© ICST Institute for Computer Sciences, Social Informatics and Telecommunications Engineering 2020
Published by Springer Nature Switzerland AG 2020. All Rights Reserved
B. Li et al. (Eds.): IoTaaS 2019, LNICST 316, pp. 489–502, 2020.
https://doi.org/10.1007/978-3-030-44751-9_41

Fog then can decide whether it should send data to Cloud for further processing or just finish the processing locally. In this way, Fog not only can reduce the load of the cloud but also can reduce processing latency of IoT/M2M applications.

In our research, in order to achieve overall system scalability while accommodating the demands from low latency applications, we propose adding a Traffic Classifier in the Fog architecture to identify IoT/M2M traffic requiring low latency. For IoT/M2M systems in Cloud and Fog, we use oneM2M, a global IoT/M2M standard, as the middleware to integrate both Cloud and Fog. Furthermore, independent scalability mechanisms are designed for them in order to dynamically scale out/in the respective oneM2M MN-CSE (Middle Node – Common Service Entity) and IN-CSE (Infrastructure Node – Common Service Entity) instances according to the IoT/M2M traffic load.

Smart Hospital [3] is an ideal use case for applying system scalability of Cloud and Fog. There are several IoT/M2M applications deployed in such a hospital and each one has different demands for latency. As the hospital grows and the patient needs evolve, the smart hospital should keep up with these demands with its system scalability design.

The rest of this paper is organized as follows. Section 2 gives a survey of related work and explains our motivation and unique contribution. Section 3 describes the high-level architecture of our proposed system. Section 4 presents our implementation details. Section 5 compares our proposed system to that with only Fog or Cloud and explains our experimental results for the smart hospital use case. Finally, Section 6 presents our conclusion and future work. The main abbreviations used throughout the paper are summarized in Table 1.

2 Related Work

Scalability research is done based on either Cloud or Fog computing. In addition, there are also research efforts to explore the collaboration between Cloud and Fog. As such, we categorize our survey into three areas in the following.

2.1 Scalability Research Based on Cloud Computing

Cerritos et al. [4] designed a Master Node in the cloud that is aware of system resources and traffic load so that it not only can decide load balancing policies but also proactively

Table 1. Summary of abbreviations

Abbreviation	Expansion
MN	Middle Node
IN	Infrastructure Node
CSE	Common Service Entity
AE	Application Entity
TC	Traffic Classifier

react to scalability needs. Bastida et al. [5] proposed a highly scalable OpenStack-based architecture for IoT/M2M platforms by taking advantage of functionalities of OpenStack and introducing a master node cooperating with a load balancing queue for fair distribution of incoming traffic among platform nodes.

2.2 Scalability Research Based on Fog Computing

As the latency demand of IoT/M2M applications becomes increasingly more important, Fog is regarded as an alternative to Cloud in this issue. Sen et al. [6] implemented an auto-scaled IoT broker Nucleus with MQTT in the fog architecture that can scale as the number of IoT devices increases. Tseng et al. [7] integrated Middle Nodes of oneM2M with highly scalable container-based Fog nodes to develop a scalable fog network that can dynamically scale in/out oneM2M instances along with Fog nodes.

2.3 Collaboration Between Cloud and Fog

By collaborating with Fog, both latency and congestion in Cloud can be greatly improved. Hence there has been active research on the collaboration between Cloud and Fog. Zhao et al. [8] proposed an approach for edge-node-assisted data transmission in the cloud-centric IoT architecture to overcome the problem of overwhelming bandwidth consumption in the cloud. Chen et al. [9] took advantage of Fog to reduce the workload of Cloud by designing an innovative scheduling mechanism to optimize the dispatch of cloud and fog computing resources.

With the heterogeneous nature of IoT applications, processing them solely in the cloud or in the fog is not sufficient to meet all their QoS requirements. Although some collaboration models between Cloud and Fog have been proposed, these models focus on load sharing between Cloud and Fog than the overall system scalability. In our research, we adopt a different approach: First, instead of collaboration we just let Cloud and Fog each handle the IoT traffic they are good at. Second, we enhance each with independent scalability mechanism to support the huge amount of IoT/M2M traffic.

To accomplish our scalability objective: (1) we design the Traffic Classifiers in the fog architecture to identify the IoT/M2M traffic that requires low latency, (2) we utilize oneM2M as a middleware to connect Cloud and Fog, and (3) we enable both Cloud and Fog to dynamically scale out/in their respective oneM2M instances according to the incoming traffic load.

3 Proposed System Architecture

In this section, we explain the high level architecture and communication interfaces of our system. As depicted in Fig. 1, starting from the bottom is Sensor Network that collects and sends the IoT traffic upward. Next above is Fog Network where each fog local area network is equipped with an embedded Traffic Classifier for identifying the IoT traffic to be processed in Fog. Finally, on the top is Cloud Network with multiple cloud nodes; each has its own IoT platform to handle the IoT Traffic.

Though not explicit in Fig. 1, oneM2M is adopted as the communication middleware of our system that will be explained below.

3.1 Sensor Network

Sensor Network consists of multiple types of sensor devices. They can be regarded as representing IoT applications and each application requires different QoS for latency. For example, the ehealth application demands low latency processing to ensure quick report of a patient's medical status, while clinic historical information can endure high latency due to its nature of information retrieval and storage.

3.2 Fog Network

Fog Network is an LAN close to Sensor Network. Traffic Classifiers, as the first points of receiving the IoT traffic, are capable of distinguishing whether an IoT application requires low latency processing or not. Then, it will decide whether the traffic should be processed immediately locally or go to the Cloud Network according to the application nature. Fog Network consists of a hierarchy of Fog Nodes as illustrated in Fig. 1. In order to build a highly scalable Fog architecture, Fog Network must not only balance the load of each Fog Node but also have the scalability mechanism to scale out/in these nodes according to the overall workload.

3.3 Cloud Network

On the other hand, Cloud Network is responsible for handling all other IoT traffic which have no low latency demand. It consists of only a single level of Cloud nodes as illustrated in Fig. 1. Similar to Fog Network, Cloud Network can distribute the load to different Cloud Nodes and scale them up/down according to the workload.

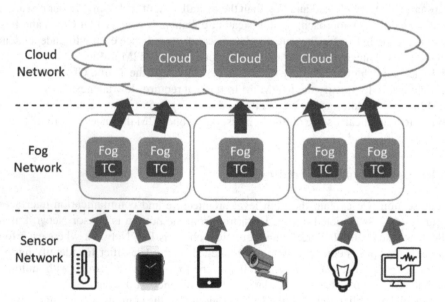

Fig. 1. Proposed system architecture

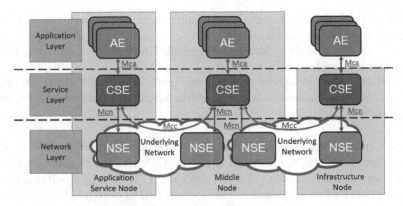

Fig. 2. oneM2M functional architecture

3.4 Communication Interface

In order to construct the above components, a middleware is required to support the communication and connection among them. Our research utilizes the standardized IoT platform, oneM2M [10], as the middleware. Figure 2 depicts the oneM2M architecture in our system which consists of a infrastructure domain and a field domain. Besides IoT/M2M devices represented by Application Service Node (ASN) and Application Dedicated Node (ADN), we focus on the other two types of nodes: Infrastructure Node (IN) and Middle Node (MN). IN is an IoT/M2M server that is normally deployed in the cloud while MN resides between IoT/M2M devices and Cloud. Both of them consist of three functional entities: Application Entity (AE), Common Service Entity (CSE) and Network Service Entity (NSE). AE is an application service. CSE provides common service functions (CSFs) which maintain communication interfaces in oneM2M. NSE is responsible for providing the interface to the underlying transport network. The oneM2M supports HTTP binding and provides Restful APIs over each layer. The oneM2M also defines several reference points among its entities: Mca between AE and CSE; Mcc between CSEs; and Mcn between CSE and NSE.

IN is related to MN as how cloud is related to Fog as there are many common features between them. In our research, MNs are thus deployed in Fog nodes and used to offload the congested IN normally deployed in the cloud. These MNs on Fog nodes support low latency required for critical IoT/M2M applications.

4 Detailed Design and Implementation

This section illustrates the implementation details of our system architecture introduced in Sect. 3, including its applications to a smart hospital use case.

4.1 Sensor Network

We assume three kinds of IoT/M2M devices deployed in the hospital. Each one produces a specific type of data traffic:

- *Heartbeat Data* - produced by the heart monitoring devices to ensure the wellness of the patients with heart disease.
- *Video Stream* - produced by video cameras installed in the hospital to monitor patients and detect any anomaly.
- *Personal and Clinic Historical Information* - produced by the hospital information system terminals to track patients' personal data and clinic historic record for reference and analytics.

To simulate the three kinds of devices above we design a multi-thread Traffic Generator configurable in terms of number of thread, data size and data frequency. Each simulated device can send IoT data to Fog Network via HTTP Post by specifying the URI address of a oneM2M AE (Application Entity) such as m2m/video_app/video_container.

4.2 Fog Network

Our design of Fog Network, as depicted in the lower part of Fig. 3, is based on the opensource container orchestration system, Kubernetes [11]. Fog Nodes are constructed as Kubernetes pods managed by kubelet and communicate with each other using Flannel Container Network Interface (CNI).

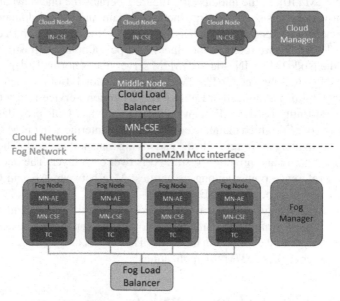

Fig. 3. Detailed system architecture

The components of Fog Network and its associated scalability mechanism are described below.

1. *Fog Manager:* Fog Manager is implemented based on Kubernetes Metrics Server [12] that can monitor the CPU utilization of Fog nodes periodically. Through API, the resource usage metrics for pods and nodes can be monitored. Fog Manager then can scale Fog nodes out and in according to the workload discovered.

2. *Fog Node:* We construct Fog nodes as a single-level architecture and each one consists of three entities: Traffic Classifier (TC), oneM2M MN-CSE and oneM2M MN-AE.

   TC is the first point of Fog Network for receiving IoT traffic from Sensor Network. It decides whether to relay the traffic to remote Cloud or keeps it locally. Assuming the kinds of IoT applications coming to the IoT/M2M system are known in advance, a mapping table is pre-provisioned in Traffic Classifier to specify the latency demand of each type of IoT applications. When Traffic Classifier receives an HTTP request, it will parse the HTTP post to get the URI of oneM2M AE and use it to determine its latency demand from the mapping table.

   Among the three IoT devices in our hospital use case, heart monitoring devices require ultra-low latency response to ensure the quick report of a patient's medical status. Video cameras also demand low latency for anomaly detection. On the other hand, personal and historical clinic information has no need of low latency because it's for information retrieval and storage. Consequently, Traffic Classifier would divert the first two types of traffic to local Fog nodes for fast processing and the last one to Cloud Network for regular processing.

   Each MN-CSE in Fog Network registers to the upper MN-CSE that acts as the load balancer in the Cloud Network. As a result, when TCs want to forward the traffic to Cloud, MN-CSEs in Fog nodes can retarget these requests to the MN-CSE Load Balancer in the cloud via the oneM2M Mcc interface. MN-AE subscribes to the MN-CSE in the same Fog node so that it can receive notification from MN-CSE when there's any new IoT traffic coming in.

   When TC forwards the IoT traffic requiring low latency to the MN-CSE in Fog node, the MN-CSE stores the incoming data and sends notification to the MN-AE. MN-AE will either analyze the heartbeat data or process the video stream to determine whether there is any anomaly. If any anomaly is detected, MN-AE will trigger an alarm for special actions.

3. *Fog Load Balancer:* Fog Load Balancer is used to distribute the incoming data traffic to each Fog node fairly. It is designed based on RabbitMQ [13], an open-source message-broker software supporting Advanced Message Queuing Protocol (AMQP). Load Balancer is implemented in Remote Procedure Call (RPC) consisting of the request channel and the response channel. The RPC client in Load Balancer forwards the HTTP requests to the RPC servers in each Fog node via the request channel. Next, the RPC server in each Fog Node translates the messages to a specific format for inserting IoT data to oneM2M; it then sends a response back to the RPC client via the response channel. The response would be forwarded through Load Balancer to IoT/M2M devices in Sensor Network.

4. *Scalability Mechanism:* We define two thresholds as depicted in Fig. 4: Scale In (10%) and Scale Out (50%). Whenever Fog Manager detects that the average CPU utilization of Fog nodes is higher than the Scale Out threshold, it will scale out one more Fog node. On the other hand, if the average CPU utilization of Fog nodes is lower than the Scale In threshold, Fog Manager will scale in one Fog node.

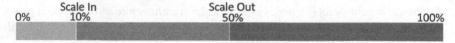

Fig. 4. The threshold of scalability mechanism

4.3 Cloud Network

We depict the architecture of our scalable Cloud Network in the upper part of Fig. 3. We use the open-source cloud operating system, OpenStack [14], to construct our Cloud Network. All the components as discussed below are virtual machines managed by OpenStack Nova and communicate with each other using OpenStack Neutron.

1. *Cloud Manager:* Cloud Manager manages the scale-out and scale-in of Cloud nodes with the following operations: (1) Cloud nodes send their CPU status to Cloud Manager periodically, (2) At CPU overload, Cloud Manager would scale Cloud nodes up while at CPU underload, it would scale Cloud nodes down.
2. *Cloud Node:* We provision a oneM2M IN-CSE into each Cloud node so that each Cloud node becomes a oneM2M server capable of processing the personal and clinic historical information. In addition, a plugin is embedded in each Cloud node for reporting its CPU utilization to Cloud Manager.
3. *Cloud Load Balancer:* Cloud Load Balancer is integrated in oneM2M Middle Node. When MN-CSE receives the data from TCs in Fog Network, it will redirect the data to Cloud Load Balancer immediately instead of processing it. Similar to Fog Network, Cloud Load Balancer for Cloud Nodes is also implemented based on RabbitMQ with RPC. The RPC client in Load Balancer forwards the HTTP requests to the RPC servers in each Cloud node via the request channel. After RPC servers send the data to IN-CSE, the response from the Cloud node is then sent back via the response channel to TCs, then to Sensor Network.
4. *Scalability Mechanism:* We define the same two thresholds: Scale In (10%) and Scale Out (50%) as depicted in Fig. 4, Once the average CPU utilization of Cloud nodes calculated by Cloud Manager exceeds Scale Out threshold, Cloud Manager will create and add one more Cloud node. Conversely, if the average CPU utilization of Cloud nodes is lower than Scale In threshold, Cloud Manager will stop and remove one Cloud node.

5 Experiment and Evaluation

In this section, we will show the experimental testing of the proposed architecture and the evaluation of testing results.

5.1 Testbed Environment

Our testbed environment is shown in Table 2. In Cloud Network, OpenStack Newton is deployed while in Fog Network, Kubernetes v1.12.1 and Docker [15] 18.06.1-ce are installed. We use OM2M [16], an open source implementation of oneM2M from LAAS-CNRS, to construct oneM2M MN and IN. Cloud Network consists of two physical machines: one for Controller and one for Compute Node. Fog Network consists of four physical machines: one for K8S Master and three for K8S Nodes. Besides, we set the minimum number of Cloud nodes to 2, the maximum number to 5 and each one runs on a virtual machine with 8CPU, 4 GB of RAM and 30 GB of HDD. On the other hand, we set the minimum number of Fog nodes to 2 and the maximum number to 7, each one running on a Kubernetes pod with 1 CPU, 2 GB of RAM and 15 GB of HDD.

Table 2. Testbed hardware information

Component	Operating system	CPU	RAM	Machine	Disk
Sensor network	Ubuntu 16.04	Inter Core i5-8400 CPU @2.80 GHz (6cores)	8 GB	1 Desktop	256 GB
Fog network		Intel Core i5-4200H CPU @ 2.80 GHz (4cores)	8 GB	4 Laptops	512 GB
Cloud network		Intel Core i7-8700 CPU @ 3.20 Ghz (12cores)	64 GB	2 Desktops	1 TB

To simulate the proximity of Fog Network and the Cloud Network to Sensor Network, we configure the network in such a way that the average response time from Fog Network is 6.7 ms while the one from Cloud Network is 210 ms with 1000 simple HTTP requests sent to each site. This simulates the distance from Sensor Network to Fog Network and Cloud Network, respectively.

5.2 Experiment Setup

We design a Traffic Generator that is a multi-thread program, to simulate the IoT traffic of heartbeat data [17], video stream [18] and clinic information [19] as described in Sect. 4.1. Traffic Generator can configure any number of devices with different data frequency and data size such as those in Table 3. used in our experiments. The settings

Table 3. Traffic generator configuration

IoT traffic	Thread number (low/high)	Data frequency	Data size
Heartbeat data	2/10	10 records/s	170 B
Video stream	2/10	10 records/s	20 KB
Clinic information	4/20	2 records/s	950 B

are chosen to reflect the relatively small size but high frequency of heartbeat data, the large data size and high frequency of video stream though our IoT/M2M system only stores the metadata of video instead of the whole media. Furthermore, we assume Personal and Clinic Historical Information is the major application data traffic in the smart hospital so its number of devices is set to be the largest. We intend to show that by letting Cloud and Fog handle the type of traffic they are good at, we can achieve better overall system scalability than sending all the traffic to either Fog or Cloud alone.

We test our system with two scenarios: high and low traffic loads. The amount of high traffic is five times than that of low traffic as indicated in Table 3. In our experiment, we send both high and low traffic loads for 5 min respectively to our proposed system and compare the scalability of our system versus those with only Fog or Cloud in terms of *latency*, *CPU usage* and *power consumption* per each IoT request. These three features can represent how well the scalability of a system has been designed. Ideally, for the system with good scalability design, when the amount of processed data increases, it would cause lower latency, lower CPU resource and lower power consumption than the ones with worse scalability.

5.3   Evaluation Result

We expect our system can leverage the benefits of dual scalability mechanisms of Fog and Cloud to outperform the other two compared systems in majority of our test cases.

- Latency

In order to explain the benefits of our proposed system, we define maximum tolerable latency of each application. For the application which would be forwarded to Fog Network, the value of heartbeat data is set at 70 ms and the one of video stream is set at 250 ms. On the other hand, the value of Personal and Clinic Historical Information is set at 4 s because it doesn't require low latency response.

The evaluation results of latency are shown in Fig. 5. Under the condition of low traffic, our proposed system and the one with only Fog can meet all the latency demands

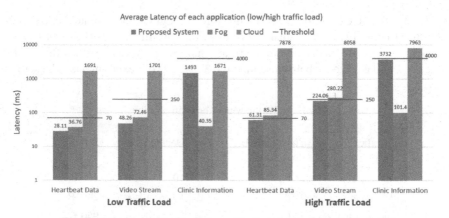

Fig. 5. Latency results for three applications in low/high traffic load

of three IoT applications. However, the one with only Cloud cannot provide low latency to heartbeat data and video stream due to the long haul communication. On the other hand, only our proposed system satisfies all latency requirements in the case of high traffic thanks to the effort of Traffic Classifier. Similar to the situation in low traffic, the system with only Cloud cannot even meet one of them. In addition, the system with only Fog has to allocate part of computing resources for Personal and Clinic Historical Information, so it cannot fully focus on handling the other traffic requiring low latency.

- CPU Usage

Figure 6 depicts the result of Average CPU usage. These results measured average CPU utilization of physical machines for computing. To calculate the overall CPU usage of our proposed Cloud-Fog system, we survey a CPU benchmark website [20] to compare the CPU of both sites so that we can get the CPU usage of our hybrid system by using the weighted average method. For the low traffic load, the system with only Fog outperforms the others due to its lightweight characteristics. On the other hand, Cloud has the highest CPU usage due to the needs to maintain heavyweight Virtual Machines even in the light traffic load.

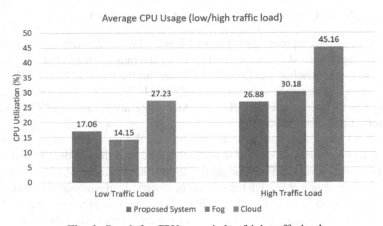

Fig. 6. Result for CPU usage in low/high traffic load

However, our proposed system shows the best result in the condition of high traffic load. That's because when the amount of data traffic increases, the value of Traffic Classifier and dual scalability mechanisms stands out. Both Fog and Cloud can fully utilize their computing resources to handle the traffic that they are good at instead of spending extra resource to process all three types of traffic.

- Power Consumption

Figure 7 shows the results of average power consumption per request for three applications. We calculate the total power consumption in the period of our experiment and

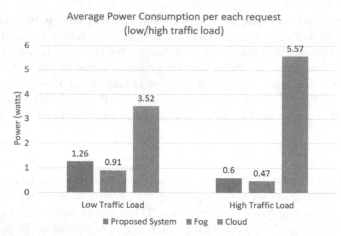

Fig. 7. Result for average power consumption per request in low/high traffic load

derive the results by dividing it by the total number of requests. We use the following formula (1) to calculate the power consumption:

$$Power\ Consumption = TDP * CPU\% + K * Memory\% \tag{1}$$

where TDP is the microprocessor's Thermal Design Power, a reference measurement of CPU running in normal conditions and given by the manufacturer. For our particular testbed, TDP for the machines in Cloud is 65 W and for the ones in Fog is 47 W. K is the common power consumption of memory modules [21], and it's 6 W for the memory in Cloud and 4 W for the one in Fog. CPU% and Memory% are the average CPU utilization and memory usage of the machines.

The results show that our proposed system and the one with only Fog consume less power consumption *per request* in the high traffic load than in the low traffic load, because both sites leverage Fog Computing to handle the traffic. Although they may consume more total power in high traffic than in low traffic, the amount of requests they can handle also largely increases due to low latency communications and scalability mechanisms. As the impact of the increase in the amount of requests is greater than the increase of total power usage, the average power consumption per request becomes dramatically lower. On the other hand, the system with only Cloud performs worse in the high traffic load than in the low traffic load because its high latency characteristics produces more impact to the average power consumption per request.

In the two conditions of traffic load, our proposed system performs better than the one with only Cloud but it doesn't perform better than the one with only Fog because we leverage both Cloud and Fog to handle the IoT traffic so it's reasonable that our proposed system consume more power than the system with only Fog.

In summary, only our proposed system can meet all the latency requirements of three applications even though it doesn't always perform the best in terms of the average power consumption per request. However, for smart hospital latency should be the first priority consideration. This verifies that our proposed architecture is indeed the best choice in the case of smart hospital applications.

6 Conclusion and Future Work

In this research, we propose the use of Fog Computing to help Cloud handle the IoT/M2M applications requiring low latency. Accordingly, we introduce a Traffic Classifier which is deployed near the Sensor Network, to divert different IoT traffic to Fog Network or Cloud Network according to their latency requirements. We also propose the use of standardized IoT/M2M platform, oneM2M, to integrate Kubernetes-based Fog Network and OpenStack-based Cloud Network. Moreover, we adopt dual scalability mechanisms in Fog and Cloud to achieve overall system scalability while accommodating the demands from low latency applications.

We compared our proposed system to the ones with only Fog or Cloud by utilizing a smart hospital use case. Three architectures are compared in terms of their latency, CPU usage and power consumption. We verify that the proposed system is the best choice for the specific use case.

In the future, we plan to apply SDN/NFV technology to our proposed system. The goal is to bring the benefits of softwarization and virtualization to system scalability such as to manage Cloud Node as VM-based VNFs and Fog Node as container-based VNFs in the NFV architecture.

Another extension in our plan is to add more layers of Fog Nodes. As more complicated IoT traffic comes in, it's necessary to distribute the task to more levels of Fog nodes and each level of Fog nodes can be equipped with scalability mechanisms to support the processing of the huge amount of incoming data requests.

Acknowledgement. This work was financially supported by the Center for Open Intelligent Connectivity from The Featured Areas Research Center Program within the framework of the Higher Education Sprout Project by the Ministry of Education (MOE) in Taiwan.

References

1. Bonomi, F., Milito, R., Zhu, J., Addepalli, S.: Fog computing and its role in the internet of things. In: Proceedings of the First Edition of the MCC Workshop on Mobile Cloud Computing, Helsinki, Finland, pp. 13–16 (2012)
2. OpenFog Consortium: OpenFog Reference Architecture for Fog Computing (2017)
3. Smart Hospital. https://www.sdglobaltech.com/blog/how-developers-must-prepare-to-create-smart-hospital-solutions. Accessed 9 Apr 2019
4. Cerritos, E., Lin, F.J., De la Bastida, D.: High scalability for cloud-based IoT/M2M systems. In: IEEE International Conference on Communications (ICC), Kuala Lumpur, Malaysia (2016)
5. De la Bastida, D., Lin, F.J.: OpenStack-based highly scalable IoT/M2M platforms. In: iThings, Exeter, England, UK, June 2017
6. Sen, S., Balasubramanian, A.: A highly resilient and scalable broker architecture for IoT applications. In: 10th International Conference on Communication Systems & Networks (COMSNETS), Bengaluru, India (2018)
7. Tseng, C.L., Lin F.J.: Extending scalability of IoT/M2M platforms with fog computing. In: IEEE World Forum on IoT, Singapore (2018)
8. Zhao, W., Liu, J., Guo, H., Hara, T.: ETC-IoT: edge-node-assisted transmitting for the cloud-centric internet of things. IEEE Netw. **32**, 101–107 (2018)

9. Chen, Y.C., Chang, Y.C., Chen, C.H., Lin, Y.S., Chen, J.L., Chang, Y.Y.: Cloud-fog computing for information-centric Internet-of-Things applications. In: 2017 International Conference on Applied System Innovation (ICASI) (2017)
10. oneM2M: Functional Architecture, oneM2M Technical SpecificationTS-0001-V.3.12.0
11. Kubernetes. https://kubernetes.io/. Accessed 9 Apr 2019
12. Metrics Server. https://github.com/kubernetes-incubator/metrics-server. Accessed 9 Apr 2019
13. RabbitMQ. https://www.rabbitmq.com/. Accessed 9 Apr 2019
14. Openstack. https://www.openstack.org. Accessed 9 Apr 2019
15. Docker. https://www.docker.com/. Accessed 9 Apr 2019
16. OM2M. https://www.eclipse.org/om2m/. Accessed 9 Apr 2019
17. Heartbeat Data. https://archive.ics.uci.edu/ml/datasets/Heart+Disease. Accessed 24 Apr 2019
18. Video Stream. https://schema.org/VideoObject. Accessed 25 Apr 2019
19. Personal and Clinic Historical Information. https://schema.org/Patient. Accessed 25 Apr 2019
20. UserBenchmark. https://cpu.userbenchmark.com/. Accessed 9 Apr 2019
21. Power Supply Calculator: https://outervision.com/power-supply-calculator. Accessed 9 Apr 2019

Towards Efficient Privacy-Preserving Personal Information in User Daily Life

Hai Wang[1](✉), Tong Feng[1], Zhe Ren[1], Ling Gao[2], and Jie Zheng[1]

[1] Northwest University, Xi'an, China
hwang@nwu.edu.cn
[2] Xi'an Polytechnic University, Xi'an, China

Abstract. The popularity of smart home has added a lot of convenience to people's lives. However, while users use these smart products, users' privacy data has also been leaked and it may cause some risks. Besides, because of untrusted third-party servers, we simply use traditional privacy-preserving methods could no longer protect users' private information effectively. In order to solve these problems, this paper proposes a privacy-preserving method for multi-private data: We first determine the privacy data format that needs to be protected, such as audio or text. Secondly, if the data format is text, we will use the local differential privacy method. We first obtain the key attributes of the user from the key information chain, and then select the appropriate localized differential privacy method according to the text characteristics of the key attributes. The user realizes the local disturbance of the data and then uploads it to the data collection center—the cloud platform. Finally, when an attacker attempts to obtain user information from the cloud platform, it uses the central differential privacy method to add noise and the noise-added data is transmitted to the attacker. If the data format is voice frequency, we first convert the voice information into binary code, then chaotically encrypt the binary code, and upload the encrypted binary code to the cloud platform. We verify the effectiveness of our methods by experiments, and it can protect users' privacy information better.

Keywords: Multi-privacy data · Key information chain · Localized differential privacy · Noise adding · Privacy-preserving

1 Introduction

As Internet of Things is deeply used in various industries, IoT devices have increased more connections with people. Smart home is a very common scene. When users want to play music, they only need to input voice commands to the smart speakers, when the users come back, the smart lock will open automatically; when the sun rises or falls, the smart curtain will follow, the smart camera allows users to keep an eye on the room and ensure the safety of the room. However, since the smart device can access very private data, for example, a smart camera can also be used by an attacker to photo the user's privacy, a smart speaker can obtain the user's voice information, and the smart

© ICST Institute for Computer Sciences, Social Informatics and Telecommunications Engineering 2020
Published by Springer Nature Switzerland AG 2020. All Rights Reserved
B. Li et al. (Eds.): IoTaaS 2019, LNICST 316, pp. 503–513, 2020.
https://doi.org/10.1007/978-3-030-44751-9_42

lock's password is related to the security of the entire room. Therefore, the Internet of Things has also raised concerns about the privacy of these digitally augmented spaces [1–3]. Most existing researches on IoT security issues focus on privacy data leakage detection. FlowFence [4] is a system that enforces streaming policies for IoT applications to protect sensitive data; ContexIoT [5] is a context-based licensing system for the IoT platform that collects contextual information to identify sensitive operations. Zawoad et al. [6] formally defined the Internet of Things forensics and proposed a forensic sensing Internet of Things (FAIoT) model to support forensic research in the Internet of Things infrastructure. ProvThings [7] seized a series of events through the security-sensitive system-level SmartThings API and used it for forensic reconstruction attacks. SAINT [8] is the first accurate system to carefully detect sensitive data streams in IoT applications to fully identify a complete set of pollution sources and sinks through analoging IoT-specific challenges, solutions for platform and specific language issues. Although the means of detection can make security personnel better understand the problems in the environment, the ultimate goal of detection is to better protect privacy. Therefore, it is also a feasible solution to solve this problem directly from the perspective of privacy protection.

Differential privacy technology [9, 10] is a hot research in the current academic world. Traditional differential privacy technology concentrates raw data into a data center and then publishes relevant statistical information that satisfies differential privacy, we call it centralized differential privacy technology. Centralized differential privacy protects sensitive information based on a premise: trusted third-party collectors, ensuring that third-party data collectors do not steal and reveal sensitive users' information. However, in practical applications, even the privacy of these trusted third-party collector users is still not guaranteed. In 2016, nearly 170 million accounts of American social networking site LinkedIn were publicly sold by hackers in the black market; personal information of nearly 5,000 W citizens in Turkey was leaked, and the President's personal information was hanged on the dark network platform; Yahoo happened the largest data breach, more than 5 billion users' account information was stolen by hackers. There are many similar examples, so it is very difficult to find a truly trusted third-party data collection platform in practical applications. Localized differential privacy [11, 12] came into being under such a background. Localized differential privacy has two major characteristics: (1) fully consider the background knowledge of any attacker and quantify the degree of privacy protection; (2) localize the perturbed data to protect against privacy attacks from untrusted third-party data collectors. In sensitive image feature extraction scenarios, localized differential privacy shows how important it is. Finn [13] took the medical images an example to illustrate the privacy problem contained in the image. Qin [14] proposes the encryption-based privacy protection method in the image feature extraction process in the cloud computing environment. Ren [15] pointed out that in the cloud computing environment local differential privacy had great potentiality in image processing. After reading much paper, we choose to apply the local differential privacy method to the smart home scene, and realize the adaptive privacy protection method for the privacy data in the smart home scene. Firstly, the user needs to judge the privacy data type, and then according to different data types user differently realizes the disturbance of ε-localized differential privacy, next transmit it to the third-party data collector.

The data collector receives the disturbed data and performs a series of queries and refinement to obtain effective statistical results.

Our contributions can be summarized as follows:

(1) Combining the differential privacy protection technology with the smart home scene, using the privacy protection method based on privacy data leakage detection method, so that the privacy of the user is better protected better.
(2) Using the localized differential privacy method to process the text type privacy data, using different methods for different text characteristics, and finally realizing the adaptive localized differential privacy protection for the text type privacy data.
(3) Using chaotic encryption algorithm to process speech type data to ensure the security of speech in the process of transmission, and using experiment to verify the effectiveness of methods we propose.

2 Model

Before implementing privacy protection, we need to understand what data needs to be protected. In the smart home scenario, this paper mainly studies text privacy data and voice privacy data. The text types include personal information (such as ID number and mobile phone number), room password, communication record and content, and whereabouts; the voice type is mainly the user's voice information, such as the voice command issued by the user to control the smart device, the voice when you call in the room or talk to other members of the family. Since these two types of private data are handled differently, we will use different privacy protection methods protect them.

2.1 Text Type Private Data

The privacy data of the text type includes two types: numerical data (such as age, telephone number) and non-numeric data (such as name and gender). For the user, the sensitive attributes are various, if users need to use the localized differential privacy method to protect every sensitive attribute, which will cause great trouble to users, and the user's sense of smart devices' convenience will be get bad. In this paper, each sensitive attribute of the user is connected to form a complete information chain of the user. In this information chain, some sensitive attributes are key attributes that can constitute the overall information of the user, while other sensitive attributes are subordinate to these key attributes. As shown in the Fig. 1 below, the blue circle represents the key sensitive attribute, and the white box represents other sensitive attributes. If all the key sensitive attributes represented by the circle are leaked, then a specific person can be located, so it is easy to infer other sensitive attributes. For example, If the text information of a user is 'age 27, Hangzhou, Zhejiang Province, China, square face, 1.9 m height', then the key information may be clearly distinguishable '1.9 m height, Hangzhou, Zhejiang Province, China'.

We can see that if we can hide the user's key sensitive attributes, the user's private information can be effectively protected. As in the above example, we blur the key

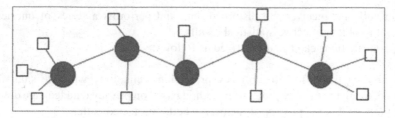

Fig. 1. Key information chain

information, then the user information becomes "age 27, a southern province in China, square face, 1.9 m height" or "age 27, Hangzhou, Zhejiang Province, China, square face", through this information it is not possible to locate a specific person, so it can be seen that the user's key attributes are very important to user privacy protection.

Through the key information chain, we can understand what are the user's key attributes, and then users can localize differential privacy protection for these key attributes, which can save users' time and make users get better service. On the other hand, the user's critical privacy is protected from the risk of data leakage. Since the sensitive attributes of user in the smart home scene are mostly discrete, this paper mainly uses the frequency statistics method based on localized differential privacy to realize the privacy protection for text type data. The frequency statistics method is divided into single value and multi value. The RAPPOR [16] method is representative of single value frequency statistics. The value of a variable is represented as a string. Suppose there are a total of n users, the i_{th} user u_i corresponds to a certain sensitive value, $x_i \in X$ and $|X| = k$, and now it is desirable to count the frequency of the value $x_i (1 \le i \le k)$, the RAPPOR method is shown as Fig. 2 shows.

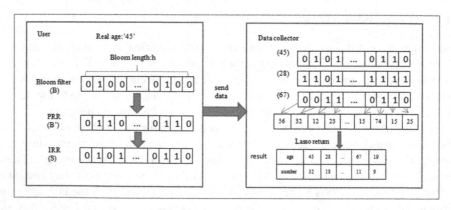

Fig. 2. Process of RAPPOR

In Fig. 2, X represents the age attribute, there is a certain value $x_i =' 45'$, we first used the Bloom Filter [17] technique to express it as a vector $B = (0, 1)^h$ that its length is h, and the mapping relationship matrix of the Bloom string is recorded at the same time. Then we perturbed to each bit of the vector B by using a random response technique to obtain a permanent random response result B', the perturbation mode is performed according to the following formula, $f \in [0, 1]$ indicates the probability value:

$$p\left(B_i' = x\right) = \begin{cases} 0.5f & x = 1 \\ 0.5f & x = 0 \\ 1 - f & x = B_i \end{cases} \tag{1}$$

Then, the second perturbation of each bit of the vector B' is performed to obtain a transient random response result S, the second perturbation mode is performed according to the following formula, where $p \in [0, 1]$ and $q \in [0, 1]$ indicates the probability that S_i is 1 when B_i' takes a value of 1 or 0:

$$P(S_i = 1) = \begin{cases} p \; if \; B_i' = 1 \\ q \; if \; B_i' = 0 \end{cases} \tag{2}$$

After each user gets the disturbance result S, it is sent to the third-party data collector. The data collector counts the number of occurrences of each bit and corrects it, and then combines the mapping matrix to complete each frequency statistics corresponding to the age value by Lasso regression method [18].

In view of the high communication cost of the RAPPOR method, also in the single-value case, each user in the S-Hist [19] method encodes a character string, randomly selects one of the bits, and uses the random response technique to perform the disturbance, then send it to the data collector, thus greatly reducing the transmission cost. K-RR [20] is a gradient response technique proposed by Kairouz et al. It mainly overcomes the problem that the random response technique is for binary variables. For the case where the variable contains $k(k > 2)$ candidate values, it can be directly make a random response. For any input $R \in X$, the response to the output $R' \in X$ is as follows:

$$P\left(R'|R\right) = \frac{1}{k - 1 + e^\epsilon} \begin{cases} e^\epsilon \; if \; R' = R \\ 1 \; if \; R' \neq R \end{cases} \tag{3}$$

That is, the probability of $\frac{e^\epsilon}{k-1+e^\epsilon}$ is used to respond to the real result, and the probability of $\frac{1}{k-1+e^\epsilon}$ is used to respond to any of the remaining $k - 1$ results. Make it satisfy ε-localized differential privacy.

Based on the K-RR method, Kairouz et al. proposed the O-RR method for the case where the value of the variable is unknown [21]. The O-RR method is an improvement of the K-RR method. Hash mapping and grouping operations are also introduced on the basis of K-RR. The hash mapping makes the method no longer pay attention to the string itself, so that no candidate characters string list need to be collected in advance. And the probability of hash map value collisions can be further reduced by grouping operations. The above describes several frequency statistics methods for localized differential privacy. In the actual situation, we will select the most suitable localized differential privacy protection method for different text types, which can reduce the communication cost and save the overhead.

After selecting the appropriate localized differential privacy method for the text, we can upload the disturbed data to the cloud platform, and the cloud platform will perform the second noise addition and then release the data by the exponential mechanism. The general idea of the exponential mechanism is to select an output value r from the output field based on the score of the usability q, and the probability of selecting the value is exponentially proportional to the score. The function q needs to be insensitive to the variation of a single record, that is, the function sensitivity is low, and its sensitivity can be expressed as $\Delta q = \max\limits_{\forall r, D1, D2} |q(D1, r) - q(D2, r)|$. The privacy protection algorithm can be designed by an exponential mechanism, as shown by the theorem.

Given a data set D and an availability function $q = (D \times R) \rightarrow R$, the privacy protection mechanism A satisfies ε-differential privacy if and only if the following expression holds:

$$A(D, q) = \left\{ reutrn\ with\ probability \propto exp\left(\frac{\epsilon q(D, r)}{\Delta q} \right) \right\} \qquad (4)$$

The exponential mechanism is the operation of the cloud platform. It is not our main research method, so it is not detailed. Through the above method, we can effectively protect the text data, and finally realize the privacy protection of the text type data.

2.2 Voice Type Private Data

The speech signal is a simple and succinct signal with a large amount of information, such as accent, language, emotion, gender identity and speech content. All kinds of information are expressed in one-dimensional signals. From the perspective of structure, human language information can be divided into three layers: the first layer is language information, including speech content and sentences; the second layer is sub-language information, including the speaker's attitude, emotion, intention, etc. Pitch, rhythm, volume, and tone, etc. can show intentions and attitudes; the third layer is non-verbal information, such as physical condition, age, and gender. The linguistic information is conducive to prevent forgery, and is also conducive to the preservation of living evidence; the paralinguistic information is useful for detecting true intentions, and the non-verbal information can be partially traced back to evidence. Therefore, we need to start from the above single layer to achieve privacy protection of voice data. Speech recognition is also a hot topic of current research, so if we want to protect the privacy of voice type data, then the starting point is speech recognition. Speech recognition includes two processes of recognition and text translation. If the user speaks a local dialect, then the approximate area of the user can be determined according to the dialect type, and the user's personal preference can be understood according to the user's speech during the translation stage. After translating the voice information into text, it can be processed according to the above-mentioned text type privacy data, so we mainly protect the privacy of the speech recognition process in this section.

The goal of speech recognition is to convert the vocabulary content in human speech into computer-readable input, such as buttons, binary codes or character sequences. This paper encrypts the digitized code of the speech signal to protect the user's voice information. Both compressed sensing and chaos can be applied to the field of data encryption. This paper combines the two methods to implement the chaotic encryption method based on compressed sensing. The mathematical model is as follows:

$$C = M(\dot{X}) \tag{5}$$

M() is Arnold map, and C is a ciphertext information that needs to be transmitted. In Eq. (5), $\dot{X}$ is the superimposed n × n dimensional matrix of X, X is:

$$X = AS + L(A\bar{S}) \tag{6}$$

A is the key matrix, we choose the random Gauss matrix as the key matrix, A is a random Gauss matrix, and $A \in R^{M \times N} (M \ll N)$, the construction process of the key matrix A: construction a matrix A of $M \times N$ size, each element in A independently obeys a Gaussian distribution with a mean of 0 and a variance of 1/M, that is:

$$A_{i,j} = N\left(0, \frac{1}{M}\right) \tag{7}$$

S is a speech signal that needs to be encrypted. According to the short-term stationary analysis of the speech signal, the speech signal needs to be pre-processed in the encryption process, that is, the encryption process is actually after the speech signal pre-processing framing, for each frame. The signal is encrypted. The voice signal frame length is selected to be 400, that is, the plaintext S length is 400, and the key matrix A has a dimension of 256 × 400. L is the Lorenz transform. This encryption model uses the third-order Lorenz equation as the transformed chaotic system, and $\bar{S}$ is the fixed random signal in the same dimension as the plaintext signal. The information is known to both parties, that is $\bar{S} \in R^N$. The key matrix A and the random signal $\bar{S}$ are transformed as parameters in the Lorenz system, and the key space is added directly to the voice signal encrypted by the compressed sensing, which has better security. The signal X processed by the Eq. (6) is a 256-dimensional column signal, which is sequentially superimposed into $\dot{X}$, $\dot{X}$ is a 16-order square matrix, and then the position of each element in the $\dot{X}$ is performed using Arnold map. Scrambling. The Arnold mapping can be expressed as:

$$\begin{bmatrix} X_{n+1} \\ Y_{n+1} \end{bmatrix} = U \begin{bmatrix} X_n \\ Y_n \end{bmatrix} (mod \ \ 1) \tag{8}$$

U is:

$$U = \begin{bmatrix} 1 & 1 \\ 1 & 2 \end{bmatrix} \tag{9}$$

As shown in Eq. (8), mod1 means that only the fractional part is taken. In order to scramble $\dot{X}$ and spread the formula (7), there is:

$$\begin{bmatrix} X_{n+1} \\ Y_{n+1} \end{bmatrix} = U \begin{bmatrix} X_n \\ Y_n \end{bmatrix} (mod \ \ N) \tag{10}$$

After the diffusion, in order to ensure its feasibility, the matrix U in Eq. (9) is processed, and the parameters a, b(a, b < N) are introduced, then the matrix U can be expressed as:

$$U_d = \begin{bmatrix} ab + 1 & a \\ b & 1 \end{bmatrix} \tag{11}$$

a, b need to satisfy the condition $0 < a < 256, 0 < b < 256$. After scrambling it with Arnold map, the encryption operation is completed, and the encrypted information becomes ciphertext, which is transmitted to the receiver through the channel. Decryption is the inverse of encryption. It is not described here. The signal is reconstructed from the decrypted code to obtain the original signal.

3 Experiment and Analysis

For the above methods, we have carried out experimental verification, and the experimental results prove the effectiveness of our proposed method.

3.1 Text Type Private Data Experiment

In this paper, experiments are carried out by adopting different privacy budgets ε. The communication cost, progressive error boundary and computational cost are compared and analyzed among the above methods. The communication cost refers to the data transmission overhead from each user to the data collector. Here, we approximate that the communication cost is proportional to the amount of data. In the progressive error boundary, n refers to the total number of users, k refers to the number of attribute candidates, and h represents the length of the Bloom Filter string. The calculation cost refers to the calculation cost when the data collector counts the user data, and it is divided into three levels: high, medium, and low.

It can be seen from Table 1 that the availability based on the RAPPOR method is higher, and it also brings higher computational overhead; The S-Hist-based method greatly reduces the communication cost, but its computational cost is positively correlated with the number of users, the computational overhead is huge, and the sampling process also brings a certain precision loss; the K-RR-based method simplifies the data perturbation process and sacrifices certain release precision.

3.2 Voice Type Private Data Experiment

This paper verifies the feasibility of the above method for speech encryption through experiments. The experiment selected a male voice from our laboratory with a total of 23,455 points and a sampling rate of 16 K. Different frame lengths and compression ratios (M/N) were chosen to test the results. The results are shown in Table 2 and Fig. 3:

The average frame signal-to-noise ratio AFSNR is used to evaluate the recovery quality of the signal. The larger the AFSNR, the smaller the difference between the signal after decryption and the original signal. It can be seen that different frame lengths

Table 1. Existing four methods of single-valued frequency estimation

Methods	Communication cost	Progressive error boundary	Computational cost
RAPPOR	$o(h)$	$o\left(\frac{k}{\epsilon\sqrt{n}}\right)$	High
S-Hist	$o(1)$	$o\left(\frac{\sqrt{\log k}}{\epsilon\sqrt{n}}\right)$	High
K-RR	$o(1)$	$o\left(\frac{\sqrt{k^2}}{\epsilon\sqrt{n}}\right)$	Low
O-RR	$o(1)$	$o\left(\frac{\sqrt{k^2}}{\epsilon\sqrt{n}}\right)$	Low

Table 2. Voice signal test

Frame length	Compression ratios M/N				
	0.2	0.3	0.4	0.5	0.6
160	5.461	8.950	13.637	17.877	20.872
240	5.822	8.154	12.554	16.928	19.296
320	6.697	9.775	13.656	17.513	18.219
400	6.767	9.954	12.037	15.952	15.972
480	6.708	9.235	11.780	13.102	24.773

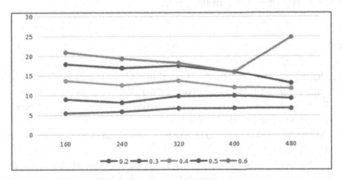

Fig. 3. Voice signal test

and compression ratios have an impact on the accuracy of the decryption. And the accuracy is best when the frame length is 400 and the compression ratio is 0.6.

Through the above experiments, we use the existing localized differential privacy method for text type private data, and select the appropriate privacy protection method according to the data characteristics (such as the number of attribute values), and can estimate the cost according to the importance of privacy, then we select the better method;

For the speech type, we use the chaotic encryption algorithm based on compressed sensing. It is verified by experiments that this method can effectively protect the privacy of users information.

4 Conclusion

This paper focuses on the privacy security issues in the smart home scene. Different from the existing privacy disclosure detection, this paper takes a different approach. We divided the privacy data types in the smart home scene into two types: text type and voice type. For the text type, we first integrate and analyze the user's text privacy data, and put forward the idea of a key information chain, so that users do not need to protect every sensitive attribute, only need to protect key attributes. In addition, considering the problem of untrusted third-party servers, it is proposed to introduce the localized differential privacy method into the scenario, and describe and analyze several existing localized differential privacy methods. The specific experiments verify our analysis. For the voice type, this paper combines the compressed sensing and chaotic encryption methods, and uses these two methods to encrypt the speech-coded binary code. The experimental results show that the proposed method can effectively protect voice information and prevent threats caused by interception of voice information.

This paper protects the user privacy from the two data types of voice and text, but the method proposed in this paper is not used in the real smart home scene, the effectiveness of the method is just verified by simulation experiments. In the case of the effect, further exploration is needed. On the other hand, the privacy in this scene also includes information such as pictures and videos, and it will be more complicated. We need to study more deeply, and we can complete the comprehensive privacy protection work under the smart home scene in the future.

References

1. Ronen, E., Shamir, A., Weingarten, A.-O., O'flynn, C.: IoT goes nuclear: creating a ZigBee chain reaction. In: IEEE Security and Privacy (SP) (2017)
2. Fernandes, E., Jung, J., Prakash, A.: Security analysis of emerging smart home applications. In: IEEE Security and Privacy (SP) (2016)
3. Celik, Z.B., Mcdaniel, P., Tan, G.: SOTERIA: automated IoT safety and security analysis. In: USENIX ATC (2018)
4. Fernandes, E., Paupore, J., Rahmati, A., Simionato, D., Conti, M., Prakash, A.: FlowFence: practical data protection for emerging IoT application frameworks. In: USENIX Security (2016)
5. Jia, Y.J., et al.: ContexIoT: towards providing contextual integrity to appified IoT platforms. In: NDSS (2017)
6. Zawoad, S., Hasan, R.: FAIoT: towards building a forensics aware eco system for the internet of things. In: SCC, pp. 279–284 (2015)
7. Wang, Q., Hassan, W.U., Bates, A., Gunter, C.: Fear and logging in the internet of things. In: NDSS (2018)
8. Celik, Z.B., et al.: Sensitive information tracking in commodity IoT. In: USENIX Security (2018)

9. Dwork, C., Lei, J.: Differential privacy and robust statistics. In: Proceedings of the 41st Annual ACM Symposium on Theory of Computing, pp. 371–380. ACM (2009). https://doi.org/10.1145/1536414.1536466

10. Smith, A.: Privacy-preserving statistical estimation with optimal convergence rates. In: Proceedings of the 43rd Annual ACM Symposium on Theory of Computing, pp. 813–822. ACM (2011). https://doi.org/10.1145/1993636.1993743

11. Kasiviswanathan, S.P., Lee, H.K., Nissim, K., Raskhodnikova, S., Smith, A.: What can we learn privately. In: Proceedings of the 49th Annual IEEE Symposium on Foundations of Computer Science (FOCS), pp. 531–540. IEEE (2008)

12. Duchi, J.C., Jordan, M.I., Wainwright, M.J.: Local privacy and statistical minimax rates. In: Proceedings of the 54th Annual IEEE Symposium on Foundations of Computer Science (FOCS), pp. 429–438. IEEE (2013). https://doi.org/10.1109/focs.2013.53

13. Finn, R.L., Wright, D., Friedewald, M.: Seven types of privacy. In: Gutwirth, S., Leenes, R., de Hert, P., Poullet, Y. (eds.) European Data Protection: Coming of Age, pp. 3–32. Springer, Dordrecht (2013). https://doi.org/10.1007/978-94-007-5170-5_1

14. Qin, Z., Yan, J., Ren, K., Chen, C.W., Wang, C.: Towards efficient privacy-preserving image feature extraction in cloud computing. In: Proceedings of the 22nd ACM International Conference on Multimedia, pp. 497–506. ACM (2014). https://doi.org/10.1145/2647868.2654941

15. Ren, K.: Privacy-preserving image processing in cloud computing. Chin. J. Netw. Inf. Secur. 1, 12–17 (2016)

16. Erlingsson, Ú., Pihur, V., Korolova, A.: RAPPOR: randomized aggregatable privacy-preserving ordinal response. In: Proceedings of the 2014 ACM SIGSAC Conference on Computer and Communications Security, pp. 1054–1067. ACM (2014). https://doi.org/10.1145/2660267.2660348

17. Bloom, B.H.: Space/time trade-offs in hash coding with allowable errors. Commun. ACM 13(7), 422–426 (1970). https://doi.org/10.1145/362686.362692

18. Tibshirani, R.: Regression shrinkage and selection via the Lasso. J. Roy. Stat. Soc. (Ser. B-Methodol.) 58, 267–288 (1996)

19. Bassily, R., Smith, A.: Local, private, efficient protocols for succinct histograms. In: Proceedings of the 47th Annual ACM on Symposium on Theory of Computing, pp. 127–135. ACM (2015). https://doi.org/10.1145/2746539.2746632

20. Kairouz, P., Oh, S., Viswanath, P.: Extremal mechanisms for local differential privacy. In: Advances in Neural Information Processing Systems, pp. 2879–2887 (2014)

21. Kairouz, P., Bonawitz, K., Ramage, D.: Discrete distribution estimation under local privacy. In: Proceedings of the 33rd International Conference on Machine Learning, New York, pp. 2436–2444 (2016)

Properties and Performance of the Orbital-Angular-Momentum Modes in Wireless Communication

Chen Feng and Jinhong Li[✉]

School of Electronics and Information,
Northwestern Polytechnical University, Xi'an, China
lijinhong@mail.nwpu.edu.cn

Abstract. The orbital-angular-momentum (OAM) mode multiplexing is one of the promising ways to improve the efficiency of the spectrum utilization of the network in the Internet of Things (IoT). In this article, the propagation properties and the communication performance of the OAM modes in radio frequency are studied. The transverse patterns for the single mode, two/three superimposed modes are discussed, while the influences of the mode number and the propagation distance on the beam width are analyzed. Based on 2FSK and 2PSK modulations the bit error rate (BER) of OAM modes are found varying with both the mode and the receiving radius of the array antennas. By analyzing the BER, it is found that when both the transmitting antenna and the transmitting power are fixed, also the noise power is the same, an OAM mode can have different optimal receiving radii in the single mode transmission and in the mode multiplexing transmission. These results will be helpful in optimizing the OAM mode receiving system and may have applications in the network of the IoT.

Keywords: Orbital angular momentum · IoT · Vortex

1 Introduction

Nowadays, we are standing on the brink of a new ubiquitous computing and communication era [1,2]. The development and application of the IoT are based on numerous micro-sensor networks, and the collected data by numerous sensors are transmitted through wireless communication [3]. As we all know, the number of wireless communication devices are growing fast, so it has led to the congestion on the available bands [4,5]. Therefore, its vital to find new methods to solve this problem.

Supported by the Seed Foundation of Innovation and Creation for Graduate Students in Northwestern Polytechnical University.

Electromagnetic (EM) vortex technology, as a new wireless communication technology, utilizes the orbital angular momentum (OAM) characteristics to transmit information efficiently. The waves with OAM has been studied a lot in optical frequency [6–10], and also is proposed to increase the spectral efficiency in optical wireless communication systems [5,11,12]. It was recently shown that the OAM can be used in the radio frequency (RF) and is not restricted to the optical frequency range [13]. In 1992, Allen et al. discovered that a helically phased light beam with the OAM property can be obtained when Laguerre-Gaussian (LG) modes were generated from Hermite-Gaussian (HG) modes through using cylindrical lenses [14,15]. By using the same principle, in 2012, Tamburini et al. [4] used a helical parabolic antenna to generate OAM modes in radio beams, and realized OAM multiplexing transmission at the radio frequency. Theoretically, an EM wave can carry an infinite number of OAM modes at the same frequency where each mode is orthogonal to each other [16]. Thus the multiplexing based on OAM modes can greatly increase the efficiency spectrum utilization in free space. Also because of the orthogonality of different OAM modes the EM waves with OAM modes have a good anti-jamming ability. Therefore the application of OAM in wireless communication is going to become a trend in EM wave studies. However, the performance of the EM beams with OAM in wireless communication channels is not quite clear.

In the paper, the theoretical background of OAM modes is introduced firstly, then the formula for generating EM wave carrying OAM modes with circular array antenna is given. The propagation properties of the EM waves with OAM modes and their performance in a wireless communication system will be analyzed in detail in Sect. 3.

2 Theory

It is well known that EM radiation can carry both linear momentum and angular momentum [6,17]. The total angular momentum is composed of spin angular momentum (SAM) and OAM, which can be described in the following expression:

$$\mathbf{J} = \epsilon_0 \int \mathbf{r} \times \mathrm{Re}\left[\mathbf{E} \times \mathbf{B}^*\right] dV. \tag{1}$$

Where $\mathbf{E}$ and $\mathbf{B}$ are the electric and magnetic vector fields, $\mathbf{r}$ is the position vector, and ϵ_0 is the vacuum permittivity, respectively. The angular momentum can be decomposed into a polarization dependent intrinsic rotation (i.e. SAM) and an extrinsic rotation (i.e. OAM) [18]. Then the total angular momentum $\mathbf{J}$ can be given by the sum [19]

$$\mathbf{J} = \mathbf{L} + \mathbf{S}, \tag{2}$$

where $\mathbf{L}$ represents the OAM of the electromagnetic radiation, and the mode number is denoted by l, while $\mathbf{S}$ is the SAM whose mode number is s with $s = \pm 1$.

An EM beam with OAM is also called an EM vortex beam, and its expression can be written as

$$E(r, \varphi, \omega) = A(r, \varphi) \exp(il\varphi) \exp(i\omega t), \tag{3}$$

Where $A(r, \varphi)$ is the amplitude of this vortex wave, r represents the radial distance, φ is the azimuth angle, and ω is the frequency of the EM wave. Here as we introduced before, l is the mode of OAM which represents how many 2π of the phase change as the φ goes from 0 to 2π in the transverse plane of the wave. It can be concluded from the formula that OAM can carry infinite topological charges theoretically. Thus unlike linear momentum, it can provide a new degree of freedom for the beams in wireless communication systems. In addition, different OAM modes are orthogonal to each other and they can be multiplexed/demultiplexed together, thus the channel capacity will be increased.

There are many ways to generate vortex waves, such as using a helicoidal parabolic antenna [4], adopting the spiral phase plate [20] and applying a uniform circular array (UCA) [19,21]. Among these methods, maybe the most common way is using a UCA in which each element is fed by the same signal, but with a successive phase element to element, such that after a full turn, the phase of the composed wave has been incremented by an integer multiple l of 2π (see Fig. 1). The N elements of this antenna array are located equidistantly around the perimeter of the circle and are phased with phase difference between each element $\Delta\phi = 2\pi l/N$. According to [13], for an array of N antenna elements, the largest OAM number l_{max} should satisfy $|l_{max}| < N/2$.

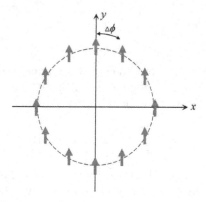

Fig. 1. Structure of the antenna array configuration.

The electric field in the far field of such an array antenna can be calculated by using the radiation theory of the array antennas, and for any detection point $P(r, \theta, \varphi)$ in this field (see Fig. 2) can be expressed as [19]:

$$E(r, \theta, \varphi) = -j \frac{\mu_0 \omega}{4\pi} \sum_{n=0}^{N-1} e^{il\varphi_n} \int \frac{e^{ik|r-r'_n|}}{|r - r'_n|} dV'_n$$

$$\approx -j \frac{\mu_0 \omega d}{4\pi} \cdot \frac{e^{ikr}}{r} \sum_{n=0}^{N-1} e^{-i(k \cdot r_n - l\varphi_n)} \tag{4}$$

$$\approx -j \frac{\mu_0 \omega d}{4\pi} \frac{e^{ikr}}{r} N i^{-l} e^{il\varphi} J_l(kR\sin\theta),$$

where j is the constant current density vector of the dipole, d is the electric dipole length, μ_0 is the magnetic conductivity in the vacuum, ω and k are the circular frequency and wave vector, respectively. $J_l(kR\sin\theta)$ is the Bessel function of the first kind, $\varphi_n = 2\pi n/N$ $(n = 0, 1, 2, \cdots, N-1)$ is the azimuthal angle of the array element position, and R is the radius of the array. Also in Eq. (4) the frequency dependence is suppressed for brevity, and from here on we will not discuss that dependence.

As an example, the intensity distribution of the radiation field from this array antennas is shown in Fig. 3, where the total number of the elements is 15, the topological charge or the OAM mode is chosen as 2 and the propagation distance is 1 m. It is clear to see that there is a dark hole (i.e. the intensity minimum) in the beam center that is the reason for another name of the beam with OAM – 'doughnut beam'.

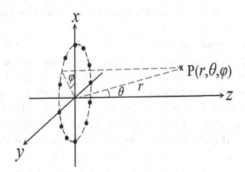

Fig. 2. Diagram of uniform circular antenna array.

3   Simulation and Discussion

In this part, the propagation properties of EM waves with OAM mode and their performance in communication systems will be analyzed. In this article the UCA is adopted to generate and receive OAM waves. The number of the antenna elements in both the transmitting and receiving ends always is set to be 15 (i.e., $l_{max} \leq 7$), and the frequency is set as $f = 3\,\text{GHz}$, i.e., $\lambda = 0.1\,\text{m}$. Here the transmit array radius is denoted by R_t and in this part R_t is chosen as λ. The receive array radius is denoted by R_r, and from here on we use n and p to represent the nth and the pth element of the transmitter and receiver, respectively.

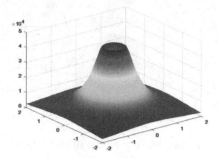

Fig. 3. Intensity distribution of EM wave with OAM mode. Here $N = 15$, $l = 2$ and $z = 1\,\mathrm{m}$.

3.1   Propagation Properties

The phase distribution in the transverse plane with $z = 10\lambda$ (propagation distance) is shown in Fig. 4 for different OAM modes, i.e. $l = 0, 1, 2$. The change in color from red to blue corresponds to a change in phase of 2π. Here $l = 0$ indicates there is no OAM, and it is clear to see that the phase does not rotate along the azimuthal angle, which means that the wave with $l = 0$ is a plane EM wave. When $l = 1$, the phase of radiation electric field changes 2π during one revolution, while $l = 2$, the phase changes 4π. The result shows that the EM wave with OAM mode has a helical phase front, and the phase variation is l times 2π.

Let us examine the propagation properties of the EM wave with one mode, and here the mode 3 is chosen. Except the propagation distance which is a variable in this part, the other parameters are the same with them in Fig. 4. The intensity distribution of electric field in the transverse plane with different propagation distances is shown in Fig. 5, where the color from blue to red corresponds to the 0 and maximum value of the intensity. From here on, in each plot of intensity, the intensity maximum is normalized to 1. We can see in Fig. 5 that there always exists a dark core in the intensity pattern, which means that the vortex or the phase singularity is located at the beam center. From this figure one can get that as the wave propagates, the beam spreads wider and wider.

Now we will look at the influence of the topological charge, i.e. OAM mode on the beam propagation. In Fig. 6 the intensity distribution of the electric field with different OAM modes are shown, where the propagation distance is $z = 10\lambda$. It can be seen that when the mode is getting bigger, the radius of the intensity pattern becomes wider and the hollow in the beam center is wider too. In another word, the bigger of l is, the stronger the wave diverges.

Therefore, we can conclude that increasing the OAM mode and/or the propagation distance, the width of the beam will be larger, which is very important in the receiving end of the wireless communication system.

When the OAM multiplexing is applied, the superposition of multi-OAM modes will occur, and since the helical phase distribution of the EM waves

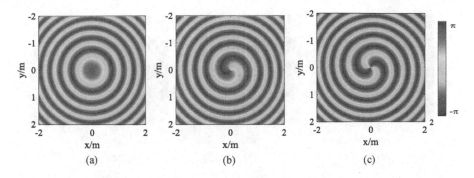

Fig. 4. Phase distribution of the OAM. (a) $l = 0$ (b) $l = 1$ (c) $l = 2$.

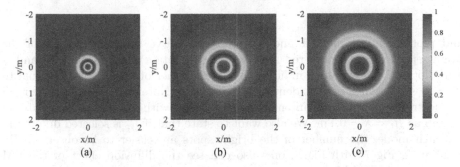

Fig. 5. Intensity distribution at the transverse planes with different propagation distances in the case of $l = 3$. (a) $z = 3\lambda$ (b) $z = 6\lambda$ (c) $z = 9\lambda$.

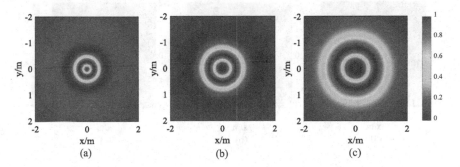

Fig. 6. Intensity distribution at the transverse planes for the different topological charges. (a) $l = 1$ (b) $l = 2$ (c) $l = 3$. Here $z = 10\lambda$

with OAM modes, the superposition patterns of different modes are usually not uniformally distributed and as we will see that they will show quite interesting patterns. First, the superposition patterns of two different modes are shown in Fig. 7 ($z = 3\lambda$) and Fig. 8 ($z = 10\lambda$). Plot (a) in these two figures is the superposition of the waves with mode 1 and 2, plot (b) is for mode 1 and 3,

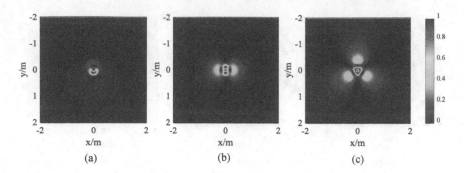

Fig. 7. Intensity distribution of the superposition of two different OAM modes. (a) $l = 1, 2$, (b) $l = 1, 3$, (c) $l = 1, 4$. Here $z = 3\lambda$.

and plot (c) is for mode 1 and 4. One can observe that the number of the bright spots (i.e. the dark red regions) is 1 in plot (a), is 2 in plot (b) and is 3 in plot (c). These results indicate that the number of bright spots is equal to $N = |l_1 - l_2|$, which is coincident with that in [22]. Note in these figures the radii of the transmitting array antennas for the waves with any OAM mode are all chosen as $R_t = \lambda = 0.1\,\text{m}$. We also want to state that if R_t is selected differently for each mode, the number of the bright spots are easier to be observed. By comparing Fig. 7 with Fig. 8, one also can see the diffusion effect of the EM waves with two OAM modes.

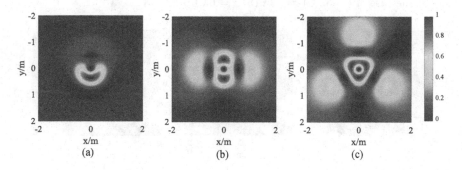

Fig. 8. Intensity distribution of the superposition of two different OAM modes. (a) $l = 1, 2$, (b) $l = 1, 3$, (c) $l = 1, 4$. Here $z = 10\lambda$.

When the number of the superimposed OAM modes is more 2, the superposition pattern will become more complicated which is not easy to describe the number of the bright spots in a simple equation. For instance when three OAM modes are superimposed, there can be 1, 2 and 3 bright spots, which is not easy to connect with their mode number difference. This is shown in Figs. 9 and 10, where the propagation distance is 3λ and 10λ respectively. Comparing the intensity distributions of single mode, two superimposed modes and three superimposed modes, it is not hard to find that at the same propagation distance the intensity maxima with more modes are closer to the beam center. This result also indicates that if a good efficiency wants to be obtained in the receiving end, the position of the receiving antenna should be adjusted with the number of the modes involved in the EM wave.

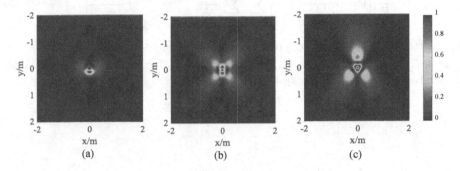

Fig. 9. Intensity distribution of the superposition of three different OAM modes. (a) $l = 1, 2$, (b) $l = 1, 3$, (c) $l = 1, 4$. Here $z = 3\lambda$. (a) $l = 1, 2, 3$, (b) $l = 1, 3, 5$, (c) $l = 1, 4, 6$. Here $z = 3\lambda$.

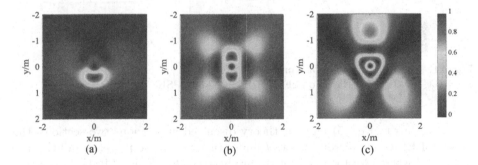

Fig. 10. Intensity distribution of the superposition of three different OAM modes. (a) $l = 1, 2, 3$, (b) $l = 1, 3, 5$, (c) $l = 1, 4, 6$. Here $z = 10\lambda$.

3.2   Performance of OAM Modes in Communication System

In the previous section, the propagation properties of the EM waves with OAM modes are discussed, here we focus our attention on the performance of the OAM modes in communication systems and the bit error rate (BER) is adopt to measure this performance.

EM waves with OAM not only diffuse during propagation, but also have a certain amount of attenuation [23]. Therefore, OAM-link budget should be considered in the OAM communication system. For the transmitting and receiving antennas are both UCA, the OAM-link budget estimation between two facing arrays can be expressed as [24]:

$$\frac{P_r}{P_t}(l) = \left| \frac{b_l^{OAM}}{a_l^{OAM}} \right|^2 = \left| \sum_{p=0}^{N-1} \sum_{n=0}^{N-1} \frac{\beta}{N} e^{-il\theta_{np}} e^{-ikr_{np}} \frac{\lambda}{4\pi r_{np}} \right|^2, \tag{5}$$

where P_r and P_t are receiving power and transmitting power, respectively. $r_{np} = \sqrt{z^2 + R_t^2 + R_r^2 - 2R_t R_r \cos \theta_{np}}$, $\theta_{np} = 2\pi(\frac{n-p}{N})$, β contains all the variables associated with the antenna system configuration.

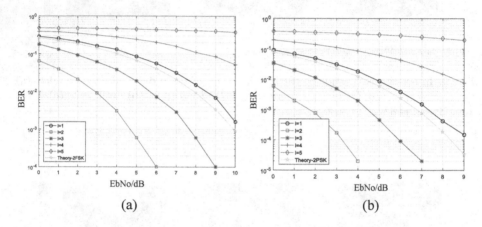

Fig. 11. The BER of different l under the same noise power. Here $N = 15$, $R_t = \lambda$, $R_r = 6\lambda$, $z = 10\lambda$. (a) Based on 2FSK, (b) Based on 2PSK.

According to Eq. (5) and the theory discussed in previous two sections, the curves of BER for different modes l under the same noise power are illustrated in Fig. 11, where plot (a) and plot (b) are based on 2FSK and 2PSK modulation respectively. Here the transmit array radius is also set as $R_t = \lambda = 0.1$ m, and the receive array radius $R_r = 6\lambda = 0.6$ m. First, one can see that two different modulations 2FSK and 2PSK do not influence the BER strongly. Second, it can be observed that the BER for each l is different with each other, and it follows this rule: $\text{BER}(l = 2) < \text{BER}(l = 3) < \text{BER}(l = 1) < \text{BER}(l = 4) < \text{BER}(l = 5)$. Also the BER for $l = 2$ and $l = 3$ is lower than the theoretical value. This can be explained as the different attenuation for each l. The different attenuation will lead to different power received at the same receiving position for different modes, which has a straight effect on the BER. The small BER for $l = 2$ and $l = 3$ is obtained because at the receiving radius $R_r = 6\lambda$ the power received for these two modes are bigger than others. This also indicates that if both the

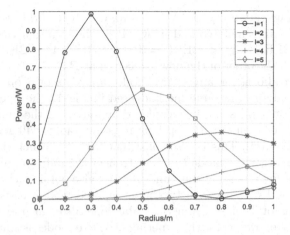

Fig. 12. The receiving power of selected l with different receiving radius. Here $N = 15$, $R_t = \lambda$, $z = 10\lambda$.

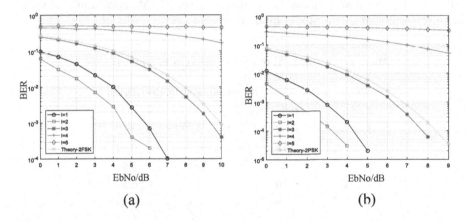

(a)   (b)

Fig. 13. The BER of different l under the same noise power. Here $N = 15$, $R_t = \lambda$, $R_r = 5\lambda$, $z = 10\lambda$. (a) Based on 2FSK, (b) Based on 2PSK.

transmitting antenna and the transmitting power are fixed and the noise in the channel also does not change, for each mode l, there exists an optimal receiving radius.

In Fig. 12 the receiving power for different l at varying receiving radius are shown. Here the transmitting power is set as $P_t = 1$ W. It is clear to see that at different receiving radius the power for different modes may follow different orders. For example when $R_r = 6\lambda = 0.6$ m, the power PW received for different modes satisfy: $PW(l = 2) > PW(l = 3) > PW(l = 1) > PW(l = 4) > PW(l = 5)$. Since the noise power is the same and the BER is inversely proportional to the receiving power, the BER in the Fig. 11 follows the rule of $\text{BER}(l = 2) < \text{BER}(l = 3) < \text{BER}(l = 1) < \text{BER}(l = 4) < \text{BER}(l = 5)$. As a test, in Fig. 13, when the receiving radius $R_r = 5\lambda = 0.5$ m, the BER of different l under the same noise power are simulated and shown. It can be seen that the BER follows: $\text{BER}(l = 2) < \text{BER}(l = 1) < \text{BER}(l = 3) < \text{BER}(l = 4) < \text{BER}(l = 5)$, which is consistent with the order of the power received at $R_r = 5\lambda = 0.5$ m in Fig. 12.

As discussed above, for any OAM mode it has its own optimal receiving radius. Here, applying the same method used in Fig. 12 the optimal receiving radius for different modes can be calculated and given in the first two columns of Table 1. It can be seen that the optimal receiving radius will get bigger as the OAM mode l increases. This is also consistent with our conclusion in previous section that the larger the mode l is, the stronger the diffusion of the EM wave gets. In addition, by repeating the same steps we also obtain the optimal receiving radius for the EM wave with two superimposed modes, as is shown in the last two columns of Table 1. From this table, one also can find that generally the optical receiving radius for the superimposed two modes is smaller than that for a single mode, which also can be illustrated in the propagation patterns in previous sections (see Figs. 5, 6, 7 and 8). This result indicates that the communication performance of an OAM mode in the OAM mode multiplexing is different from that in the single mode transmission.

Table 1. The optimal receiving radius of different modes.

Single mode	R_r/m	Superimposed modes	R_r/m
$l = 1$	0.29	$l_1 = 1,\ l_2 = 2$	0.38
$l = 2$	0.52	$l_1 = 1,\ l_2 = 3$	0.37
$l = 3$	0.78	$l_1 = 1,\ l_2 = 4$	0.32
$l = 4$	1.12	$l_1 = 2,\ l_2 = 4$	0.61
$l = 5$	1.50	$l_1 = 2,\ l_2 = 5$	0.57
$l = 6$	1.88	$l_1 = 2,\ l_2 = 6$	0.53

4   Conclusions

In this article the UCA is used for both the transmitting and receiving the EM waves with OAM modes, and the propagation properties and the communication performance of the OAM modes are studied. First, it is found that the increasing the OAM mode and/or the propagation distance will enlarge the width of the beam with OAM. Second, when the number of the superimposed OAM modes is more 2, the superposition pattern will become more complicated and its bright spots number can not be described by the mode number difference. Third, two different modulations 2FSK and 2PSK do not have strong effect on the BER of OAM modes, but the mode l does. For each mode, it has its own attenuation during the mode propagation, which leads to the difference BER for different modes. At last, the optimal receiving radii for the OAM modes are proposed and calculated for both the different single modes and the different superimposed modes. Our result shows that the communication performance of an OAM mode relies on whether it is in the mode multiplexing or not, and also depends on how many modes are used in the multiplexing. We believe that our findings will be quite useful in improving the receiving techniques for OAM modes, and can be applied to the IoT. For example, smart home connects all kinds of devices through the IoT technology to realize the full-ranged information interaction and Intelligent Transportation System also integrates different installations to ensuretrafficsafety. The large amount of data generated during these devices makes it difficult to transfer data efficiently. The orthogonality between different modes of OAM can deal with this problem and improve information interaction capability.

References

1. Peña-López, I., et al.: ITU internet report 2005: the internet of things (2005)
2. Lin, J., Yu, W., Zhang, N., Yang, X., Zhang, H., Zhao, W.: A survey on internet of things: architecture, enabling technologies, security and privacy, and applications. IEEE Internet Things J. **4**(5), 1125–1142 (2017)
3. Ashton, K.: That internet of things. RFID J. **22**(7), 97–114 (2009)
4. Tamburini, F., Mari, E., Sponselli, A., Thidé, B., Bianchini, A., Romanato, F.: Encoding many channels on the same frequency through radio vorticity: first experimental test. New J. Phys. **14**(3), 033001 (2012)
5. Chen, C., Wang, W., Wu, J., et al.: Visible light communications for the implementation of internet-of-things. Opt. Eng. **55**(6), 060501 (2016)
6. Allen, L., Barnett, S.M., Padgett, M.J.: Optical Angular Momentum. IoP Publishing, Bristol (2003)
7. Pang, X.: Gouy phase and phase singularities of tightly focused, circularly polarized vortex beams. Opt. Commun. **338**, 534–539 (2015)
8. Zhao, X., Zhang, J., Pang, X., Wan, G.: Properties of a strongly focused gaussian beam with an off-axis vortex. Opt. Commun. **389**, 275–282 (2017)
9. Pang, X., Miao, W.: Spinning spin density vectors along the propagation direction. Opt. Lett. **43**(19), 4831–4834 (2018)
10. Li, J., Zhang, J., Li, J.: Optical twists and transverse focal shift in a strongly focused, circularly polarized vortex field. Opt. Commun. **439**, 284–289 (2019)
11. Wang, J., et al.: Terabit free-space data transmission employing orbital angular momentum multiplexing. Nat. Photon. **6**(7), 488 (2012)
12. Li, M.: Orbital-angular-momentum multiplexing optical wireless communications with adaptive modes adjustment in internet of things networks. IEEE Internet Things J. **6**, 6134–6139 (2019)
13. Thidé, B., et al.: Utilization of photon orbital angular momentum in the low-frequency radio domain. Phys. Rev. Lett. **99**(8), 087701 (2007)
14. Allen, L., Beijersbergen, M.W., Spreeuw, R., Woerdman, J.: Orbital angular momentum of light and the transformation of laguerre-gaussian laser modes. Phys. Rev. A **45**(11), 8185 (1992)
15. Demeter, Á., Kertész, C.Z.: Simulation of free-space communication using the orbital angular momentum of radio waves. In: 2014 International Conference on Optimization of Electrical and Electronic Equipment (OPTIM), pp. 846–851. IEEE (2014)

16. Molina-Terriza, G., Torres, J.P., Torner, L.: Management of the angular momentum of light: preparation of photons in multidimensional vector states of angular momentum. Phys. Rev. Lett. **88**(1), 013601 (2001)
17. Loudon, R., Baxter, C.: Contributions of john henry poynting to the understanding of radiation pressure. Proc. R. Soc. Lond. A **468**(2143), 1825–1838 (2012)
18. Barnett, S.M.: Optical angular-momentum flux. J. Opt. B: Quantum Semiclass. Opt. **4**(2), S7 (2001)
19. Mohammadi, S.M., et al.: Orbital angular momentum in radio-a system study. IEEE Trans. Antennas Propag. **58**(2), 565–572 (2009)
20. Tamburini, F., Mari, E., Bo, T., Barbieri, C., Romanato, F.: Experimental verification of photon angular momentum and vorticity with radio techniques. Appl. Phys. Lett. **99**(20), 321 (2011)
21. Gong, Y., et al.: Generation and transmission of OAM-carrying vortex beams using circular antenna array. IEEE Trans. Antennas Propag. **65**(6), 2940–2949 (2017)
22. Ke, X., Pu, X.: Generation of orbital angular momentum superpositions and its test. Infrared Laser Eng. **47**(4), 56–61 (2018)
23. Cagliero, A., De Vita, A., Gaffoglio, R., Sacco, B.: A new approach to the link budget concept for an oam communication link. IEEE Antennas Wireless Propag. Lett. **15**, 568–571 (2015)
24. Nguyen, D.K., Pascal, O., Sokoloff, J., Chabory, A., Palacin, B., Capet, N.: Antenna gain and link budget for waves carrying orbital angular momentum. Radio Sci. **50**(11), 1165–1175 (2015)

Vehicle Re-identification Using Joint Pyramid Feature Representation Network

Xiangwei Lin[1], Huanqiang Zeng[1(✉)], Jinhui Hou[1], Jianqing Zhu[2], Jing Chen[1], and Kai-Kuang Ma[3]

[1] School of Information Science and Engineering, Huaqiao University,
Xiamen 361021, China
zeng0043@hqu.edu.cn
[2] School of Engineering, Huaqiao University, Quanzhou 362021, China
[3] School of Electrical and Electronic Engineering, Nanyang Technological University,
Singapore 639798, Singapore

Abstract. Vehicle re-identification (Re-ID) technology plays an important role in intelligent video surveillance systems. Due to various factors, e.g., resolution variation, viewpoint variation, illumination changes, occlusion, etc., vehicle Re-ID is a very challenging computer vision task. In order to solve this problem, a joint pyramid feature representation network (JPFRN) is proposed in this paper. Based on the consideration that various convolution blocks with different depths hold various resolution and semantic information of the vehicle image, which can help to effectively identify the vehicle, the proposed JPFRN method obtains four vehicle feature blocks with different depths by designing pyramidal feature fusion of each convolution block in a basic network. After that, a joint representation of these pyramidal features is feed into the loss function for learning discriminative features for vehicle Re-ID. We validated the proposed approach on a commonly used vehicle database i.e., VehicleID. Extensive experimental results show that the proposed method is superior to multiple state-of-the-art vehicle Re-ID methods.

Keywords: Vehicle re-identification · Joint pyramid feature representation · Deep learning

This work was supported in part by the National Natural Science Foundation of China under the grants 61871434, 61602191, and 61802136, in part by the Natural Science Foundation for Outstanding Young Scholars of Fujian Province under the grant 2019J06017, in part by the Natural Science Foundation of Fujian Province under the grant 2017J05103, in part by the Fujian-100 Talented People Program, in part by High-level Talent Innovation Program of Quanzhou City under the grant 2017G027, in part by the Promotion Program for Young and Middle-aged Teacher in Science and Technology Research of Huaqiao University under the grants ZQN-YX403 and ZQN-PY418, and in part by the High-Level Talent Project Foundation of Huaqiao University under the grants 14BS201, 14BS204 and 16BS108, and in part by the Subsidized Project for Postgraduates Innovative Fund in Scientific Research of Huaqiao University.

© ICST Institute for Computer Sciences, Social Informatics and Telecommunications Engineering 2020
Published by Springer Nature Switzerland AG 2020. All Rights Reserved
B. Li et al. (Eds.): IoTaaS 2019, LNICST 316, pp. 527–536, 2020.
https://doi.org/10.1007/978-3-030-44751-9_44

1   Introduction

Similar to pedestrians, vehicle has become an important target in the intelligent video surveillance systems, because vehicle has been an indispensable part of human daily life. Some related researches on vehicles, such as vehicle classification [1,2], vehicle tracking [3,4], vehicle detection [5,6], vehicle re-identification (Re-ID) [7] draw increasing attentions from both academic and industry. Among these related tasks, vehicle Re-ID is a significant but a frontier area that aims to match all the same vehicles captured by different cameras under various viewing angles. Therefore, vehicle Re-ID can be widely used in many fields, such as intelligent transportation, urban computing, criminal tracking for public safety, to name a few.

In the practical situation, vehicle Re-ID is a very challenging task, due to the influences of many uncertain factors, such as blur, resolution variation, illumination change and viewpoint variation, which can be referred to Fig. 1. It is worthwhile of mentioning that among all the influencing factors, the large varying resolutions of vehicle images collected by different kinds of cameras under different distances is the primary factor needed to be solved in vehicle Re-ID tasks. In practice, vehicle images have different resolutions that tend to make the vehicle target appear larger or smaller, seriously affecting the accuracy of the vehicle recognition. Therefore, matching vehicle images only based on a single resolution has certain limitations. Based on this motivation, by considering the correlation between high resolution and low resolution images in the feature space of convolutional neural networks, we propose a joint pyramidal feature representation network (JPFRN), which integrates vehicle features with different resolutions and different strengths of semantic information to achieve the more rich representation of vehicle targets. Extensive experiments are conducted on large vehicle database VehicleID [7] to evaluate the performance of the proposed method. The corresponding results show that the proposed JPFRN method consistently outperforms multiple state-of-the-art related works.

The rest of this paper is organized as follows: Sect. 2 introduces the related work, Sect. 3 describes the proposed method JPFRN, Sect. 4 presents the experimental results to validate the superiority of the proposed method, Sect. 5 concludes this paper.

2   Related Work

In this section, the existing vehicle Re-ID methods will be briefly reviewed. They can be roughly classified into two categorizes: sensor/clue based method and vehicle appearance feature based method.

2.1   Sensor Based Method/Clue Based Method

The traditional vehicle Re-ID methods mainly relied on the sensor data or clues. In the early research phase of vehicle Re-ID works, most researchers worked

Fig. 1. The vehicle images are from the VehicleID [7] database. The images of the vehicles in each row are collected by the same vehicle, but the appearance is different under different cameras, such as blur, illumination, resolution and occlusion.

with different types of sensor data and multiple clues due to database shortages, such as the vehicle passing time [8], wireless magnetic sensors [9], and license plate, etc. Among them, the license plate number is the most important clue of vehicle and contains all the useful information about the vehicle. Therefore, the Re-ID method based on the license plate number becomes an accurate and effective solution. But in some cases, the license plate number is easily obscured, modified, or blurred. In addition, sensors-based and clue-based methods require additional hardware costs and are very sensitive to complex real-world environments. In contrast, the vehicle Re-ID method based on appearance features has more practical application scenarios.

2.2 Appearance Feature Based Method

For the appearance feature representation, the earlier approach used low-level features, such as SIFT [10], LOMO [11], BOW-CN [12]. And the recent-developed approach is to take advantage of the depth features of the image. Farenzena [13] proposed a joint representation method based on pedestrian global appearance features and local appearance features can directly employed for vehicle Re-ID. Furthermore, Liu et al. [14] proposed a coarse-to-fine vehicle Re-ID method that filters out potential matches by manual features (color, shape) and depth features, then reconstructs the rankings with license plate information and spatiotemporal information. In addition, some classic network models [15–18] are widely used as vehicle feature extractors in vehicle Re-ID tasks, such as VGGNet [17] and ResNet [18], which greatly convenient for features extraction. Furthermore, in order to improve the robustness of vehicle Re-ID, Bai et al. [19] proposed a novel depth metric learning method, triple loss function metric (the distance between features of the same class should be as small as possible). This method fully considers the inter-class similarity and intra-class variance of vehicle shape in the vehicle model. Zhang et al. [20] proposed an improved

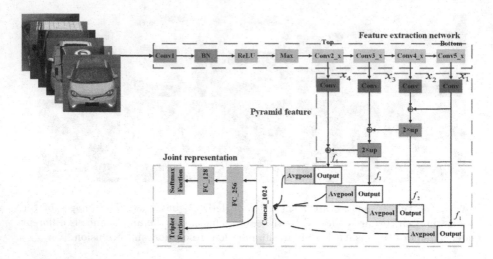

Fig. 2. The proposed network structure diagram using joint pyramid feature representation. Here, x_1, x_2, x_3, and x_4 respectively represent the output of each convolution block of ResNet, and f_1, f_2, f_3, and f_4 respectively represent the outputs of the respective reconstructed feature blocks.

training method for triple loss, the method takes three samples as a group and ensures that the distance between similar samples in the mapped space is less than the distance between different types of samples. Zhou et al. [21] focused on multi-view feature representation, proposed a viewpoint-aware attention model to select the core regions of different viewpoints, and then combined the regions of interest from multiple views by adversarial learning ideas to improve vehicle Re-ID performance. Zhou et al. [22] proposed a long-short-term memory network model to simulate the appearance transformation of different viewpoints of vehicles to increase the diversity of data under different viewpoints, so as to learn more robust and more differentiated vehicle characteristics. Through the above reviewing, we can know that the vehicle Re-ID task has made some progress. However, in the actual monitoring scenario, due to various factors such as vehicle viewpoint change, resolution change, illumination change, and occlusion, etc, the vehicle Re-ID tasks still face enormous challenges, and there is a large room for improvement.

3 Vehicle Re-ID Using Joint Pyramid Feature Representation Network

As shown in Fig. 2, the proposed joint pyramid feature representation network method consists of three parts: baseline network, feature pyramid network, and a joint representation network.

Fig. 3. The vehicle images are from the VehicleID [7] database. The images are collected by the same vehicle, but the resolution is different under different cameras.

3.1 Baseline Deep Learning Network

In this work, we use the ResNet-50 [18] architecture as a feature extractor in our experiments. ResNet-50 [18] is a particularly popular network because it is closely monitored during the training process. Among each residual block, the output of each residual block contains the output of the previous block, so it combines the low-level and high-level features of the input image. Specifically, the training images are resized into $256 \times 256 \times 3$ to adapt the baseline model. We replace the fully-connected layer in the original network with two other fully-connected layers and a classification layer. The first fully-connected layer has 1024 units, and the second fully-connected layer has 128 units. The classification layer has K neurons to predict the K classes, where K is the number of classes in the training set.

3.2 Pyramid Feature Extraction

The human visual system has different perceptions of different resolution images, that is, the human eyes can acquire more image features for high-resolution images, and less for low-resolution images. As shown in Fig. 3, these vehicle images are of the same vehicle, but their resolutions are different due to diversifying capture distances, so the features obtained by the visual system are different. Ultimately, the visual system recognizes the target by combining the different scale features acquired. Similarly, in computer vision, after extracting features from the basic network, the image at the bottom of the network has lower resolution, the implicit semantic information is richer, while the image at the top of the network has higher resolution, but its semantic information is relatively less. Therefore, we give full consideration to the characteristics of the bottom convolutional block and the top convolutional block, propose a pyramidal feature reconstruct method, which can combine vehicle image features with different resolution and semantic information to achieve unified representation and make the task of vehicle Re-ID more robust. The specific network as shown in Fig. 2, the bottom layer, convolutional block $Conv5_x$, first goes through a dimensionality reduction operation and then adds with convolutional block $Conv4_x$ after an up-sampling operation. It is worth noting that $Conv4_x$, the convolutional block, also goes through a descending dimension operation. Repeatedly, the reconstructed image block is continuously up-sample and added to the last block, so as to fuse the semantic information and resolution information of all convolutional blocks. This feature pyramid can be represented as:

$$F_n = \sigma(W_n * x_n + b_n) \qquad n = 1, 2, 3, 4 \tag{1}$$

$$f_1 = F_1 \tag{2}$$

$$f_n = F_n + upsample(f_{n-1}) \qquad n = 2, 3, 4 \tag{3}$$

where F_n refers to dimensionality reduction of convolution block. The W and b represent weight and bias respectively. Upsample() represents up-sampling operation of the target (no up-sampling for features with the same resolution), and f_n refers to feature blocks at all levels after pyramid reconstruction.

3.3   Joint Representation Network

In the previous section, we proposed a method to reconstruct vehicle features from the bottom layer of the network to the top layer through up-sampling. However, there are still limitations of single resolution vehicle images after reconstruction for complex identification tasks. Since the resolution of the vehicle images collected by different cameras is different, and vehicle size of the vehicle is also inconsistent. For this problem, we consider the correlation between the reconstructed convolutional blocks, and combine the four feature blocks with different resolutions after reconstruction to realize the joint representation. Therefore, our model can contain multiple resolution vehicle features and identify vehicle images with different target sizes at different resolutions. As shown in Fig. 2, the reconstructed fused feature blocks f_1, f_2, f_3, f_4 are respectively aggregated into a (36×1024) feature vector for joint representation after Avgpooling layer. One branch connects the triplet loss function, and the other connects the Softmax loss function through two full connection layers.

4   Experiment and Analysis

4.1   Databases and Evaluation Index

In order to verify the superiority of the proposed joint pyramid feature representation network, we compare it with multiple state-of-the-art methods. The corresponding database and evaluation indexes used in our experiment are described as follows.

The VehicleID database contains 221763 vehicle images collected from multiple non-overlapping cameras in 26267 vehicles, each with its own front and back viewpoint images. And in the database, all vehicles are marked with their

Table 1. Network parameters for JPFRN.

Name	Channels	Conv window	Stride	Output size
Conv1	64	7×7	2	$64 \times 128 \times 128$
Maxpooling	64	3×3	2	$64 \times 64 \times 64$
$Conv2_x$	256	–	1	$256 \times 64 \times 64$
$Conv2_{x-}$	256	1×1	1	$256 \times 64 \times 64$
$Conv3_x$	512	–	2	$512 \times 32 \times 32$
$Conv3_{x-}$	256	1×1	1	$256 \times 32 \times 32$
$Conv4_x$	1024	–	2	$1024 \times 16 \times 16$
$Conv4_{x-}$	256	1×1	1	$256 \times 16 \times 16$
$Conv5_x$	1024	–	2	$2048 \times 16 \times 16$
$Conv5_{x-}$	256	1×1	1	$256 \times 16 \times 16$
$Pyramid_{f1}$	256	1×1	1	$256 \times 16 \times 16$
$Pyramid_{f1}$	256	1×1	1	$256 \times 16 \times 16$
$Pyramid_{f1}$	256	1×1	1	$256 \times 32 \times 32$
$Pyramid_{f1}$	256	1×1	1	$256 \times 64 \times 64$

matching ID information, most of which have color and vehicle type information. In addition, the database is divided into two parts: training subset and testing subset. The training subset contains 110178 vehicle images collected by 13134 vehicles. The testing subset can be divided into three sub-tests, test-800, test-1600, test-2400. The test-800 contains 6532 vehicle images collected by 800 vehicles, the test-1600 contains 11395 vehicle images collected by 1600 vehicles, and the test-2400 contains 17638 vehicle images collected by 2400 vehicles.

In the research of vehicle Re-ID, average precision (mAP) and cumulative matching characteristic (CMC) are generally adopted. Where the cumulative matching feature curve represents the probability of query target appearing in candidate sets of different size, that is, the curve represents the probability of finding the matching target in the candidate sets with the first k ranks. In other words, assume that there are N query targets in total and conduct N queries, $k = (k_1, k_2 ..., k_n)$ represents the ranking result of matching targets in each query, and set k as the size of the candidate set. The calculation formula of CMC is as follow:

$$CMC@k = \frac{\sum_{q=1}^{Q} gt(1, k)}{Q} \qquad (4)$$

The average precision evaluates the overall performance of Re-ID and calculates the average precision of each query image. The formula is:

$$mAP = \frac{\sum_{q=1}^{Q} AP(q)}{Q} \qquad (5)$$

Q is the number of vehicle images to be queried, and $AP(q)$ is the accuracy of each query vehicle image. In addition to CMC and mAP, Rank-N also adopted as auxiliary means in vehicle Re-ID tasks. Rank-N can represent the real performance of vehicle Re-ID. For example, Rank-1 means the first target to be matched in the return list. In particular, the greater the number of vehicle types in the candidate set, the lower the probability of finding an accurate match.

4.2   Training Configuration

In our experiments, the software tools are PyTorch, CUDA10.0, CUDNN V7.6.0. The hardware device is a workstation equipped with Inter(R) Xeon(R) CPU E5-2643 v4 @ 3.40 GHZ, two NVIDIA GeForce 2080Ti and 256 GB of memory. We adopted the following training setting: the size of all images in the database was set to 256 × 256, and each image was randomly flipped horizontally with a probability of flipping 0.5. The ResNet pertaining model is used in the training to initialize the parameters of the network. The number of small batches is 18, the initial learning rate is 0.0003, and the number of training sessions is 50000 and the learning rate begins to decline after 25000 training sessions. Network parameters are shown in Table 1.

4.3   Experimental Evaluation

The experimental results on VehicleID are shown in Table 2, where the performance of the proposed method is compared with multiple existing methods,

Table 2. The performance comparison on VehicleID.

Method	Test-800			Test-1600			Test-2400		
	mAP	Rank-1	Rank-5	mAP	Rank-1	Rank-5	mAP	Rank-1	Rank-5
DRDL [7]	N/A	48.91	66.71	N/A	46.36	64.38	N/A	40.97	60.02
FACT [24]	N/A	49.53	67.96	N/A	44.63	64.19	N/A	39.91	60.49
Zhu [23]	76.54	72.32	92.48	74.63	70.66	88.90	68.41	64.14	83.37
JPFRN	**79.91**	**74.68**	**94.93**	**74.32**	**68.75**	**90.40**	**70.38**	**63.34**	**86.68**

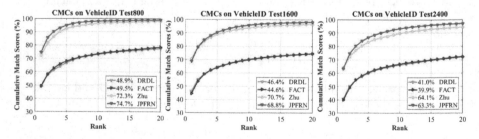

Fig. 4. The CMC curve comparisons of the proposed methods and state-of-the-art methods on VehicleID-Test800, VehicleID-Test1600, and VehicleID-Test2400 dataset, respectively.

including Zhu [23], DRDL [7], and FACT [24]. In order to ensure the stability of the experimental results, we performed ten tests on the model and took the average of ten test results as the final result. Obviously, the proposed method, including mAP, Rank-1, and Rank-5 in test-800, Rank-5 in test-1600, mAP and Rank-5 in test-2400, are slightly better than Zhu's [23] method, and far better than that of DRDL [7] and FACT [24]. Moreover, the CMC curves of various methods are further shown in the Fig. 4. One can see that the proposed method has achieved better results than other methods under comparison.

5   Conclusion

In this paper, a joint pyramid feature representation network is designed for vehicle Re-ID. In the proposed method, each convolution block in base network has vehicle features with different resolutions and intensity semantic information. By combining the bottom-layer convolutional block with the previous level of convolutional block, we obtain the pyramid feature block that fusing the bottom-layer high intensity semantic information and the top-layer high resolution. These pyramid vehicle features are then jointly represented by concatenating the feature blocks at each level. Since the proposed JPFRN method effectively resists the adverse effects of resolution variations in vehicle images, the performance of vehicle Re-ID is improved. Experimental results shown that the proposed method is obviously superior to multiple recently-developed vehicle Re-ID methods.

References

1. Yang, L., Luo, P., Loy, C.C., Tang, X., Huang, T.: A largescale car dataset for finegrained categorization and verification. In: IEEE International Conference on Computer Vision and Pattern Recognition, pp. 3973–3981 (2015)
2. Sochor, J., Herout, A., Boxcars, J.H., Huang, T.: 3D boxes as CNN input for improved finegrained vehicle recognition. In: IEEE International Conference on Computer Vision and Pattern Recognition, pp. 3006–3015 (2016)
3. Matei, B.C., Sawhney, H.S., Samarasekera, S.: Vehicle tracking across nonoverlapping cameras using joint kinematic and appearance features. In: IEEE International Conference on Computer Vision and Pattern Recognition, pp. 3465–3472 (2011)
4. Guo, J.-M., Hsia, C.-H., Wong, K., Wu, J.-Y., Wu, Y.-T., Wan, N.-J.: Nighttime vehicle lamp detection and tracking with adaptive mask training. IEEE Trans. Veh. Technol. **65**(6), 4023–4032 (2016)
5. Chen, X., Xiang, S., Liu, C.L., Pan, C.H.: Vehicle detection in satellite images by hybrid deep convolutional neural networks. IEEE Geosci. Remote Sens. Lett. **11**(10), 1797–1801 (2017)
6. Fan, Q.F., Brown, L., Smith, J.: A closer look at Faster R-CNN for vehicle detection. In: IEEE Intelligent Vehicles Symposium (IV), pp. 124–129 (2016)
7. Liu, H., Tian, Y., Wang, Y., Pang, L., Huang, T.: Deep relative distance learning: tell the difference between similar vehicles. In: IEEE International Conference on Computer Vision and Pattern Recognition, pp. 2167–2175 (2016)

8. Lin, W.H., Tong, D.: Vehicle re-identification with dynamic time windows for vehicle passage time estimation. IEEE Trans. Intell. Transp. Syst. **12**(4), 1057–1063 (2011)
9. Kwong, K., Kavaler, R., Rajagopal, R., Varaiya, P.: Arterial travel time estimation based on vehicle re-identification using wireless magnetic sensors. Transp. Res. Part C Emerg. Technol. **17**(6), 586–606 (2009)
10. Zhao, R., Ouyang, W., Wang, X.: Unsupervised salience learning for person re-identification. In: IEEE International Conference on Computer Vision and Pattern Recognition, pp. 3586–3593 (2013)
11. Liao, S., Hu, Y., Zhu, X., Li, S.Z.: Person re-identification by local maximal occurrence representation and metric learning. In: IEEE International Conference on Computer Vision and Pattern Recognition, pp. 2197–2206 (2015)
12. Zheng, L., Shen, L., Tian, L., Wang, S., Wang, J., Tian, Q.: Scalable person re-identification: a benchmark. In: European Conference on Computer Vision, pp. 1116–1124 (2016)
13. Farenzena, M., Bazzani, L., Perina, A., Murino, V., Cristani, M.: Person re-identification by symmetry driven accumulation of local features. In: IEEE International Conference on Computer Vision and Pattern Recognition, pp. 2360–2367 (2010)
14. Liu, X., Liu, W., Mei, T., Ma, H.: A deep learning-based approach to progressive vehicle re-identification for urban surveillance. In: Leibe, B., Matas, J., Sebe, N., Welling, M. (eds.) ECCV 2016. LNCS, vol. 9906, pp. 869–884. Springer, Cham (2016). https://doi.org/10.1007/978-3-319-46475-6_53
15. Krizhevsky, A., Sutskever, I., Hinton, G.E.: Imagenet classification with deep convolutional neural networks. In: Neural Information Processing Systems, pp. 1097–1105 (2012)
16. Simonyan, K., Zisserman, A.: Very deep convolutional networks for largescale image recognition. arXiv:1409.1556 (2014)
17. Szegedy, C., et al.: Going deeper with convolutions. In: IEEE International Conference on Computer Vision and Pattern Recognition, pp. 1–9 (2015)
18. He, K., Zhang, X., Ren, S., Sun, J.: Deep residual learning for image recognition. In: IEEE International Conference on Computer Vision and Pattern Recognition, pp. 770–778 (2016)
19. Bai, Y., Lou, Y., Gao, F., Wang, S., Wu, Y., Duan, L.: Group-sensitive triplet embedding for vehicle reidentification. IEEE Trans. Multimedia **20**(9), 2385–2399 (2018)
20. Zhang, Y., Liu, D., Zha, Z.J.: Improving triplet wise training of convolutional neural network for vehicle re-identification. In: IEEE International Conference on Multimedia and Expo, pp. 1386–1391 (2017)
21. Zhou, Y., Shao, L.: Viewpoint-aware attentive multi-view inference for vehicle re-identification. In: IEEE International Conference on Computer Vision and Pattern Recognition, pp. 6489–6498 (2018)
22. Zhou, Y., Liu, L., Shao, L.: Vehicle re-identification by deep hidden multi-view inference. IEEE Trans. Image Process. **27**(7), 3275–3287 (2018)
23. Zhu, J., et al.: Vehicle re-identification using quadruple directional deep learning features. IEEE Trans. Intell. Transp. Syst. **21**(1), 410–420 (2020)
24. Liu, X., Liu, W., Ma, H., Fu, H.: Large-scale vehicle re-identification in urban surveillance videos. In: IEEE International Conference on Multimedia and Expo, pp. 1–6 (2016)

Generation and Performance Evaluation of Distributed Interference Based on Multiple-Wavelet

Xiaozhu Shi[1]($\boxtimes$) and Zichun Zhang[2]

[1] State Key Laboratory of Air Traffic Management System and Technology, Nanjing, China
xidianshi1998@163.com
[2] School of Electronics and Information, Northwestern Polytechnical University, Xi'an, China

Abstract. Sensor networks are groups of specialized transducers that have a communications infrastructure which is intended to record and monitor conditions at different locations. Sensor network are widely adopted in distributed interference because they are lightweight, small and extremely portable. In order to ensure the safety of civil aviation, it is necessary to control and disperse the unmanned aerial vehicle (UAV). This paper proposed the precise distributed interference for the UAV management and control by aggregating interference signal energy at the specific point and in the specific area. First, the distance between the distributed jammers and the target point is given, and the time of different wavelets reach the target point is calculated. Then the initial phases of all the wavelets are adjusted so as to ensure all the wavelets reaching the peak value at the specific point. Finally, the interference generated in specific area is proposed to meet practical application requirements. The experiment results demonstrate that the proposed distributed interference method can be used for precise interference under UAV management and control and even in the dynamic warfare environments.

Keywords: Distributed interference · Unmanned aerial vehicle (UAV) management and control · Energy aggregating · Wavelets cooperate

1 Introduction

Sensor networking technology is widely used in unmanned aerial vehicle (UAV) and electronic warfare, where a certain number of sensors are placed on the sea, on the ground or in the air with certain criteria to cooperate for a certain purpose [1]. As the civil unmanned aerial vehicles are used in various fields, Low-altitude and ultra-low-altitude airspace are becoming smaller and more complex, which brings huge security risks for other military and civilian aircraft [2, 3]. Therefore, the demand for precise air flight control system for civil UAVs is more urgent. Distributed precise interference is designed based on Multiple-wavelet system for the UAV management and control. Furthermore, in modern electronic warfare, the traditional conflict is changed into a struggle to seize the electromagnetic advantage in wireless confrontation [4, 5]. In order

© ICST Institute for Computer Sciences, Social Informatics and Telecommunications Engineering 2020
Published by Springer Nature Switzerland AG 2020. All Rights Reserved
B. Li et al. (Eds.): IoTaaS 2019, LNICST 316, pp. 537–548, 2020.
https://doi.org/10.1007/978-3-030-44751-9_45

to ensure the electronic equipment of the cooperative targets normally operating and non-cooperative targets are effectively interfered, we need to perform accurate interference [6]. The principle of electronic interference is to transmit an electromagnetic signal. That is, the transmitter transmits an interference signal with enough power and it is received by the non-cooperative target receiver. If the non-cooperative target is effectively interfered, it will inevitably lead to the loss of operational capability and even paralysis [7, 8]. As the rapid changes in the electronic warfare environment, we have to develop a technology that can adapt to the characteristics of electronic warfare [9]. It can dynamically make the interference signal energy aggregate in a specific area to achieve precise interference. How to arrange various types of reconnaissance and interference units according to the operational tasks in practical applications is a key technology in distributed precision interference [10, 11]. Through the arrangements of various interference sources in the air, on the ground and on the sea, theoretically the interference can operate at the target area and artificially implement accurate interference [12]. In distributed interference, the coherent signals are transmitted through the transmit antennas to accurately aggregate energy into a specific target area while ensuring that the cooperative targets are not affected [13]. Existing interference technologies mainly include: beamforming technology, sidelobe cancellation technology and waveform diversity technique. In the beamforming technology, the useful signal and the useless signal are considered to be separated, so that a beam with better performance can be formed in the direction of the enemy [14, 15]. However, in practical environment, useful and useless signals always intertwined and the useful signal is also affected while suppressing the useless signal, thereby the performance of beamforming technology is reduced. In the sidelobe cancellation technology, the performance of sidelobe cancellation system is related to the signal-to-noise ratio of the input signal under stable conditions. The larger the signal-to-noise ratio is, the deeper the depression is. Therefore, when the noise is relatively large and the signal-to-noise ratio is low, the suppression of useless signal effect is degenerated [16, 17]. In the waveform diversity techniques, the accuracy is improved at the expense of reducing the effective interference area. In addition, the algorithm of waveform diversity technology is quite complex and requires strong mathematical and computational ability [18, 19]. Therefore, in the practical applications, more realistic influencing factors need to be considered and the research is more complicated [20]. Aimed at the precise UAV management and control and the modern electronic warfare, this paper proposes a novel generation method of accurate interference at specific points and specific areas by aggregating coherent multi-frequency signals.

2 Distributed Interference

Wireless communication spreads signals through open structure, breaks the limitation of traditional closed transmission of wired structure and overcomes the lack of dynamics of wired structure, thereby meeting the demand for rapid information interaction. The distributed interference has two distinct advantages: one is that the cooperation capability between the devices is improved and the other is that the usage of energy is greatly improved.

2.1 Distributed Jammer Structure

The distributed jammer is mainly composed of a power supply, an interference signal generator, a power amplifier and transmitting antennas. Controllers can control the timing and combination of the generation of interference signals. Compared with the centralized interference system, it can effectively solve the problem that the interference signal interferes the cooperate targets when the transmission power of the interference signal is very strong. In addition, the distributed jammer is light and convenient, so it can be placed in the enemy's deep area, away from the radar and other reconnaissance communication equipment of cooperator. Therefore, the distributed interference technology effectively solves the problem that the interference signals interfere the enemy and interfere the cooperator at the same time. Following is the structure of the distributed jammer (Fig. 1).

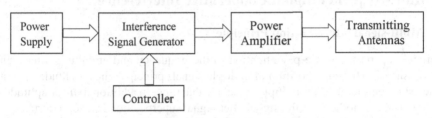

Fig. 1. Structure of the distributed jammer

According to the signal strength of distributed interference signals, we divide the interference into three broad categories: repressive interference, strong interference and weak interference.

Repressive interference: the power of the interfered signal is far less than the power of the interference signal, and the interfered target generally cannot work normally in the frequency band of the interference effect and the error rate is higher than 50%.

Strong interference: The distributed jammer uses a strong power interference signal to interfere the electronic equipment of non-cooperative targets. The power of the interfered signal is less than the power of the interfered signal. Therefore, the interfered equipment is basically difficult to work normally at the interference frequency, and the error rate is between 15% and 20%.

Weak interference: The distributed jammer adopts a low power electromagnetic interference to interfere the electronic equipment of non-cooperative targets. The signal received by the non-cooperative targets is mixed with the interference signal. Because the strength of the interference signal is low, it is impossible to completely suppress the signal and the error rate is about 3%–5%.

2.2 Distributed Interference Characteristics

Compared with traditional centralized jammers, distributed interference has clear advantages in three areas:

First of all, in terms of distribution, the traditional interference adopts the high-power interference jammer, which causes it easily detected and treated as an attack target by enemy equipment while interfering with the enemy. When the number of interference sources is large, and the distribution is very wide, the distributed interference will not be damaged even if they are attacked.

In terms of cost, the distributed interference cost is low for its circuit hardware is simple. Since only certain targets that interfere with the enemy are required during the interference process, there is no strict requirement for the power and form of the interference signal released by the interference source.

In terms of distance, the distance of distributed interference is close for its structure and other problems, generally belonging to near-field interference. The power lose is small for short interference distance, and the interference power entering the interfered radar is large, so the probability of effective interference is greatly improved.

3 Multi-frequency Signal Cooperative Interference

3.1 Multi-signal Superposition Principle

In signal superposition, we pay attention to the frequency and amplitude after signal superposition. In the superposition of multiple signals principle, the amplitude of signal is the arithmetic addition of multiple signals at that time. In addition to the amplitude of the signal, the periodicity of the signal after signal superposition is also important.

For the latter introduction of multi-signal superposition theory, we first introduce the superposition principle of a simple sinusoidal signal, that is to give the further introduction of periodic signals superposition. The periodic signal has some properties: the periodicity is not affected by the multiplication effect but after the addition the periodic uncertainty is generated. According to the knowledge in digital signal processing, we know that if the ratio of the two periodic signal period is a rational number, after the addition the two periodic signal is 100% of the periodic signal. The period of the new signal is the least common multiple of the initial signal period.

For the sake of intuition, it is assumed that the period of the periodic signal $f(t)$ is T_0, the period of the periodic signal $g(t)$ is T_1, when the ratio between the T_0 and T_1 is a rational number, the new signal period T is a multiple of their period, that is, T is both the integral multiple of the period T_0 and the period T_1, and certainly $f(t)+g(t)$ satisfies the regularity of the period. Furthermore, from the perspective of the frequency domain, the Fourier transform of the periodic signal is equivalent to equally spaced sampling of its spectrum, and the sampling interval of the frequency domain is $\frac{2\pi}{T}$, and the spectrum of the superposed signal is the accumulation of the impact sequence generated by the initial signal sampling. When the initial signal period ratio is a rational number, the ratio of the interval sampling is a rational number. The new spectral interval formed by the superimposed impact sequence is uniform, otherwise the interval changes with frequency.

The simulation parameters are set to simulate the superposition of multiple sinusoidal signals with different initial frequencies and zero sinusoidal signals in the same frequency at different frequencies. The superposition of multiple signals with the same frequency interval is also simulated. Their respective periods are 2π, π, $\frac{2}{3}\pi$, $\frac{1}{2}\pi$, $\frac{2\pi}{n}$, n is the number of the superposition signals (Figs. 2 and 3).

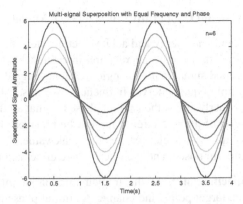

Fig. 2. Multi-signal superposition with equal frequency and phase

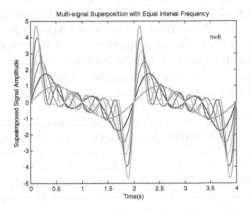

Fig. 3. Multi-signal superposition with equal interval frequency

It can be seen form the comparison of the simulation diagrams that as the number of superimposed signals increases, the amplitude of the superimposed signal increases, and the directivity of the signal increases. When the number of superposition signals is the same, in the simulation based on the superposition of multiple signals with same frequency, the amplitude after signal superposition is multiplied, but its main lobe width is wide and the directivity is poor. In the simulation based on the superposition of multiple signals with equal interval frequency, the amplitude is not multiplied increasing after the signal superposition, but the directivity of the superimposed signal is significantly enhanced. We are eager to find a way to equalize the amplitude and directivity, where the peaks of all the signals at the target point are superimposed. After adjusting the initial phases of the wavelets, the peak of each wavelet signal arriving is superimposed at the target point. This method is named as multi-signal superposition energy aggregation.

3.2 Multi-frequency Signal Cooperative Interference Model

In order to better aggregate the energy and achieve better interference effect, the multi-frequency signal superposition energy aggregation interference strategy is adopted. In this section, the transmitted signal is not a single frequency signal, and the transmitted signal consists of multiple equal interval frequency wavelets. All the wavelets with different frequencies properly adjust their initial phases so that all the wavelet reach the peak value at the position of the interference target (the receiver of the other party). In this way, the energy of all the wavelet reaches the peak value, the interference signal energy is coherently superimposed, and the interference effect achieves better.

Interference at the Specific Point. In the implementation of interference, we must clear the position of the target point, and change the initial phase of the wavelets with different frequencies according to the distance between our transmitter and the enemy receiver, so that when the wavelets of different frequencies arrive at the enemy receiver, the energy reaches the peak value. The energy of each wavelet is fully utilized and plays a positive role in the interference. Interference cancellation occurs at non-target points for the cooperative of wavelets of different frequencies in this process, so that the energy of the wavelets of different frequencies is maintained at zero in the non-target position. We can place our own equipment at these positions, which has a good application prospect. We summarize the above process in the following steps (Fig. 4):

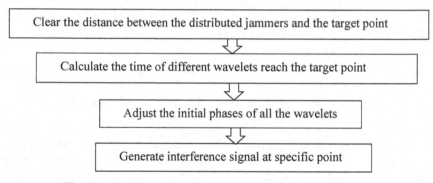

Fig. 4. The process of interference generated at the specific point

Firstly, we should clear the distance D between the distributed jammers and the target point, then calculate the time of different wavelets reach the target point with the formula $\Delta t = \frac{D}{C}$, where C is the electromagnetic wave transmission speed and $c = 3.0 \times 10^8$. Adjust the initial phase according the formula $\Delta \varphi_n = -2\pi f_n \Delta t$, in this way, the energy of different frequency wavelets arrives at the target point with peak energy value.

Interference in Specific Area. In practical applications, the actual interference area is not just a point. Therefore, interference at the specific point often cannot meet the actual requirements. We hope that the interference area can be flexibly adjusted according to the actual requirements, in addition to the peak energy aggregate at the fixed point. Interference in specific area can accurately interfere with the destruction of enemy equipment in small areas, while protecting our own equipment in the nearby area to work properly, improving the efficiency and accuracy of interference. Therefore, compared with the interference at the specific point, the interference in specific area with adjustable interference area is more applicable in engineering. We summarize the process in the following steps (Fig. 5):

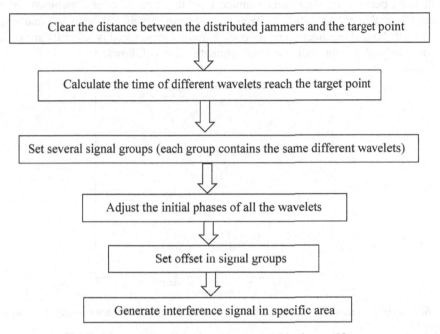

Fig. 5. The process of interference generated in the specific area

Firstly, we should clear the distance D between the distributed jammers and the target point according to the positioning reconnaissance equipment. It is assumed that all wavelets travel at the same speed in the air and equal to the speed of light. The time of different wavelets reach the target point with the formula $\Delta t = \frac{D}{C}$, where C is the electromagnetic wave transmission speed. In order to implement interference in specific area, we set several groups of signals, each group containing the same different frequency wavelets. The number of wavelet groups N is uncertain, but the more groups, the better interference accuracy. Adjust the initial phase according the formula $\Delta\varphi_n = -2\pi f_n \Delta t$, when the wavelets reach the target point, adjust the initial phase of the wavelets to form a peak. Finally, at the receiver position, each signal group slightly adjusted the wavelets phase so that the aggregate points of the plurality of wavelet groups are evenly distributed around the interference point.

4 Simulation and Analysis

4.1 Interference at the Specific Point

Set the parameters for simulation is as following: The principle for UAV management and control is to generate precise interference. Considering the actual application scenarios, the distance between the interference jammers and the target receiver is assumed 700 m. 16 and 48 equal interval frequency wavelets are set respectively and the lowest frequency is 2.0×10^5 Hz and the electromagnetic wave transmission speed is 3.0×10^8 m/s. The one-dimensional and three-dimensional simulation are as follows:

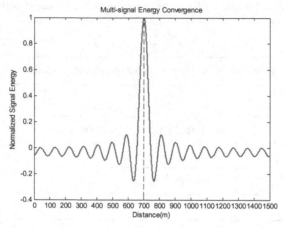

Fig. 6. The one-dimensional figure of energy convergence with 16 equal interval frequency wavelets

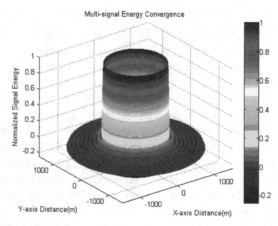

Fig. 7. The three-dimensional figure of energy convergence with 16 equal interval frequency wavelets

It can be seen from the Figs. 6 and 7 that multiple wavelets can interfere with the equipment at the specific points according to requirements. However, the interference is not accurate for the main lobe of the interference energy is relatively fat and the directivity is poor.

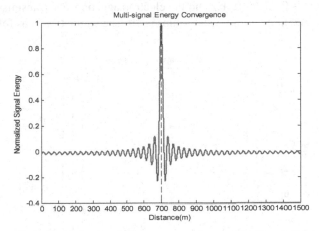

Fig. 8. The one-dimensional figure of energy convergence with 48 equal interval frequency wavelets

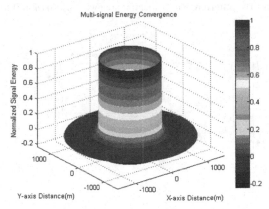

Fig. 9. The three-dimensional figure of energy convergence with 48 equal interval frequency wavelets

It can be seen from the Figs. 8 and 9 that multiple wavelets can interfere with the equipment at the specific points according to requirements. When the number of the wavelets is 16, the accuracy of interference is relatively poor, and the main lobe is relatively fat. When the number of the wavelets is 48, the interference is more accurate and the main lobe is thinner. That is to say, as the number of wavelets increases, the interference becomes more and more accurate, and the effect of interference becomes stronger and stronger. However, as the number of wavelets increases, the calculated amount increases and the speed of interference is slowed down.

4.2   Interference in Specific Area

Set the parameters for simulation is as following: It is assumed that the distance between the interference jammers and the target receiver is 800 m and the interference area is 400 m and 600 m respectively. 48 equal interval frequency wavelets are set and the lowest frequency is 0.75×10^5 Hz and the electromagnetic wave transmission speed is 3.0×10^8 m/s. The number of signal groups is 10. The simulation is as follows:

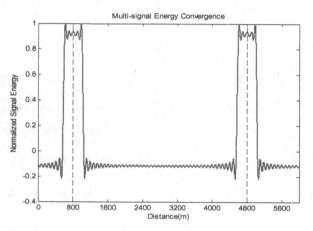

Fig. 10. Interference in specific area with width of 400 m

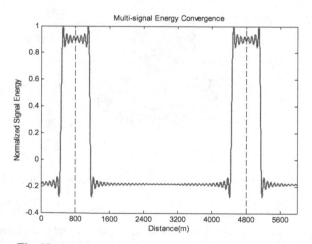

Fig. 11. Interference in specific area with width of 600 m

It can be seen from the Figs. 10 and 11 that interference with the width of 400 m and 600 m is generated near the target point of 800 m. We can see that in the interference region, the interference energy is aggregated, while the energy of interference at other locations is relatively weak. In practical applications, the cooperative interference parameters can be set according to the distance and distribution of the other devices, thereby implementing accurate interference based on interference regions.

5 Conclusion

Under the background of urgent demand of air flight control system for civil UAVs and precise electronic warfare, this paper proposed the accurate interference method, which can effectively interfere non-cooperative targets in a certain area, and cooperative targets in other areas are not affected. In this paper, a method of superimposing interference with multiple equal interval frequency wavelets is adopted to generate accurate interference at the specific point and in the specific area. The distance between the distributed jammers and the target point is provided by the cooperative device and the initial phase of the plurality of wavelets is adjusted so that the energy of the interference signal reaches the peak value. When different interference wavelets reach the target point, the energy of the multiple wavelets is aggregated to obtain accurate suppression interference. The simulation shows that the interference method proposed in this paper can generate effective interference at the target point and around the target point. Therefore, the distributed interference method proposed in this paper can be applied to practical applications.

References

1. Choi, K.W., Ginting, L., Rosyady, P.A., Aziz, A.A., Dong, I.K.: Wireless-powered sensor networks: how to realize. IEEE Trans. Wireless Commun. **16**(1), 221–234 (2017)
2. Liu, G., Zhang, X., Qin, W., et al.: Construction of air flight regulatory system for civil unmanned aerial vehicles. Command Inf. Syst. Technol. **9**(3), 23–27 (2018)
3. Shi, L., Liu, W.: UAV management and control technology based on satellite navigation spoofing jamming. Command Inf. Syst. Technol. **8**(1), 22–26 (2017)
4. Bo, L.I., Gao, X.G.: Integrated decision for airborne weapon systems based on Bayesian networks. J. Syst. Simul. **19**(4), 886–889 (2007)
5. Spezio, A.E.: Electronic warfare systems. IEEE Trans. Microw. Theory Tech. **50**(3), 633–644 (2002)
6. Wang, Y., Huang, G., Wei, L.I.: Waveform design for radar and extended target in the environment of electronic warfare. J. Syst. Eng. Electron. **29**(1), 48–57 (2018)
7. Miao, G., Himayat, N., Li, G.Y., Talwar, S.: Distributed interference-aware energy-efficient power optimization. IEEE Trans. Wireless Commun. **10**(4), 1323–1333 (2011)
8. Hsu, F., Giordano, A.: Digital whitening techniques for improving spread spectrum communications performance in the presence of narrowband jamming and interference. IEEE Trans. Commun. **26**(2), 209–216 (1978)
9. Shi, C., Berry, R.A., Honig, M.L.: Monotonic convergence of distributed interference pricing in wireless networks. In: IEEE International Symposium on Information Theory (2009)
10. Huang, J., Berry, R.A., Honig, M.L.: Distributed interference compensation for wireless networks. IEEE J. Sel. Areas Commun. **24**(5), 1074–1084 (2006)
11. Gomadam, K., Cadambe, V.R., Jafar, S.A.: A distributed numerical approach to interference alignment and applications to wireless interference networks. IEEE Trans. Inf. Theory **57**(6), 3309–3322 (2011)
12. Xia, Y., Shi, W., Wang, H.: Design and implementation of efficient distributed operational application framework. Command Inf. Syst. Technol. **8**(3), 49–53 (2017)

13. Ngo, D.T., Long, B.L., Le-Ngoc, T., Hossain, E., Dong, I.K.: Distributed interference management in two-tier CDMA femtocell networks. IEEE Trans. Wireless Commun. **11**(3), 979–989 (2012)
14. Xu, Y., et al.: Joint beamforming and power-splitting control in downlink cooperative SWIPT NOMA systems. IEEE Trans. Signal Process. **65**(18), 4874–4886 (2017)
15. Nasir, A.A., Tuan, H.D., Ngo, D.T., Duong, T.Q., Poor, H.V.: Beamforming design for wireless information and power transfer systems: receive power-splitting versus transmit time-switching. IEEE Trans. Commun. **65**(2), 876–889 (2017)
16. Mohammed, J.R., Sayidmarie, K.H.: Performance evaluation of the adaptive sidelobe canceller system with various auxiliary configurations. AEU Int. J. Electron. Commun. **80**, 179–185 (2017)
17. Wang, X., Xie, J., He, Z., Zhang, Q.: Performance analysis of the generalized sidelobe canceller in finite sample size and correlative interference situations. IEICE Trans. Fundam. Electron. Commun. Comput. Sci. **100**(11), 2358–2369 (2017)
18. Krieger, G., Gebert, N., Younis, M., Moreira, A.: Advanced synthetic aperture radar based on digital beamforming and waveform diversity. In: IEEE Radar Conference (2008)
19. Wang, W.Q.: Mitigating range ambiguities in high-PRF SAR with OFDM waveform diversity. IEEE Geosci. Remote Sens. Lett. **10**(1), 101–105 (2013)
20. Dan, S., Wei, W., Xu, Z., Xiong, Z., Kirubarajan, T.: Focused energy delivery with protection for precision electronic warfare. IEEE Trans. Aerosp. Electron. Syst. **52**(6), 3053–3064 (2017)

Analysis of ADAS Technology Principle and Application Scenario

Yao Tang[1,2], Bo Li[1], Zhongjiang Yan[1(✉)], and Mao Yang[1]

[1] School of Electronics and Information, Northwestern Polytechnical University,
Xi'an, China
confusedty@163.com,
{libo.npu,zhjyan,yangmao}@nwpu.edu.cn
[2] Xi'an Electronic Engineering Research Institute, Xi'an, People's Republic of China

Abstract. With the development of vehicle sensors, artificial intelligence and vehicle network technique, Advanced Driving Assistant System (ADAS) technology is now experiencing a rapid development. However the interaction of the sensors' data in the real scene is seldom discussed. This paper firstly describes the application scenarios and typical working mechanism of ADAS. Then it analyses the advantages and deficiencies of the environment perception only based on vehicle-self sensors. Secondly, it describes the main research of vehicle networking. Lastly through two typical scenes it analyses the possibility and problem of communicating the sensors' data via vehicle networking. Through the application scenarios analysis, it proposes a new potential research route for the ADAS.

Keywords: Advanced Driving Assistant System (ADAS) ·
Vehicle-mounted sensors · Vehicle to Everything (V2X) · Vehicular
Ad-hoc Network (VANET)

1 Introduction

At present ADAS [1–4] is mainly to use the vehicle-mounted sensors to perceive the surrounding environment and to make the identification of static or dynamic targets. To track the surrounding objects, and combine with the navigation map, it finally can make the automatic driving decision. This effectively increase the car driving comfort and safety.

In recent years, V2X technology represented by Long Term Evolution for Vehicle (LTE-V) and Dedicated Short Range Communications (DSRC) have brought new opportunities for ADAS [5–8] which provides the possibilities for communication between vehicles, road units, pedestrians and so on. However its design did not provide a reliable enough mechanism for vehicle-mounted sensor data interaction.

This paper introduces the main achievements of ADAS. Through the construction of typical scenarios, it indicates the defect of ADAS only make the usage of its own vehicle-mounted sensor information. Further it illustrates the potential threat caused by the vehicle-mounted sensor data collision and points out that it may be an important development direction of ADAS technology to take the transmission efficiency of sensor data into the design consideration of V2X.

2   ADAS Technology Principle

At present, the main approach of the ADAS system is to perceive the surrounding environment through the vehicle-mounted sensors, so as to track the obstacles and realize the safe driving of vehicles. This section explains the advantages and limitations of the current ADAS approach through the introduction and comparison of different vehicle-mounted sensors and related technologies.

2.1   Camera Sensors

Vehicle-mounted camera is the eye of this system, and the environment perception technology based on image recognition is the mainstream of ADAS technology at present [9,10]. In addition, vehicle-mounted cameras play an irreplaceable role in realizing automatic driving, such as identifying traffic signs and traffic lights. The basic principle of camera imaging is as follows:

$$\frac{Z}{f} = \frac{W}{W'} \tag{1}$$

Where Z is the distance from the target to the camera, f is the focal length of the camera, W is the width of the transverse scene, W' is the imaging width. It can be seen that the shorter the focal length, the smaller the magnification, and the larger the field of view. That is, the wider the camera Angle is, the shorter the length of the accurate detection distance will be; and the narrower the Angle is, the longer the detection distance will be. Therefore, to perceive the surrounding environment, different types of cameras need to be installed around the vehicle. A typical car camera layout is shown in the following figure:

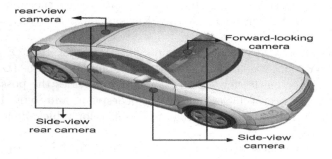

Fig. 1. Vehicle camera sensors distribution diagram

In Fig. 1, the forward-looking-camera is usually a combination of binocular or trinocular camera, including a fish-eye camera, a narrow-angle camera (and a medium-range camera). Side-view-camera is made of two wide-angle cameras, side-view-rear-camera is a medium-range camera, and rear-view-camera is a fish-eye camera.

Night vision function and AI automatic recognition function applying to vehicle-mounted cameras will be the foreseeable trend in the future [11, 12]. But relying solely on cameras as ADAS sensors still has obvious defects, that is in extreme weather conditions such as strong light, sudden illumination or fog and haze, the environmental perception ability of the camera will be greatly hindered, and it is easy to cause misjudgment.

2.2   Radar Sensors

Radar is a sensor that determines the target distance through time delay. The vehicle-mounted radar sensors can be divided into three main categories: ultrasonic radar, millimeter-wave radar and lidar. Its ranging formula is as follows:

$$R = V_c \cdot T/2 \tag{2}$$

Where, R is the target's distance, V_c is the propagation speed of the wave emitted by the sensor in the air, and T is time delay. The frequency of the vehicle-mounted ultrasonic wave is about $f_S \approx 40\,\text{KHz}$, and the propagation speed of the ultrasonic wave is $V_S \approx 340\,\text{m/s}$. The vehicle-mounted millimeter-wave radar is mainly constrained in $f_{R1} = 24\,\text{GHz}$ and $f_{R2} = 77\,\text{GHz}$ frequency bands. The wavelength of the vehicle-mounted laser sensor is about $\lambda_L = 900\,\text{nm}$, and the propagation speed of the millimeter-wave and optical-wave is $V_{RL} \approx 3 \times 10^8\,\text{m/s}$. Among these three kinds of radar sensors, ultrasonic radar has the lowest cost and the highest assembly amount in the automobile market. However, because ultrasonic wave attenuates too fast in the air [13], it is mainly used for obstacle detection for $R < 3\,\text{m}$.

The vehicle-mounted millimeter-wave radar is almost unaffected by rain, snow and other weather conditions [14]. Due to these all-weather fits and doppler measurement characteristics, millimeter-wave radar has become an important vehicle-mounted sensor recently. However although the spatial beam scanning can be realized by Digital Beam Forming (DBF) through coherent processing [15], its angular resolution is limited by wavelength and aperture, that is:

$$\theta \approx \lambda/D \tag{3}$$

Where θ is the angular resolution, λ is the transmitting wavelength of the sensor, and D is the radar aperture size.

Because of its small wavelength, lidar has the highest resolution and accuracy in these three radar systems, the resolution of the beam can be controlled within 0.1°. By means of multi-line scanning or phased array [16], it is possible to accurately construct the surrounding scenes. However the disadvantage is that the cost of multi-line lidar is too high to be used in consumer electronics. On the other hand, the use of laser is limited by rain, snow, fog and other weather effects.

For different sensors have diverse feature, it always has a combination of different sensors in ADAS as below [17].

Table 1. Typical sensors installation in ADAS system

	L2	L3	L4 and L5
MMW radar	≥3	≥6	≥10
Camera	≥1	≥4	≥8
LIDAR	0	≥1	≥1
Others	Ultrasonic	Ultrasonic interior camera	Ultrasonic interior camera V2x

As can be seen from Table 1, the number of cameras and millimeter-wave radars increases from low to high with the level of autonomous driving rank, and they are complemented for each other.

2.3   SLAM

Simultaneous Localization and Mapping (SLAM) as an environment model built technique, is a high-order technology in recent years. It emerges the image recognition, remote sensing, digital map and other technologies [18,19].

Through GPS the vehicle can obtain its own general position information, but the accuracy is poor, the accuracy of urban environment is about 3–10 m. For unmanned usage, digital map positioning accuracy is often required within 1m. SLAM accurately calibrates its position by matching the data acquired by the camera or lidar sensor with high-precision digital map information.

SLAM technology can well realize the high-precision map under the known scenes. Thus, it can assist vehicles to make driving decisions to achieve autonomous driving. However, the problem of multi-vehicle collaborative driving in complex environment still brings safety risks for ADAS.

3   V2X Communication

V2X technology supports the communication between vehicles and the surrounding environment, which enables real-time interaction of road traffic environment information. V2X is currently the route of the smart transportation system predetermined by the governments of various countries, making the ADAS technology transform from autonomous mode to network connected mode.

This section summarizes the advantages and disadvantages of the current V2X technology by explaining and comparing the current mainstream of LTEV & DSRC and the research hotspot of VANET.

3.1   LTE-V and DSRC

At present, the two main standardization development ways of V2X in the world are LTE-V and DSRC. The former is mainly supported by 4G/5G mobile communication technology of 3GPP, while the latter is mainly supported by 802.11 technology of IEEE.

DSRC's standardization can retrospect back to 2004. At that time, IEEE began to develop new vehicle-mounted communication standards under its 802.11 (Wireless Local Area Networks) WLAN standard series. This standard is known as 802.11p. Around 2007, the IEEE 802.11p standard had been stabilized. IEEE then proceeded to develop the 1609.x family of standards as a security framework for V2X. Around the same time, the Society of Automotive Engineers (SAE) began to develop standards for vehicle to vehicle (V2V) applications based on the needs of the automotive industry and named DSRC. The communication standards adopted by DSRC are IEEE 802.11p and 1609.x. The technology allows all traffic participants to interact with their dynamic information at a rate of 10 to 20 times per second.

The LTE-V was newly released by 3GPP in 2017. Unlike the IEEE 802.11 WLAN standard, LTE-V is a set of vehicle-to-infrastructure (V2I) and V2V communication physical layer protocols based on cellular communication networks. LTE-V technology is considered as an important cornerstone for realizing the Internet of vehicles, and is valued by people in the field of Intelligent Transport System (ITS). LTE-V is based on 4.5 G network to LTE cellular networks as the basis of V2X, the key research direction of the 5G. It is the exclusive vehicle networking protocol, networking application scenario for V2V, V2I, vehicle-to-pedestrian (V2P), vehicle-to-network (V2N). The core of these set of V2X protocols is V2V interconnection. In order to meet the multi-scene business requirements of vehicle safety, driving efficiency and on-board entertainment, LTE-V adopts "LTE-V-Cell" and "LTE-V-Direct". The former is based on the expansion of the existing cellular technology, mainly carrying the traditional Internet business of vehicles. The latter introduces LTE device-to-device (D2D) to realize the direct communication of V2V and V2I, and carries active security services of vehicles, mainly meeting the requirements of low delay and high reliability of terminal security.

The main differences between DSRC and LTE-V are shown in the table below [20].

Table 2. Difference between DSRC and LTE-V design parameters

	DSRC (IEEE802.11p)	LTE-V
Multi-user allocation	Single user per symbol	Multiple users share the same symbol
Synchronization requirements	Asynchronous	Tight synchronization
OFDM parameters	Short symbol duration	Long symbol duration
Channel access mechanism	(Carrier Sense Multiple Access with Collision Avoidance) CSMA-CA	Sensing based Semi-Persistent Scheduling (SPS)

As can be seen from Table 2, the symbol duration of OFDM in DSRC is much shorter than that in LTE-V. That result in the OFDM subcarriers are 10 times closer in LTE-V than in IEEE802.11p. Eventually LTE-V application is strictly limited to speeds below 140 km/h by doppler effect, however IEEE802.11p can perform well at speeds of 250 km/h. Nevertheless the channel scheduling mechanism of LTE-V is more flexible, cause OFDM subcarrier is divided in much more detail. Another difference between LTE-V and DSRC is that the former requires network time synchronization mechanism, and Media Access Control (MAC) layer adopts SPS mechanism so it requires coordination of base station terminal. That makes LTE-V's application environment is more subject to the base station coverage.

Due to the periodic and real-time characteristics of the data generated by vehicle sensors, the data of vehicle sensors is usually communicated in the broadcasted way [21]. However, CSMA-CA in DSRC is difficult to apply in broadcast mode. And in the absence of base station coverage, it is difficult to make channel reservation based on SPS in LTE-V. For the above problems, the application of VANET in the field of intelligent transportation has attracted extensive attention.

3.2 VANET Protocols

Since LTE-V and DSRC protocols do not involve the concept of clustering, and vehicle networking is characterized by high mobility, if vehicles traveling in different directions are grouped in the same cluster, it will create a lot of clustering overhead for re-clustering frequently. So it is feasible to divide different clusters by driving directions [22].

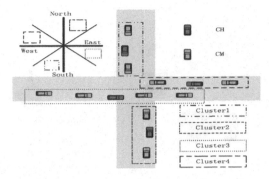

Fig. 2. Basic vehicle cluster diagram

As shown in Fig. 2, the vehicles are divided into four clusters according to different driving orientations. The specific dividing basis is as follows:

$$
\begin{cases}
\alpha \in [-45°, 45°), \ m \in C_1 \\
\alpha \in [45°, 135°), \ m \in C_2 \\
\alpha \in [135°, -135°), \ m \in C_3 \\
\alpha \in [-135°, 45°), \ m \in C_4
\end{cases}
\tag{4}
$$

Where, m represents the vehicle, and α is the north-to-east angle value of vehicle's orientation, and there are four basic classes $C_1 \sim C_4$ divided according to driving direction. The advantage of cluster-based VANET is that, the information interaction within the cluster can be carried out under the coordination of the cluster header. The cluster header can make MAC layer channel reservation and division mechanism like TDMA for each cluster member, that can avoid the data collision effectively in the cluster [23]. Meanwhile, the cluster head can acts as the gateway node for information interaction between clusters.

The use of cluster-based VANET protocol for sensor-based information exchange can effectively avoid information collision, but this kind of protocol is still in the research stage, and the corresponding V2X standard has not been carried out yet.

4 Typical Scenarios

This section illustrates the necessity of sensor data interaction through two typical scenarios. Further more points out the potential danger of sensor data collision in the free broadcast way.

As shown in Fig. 3, when the pedestrian is crossing the road in this scenario, Car1 can detect the pedestrian by its vehicle-mounted sensor like millimeter-wave radar, but the electromagnetic wave emitted by Car2's radar is blocked by Car1, so it can't detect this pedestrian in time.

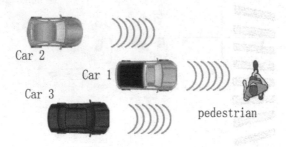

Fig. 3. The pedestrian crossing scenario

When Car1 or Car2 senses the pedestrian, friction is used to slow down the moving vehicle. That is:

$$F_f \cdot d = \mu \cdot m \cdot g \cdot d = 0.5m \cdot v_o^2 \tag{5}$$

Where F_f is the friction force, d is the braking distance, μ is the friction coefficient of road surface, m is the vehicle quality, v_o is the speed before braking. The braking distance is:

$$d = \frac{v_o^2}{2\mu g} \tag{6}$$

Take $\mu = 0.5$ (wet asphalt pavement) and $\mu = 0.8$ (dry asphalt pavement), then the relationship between braking distance and speed is shown in the figure below.

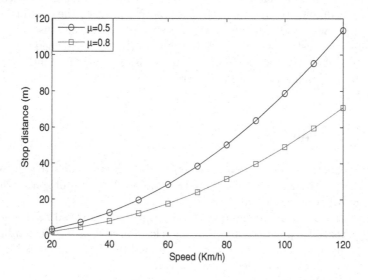

Fig. 4. Relationship between stop distance and speed

As shown in Fig. 4, when the driving speed is under 120 Km/h, the braking distance of the car is lower than 120 m, while the detection distance of the front anti-collision laser or millimeter-wave radar is generally greater than 150 m. Therefore, in Fig. 3, the braking distance of Car1 is sufficient, and the key for Car2 to break in time, is that Car2 can timely get the pedestrian's information. The braking time of the vehicle is:

$$t = \frac{v_\circ}{\mu g} \tag{7}$$

Therefore, the average sensor data transmission delay and collision probability of vehicle-mounted sensor data is the key of the problem. To illustrate this further, introduce the scenario shown below.

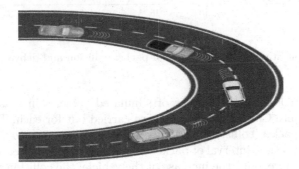

Fig. 5. Mountain road roundabout

Figure 5 constructs the scene of vehicles trudging on the mountain road. Due to the block in sight of the mountain road, it is difficult to detect the coming vehicle. In order to prevent collision, vehicles in both orientations need to detect each other in advance. That means the vehicles' GPS/INS information should be known by the opposite side vehicles. In Fig. 5, Car1 and Car3 need to receive the position information sent by each other in advance to effectively slow down and control the driving path, so as to avoid the collision when they meet.

It is assumed that all vehicles are equipped with vehicle-mounted sensor, and vehicles transmit sensor data packets by broadcast, with random time interval between 50 ms to 100 ms (update frequency of vehicle-mounted sensor data is between 10–20 Hz), and the data packets' duration is 1 ms (LTE-V Fixed Transmission duration). The collision probability (collision packet number/total number of packets sent) and the average delivery delay (non-collision packet sending time interval) are counted.

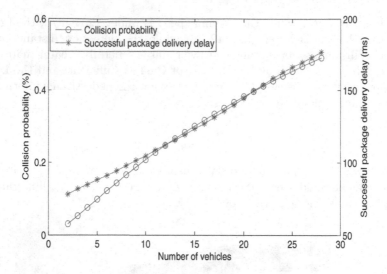

Fig. 6. The statistical probability of packet collision and delivery delay

As shown in Fig. 6, the number of simulated vehicles increases from 2 to 28, and 500 Monte Carlo experiments were carried out for each. The statistical probability of packet collision gradually increases from 3% *to* 49%, and the average successful time interval of packet delivery gradually increases from 78 ms to 176 ms. Therefore, with the increase of the vehicle, the collision probability of sensor data packets increases, and the average packet arrival delay increases too. However if the TDMA channel is allocated to the cluster-member and different clusters work in different frequency channel in the way of clustering network, the collision of data packets can be avoided and the effective delivery of sensor data packets can be guaranteed. Therefore, fusing the VANET technology of cluster communication into the mainstream of LTE-V and DSRC technologies will effectively promote the interaction ability of the sensor data in V2X network.

5   Conclusion

This paper summarizes the current ADAS technology development on vehicle-mounted sensors and V2X communication. It points out the defects of the recent ADAS technology only relies on vehicle-mounted sensors for environmental perception, and asserts the interaction of vehicle-mounted sensor information through V2X technology is an important direction for the development of ADAS in the future. Through the analysis of specific scenarios, it points out that to apply the broadcast random competition way to the current LTE-V or DSRC standard has some disadvantages. It predicts that to introduce the cluster-based channel allocation method in VANET into LTE-V and DSRC may be the next technical development direction of V2X.

Acknowledgement. This work was supported in part by the National Natural Science Foundations of CHINA (Grant No. 61771392, 61771390, 61871322, 61501373 and 61271279), the National Science and Technology Major Project (Grant No. 2015ZX03002006-004 and 2016ZX03001018-004), and Science and Technology on Avionics Integration Laboratory (Grant No. 20185553035).

References

1. Reichenbach, M., Liebischer, L., Vaas, S., et al.: Comparison of lane detection algorithms for ADAS using embedded hardware architectures. In: 2018 Conference on Design and Architectures for Signal and Image Processing (DASIP), pp. 48–53 (2018)
2. Lyu, N., Duan, Z., Xie, L., et al.: Driving experience on the effectiveness of advanced driving assistant systems. In: 2017 4th International Conference on Transportation Information and Safety (ICTIS), pp. 987–992 (2017)
3. Rommerskirchen, C.P., Helmbrecht, M., Bengler, K.J.: The impact of an anticipatory eco-driver assistant system in different complex driving situations on the driver behavior. IEEE Intell. Transp. Syst. Mag. **6**(2), 45–56 (2014)
4. Xiao, L., Gao, F.: Practical string stability of platoon of adaptive cruise control vehicles. IEEE Trans. Intell. Transp. Syst. **12**(4), 1184–1194 (2011)
5. Shi, M., Zhang, Y., Yao, D.: Application-oriented performance comparison of 802.11p and LTE-V in a V2V communication system. Tsinghua Sci. Technol. **24**(2), 123–133 (2019)
6. Gonzalez-Martn, M., Sepulcre, M., Molina-Masegosa, R.: Analytical models of the performance of C-V2X mode 4 vehicular communications. IEEE Trans. Veh. Technol. **68**(2), 1155–1166 (2019)
7. Abboud, K., Omar, H.A., Zhuang, W.: Interworking of DSRC and cellular network technologies for V2X communications: a survey. IEEE Trans. Veh. Technol. **65**(12), 9457–9470 (2016)
8. Bey, T., Tewolde, G.: Evaluation of DSRC and LTE for V2X. In: 2019 IEEE 9th Annual Computing and Communication Workshop and Conference (CCWC), pp. 1032–1035 (2019)
9. Zhang, X., Gao, Y., Chen, J.: An efficient method to recover relative pose for vehicle-mounted cameras under planar motion. IEEE Trans. Syst. Man. Cybern. Syst. (Early Access), 1–11 (2019)
10. Wang, Y., Lu, X., Ling, Z., et al.: A method to calibrate vehicle-mounted cameras under urban traffic scenes. IEEE Trans. Intell. Transp. Syst. **16**(6), 3270–3279 (2015)
11. Wang, H., Duan, W., Zhao, H., et al.: Research of night vision image denoising method based on the improved FastICA. In: 2017 IEEE International Conference on Mechatronics and Automation (ICMA), pp. 332–336 (2017)
12. Ruili, J., Haocong, W., Han, W., et al.: Smart parking system using image processing and artificial intelligence. In: 2018 12th International Conference on Sensing Technology (ICST), pp. 232–235 (2017)
13. Paulet, M.V., Salceanu, A., Neacsu, O.M.: Ultrasonic radar. In: 2016 International Conference and Exposition on Electrical and Power Engineering (EPE), pp. 551–554 (2016)
14. Zhang, Y., Wang, G.: Application of compressed sensing in vehicular LFMCW millimeter wave radar ranging. In: 2018 International Conference on Microwave and Millimeter Wave Technology (ICMMT), pp. 1–3 (2018)

15. Steinhauer, M., Ruob, H.-O., Irion, H., et al.: Millimeter-wave-radar sensor based on a transceiver array for automotive applications. IEEE Trans. Microw. Theory Tech. **56**(2), 261–269 (2008)
16. Poulton, C.V., Byrd, M.J., Timurdogan, E., et al.: Optical phased arrays for integrated beam steering. In: 2018 IEEE 15th International Conference on Group IV Photonics (GFP), pp. 1–2 (2018)
17. Three types of autonomous vehicle sensors in L1-L5 self-driving cars. https://www.itransition.com/blog/three-types-of-autonomous-vehicle-sensors-in-self-driving-cars
18. Qiu, K., Qin, T., Gao, W., et al.: Tracking 3-D motion of dynamic objects using monocular visual-inertial sensing. IEEE Trans. Rob. **35**(4), 799–816 (2019)
19. Wang, D., Liang, H., Mei, T., et al.: Lidar Scan matching EKF-SLAM using the differential model of vehicle motion. In: 2013 IEEE Intelligent Vehicles Symposium (IV), pp. 908–912 (2013)
20. IEEE802.11p ahead of LTE-V2V for safety applications. https://www.auto-talks.com/wp-content/uploads/2017/09/Whitepaper-LTE-V2V-USletter-05.pdf
21. Tonguz, O.K., Zhang, R.: Harnessing vehicular broadcast communications: DSRC-actuated traffic control. IEEE Trans. Intell. Transp. Syst. **21**(2), 509–520 (2020)
22. Shahen Shah, A.F.M., Ilhan, H., Tureli, U.: CB-MAC: a novel cluster-based MAC protocol for VANETs. IET Intel. Transport Syst. **13**(4), 587–595 (2019)
23. Haq, A.U., Liu, K.: Review of TDMA-based MAC protocols for vehicular ad hoc networks. In: 2018 IEEE 18th International Conference on Communication Technology (ICCT), pp. 459–467 (2018)

Electromagnetic Wave with OAM and Its Potential Applications in IoT

Jinhong Li, Xiaoyan Pang$^{(\boxtimes)}$, and Chen Feng

School of Electronics and Information, Northwestern Polytechnical University,
Xi'an, China
xypang@nwpu.edu.cn

Abstract. As one of the hot techniques, the Internet of Things (IoT) is gradually penetrating all aspects of human life. The limitation of the spectrum resources has limited the development of the IoT, which forces us to look for new ways to increase the efficiency of the spectrum utilization. The Electromagnetic (EM) wave with orbital angular momentum (OAM), also called the EM vortex wave is a promising method to solve this problem. In this article, the basic theory of EM wave with OAM in radio frequency (RF) is introduced and the main techniques in the OAM radio beam, including the generation of the EM with OAM, the receive, the multiplexing based on OAM mode are summarized. Based on the main properties of EM wave with OAM in RF, the potential applications of EM vortex beam in the IoT are discussed.

Keywords: Orbital angular momentum · Vortex beam · IoT

1 Introduction

Since it was first introduced in 1999, the IoT has received a lot attention from all over the world and has been developed extensively in many areas [1]. The IoT has become the third tide of development after computers, the Internet and mobile communication networks. Communication technology enables the IoT to efficiently collect and exchange the perceived information data between different terminals, and realize the interworking and sharing of information resources, which is the key support for various application functions of the IoT. However, in a wireless communication system of IoT, there may be trillions of devices, which may congest the network because the limitation of the bandwidth. That may limit the development of the IoT and need novel techniques to overcome this problem.

Since wireless communication has spread to all aspects of our lives, there is always an increasing demand of new ways for using the existing spectrum

Supported by the Seed Foundation of Innovation and Creation for Graduate Students in Northwestern Polytechnical University.

efficiently. Various technologies such as the Orthogonal Frequency Division Multiplexing (OFDM) and the Code Division Multiple Access (CDMA) have been used to increase the efficiency of the available bandwidth [2], but they are still far from being sufficient. It has been known that the EM wave can carry both linear momentum and angular momentum [3]. When an EM wave has a helical phasefront, it has OAM [4]. The waves with OAM are also called 'vortex waves' and have been studied extensively in optical frequency [5–8] and have many applications in optics, for instance in optical manipulation [9], and microscopy [10]. However, the EM waves with OAM in RF is still quite new and a lot of their properties have not been clarified. One of the main researches on OAM in RF is how to using OAM modes in multiplexing in free-space communication. Theoretically, an EM wave can carry an infinite number of OAM modes on the same frequency, and each mode is orthogonal to each other [11]. Thus the multiplexing based on OAM modes can greatly increase the efficiency spectrum utilization in free space, while the EM waves with different OAM modes have a good anti-jamming ability due to the orthogonality of different OAM modes. In modern wireless communication systems, all the EM waves are plane waves, which means that their OAM modes are 0. Thus the EM waves carrying any OAM mode are orthogonal to the plane waves. Although the EM waves with OAM have not been studied extensively in wireless communications of RF, they were even paid less attention in the development of the IoT. Since their advantages over common EM waves, we believe that the EM waves with OAM will supply a quite new perspective in studying IoT and can support new ways to increase the efficiency of spectrum utilization for the IoT network.

In this article, we will first have a review of the main characteristics of the EM waves with OAM in RF and summarize the current key techniques in studying OAM in RF, then the potential applications of EM waves with OAM in the IoT will be discussed.

2   Basic Theory of OAM

As described in the standard electrodynamics literature, an EM wave will not only radiate energy (linear momentum) but also angular momentum (AM) into the far field [12]. The angular momentum of an EM wave is composed of two parts: the spin angular momentum (SAM) and OAM [13]. The SAM is associated with the photon spin which is manifested as circular polarization, and, in contrast, the OAM is shown as a result of a beam possessing helical phase fronts [14].

Let SAM be denoted by S and OAM be L, then the total angular momentum of J can given by the sum [15]

$$J = L + S, \tag{1}$$

where,

$$L = \varepsilon_0 \int Re(\mathrm{i}E^*(\widehat{L} \cdot A))\mathrm{d}V, \tag{2}$$

$$S = \varepsilon_0 \int \boldsymbol{Re}(\boldsymbol{E}^* \times \boldsymbol{A}) dV, \qquad (3)$$

note the occurrence of the OAM operator $\widehat{\boldsymbol{L}} = -i(r \times \nabla)$, $\boldsymbol{A}$ is the vector potential, $\boldsymbol{E}$ is the electric vector field, ε_0 is the vacuum permittivity.

OAM is one basic physical property of EM wave [16]. It describes the orbital property of an EM wave and supplies an rotational degree of freedom in EM field. The EM wave carrying OAM can be generated by an plane wave with one phase rotation factor $\exp(il\varphi)$, where l is the topological charge representing the state of OAM, and φ is the azimuthal angle. Because of the phase rotation factor, the wavefront phase or the phase-front has an spiral structure instead of a planar structure. The wavefront phase rotates around the beam propagation direction and the phase changes $2\pi l$ after a full turn.

The complex amplitude $U(r, \varphi)$ [17] of an electric field with OAM is a common EM wave with a phase rotation factor $\exp(il\varphi)$, which can be described as

$$U(r, \varphi) = A(r) \cdot \exp(il\varphi), \qquad (4)$$

where r is the radial distance from the beam axis to the field point, and $A(r)$ represents the magnitude of the electromagnetic field. Figure 1 shows the phase structure distribution of four OAM radio waves with mode numbers 0, 1, 2, and 3 [18], where $l = 0$ represents the plane wave. It can be seen that if the topological charge of the OAM is different, the corresponding radiation mode is also different. As the topological charge l increases, the helicity of the wavefront for that EM waves become complicated, and the variation of the phase becomes more dramatic.

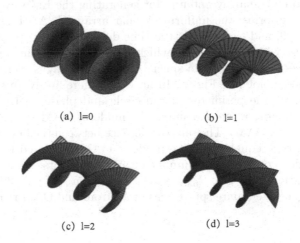

(a) l=0   (b) l=1

(c) l=2   (d) l=3

Fig. 1. The phase front structure of the EM vortex [18].

It is easy to demonstrate that the topological charge l can take any non-zero integer value, each value corresponds to an OAM mode, so the OAM modes have infinite states, and all these states are orthogonal to each other. Only two OAM modes with the same topological charge, i.e. two identical modes, have an inner product result of 1, and the OAM modes with different topological charge values has an inner product of 0. The OAM modes with different topological charge can be used as a series of channels, and theoretically such channels can be infinite, which means that using the OAM modes can greatly improve the transmission capacity and spectrum utilization. The orthogonality of the OAM modes also ensures that under ideal conditions, the crosstalk will not occur between channels, and the different modes can be easily separated at the receiving end to perform signal reading and processing. Therefore, the OAM technique can provide a potential solution for improving the transmission capacity and spectrum utilization of communication systems.

3   Techniques of OAM in RF

3.1   Generation

The EM waves carrying OAM can be generated in many different ways, and the most common methods include the array antenna method, the spiral phase plate (SPP) method, the helicoidal parabolic antenna method, etc. These methods allow the traditional plane wave to carry a spiral phase wavefront from different perspectives, thereby generating an OAM radio wave.

Array Antenna. The array antenna for generating the EM waves with OAM mainly have three forms: the uniform circular array (UCA) [15,19], the time-switched array [20] and the optical true time delay unit [21]. Among them, the UCA is the most widely used form, which is based on an unit antenna and is arranged with certain number in a special form. The array is evenly distributed around the center point (see Fig. 2). In an UCA, there are N antennas located equidistantly along the perimeter of the circle and phased with $\delta\phi = 2\pi l/N$ between two elements, where l denotes the mode of OAM (or the topological charge of waves with OAM). The phase difference between the first array element and the last element equals $2\pi l$. The mode of OAM generated by the antenna array is dependent on the total number of array elements N, i.e. they should satisfy this relation: $-N/2 < l_{max} < +N/2$. When $|l| \geq N/2$, the antenna array will not generate a pure spiral phase wavefront and OAM mode cannot be obtained.

Spiral Phase Plate. The SPP is one of the common devices generating OAM radio waves. In 1996, Turnbull explained how the beams carrying OAM arise from the SPP by using an optical model [22]. The SPP is a media disk with a spiral shape whose thickness varies with azimuthal angle (see Fig. 3). To generate an OAM radio wave with mode l, the phase of the EM field rotation should change by $2\pi l$. Assuming that number of discrete jumps is N, surface pitch is h, wavelength is λ, then the mode l is generated as shown in the following equation [23]:

$$l = \frac{2h}{\lambda}\left(\frac{N+1}{N}\right).$$ (5)

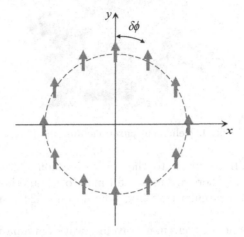

Fig. 2. Structure of circular array antenna [15].

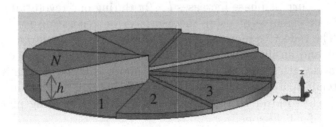

Fig. 3. Structure of SPP [23].

Helicoidal Parabolic Antenna. Using the helicoidal parabolic antenna is an early method of generating EM waves with OAM in RF. The first OAM wireless communication field experiment used a parabolic antenna as a reflective surface. The antenna was a 26 dBi commercial off-axis parabolic antenna, with diameter of 80 cm, which produced a vortex beam with $l = 1$ (see Fig. 4) [2]. Because the discontinuity of the phases in each element for the UCA and the SPP, the vortices generated in these two methods are not quite 'perfect', while the vortex beam produced in the helicoidal parabolic antenna usually has a very good helical shape. However the mode of OAM is hard to change in the helicoidal parabolic antenna, and it can be adjusted according to the need in the other two methods.

Fig. 4. Helicoidal parabolic antenna [2].

Other Methods. In addition to the more common methods of generating OAM described above, there are more and more other methods proposed these years, such as using the circular traveling-wave antenna [24], and the metasurface method [25–28].

Mathematical model of a circular traveling-wave antenna is shown in Fig. 5. It is a wire bent in a circle of radius a in the xOy plane, fed with a constant electric current amplitude I_0, which can ensure that the phase distribution on the ring is $\exp(il\varphi)$, where φ is the azimuthal angle. This current distribution means that the current phase increases $l \times 2\pi$ during one revolution.

In Fig. 6, an example of using metasurface for generating OAM modes is illustrated. The reflective metasurface is composed of a metasurface, a metallic ground plate, and an illuminating feed antenna. On the metasurface, there are some sub-wavelength elements without any power division transmission lines. The feed antenna spatially illuminates these elements that are designed to scatter the incident field to produce the reflective wave with a rotating phase front of $\exp(il\varphi)$ in the far-field zone.

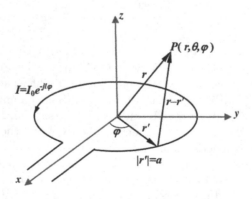

Fig. 5. Mathematical model of a circular traveling-wave antenna [24].

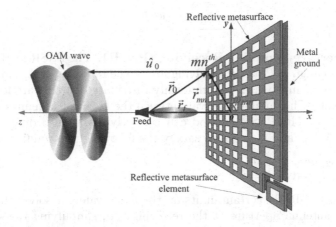

Fig. 6. Configuration of OAM generating reflective metasurface [25].

3.2 Receive

At the receiver, the phase detection is a key to distinguish the value of different OAM modes [29]. In this section we present two different methods for estimating the OAM of a radio wave.

Phase Gradient Method. An obvious feature of the OAM radio waves is that it has a spiral wavefront phase, so the phase gradient method uses phase differences at different receiving locations to identify different OAM modes. An approximation to the phase gradient would be to measure the phase difference between two points on a circle or a circle segment with the circle center on the beam axis [30]. As Fig. 7 shows, $\phi_1^{electric}$, $\phi_2^{electric}$ are phase samples, β is the angle of the circle segment, then the estimated OAM mode can be calculated as

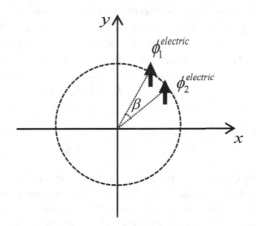

Fig. 7. Schematic of phase gradient method [30].

$$\frac{\phi_1^{\text{electric}} - \phi_2^{\text{electric}}}{\beta} = l. \tag{6}$$

Partial Aperture Sampling Receiving (PASR). The PASR method selects a part of the circle, $1/P$ as the receiving arc at the receiving end, and then uses M receiving antennas which are uniformly distributed on this arc for M-point signal sampling. The angular interval between the adjacent antennas is $2\pi/MP$ (see Fig. 8) [31]. The PASR method can correctly distinguish different modes, and the modes l_{n1} and l_{n2} need to satisfy the following two conditions:

(1) $|l_{n1} - l_{n2}| \bmod P = 0$,
(2) $|l_{n1} - l_{n2}| \bmod MP \neq 0$,

Although PASR has certain limits on the mode value, it solves the problem of excessive antenna aperture at the receiving end, simplifying the size of the receiving end.

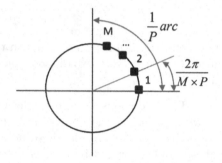

Fig. 8. Schematic of partial aperture sampling receiving [31].

3.3 Multiplexing

Without considering other factors, theoretically the number of OAM modes can be infinite. By using the orthogonality between the OAM radio waves with different modes and anti-interference characteristics, it is possible to transmit more information on the same carrier frequency without any interference, which greatly increase the rate of wireless communication and spectrum utilization [32]. For OAM radio waves in any two different OAM modes (l_1, l_2), the orthogonality equation can be expressed as:

$$\int_0^{2\pi} \exp[il_1\varphi_1]\exp^*[il_2\varphi_2]\mathrm{d}\varphi = \begin{cases} 2\pi & l_1 = l_2 \\ 0 & l_1 \neq l_2, \end{cases} \tag{7}$$

where $*$ means complex conjugate. As it is shown in the Eq. (7), if the modes of the OAM radio waves are different, they are orthogonal to each other, which ensures that the EM waves carrying different OAM modes do not interfere with each other during propagation. In theory, the information carried by the OAM radio waves is proportional to the amount of the topological charges, which can increase the channel capacity.

3.4 Existing Problems

In the field of wireless communication, since the multipath effect has a large influence on the vortex waves, this limits the propagation distance of the EM waves with OAM, and makes the distance basically only for line-of-sight communication. In addition, the current methods of generating OAM commonly used generally has the problem of energy divergence, that is, when the transmitting end radiates the vortex wave outwardly by using a certain aperture antenna, the energy divergence angle is obtained on the premise of receiving the complete electromagnetic vortex information. The existence of the receiving antenna will increase with the increase of the transmission distance. Whether these problems can be effectively solved will be crucial for realizing vortex waves long-distance communication.

4 Potential Applications in the IoT

With the development of the IoT, the user types, scenarios, and scales of the communications industry have also undergone very big changes, highlighting the complexity and changes in the IoT [33]. The principle of the IoT is to use a combination of sensors and the Internet to create new technologies. During this period, the sensor generates massive data. However, due to the lack of spectrum resources, it is very hard to allocate large amounts of spectrum for transmitting these data, thus it is of great significance to apply OAM technology to the IoT. The possible applications of OAM in the IoT are discussed below.

4.1 Increasing Channel Capacity

Through the techniques of sensors, RF identification, and global positioning system, the IoT needs to collect data or process data in real time. The IoT collects all kinds of required information such as sound, light, heat, electricity, mechanics, chemistry, biology, location, etc. Through various types of possible network accesses, the IoT can realize the ubiquitous link between objects and objects, objects and people, and realize the goods and intelligent awareness, identification and management of processes. While during this period, a large amount of data will be generated, and the data generated by different access networks usually have the characteristics of large scale, multiple types, high speed, and complicated structure, which will affect the storage, processing and transmission of data. This problem can be solved by using the orthogonal properties of different modes of OAM. The radio beams carrying different OAM modes do not interfere with each other. Theoretically, the information carried by the OAM radio waves is proportional to the amount of topological charges, which makes it possible to multiply the channel capacity.

4.2 Potential Application Areas

The IoT can find its applications in almost every aspect of our daily life [34]. Below are some examples of applying OAM technique to IoT.

Wi-Fi Technology. Wi-Fi technology is a kind of near-field wireless communication technology, and also is a key technology in the IoT. Users connect Wi-Fi through different ways like mobile phones, laptops and other devices to achieve the purpose of browsing network information. The Wi-Fi transmission rate is from 1 Mb/s to 6.75 Gb/s [35]. However, if the amount of accessing users is too large, the transmission rate will be reduced sharply, which will strongly affect the user's communication experience. OAM can provide a novel multiple access method, like Mode Division Multiple Access (MDMA). The MDMA used the orthogonality property of the OAM modes instead of using the power domain to distinguish non-orthogonal multiple accesses for multiple users, thus it can be realized without consuming excessive frequency and time resources. With MDMA, different users can use different OAM modes to access the wireless network without interference.

Smart Agriculture. The effective combination of agricultural technology and IoT technology has greatly promoted the modernization of agriculture and realized the automation and intelligence of agriculture. At present, agriculture has used a large number of sensors in greenhouses and breeding ponds to obtain current temperature, humidity, PH, carbon dioxide concentration, etc. Through using these sensors, the data can be collected and sent to the management center of agricultural production through the communication system. The large amount of data generated during this period makes it difficult to transmit data efficiently. The orthogonality between different modes of OAM can solve this problem and effectively improve the transmission capacity.

Smart Logistics. The smart logistics is an important result of the application of IoT technology and meets the expectations and requirements of modern people. However, it is still in its early stage of development and a lot of problems need to be solved. The concept of smart logistics may refer to the intelligent supply chain, which contains various information about products and process indicators. All the parts in the smart logistics, such as product storage, delivery, distribution, and the construction of information management systems all are connected and processed through wireless sensing technology. A large amount of data will be generated during this period, and the transmission of this information can be achieved by OAM multiplexing technology, which will be helpful for developing the smart logistics.

5   Conclusion

In this article the EM waves with OAM and their potential applications are discussed. The basic theory including the physical meaning and the principle of the OAM of EM waves is explained firstly. The main techniques or methods of the generation, the receive and the OAM mode multiplexing for the OAM radio beams are analyzed. Through our analysis, one can find that applying the EM waves with OAM into the IoT may greatly improve the efficiency of the spectrum utilization, which will give a boost in the development of the IoT. Based on this theory, the potential applications of the OAM radio beams in the IoT, such as the Wi-Fi technology, smart agriculture and smart logistics are proposed. We believe that adopting the EM waves with OAM is a very promising way to greatly improve the utilization of the IoT, and the IoT with the technique of the OAM radio beams will have a very brilliant future.

References

1. Ashton, K.: That 'Internet of Things' thing. RFID J. **22**(7), 97–114 (2009)
2. Tamburini, F., Mari, E., Sponselli, A., Thidé, B., Bianchini, A., Romanato, F.: Encoding many channels on the same frequency through radio vorticity: first experimental test. New J. Phys. **14**(3), 033001 (2012)
3. Loudon, R., Baxter, C.: Contributions of John Henry Poynting to the understanding of radiation pressure. Proc. Math. Phys. Eng. Sci. **468**(2143), 1825–1838 (2012)
4. Allen, L., Barnett, S.M., Padgett, M.J.: Optical Angular Momentum. IoP Publishing, Bristol (2003)
5. Indebetouw, G.: Optical vortices and their propagation. J. Mod. Opt. **40**, 73–87 (1993)
6. Zhao, X., Zhang, J., Pang, X., Wan, G.: Properties of a strongly focused Gaussian beam with an off-axis vortex. Opt. Commun. **389**, 275–282 (2017)
7. Pang, X., Miao, W.: Spinning spin density vectors along the propagation direction. Opt. Lett. **43**(19), 4831–4834 (2018)
8. Li, J., Zhang, J., Li, J.: Optical twists and transverse focal shift in a strongly focused, circularly polarized vortex field. Opt. Commun. **439**, 284–289 (2019)
9. Dholakia, K., Čižmár, T.: Shaping the future of manipulation. Nat. Photon. **5**(6), 335–342 (2011)
10. Rittweger, E., Han, K.Y., Irvine, S.E., Eggeling, C., Hell, S.W.: Sted microscopy reveals crystal colour centres with nanometric resolution. Nat. Photon. **3**(3), 144–147 (2009)
11. Molina-Terriza, G., Torres, J.P., Torner, L.: Management of the angular momentum of light: preparation of photons in multidimensional vector states of angular momentum. Phys. Rev. Lett. **88**(1), 013601 (2001)
12. Jackson, J.D., Fox, R.F.: Classical Electrodynamics, 3rd ed. Wiley, New york (1999). American Journal of Physics, 67(9), 841–842
13. Thidé, B., et al.: Utilization of photon orbital angular momentum in the low-frequency radio domain. Phys. Rev. Lett. **99**(8), 087701 (2007)
14. Courtial, J., Zambrini, R., Dennis, M.R., Vasnetsov, M.: Angular momentum of optical vortex arrays. Opt. Express **14**(2), 938–949 (2006)
15. Mohammadi, S.M., et al.: Orbital angular momentum in radio—a system study. IEEE Trans. Antennas Propag. **58**(2), 565–572 (2009)
16. Yao, A.M., Padgett, M.J.: Orbital angular momentum: origins, behavior and applications. Adv. Opt. Photonics **3**(2), 161–204 (2011)
17. Wang, J., et al.: Terabit free-space data transmission employing orbital angular momentum multiplexing. Nat. Photon. **6**(7), 488 (2012)
18. Cheng, W., Zhang, W., Jing, H., Gao, S., Zhang, H.: Orbital angular momentum for wireless communications. IEEE Wireless Commun. **26**(1), 100–107 (2018)
19. Gong, Y., et al.: Generation and transmission of OAM-carrying vortex beams using circular antenna array. IEEE Trans. Antennas Propag. **65**(6), 2940–2949 (2017)

572   J. Li et al.

20. Tennant, A., Allen, B.: Generation of OAM radio waves using circular time-switched array antenna. Electron. Lett. **48**(21), 1365–1366 (2012)
21. Gao, X., et al.: Generating, multiplexing/demultiplexing and receiving the orbital angular momentum of radio frequency signals using an optical true time delay unit. J. Opt. **15**(10), 105401 (2013)
22. Turnbull, G., Robertson, D., Smith, G., Allen, L., Padgett, M.: The generation of free-space Laguerre-Gaussian modes at millimetre-wave frequencies by use of a spiral phaseplate. Opt. Commun. **127**(4–6), 183–188 (1996)
23. Huang, W.Y., Li, J.L., Wang, H.Z., Wang, J.P., Gao, S.S.: Vortex electromagnetic waves generated by using a laddered spiral phase plate and a microstrip antenna. Electromagnetics **36**(2), 102–110 (2016)
24. Zheng, S., Hui, X., Jin, X., Chi, H., Zhang, X.: Transmission characteristics of a twisted radio wave based on circular traveling-wave antenna. IEEE Trans. Antennas Propag. **63**(4), 1530–1536 (2015)
25. Yu, S., Li, L., Shi, G., Zhu, C., Zhou, X., Shi, Y.: Design, fabrication, and measurement of reflective metasurface for orbital angular momentum vortex wave in radio frequency domain. Appl. Phys. Lett. **108**(12), 121903 (2016)
26. Shen, Y., Yang, J., Meng, H., Dou, W., Hu, S.: Generating millimeter-wave bessel beam with orbital angular momentum using reflective-type metasurface inherently integrated with source. Appl. Phys. Lett. **112**(14), 141901 (2018)
27. Veysi, M., Guclu, C., Capolino, F., Rahmat-Samii, Y.: Revisiting orbital angular momentum beams: fundamentals, reflectarray generation, and novel antenna applications. IEEE Antennas Propag. Mag. **60**(2), 68–81 (2018)
28. Zhang, Y., Lyu, Y., Wang, H., Zhang, X., Jin, X.: Transforming surface wave to propagating oam vortex wave via flat dispersive metasurface in radio frequency. IEEE Antennas Wireless Propag. Lett. **17**(1), 172–175 (2017)
29. Uchida, M., Tonomura, A.: Generation of electron beams carrying orbital angular momentum. Nature **464**(7289), 737 (2010)
30. Mohammadi, S.M., et al.: Orbital angular momentum in radio: measurement methods. Radio Sci. **45**(4), 1–14 (2010)
31. Hu, Y., Zheng, S., Zhang, Z., Chi, H., Jin, X., Zhang, X.: Simulation of orbital angular momentum radio communication systems based on partial aperture sampling receiving scheme. IET Microw. Antennas Propag. **10**(10), 1043–1047 (2016)
32. Feng, Q., Xue, H., Liu, Y., Li, L.: Multiple orbital angular momentum vortex electromagnetic waves multiplex transmission and demultiplex reception analysis. In: 2018 IEEE International Conference on Computational Electromagnetics (ICCEM), pp. 1–3. IEEE (2018)
33. Sundmaeker, H., Guillemin, P., Friess, P., Woelfflé, S.: Vision and Challenges for Realising the Internet of Things. Cluster of European Research Projects on the Internet of Things, European Commision, vol. 3, no. 3, pp. 34–36 (2010)
34. Lin, J., Yu, W., Zhang, N., Yang, X., Zhang, H., Zhao, W.: A survey on Internet of Things: architecture, enabling technologies, security and privacy, and applications. IEEE Internet Things J. **4**(5), 1125–1142 (2017)
35. Ray, P.P.: A survey on Internet of Things architectures. J. King Saud Univ. Comput. Inf. Sci. **30**(3), 291–319 (2018)

Propagation Properties of Optical Beams with Multi-OAM Modes: Effect of the Off-Axis Vortex

Ying Dang[1] and Wenrui Miao[2(✉)]

[1] No. 365 Institute of Northwestern Polytechnical University
(Xi'an ASN Technology), Xi'an, China
snow365dy@163.com

[2] School of Electronics and Information, Northwestern Polytechnical University,
Xi'an, China
wenruimiaonpu@163.com

Abstract. As one of the promising techniques to improve the spectral efficiency of the network in the Internet of Things (IoT), the orbital-angular-momentum (OAM) multiplexing optical wireless communication has been studied a lot. In the optical beams with multi-OAM modes, the vortices deviating from the beam center sometimes cannot be avoidable, and they will strongly influence the transverse patterns during the beam propagation. In this article, the expressions of optical beams with off-axis vortices are derived in a commonly used focusing system, and the effect of the vortices deviating from the beam center on the propagation properties of the optical beam is discussed. We find that the number of the bright spots in the transverse patterns of the superposition of two OAM modes with off-axis vortices is not always equal to the absolute value of the mode difference which is observed in the field with only on-axis vortices. The bright spot can also be found to rotate during the beam propagating, and as the number of the modes increases in the overlapping, the superposition patterns become more complicated and these patterns can be adjusted by the off-axis distance and the topological charge of the vortices. Our result will be helpful in developing the network of the IoT.

Keywords: Orbital angular momentum · Off-axis vortices · Multiplexing

1 Introduction

The term of Internet of Things (IoT) was first proposed in 1998 [1], after that, the IoT has been developing extensively in various areas, and will realize the goal of intelligent identifying, locating, tracking, monitoring, and managing things [2, 3]. However, as the developing of the IoT, trillions of devices will be involved into

© ICST Institute for Computer Sciences, Social Informatics and Telecommunications Engineering 2020
Published by Springer Nature Switzerland AG 2020. All Rights Reserved
B. Li et al. (Eds.): IoTaaS 2019, LNICST 316, pp. 573–581, 2020.
https://doi.org/10.1007/978-3-030-44751-9_48

the IoT, therefore the network of the IoT will be congested. The orbital-angular-momentum (OAM) multiplexing optical wireless communication is a promising technique to overcome this problem [4,5].

In most of researches on the OAM mode multiplexing, only the vortices embedded in the beam center are considered [6,7] and many results are obtained based on the assumption of the axial vortices (i.e. located in the beam center) [8]. However, the off-axis vortices sometimes are inevitable in the generation of the beams with OAM modes, like in generating on-axis vortex with misalignment [9–11]. In another perspective, the vortices deviating from the beam center also have very interesting properties during the beam propagation, such as decreasing the total OAM of the beam [12,13], improving the acceleration of the beams [14], generating transverse focal shift [15] and having rotating trajectories in the focused fields [16–23], and also can lead to some special polarization structures [24,25]. In the OAM multiplexing optical wireless communication system, the off-axis vortices are also not avoidable in many circumstances, and these vortices will change the superposition patterns of multi-OAM modes, which will influence the efficiency at the receiving end. In this article, the expressions of the propagating optical beams with vortices off the beam center will be derived, and the influence of these vortices on the propagation properties of the beam with multi-OAM modes will be discussed.

2   Theory

In practical experiments or applications, in order to concentrate more energy in the propagation direction, a thin lens is usually used to focus the light before its propagation. Even if the thin lens is absent, the diffraction effect should also be considered in the propagation of the optical wave. The far field of the diffracted light is actually equivalent to the field at the focal plane of the wave going through a thin lens [26]. Generally an optical beam with OAM mode N means an optical vortex beam with topological charge N. In this article, we are considering the propagation of optical beams with multi-OAM modes, therefore, we first derive the field distribution along the propagation in the focal region of optical beams with different OAM mode.

Assume that there are N vortices with topological charge m_k located at $r = r_k$, $\phi = \phi_k$, embedded in a Gaussian beam. The amplitude distribution of the electric field V_0, according to [16] at the beam waist w_0 can be expressed as

$$V_0(r, \phi) = \prod_{k=1}^{N} e^{-r^2/w_0^2} \left(re^{\pm i\phi} - r_k e^{\pm i\phi_k} \right)^{|m_k|}, \tag{1}$$

where r denotes the radial distance and ϕ is the azimuthal angle. If m_k is positive, the sign of ϕ and ϕ_k is positive and vice versa.

Let us then consider a converging, monochromatic wave whose amplitude at the entrance plane can be expressed by Eq. (1), and this wave emerges from a circular aperture (which can be treated as passing through a thin lens) with its radius a. The geometrical focus is located at the origin of the Coordinates (see Fig. 1) and f is the focal length or the radius of a Gaussian reference sphere S. The electric field at point P in the focal region can be given by the expression [26]

$$E(P) = -\frac{i}{\lambda}\frac{e^{-ikf}}{f} \iint_S V_0 \frac{e^{iks}}{s} dS, \tag{2}$$

where k is the wave-number. $k = 2\pi/\lambda$ and λ is the wavelength in free space.

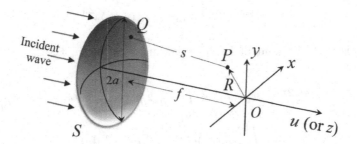

Fig. 1. Illustrating the notation.

When the vortex is located at $(a_1, 0)$ and its topological charge is $m = 1$ (i.e., the mode is 1), the complex amplitude at the entrance plane is expressed as

$$V_0(\rho, \phi) = e^{-(a\rho/w_0)^2}(a\rho e^{i\phi} - a_1), \tag{3}$$

here $a\rho = r$. Substituting Eq. (3) into Eq. (2), we can get

$$E_1(P) = -\frac{i}{\lambda}\frac{e^{-ikf}}{f} \iint_S e^{-(a\rho/w_0)^2}(a\rho e^{i\phi} - a_1)\frac{e^{iks}}{s} dS, \tag{4}$$

where the subscript 1 of U_1 means that the mode is 1. In this article, we will adopt the dimensionless Lommel variables u and v instead of x, y, z, i.e.,

$$u = \frac{2\pi}{\lambda}\left(\frac{a}{f}\right)^2 z \tag{5}$$

$$v = \frac{2\pi a^2 \rho}{\lambda f} = \frac{2\pi a}{\lambda f}\sqrt{x^2 + y^2}. \tag{6}$$

In order to get the explicit expression of Eq. (4), we will use some approximations. First the factor $1/s$ can be approximated as $1/f$, second the Debye approximation is also applied, i.e.,

$$s - f = -q \cdot R, \tag{7}$$

where q is a unit vector in the direction of OQ and R is the vector from the focus to the point P (see Fig. 1). Then Eq. (7) can be written as

$$kq \cdot R = v\rho\cos(\phi - \psi) - (f/a)^2 u + \frac{1}{2}u\rho^2, \tag{8}$$

with $\psi = \arctan(y/x)$. By applying Eq. (8) and $dS = a^2 \rho d\rho d\phi$, we can re-write Eq. (4) as

$$E_1(u,v,\psi) = -\frac{i}{\lambda}\frac{a^2}{f^2}e^{i(\frac{f}{a})^2 u}\int_0^1\int_0^{2\pi} e^{-i[v\rho\cos(\phi-\psi)+\frac{1}{2}u\rho^2]}$$
$$\times e^{-(a\rho/w_0)^2}(a\rho e^{i\phi} - a_1)\rho d\rho d\phi \tag{9}$$

Because of the following identity

$$\int_0^{2\pi} e^{i[-v\rho\cos(\phi-\psi)]}e^{im\phi}d\phi = J_m(-v\rho)\frac{2\pi}{i^{-m}}e^{im\psi}, \tag{10}$$

where J_m is the first kind of Bessel function of order m, the Eq. (9) can be simplified as

$$E_1(u,v,\psi) = \frac{2\pi a^2}{\lambda f^2}e^{i(\frac{f}{a})^2 u}\left[e^{i\psi}\int_0^1 -a\rho^2 J_1(v\rho)e^{-(a\rho/w_0)^2}e^{-\frac{1}{2}u\rho^2}d\rho\right.$$
$$\left.+ia_1\int_0^1 \rho J_0(v\rho)e^{-(a\rho/w_0)^2}e^{-\frac{1}{2}u\rho^2}d\rho\right]. \tag{11}$$

Using the same steps, one can derive the expressions of the electric fields for arbitrary modes, and here the expressions for mode 2, 3 and −1 are presented, as

$$E_2(u,v,\psi) = \frac{2\pi a^2}{\lambda f^2}e^{i(\frac{f}{a})^2 u}\left[ie^{i2\psi}\int_0^1 a^2\rho^3 J_2(v\rho)e^{-(a\rho/w_0)^2}e^{-\frac{1}{2}u\rho^2}d\rho\right.$$
$$+2a_2 e^{i\psi}\int_0^1 a\rho^2 J_1(v\rho)e^{-(a\rho/w_0)^2}e^{-\frac{1}{2}u\rho^2}d$$
$$\left.-ia_2^2\int_0^1 \rho J_0(v\rho)e^{-(a\rho/w_0)^2}e^{-\frac{1}{2}u\rho^2}d\rho\right], \tag{12}$$

$$E_3(u,v,\psi) = \frac{2\pi a^2}{\lambda f^2}e^{i(\frac{f}{a})^2 u}\left[e^{i3\psi}\int_0^1 a^3\rho^4 J_3(v\rho)e^{-(a\rho/w_0)^2}e^{-\frac{1}{2}u\rho^2}d\rho\right.$$
$$-i3a_3 e^{i2\psi}\int_0^1 a^2\rho^3 J_2(v\rho)e^{-(a\rho/w_0)^2}e^{-\frac{1}{2}u\rho^2}d\rho$$
$$-3a_3^2 e^{i\psi}\int_0^1 a\rho^2 J_1(v\rho)e^{-(a\rho/w_0)^2}e^{-\frac{1}{2}u\rho^2}d\rho$$
$$\left.+ia_3^3\int_0^1 \rho J_0(v\rho)e^{-(a\rho/w_0)^2}e^{-\frac{1}{2}u\rho^2}d\rho\right], \tag{13}$$

$$E_{-1}(u,v,\psi) = \frac{2\pi a^2}{\lambda f^2}e^{i(\frac{f}{a})^2 u}\left[e^{-i\psi}\int_0^1 -a\rho^2 J_1(v\rho)e^{-(a\rho/w_0)^2}e^{-\frac{1}{2}u\rho^2}d\rho\right.$$
$$\left.+ia_{-1}\int_0^1 \rho J_0(v\rho)e^{-(a\rho/w_0)^2}e^{-\frac{1}{2}u\rho^2}d\rho\right], \tag{14}$$

where the subscript n of E_n $(n = 1, 2, 3, -1)$ indicates the mode of the beam (or the topological charge of the vortex), and a_n presents the off-axis distance of the vortex with charge n in the entrance plane.

3   Result and Discussion

In this section, we will use the expressions derived in the previous section to discuss the propagation properties of the focused optical beams with multi-OAM modes. In our research, only the case of perfect superimposed beams are considered, which means that the beams with different modes are overlapped with their beam centers and propagating directions coincident with each other.

First of all, the superposition of the mode $m = 1$ and mode $m = 2$ are considered. When the off-axis distances a_1 and a_2 are both equals to 0, i.e., the vortices are perfectly in the beam center, the superimposed pattern in the transverse planes during the propagation of the beam usually has one bright spot because of their phase distributions. It is shown in Fig. 2 that in the focal plane and in the transverse planes along the propagation direction there is only one diffraction spot (i.e. the bright spot), which is coincident with the result in [5]. Moreover, it also can be found that this bright spot rotates during its propagation.

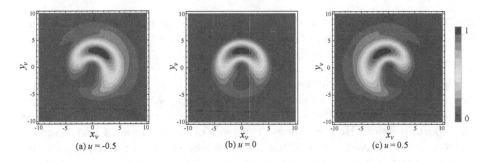

Fig. 2. Intensity distribution in the transverse planes along the propagation direction. Here $a = w_0$, $a/f = 10$, $a1 = a2 = 0$.

When there is one vortex moving away from the beam center, i.e., $a_N \neq 0$ $(N = 1, 2)$, the number of the bright spots in the superimposed pattern will not always equal $|N_1 - N_2|$ $(N_1, N_2$ are the numbers of the modes). It is shown in Fig. 3 that as the vortex of mode 2 is leaving off the beam center with $a_2 = 0.25w_0$, there appear two bright spots during the beam propagation and also these two spots rotate with the distance.

If the vortices in both two modes are placed at a very short distance from the beam center, i.e., $a_1 \neq 0$ and $a_2 \neq 0$, the superimposed field can also be quite different. In Fig. 4, it is clear to see that when $a_1 = a_2 = 0.25w_0$, although there are also two bright spots, the pattern in this case is perpendicular to that

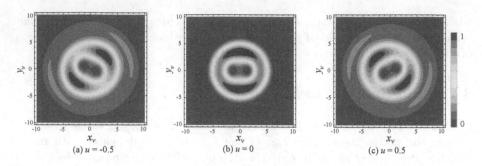

Fig. 3. Intensity distribution in the transverse planes along the propagation direction. Here $a = w_0$, $a/f = 10$, $a1 = 0$, $a2 = 0.25w_0$.

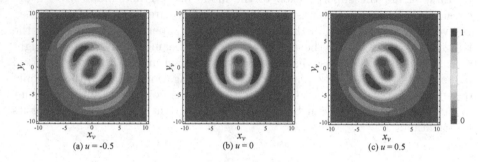

Fig. 4. Intensity distribution in the transverse planes along the propagation direction. Here $a = w_0$, $a/f = 10$, $a_1 = 0.25w_0$, $a_2 = 0.25w_0$.

in Fig. 3, for instance in the focal plane the bright spots are located along the y axis in Fig. 3, while they appear on the x axis in Fig. 4.

Secondly, the mode difference of two modes which is more than 1 is considered for superimposition. Here we choose two pairs of modes: mode 1 and 3, mode 1 and -1. It is displayed in Fig. 5 that since the mode difference in these two cases are both equal to 2, there exist two bright spots when $a_1 = a_3 = a_{-1} = 0$. When there is one vortex embedded away from the beam center, one can see that in the superposition of mode 1 and 3, the number of the bright spots becomes 1 [see plot (a) and (a') in Fig. 6], whereas in the case of mode 1 and -1, this number can be different in the focal plane and other transverse planes during the beam propagation [see plot (b) and (b') in Fig. 6].

At last, we will look at the superposition of three different modes. Here the mode 1, 2 and 3 are overlapped in one beam. There has not been any theoretical formula to describe the superposition pattern of the modes more than 2, thus it is hard to say how many bright spots will exist there. As it shows in Fig. 7, for the superposition of mode 1, 2 and 3, the number of the bright spots can be 1 or 2, and the position of the bright spot is dependent on the position of the vortices in the initial beams.

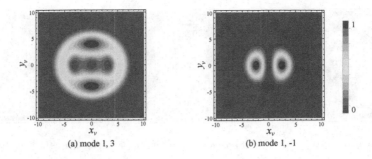

(a) mode 1, 3   (b) mode 1, -1

Fig. 5. Intensity distribution in the focal planes for (a) the superposition of mode 1 and 3, (b) the superposition of mode 1 and −1. Here $a = w_0$, $a/f = 10$, $a_1 = a_2 = 0$.

In summary, from the discussions in this section, we can see that if there exists any off-axis vortex in the beam with multi-OAM modes, it is hardly to define the superposition patterns during the propagation. When two different modes are superimposed, the number of the bright spots is not always equal to the absolute value of the mode difference. The positions of the bright spots also can be changed as the beam propagates. Even if there is no off-axis vortice, the position of the bright spots can rotate along its propagation direction. The

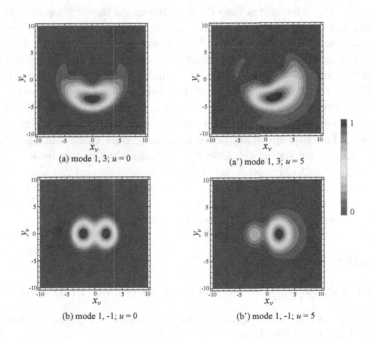

(a) mode 1, 3; $u = 0$ (a') mode 1, 3; $u = 5$

(b) mode 1, -1; $u = 0$ (b') mode 1, -1; $u = 5$

Fig. 6. Intensity distribution in the transverse planes. The superposition of mode 1 and 3 are shown in (a) $u = 0$ and (a') $u = 5$; The superposition of mode 1 and −1 are shown in (b) $u = 0$ and (a') $u = 5$; Here $a = w_0$, $a/f = 10$, $a_1 = 0$, $a_3 = 0.25w_0$, $a_{-1} = 0.50w_0$.

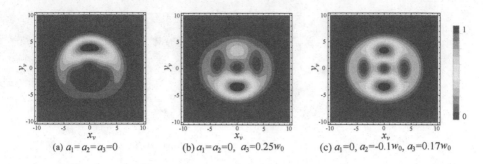

(a) $a_1 = a_2 = a_3 = 0$ (b) $a_1 = a_2 = 0$, $a_3 = 0.25w_0$ (c) $a_1 = 0$, $a_2 = -0.1w_0$, $a_3 = 0.17w_0$

Fig. 7. Intensity distribution in the focal planes for the superposition of mode 1, 2 and 3. In plot (b) $a_2 = -0.10w_0$ means that the vortex is embedded in the $-x$ axis with the distance $0.10w_0$. Here $a = w_0$ and $a/f = 10$.

superposition pattern will become more complicated as the number of modes increases. In this case the number and positions of the bright spots are also dependent on the topological charges, the off-axis distances of the vortices in the input field.

4   Conclusion

In this article, the influence of the off-axis vortices on the propagation properties of the optical beam with multi-OAM modes is discussed. The expressions for the optical beams with different OAM modes (including the on-axis/off-axis vortices) passing through a thin lens are derived. Based on the derivation, the superposition fields of different modes are analyzed. It is found that when there is any off-axis vortices, the number of the bright spots is not always equal to that in the superimposed field with only on axis vortices. The superposition patterns can rotate and the bright spots can split or combine during the beam propagation. The superposition patterns will become more complicated if the combined modes are increased. Our result shows that in a telecommunication system with multi-OAM modes the effect of the off-axis vortices should be taken into consideration seriously, and our finding will give implications in the receiving end of the telecommunication system with multi-OAM modes where an antenna needs to be adjusted according to the superposition pattern.

References

1. Ashton, Kevin, et al.: That Internet of Things of thing. RFID J. **22**(7), 97–114 (2009)
2. Stankovic, J.A.: Research directions for the Internet of Things. IEEE Internet Things J. **1**(1), 3–9 (2014)
3. Chen, S., Xu, H., Liu, D., Hu, B., Wang, H.: A vision of IoT: applications, challenges, and opportunities with china perspective. IEEE Internet Things J. **1**(4), 349–359 (2014)
4. Chen, C., Wang, W., Wu, J., et al.: Visible light communications for the implementation of internet-of-things. Opt. Eng. **55**(6), 060501 (2016)

5. Li, M.: Orbital-angular-momentum multiplexing optical wireless communications with adaptive modes adjustment in Internet of Things networks. IEEE Internet Things J. **6**(4), 6134–6139 (2018)
6. Wang, J., et al.: Terabit free-space data transmission employing orbital angular momentum multiplexing. Nat. Photonics **6**(7), 488 (2012)
7. Feng, Q., Xue, H., Liu, Y., Li, L.: Multiple orbital angular momentum vortex electromagnetic waves multiplex transmission and demultiplex reception analysis. In: 2018 IEEE International Conference on Computational Electromagnetics (ICCEM), pp. 1–3. IEEE (2018)
8. Ke, X., Pu, X.: Generation of orbital angular momentum superpositions and its test. Infrared Laser Eng. **47**(4), 56–61 (2018)
9. Almazov, A.A., Elfstrom, H., Turunen, J., Khonina, S.N., Soifer, V.A., Kotlyar, V.V.: Generation of phase singularity through diffracting a plane or gaussian beam by a spiral phase plate. J. Opt. Soc. Am. A **22**(5), 849–861 (2005)
10. Anzolin, G., Tamburini, F., Bianchini, A., Barbieri, C.: Method to measure off-axis displacements based on the analysis of the intensity distribution of a vortex beam. Phy. Rev. A **79**(3), 033845 (2009)
11. Bekshaev, A.Ya., Sviridova, S.V.: Effects of misalignments in the optical vortex transformation performed by holograms with embedded phase singularity. Opt. Commun. **283**(24), 4866–4876 (2010)
12. Oemrawsingh, S.S.R., Eliel, E.R., Nienhuis, G., Woerdman, J.P.: Intrinsic orbital angular momentum of paraxial beams with off-axis imprinted vortices. J. Opt. Soc. Am. A **21**(11), 2089–2096 (2004)
13. Kotlyar, V.V., Kovalev, A.A., Porfirev, A.P.: Asymmetric gaussian optical vortex. Opt. Lett. **42**(1), 139–142 (2017)
14. Zhu, W., She, W.: Improved nonparaxial accelerating beams due to additional off-axis spiral phases. J. Opt. Soc. Am. A **31**(11), 2365–2369 (2014)
15. Zhao, X., Pang, X., Zhang, J., Wan, G.: Transverse focal shift in vortex beams. IEEE Photonics J. **10**(1), 1–17 (2018)
16. Indebetouw, G.: Optical vortices and their propagation. J. Mod. Opt. **40**, 73–87 (1993)
17. Molina-Terriza, G., Torner, L., Wright, E.M., García-Ripoll, J.J., Pérez-García, V.M.: Vortex revivals with trapped light. Opt. lett. **26**, 1601–1603 (2001)
18. Molina-Terriza, G., Wright, E.M., Torner, L.: Propagation and control of non-canonical optical vortices. Opt. lett. **26**(3), 163–165 (2001)
19. Roux, F.S.: Canonical vortex dipole dynamics. J. Opt. Soc. Am. B **21**, 655–663 (2004)
20. Toda, Y., Honda, S., Morita, R.: Dynamics of a paired optical vortex generated by second-harmonic generation. Opt. Express **18**(17), 17796–17804 (2010)
21. Chen, Z., Pu, J., Zhao, D.: Tight focusing properties of linearly polarized gaussian beam with a pair of vortices. Phys. Lett. A **375**(32), 2958–2963 (2011)
22. Zhao, X., Zhang, J., Pang, X., Wan, G.: Properties of a strongly focused gaussian beam with an off-axis vortex. Opt. Commun. **389**, 275–282 (2017)
23. Li, J., Zhang, J., Li, J.: Optical twists and transverse focal shift in a strongly focused, circularly polarized vortex field. Opt. Commun. **439**, 284–289 (2019)
24. Pang, X., Zhang, J., Zhao, X.: Polarization dynamics on optical axis. Opt. Commun. **421**, 50–55 (2018)
25. Pang, X., Miao, W.: Spinning spin density vectors along the propagation direction. Opt. Lett. **43**(19), 4831–4834 (2018)
26. Born, M., Wolf, E.: Principles of Optics: Electromagnetic Theory of Propagation, Interference and Diffraction of Light, 7th (expanded) edn. Cambridge University Press, Cambridge (1999)

Unequally Weighted Sliding-Window Belief Propagation for Binary LDPC Codes

Zhaotun Feng, Bowei Shan(iD), and Yong Fang(✉)(iD)

School of Information Engineering, Chang'an University,
Xi'an, People's Republic of China
{2018124076,bwshan,fy}@chd.edu.cn

Abstract. In this paper, an Unequally Weighted Sliding-Window Belief Propagation (UW-SWBP) algorithm was proposed to decode the binary LDPC code. We model the important of overall beliefs of variable nodes in a sliding window as Gaussian distribution, which means central nodes play a more importance role than the nodes on both sides. The UW-SWBP demonstrates better performance than SWBP algorithm in both BER and FER metrics.

Keywords: UW-SWBP · LDPC · Overall belief

1 Introduction

Thanks to extremely fast data speed, very low latency and ubiquitous coverage, the Fifth Generation (5G) technology promises a fundamental ecosystem for the Internet of Things as a Services (IoTaaS). In 2018, 5G New Radio (NR) has used Low-Density Parity Check (LDPC) Codes as the code for forward error correction [1]. LDPC codes was originally invented by Gallager [2] in 1962. Due to lack of high computing ability at that time, it was not recognized by information community for nearly thirty years. In 1990s, MacKay at Cambridge [3] and Spielman at MIT [4] independently rediscovered the LDPC codes and showed its near-Shannon-limit performance.

In today's communication society, LDPC codes play a key role in many different areas. Thereafter, how to design a LDPC decoder with best performance is an important issue. In 2012, a Sliding-Window Belief Propagation (SWBP) algorithm [5] for decoding binary LDPC codes was introduced by Fang. Many experiments [6,7] shows that SWBP can outperform standard belief propagation (BP) algorithm. As the state-of-the-art LDPC decoder, SWBP can be easily accelerated by GPU as well [8].

The idea of SWBP is based on belief propagation between variable nodes and check nodes of LDPC, while SWBP initialize the variable nodes with the

Supported by organization x.

optimum seeds which are computed by averaging the overall beliefs of the variable nodes in a well-chosen window size. Experiments results demonstrated that, as long as the window size is selected properly, this technique is highly effective [5–7]. With the advance of this research, we discover that some improvement can be made in the basic SWBP algorithm, which regards all the variable nodes as same weights. In fact, different variable nodes in the window should have different importance. The closer to the central nodes, the more important the nodes should be. In this paper, we present an Unequally Weighted Sliding-Window Belief Propagation (UW-SWBP) algorithm. In this algorithm, the optimum seeds are obtained by weighted averaging overall beliefs, and the weights decreases from the center node to the nodes on both sides. The experiment results show that UW-SWBP outperforms standard SWBP for decoding binary LDPC codes.

This paper is organized as follow. Section 2 reviews the SWBP algorithm. Our proposed UW-SWBP is introduced in Sect. 3. Section 4 presentes the experiment results and Sect. 5 concludes this work.

2   Review on Related Works

2.1   Notations

Let $\mathbf{x} = (x_1, \ldots, x_n)^T$ be the binary source codeword and $\mathbf{y} = (y_1, \ldots, y_n)^T$ be the binary received codeword, where n is the length of the LDPC code. Let $\mathbf{H}$ be an $m \times n$ parity check matrix, and $\mathbf{s} = (s_1, \ldots, s_n)^T = \mathbf{Hx}$ be the syndrome. In this paper, we only consider Binary Symmetric Channel (BSC) with cross probability $\mathbf{p} = (p_1, \ldots, p_n)$, where $p_i = \Pr(x_i \neq y_i)$.

2.2   SWBP Algorithm

SWBP algorithm is consisted of two steps: standard BP algorithm and computing the optimum seeds. Standard BP algorithm has been depicted in many articles. Reader nay refer to [5] for details.

The optimum seeds $\tilde{\mathbf{p}} = (\tilde{p}_1, \ldots, \tilde{p}_n)^T$ of variable nodes can be computed by averaging the overall beliefs of neighboring variable nodes in a size-l (an odd) window around x_i.

$$\tilde{p}_i = \frac{-r_i + \sum_{i'=\max(1,i-u)}^{\min(i+u,n)} r_{i'}}{\min(i+u,n) - \max(1, i-u)}, \tag{1}$$

where $\mathbf{r} = (r_1, \ldots, r_n)^T$ is the overall belief of variable node i, and $u = \lfloor l/2 \rfloor$. Ref. [5] also presented an stepwise form of Eq. (1):

$$\tilde{p}_i = \begin{cases} \tilde{p}_{i-1} + \dfrac{r_{i-1} - r_i + r_{i+u} - \tilde{p}_{i-1}}{i + u - 1}, & 2 \leq i \leq (1+u) \\[2mm] \tilde{p}_{i-1} + \dfrac{r_{i-1} - r_i + r_{i+u} - r_{i-u-1}}{h - 1}, & (2+u) \leq i \leq (n-u) \\[2mm] \tilde{p}_{i-1} + \dfrac{r_{i-1} - r_i + r_{i-u-1} - \tilde{p}_{i-1}}{n - i + u}, & (n-u+1) \leq i \leq n \end{cases} \tag{2}$$

How to determine a proper window size l^* is the key task in SWBP. In [5,6], the mean squared error (MSE) τ^2 between r and $\tilde{p}$ is calculated.

$$\tau^2 = \frac{1}{n}\sum_{i=1}^{n}(r_i - \tilde{p}_i)^2. \tag{3}$$

Then we search all l one by one from 1 to n and only that gives the smallest τ^2 is selected as l^*.

The complexity of above algorithm is $\mathcal{O}(n^2)$. To reduce it, a fast window size algorithm is presented in [7]. This search-free algorithm first calculates the Fast Fourier Transform (FFT) of $\mathbf{r}$ as $f(\theta)$, where $\theta \in [1 : n]$. Then let

$$A = \sum_{\theta=1}^{n}|f(\theta)|, \tag{4}$$

where $|f(\theta)|$ is the modulus of $f(\theta)$. Then the proper window size

$$l^* \approx \frac{n}{A}\sum_{\theta=1}^{n}|f(\theta)|/\theta, \tag{5}$$

Obviously, the complexity of this new algorithm is reduced to $\mathcal{O}(n\log_2 n)$.

3   UW-SWBP Algorithm

Our proposed UW-SWBP is based on SWBP. The step of Standard BP of these two are identical, while the step of computing the optimum seeds is improved in UW-SWBP to achieve better performance. In Eq. (1), every overall beliefs of variable nodes r_i in window have the same importance account for $\tilde{p}_i$. In fact, when we want to calculate the optimum seeds of a node, a natural idea is to highlight the characteristics of the node, so we believe that nodes in different locations should play different degrees of importance.In other words, the central node should play a more important role than the nodes on both sides of the window. As a result, we modify Eq. (1) to a weighted form.

$$\tilde{p}_i = \frac{-r_i * w_i + \sum_{i'=1}^{n}(r_{i'} * w_{i'})}{\sum_{i'=1}^{n}w_{i'}}, \tag{6}$$

where the weight of variable nodes $w(x)$ follows Gaussian distribution

$$w(x) = \frac{1}{\sqrt{2\pi\sigma^2}}e^{-\frac{|x-\mu|}{2\sigma^2}}. \tag{7}$$

We illustrate equal and unequal weights distribution in Fig. 1. Obviously unequal weights distribution fulfills our expectations of the importance of different nodes.

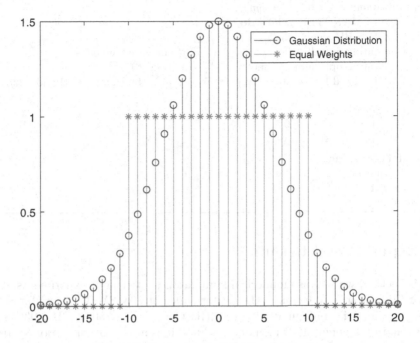

Fig. 1. Different type of weight distribution.

We can find that parameter σ plays an key role in computing the optimum seeds. Because σ determines the size of the window and the importance of each node. The main task of UW-SWBP is to estimate an optimum σ^*. Same as SWBP algorithm, we first calculate the MSE τ^2 between r_i and $\tilde{p}_i$ by Eq. (3). Then we calculate the following problem:

$$\sigma^* = \arg\min_{\sigma} \tau^2, \tag{8}$$

which can be solved by searching all σ from 1 to n and only that gives the smallest τ^2 is choosed as σ^*. We show the UW-SWBP algorithm as follow.

Algorithm 1. UW-SWBP Algorithm.

Input: Overall beliefs, $\mathbf{r}$; Side information, $\mathbf{y}$; Syndrome, $\mathbf{s}$;

Output: Estimated source, $\tilde{x}$;

1: Initialization: $b_i^{(0)} = 0$, $q_{ij}^{(0)} = pmf_{ij}$

2: **for** $l = 1 : \text{MAX\_ITERATION}$ **do**

3:    Standard BP algorithm [5]

4:    Computing overall beliefs $\mathbf{r} = (r_1, \ldots, r_n)^T$ for variable nodes:

5:    Computing optimum parameter σ^* by equation (6)

6:    Refining local bias probability $\tilde{\mathbf{p}} = (\tilde{p}_1, \ldots, \tilde{p}_n)^T$ by equation (4) and equation (5)

7:    Hard decision:

8:    $\tilde{x}_i = \begin{cases} 0, & \text{if } r_i \leq 0.5 \\ 1, & \text{if } r_i > 0.5 \end{cases}$

9:    **if** $\mathbf{H\tilde{x}} = \mathbf{s}$ **then**

10:       quit loop

11:    **end if**

12: **end for**

---

4 Experimental Results

In this section, we will use numerical simulation to carry out experiments. The aim of this paper is to evaluate the performance of UW-SWBP algorithm. Our testing platform is configured with Intel(R) Core(TM) E7500 CPU 2.93GHz(2 Cores) main frequency, 4GB memory, and 64-bit Windows-10 operation system. All algorithms are developed in MATLAB 2017b environment.

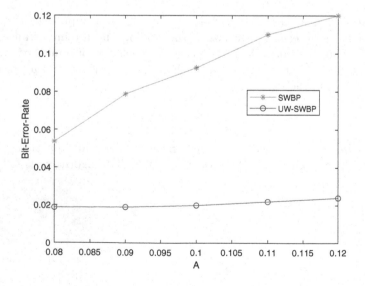

Fig. 2. Bit-Error-Rate under two algorithms

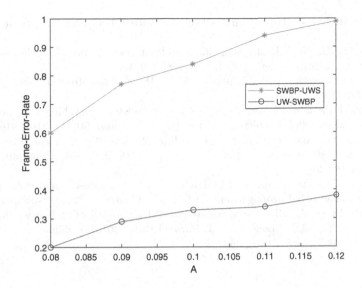

Fig. 3. Frame-Error-Rate under two algorithms

We construct a LDPC code with codeword length $n = 1024$ and information bit number $k = 512$. The local bias probability varies according to $p_i = A(1 + \sin(2\pi i/n))$. We test five value of A, *i.e.*, $A \in \{0.08, 0.09, 1.00, 1.05, 1.10\}$ in our experiment. The Bit-Error-Rate (BER) and Frame-Error-Rate (FER) are used as the metrics to compare these two algorithms. The experimental results are illustrated in Figs. 2 and 3. We can see that the BER and FER of UW-SWBP are much lower than SWBP when the initial value $A=0.08$. Moreover, with the increase of A value, the BER and FER of SWBP show unstable and drastic changes, and the increase trend of UW-SWBP has been very flat. We find that under different A, UW-SWBP outperforms SWBP in both BER and FER.

5   Conclusion

In this paper, we propose a unequally weighted Sliding-Window Belief Propagation (UW-SWBP) algorithm to decode binary LDCP codes. We assume that the importance of the overall belief of a variable node is subject to a Gaussian distribution. The UW-SWBP algorithm can improve the local deviation probability with higher precision. Experiment results show that UW-SWBP has better performance that SWBP algorithm.

References

1. Richardson, T., Kudekar, S.: Design of low-density parity check codes for 5G new radio. IEEE Commun. Mag. **56**(3), 28–34 (2018)

2. Gallager, R.G.: Low-density parity-check codes. IRE Trans. Inf. Theory **8**(1), 21–28 (1962)
3. Mackay, D.J.C., Neal, R.M.: Near Shannon limit performance of low density parity check codes. Electron. Lett. **32**(6), 457–458 (1997)
4. Sipser, M., Spielman, D.A.: Expander codes. IEEE Trans. Inform. Theory **42**(11), 1710–1722 (1996)
5. Fang, Y.: Ldpc-based lossless compression of nonstationary binary sources using sliding-window belief propagation. IEEE Trans. Commun. **60**(11), 3161–3166 (2012)
6. Fang, Y.: Asymmetric Slepian-Wolf coding of nonstationarily-correlated M-ary sources with sliding-window belief propagation. IEEE Trans. Commun. **61**(12), 5114–5124 (2013)
7. Fang, Y., Yang, Y., Shan, B., Stankovic, V.: Joint source-channel estimation via sliding-window belief propagation. IEEE Trans. Commun (2019). (submitted)
8. Shan, B., Fang, Y.: GPU Accelerated parallel algorithm of sliding-window belief propagation for LDPC codes. Int. J. Parallel Prog (2019). (Online First). https://doi.org/10.1007/s10766-019-00632-3

Direction of Arrival Estimation of Spread Spectrum Signal

Hongwei Zhao$^{(\boxtimes)}$ and Zichun Zhang

School of Electronics and Information, Northwestern Polytechnical University,
Xi'an 710072, China
hongvi_zhao@126.com, 2244247525@qq.com

Abstract. The sensor networking based on multi-source information fusion can significantly improve direction accuracy, and the sensor networking is always used in direction of spread spectrum signals. Aimed at eliminating the phase ambiguity of the phase-comparison method, this paper proposed a direction-finding method based on ISM (Incoherent Signal Subspace Method) and CSM (Coherent Signal Subspace Method) algorithms. Firstly, the wideband spread spectrum signal is divided into narrowband at different time points. Then perform the DCT (Discrete Cosine Transform) and obtain the covariance matrix at different frequency points. Finally, the narrowband signal power spectrums at independent frequency points are synthesized to obtain the total power spectrum of spread spectrum signal. The simulation results demonstrate that the ISM and CSM algorithms can accurately determine the direction of the spread spectrum signal, and the direction error is kept within 1° when the signal-to-noise ratio (SNR) is higher than 5 dB, which satisfy the accurate direction-finding requirement. Therefore, the ISM and CSM algorithms based on sensor networking is a necessary solution in high-precision direction of spread spectrum signals.

Keywords: Spread spectrum signal · DOA · ISM · CSM

1 Introduction

The DOA (direction of arrival) of the signal based on multi-source information fusion can significantly improve direction accuracy, and the multi-source information is always obtained through sensor networking. The spread spectrum signal has good anti-interference, low interception and strong networking capability, and it is widely used in military communication and GNSS navigation and positioning [1, 2]. It directly modulates the information code through a pseudo-random spread spectrum sequence, so that the used bandwidth of the transmission signal is greatly increased. For the signal transmitter, since the energy of transmitting information is extended to a wider spectrum, the signal radiated power per unit bandwidth is reduced, and the system capacity is improved [3]. For the cooperative receiver, the received signal increases the anti-interference ability of the system. Because the signal is despreaded by the known spread spectrum sequence, and the channel noise and the narrowband interference signal are extended to a wider frequency band [4].

The estimation of the DOA of the spread spectrum signal plays an important role in various military and civilian fields such as GNSS and GPS navigation, as well as sonar and radar. The spread spectrum signal is essentially a wideband signal. Compared with wideband DOA, the narrowband DOA estimation algorithm developed earlier [5]. In 1967, Burg proposed the MEM algorithm (Maximum Entropy Method) and 1969 Capon proposed the MVM algorithm (Minimum Variance Method). In these methods, the resolution ratio and accuracy of DOA estimation are improved, but in low signal-to-noise ratio the estimation performance is not good, and the high resolution in the true sense is not realized [6, 7]. The classification algorithm appeared in the 1970s, such as the MUSIC algorithm (Multiple Signal Classification) proposed by Schmidt in 1979 [8, 9]. It is the first algorithm to realize signal DOA estimation by using subspace. The resolution ratio of the array signal direction-finding is greatly improved, and it is an important node in the history of high resolution ratio direction-finding algorithm [10, 11]. The broadband high-resolution direction-finding algorithm is developed on the basis of narrowband signal direction-finding algorithm. The DOA estimation of narrow-band signals has been developed for several decades, and the technology has been relatively mature [12, 13]. However, direction-finding algorithm for wideband signals, especially for spread-spectrum signals, there are few studies on DOA estimation. The existed direction-finding technology of wideband signals is mainly based on the phase comparison method [14, 15]. However, in the phase comparison method, the phase ambiguity occurs with a period of multiple of 2π and it is difficult to eliminate, which limits the direction-finding accuracy [16, 17]. In this paper, aiming at solving the above problems, this paper proposes the ISM (Incoherent Signal Subspace Method) and CSM (Coherent Signal Subspace Method) methods to determine the direction of the wideband spread spectrum signal.

2 DOA Estimation

2.1 Mathematical Model of the Signal

In the narrowband signal model, a phase delay is used to approximately represent the time delay, which is obviously no longer applicable for wideband signals. In this case, Fourier transform is used. Each wideband signal is distributed within $[\omega_L, \omega_H]$ and use the following formula to express the output of the m element:

$$x_m(t) = \sum_{l=1}^{P} \alpha_l s_l(t - \tau_{lm}) + n_m(t), m = 1, 2, \cdots, M \tag{1}$$

Where, α_l is the gain of the m th element for the l th signal; $n_m(t)$ is additive noise at the m th element; τ_{lm} is the delay generated by the m th signal when it reaches the l th element.

For the uniform linear array; $\tau_{lm} = v_m \sin \theta_l$, $v_m = d_m/c$; d is the array space; c is the speed of the signal in the propagation medium; θ_i is the target angle to estimate. Assuming α_l is 1, and the array is sampled at time t. The output vector of the array is as follows:

$$X(t) = \begin{bmatrix} \sum_{l=1}^{P} s_l(t - \tau_{l1}) \\ \sum_{l=1}^{P} s_l(t - \tau_{l2}) \\ \vdots \\ \sum_{l=1}^{P} s_l(t - \tau_{lM}) \end{bmatrix} + \begin{bmatrix} n_1(t) \\ n_2(t) \\ \vdots \\ n_M(t) \end{bmatrix} \tag{2}$$

Adopt DFT for Eq. (1), we can get:

$$X_m(\omega) = \sum_{l=1}^{P} S_l(\omega) \exp(-j\omega\tau_{lm}) + N_m(\omega) \tag{3}$$

When the frequency is f_n, rewrite the above equation into a matrix equation:

$$X(f_n) = A(f_n)S(f_n) + N(f_n) \tag{4}$$

Where, $A(f_n)$ is $M \times P$ matrix, represents a flow matrix of the spatial array.

$$\begin{aligned} X(f_n) &= \left[X_1(f_n) \; X_2(f_n) \cdots X_M(f_n) \right]^T \\ N(f_n) &= \left[N_1(f_n) \; N_2(f_n) \cdots N_M(f_n) \right]^T \\ S(f_n) &= \left[S_1(f_n) \; S_2(f_n) \cdots S_P(f_n) \right]^T \end{aligned} \tag{5}$$

$$A(f_n) = \begin{bmatrix} \exp(-j2\pi f_n\tau_{11}) & \exp(-j2\pi f_n\tau_{12}) & \cdots & \exp(-j2\pi f_n\tau_{1P}) \\ \exp(-j2\pi f_n\tau_{21}) & \exp(-j2\pi f_n\tau_{22}) & \cdots & \exp(-j2\pi f_n\tau_{2P}) \\ \vdots & \vdots & \ddots & \vdots \\ \exp(-j2\pi f_n\tau_{M1}) & \exp(-j2\pi f_n\tau_{M2}) & \cdots & \exp(-j2\pi f_n\tau_{MP}) \end{bmatrix} \tag{6}$$

The covariance matrix corresponding to Eq. (4) is as follows:

$$\begin{aligned} R(f_n) &= A(f_n)E\left[S(f_n)S^H(f_n) \right]A^H(f_n) + \sigma_n{}^2 I \\ &= A(f_n)R_s(f_n)A^H(f_n) + \sigma_n{}^2 I \end{aligned} \tag{7}$$

It is represented at different frequency points. Where, $R_s(f_n) = E\left[S(f_n)S^H(f_n)\right]$ represents the covariance matrix of the wideband signal at f_n.

2.2 ISM (Incoherent Signal Subspace Method)

From Eq. (7), we obtain the covariance matrix $R(f_n)$ of the wideband signal. During this part, the wideband signals involved are incoherent wideband signals. Assuming there are J frequency points in the signal bandwidth, and the covariance matrix is $R(f_j), j = 1, 2, \cdots, J$. Decompose this matrix to obtain the M eigenvalues: $\lambda_1(f_j) \geq \lambda_2(f_j) \geq \cdots \geq \lambda_M(f_j)$ in descending order and the corresponding eigenvectors is $e_m(f_j), m = 1, 2, \cdots M$. The eigenvectors corresponding to the large P eigenvalues and the eigenvectors corresponding to the small $M - P$ eigenvalues are constructed into matrixes respectively.

$$
\begin{aligned}
US(f_j) &= [e_1(f_j), e_2(f_j), \cdots, e_P(f_j)] \\
UN(f_j) &= [e_{P+1}(f_j), e_{P+2}(f_j), \cdots, e_M(f_j)]
\end{aligned}
\tag{8}
$$

The signal subspace constructed at f_j is the same as the space formed by the array flow matrix, and the signal subspace is orthogonal to the noise subspace. That is, $span\{U_S(f_j)\} = span\{A(f_j, \theta)\} span\{U_S(f_j)\} \perp span\{U_N(f_j)\}$.

We can firstly obtain the covariance matrix of each frequency point in the bandwidth of the wideband signal. Then the weighted average of these spatial spectrum is obtained to get the total ISM spatial spectrum. Finally, DOA estimation is performed. There are two different weighted averaging methods: the arithmetic averaging method and the geometric averaging method. The arithmetic average method calculates the ISM spatial spectrum:

$$
P_{ISSM1}(\theta) = \left(\frac{1}{J} \sum_{j=1}^{1} \frac{1}{P_{MUSIC}(f_j, \theta)} \right)^{-1}
\tag{9}
$$

The geometric mean method calculates the ISM spatial spectrum:

$$
P_{ISSM2}(\theta) = \left(\prod_{j=1}^{J} \frac{1}{P_{MUSIC}(f_j, \theta)} \right)^{-\frac{1}{J}}
\tag{10}
$$

Here, $P_{MUSIC}(f_j, \theta)$ represents the MUSIC spatial spectrum at j th frequency:

$$
P_{MUSIC}(f_j, \theta) = \frac{1}{a^H(f_j, \theta) U_n(f_j) U_n^H(f_j) a(f_j, \theta)}
\tag{11}
$$

2.3   CSM (Coherent Signal Subspace Method)

In ISM algorithm for wideband DOA estimation, we need to select the frequency point with high SNR, and also carry out plenty of snapshots. In this case, the DOA calculation is greatly increased. Besides, the ISM algorithm cannot perform in DOA estimation of coherent wideband signals. The CSM algorithm constructs a focusing matrix by aligning the array flow matrix of each frequency point at the predicted angle to the same array flow matrix at the focus frequency. Then the array covariance matrix corresponding to each frequency of the signal is focused transform under this focus matrix.

Assuming $s_1(t)$ and $s_2(t)$ $(s_2(t) = s_1(t - t_0))$ are two coherent broadband signals, let $s(t) = \begin{bmatrix} s_1(t) \\ s_2(t) \end{bmatrix}$ and its covariance matrix can be expressed as:

$$R_s(\tau) = E\left\{s(t)s^H(t + \tau)\right\}$$
$$= \begin{bmatrix} R_1(\tau) & R_1(\tau - t_0) \\ R_1(\tau + t_0) & R_1(\tau) \end{bmatrix} \tag{12}$$

Where, $R_1(\tau)$ is the correlation function of $s_1(t)$. The spectral matrix can be obtained by performing a Fourier transform on both sides of the above formula:

$$P_s(f) = \begin{bmatrix} P_1(f) & P_1(f)\exp(-j2\pi f t_0) \\ P_1(f)\exp(j2\pi f t_0) & P_1(f) \end{bmatrix} \tag{13}$$

The spectral matrix $P_s(f)$ of $s_1(t)$ is always a singular matrix and the signal subspace and the noise subspace cannot be completely orthogonal. In order to solve this problem, it needs to make $P_s(f)$ be non-singular. Smoothing the spectral matrices in frequency at individual J frequency points:

$$P(f) = \frac{1}{J}\sum_{j=1}^{J} P(f_j)$$
$$= \begin{bmatrix} P(f_0) & P(f_0)\frac{1}{J}\sum_{j=1}^{J}\exp(-j2\pi f_j t_0) \\ P(f_0)\frac{1}{J}\sum_{j=1}^{J}\exp(j2\pi f_j t_0) & P(f_0) \end{bmatrix} \tag{14}$$

The construction of the focusing matrix is described in the following. Assuming that the rank of the array $A(f_j)$ flow matrix at the frequency point f_j is P, the focusing matrix should satisfy:

$$T(f_j)A(f_j) = A(f_0), j = 1, 2, \cdots, J \tag{15}$$

Here, f_0 is the reference frequency and also the focus frequency. $T(f_j)$ is a dimensional non-singular $M \times M$ matrix. Because the rank of $A(f_j)$ and $A(f_0)$ is P, we can construct $M \times (M - P)$ matrixes $B(f_j)$ and $B(f_0)$ to make $[A(f_j)|B(f_j)]$ and $[A(f_0)|B(f_0)]$ be both non-singular matrixes. We can get the focusing matrix as following:

$$T(f_j) = [A(f_0)|B(f_0)][A(f_j)|B(f_j)]^{-1} \tag{16}$$

After the focus matrix transformation, the array output vector is:

$$Y(f_j) = T(f_j)X(f_j) = A(f_0)S(f_j) + T(f_j)N(f_j), j = 1, 2, \cdots, J \tag{17}$$

We can get the following:

$$\sum_{j=1}^{J} w_j \mathrm{cov}(Y(f_j)) = A(f_0)\left[\sum_{j=1}^{J} w_j P_s(f_j)\right] A^H(f_0)$$

$$+ \sigma_n^2 \sum_{j=1}^{J} w_j T(f_j) P_n(f_j) T^H(f_j) \qquad (18)$$

Where,

$$R = A(f_0) R_s A^H(f_0) + \sigma_n^2 R_n$$
$$R = \sum_{j=1}^{J} w_j \mathrm{cov}(Y(f_j))$$
$$R_s = \sum_{j=1}^{J} w_j P_s(f_j) \qquad (19)$$
$$R_n = \sum_{j=1}^{J} w_j T(f_j) P_n(f_j) T^H(f_j)$$

w_j is the normalized weighted value, which is proportional to the SNR of the frequency f_j. Here, take it as 1.

Decompose the matrix (R, R_n) to obtain the M eigenvalues: $\lambda_1(f_j) \geq \lambda_2(f_j) \geq \cdots \geq \lambda_M(f_j)$ in descending order and the corresponding eigenvectors is $e_m(f_j)$, $m = 1, 2, \cdots M$. The subspace formed by the column vector of $E_s = [e_1, e_2, \cdots, e_P]$ is called the signal subspace, and the subspace formed by the column vector of $E_n = [e_{P+1}, e_{P+2}, \cdots, e_M]$ is called the noise subspace, and then the signal subspace and the noise subspace are orthogonal to each other.

$$\lambda_P = \lambda_{P+1} = \cdots = \lambda$$
$$A^H(f_0) E_n = 0$$
$$Es^H R_n E_n = OP \times (M - P) \qquad (20)$$
$$Es^H R_s E_s = IP$$
$$En^H R_n E_n = I(M - P)$$

We can get the CSM spatial spectrum as the following:

$$P_{MUSIC}(f_0, \theta) = \frac{1}{a^H(f_0, \theta) Un(f_0) Un^H(f_0) a(f_0, \theta)} \qquad (21)$$

3 Simulation Analysis

3.1 Spatial Spectrum Analysis

The distribution of energy of the target signal in all directions in space is the spatial spectrum. This is a intuitive indicator of the performance of the DOA estimation algorithm. In the experiment, it is assumed that the receiving antenna array is a 10 elements uniform linear array, snapshots are performed 128 times and the array element spacing is half of wavelength. The target wideband spread spectrum signals wave come from 20° and 26°. Perform the ISM and CSM algorithm with signal-to-noise ratio of −5db and 5db respectively and following is the spatial spectrum of ISM and CSM.

It can be seen from Figs. 1 and 2 that the power spectrum formed the peak in 20° and 26°, which are the directions of target signal and it almost maintained nearly zero in other directions. That is both the ISM and CSM algorithms can find the direction of the wideband spread spectrum signals. But in the condition with lower SNR, the ISM impossible to find the direction accurately and the CSM has higher resolution ratio. Besides, with the SNR becoming higher, the power spectrum in the target direction is sharper. In practical engineering applications, the resolution of the peaks can be increased by increasing the number of receiving antenna elements and the number of fast snapshots.

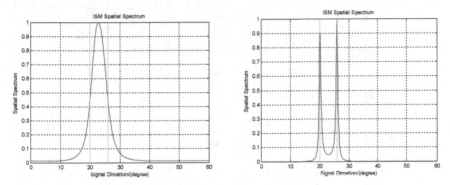

Fig. 1. ISM Spatial Spectrum with SNR of −5 dB and 5 dB.

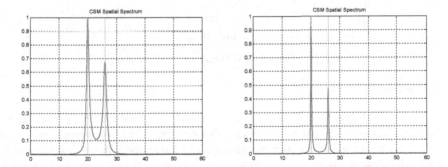

Fig. 2. CSM Spatial Spectrum with SNR of −5 dB and 5 dB.

3.2 Direction Correct Rate

The correct rate of direction-finding refers to the ratio of the number of successful direction-findings to the total number of experiments (monte carlo number). In the experiment, it is assumed that the wideband spread spectrum signals are received by the 10-element antenna. The direction is successfully determined if the difference between the direction-finding angle and the true angle is within 1°. ISM and CSM algorithm are performed 100 monte carlo simulations respectively and following is the result.

It can be seen from Fig. 3 that as the signal-to-noise ratio increases, the direction-finding correct rate of both ISM and CSM algorithms will increase. However, in the case of SNR within −10 dB and 5 dB, the CSM algorithm has a higher direction-finding correct rate. The correct rate of the direction-finding is almost maintained at around 1 after the SNR reaching a certain value. That is, the ISM and CSM direction-finding algorithms proposed in this paper can effectively reduce the influence of interference on the direction-finding result and achieve accurate direction-finding. Therefore, in practical engineering applications, we can use the ISM algorithm for incoherent wideband signals direction and CSM algorithm for coherent wideband signals direction.

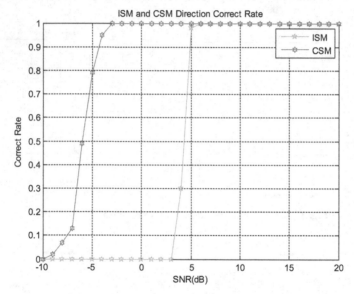

Fig. 3. ISM and CSM Direction Correct Rate.

4   Conclusion

The ISM and CSM algorithms based on sensor networking for the spread spectrum signal direction finding are proposed in this paper. After dividing the received spread spectrum signal into multiple time segments and performing DFT transform, the covariance matrix is obtained at different frequency points according to the different constraint criteria of ISM and CSM. Then, the mentioned covariance matrixes are decomposed into eigen-values to obtain the corresponding signal subspace and noise subspace. Meanwhile, the narrowband MUSIC direction finding is applied independently at different frequency points. Finally, the geometric power average or arithmetic average method is adopted to synthesize the final power spectrum in order to implement the direction finding of wideband spread spectrum signal. When the SNR is higher than 5 dB, the proposed algorithm performance satisfies accurate and low error direction finding, which should be better for engineering direction finding of spread spectrum signals.

Acknowledgements. This work was supported by the National Natural Science Foundation of China (Grant No. 61771393 and 61571368), and the seed Foundation of Innovation and Creation for Graduate students in Northwestern Polytechnical University.

References

1. Ren, H.P., et al.: A chaotic spread spectrum system for underwater acoustic communication. Physica A Stat. Mech. Appl. **478**, 77–92 (2017)
2. Bo, L.I., Gao, X.G.: Integrated decision for airborne weapon systems based on bayesian networks. J. Syst. Simul. **19**(4), 886–889 (2007)
3. Zhang, Y.-S., et al.: Comb jamming mitigation in frequency-hopping spread spectrum communications via block sparse bayesian learning. Acta Armamentarii **39**(9), 1864–1872 (2018)
4. Park, H.P., Kim, M., Jung, J.H.: Spread-spectrum technique employing phase-shift modulation to reduce EM noise for parallel–series LLC resonant converter. IEEE Trans. Power Electron. **34**(2), 1026–1031 (2018)
5. Yang, T.C., Yang, W.B.: Performance analysis of direct-sequence spread-spectrum underwater acoustic communications with low signal-to-noise-ratio input signals. J. Acoust. Soc. Am. **123**(2), 842 (2008)
6. Cadzow, J.A.: A high resolution direction-of-arrival algorithm for narrow-band coherent and incoherent sources. IEEE Trans. Acoust. Speech Signal Process. **36**(7), 965–979 (1988)
7. Uddin, M.A., et al.: Direction of arrival of narrowband signals based on virtual phased antennas. Communications (2018)
8. Hassen, S.B., et al.: DOA estimation of temporally and spatially correlated narrowband noncircular sources in spatially correlated white noise. IEEE Trans. Signal Process. **59**(9), 4108–4121 (2011)
9. Nunes, L.O., et al.: A steered-response power algorithm employing hierarchical search for acoustic source localization using microphone arrays. IEEE Trans. Signal Process. **62**(19), 5171–5183 (2014)
10. Zhang, D., et al.: Improved DOA estimation algorithm for co-prime linear arrays using root-MUSIC algorithm. Electron. Lett. **53**(18), 1277–1279 (2017)
11. Chen, Z., et al.: A novel noncircular MUSIC algorithm based on the concept of the difference and sum coarray. Sensors **18**(2), 344 (2018)
12. Cui, K.B., et al.: DOA estimation of multiple LFM sources using a STFT-based and FBSS-based MUSIC algorithm. Radioengineering **26**(4), 1126–1137 (2017)
13. Wang, J., et al.: DOA estimation of excavation devices with ELM and MUSIC-based hybrid algorithm. Cogn. Comput. **9**(4), 1–17 (2017)
14. Altarifi, M., Filipovic, D.S.: On the assessment of antenna patterns for wideband amplitude-only direction finding. IEEE Antennas Wireless Propag. Lett. **17**, 385–388 (2018)
15. Lee, J.H., Lee, J., Woo, J.: Method for obtaining three- and four element array spacing for interferometer direction-finding system. IEEE Antennas Wireless Propag. Lett. **15**, 897–900 (2016)
16. Wang, C., Mu, J.: Direction-finding via phase comparison using orthogonally cross dipole antenna. Chin. J. Sci. Instrum. **32**(5), 976–982 (2011)
17. Zhang, T., et al.: Resolving phase ambiguity in dual-echo dixon imaging using a projected power method. Magn. Reson. Med. **77**(5), 2066–2076 (2017)

A Trigger-Free Multi-user Full Duplex User-Pairing Optimizing MAC Protocol

Meiping Peng, Bo Li, Zhongjiang Yan$^{(\boxtimes)}$, and Mao Yang

School of Electronics and Information, Northwestern Polytechnical University,
Xi'an, China
meiping@mail.nwpu.edu.cn, {libo.npu,zhjyan,yangmao}@nwpu.edu.cn

Abstract. In the high-density deployment scenario of the next generation wireless local area network (WLAN), the intensification of conflict
makes spectrum utilization low. In order to improve the spectrum efficiency, the academia and industry will introduce Co-frequency Co-time
Full Duplex (CCFD) technology into MAC as a key technology. However, the existing full-duplex Medium Access Control (MAC) protocol
based on access point (AP) scheduling has the problem of low success
rate in establishing full-duplex links. In order to solve this problem, a
dynamic full-duplex link matching algorithm based on Binary-Graph is
proposed, which is based on the author's earlier research on FD-OMAX
[16]. This algorithm uses bipartite graph to establish the relationship
model between full-duplex link and Resource Unit (RU). In each round
of full-duplex transmission, AP establishes the optimal full-duplex link
transmission based on the user's dynamic interference information on
RU resources. In order to improve the success probability of establishing full-duplex links and spectrum efficiency, an enhanced trigger-free
full-duplex MAC protocol, EnFD-OMAX, is designed on the basis of
FD-OMAX protocol. The simulation results show that compared with
FD-OMAX protocol, MuFuPlex protocol, OMAX protocol and FuPlex
protocol, the throughput distribution of EnFD-OMAX protocol increases
by 26.5%, 56.60%, 88.37% and 118.4% under saturated traffic. In high-
density deployment scenarios, the probability of full duplex link to successful transmission and MAC efficiency are increased by 88.98% and
149.9% respectively compared with OMAX protocol.

Keywords: Next generation WLAN · MAC · CCFD · Bipartite graph

1 Introduction

Wireless Local Area Network (WLAN) has become the main carrier of wireless
network services because of its low cost and flexible deployment. According to
Cisco's analysis and forecast, the wireless business carried by WLAN will reach
49% in 2021 [1]. However, limited spectrum resources and low spectrum utilization have become a problem that hinders the development of WLAN. Therefore,

© ICST Institute for Computer Sciences, Social Informatics and Telecommunications Engineering 2020
Published by Springer Nature Switzerland AG 2020. All Rights Reserved
B. Li et al. (Eds.): IoTaaS 2019, LNICST 316, pp. 598–610, 2020.
https://doi.org/10.1007/978-3-030-44751-9_51

how to improve the spectrum efficiency of WLAN system has become a hot research issue in industry and academia. IEEE 802.11 Standards Committee is working on the next generation of high-efficiency WLAN standards: IEEE 802.11ax [2], to further improve the data transmission efficiency and multiple access efficiency of WLAN.

IEEE 802.11ax standard introduces multi-user random competitive access and multi-user scheduling access into the MAC protocol. It combines two channel access modes to improve MAC efficiency. At the same time, the CCFD technology [3,4] is introduced into the next generation WLAN as the key technology to improve the spectrum efficiency under high-density deployment. In recent years, the maturity of self-interference cancellation technology [5–7] provides physical layer technical support for simultaneous full-duplex transmission at the same frequency. However, the traditional MAC protocol can not meet the requirements of full-duplex transmission. Designing an efficient full-duplex MAC protocol has become a hot research issue for researchers. H. Ah et al. proposed a frequency-domain coordinated full-duplex MAC protocol for AP scheduling [8]. This protocol reports channel information on designated subchannels by designated Station (STA). AP only schedules full-duplex link transmission, and the protocol STA has full-duplex capability. Document [9] proposes a multi-user full-duplex MAC protocol based on Orthogonal Frequency Division Multiple Access (OFDMA) with random competition in subchannels, which requires all users to have full-duplex capability. This protocol increases the complexity of equipment. Q. Qu et al. proposed a full-duplex transmission framework for the next generation WLAN [10], that is, AP has full-duplex capability, STA does not have full-duplex capability, and designed a full-duplex MAC protocol compatible with the standard protocol of IEEE 802.11. Subsequently, based on AP scheduling, multi-user full-duplex MAC protocol: MuFuPlex protocol [11], PCMu-FuPlex protocol [12] is designed and applied to the next generation of high-density deployment WLAN scenarios.

In summary, most of the existing full-duplex MAC protocols are focused on single-user random access and Scheduling-based multi-user access. However, the collision probability of simple random access protocol is high, which leads to low efficiency of MAC. Service collection based on scheduling multi-user MAC protocol results in high system overhead and poor real-time traffic transmission. Moreover, the existing Scheduling-based multi-user full-duplex MAC protocol has non-real-time link channel information, which results in low probability of successful transmission of full-duplex links. OMAX [13] first proposed the trigger-free upstream multi-user access MAC protocol for the next generation WLAN. The advantages of demand-based upstream multi-user access were expounded, and the feasibility was proved by theoretical analysis. Therefore, based on the framework of OMAX protocol, this paper designs a multi-user full-duplex OFDMA MAC protocol: EnFD-OMAX protocol, which is initiated by STA to establish full-duplex link transmission and report the channel state information of full-duplex link in real time. The protocol assumes that STA has the ability to detect subchannel power intensity. Through performance simulation, compared with FD-OMAX protocol, MuFuPlex protocol, OMAX protocol and FuPlex protocol, EnFD-OMAX protocol improves the system throughput distribution by 26.5%, 56.60%, 88.37% and 118.4%. In high-density deployment scenarios, the probability of successful transmission and MAC efficiency of full-duplex links are increased by 88.98% and 149.9% respectively compared with OMAX protocol.

The main contributions of this paper are summarized as follows:

(1) A dynamic full-duplex link pair matching algorithm based on bipartite graph is proposed. In each round of transmission, AP establishes the optimal full-duplex link pair according to the real-time dynamic interference information of STAs on RU to improve the success probability of full-duplex link.

(2) Based on the FD-OMAX protocol, an enhanced trigger-free multi-user full-duplex multiple access protocol, EnFD-OMAX, is designed, which supports upstream multi-user parallel channel access and real-time reporting of link status information. In order to realize the complete flow of the protocol, the corresponding Group Clear to Send (G-CTS) frame and Full-Duplex Clear to Send (F-CTS) frame structures are designed.

(3) Build NS-2 simulation platform, and simulate and verify the network performance and MAC efficiency of EnFD-OMAX protocol and FD-OMAX protocol, MuFuPlex protocol, OMAX protocol and FuPlex protocol.

The rest of this paper is structured as follows: Sect. 2 describes the full-duplex network scenario model and system model considered in this paper. Section 3 analyses the full duplex link pair matching scheme based on bipartite graph and the design of EnFD-OMAX protocol flow. Section 4 simulates and verifies the network performance of EnFD-OMAX protocol and existing MAC protocol. Finally, this paper summarizes.

2   System Model

A single Basic Service Set (BSS) is considered in the proposed protocol for the next generation WLAN and the performance of proposed MAC protocol is studied for different network scales with serious changes in channel state. As shown in Fig. 1, AP is located at the geometric center of the cell, STA is randomly distributed within the signal coverage of AP, and N semi-duplex STAs are associated with an AP with full duplex capability.

For the network scenario in Fig. 1, $UL = \{1, 2, \cdots K\}$ and $DL = \{1, 2, \cdots M\}$ are used to represent the upstream and downstream STAs set in a full-duplex transmission process, where $K, M \in [0, RU_{\max}]$, i.e. the total number of full-duplex link pairs established each time does not exceed the maximum RU, are determined by the upstream random access stage. According to EnFD-OMX protocol design, the target association in the set of uplink/downlink STAs is disorderly and $K \geq M$. Define the weights of the edges of UL_i and DL_j of any two vertices in the uplink/downlink STAs sets UL and DL as the signal-to-noise ratio strength of downlink DL_j in the case of uplink UL_i interference, as shown in Eq. (1).

$$\Gamma_{i,j} = \frac{P_{r,j}}{I_{i,j} + N_0} \tag{1}$$

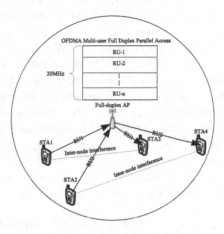

Fig. 1. Full duplex network scenario

Among them: $P_{r,j}$ is the downlink receiving power, N_0 is the additive white Gauss noise, $I_{i,j}$ is the interference power of uplink $I_{i,j}$ to downlink DL_j. According to Eq. (1), the weight $\Gamma_{i,j}$ of the edges of any two vertices in UL and DL can be calculated in one transmission, thus forming the correlation strength matrix. The larger the weight $\Gamma_{i,j}$ between vertices and edges, the higher the degree of target correlation; the lower the intensity of correlation. In this paper, in order to simplify the computational strength, $\Gamma_{i,j} \geq SINR_{throld}$ is considered to indicate that the objectives are interrelated, otherwise the objectives are not interrelated. According to the theory of bipartite graph matching, the optimal full duplex link pairs problem for one transmission can be modeled as a linear programming problem based on the correlation intensity matrix,as shown in Eq. (2).

$$\begin{cases} \max \sum_{i=1}^{M} \sum_{j=1}^{K} \Gamma_{i,j} H(i,j) \\ s.t \ \sum_{i} H(i,m) = 1 \quad m = 1, 2, \cdots M \\ \sum_{j} H(n,j) = 1 \quad n = 1, 2, \cdots K \\ \Gamma_{i,j} \geq SINR_{throld} \quad \forall i \in DL, \forall j \in DL \end{cases} \tag{2}$$

Among them: $H(i,j) = 1$ or 0, when $H(i,j) = 1$, it means that the two target vertices can form a matching relationship, and when $H(i,j) = 0$, it means that the two target vertices can not form a matching relationship.

3   Multiuser Full Duplex User Pair Optimizing MAC Protocol

The design of full-duplex MAC protocol for next generation WLAN can be divided into symmetric full-duplex MAC protocol and asymmetric full-duplex MAC protocol. Symmetric full-duplex MAC protocol requires full duplex capability of STA, while asymmetric full-duplex MAC protocol conforms to the trend of miniaturization and low complexity of the next generation WLAN terminal equipment. To meet the low complexity of WLAN terminal devices, the proposed protocol is asymmetric full-duplex MAC protocol. Firstly, according to OMAX upstream random competitive access mechanism, AP allocates RU channel resources and initiates downstream transmission requests according to the number of successful upstream access nodes. STA receives downstream requests to reply to the interference information of this upstream STA to this node. AP collects the interference information between this upstream and downstream STAs, and redistributes full-duplex link pairs based on Dichotomy theory to enhance the performance. Full duplex links improve the overall throughput of the system for the probability of successful transmission.

As shown in Fig. 2, EnFD-OMAX protocol is divided into three stages: upstream random competitive access stage, full-duplex transmission link pair establishment stage and full-duplex data transmission stage.

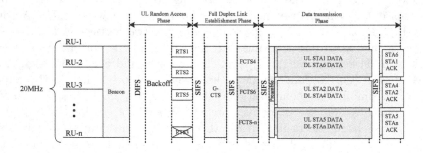

Fig. 2. A trigger-free multi-user full-duplex MAC protocol

3.1   Bipartite Graph-Based Resource Allocation Algorithms for Full Duplex Links

For the full duplex MAC protocol proposed in this paper, it can be understood as spectrum resource reuse of downlink transmission on upstream transmission RU. However, the EnFD-OMAX protocol is designed as an asymmetric full-duplex MAC protocol. During the establishment of a full-duplex transmission link pair, the upstream/downstream STAs set is a set of two sets of disjoint vertices. In order to better describe the maximum full-duplex link logarithm in a full-duplex transmission, a bipartite graph $G = \langle V, E \rangle$ is used to model it. For V is a set of node, it can be divided into two disjoint vertex sets A and B ;E is the edge set, and the vertex distribution associated with each edge belongs to A and B set. As shown in Fig. 3, let $A = UL$ be an upstream STA set and $B = DL$ is the downstream STA set, E set represents the frequency resource reuse relationship between the downstream STA and the upstream STA on the same RU. In this paper, only considering the optimization of full duplex transmission link pairs, Eq. (2) can be transformed into a bipartite graph for modeling, thus, the Hungarian algorithm [17] can be used as shown in Algorithm 1 to obtain the optimal solution for forming full duplex link pairs.

According to the protocol and bipartite graph algorithm proposed in this paper, it can be seen that in each iteration, the upstream STA contests for downstream STA to establish full-duplex transmission. At this time, the algorithm can only elect one downstream STA to establish full-duplex link. Therefore, the time complexity of the bipartite graph algorithm is $\Theta(n^2)$, and it has the advantage of low complexity.

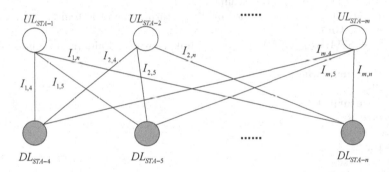

Fig. 3. Bipartite graph model

3.2 Uplink Random Access

In order to ensure the backward compatibility of the protocol, STA in BSS adopts the traditional DCF channel access mechanism, and the backoff process must be executed before data service is sent. When the channel is detected to be idle in DCF Inter-frame Space (DIFS), the backoff process is executed. STA with service delivery needs selects random values as backoff counts between Contention Windows (CW), and the backoff counts are reduced by 1 for each idle time slot. EnFD-OMAX protocol follows the OMAX protocol framework and adopts the time-frequency two-dimensional backoff mechanism [14] with the maximum resource block of 20 MHz bandwidth defined by the next generation WLAN standard. After backoff is completed, STA selects RU to send Request To Send (RTS) frames independently and randomly.

Algorithm 1. Full Duplex Link Pairs Matching Algorithm

Require: $UL = \{UL_0, UL_1 \cdots UL_k\}$, $DL = \{DL_0, DL_1 \cdots DL_h\}$;   /* UL represents the set of uplink STAs,DL represents the set of downlink STAs*/

Ensure: $FD = \{< UL_{ulIndex}, DL_{dlIndex} >, \cdots\}$;   /* Full duplex link pairs established by this transmission */

1: initialization
2: $M = k, N = h$
3: **for** $dlIndex = 0$ to $N - 1$ **do**
4:    Initialize all vertices of DL to unscanned
5:    **if** FDPair(dlIndex) **then**
6:       Loop the next value
7:    **end if**
8: **end for**
9: **print** /*************** FDPair (int dlIndex) start ******************/
10: **function** FDPair(dlIndex)
11: Mark the $STA_{dlIndex}$ as scanned
12: **for** $ulIndex = 0$ to $M - 1$ **do**
13:
14:    **if** $STA_{ulIndex}$ isn't scanned and $SINR_{ulIndex,dlIndex} > SINR_{throld}$ **then**
15:       Mark the $STA_{ulIndex}$ as scanned
16:       **if** $STA_{ulIndex}$ isn't matched or The return value of FDPair($FD_{dlIndex}.DL$) is true **then**
17:          $< STA_{ulIndex}, STA_{dlIndex} >$ Uplink/Downlink Pairs Inserted into Set FD

18:          **return** true
19:       **else**
20:          **return** false
21:       **end if**
22:    **end if**
23: **end for**
24: **return** false
25: **end function**
26: **print** /*************** FDPair (int dlIndex) end *******************/

3.3   Full Duplex Link Establishment Process

First, each STA maintains an inter-node interference information table, dynamically updates the interference intensity after receiving RTS frames of other STAs; AP maintains a full-duplex link-to-information table, and dynamically updates full-duplex link-to-history information after receiving F-CTS frames. After the access of the upstream STA random competitive channel is completed, AP records the STA number of the channel successfully accessed on each RU. AP pre-selects downlink STAs that may form full-duplex links based on full-duplex links to historical information tables, and replies to G-CTS frames. As shown in Fig. 4, if there is no downlink link pair between the successful competitive access upstream STAs and the full-duplex link pair, the full-duplex transmission opportunity will be abandoned to enter the OMAX protocol transmission process; otherwise, the full-duplex transmission process will be entered and F-CTS frames will be received. AP receives F-CTS frames. Based on the latest inter-node interference information, full-duplex link pairs are redistributed to establish the algorithm by using full-duplex link pairs based on bipartite graph.

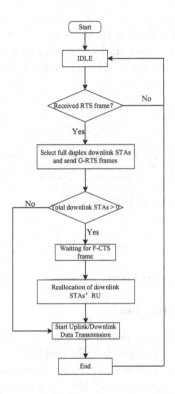

Fig. 4. AP establishes full duplex link pair processing flow

3.4   Frame Format

In EnFD-OMAX, RTS, DATA and ACK frames are defined by traditional WLAN standards. In order to improve the process integrity of EnFD-OMAX protocol, we need to extend G-CTS and F-CTS frames on the basis of CTS frames defined by traditional WLAN standard.

As shown in Fig. 5, the G-CTS frame contains downlink request receiving address and RU resource scheduling information, which takes up 2 bytes (16 bits), and each bit corresponds to one RU resource, i.e. it can support up to 16 full-duplex link allocation information. When RU resource scheduling bit position 1, it means that the upstream STA transmits DATA frames on this RU, and the downstream STA replies to F-CTS frames on this STA.

Fig. 5. G-CTS frame structure

As shown in Fig. 6, the F-CTS frame adds all the upstream STA address information in the G-CTS frame, and corresponds to the interference intensity information of the STA to the node. The interference intensity domain is 2 bytes long (16 bits).

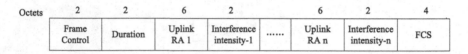

Fig. 6. F-CTS frame structure

4 Performance Evaluation

4.1 Simulation Configuration

In order to verify the network performance of EnFD-OMAX protocol, a link-system network simulation platform is built under NS2 network simulation software. The simulation scenario is set as a single basic service set (BSS) scenario, that is, AP is located in the center of the simulation area; STA is randomly distributed in the region, and the number of STAs increases gradually from 10 to 50 with a growth base of 5. The simulation time is 50 s, and the final simulation result is the average of 5 repeated simulation results. In order to fairly verify the network performance of the proposed protocol and the existing protocols, the traffic of AP and STA is set to saturated traffic, and there is a data packet waiting to be sent at any time. The draft 802.11ax protocol divides the 20 MHz channel into nine RUs by OFDMA technology, allowing simultaneous access of nine STAs to parallel channels with different RU resources. Channel is a time-varying channel model. Other network parameters are set as shown in Table 1.

Table 1. Parameters

Parameters	Value
Preamble time	20 us
Control packet PHY rate	6 Mbps
DATA packet PHY rate	54 Mbps
$CW_{\min}$	15
$CW_{\max}$	1023
$DIFS$	34 us
$SIFS$	16 us
$Slot$	9 us
$RU_{\max}$	9
$SINR_{Throld}$	3.16 dB
Channel bandwidth	20 MHz
TXOP	3 ms

4.2 Simulation Results

In order to verify the performance of EnFD-OMAX protocol, this paper compares the network performance with OMAX, FuPlex and MuFuPlex.

The total system throughput is an important performance index to measure the design of MAC protocol. To fairly verify the FD-OMAX protocol, MuFuPlex protocol, OMAX protocol, FuPlex and EnFD-OMAX protocol, both upstream and downstream are set to saturate traffic, ensuring that at least one packet needs to be sent at any time. As shown in Fig. 7, the total throughput of the proposed EnFD-OMAX protocol is 26.5% higher than that of the FD-OMAX protocol system, because the optimal pairing algorithm of full-duplex transmission link pairs based on bipartite graph is adopted in each full-duplex establishment process. FuPlex protocol is lower than OMAX protocol in total system throughput, which proves that the performance of multi-user access protocol is obviously due to single-user access protocol. MuFuPlex protocol and EnFD-OMAX protocol are multi-user MAC access protocols. With the increase of deployment nodes, system throughput tends to be balanced, while EnFD-OMAX protocol has obvious advantages in system throughput.

In full-duplex network system, the success probability of full-duplex transmission link is an important performance index to measure the design of full-duplex MAC protocol. Successful transmission probability of full duplex link directly affects the total throughput of the system. As can be seen from in Fig. 8, the EnFD-OMAX protocol combines real-time reporting of full-duplex link information with full-duplex link history information, and the full-duplex link allocation algorithm based on the bipartite graph is reconfigured twice with full-duplex link pairs, which greatly improves the probability of successful transmission of full-duplex links. At a certain degree of node size, the probability of success is more than 80%.

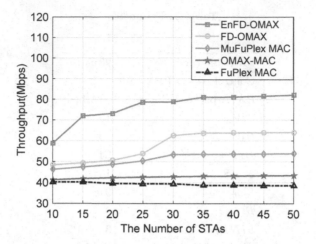

Fig. 7. System effective throughput (saturated traffic)

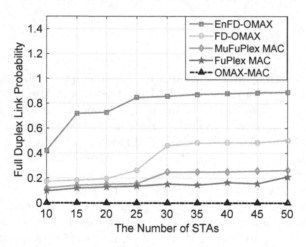

Fig. 8. Full duplex link probability

MAC efficiency has been considered as an important indicator to evaluate the performance of MAC protocol design in academia and industry [15]. CCFD is an important means to improve MAC efficiency. As shown in Fig. 9, the efficiency of multi-user MAC protocol is higher than that of single-user MAC protocol, while the EnFD-OMAX protocol improves significantly the efficiency of MAC due to the improvement of the probability of successful transmission of full-duplex links, especially in large-scale network scenarios, which is in line with the next generation of WLAN high-density network deployment scenarios.

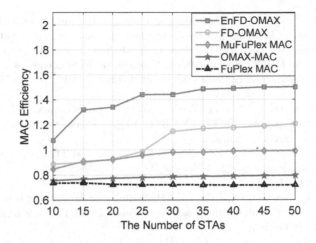

Fig. 9. MAC efficiency

5 Conclusion

In view of the low probability of success of full-duplex link establishment under the high-density deployment of the next generation WLAN, this paper proposes a trigger-free multi-user full-duplex MAC protocol initiated by the STA competitive access channel to report the full-duplex link information in real time, and optimizes the maximum full-duplex transmission by referring to the full-duplex link allocation algorithm based on the bipartite graph. The simulation results show that compared with FD-OMAX protocol, MuFuPlex protocol, OMAX protocol and FuPlex protocol, EnFD-OMAX protocol improves the system throughput distribution by 26.5%, 56.60%, 88.37% and 118.4%. In high-density deployment scenario, the probability of successful transmission and MAC efficiency of full duplex link are increased by 88.98% and 149.9% respectively compared with OMAX protocol. Follow-up research will optimize the allocation of full-duplex spectrum resources, so as to further improve system throughput.

Acknowledgment. This work was supported in part by the National Natural Science Foundations of CHINA (Grant No. 61771392, No. 61771390, No. 61871322, No. 61271279, No. 61501373), and the National Science and Technology Major Project (Grant No. 2015ZX03002006-004, 2016ZX03001018-004).

References

1. Cisco. Cisco Visual Networking Index: Global mobile data traffic forecast update 2016–2021. Cisco White Paper (2017)

2. IEEE Draft Standard for Information Technology - Telecommunications and Information Exchange Between Systems Local and Metropolitan Area Networks - Specific Requirements Part 11: Wireless LAN Medium Access Control (MAC) and Physical Layer (PHY) Specifications Amendment Enhancements for High Efficiency WLAN. In: IEEE P802.11ax/D4.0, February 2019, pp. 1–746, 12 March 2019

3. China Telecom: IEEE P802.11 Wireless LANs Proposed TGax draft specification. https://mentor.ieee.org/802.11/dcn/13/11-13-0765-02-0hew-co-time-co-frequency-full-duplex-for-802-11-wlan.ppt

4. Wang, P., et al.: IEEE P802.11 wireless LANs proposed TGax draft specification. https://mentor.ieee.org/802.11/dcn/18/11-18-1588-02-00fd-prototype-of-full-duplex-for-802-11.pptx

5. Shende, N.V., Gürbüz, Ö., Erkip, E.: Half-duplex or full-duplex communications: degrees of freedom analysis under self-interference. IEEE Trans. Wireless Commun. **17**(2), 1081–1093 (2018)

6. Han, S., Zhang, Y., Meng, W., Chen, H.: Self-interference-cancellation-based SLNR precoding design for full-duplex relay-assisted system. IEEE Trans. Veh. Technol. **67**(9), 8249–8262 (2018)

7. Hong, S., Mehlman, J., Katti, S.: Picasso: flexible RF and spectrum slicing. In: ACM SIGCOMM Conference on Applications (2012)

8. Ahn, H., Lee, J., Kim, C., Suh, Y.: Frequency domain coordination MAC protocol for full-duplex wireless networks. IEEE Commun. Lett. **23**(3), 518–521 (2019)

9. Wang, X., Tang, A., Huang, P.: Full duplex random access for multi-user OFDMA communication systems. Ad Hoc Netw. **24**, 200–213 (2015)

10. Qu, Q., Li, B., Yang, M., et al.: FuPlex: a full duplex MAC for the next generation WLAN. In: 11th EAI International Conference on Heterogeneous Networking for Quality, Reliability, Security and Robustness. IEEE (2015)

11. Qu, Q., Li, B., Yang, M., et al.: MU-FuPlex: a multiuser full-duplex MAC protocol for the next generation wireless networks. In: Wireless Communications & Networking Conference. IEEE (2017)

12. Qu, Q., Li, B., Yang, M., Yan, Z.: Power control based multiuser full-duplex MAC protocol for the next generation wireless networks. Mob. Netw. Appl. **23**(4), 1008–1019 (2017). https://doi.org/10.1007/s11036-017-0966-y

13. Qu, Q., Li, B., Yang, M., et al.: An OFDMA based concurrent multiuser MAC for upcoming IEEE 802.11 ax. In: Wireless Communications and Networking Conference Workshops (WCNCW), pp. 136–141. IEEE (2015)

14. Kwon, H., Seo, H., Kim, S., Lee, B.G.: Generalized CSMA/CA for OFDMA systems: protocol design, throughput analysis, and implementation issues. IEEE Trans. Wireless Commun. **8**(8), 4176–4187 (2009)

15. IEEE Technical Presentations: Analysis on IEEE 802.11n MAC Efficiency. IEEE 802.11-07/2431r0

16. Peng, M., Li, B., Yan, Z., et al.: Research on a trigger-free multi-user full-duplex MAC protocol. Submitted to Journal of Northwestern Polytechnical University

17. Wright, M.B.: Speeding up the Hungarian algorithm. Comput. Oper. Res. **17**(1), 95–96 (1990)

Adaptive Block ACK for Large Delay of Space-Terrestrial Integrated Network

Tianjiao Xie[1,2], Bo Li[1], Mao Yang[1(✉)], Zhongjiang Yan[1], and Zhaozhe Jiang[1]

[1] School of Electronics and Information, Northwestern Polytechnical University,
Xi'an, China
xiexietianjiao@163.com, yangmao@nwpu.edu.cn
[2] China Academy of Space Technology (Xi'an), Xi'an, People's Republic of China

Abstract. Aiming at the large delay characteristics of space-terrestrial integrated network, an efficient MAC protocol based on TDMA adaptive block ACK is proposed in this paper. Among them, the adaptive block ACK can effectively reduce the delay of the space-terrestrial integrated network by reducing the probability of retransmitting, at the same time, it can reduce the overhead of the MAC layer and help to achieve high throughput of the Space-Terrestrial integrated network. The simulation results with different access strategies show that the proposed efficient MAC access protocol has great advantages over the traditional ACK and block ACK access methods in system delay and network throughput, and has certain guiding significance for Space-Terrestrial integrated network.

Keywords: Space-Terrestrial integrated network · Adaptive · Block ACK · MAC protocol

1 Introduction

With the rapid development of rocket launching technology, satellite platform technology and payload technology, satellite-centric or integrated satellite space-terrestrial network [1] has attracted worldwide attention. Satellite constellations based on space-based information sharing can provide a variety of services covering the world. For example, the Space-Terrestrial integrated network can not only provide network access services for ground base stations in remote areas, but also provide low-latency and high-reliability satellite network connection services for customers such as automobiles, airplanes, maritime transport, and land transportation in remote areas. In addition, it can meet the needs of Regional Disasters and temporary communications, and achieve real-time seamless access, monitoring, transmission and sharing of the status information of the Internet of Things worldwide [7]. Moreover, the space-terrestrial integrated satellite network can also meet the network requirements of scientific investigation, exploration and other activities in extreme and harsh environments.

© ICST Institute for Computer Sciences, Social Informatics and Telecommunications Engineering 2020
Published by Springer Nature Switzerland AG 2020. All Rights Reserved
B. Li et al. (Eds.): IoTaaS 2019, LNICST 316, pp. 611–620, 2020.
https://doi.org/10.1007/978-3-030-44751-9_52

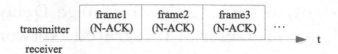

Fig. 1. N-ACK mechanism.

Terminals of space-terrestrial integrated network are widely distributed in the areas of sky, land, sea and so on. For GEO satellites in geosynchronous orbit, the one-way propagation delay between satellites and ground is more than 100 ms. Even LEO satellites in low orbit have several milliseconds of total propagation delay. Compared with the ground communication network, the inherent long propagation delay is a huge technical problem faced by satellite network [2]. Nowadays, the technology of ground network access [3–5] cannot solve the problem of large delay of space-terrestrial integrated network transmission. Therefore, the integration of space and earth network should adopt a new and efficient MAC access strategy.

In order to avoid the long delay caused by retransmit, improving the efficiency of random access channel is a key issue in the MAC strategy of space-terrestrial integrated network. An adaptive block ACK MAC access protocol based on TDMA is presented in this paper. It is proposed to overcome the problem of retransmit caused by inherent propagation delay of satellite communication by considering the use of adaptive block ACK, so as to solve the problem of large link delay in the space-terrestrial integrated network access.

2   Existing ACK Strategy

In terrestrial wireless communication systems, confirmation and retransmit mechanisms are commonly used to improve the reliability of the system, which is implemented through the MAC layer. There are three ACK mechanisms in the ground network. They are N-ACK mechanism, I-ACK mechanism and B-ACK mechanism respectively.

N-ACK means that the sender does not need to confirm that the receiver has received the data, but directly transmits the data. As shown in Fig. 1, this method has low latency and ensures high throughput, which is suitable for good communication link quality. It is often used in streaming media, etc. of course, because broadcast and multicast data cannot be confirmed, only N-ACK mechanism can be adopted.

I-ACK means that each received frame needs to immediately send a response frame (ACK frame) to the sender. The sender will continue to send the next frame only after receiving the correct response frame sent by the receiver. Otherwise, the previous frame will be retransmitted, as shown in Fig. 2. I-ACK mechanism can ensure the correctness of data service reception, but its delay is large and throughput is low. It is suitable for high reliability services.

The operation of B-ACK was introduced in IEEE 802.11e, which was further enhanced in IEEE 802.11n and applied with frame aggregation mechanism [6]. It

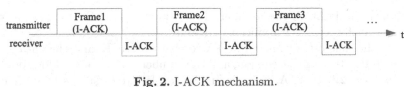

Fig. 2. I-ACK mechanism.

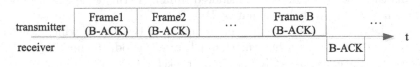

Fig. 3. B-ACK mechanism.

is a mechanism between N-ACK and I-ACK. This mechanism allows the sender to receive a confirmation frame to get which frames are received correctly and which frames need to be retransmitted after sending a certain frame. The specific process is as follows: the sending device first sends a B-ACK request frame, and if the receiving device can support the B-ACK mechanism, it will indicate the maximum frame size and the maximum number of frames that its cache can receive in the response frame. The first frame in this sequence needs to refer to the ACK domain as B-ACK, and the last frame needs to assign the ACK domain to the B-ACK request. In this way, when the receiving device receives the last frame, it will send a B-ACK frame, indicating which frames were received correctly and which ones were not received correctly. According to the instructions of B-ACK frame, the sender retransmits the frame that the receiver has not received correctly. As shown in Fig. 3, block validation mechanism improves reliability while maintaining high throughput.

3   Proposed Adaptive B-ACK Strategy

Because of the long distance and long propagation delay of satellite-earth link in Space-Terrestrial integrated satellite access network, B-ACK is considered to reduce the system delay. Considering the large link delay of Space-Terrestrial integrated network, the free space propagation is large, which leads to the high bit error rate of the system, i.e. "link unreliable problem", which may cause ACK loss, as shown in Fig. 4, so a large number of frames will be retransmitted. Because of the large propagation delay, the retransmit will further increase the system delay. Therefore, the current B-ACK cannot be directly applied to Space-Terrestrial integrated space-based access network system.

In order to reduce end-to-end delay, an adaptive B-ACK low-delay MAC access method based on TDMA is proposed in this paper. When the terrestrial integration network terminal (STA) needs to access the satellite (AP) uplink, the sender STA adaptively adjusts the length of Data B in the next block according to the received B-ACK. The steps of the adaptive B-ACK algorithm proposed in this paper are as follows:

1. Initialization: B-ACK, the number of data in the block B = 1, that is, each packet sent by STA, AP replies to an ACK.
2. During the time-out retransmit, STA receives the ACK that the data is sent successfully t times in succession, and the number of data in the block doubles, that is, B = 2B. In STA, there is one packet failure in successive t times, it means that the Block data is considered to fail. At this time, the number of Data in the Block is halved, that is, B = B/2.
3. When the channel state is poor, the minimum of B is Bmin, which keeps one ACK per Bmin packet; when the channel state is good, the maximum of B is Bmax, which keeps one ACK per Bmax packet.
4. STA needs to retransmit the wrong packet when it does not receive the ACK or the wrong ACK during the timeout of the retransmit.

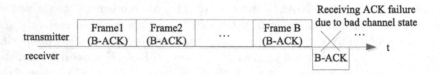

Fig. 4. Receiving ACK failure due to bad channel state.

The MAC access mode based on adaptive B-ACK strategy can overcome the loss of ACK caused by channel state difference, effectively reduce the probability of data frame retransmit, and thus improve the delay performance of data packet transmission. For each B packet, only one ACK is replied. This adaptive B-ACK strategy can also reduce the overhead of the MAC layer and help to achieve high throughput of the Space-Terrestrial integrated network. In order to achieve simplicity, TDMA access mode is adopted. For each slot, the data of different access nodes may be transmitted. The function of uplink low-latency multiple access is implemented simply and efficiently. It is very suitable for the application scenario of long time delay in Space-Terrestrial integrated network.

4   Simulation and Performance Analysis

4.1   Space-Terrestrial Integration Access Network Simulation Scenario

Space-based access network [6] refers to the terminal equipment of ships, vehicles, people, aircraft and UAV waiting for access to space-based satellite network in the sea, land, air and space domains. Unlike the ground network, the node-to-satellite transmission in the space-based access network is greater, and the delay from each node to the satellite is diversity. End-to-end two-way communication can be achieved through satellite access network for terminal nodes in space-terrestrial integrated network. This kind of service is widely used in various application scenarios and is the most important typical service type. As shown in Fig. 5.

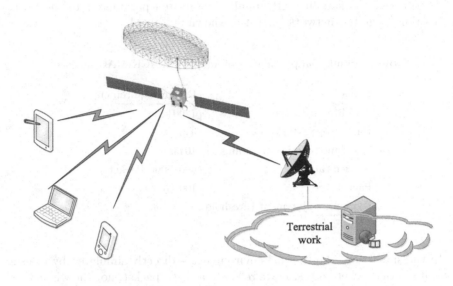

Fig. 5. Sketch of satellite access service.

The link characteristic of satellite access network is that the propagation time is prolonged and the delay deviation between the access nodes is large. Because of the large space span of satellite network, the link length between satellite and ground is much longer than the link length of ground network, which will bring significant propagation delay. And for different user terminals, due to the wide types of terminals, including land, sea, air and sky users, the transmission delay deviation from terminal to access node satellite will be very large.

The mobile access service of satellite communication means that the terminal nodes can directly communicate with the satellite through the satellite communication device under any state, including the mobile state and the stationary state, and realize the two-way communication service through the satellite communication system. In order to meet the access requirements in the mobile state, mobile communication satellites are usually used to provide services for mobile access services. Using satellite systems to provide mobile access services to end users, a scenario where there is no terrestrial network coverage, such as in areas such as countryside, desert islands, deserts, oceans, adjacent spaces, etc. and the civil servants have certain service target users; the other scenario is to support the high-speed mobile state of the end users, such as high-speed targets in subsonic or supersonic motion states, which are mainly targeted at military applications in the current state.

Assuming that the algorithm runs on the TDMA protocol and does not consider the synchronization problem, the algorithm only schedules the adaptive B-ACK strategy when the space-terrestrial integration network terminal STA needs to access the satellite AP uplink. The related parameters of the Space-Terrestrial integrated network are set as shown in Table 1.

Table 1. Simulation parameters of adaptive B-ACK MAC protocol

Items	Design requirement
Satellite altitude	1200 km
Data propagation time	4 ms
Overtime retransmit timing	10 ms
Service rate	500–5000 Packets/s
Packet size	100 Bytes
Dynamic adjustment threshold	3

In the simulation, the channel environment is directly simulated by the success rate of the packet (success rate refers to a single packet, not the whole block packet). The change of the success rate of the packet is used to simulate the change of the channel environment. The success rate varies from 10% to 100% with time, once per second. When the end of time is 0, that is, 0.0–1.0, the success rate is 100%; when the end of time is 1, that is, 1.0–2.0, the success rate is 90%; when the end of time is 2, that is, 2.0–3.0, the success rate is 80%, and so on.

4.2   Simulation Results and Analysis

The adaptive B-ACK algorithm proposed in this paper is used to simulate the throughput and average delay of data packets, and compared with the traditional I-ACK and B-ACK.

In this paper, Block ACK simulates three situations:

The first is I-ACK mode. Send a Data back to an ACK. (B = 1)

The second is B-ACK mode. Send multiple data back to an ACK. (B > 1)

The third is adaptive B-ACK. That is to say, according to the current transmission status, adjust the number of Data in the Block. (B Dynamic Adjustment)

The adaptive B-ACK dynamic adjustment method is as follows:

If Block data succeeds three times, the number of Data in Block doubles (B doubles). If Block data fails three times in a row, the number of Data in Block will be halved (B halved). In the simulation configuration, it is considered that there is a packet failure in Block data block, that is, Block data failure. The minimum and maximum of B is 1 and 128 individually.

(1) System throughput [8]

The purpose of MAC protocol is to maximize throughput under the condition of minimal access delay. Throughput is the transmission rate per unit time. It is defined as follows: assuming that the frame length is fixed L bits and the number of frames successfully transmitted within a unit time (s) is n, the throughput is nL (b/s). If the transmission rate of the channel is $R(b/s)$, then the normalized throughput $S = nL/R$. Define the transmission time of each frame on the channel as $T = L/R$, then S can be expressed as nT.

Throughput results are divided into two types: data volume per unit time (MB/s), data packet number per unit time (Packets/s). The simulation results are shown in Figs. 6 and 7 respectively.

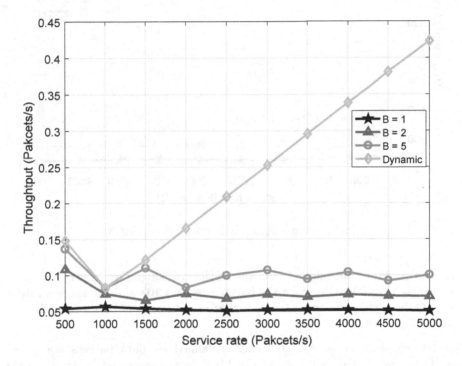

Fig. 6. Average throughput 1 for different ACK

From the above results, the two are basically the same, but the units of statistics are different, according to the size of the data packet, the two can be converted to each other. The average throughput of adaptive B-ACK is the highest, the average throughput of I-ACK mode is the worst, and the performance of B-ACK mode is in the middle. The performance of N = 5 is better than that of N = 2. At the service rate of the simulation configuration, the adaptive B-ACK mode has not reached the saturation state, and other modes have reached the saturation state.

The throughput decreases at 1000 Packets/s: it is related to the channel change of simulation configuration. At 500, the simulation time is 2.69802 s, and 500 packets can be sent successfully. At this time, the success rate of a single packet is 90%–70%, which is acceptable; at 1000, the simulation time is

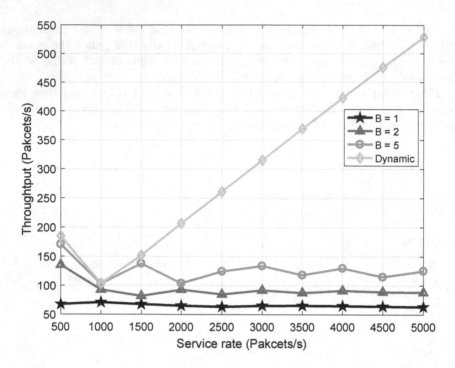

Fig. 7. Average throughput 2 for different ACK

9.14704 s, and the transmission efficiency of the last 500 packets is very low when the success rate is low, so when the backlog reaches 10 s and the success rate is 100%. Only in this way can a large number of data packets be successfully sent out.

(2) Average delay of packet [8] Delay is defined as: data packets are generated from the source, buffered by the MAC layer, processed by transmitters and receivers, and propagation delay. Because the propagation delay of Space-Terrestrial integrated network is much longer than other delays, other delays are ignored in the algorithm, which can be recorded as:

$$T_{delay} = 2T_{transmission} \tag{1}$$

Then the average delay of data packet is defined as the ratio of the total delay value of the successfully received data packet to the total number of data packets. The formula is as follows:

$$T_{average-delay} = \sum_{i=1}^{n} T_{delay}^{i} / n \tag{2}$$

The average delay from packet generation to successful reception simulated in this paper is shown in Fig. 8.

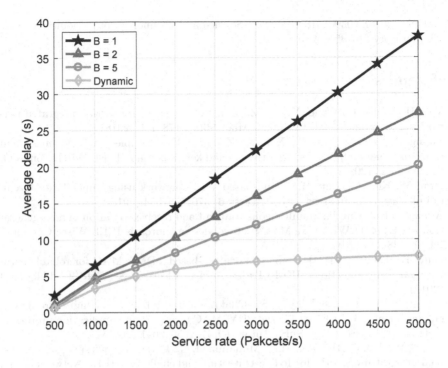

Fig. 8. Average delay of packet

In terms of time delay, the adaptive Block ACK mode has the smallest time delay, the I-ACK mode has the largest time delay, and the fixed B-ACK mode has the middle time delay. The time delay in the case of B = 5 is smaller than that in the case of B = 2. Generally speaking, the results of average delay and average throughput show that the adaptive Block ACK mode has the best performance.

5   Conclusion

In order to achieve low delay transmission in Space-Terrestrial integrated network, an adaptive B-ACK MAC protocol is proposed based on TDMA. The adaptive B-ACK not only improves the transmission delay, but also reduces the overhead of MAC layer, which is helpful to achieve high throughput of space network. The simulation results of adaptive B-ACK access strategies with different channel characteristics show that this MAC mode has great advantages in network system delay and throughput compared with the access mode without adaptive reservation B-ACK, which has certain guiding significance for the integration of heaven and earth.

Acknowledgement. This work was supported in part by the National Natural Science Foundations of CHINA (Grant No. 61871322, No. 61771390, No. 61771392, No. 61501373, and No. 61271279), the National Science and Technology Major Project

(Grant No. 2016ZX03001018-004), and Science and Technology on Avionics Integration Laboratory (20185553035).

References

1. Yao, H., Wang, L., Wang, X., Lu, Z., Liu, Y.: The space-terrestrial integrated network: an overview. IEEE Commun. Mag. **56**(9), 178–185 (2018)
2. Zhang, X., Zhu, L., Li, T., Xia, Y., Zhuang, W.: Multiple-user transmission in space information networks: architecture and key techniques. IEEE Wirel. Commun. **26**(2), 17–23 (2019)
3. Kim, Y., Kim, G., Lim, H.: Cloud-based Wi-Fi network using immediate ACK in uplink data transmissions. IEEE Access **6**, 37045–37054 (2018)
4. Aijaz, A., Kulkarni, P.: Simultaneous transmit and receive operation in next generation IEEE 802.11 WLANs: a MAC protocol design approach. IEEE Wirel. Commun. **24**(6), 128–135 (2017)
5. Jang, H., Kim, E., Lee, J., Lim, J.: Location-based TDMA MAC for reliable aeronautical communications. IEEE Trans. Aerosp. Electron. Syst. **48**(2), 1848–1854 (2012)
6. Karmakar, R., Chattopadhyay, S., Chakraborty, S.: Impact of high throughput enhancements on IEEE 802.11n/ac PHY/MAC transport and application protocols-a survey. IEEE Commun. Surv. Tutor. **19**(4), 2050–2091 (2017)
7. Chien, W., Lai, C., Hossain, M.S., Muhammad, G.: Heterogeneous space and terrestrial integrated networks for IoT: architecture and challenges. IEEE Network **33**(1), 15–21 (2019)
8. Li, P., Fang, Y., Li, J., Huang, X.: Smooth trade-offs between throughput and delay in mobile ad hoc networks. IEEE Trans. Mob. Comput. **11**(3), 427–438 (2012)

Design and Implementation of Tunnel Environment Monitoring System Based on LoRa

Gui Zhu, Honggang Zhao$^{(\boxtimes)}$, Zuobin Liu, and Chen Shi

College of Information and Communication,
National University of Defense Technology, Xi'an, China
zhugui53@163.com, hgz_nwpu@163.com, 2551105254@qq.com,
shishen26@163.com

Abstract. Tunnel is the basic construction project to construct underground, underwater, and mountain buildings, such as mines, subways, and so on. Effective monitoring of tunnel environment plays on important part in the tunnel management, it can provide early warning before the accidents and minimize the hazard of the accident. Compared with the traditional IoT technologies such as ZigBee, Wi-Fi, and so on, the LoRa (Long Range) technology emerging in recent years performs better in terms of coverage range, connection number, and energy consumption, etc. It is foreseeable that the LoRa technology will certainly make a tremendous promotion in the field of tunnel environment monitoring. In this paper, A Lora-based tunnel environment monitoring system is designed and implemented. Firstly, the system architecture is described. Then, the detailed design and implementation of LoRa terminal hardware, LoRa terminal embedded software, LoRa server and monitoring App is given respectively. Finally, the experimental results show that the system has good network coverage capacity and communication reliability, can accurately monitor the tunnel environment and have low power consumption. This system has good promotion and application value.

Keywords: Tunnel · Environment monitoring · LoRa · Internet of Things

1 Introduction

Tunnel is the basic construction project to construct underground, underwater, and mountain buildings, such as mines, subways, and so on. With the wide application of IoT technologies in different areas, it has become an inevitable trend that the IoT technologies are used in the tunnel construction and maintenance, in order to improve the reliability of transmission and the intelligent level of data processing.

The main factors affecting tunnel include: toxic gas concentration, temperature and humidity, carbon dioxide concentration, and water leakage which may lead to the collapse. In literature [1], temperature, humidity, PM2.5 concentration and combustible gas concentration are monitored, then transmitted to the mobile terminal simultaneously by Bluetooth. Besides, the SMS alarm message is generated when gas concentration exceeds the threshold. In literature [2], the ZigBee technology is used, then the early

© ICST Institute for Computer Sciences, Social Informatics and Telecommunications Engineering 2020
Published by Springer Nature Switzerland AG 2020. All Rights Reserved
B. Li et al. (Eds.): IoTaaS 2019, LNICST 316, pp. 621–638, 2020.
https://doi.org/10.1007/978-3-030-44751-9_53

warning and judgment information from distributed gas sensor nodes, can be transmitted to the ground monitoring stations through the relay nodes. In literature [3], a ZigBee network is deployed, not only the mine's temperature, gas concentration but also the personnel information such as pulse, are monitored and transmitted to the server in real time.

Obviously, the traditional IoT technology has greatly promoted the tunnel environment monitoring system. However, due to the complexity of tunnel environment, it is difficult to solve the contradiction between low power consumption and wide coverage. By contrast, the LoRa technology emerging in recent years performs better in terms of coverage range, connection number and energy consumption, etc. It is foreseeable that the LoRa technology will certainly make a tremendous promotion in the field of tunnel environment monitoring (Table 1).

Table 1. The comparison between LoRa and traditional IoT technologies such as ZigBee [4]

Performance	Technologies			
	LoRa	ZigBee [5]	Wi-Fi [6]	GSM/GPRS [7]
Distance	5–15 km	10–75 m	100 m	10 km
Rate	300 Kbps	250 Kbps	11 Mbps	2 Mbps
Low-power	Ultra-low	Support	No support	No support

In this paper, the architecture of the tunnel environment monitoring system based on LoRa is proposed. It consists of LoRa terminal, LoRa gateway, LoRa server and monitoring App. The detail of LoRa terminal hardware, embedded software and monitoring App is given. The LoRa server is deployed on Aliyun. Finally, the communication performance, monitoring performance and terminal power consumption are tested. The experimental results show that the system has good network coverage capacity and communication reliability, can accurately monitor the tunnel environment and have low power consumption. This system has good promotion and application value.

2   LoRa-Based Tunnel Environment Monitoring System Architecture

In this paper, the problem that may be encountered during tunnel construction and maintenance, and the advantages of LoRa [8, 9, 10] technology, are fully taken into consideration, then the architecture of tunnel environment monitoring system based on LoRa is proposed, which is shown in Fig. 1.

The system consists of four parts: LoRa terminal, LoRa gateway, LoRa server and monitoring App. The tunnel environment is monitored by LoRa terminal, then the collected information is transmitted to the monitoring App via LoRa gateway and LoRa server.

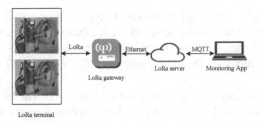

Fig. 1. LoRa-based tunnel environment monitoring system architecture.

The LoRa terminal is deployed in the tunnel to collect carbon dioxide concentration, toxic gas concentration, temperature, humidity, and water leakage. The number and location of LoRa terminals are determined by the actual tunnel environment. The LoRa terminal consists of 7 hardware parts: MCU module, leakage monitoring module, Temperature and humidity monitoring module, gas monitoring module, alarm function module, LoRa transmission module and power management module. The software contains of 8 parts: serial communication module, stop mode, external interruption, temperature and humidity acquisition, RTC clock wake-up, carbon dioxide concentration acquisition, alarm control, LoRa transmission. In order to reduce energy consumption as much as possible, the LoRa terminal periodically wakes up, then it collects the tunnel environment information and send it to the monitoring App by LoRa technology (Figs. 2 and 3).

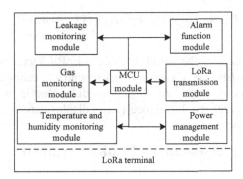

Fig. 2. The hardware structure diagram of LoRa terminal.

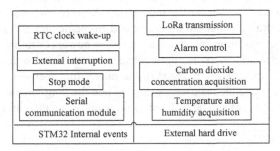

Fig. 3. The software structure diagram of LoRa terminal.

LoRa gateway collects the uplink data of LoRa terminal within the coverage, and establishes a connection with LoRa server through Ethernet or wireless communication. Then it sends the uplink data frame and the status frame to LoRa server through UDP. In this paper, the system uses the indoor gateway RGWC490LA-G of Changsha Rime Company.

LoRa server manages LoRa gateway and LoRa terminal. The LoRa server is set up based on the open source LoRa Server project. LoRa Server consists of a set of programs, including lora-gateway-bridge, loraserver, lora-geo-server and lora-app-server (Fig. 4).

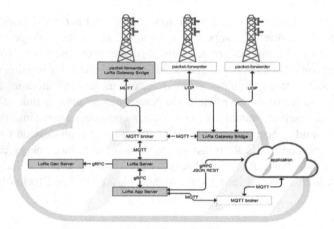

Fig. 4. The structure diagram of LoRa Server.

Monitoring App receives the uplink data from LoRa Server and stores it in SQL Server database. It consists of receiving data background, collecting data display module, management node module and alarm display module. Parallel processing of a large number of terminals is realized. It can receive and display data in real time.

3   Design and Implementation of LoRa Terminal

The LoRa terminal collects carbon dioxide concentration, temperature and humidity, toxic gas concentration and water leakage in the tunnel. It joins the LoRa network, and periodically sends the data to the monitoring App. In this section, the hardware and software of LoRa terminal are designed and implemented according to terminal requirements. At the same time, in order to achieve low power consumption performance, not only the power source classification control method, but also the periodical sleep and monitoring mechanism, are realized in the power management module hardware design and terminal embedded software design. Then the long-term stable operation of terminal power supply [11] can be realized through above method and mechanism.

3.1 LoRa Terminal Hardware Design and Implementation

LoRa terminal hardware consists of 7 modules, including MCU module, leakage monitoring module, gas monitoring module, alarm function module, temperature and humidity monitoring module, LoRa transmission module, and power management module. Detailed schematic diagram of LoRa terminal hardware is shown in Fig. 5.

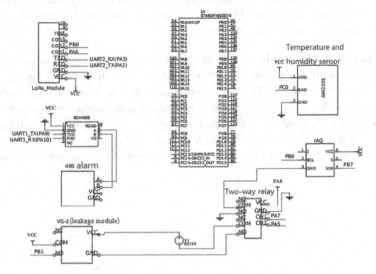

Fig. 5. LoRa terminal hardware schematic diagram.

MCU Module. In order to reduce the node's power consumption, this system uses STM32 [12] as the MCU module. STM32 is popular in the field of low-power IoT. MCU module communicates with temperature and humidity monitoring module and gas monitoring module through IIC protocol, with LoRa transmission module and alarm function module through serial port, and with water leakage monitoring module through interruption input.

Leakage Monitoring Module. The leakage monitoring module is composed of a water leakage monitoring controller VG-2 and a rope [13]. The leakage monitoring module is used to monitor the leakage within the coverage range of the rope. When the leakage is perceived, the leakage monitoring module pulls up the PB1 of STM32.

Gas Monitoring Module. Gas monitoring sensor [14, 15] uses iaq-core c. Its power supply voltage is 3.3 V. Iaq-core c is used to monitor carbon dioxide and toxic gas concentration. Its preheating time lasts 5 min. And the preheating process doesn't affect other module's operation, so the terminal's monitoring time can be minimize as much as possible.

Alarm Function Module. The alarm function module uses rs485 sound-light alarm equipment. It communicates with MCU module through TTL to 485 chip (SC4450S). It gives an alarm signal when toxic gas concentration exceeds the threshold.

Temperature and Humidity Monitoring Module. AM2301 is used as the temperature and humidity sensor [16]. Its precision for humidity is ±3% RH, and for temperature is ±0.3 °C. Its current consumption in sleep mode is 15 uA, and its current consumption in working mode is 500 uA.

LoRa Transmission Module. RNDU490L is used as the LoRa transmission module, and communication with the MCU module through serial port (TTL level). It is used to transmit the acquired carbon dioxide and toxic gas concentration, temperature, humidity and water leakage to the LoRa server.

Power Management Module. In the design of power management module [17], the power source classification control method is adopted to satisfy power supply requirements of different modules. The main power module consist of: leakage monitoring module for 9–30 V power supply without low power consumption mode, gas monitoring module for 3.3 V power supply without low power consumption mode, temperature and humidity monitoring module for 3.3 V power supply with low power consumption mode, LoRa transmission module for 3.3 V power supply with low power consumption mode.

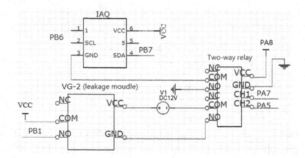

Fig. 6. Power management module.

As shown in the Fig. 6, the four modules can be divided into two types, according to the voltage levels of their power supplies. One is the leakage monitoring module, it is the only module that uses 12 V battery for power supply. The other three modules use the 3.3 V power supply, and they share the stabilized power source with STM32.

According to the working mode, the four modules can also be divided into two types. One is the LoRa transmission module, temperature and humidity module. They both have low power consumption mode. The other is the leakage monitoring module and gas monitoring module. They don't have low power consumption mode. So a relay is adopted to control their power supply, and the power supply is provided when needed. It is ensured that the unnecessary energy consumption is reduced when the leakage monitoring module and gas monitoring module don't work.

The RTC clock is used to wake up the STM32 periodically. After STM32 wakes up, the pin PA7 and pin PA5 are checked. If the pins are in high level, the MCU module reads the carbon dioxide and toxic gas concentration, temperature, humidity, and water leakage, then transmits it to the LoRa module. If the pins are in low level, the pin PA7 and pin PA5 are set to turn on the power supply of gas monitoring module and leakage monitoring module. Then the gas monitoring module preheats for 5 min, and the leakage monitoring module continuously monitors the water leakage.

3.2 Design and Implementation of LoRa Terminal Software

LoRa terminal software is the executive program of MCU module, which is used to realize the LoRa terminal workflow. It consists of the implementation of internal execution events and the preparation of external sensor drivers. According to the hardware design and software functional requirements, LoRa terminal software's workflow is divided into three working stages. The first stage is the 55 min sleep stage. The second stage is 5 min preheating stage. The third stage is acquisition and transmission stage of about 30 s [18].

Two issues should be fully taken into consideration in the LoRa terminal software design. One is to collect data correctly and transmit it through LoRa module. The other is to preheat the gas monitoring module for 5 min before it can be used.

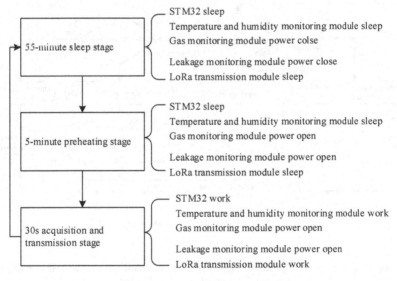

Fig. 7. LoRa terminal work phase.

According to the above consideration and the hardware design, the workflow of LoRa terminal is divided into three stages as shown in the Fig. 7. During the first stage, all modules running at the lowest power consumption. During the second stage, except for the gas monitoring module and leakage monitoring module, the other three modules are still running at low power consumption. During the third stage, all modules are working [19] (Fig. 8).

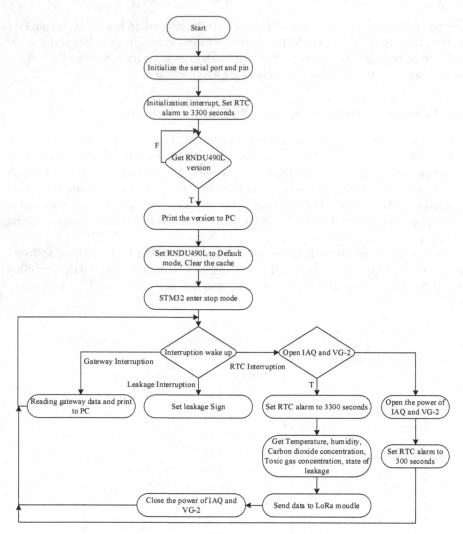

Fig. 8. Software flow chart.

The operation of software starts with a series of initialization, which consist of the initialization of three serial ports, input/output pin, delay function, interrupt function, iaq driver, and RTC clock.

The second serial port sends a command to RNDU490L to get the version, which verifies that RNDU490L is working properly. If the version is correctly obtained, execute the following procedure. Otherwise, the program delay 0.5 s, then send the command again.

Set RNDU490L as the default working mode. The default working mode means starting ADR (rate adaptive), setting the data rate to SF12, and sending power to 17 dBm.

STM32 enter stop mode.

Exit low power mode by three interrupts: ① Timer interruption: determine whether the power of iaq and VG-2 are on. If not, turn on and set the RTC clock for 300 s next time. If it is turned on, set the RTC clock to 3300 s next time, then read the temperature, humidity, and the concentration of toxic gas and carbon dioxide. Send it to the LoRa server. If the toxic gas content exceeds the limit, send a signal to alarm; ② Interruption of LoRa module: when the gateway has downlink data, LoRa module will send a rising edge to trigger the interrupt. In this interrupt processing event, STM32 prints the downlink data received from the LoRa module to the PC. ③ VG-2 leakage interruption: set the water leakage flag bit.

4   Design and Implementation of LoRa Server and Monitoring App

The LoRa server manages gateways, LoRa nodes, and data transmission within LoRa network. The monitoring App receives data from LoRa server and conducts analysis, processing and usage. According to the system requirements, it is divided into four parts: receiving platform, data display module, manage node module and alarm display module. Meanwhile, in order to realize multi-node monitoring, two mechanisms are designed and implemented in the receiving platform. One is "thread programming" and the other is "data receiving and processing separation".

4.1   LoRa Server Software

LoRa server software is based on the open source LoRa Server project, and the usage of OS is 64-bit ubuntu system (Fig. 9).

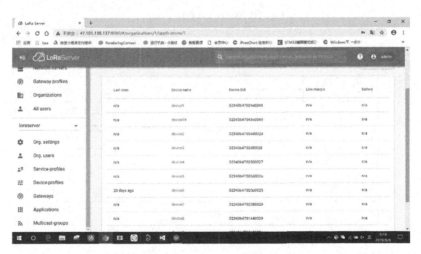

Fig. 9. The LoRa server Deployed on aliyun ubuntu platform.

After the deployment of LoRa server on aliyun ubuntu, it is necessary to open some ports of the cloud server, including the 1700 port which is used to communicate with the gateway through UDP, and the 8080 port which is used by Lora-app-server to provide web access services.

4.2 Monitoring App Design and Implementation

The function of monitoring App can be divided into four parts. Firstly, collect and store the uplink data. Secondly, display trends of various types of information. Thirdly, alarm when carbon dioxide concentration exceeds the threshold, or toxic gas concentration exceeds the threshold, or water leakage happens. Finally, manage node information [20] (Figs. 10 and 11).

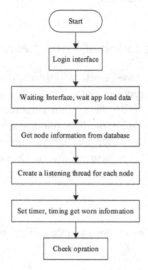

Fig. 10. Software flow chart.

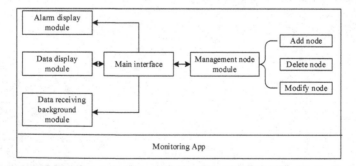

Fig. 11. Monitoring App functional structure.

Database. The database uses SQL server. We create a database named 'server' and a user. In 'server', there are three types of tables: node table, warning_log table, and each node's table (Fig. 12).

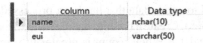

Fig. 12. Node table.

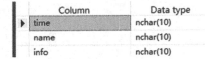

Fig. 13. Worning_log table.

The node table is used to store the name of the node and its corresponding eui. The node name is set by the user. Eui is a fixed value of each node, which is provided by the manufacturer (Fig. 13).

The Warning_log table is used to store details of each alarm, with columns 'time', 'name', and 'info'. The column 'info' is used to indicate the pre-agreed event, and the alarm information can be shown by 'check log' button of the monitoring App.

month	nchar(10)
day	nchar(10)
hour	int
co2	nchar(10)
temp	nchar(10)
humi	nchar(10)
c2tn	char(10)

Fig. 14. Each node's table.

Each node table is named according to the node name, for example, the table name of the Fig. 14 is "node 1". Since the terminal program is designed to send uplink data every one hour, the columns of table are 'month', 'day', 'hour', 'co2', 'temp', 'humi' and 'c2tn' (toxic gas). The primary key of node table is (month, day, hour).

Receiving Platform. The Receiving Platform is used to acquire and store the terminal data. Due to the large number of terminals, two concurrency problems need to be taken into consideration in the design. Firstly, it is needed to solve how to promote the platform's efficiency. Secondly, it is needed to solve how to receive data accurately.

To solve the above problems, two mechanisms are proposed. One is "thread programming". The other is "data receiving and processing separation" [21].

The "thread programming" mechanism means creating new thread listening to each node. When a terminal does not report information, the listening thread is blocked. It realizes that the receiving platform does not occupy the CPU resources of PC during the long period of terminal sleep.

The mechanism of "data receiving and processing separation" means storing all data into a buff array without doing any processing. The buff array has two variables, rcount and scount. Rcount is used to count data that has been processed, and scount is used to count data that has been stored. Create a timer to handle the buff array, judging the values of rcount and scount every 10 s. When rcount is greater than or equal to the value of scount, it is proved that no new data needs to be processed. Otherwise, start processing the buff array data from rcount until the scount, then update the values of rcount and scount.

Data Display Module
After selecting node name, information and time interval in the main interface, click "ok" button to display broken line graph of information change. Click the "save as picture" button to output the graph as an image and save it to the file system (Fig. 15).

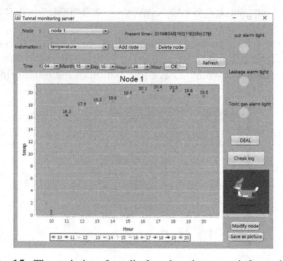

Fig. 15. The main interface displayed environment information.

Manage Node Module. The manage node module consists of the addition, modification and deletion of the node name and eui mapping.

5   System Test and Result Analysis

In this paper, three types of system tests are conducted, which consist of communication performance test, monitoring performance test and terminal power consumption test. The first test mainly tests the packet loss rate between LoRa terminal and gateway. The second test mainly tests whether the data uplinked by the LoRa terminal are consistent with the actual situation. The third test mainly measures the average power consumption of LoRa terminal.

5.1 Communication Performance Test

Communication distance has a great impact on the management of LoRa terminal, deployment costs and the performance of the system. In this test, the communication performance was tested in two experimental environments. Firstly, the gateway is deployed at the tunnel gate, and the LoRa terminal is placed deep in the tunnel. Secondly, the gateway and the LoRa terminal are deployed in an open environment [22].

In the first case, the LoRa terminal transmitted 100 uplink packets to the gateway. And the average communication success rate is 99%.

In the second case, the distance between gateways and the terminal are shown in Fig. 16.

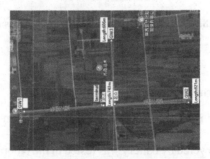

Fig. 16. Terminal communication performance test topology.

The distance between the gateway 1 and terminal is 743 m. The terminal transmitted 50 uplink packets to the gateway 1. And average packet loss rate is 14%. Besides, the RSSI obtained from the gateway 1 fluctuates very little, its average value is −107 dbm (Fig. 17).

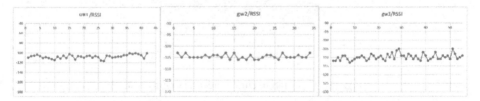

Fig. 17. Gateway 1, 2, 3's received signal strength fluctuates.

The distance between the gateway 2 and terminal is 821 m. The terminal transmitted 50 uplink packets to the gateway 2. And average packet loss rate is 20%. Besides, the RSSI obtained from the gateway 2 fluctuates very little, its average value is −104 dbm.

The distance between the gateway 3 and terminal is 606 m. The terminal transmitted 50 uplink packets to the gateway 3. And average packet loss rate is 2%. Besides, the RSSI obtained from the third gateway 3 fluctuates very little, its average value is −109 dbm.

The packet loss rate varies with the communication distance as shown in Fig. 18. And the packet loss rate apparently varies linearly with the change in communication distance.

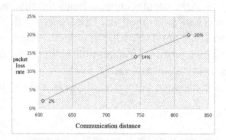

Fig. 18. Communication distance vs packet loss rate.

5.2 Monitoring Performance Test

Monitoring performance is tested to verify that the system can accurately monitor the tunnel environment.

Firstly, the system powered by battery was tested in the laboratory for 2 days, and the carbon dioxide concentration, temperature, humidity, toxic gas concentration and water leakage are monitored continuously. The temperature acquired is shown in Fig. 19.

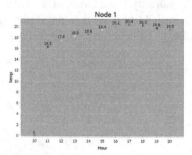

Fig. 19. Temperature curve under laboratory test.

In the tunnel test, the terminal is deployed to the actual tunnel, and collect tunnel environment every 10 s. Secondly, the system powered by battery was tested in the actual tunnel, and the tunnel information was collected every 10 s. Parts of the data are shown in Table 2. The average humidity was 72.18%, the average temperature was 17.94 °C, the average carbon dioxide concentration was 317 ppm (3.17% of the air), and the average toxic gas concentration was 125 ppb (1.25×10^{-3}% of the air).

In Table 2, the first column 'node eui' indicates the hardware number of LoRa transmission module in LoRa terminal. The format of 'time' is 'minutes-seconds'. 'Humidity' refers to the humidity in the air. Column 'temperature' indicates the temperature in

Table 2. The first ten groups of test data under pit test.

node eui	Time	Humidity	Temperature	CO_2	Tvoc	FCnt	Isleak
32343647034d0029	26–30	71.3	18.8	318	125	0	N
32343647034d0029	26–40	71.2	18.2	318	125	1	N
32343647034d0029	26–53	69.5	18.1	318	125	2	N
32343647034d0029	27–04	71	18.1	318	125	3	N
32343647034d0029	27–15	70	18.1	318	125	4	N
32343647034d0029	27–27	70.2	18.1	318	125	5	N
32343647034d0029	27–39	71.4	18.1	317	126	6	N
32343647034d0029	27–51	71.5	18.1	318	125	7	N
32343647034d0029	27–51	71.6	18.1	318	125	8	N
32343647034d0029	28–14	70.4	18.1	318	125	9	N

degrees Celsius. 'CO_2' refers to the concentration of carbon dioxide in ppm (parts per million). 'Tvoc' refers to the concentration of toxic gases in ppb (concentration per billion parts). 'FCnt' is the frame count between the gateway and LoRa terminal. 'Isleak', 'Y' is leakage and 'N' is no leakage.

5.3 Terminal Power Consumption Test

Only LoRa terminal power consumption needs to be considered. Therefore, the power consumption of LoRa terminal is the key factor to determine the working life of the system, and it is also the advantage of the tunnel environment monitoring system designed based on LoRa. It is of great significance to the promotion and application of the system. This test uses oscilloscope method. As shown in Fig. 20, the high precision resistor is connected in series between the LoRa terminal and the power supply. The voltage difference across the resistor in the three working stages is measured by an oscilloscope. According to ohm's law, the working current of the LoRa terminal can be calculated. The resistance value of the test resistor is 10 Ω.

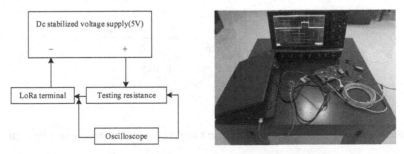

Fig. 20. Schematic diagram of oscilloscope method.

During the 55 min sleep stage, the voltage difference measured by the oscilloscope is 23 mV. According to Fig. 21, the voltage difference across the LED is 15 mV, so the voltage difference across the necessary circuit is 8 mV. That is to say that the system current consumption is 0.8 mA.

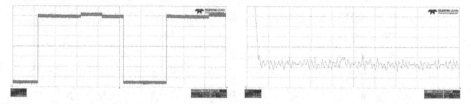

Fig. 21. The first stage is the voltage change of oscilloscope.

During the 5 min preheating stage, the voltage difference measured by the oscilloscope is about 400 mV. That is to say that the system current consumption is 40 mA (Fig. 22).

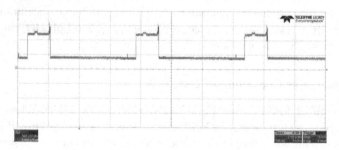

Fig. 22. The second and third stage voltage.

During the reading and transmission stage, the voltage difference measured by the oscilloscope is about 1.2 V. That is to say that the system current consumption is 120 mA.

Table 3. LoRa terminal power consumption.

Stage	Plate on the current
The first stage lasts 55 min	0.8 mA
The second phase lasts 5 min	40 mA
The third stage takes about 30 s	120 mA

Then the average current consumption in one period, can be represented by formula 1.

$$I_h = \sum_i^3 \frac{T_i}{T_h} \times I_i \tag{1}$$

T_i is the duration of working stage i, and T_h is 60 min which is the duration of one period. Substitute data from Table 3 into formula 1, the calculated I_h is 5.06 mA. The capacity of two AA batteries is about 3000 mAh, which means the LoRa terminal power by two AA batteries in this system can run for up to 592 h.

6 Conclusion

Compared with the traditional IoT technologies such as ZigBee, LoRa technology performs better in terms of coverage range, connection number, and energy consumption, etc. It is foreseeable that the LoRa technology will certainly make a tremendous promotion in the field of tunnel environment monitoring. In this paper, A Lora-based tunnel environment monitoring system is designed and implemented. The system architecture is described, and the detailed design and implementation of hardware and software are also described. The experimental results show that the system has good network coverage capacity and communication reliability, can accurately monitor the tunnel environment and have low power consumption. This system has good promotion and application value.

References

1. Tao, X., Yan, Z., Yong, M.: Underground tunnel environment wireless monitoring system. Inf. Technol. (8), 46–49 (2017)
2. Liu, W., Li, Q.: Research on mine explosion-proof monitoring system based on ZigBee. Autom. Instrum. (4), 26–29 (2009)
3. Yun, H.: Research on mine personnel sign monitoring system based on ZigBee. Chang'an University, Xian (2011)
4. Feng, W.: LoRa Internet of Things technology and application. Telecom World (2), 91–92 (2017)
5. Guo, C.: Discuss the advantages and applications of short distance wireless communication technology. China New Telecommun. 19(5), 94 (2017)
6. Lee, K., Lee, J., Yi, Y.: Mobile data offloading: how much can WiFi deliver. In: International Conference, vol. 21. ACM (2010)
7. Lin, S.: Characteristics and application of GPRS technology. Telecommun. Technol. (3), 2–5 (2002)
8. Aref, M., Sikora, A.: Free space range measurements with Semtech Lora^{TM} technology. In: 2014 2nd International Symposium on Wireless Systems within the Conferences on Intelligent Data Acquisition and Advanced Computing Systems: Technology and Applications (IDAACS-SWS) (2014)
9. Won, Y.-Y., Yoon, S.M., Seo, D.: Optical access transmission with improved channel capacity using non-orthogonal frequency quadrature amplitude modulation. Opt. Quant. Electron. 49(2), 1–13 (2017)
10. Akhlaghi, M.: High-speed optical FSK demodulator using plasmonicnano bi-dome. Optik Int. J. Light Electron Optics 127(19), 8030–8035 (2016)
11. Chung, Y.W., Chung, M.Y., Sung, D.K.: Adaptive algorithm for mobile terminal power on/off state management. Comput. Commun. 24(14), 1411–1424 (2001)
12. Zhang, H., Kang, W.: Design of the data acquisition system based on STM32. Procedia Comput. Sci. 17, 222–228 (2013)

13. Mei, G., G-H., Cai, L.: Design of water leakage detection device in computer room based on Hetai single chip microcomputer. Electron. Instrum. Cust. **24**(3), 34–40 (2017)
14. Patel, N.G., Panchal, C.J., Makhija, K.K.: Use of cadmium selenide thin films as a carbon dioxide gas sensor. Cryst. Res. Technol. **29**, 1013–1020 (1994)
15. Xiao, B., Jian, F., Fan, L.: Design and development of remote indoor air monitoring system based on Yeelink. Comput. Program. Skills Maint. **10**, 26–27 (2015)
16. Arshak, K.I., Twomey, K.: Investigation into a novel humidity sensor operating at room temperature. Microelectron. J. **33**(3), 213–220 (2002)
17. Xing, F., Fei, T., Yan, L.: Design of low power consumption wireless Internet of Things terminal power management system. Semicond. Technol. **43**(12), 883–886 (2018)
18. Yu, Z., Rui, S., Kun, W.: Development of greenhouse environment monitoring system based on Proteus and Keil software. Trans. Chin. Soc. Agric. Eng. **28**(14), 177–183 (2012)
19. Ning, L., Qiong, C., Lei, Y.: Design of serial communication display system based on STM32 minimum system. Ind. Control Comput. **30**(8), 33–36 (2017)
20. Lin, Y.: Student achievement information management system based on Java Web. Jilin University (2015)
21. Hua, W., Yun, X.: Java multithreading mechanism and its application. Comput. Mod. **1**, 1–6 (2000)
22. Tao, S.: Computer application system performance test technology and application research. Electron. Test (8), 69–70+66 (2019)

Wyner-Ziv Video Coding for Highway Traffic Surveillance Using LDPC Codes

Linlong Guo, Bowei Shan(ID), and Yong Fang(✉)(ID)

School of Information Engineering, Chang'an University,
Xi'an, People's Republic of China
{2018124070,bwshan,fy}@chd.edu.cn

Abstract. This paper presents a 2D Q-ary Sliding-Window Belief Propagation (2DQSWBP) algorithm to decode Low-density Parity-check (LDPC) code which is utilized to compress highway traffic surveillance video under Wyner-Ziv video framework. This framework is beneficial for camera device with limited memory and computing ability. The differences of successive frames is modeled as Truncated Discrete Laplace (TDL) distribution. The experimental result shows the 2DQSWBP outperforms the Q-ary Belief Propagation (QBP) algorithm in both Bit-Error-Rate and computing time.

Keywords: 2DQSWBP algorithm · LDPC code · QBP algorithm · Wyner-Ziv video coding

1 Introduction

Recent advances in the Fifth Generation (5G) telecommunication and Internet of Things as a Service (IoTaaS) enables real-time video surveillance of highway traffic using mobile camera device. In this scenario, the video codes at the camera usually has limited memory and computing ability, therefore a low-complexity encoder is always required.

The successive frames in a video sequence typically are very similar, and current video coding standards, such as MPEG or ITU-T H.26x, take advantage of this similarity to make compression efficient. The implementation of traditional video codes requires encoder 5 to 10 times more computational complex than the decoder, which is well suited for streaming video-on-demand system instead of surveillance system.

The Wyner-Ziv video coding [1,2] (also known as distributed video coding) is an asymmetric compression scheme which encodes individual frame independently while decodes them conditionally. The theoretical foundation of the Wyner-Ziv video coding is the Slepian-Wolf theorem [3] on distributed source coding and the Wyner-Ziv [4] theorem for lossy source coding. These theorems state an astonishing result that for two statistically dependent discrete signals,

© ICST Institute for Computer Sciences, Social Informatics and Telecommunications Engineering 2020
Published by Springer Nature Switzerland AG 2020. All Rights Reserved
B. Li et al. (Eds.): IoTaaS 2019, LNICST 316, pp. 639–645, 2020.
https://doi.org/10.1007/978-3-030-44751-9_54

X and Y, with entropies $H(X)$ and $H(Y)$, even if the encoders are independent, the achievable rate region for a joint decoder is

$$R_X \geq H(X|Y), R_Y \geq H(Y|X),$$
$$R_X + R_Y \geq H(X,Y). \tag{1}$$

In this paper, the Wyner-Ziv video coding is implemented by Low-density Parity-check (LDPC) codes for highway traffic surveillance video compression. The difference between the successive frames are modeled as Truncated Discreate Laplacian (TDL) distribution. The 2D Q-ary Sliding-Windows Belief Propagation (2DQSWBP) algorithm is proposed to decode LDPC codes. The experiment result shows that 2DQSWBP outperforms Belief Propagation (BP) algorithm for decoding the traffic video.

2   Wyner-Ziv Video Coding

2.1   Framework

In the Wyner-Ziv video coding, the encoder is implemented by Pixel-Domain and Transform-Domain (PDTD) scheme. The framework of PDTD is illustrated in Fig. 1

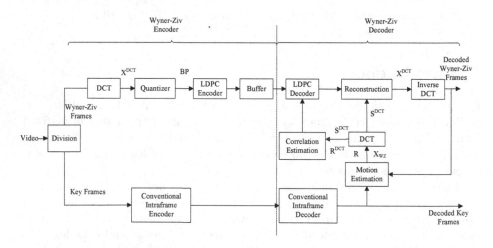

Fig. 1. Framework of Wyner-Ziv video coding.

PDTD divides video frames into two parts: the first frame is named as Key Frame, and the rest are named as Wyner-Ziv Frames. Key Frame is encoded and decoded using a conventional intraframe codec. For Wyner-Ziv Frames, A blockwise Discrete Cosine Transformation (DCT) is performed to obtain the transform coefficients X^{DCT} which are independently quantized and grouped into coefficient bands. These bands are compressed by LDPC encoder. At the decoder, the side information frame X_{WZ} and motion compensation residual frame R are generated by previously reconstructed frames with the help of motion compensation. Then a block-wise DCT is applied to them, resulting in side information S^{DCT} and residual frame R^{DCT}. The correlation between X^{DCT} and S^{DCT} is modeled as a Laplacian distribution. LDPC decoder reconstructs the coefficient bands with the corresponding side information and performs a inverse DCT to generate the reconstructed Wyner-Ziv frames.

Above coding paradigm has many advantages. First, it makes it possible to shift the computational complexity from encoder to decoder. This is beneficial for many wireless camera devices which normally have limited computing ability and battery life. Second, since there is no side information at the encoder, the frame error will not be propagated and the recovered videos appear to be more robust.

2.2   2DQSWBP Algorithm

In 2013, Fang [5] proposed a 2D SWBP algorithm for binary LDPC codes, and a Q-ary SWBP [6] in 1D form is introduced in 2019. As what we have known, the 2D Q-ary SWBP algorithm has not been presented. The video is consisted of successive 2D frames. Each frame has many pixels and each pixel is represented by a q bit value which varies from 0 to $Q = 2^q - 1$. In this paper, we will use 2DQSWBP to decode Wyner-Ziv video, and the flowchart of 2DQSWBP is illustrated in Fig. 2

For 2D paradigm, Let

$$x^{n,n} \triangleq \begin{pmatrix} x_{0,0} & \cdots & x_{0,n-1} \\ \vdots & \ddots & \vdots \\ x_{n-1,0} & \cdots & x_{n-1,n-1} \end{pmatrix}, \tag{2}$$

$y^{n,n}$ be two $n \times n$ 2D sources, where $x_{i,j} \in [0 : Q)$. Let the correlation between them be $z^{n,n} = x^{n,n} - y^{n,n}$.

$$p_{z^{n,n}}(z^{n,n}) = \prod_{i=0}^{n-1} \prod_{j=0}^{n-1} p_{z_{i,j}}(z_{i,j}), \tag{3}$$

where $p_{z_{i,j}}(z_{i,j})$ obeys Truncated Discreate Laplacian (TDL) distribution

$$p_{z_{i,j}}(a|y_{i,j}, \sigma_{i,j}^2) = \frac{\exp\left(-\sqrt{\frac{2}{\sigma_{i,j}^2}}|a|\right)}{\sum_{a'=-y_{i,j}}^{M-1-y_{i,j}} \exp\left(-\sqrt{\frac{2}{\sigma_{i,j}^2}}|a'|\right)}. \tag{4}$$

We call $\sigma_{i,j}^2$ the local nominal variance of $Z_{i,j}$ and define the global nominal variance of $z^{n,n}$ as

$$\sigma^2 \triangleq \frac{1}{n \times n} \sum_{i=0}^{n-1} \sum_{j=0}^{n-1} \sigma_{i,j}^2. \tag{5}$$

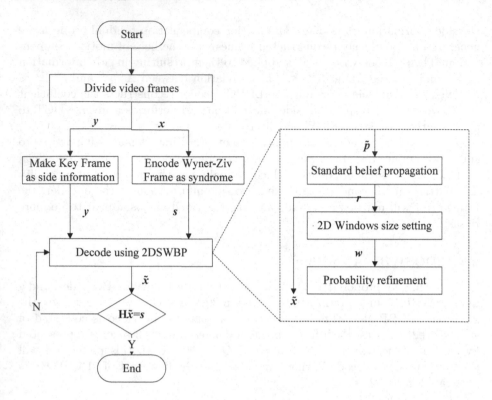

Fig. 2. Flowchart of 2DQSWBP.

At the encoder, $x^{n,n}$ is first vectorized into an Q-ary temporary vector $v^{n,n}$. Then $v^{n,n}$ is performed a matrix-vector multiplication over the finite field $GF(Q)$ to compress source to syndrome s^m:

$$s^m = \mathbf{H}v^{n,n}, \tag{6}$$

where $\mathbf{H}$ is an $m \times (n \times n)$ sparse parity-check matrix.

At the decoder, standard Q-ary BP algorithm (QBP) utilize side information $y^{n,n}$ to recover $x^{n,n}$, which has been introduced in [6]. After each QBP iteration, the local nominal variances of symbol nodes are reestimated according to their overall probability mass functions (pmf). Let $r_{i,j}(a)$ for $a \in [0:Q)]$ be the overall pmf of symbol node $x_{i,j}$. The Expected Squared Euclidean Distance (ESED) between each source symbol and its corresponding side information symbol is computed by

$$d_{i,j} = \sum_{a=0}^{Q-1} r_{i,j}(a)|a - y_{i,j}|^2. \tag{7}$$

The optimal half window size u^* is determined by

$$u^* = \arg\max_u d_{i,j}(u). \tag{8}$$

Then, $\sigma_{i,j}^2$ is computed by averaging $d_{r',c'}$ over a $(2u^* + 1) \times (2u^* + 1)$ 2D window around $x_{i,j}$, i.e.,

$$\hat{\sigma}_{i,j}^2(u^*) = \frac{\sum_{i',j' \in \mathcal{W}_{i,j} \backslash (i,j)} d_{i,j}}{|\mathcal{W}_{i,j}| - 1}, \tag{9}$$

where

$$\mathcal{W}_{i,j} \triangleq \{(i',j') : i' \in \mathcal{W}_i \cap j' \in \mathcal{W}_j\}, \tag{10}$$

where

$$\mathcal{W}_i \triangleq [\max(0, i - u) : \min(i + u, n - 1)], \tag{11}$$

and $|\cdot|$ denotes set cardinality. Finally, $r_{i,j}(a)$ is updated with the refined $\sigma_{i,j}^2(u^*)$

3   Experimental Results

A highway traffic surveillance video is used to perform our tests. Each frame in the video has 128×128 pixels. We construct a regular LDPC code with codeword length 16384, and information bit number 8192. Then the rate is $1/2$. Our experimental platform is configured with Intel(R) Core(TM) i7-7700 CPU 3.60 GHz(4 Cores) main frequency, 8 GB memory, and 64-bit Windows-10 operation system. All above algorithms are developed in MATLAB 2017a environment.

The aim of the experiment is to compare the performance between the 2DQSWPB and QBP algorithm. The alphabet cardinality Q is fixed to $2^8 = 256$. The source size $n \times n$ is fixed to 128×128. The LDPC code is used to compress the source. The local nominal variance of $z^{n,n}$ varies according to $\sigma_{i,j}^2 = 2b^2$. Five value of b are tested, i.e., $b \in \{1.2, 1.4, 1.5, 2, 2.5\}$.

Two metrics, i.e., Bit-Error-Rate (BER) and running time, are used to evaluate the performance of proposed algorithms. The results are plotted in Fig. 3, from which we find that 2DQSWBP outperforms QBP with less computing time (Fig. 4).

From the results we can conclude that:

We select a frame from the highway traffic surveillance video and depict it for $b = 1.4$ in Fig. 5(a). The recover frame by 2DQSWBP is depicted in Fig. 5(b). We find 2DDSWBP can successfully recover the video and when $b > 1.4$, QBP cannot recover the video.

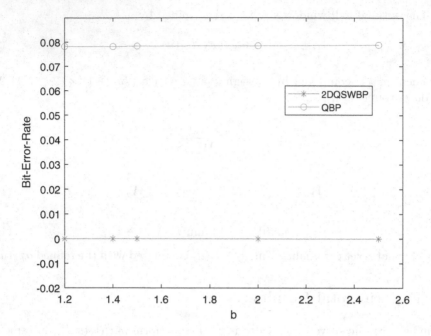

Fig. 3. Bit-Error-Rate under two algorithms.

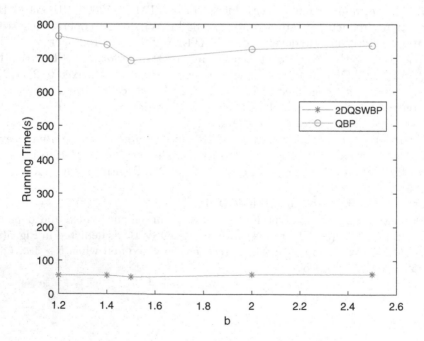

Fig. 4. Running time under two algorithms.

(a)   (b)

Fig. 5. A frame from the highway traffic surveillance video (a) Orignal Frame (b) Recovered Frame by 2DQSWBP

4   Conclusion

To deal with highway traffic surveillance video, the innovation of this paper is using the LDPC code to compress video frame under Wyner-Ziv video coding framework and proposing a 2DQSWBP algorithm to decode corresponding LDPC codes. The correlation between the successive frames are modeled as TDL distribution. Experimental results show that this algorithm can successfully recover the orignal video and 2DQSWBP outperforms QBP algorithm in both BER and computing time.

References

1. Aaron, A., Zhang, R. Girod, B.: Wyner-Ziv coding of motion video. In: Conference Record of the Thirty-Sixth Asilomar Conference on Signals, Systems and Computers, Pacific Grove, CA, USA, vol. 1, pp. 240 244 (2002). https://doi.org/10.1109/ACSSC.2002.1197184
2. Girod, B., Aaron, A.M., Rane, S., Rebollo-Monedero, D.: Distributed video coding. Proc. IEEE **93**(1), 71–83 (2005). https://doi.org/10.1109/jproc.2004.839619
3. Slepian, D., Wolf, J.K.: Noiseless coding of correlated information sources. IEEE Trans. Inf. Theory **19**(4), 471–480 (1973). https://doi.org/10.1109/TIT.1973.1055037
4. Wyner, A.D., Ziv, J.: The rate-distortion function for source coding with side information at the decoder. IEEE Trans. Inf. Theory **22**(1), 1–10 (1976). https://doi.org/10.1109/TIT.1976.1055508
5. Fang, Y.: Asymmetric Slepian-Wolf coding of nonstationarily-correlated M-ary sources with sliding-window belief propagation. IEEE Trans. Commun. **61**(12), 5114–5124 (2013). https://doi.org/10.1109/TCOMM.2013.111313.130230
6. Fang, Y., Yang, Y., Shan, B., Stankovic, V.: Joint source-channel estimation via sliding-window belief propagation. IEEE Trans. Commun. (2019, submitted)

Author Index